CHICAGO PUBLIC LIBRARY
R06003 43218

CHICAGO
C
P
L
PUBLIC LIBRARY
Form 178 rev. 01-07

D1060714

THE PROCESS OF PLANNING

The Royal Institute of International Affairs is an unofficial body which promotes the scientific study of international questions and does not express opinions of its own. The opinions expressed in this publication are the responsibility of the author.

The Institute gratefully acknowledges the comments and suggestions of the following who read the manuscript on behalf of the Research Committee: I. M. D. Little, Geoffrey Tyson, and Maurice Zinkin.

THE PROCESS OF PLANNING

A STUDY
OF INDIA'S FIVE-YEAR PLANS
1950-1964

A. H. HANSON

Professor of Politics, University of Leeds

Issued under the auspices of the Royal Institute of International Affairs

OXFORD UNIVERSITY PRESS
LONDON NEW YORK TORONTO BOMBAY
1966

Oxford University Press, Ely House, London W.1

GLASGOW NEW YORK TORONTO MELBOURNE WELLINGTON
CAPE TOWN SALISBURY IBADAN NAIROBI LUSAKA ADDIS ABABA
BOMBAY CALCUTTA MADRAS KARACHI LAHORE DACCA
KUALA LUMPUR HONG KONG

Printed in Northern Ireland at the Universities Press, Belfast

To Norman Chester
in friendship and gratitude

PREFACE

If justification be needed for this addition to the growing body of literature on Indian planning, it is to be found in the fact that I am not an economist. There are now several very competent books, such as Professor Malenbaum's and Dr Reddaway's, which subject the Indian planning process to economic analysis; but this, to my knowledge, is the first book to look at it primarily from the point of view of the student of politics and public administration. As an Indian plan, like any other plan, is the product of a given socio-political situation, and as its successful implementation largely depends on the honesty, competence, and public spirit of those who constitute what is sometimes miscalled the administrative machine, I can reasonably claim that a study of this type is needed.

Yet the misgivings of an author confronted with so large a task need hardly be stressed. The work completed, these are not allayed. I have undertaken a documentary study the thoroughness of which has been limited only by the need to complete an assignment without grossly exceeding the agreed dead-line; I have packed into a few months as many interviews with Indian politicians, planners, and administrators as could be uncomfortably accommodated therein. But I have not succeeded in producing anything that can be dignified as definitive. My excuse for this failure is that only at the cost of some superficiality can one hope to keep up, panting along several paces behind, with the precipitate rush of events.

What merits this book possesses are largely due to the unstinting help I have received. Fully to acknowledge it would be impossible; but my very special thanks are due to the Royal Institute of International Affairs, which commissioned this study and financed my research trip to India; to the Warden and Fellows of Nuffield College, Oxford, who elected me to a Research Fellowship for the year 1960–1; to the University of Leeds, which granted me generous leaves of absence; and to the Indian Institute of Public Administration and the Indian Planning Commission, which placed full facilities for study at my disposal. Of the many members and officers of the Commission who freely gave me their time and patiently answered my questions, I should like to mention Mr Tarlok Singh, whose experience of the Indian planning process is unrivalled, Dr S. R. Sen, with whom discussion is a rare intellectual pleasure, Mr R. S. Chadda, whose knowledge of India's plan projects is equalled only by his kindness, and Messrs U. S. Rana and R. P. Sachdev, who were indefatigable in arranging interviews and itineraries and in hunting up documents. By the state governments of Uttar Pradesh, Rajasthan, Maharashtra, Andhra Pradesh, and Madras I was given help far beyond my expectations. Among the Indian academics from whose writings and conversation I derived great benefit, I must make special mention of two of my old friends, Professor H. K. Paranjape, of the Indian Institute of Public Administration, and Professor V. V. Ramanadham, of Osmania University, Hyderabad, and two of my newer but not less valued ones, Professor K. N. Raj, of the Delhi School of Economics, and Dr Jagdish Bhagwati, of the Central Statistical Organization. As a further tribute to the consideration and patience shown by all my hosts and informants, I should add that many of my inquiries were being made at a time when Indians were preoccupied with Chinese aggression and could therefore have been fully forgiven if they had regarded a peripatetic research worker as an irrelevant nuisance.

Of recent writings on Indian politics and economics that have aroused my admiration and helped to crystallize my thoughts, those of Lady Jackson (Miss Barbara Ward), Professor W. H. Morris-Jones, Professor Hugh Tinker, Professor Wilfred Malenbaum, Professor Myron Weiner, Dr Selig Harrison, and Drs Lloyd and Suzanne Rudolph are outstanding. For listening patiently and critically to my over-lengthy and sometimes disorderly thinking aloud, I must thank my youthful and vigorous-minded friends, Warren and Alice Ilchman, for whom I confidently predict a brilliant future as American students of Indian politics. The long evenings of conversation in their apartment in Old Delhi were a great joy to me. I owe a special debt to Mr Ian Little, Mr Peter Nettl, Mr Geoffrey Tyson, and Mr Maurice Zinkin, whose detailed, acute, and occasionally barbed comments on the typescript of this book were of the utmost value. I am also deeply grateful to Miss Hermia Oliver and her colleagues at Chatham House, whose superbly competent editorial services smoothed the passage of this book from typescript to print, and to Mrs Jean Brayshaw, Miss Judith Overend, and Miss Hazel Wilson, who shared the burden of the typing. Miss Ingrid Hudson gave valuable assistance in the compilation of the index.

My opinions, of course, are not necessarily endorsed by those who have helped me. The most I can hope is that some of them will agree with me for some of the time. To those who feel that I have gone badly astray I apologize for what must seem my obtusensss, with the reminder that even mistaken views, if sincerely held and honestly presented, can make their contribution towards the discovery of the truth. I would also remind them that it is as a friend of India and an admirer of Indian planning, with all its faults, that I write.

Leeds, *1965* A. H. H.

CONTENTS

TABLES

PRINCIPAL ABBREVIATIONS

AICC:	All-India Congress Committee
AR:	*Asian Recorder*
BDO:	Block Development Officer
CD:	Community Development
COPP:	Committee on Plan Projects
CSO:	Central Statistical Office
EC (date): no.:	Estimates Committee of the Lok Sabha (session, no. of report).
EE:	*Eastern Economist*
EW:	*Economic Weekly*
DO(*1*), *DO*(*2*), *DO* (*3*)	Planning Commission, *First/Second/Third Five-Year Plan, a Draft Outline* (1951, 1956 and 1960 respectively)
FC (*2*):	Report of Second Finance Commission (1957)
FC (*3*):	Report of Third Finance Commission (1961)
FYP(*1*), *FYP*(*2*), *FYP* (*3*)	Planning Commission, *First/Second/Third Five-Year Plan* (1952, 1956 and 1961 respectively). State plans are similarly abbreviated but are prefaced by the name of the state.
IAS:	Indian Administrative Service
ICIC:	Industrial Credit and Investment Corporation
IFC:	Industrial Finance Corporation
IIPA:	Indian Institute of Public Administration
IJPA:	*Indian Journal of Public Administration*
IISCO:	Indian Iron and Steel Company
IN:	*India News*
LSD:	Lok Sabha Debates (small roman figures denote volumes, arabic figures columns)
MTA:	Planning Commission, *The Third Plan—a Mid-Term Appraisal* (1963)
NDC:	National Development Council

NES:	National Extension Service
NIDC:	National Industrial Development Corporation
NPC:	National Planning Committee
PANL:	Indian Institute of Public Administration *Monthly Newsletter*
PD:	Parliamentary Debates
PEO:	Programme Evaluation Organization
PR (date):	Planning Commission, *Progress Report* (date)
RBIB:	*Reserve Bank of India Bulletin*
Rep.:	*Report*
TISCO:	Tata Iron and Steel Company
RFYP(1):	Planning Commission, *Review of the First Five-Year Plan* (1957)

Note on Sources

Official publications of the central government are all published in New Delhi; those of the state governments are published in the respective state capitals. The place of publication is not given for works published in the UK or the USA. All publications that are not included in the Abbreviations are referred to more briefly after the first reference to them.

I

INTRODUCTION

(i)

AFTER controversial and spectacular beginnings in the Russia of the 1920s and a rather chequered history, the idea of economic planning has become generally accepted. It now excites comparatively little enthusiasm and provokes intransigent opposition only from a few die-hards. Even countries which have formulated no five-year plans and established no planning commissions generally claim that they are guiding or controlling their economic development; and guidance and control imply the formulation of objectives for the economy as a whole. Few now believe that a government can confine itself to the encouragement of the spontaneous economic efforts of individuals and private associations; still fewer that it can passively accept the version of economic welfare to which such efforts give birth. However strong its theoretical commitment to *laissez-faire*, it is in the last resort dependent upon a public opinion which is fundamentally interventionist, in the sense of holding that those who possess political power are responsible for determining the rate of economic growth and for arranging the distribution of its fruits. Even if this were not so, the size of a government's expenditure on 'defence' and on other unavoidable forms of collective provision tends to compel it to accept political responsibility. The sheer pace of technological advance, particularly since the advent of automation, has further added to the interventionist pressures. The impact of technology on human welfare cannot, it is argued, be left to chance, and if it is to be regulated there is a strong case for regulating it in the light of coherently-formulated and politically-acceptable objectives, rather than by way of a series of *ad hoc* responses to specific emergencies.

The popularity of planning, however, proves neither its desirability nor its necessity, particularly as there is no general correlation, either positive or negative, between the extent of economic planning and the rate of economic growth. All planning aims at stepping up the rate of growth; but it does not necessarily succeed in doing so. Indeed, one might argue that in some cases the attempt to plan has actually retarded the rate of growth and that greater reliance on spontaneity would have brought much nearer the attainment of the planners' proclaimed objectives. Except in a completely socialized society, where virtually all economic initiative comes from the government, the variables responsible for growth, stagnation, or regression are difficult to isolate. It cannot be held, for instance, that France's coherent, carefully-drafted, and efficiently-executed post-war plans are *responsible* for the remarkable economic upsurge she has experienced since the middle 1950s. She might conceivably have achieved better results with less planning; for it is well known that Western Germany and Italy, both relatively unplanned countries, have made at least comparable advances. Nor can it be argued that Britain's relative stagnation during the 1950s was the inevitable result of an unplanned, or imperfectly-planned, economy. It may be that only by vigorous planning can we now emerge from stagnation; but it is fairly obvious that other methods *might* have been successfully employed at an earlier stage. If, for instance, the road-building and educational programmes had been considerably stepped up and a genuine assault made on Britain's ossified class structure, stagnation might have been avoided. The requirements for economic advance were, after all, fairly evident to intelligent and impartial people, and nothing in the nature of a *Commissariat du Plan* or a series of *Commissions de Modernisation* was needed to discover them.

Such scepticism about the value of planning as a stimulus to growth, tends, *prima facie*, to be reinforced by the experience of the underdeveloped countries. Most of these countries have plans, but there is no positive correlation between their rates of economic growth and the intelligence, vigour, and consistency with which their plans are formulated and executed. Both Thailand and the Philippines, where economic planning is rather a bad joke, have achieved comparatively high rates of growth. India, which has treated economic planning very seriously, is having a grim race between productivity and population. But this chance inverse correlation offers no basis for arguing that India's growth-rate would have been improved if she had taken planning *less* seriously. It may well be that, inadequate as her growth achievements have proved, they would have been even less adequate if the three Five-Year Plans had been jettisoned.

Moreover, as all governments, even in those countries which have made little attempt at coherent economic planning, are pursuing interventionist policies of one kind or another, it may be reasonable to suggest that these are likely to be more successful in promoting economic growth the better they are co-ordinated and the more broadly they are conceived. Alternatively, one may regard such interventionism as itself a variety of planning, in so far as each act of intervention is aimed—or so the government would claim—at widening some bottleneck which is currently restricting a desired economic flow. 'Bottleneck planning', in fact, has distinguished advocates.[1] However, to judge whether a specific act of

[1] See Albert O. Hirschman, *The Strategy of Economic Development* (1958).

intervention, or a series of such acts, has contributed to or detracted from economic growth is an exercise of some difficulty. It can of course be argued, even in these days, that nearly all the forms of interventionism of which the classical economists would have disapproved are deleterious to growth, which flourishes best in conditions of economic freedom. But what 'freedom' really means in this context can be discovered neither by poring over the classical texts nor by consulting the historical record.

Another view is that the positive correlation between planning and growth becomes manifest only when planning is total. This is the Communist argument. The half-planning characteristic of a mixed economy, it holds, inevitably gets involved in contradictions. The planners cannot tell private owners what to do with their resources, but only subject them to incentives, disincentives, and controls. Their response is always problematical, and the tendency is for the disincentives (e.g. taxation) and the controls (e.g. licences) to get seriously in the way of the only incentive that the private entrepreneur understands, i.e. profit. Furthermore, rapid economic advance is impossible unless the state has the means of organizing and co-ordinating the efforts of the mass of 'small men', i.e. peasants and artisans, who for that purpose must be detached from their individually-owned means of production and dragooned into collective farms and 'co-operatives'. Unless, therefore, industry is nationalized and agriculture collectivized, genuine economic planning remains a dream. Some economic advance, of course, may be achieved within the limits of capitalist society, but it will not be long before this is brought to a halt by the frictions generated by the class struggle.

This argument, although over-stated, is not entirely untrue. Mixed-economy planning does *tend* to experience precisely the contradictions predicted for it by the Communists. It is also a fact that a high rate of economic development can be achieved under 'total' planning—at human costs that vary from country to country and reached their horrifying zenith (or so one hopes) in the Soviet Union of the 1930s. But equally high rates have been achieved elsewhere by very different methods, as in Japan during the first two decades of this century. Even in the post-war period, the growth-rate of the Soviet Union has been rivalled, at times, by that of countries such as Japan and Mexico, and in the 1950s and early 1960s the leading countries of Western Europe have not been lagging far behind. It is only the persistent international self-advertisement of the Communist countries that has obscured these facts.

Economic planning, as such, offers no infallible recipe for achieving a high rate of growth. Nor, on the other hand, does lack of economic planning. In every case, the specific characteristics of growth—or of stagnation or retrogression—must be carefully studied, in an attempt to isolate causal factors. For a totally planned economy, this is comparatively easy, as the number of variables is drastically reduced. For a less-than-totally planned economy it is more difficult. In such an economy neither the impact of planning nor the efficiency of the planning apparatus can be assessed with more than approximate accuracy.

One would be wrong, however, to suggest that planning is of no importance except to the extent that it contributes to the growth of the economy. In conditions of underdevelopment, particularly when these are combined with rapid increases in population, economic growth is obviously the first priority; but it is not the only one. There may be a choice between two or more methods of economic growth, more or less equally rapid (as far as one can judge in advance), but very different in their social and political implications. There may even be a case for adopting methods which yield a less-than-optimum growth-rate, on the grounds that these are likely to secure a more equitable distribution of the fruits of growth or to ensure that economic power does not become dangerously concentrated in a few hands. Every government must have some regard for the type of society that its policies for the promotion of economic growth are tending to create—if only from the standpoint of securing its own base, i.e. maintaining the political system upon which it depends. A government which, in its single-minded concentration on annual percentage increases in the gross national product, makes no attempt to foresee the socio-political tensions which growth stimulates, and to develop policies for their containment, may be signing its own death-warrant. Through its neglect, moreover, it may well inaugurate a period of political chaos in which economic growth itself is brought to an end. One should add that even the apparently simple criterion of rapidity is by no means unambiguous. Fast growth now may, for a variety of reasons, mean slow growth later, and vice versa. It is therefore no conclusive criticism of a particular method of planning to allege that more rapid growth, long-term or short-term, might be achieved by the employment of other methods.

The effect of these rather obvious general considerations is to emphasize the need, in one's approach to economic planning problems, of an open-mindedness not always characteristic of planners, who tend to develop one-track minds and to fall in love with their own unilinear creations. This tendency is particularly marked in econometricians, who sometimes imagine that they possess a master-science capable of providing objective answers to questions which can be answered only tentatively and provisionally, by the addition to econometric calculation of sociological insight and political judgement.

This does not mean, however, that one has to adopt the position of the small but distinguished group of dogmatic anti-planners, represented in England by Professor P. T. Bauer, in the United States by Professor Milton

Friedmann, and in India by Professor B. R. Shenoy.[2] Indeed, it would appear that these are guilty of an 'economism' quite as serious as that sometimes displayed by the econometrician-planner and far more deleterious in its potential consequences. Nevertheless, a brief examination of their point of view may usefully preface a discussion of the kinds of planning that may conceivably be adopted.

Essentially, their argument is that attempts to plan an economy—at least by the methods now popular—have the effect of stultifying rather than stimulating economic development. They admit, of course, that economic growth *has* been achieved under planned economies, but consider that the real cost of such growth, both economically and politically, has been excessive. All planning, they believe, has a natural tendency to move towards those totalitarian forms which are the *sine qua non* for the realization of that effective centralized economic control which is the planner's ideal. As politics and economics are two sides of the same coin, economic totalitarianism implies political totalitarianism, which is an evil in itself, irrespective of whatever economic achievements it may be able to display. But these achievements themselves are less than optimum, as they are the product of a wasteful and therefore irrational kind of economic policy. A free economy, in fact, will always have a more favourable input-output ratio and attain a higher level of consumer satisfaction than even the most competently planned one. Therefore governments which wish to attain the highest possible rate of growth—particularly if they are anxious to combine this with the preservation or creation of an open society—must abjure planning as it is currently understood and practised. This warning applies no less to the underdeveloped countries than to the developed ones. Indeed, they need to take it even more seriously. Most of them already are subject to powerful totalitarian urges, to which planning can give dangerous and perhaps irresistible impetus; and most of them find the siren song of the planner peculiarly attractive, because it promises them a speedy advance to an affluence which seems unattainable by less heroic and spectacular methods.

The bogey of the anti-planners, the *fons et origo* of all the evils they denounce, is the concentration of economic decision-making (or at least the making of all key economic decisions) in the hands of the state. It is this that they find inherently incompatible with true economic rationality. Decentralization by the top-level authority to subordinate authorities in no way improves matters; for this is no more than a practice designed to endow an otherwise unworkable system with tolerable efficiency. Nor

[2] See P. T. Bauer and B. S. Yamey, *The Economics of Underdeveloped Countries* (1957); P. T. Bauer, *Indian Economic Policy and Development* (1961); B. R. Shenoy, 'A Note of Dissent on the Memorandum of the Panel of Economists', in *FYP(2): Basic Considerations Relating to the Plan Frame* (1955); Milton Friedmann, *Capitalism and Freedom* (1962).

is salvation to be found in limiting the top-level authority to the formulation of certain parameters, with which the lower echelons are induced to conform by the manipulation of the capital market, price structure, credit facilities, &c. This, again, is no more than a method of ensuring that, with a minimum expenditure of administrative energy, the essentially arbitrary decisions taken at the centre are duly executed. One method of planning may be better than another, but only to the extent that all forms of economic sin are not equally reprehensible. So long as a government remains committed to planning, it *ipso facto* commits itself to the basic evil of centralized economic decision-taking.

According to this view, economic rationality and political freedom alike demand that decision-taking responsibilities shall be widely dispersed among individuals and voluntary groups, and that ultimate sovereignty shall be exercised by the consumer, through the communication of his preferences via the complex nerve-system of the free market. This does not mean the total elimination of the state as a factor in economic development. The government still has important, indeed essential, things to do. It must maintain a framework of law and order which, among other things, ensures that competition is both free and fair and that obstacles to entrepreneurship are removed; and it must provide such essential infrastructural services as the individual entrepreneur is unwilling to provide or incapable of providing, or as can be provided more efficiently, economically, and conveniently by collective public effort. But it must not attempt to usurp the entrepreneurial function, or to decide, either in general or in particular, on the direction that economic development is to take.

Admittedly, by dint of some stretching of the meaning of words, one could present these limited state activities as a form of planning. After all, the creation or extension of the infrastructure involves some degree—and, in underdeveloped countries, a considerable degree—of public mobilization of the factors of production. So, indeed, does the maintenance of law and order, in so far as this makes calls on factors which could otherwise be allocated to direct productive uses. Moreover, it is inevitable that to some extent the state's provision of services will anticipate the predicted demands rather than follow the actual demands of the private entrepreneur. Even more significantly, entrepreneurship will itself be created or stimulated by the placing of government contracts, while the location and nature of the new infrastructural services will exercise a directive influence on entrepreneurial ambitions and choices. The state's own activities, however limited, will therefore help to determine the general direction of economic development; and hence the government, however committed it may be to economic freedom, must necessarily make a series of choices that can be regarded as adding up to something in the nature of planning.

At least, it is difficult to make a clear distinction, either theoretically or practically, between stimulatory activity of this sort and the more positive forms of intervention which the anti-planners so vigorously condemn.

Few of the anti-planners, however, would deny to the state a role in influencing the direction of economic development, and most would claim that a general distinction (however fuzzy it may be at the edges) can be drawn between this and the actual taking over and/or regulation by the state of the entrepreneurial function. In common parlance, and in actual practice, economic planning involves something more than maintaining order, enforcing a commercial code, preserving the soundness of the currency, providing (or paying others to provide) a system of communications, supplying electric power (either directly or by concession), making available (or supplementing) facilities for general and technical education, and—perhaps—offering the farmer the benefits of an agricultural extension service. These are minimal services, without which significant economic development is hardly conceivable. The possibilities of any kind of growth, planned or unplanned, overwhelmingly depend on the quantity and quality of such provision. The planning, as distinct from the mere stimulation, of growth involves the formulation of economic goals and the manipulation of the factors of production to secure their attainment. For the formulation of goals some kind of planning agency, however rudimentary, is required; for their attainment, the government must be prepared to adopt a variety of means, ranging from industrial licensing to public entrepreneurship, all of which involve interference with the mechanism of the free market.

It is institutions and measures of this kind that are regarded by the anti-planners as the quintessence of economic irrationality and the substructure of political illiberalism. That they should be adopted anywhere can be attributed only to ignorance or to malice. Many of the anti-planners show a strong preference for the latter explanation, tending to regard a predilection for economic planning as an expression of the sinister political ambitions of a power-hungry élite. The extreme view, which is constantly approached by P. T. Bauer, is to see the hand of Communism behind almost every essay in economic regulation, just as Walter Laqueur sees it—or used to—behind almost every expression of Arab nationalism.[3]

If we reject such views as more fitted for the nursery than for the study, we must try to find some more rational explanation of the fact that the advice of the anti-planners is so consistently disregarded, particularly by the governments of underdeveloped countries. Apart from the Soviet

[3] Bauer, *Ind. Econ. Pol.*, ch. 7; W. Z. Laqueur, *Communism and Nationalism in the Middle East* (1956).

Union and the more advanced of the 'people's democracies', these are the countries where belief in the virtues of planning is most strongly held. There are few which have not undertaken some form of planning exercise or at least recognized the need to do so, as soon as the necessary governmental apparatus can be created and the necessary administrative and technical skills mobilized. Some, indeed, take planning more seriously than others. In Morocco and in the Philippines[4] plans tend to be mere pieces of paper setting forth targets which are largely disregarded by the political and administrative authorities. In Turkey, 'commitment' to a plan does not mean much, as the ministries and other governmental agencies supposed to be implementing it usually insist on going their own empire-building ways. In Burma, political chaos makes any plan, however seriously intended, virtually inoperable; in Ceylon, racial and linguistic struggle has a not dissimilar effect. But all—even the Latin Americans—recognize the desirability of planning, and there are at least some underdeveloped countries outside the Communist bloc, such as India, Egypt, and Ghana, which are making a determined attempt to realize their desire.

The reasons for this near-unanimity are not far to seek. They have little to do with sinister political ambitions, the intensity of which is not positively correlated with that of enthusiasm for economic planning. In most of the underdeveloped countries, the placing of major reliance on individuals or voluntary associations spontaneously to initiate or carry forward economic development appears an unviable policy, particularly where economies have assumed a lop-sided position as a result of colonial or colonial-type relationships with the developed countries. Where effective and comparatively cheap public health measures have stimulated an unprecedentedly rapid population increase, heroic measures to augment agricultural production, step up the rate of capital formation, and find employment for the growing body of unemployed seem essential. Everywhere the 'revolution of rising expectations' pushes governments in the same direction. Opposition, both internal and external, to 'forced-draft' economic development has reached a low ebb. The vast majority of economists believe in its possibility and necessity, and even the United States administration has ceased to regard those countries which practise it as virtually lost to the free world. Ironically enough, the government of the world's greatest free-enterprise country now tries to persuade the underdeveloped recipients of its assistance to plan their economies more efficiently and coherently. The examples of the Soviet Union and Communist China, of course, continue to be influential, even in resolutely non-communist countries, if only because these provide the most recent

[4] R. S. Milne, ed., *Planning for Progress; the Administration of Economic Planning in the Philippines* (Manila, 1960); Albert Waterston, *Planning in Morocco* (1962).

and most successful illustrations of 'operation bootstrap'; and it is also realized that the free economic development which brought prosperity to Britain and the United States was made possible by the presence of certain unique and unrepeatable circumstances, such as the priority of the former and the frontier mentality of the latter, and that elsewhere the state necessarily played a more positive and creative role. Another factor is the determination of the underdeveloped countries to become powerful nation-states, capable of negotiating with their former masters on terms of equality. This, like population pressure, demands a speed of economic development which seems unlikely to be attained if the state confines itself to the normal infrastructure-providing and order-maintaining functions. Finally, it must be noted that many of the governing élites of the underdeveloped countries have little affection for capitalism or fear of authoritarianism. Although this may shock devotees of free institutions, it is deeply rooted in experience. Usually, the élite is drawn from social strata which lack sympathy with the mentality of the individual entrepreneur. For them, small free enterprise is identified with petty trade and and money-lending, while big free enterprise is tarred with the brush of colonialism. Further experience may modify these attitudes, but it is unlikely to eliminate them. As for the identification of economic planning with authoritarian or totalitarian politics, one can hardly expect this to evoke much pallor in the countenances of those who have never known effective democratic institutions and who regard the elimination of primary poverty, by whatever means may lie to hand, as their basic political problem.

These considerations do not offer a decisive answer to the arguments of the anti-planners;[5] but they indicate that any attempt, in any underdeveloped country, to pursue policies based on neo-*laissez-faire* theory is likely to encounter insuperable economic, social, and political obstacles. It may be taken for granted, therefore, that underdeveloped countries whose governments are sufficiently stable, determined, and competent will embark, or attempt to embark, on planned, forced-draft, economic development. In view of this, it is futile to put the question, 'Plan or no plan?' The only realistic question is 'What kind of planning?'

(ii)

The answer depends on factors which not only vary from country to country but display considerable fluidity, in so far as they are being constantly modified by the process of economic development itself.

[5] Such an answer may be found in e.g. Gunnar Myrdal, *Economic Theory and Underdeveloped Regions* (1957); *An International Economy* (1956); Raúl Prebisch, 'The Role of Commercial Policies in Underdeveloped Countries', in *Amer. Econ. R. Papers & Proc.*, May 1959; Thomas Balogh, *Unequal Partners* (1963); Benjamin Higgins, *Economic Development* (1959).

Socio-economic and political in character, they may be provisionally classified under six heads.

1. The first is the degree to which, in a given community, traditional social institutions and attitudes constitute a barrier to economic progress or impose limitations on it. This will obviously affect the approach to planning. Decisions in this area are both crucial and chancy. Mistakes frequently arise from the relative social isolation of the decision-takers, who form a would-be modern élite, more than half-committed to 'western' values and hence more than half-alienated from the majority of their fellow countrymen.[6] Where the traditional structure of thought and action appears irredeemably hostile to all useful forms of economic growth, and where the élite is endowed with exceptional power and authority, a thorough-going 'modernization' assault may be possible. Such was the policy Atatürk attempted in the Turkey of the 1920s and 1930s, with spectacular but rather superficial results. Neither his *charisma* nor the disciplined effort of his People's Republican Party was sufficient to do more than strengthen the rather rickety modern sector of the economy and the society, without disturbing the ancient one except by temporarily inhibiting its opportunities for self-expression. Normally, such an assault can be constructed with reasonable hopes of success only by a Communist Party which has put itself at the head of a victorious revolutionary movement and established its own political monopoly. Only then do the human costs of such an upheaval become politically tolerable. But even Communist Parties rarely attempt to rush the defences of the old society. Their strategy can be subtle as well as brutal. They have learnt from some forty years of experience that it is often better to try to use old institutions and attitudes for new purposes than to batter them down, leaving the human material too crushed and resentful to be able to make any significant contribution to socialist construction. If Communists have learnt this lesson, those élites who wield no more than a fraction of their power need to be even better pupils. The type of piecemeal social engineering, which aims at bending old institutions in new directions and mobilizing traditional motivations for non-traditional tasks, would seem to offer the more promising way forward, provided that gradualism does not become so gradual as to be self-defeating. It is perhaps significant that President Nasser, who could become one of the more successful of economic developers, and who is quite capable when the need arises of virtually destroying whole social classes, has not chosen to follow Kemal Atatürk in an assault on Islamic institutions. *Par excellence* in the Arabic world, he is the protagonist of a modernized Islam. The Indians, as we shall see, might

[6] See Edward Shils, 'The Intellectual, Public Opinion and Economic Development', in *Econ. Dev. & Cult. Change*, Oct. 1957; G. Morris Carstairs, *The Twice-Born: a Study of a Community of High-Caste Hindus* (1957).

well learn from his example to cope more effectively, if less noisily, with their own religiously-based social institutions.

2. A second and more specific variable, closely dependent on the social factors we have briefly glanced at, is the type, extent, and distribution of entrepreneurial talent in the community. This will influence, although not necessarily determine, the mode of economic development for which the government chooses to plan. Not to take advantage of the services of any group of entrepreneurs, industrial or agricultural, would appear to be the product of a sad sort of socialist dogmatism. On the other hand, nothing could be more futile than to try to stimulate an entrepreneurship which does not exist. Happily, there are signs that many governments of underdeveloped countries, whatever their ideological commitments, are approaching the 'public versus private' issue in a more empirical way than they are always prepared to admit. Here the example of the Turkey of the 1920s and 1930s is a positive one. Atatürk's government, arguing that if private developers could be persuaded to take the strain more would be achieved than if entrepreneurial responsibility were given to an ill-equipped and unenterprising administration, passed a variety of laws for the encouragement of industry. They failed, because there was virtually no one to encourage. The government then thought again and, stimulated but not dominated by the example of the USSR, went over to a policy of etatism, not because it wanted to 'build socialism' but because it wanted to build industry. The job was not well done, as the people available for doing it were poorly qualified and inadequately motivated; but at least the foundations of an industrial structure were laid.[7]

The Turks could make this necessary transition comparatively easily, because their ruling élite was empiricist in economic matters and dogmatic only in its nationalism and secularism. But even ideologically-committed governments may bow to the claims of reality. The Polish and Yugoslav governments, for instance, by halting and reversing the process of collectivization, have recognized the value of small-scale peasant entrepreneurship, theoretically unacceptable as it may be to the orthodox communist. The Pakistan government, in common with many others ideologically oriented towards free enterprise, has bowed to a reality of a different kind. Like the Turkish government, it found that stimulatory policies were achieving little, and hence went into business on its own account, through the Pakistan Industrial Development Corporation.[8] By contrast, the Indian government, committed to a 'socialist pattern'

[7] See Hanson and others, *The Structure and Control of State Enterprises in Turkey*, 2nd ed. (Ankara, Public Admin. Inst., mimeo., 1959).

[8] See 'The Pakistan Industrial Development Corporation', in U.N. Technical Assistance Programme, *Public Industrial Management in Asia and the Far East* (1960); Hanson, 'Public Authorities in Underdeveloped Countries', *Law and Contemporary Problems* (Durham, N.C.), Autumn 1961.

but finding free enterprise unexpectedly resilient, has given the private entrepreneur opportunities which were hardly envisaged by the Industrial Policy Resolution of 1956.

There are, of course, limits to such empiricism. Like Russia during the period of the New Economic Policy, Poland and Yugoslavia regard concessions to private enterprise as part of a policy of *reculer pour mieux sauter*. Like Japan in the late nineteenth century, Pakistan builds public enterprises only to sell them out to private investors when the time is ripe—a policy which she has already begun to operate. Moreover, any country with a plan that envisages the long-term development of the economy in specific directions is compelled to adopt a selective attitude towards private enterprise. The Turkish Law for the Encouragement of Industry did not provide its benefits to any industrialist who proposed to erect any kind of factory in any place; the Pakistan Industrial Finance Corporation does not offer its facilities to all and sundry. In India, no encouragement is given to the village money-lender, vigorous entrepreneur as he may be; while in Egypt large-scale landowning, however enterprising, is forbidden by law. Where plans do not discourage private enterprise on principle, they encourage it only to the extent that it presents the country with what are sometimes ambiguously described as 'new and necesssary' assets.

There are also limitations of a different sort, imposed by hard political necessity. Where, for instance, the greater part of the community's entrepreneurial talent is concentrated in the hands of a small, unpopular, and perhaps racially-distinct group, a government which attempts economic development by fostering its efforts may be heading for the kind of political chaos which may well bring any kind of growth prematurely to an end. Hence the distribution of entrepreneurship, in this sense, cannot be disregarded. It may be that Indians could undertake the commercial and industrial development of East Africa, Syrians and Lebanese that of West Africa, Copts that of Egypt, Hindus that of Pakistan, Chinese that of Indonesia, and Americans and Russians that of the whole world. Historically, such 'creative minorities' have often played a decisive role, and there is no reason to suppose that their magic has diminished. But in a world of intense nationalism, where 'exploitation' by the foreigner is more bitterly resented than 'exploitation' by the native, this path of economic advance is partly closed. The Armenians and the Greeks might have developed Turkey more effectively than the Sümerbank and the Etibank; but the Armenians were massacred and the Greeks expelled. If, therefore, the alternative is between development by private enterprise under the control of a foreign minority and development by public enterprise under indigenous control, the latter will often be chosen, even though it may be less efficient.

3. The third variable is the level of economic development already reached, and the pattern that it has assumed. This will largely determine the points of concentration in economic planning and also effect the initial balance between public and private effort. A country which is beginning its planned economic development from a very low level will have to give priority to certain kinds of infrastructural investment. In Somalia, for instance, economic growth must be based on improvements in education, public health, and communications. Neglect of such prerequisites brings its own punishment: at best, stagnation continues; at worst, the country is presented with a collection of expensive white elephants, like Riza Shah's notorious factories in the Iran of the 1930s. It is perhaps fortunate for such countries that the initial forms of investment, being fairly obvious, do not require very precise calculation, and that their potential yield is often sufficient to offset the wasteful utilization which is the result of low administrative capacity and widespread corruption. Not until comparatively high levels of economic development have been reached does the problem of finding the right investment mix become acute; and by that time there is at least the possibility, if 'investment in people' has been done with reasonable intelligence, that the means to its solution will be available.[9]

It follows that the higher the level of economic development the wider the area of choice for the planners. How far should resources be devoted to the intensification of activities for which the country concerned possesses 'natural' advantages, reinforced by experience, and how far to the diversification of the economy? Should a pattern of economic life which involves heavy dependence on overseas markets be continued, or should this be replaced by one based on greater self-sufficiency? What is the 'right' balance, in a given constellation of circumstances, between industrial, agricultural, and infrastructural investment? What relative emphasis should be placed, in the light of comparative factor costs and long-term objectives, on labour-intensive and capital-intensive forms of production? How are the frequently contradictory objectives of maximum speed of development and maximum provision of employment to be reconciled? What degree of priority, if any, should be given to the establishment of a heavy industrial 'base'? How much satisfaction is to be given to the clamant demand for investment in people (e.g. education, training, housing, and health) as against the equally clamant demand for investment in things (e.g. factories, dams, powerhouses, fertilizers, soil conservation, afforestation, fisheries, transport and communications, &c.)? Is a heavy investment in birth-control worth-while, in the light of possible alternative uses of the resources concerned? These are some of the choices which confront planners in a country which has reached the

[9] See S. Kuznets and others, *Economic Growth: Brazil, India, Japan* (1955), pp. 378–9.

developmental level of Egypt, Turkey, Ghana, India, Ceylon, or Chile.

At this stage, too, the 'public versus private' controversy begins to have real meaning. Up to a point, the state has neither the resources nor the administrative capacity to undertake much more than infrastructural investment, which in any case has very nearly absolute priority. Beyond that point, and dependent on the response shown by the private sector to the stimulus of infrastructural improvements, there are choices to be made between public and private investment. To some extent, these will be influenced by ideology, but less so, particularly in the non-communist countries, than is generally imagined. Whatever decisions are made in this area, and from whatever motive, their implications for financial and fiscal policy and for administrative organization are immense. Heavy reliance on the public sector involves a correspondingly heavy use of taxation and of borrowing as a means of capital accumulation. This has effects on the private sector's capacity to develop. It also engages the government in an effort to diversify the administrative and managerial ability at its disposal. The planners must therefore inquire to what extent and how quickly the necessary resources, material and human, can be mobilized and organized, and what effect the public use of these resources is likely to have on private incentives and opportunities. If, on the other hand, free enterprise is being called upon to carry a major share of the development burden, there is the problem of directing and regulating its efforts without simultaneously stultifying them.[10] In general, the puzzle is to devise policies which will enable each sector, whatever relative weight it may be given, to make its planned contribution.

4. In making such decisions, the planners confront a fourth variable: the existing political structure and the prevalent modes of political behaviour. The constitutional framework, the kind of government, and group interests: these will both create opportunities and impose limitations. Contradictions can easily arise between the facts of a political culture and the ideals of the planners. Such contradictions indeed will provide one of the themes of our subsequent analysis of the Indian planning process.

Where civil liberties prevail, the planner must walk warily among the jostling pressure groups and will be unable to use certain methods available to a regime in which such groups are held under firmer control. Indeed, in extreme circumstances there may be complete incompatibility between any kind of economic planning worthy of the name and any kind of political democracy that is more than a charade. For although planning and democracy are not necessarily antagonistic, democracy, 'the most sophisticated of all types of government and by far the most difficult to

[10] See W. Arthur Lewis, *The Theory of Economic Growth* (1955), ch. 7.

work', does not invariably offer the most favourable environment for the pursuit of economic growth. This is now somewhat reluctantly recognized even by those most devoted to democratic values. Thus, apropos the almost universal tendency in black Africa to create one-party systems, the editor of *Socialist Commentary* (February 1964) writes:

> There is no need to accept the fallacious argument that planning, on which speedy development now depends, thrives best in the absence of democratic freedoms, to appreciate the temptations with which these new governments are beset to suppress sectional opposition. Knowing our own difficulties in devising a workable incomes policy, we cannot be surprised when African leaders do not share our inbuilt enthusiasm for free trade unions and collective bargaining; or when, given the difficulties of curbing consumer expenditure, they prefer to dispense with an opposition demanding more consumption in preference to the sacrifices which more investment entails.

Federal institutions can also put a sizeable road-block in the path. The division of powers between a central government and regional governments is itself evidence of the existence of a rift in the political culture sufficiently serious to inhibit even formal unification. While in theory the existence of strong regional authorities could introduce a healthy element of decentralization into the process of economic planning, in practice the institutionalization of regional pressures tends to make it incoherent and even chaotic. This tendency may, to some extent, be offset by the reluctance of the regional governments (which are closer to the people than the central government) to impose taxation, and their consequent high degree of financial dependence on the centre; it will also be mitigated if the same political party holds office at both levels. In India, where both of these conditions are present, a system which makes economic planning a 'concurrent' function has proved workable. It nevertheless operates under very serious strains, as we shall see. In Nigeria, where the three major political parties are almost exclusively region-based, the problem of formulating and implementing a national economic plan is much more serious.

The relationship between political culture, political system, and mode of economic development is a very complex one, of which we possess insufficient knowledge. A useful advance towards the formulation of hypotheses in this field is made by Professor David E. Apter's seminal essay entitled 'System, Process and Politics of Economic Development'.[11] This author uses the comparative method first to 'specify the differences, from the range of characteristics distributed among the rapidly growing number of new nations, in the natures of political systems'; and secondly to 'investigate the kinds of response to the problems of technological innovation that these differing systems evoke'. By doing so, he hopes to

[11] B. F. Hoselitz and W. E. Moore, eds., *Industrialization and Society* (The Hague, 1963).

provide a 'more systematic basis' for assessing the capacity of each system 'to absorb change and generate further innovation' and for indicating what types of economic development are in practice available to it.

His model is based on a threefold classification of political systems, viz. (1) the mobilization system; (2) the reconciliation system; and (3) the modernizing autocracy. The first embodies a new leadership's determination to create 'a new system of loyalties and ideas, . . . focused around the concept that economic progress is the basis for modern society', and distinguishes itself by five characteristics: '(*a*) hierarchical authority; (*b*) total allegiance; (*c*) tactical flexibility; (*d*) unitarism; and (*e*) ideological specialization.' The Soviet Union is the best example of such a system, while among the new non-Communist states those that exhibit its features most clearly are Ghana and Guinea.

The second type, the 'reconciliation system', is notable for the 'high value it places on compromises between groups which express prevailing political objectives and views', and characterized by '(*a*) pyramidal authority; (*b*) multiple loyalties; (*c*) necessity for compromise; (*d*) pluralism; and (*e*) ideological diffuseness'. Among the underdeveloped countries, India and Nigeria provide obvious if widely dissimilar examples.

The third type, the 'modernizing autocracy', which Professor Apter illustrates from the Kingdom of Buganda, is rather less clearly defined. Somewhat tautologically, he suggests that one of its 'crucial typical features' is 'its ability to absorb change so long as the system of authority is not affected by it'—surely a capacity which any political system, almost by definition, possesses. The characteristics of a 'modernizing autocracy' are set down as '(*a*) hierarchical authority; (*b*) exclusivism; (*c*) strategic flexibility; (*d*) unitarism; and (*e*) neo-traditionalism.'

The provisional nature of this classification will be obvious from the imperfect comparability of the five characteristics listed for each of the three types. Nevertheless, as a conceptual framework designed to illuminate the impact of political organization on economic development and vice versa it has merits which become apparent when Professor Apter moves on from the 'developmental types' to the 'process variables'.

Of 'process' in the 'mobilization type' of system he writes:

> First, government becomes progressively more enmeshed in investment and in seeking to control its side-effects in the society. Furthermore, the costs of coercion result in diverting revenue, hitherto available for investment, into military and police activities and other punitive institutions. Third, bargaining in external relations intensifies the need for stronger standing armies and better military technology . . . . Consequently, the costs of government rise continuously, and difficulties in spending investment funds for the expansion of government enterprises are met by raising public revenues and by the intensification of the mobilization process. Simultaneously, an increasing proportion of

revenue is diverted to non-productive enterprise, i.e. to system-maintenance rather than to development.

In a 'reconciliation system', on the other hand,

> The government's need is to reconcile diverse interests; it is mediating, integrating, and above all, coordinating, rather than organizing and mobilizing. The mobilization system fights society; the reconciliation system is a prisoner of society. Government may show that goals required by public expectations cannot, in the absence of forced measures, be achieved. The public are unwilling to sacrifice current consumption for the sake of future consumption and otherwise to modify their behaviour in order to attain these goals. For this reason, while the government may be democratic, it may break down in unfulfilment, corruption and compromise.

As for the 'modernizing autocracy', although this 'can experiment with goals without paying the penalties of immediate instability', it nevertheless 'confronts . . . the possibility that changes effected in the economic sphere may eventually threaten the principle of hierarchical authority, with consequent demands for the substantial alteration of the system'. Indeed, 'modernizing autocracies' in the new nations 'can promote economic development with stability only in the short run, because they cannot absorb the new élites sufficiently into the traditional hierarchy'.

It may be that Professor Apter's classifications and correlations are too simple and rigid, but one can hardly quarrel with his conclusion, viz:

> Each type of system under discussion represents a different set of relationships between goals, costs, coercion and information. The evaluation of data about these variables should indicate the limits within which economic development and technological change can occur in each nation. Consideration of these variables should elicit the preferences which decision-makers will demonstrate by virtue of the system variables within which they must operate. It should indicate the effects that economic development will have on the systems themselves—including the transformation of one type into another.

This general approach offers the key to an understanding of many of the problems of Indian planning with which we shall later be concerned. It is one of the major themes of this study that many of the difficulties that the Indian planners have encountered spring from the fact that they are constantly attempting to transcend the limitations of the 'reconciliation system' within which they have to operate and tending to assume the existence of attitudes and the viability of techniques which are meaningful only within the framework of a 'mobilization system'.

5. Professor Apter's classification roughly corresponds with Professor Sigmund's distinction between radical, reformist, and traditional regimes.[12] These adjectives emphasize the link between system and *ideology*, which is

[12] P. E. Sigmund, Jr., *The Ideologies of the Developing Nations* (1963), p. 9.

the fifth of the variables here to be considered. An ideology, says Professor Sigmund, quoting the dictionary, is 'a systematic scheme or coordinated body of ideas about human life or culture'. To this he adds the connotations of commitment, of action-orientation, and 'even of conscious or unconscious distortion of the facts to fit a pre-established doctrine'. In the context of economic planning, an ideology normally has three interrelated roles to play, viz. (1) to indicate objectives and prescribe the general strategic lines of advance; (2) to persuade the masses that these represent a 'general will' and should therefore be supported as a matter of moral duty as well as one of self-interest; and (3) to give the élite that has conceived the plan and accepted responsibility for its implementation a self-confidence and a capacity for dynamic action based on a sense of its own 'historic mission'.

The importance of ideology varies directly with the degree of conscious involvement in the planning process that the government is demanding of its subjects. If planning requires a deliberate reorientation of individual and collective objectives, the replacement of old 'world views' by new ones of the appropriate sort is very important. It is also very difficult—perhaps impossible—in the absence of a charismatic leader to act as the ideological fountain-head and a disciplined party to keep his ideas flowing throughout the community. If, on the other hand, the élite has placed its faith in a less heroic kind of planning, relying more on existing motivations, the need to do battle on the ideological front will be correspondingly diminished. This does not mean that the latter kind of planning is easier than the former—indeed, it may be much more difficult—but simply that it demands less effort directed towards changing public opinion.

It would be a mistake, however, to imagine that the élite is free to select, *à la carte*, the kind of ideology that fits in best with the kind of planning it has chosen to adopt. On the contrary, the élite's ideology has usually already acquired its general shape from experiences—such as the struggle for national liberation—that have little or nothing to do with planning. The pattern of planning, therefore, will itself be to some extent ideologically determined. This means that ideology, like the rest of the variables here under consideration, will impose limitations as well as offer opportunities. Perhaps the most widespread ideology among the leaders of the 'new' nations is that which might be described—if the expression did not have such unfortunate connotations—as 'national socialism'. This is a product of the fight for national freedom and against 'foreign exploitation', during the course of which the importance of solidarity and of disciplined activity is emphasized and opinion tends to harden against indigenous capitalism, which is suspected, at best, of lukewarmness in its support for the national movement, and at worst of collaboration with the foreign enemy. These experiences predispose the nationalist élite, once it has acquired political power, to think in terms of carrying over the techniques of the anti-foreign struggle into the struggle for economic development. Hence the emphasis on public enterprise, the predilection for centralized control of production and distribution, and the suspicion of foreign capital, particularly when it comes from private sources.

For ideological reasons, therefore, the élite has already made an implicit choice among the various modes of economic planning that are available. Whether that choice corresponds with needs and possibilities can be discovered only by further experience. As Professor Sigmund says, 'problems may be created . . . if ideological preconceptions interfere with a realistic assessment of the best method to achieve the goal of maximum economic growth'.

Guinea, for instance, has already been forced to dismantle its State Trading Commission, through which it attempted to nationalize all import and export activity and to control most of the distribution of goods. The Guineans learnt that it was difficult, if not impossible, to centralize in a government bureau in Conakry all the countless decisions involved in distribution; while retaining a centralized development plan, they have now substantially decentralized decision-making in this area.

Generalizing, he suggests that 'the difficulty with the nationalist ideology of economic development is that it does not distinguish between the new-style economically productive business innovators and the old-style non-productive absentee landlords and money-lenders'.[13] One might add that if the former class is non-existent or too weak to be of significance, this lack of distinction may be of no practical importance, at least in the short run. If, on the other hand, it is all ready to be up and doing but receives nothing but discouragement from the government, economic development will be held back, unless the government itself is well enough organized to undertake the entrepreneurial role with equal effectiveness—an unlikely contingency.

A different kind of ideological presupposition, however, can have equally deleterious consequences. There are some governments which, dominated by classes solely interested in the protection of their private property rights, carry devotion to free enterprise to the point of economic absurdity. Committed to the stimulation of something that is virtually non-existent, they have encouraged corruption rather than production—to quote the words of Sutan Sjariar. Significantly, many of these have been within the American sphere of influence—a fact which has made the 'new' countries outside that sphere reluctant to accept economic advice from the United States, even when it is perfectly sound.

[13] Ibid. p. 19.

As 'a set of doctrines about the proper methods to attain economic progress', an ideology of some kind is indispensable. Pure empiricism is an unattainable and unacceptable ideal. The essential function of ideology, as Professor Sigmund says, is 'to carry the nation through the period of modernization of traditional society and to justify the ensuing sacrifices and dislocations'.[14] If it succeeds, its long-term contribution to development may be positive, even though some of its shorter-term impacts are negative. The main danger lies not in having certain ideological preconceptions, but in refusing to modify them when experience has proved them inadequately realistic, or in maintaining an ideological 'purity' which contradicts the policies actually being pursued. Ideology then ceases to be an accelerator and becomes a brake. This often happens, for an ideology has a certain built-in rigidity, like a religion.

6. The sixth and last variable, the administrative capacity of the state, has obvious implications for economic planning. Here the contradictions between ideological prescriptions and practical possibilities are liable to be most acute; for 'new' governments are rarely sufficiently aware of the inadequacies of their administrative machines, and are typically prone to imagine that the problems of policy implementation can be solved by enthusiastic improvisation.

That the structure and quality of the administration are limiting factors has received plenty of emphasis in recent years. Planning is essentially a series of consecutive and interlinked administrative acts, which require for their efficient performance a rationally organized, properly trained, and adequately motivated bureaucracy. The basic Weberian characteristics of hierarchy, discipline, impartiality, and functional specificity are, of course, vital prerequisites, whatever the type of economic planning a country has chosen to adopt. Many countries have inherited from a previous political order bureaucracies which display at least some of these characteristics, albeit imperfectly. Kemal Atatürk's government, for instance, had at its disposal an Ottoman bureaucracy which, wooden and unimaginative as it may have been, was at least hierarchically organized and adequately disciplined. Without it, even the comparatively modest etatist achievements of the 1930s would have been impossible. The Indians, more fortunate, carried with the minto independence a bureaucracy which was not only 'rational' in the Weberian sense but headed by an élite corps of first-rate ability and almost unique adaptability. At the other end of the scale there are countries, of which the Congo is the most distressing example, that are faced with the task of building up an entirely new bureaucracy from pitifully inadequate material. Clearly, the kind of economic planning in which an economically underdeveloped country can engage—and indeed the very possibility of its undertaking

[14] Ibid. p. 37.

any kind of plan—will depend on the position which it occupies in the bureaucratic spectrum between India at the one extreme and the Congo at the other.

It will also depend on bureaucratic motivations and on the relationship between bureaucracy and society. To those familiar with underdeveloped countries, the prevalence of a contradiction between the formal organization and the inner dynamism of a bureaucracy is taken for granted. In a society where social relationships are highly personalized, where the ethos of the tribe or joint family prevails, where paternalistic attitudes predominate, where status is more important than achievement, and where function is characterized by diffuseness rather than by specificity, the scales are weighted against 'rationality' in bureaucratic behaviour-patterns; for the man who becomes a bureaucrat does not contract out of society and cannot bring to his work a set of values and criteria which are totally alien to his non-working hours. A totalitarian dictatorship, of course, can *impose* rationality, up to a point, by intensive training and indoctrination supplemented by a judicious mixture of stick and carrot; but even such a regime is often compelled to admit defeat, in respect of specific if not of general objectives, by 'bad administrative habits, a legacy from the old social order'.

The 'social relations' of the bureaucracy are also important in another sense. If economic planning relies heavily on co-operation and mutual understanding between administration and people, a revolution both in bureaucratic attitudes towards the populace and in popular attitudes towards the bureaucracy is required. For if any single quality may be regarded as characteristic of the 'classical' bureaucrat, it is exclusiveness or casteism; to which the prevalent response among the victims of bureaucratic malpractice (for as such do those who have regular dealings with the bureaucracy normally regard themselves) is compounded, in various proportions, of fear, suspicion, and hatred. To break down these barriers is a difficult task in any country; it is positively daunting in most of the underdeveloped countries, where the bureaucrat, as a literate and comparatively sophisticated city dweller, belongs to a different culture from the majority of his clients, who are illiterate and superstitious villagers. The problem here is not merely one of breaking down the barriers to communication; it is one of persuading both parties of the *need* to communicate. The bureaucrat is determined to avoid rural dirt, and his steps up the hierarchical ladder are not likely to be accelerated by his becoming the 'father' of a community of mud-hut dwellers; the peasant, for his part, tends to associate anything that comes from an urban-oriented government with the tax-gatherer and the policeman, neither of them popular figures. So the village wallows in its squalor and superstition, while the bureaucrat goes off to the capital city, where, if not lucky enough to get into the Atomic Energy Authority or the Hydro-Electric Commission, he may find himself concerned with the drafting of plans for rural uplift. Thus the bureaucracy acts simultaneously as a promoter of economic growth and as an obstacle to it.

To establish communication, the initiative must come from the bureaucracy; and this implies a change in its attitudes. With economic development at the top of the agenda, the bureaucrat is expected to show concern for the popular welfare, to exercise initiative, to become action-minded and achievement-oriented. Schools of public administration are established, not merely to teach him new methods but to provide him with a new vision. Ideological commitment as well as technical competence is demanded of him.

This change is difficult to make. Even where the bureaucrat has nothing to lose, and perhaps something to gain, by adopting a 'modern' outlook, he is subject to the powerful forces of inertia associated with routine, the very life-blood of officialdom. But all too often the bureaucratic corps has developed a vested interest in the maintenance of the existing system, which by multiplying formalities multiplies employment, and which guarantees to its personnel certain expectations which the transition to 'action-mindedness' can scarcely fail to undermine, in so far as merit measured by achievement will replace seniority and blamelessness as the main criterion for promotion. Hence the persistent, unpublicized, and frequently successful struggle of the bureaucracy to preserve intact the old rules of business and conduct, which even in a country such as India have suffered surprisingly few changes since pre-independence days, when law and order were the government's principal concerns and economic planning was unknown.

Even the most determined government is perplexed by the bureaucracy' sresistance to modernization, which confronts it with the unenviable alternative of leaving things more or less as they are or undermining the morale of the officials upon whom it depends. Perhaps the most useful thing it can do, without danger to itself, is to improve bureaucratic skills and increase bureaucratic diversity. The latter, of course, is particularly important when the government has assumed a major share of the responsibility for promoting economic growth. The official appointed to manage a steel-mill, to vet applications for industrial licences, or to supervise the administration of co-operative credit societies needs different qualifications from those of the district officer, chief of police, or departmental accountant. In theory, this is universally recognized, but the practice of regarding the 'generalist' as omnicompetent dies hard, particularly in countries influenced by the traditions of the British Civil Service. What is more serious is the capacity of the existing system to 'absorb' the possessors of new skills. Forcibly subjected to the normal bureaucratic routine, they either submit and become conformists or seize their first opportunity to escape to the private sector, either at home or abroad. Those who choose the latter course are usually the more able.

(iii)

This brief account of the limitations imposed on the economic planner by the nature of the administrative system through which he has to work inevitably sounds pessimistic. When these limitations are added to the others, it seems unlikely that any plan for economic growth, however subtly devised, stands much chance of success. Such pessimism would appear to be confirmed by the fact that the underdeveloped world is now strewn with the wreckage of economic plans which were begun amid great enthusiasm and high hopes. The correct conclusion, however, is not that all these were foredoomed to failure, but rather that their chances of success would have been much greater if the obstacles had been more clearly foreseen and more correctly assessed, and that the first task of the planner is not to do exercises in economic arithmetic, essential as these may be, but to understand the social and political structure of his community.

All that has hitherto been said may be condensed into one simple proposition: that, assuming a country's socio-political system makes planned economic development possible, and also assuming an adequate quantum of foreign aid (an indispensable prerequisite for any economy which is not already on the verge of 'take-off') becomes available, the main reasons for failure or for inadequate performance are haste and ignorance. When these dominate political counsels, and particularly when they are reinforced by corruption and by a predilection for prestigious display, the usual result is the familiar phenomenon of façade development, which can equally well be illustrated by the erection of a palatial headquarters for the administratively feeble Development Corporation in the Western Region of Nigeria, by the creation of a totally uneconomic iron and steel plant in Colombia, or by the building of impressive but redundant sugar refineries in Turkey, as by Riza Shah's notorious factories to which reference has already been made. There is hardly a country so underdeveloped that it cannot build factories, hospitals, schools, offices, roads, and even dams, if sufficient foreign assistance, financial and technical, is made available to it. All this is 'easy'. It creates an impression of governmental vigour and achieves nothing but the unproductive consumption of scarce resources. The real test of a government's capacity to plan economic development is its success in creating a balanced, self-sustaining, and dynamic productive system; in building up a stable and committed labour force; in training teachers, doctors, nurses, and technicians and providing them with adequate motivations and opportunities; in phasing the provision of the necessary overheads; and in ensuring that expensive collectively-provided benefits, such as irrigation waters, are adequately used. All this is difficult, and the most difficult thing of all is the least spectacular but most important: the implanting of developmental potential in a stagnant, tradition-bound system of agriculture. Compared with this, putting up and even operating a steel mill is child's play.

These are the *economic* problems which, for their solution, demand *social* changes triggered off by *political* action. In this sense, planning is a total process, and it is as such that its Indian version will be discussed here. Ideally, one should be able to bring to Indian planning a series of widely-verified propositions, purporting to establish universally-valid correlations between the economic, social, and political variables, so that the specific phenomena could be significantly located within a general planning typology. This, indeed, is the distant goal on which the eyes of all serious students of planning are fixed. As the summary of Professor Apter's theories has shown, some advance towards it has already been made; but as yet our knowledge is too incomplete, our experience too short, and our weapons of conceptualization too blunt to permit the formulation of any but the most primitive and tentative of classificatory and explicatory schemes. The immediate need is to bring our various fragmentary hypotheses to bear on the planning experiences of individual countries, with the object of writing descriptive studies which will at least contain some of the material required for answering the more general questions, particularly those which are of urgent practical interest to the countries concerned. The present study is one of many contributions towards such an accumulation of knowledge.

In the first part, after a summary of what might be called the prehistory of Indian planning, there is a description of the present planning machinery, followed by a detailed account of the making and implementing of the three Five-Year Plans. In the second part, attention is shifted to specific political and administrative problems, in order to elucidate some of the reasons for the successes and failures of the Indian planners in the pursuit of their objectives. It is in this part, one hopes, that certain conclusions of fairly general applicability will emerge.

PART 1

THE PLANNERS AND THE PLANS

II

THE PRECURSORS

(i)

THE literature on Indian planning contains only scattered references to the efforts made before independence to draw up blueprints for economic development. In comparison with the plan reports of the 1950s and 1960s, these documents were crude enough. They lacked statistical foundation; their attempts at economic calculation were rudimentary; they evaded rather than faced a host of social and administrative problems; and some of them were wildly over-optimistic. Nevertheless they are worth studying; for they familiarized educated people with the *idea* of planning, revealed the scale of the tasks that had to be attempted, defined some of the areas where concentrated effort was required, sketched out many specific projects which were subsequently taken up, and indicated some of the decisions that had to be made before planning could become a practical as distinct from a theoretical exercise.

The popularization of the planning idea was perhaps their most significant achievement; for in the 1930s the need for planning was by no means self-evident, particularly in India. Although the two Russian Five-Year Plans were evoking wide international interest, they also created the suspicion that economic planning and political totalitarianism might be inseparably allied. Even Nehru, convinced planner as he was, occasionally argued with himself about the extent to which political liberty might justifiably be sacrificed on the altar of economic development.[1] In India moreover, it was difficult for the national movement to give any sustained attention to problems of post-independence economic organization. Many patriots felt that even to discuss them distracted effort from the national struggle, and considered that once the stranglehold of British imperialism had been broken the forces of economic development would be spontaneously released. Even on the extreme left, where commitment to planning was most firm, there was some suspicion of economic scheme-making. Had Marx attempted to blueprint Communism? Did the Bolsheviks waste their time, before the Revolution, on theoretical planning exercises?

A further discouragement to those who thought that Congress ought not to wait for independence before taking planning seriously was the fact

[1] See, for instance, *The Discovery of India* (1956), p. 406.

that discussions of economic policy tended to divide rather than to unite the national movement. The two most influential congressmen, Mahatma Gandhi and Jawaharlal Nehru, saw eye to eye on very few social and economic questions, and among the mass of Congress supporters there was a variety of opinion on such fundamental matters as socialism versus capitalism, factory industry versus cottage industry, and centralization versus decentralization. Big business, influential in Congress policy-making circles if only because of the financial support which it provided, was 'definitely apprehensive and critical'[2] about planning itself, and many Gandhians, suspecting that planning and centralized industrialization were but two sides of the same coin, showed an equal lack of enthusiasm, although for quite different reasons.[3] These differences of approach became acute during the discussions of Congress's National Planning Committee (NPC), appointed in 1938.

That this Committee came into existence, however, is testimony to the force of the arguments on the other side. These were given political influence by the development of a socialist-minded left wing within the national movement. Jawaharlal Nehru and Subhas Chandra Bose, successively Congress Presidents, were both socialists, and the former had particularly close relations with the Congress Socialist Party (founded in 1934), which headed the list of its economic objectives with: 'Development of economic life of the country to be planned and controlled by the State'.[4] These leftist tendencies, which reflected growing industrial and agrarian unrest and were stimulated by the apparent successes of socialist economic planning in the Soviet Union, found expression in official Congress policy resolutions, beginning with the Lahore resolution of 1929, which stated that 'in order to remove the poverty and misery of the Indian people and to ameliorate the conditions of the masses, it is essential to make revolutionary changes in the present economic and social structure of society and to remove gross inequalities'. This was followed by the famous Karachi resolution which, although making no overt declaration in favour of national planning, included the following items:

> Currency and exchange shall be regulated in the national interest. . . .
>
> The State shall own or control key industries and services, mineral resources, railways, waterways, shipping and other means of public transport.

[2] Ibid. pp. 400–1.

[3] The differences between Gandhi and Nehru on the subject of economic planning were recently the subject of exchanges in the Lok Sabha. Minoo Masani, Swatantra leader and self-styled Gandhian, quoted a letter written by Gandhi on 29 June 1939 to Rajkumari Amrit Kaur, which included the following passage: 'I have advised you about Jawaharlal's invitation. In my opinion, the whole of his planning is a waste of effort. But he cannot be satisfied with anything that is not big' (LSD, 21 Aug. 1961, lvii, 4302).

[4] For the full list, see Saul Rose, *Socialism in Southern Asia* (1959), p. 16.

In 1936 the Lucknow resolution on the agrarian programme recognized that the state had a duty 'to provide work for the rural unemployed masses' and instructed the Working Committee to consult provincial Congress committees, together with 'such peasant organisations as the Working Committee thought fit', in drawing up an all-India programme of agrarian reform. The subjects on which provincial committees were called upon to make recommendations included 'fostering industries for relieving rural unemployment'. The agrarian programme eventually formulated, although disappointing to the socialist elements in the national movement, made an important contribution towards the popularization of the Congress cause in the elections of 1937.

In the same year, the Working Committee passed a resolution recommending that the Congress ministries which had taken office in eight of the provinces should appoint a 'Committee of Experts to consider urgent and vital problems the solution of which is necessary to any scheme of national reconstruction and social planning'. It followed this up, nearly a year later, by authorizing the President of Congress, as a 'preliminary step', to assemble a conference of Ministers of Industry. This conference, duly called together by Subhas Chandra Bose in October 1938, was responsible for the creation of the Congress's NPC.[5]

In this recital of events we see another reason for the national movement's enhanced interest in economic matters. Although condemning the 1935 constitution as a 'slave constitution' and a 'charter of bondage', Congress decided to fight the provincial elections, emerged as the strongest party in eight provinces, and, after certain 'assurances' had been fought for and won, took office. Its object in doing so was not to bring about a breakdown of the constitution, as some of the leftist elements proposed, but to use the powers of provincial government in what were considered the interests of the masses. As Professor Morris-Jones has said, the Congress Governments 'did take the lead and did govern'.[6] It was this acceptance of ministerial responsibility that gave immediacy to questions of economic policy and underlined the need for planning. In addition to 'a full plan which would apply to a free India', Congress required some indication of 'what should be done now, and under present conditions, in the various departments of national activity'.[7] This need was emphasized by the realization that there were many problems, such as irrigation, soil conservation, the prevention of flooding, the distribution of hydraulically-generated electricity, and the eradication of malaria, which could not be effectively dealt with by isolated action on the part of the various

[5] All these resolutions are conveniently set out in K. T. Shah, ed., *Report of the National Planning Committee* (Bombay, June 1949).

[6] W. H. Morris-Jones, *Parliament in India* (1957), p. 66.

[7] Chairman Nehru's Memo. of 4 June 1939, in Shah, *Rep. NPC.*

provinces.[8] Hence the Congress's understanding of the importance of economic planning may be regarded, in part, as one of the fruits of its brief experience of provincial office under the 1935 constitution. It should be noted, nevertheless, that such understanding was far more evident at the national level of the Congress organization than at the provincial levels themselves, where leading personalities had little opportunity—and sometimes little capacity—to think seriously about the wider and longer-term aspects of their responsibilities.

This, indeed, was one of the formidable list of difficulties that the newly-fledged NPC faced. As catalogued by its Chairman, Jawaharlal Nehru, they included (1) lack of data and statistics; (2) lack of co-operation from the government of India; (3) lack of real interest in all-India planning on the part of the provincial governments; (4) lack of enthusiasm among 'important elements in the Congress'; and (5) the apprehensions of big business, whose representatives participated in the Committee because they felt that they could look after their interests 'better from inside . . . than from outside'.[9] To these should be added the vagueness and ambiguity of the Congress's economic policy resolutions which the Committee had to take as its frame of reference.

On the other hand, the NPC was not tilling completely virgin soil. One previous attempt had been made to produce an Indian economic plan. In 1934 that distinguished and far-seeing engineer, Sir M. Visvesvarayya, had published his *Planned Economy for India.*[10] As Visvesvarayya was himself a member of the NPC, the ideas he had then expressed must have had some influence on its deliberations. In any case, these ideas are important enough in themselves to detain us briefly before passing on to the Committee's work.

For Visvesvarayya the essence of planning was industrialization. His proposed doubling of the national income over a period of ten years involved an increase of only Rs500 crores in agricultural production, while industrial production was to go up from Rs400 crores to Rs2,000 crores. Simultaneously the total population supported by agriculture was to decrease by 50 million, while that employed in industry was to increase by 35 million.[11] In the light of subsequent experience, so rapid an industrial revolution, supported by so inadequate an agricultural base,

[8] See Pattabhi Sitaramayya, *History of the Indian National Congress* (Bombay, 1947), ii. 96.

[9] Nehru, *Discovery of India*, pp. 400–1.

[10] Bangalore City. Quotations are from the 2nd ed. of 1936. Visvesvarayya had a profound influence on the industrial development of his native Mysore, the most go-ahead of all the princely states. 'The decade from 1931–41 witnessed the largest growth of industrial enterprises in the State.' By 1944 'almost all the industries mentioned by Sir M. Visvesvarayya—under medium and small—in his book 'Planned Economy for India' [were] 'practised in Mysore' (Mysore, Commissioner of Econ. Dev. & Planning, *Introduction to the Development Schemes of Mysore* (1946), pp. 6–7).

[11] pp. 196–7.

seems visionary particularly as private enterprise, loan financed, was apparently expected to provide most of the impetus. But similar criticism may be made of most pre-independence plans, and Visvesvarayya's looked timid enough in comparison with those that appeared in the 1940s. The NPC was to envisage a 200–300 per cent increase in national wealth over ten years; the 'Bombay' planners thought that total income could be trebled and per capita income doubled over fifteen years; S. N. Agarwal's 'Gandhian' plan was to project a 300 per cent rise in per capita income over ten years; and M. N. Roy's 'People's' plan was to consider feasible, over a similar period, a 400 per cent increase in agricultural output, a 600 per cent increase in industrial output, and a 300 per cent increase in the standard of living.[12] Such were the miracles of productivity that the ending of imperialism was to make possible. Visvesvarayya was at least free from the grosser of these illusions.

More interesting than his economic projections is his suggested planning machinery, to which he gave some detailed thought. At the centre he envisaged an Economic Council consisting mainly of expert economists and representative businessmen. This and its Standing Committee would play an advisory and supervisory role in co-operation with an official body called the Development Committee. Operational responsibility would rest with a Central Development Department, headed by a Cabinet Minister who would have at his disposal the 'brains-trusting' services of a General Economic Staff, whose expert membership would overlap with that of the Development Committee, with which it would work in close co-operation. Similar bodies with similar relationships were to be established at the provincial level, while in the districts and the cities Local Economic Councils would function as 'both thinking and executive bodies'.[13]

This scheme sounds more clumsy than it actually was, and in any case its purpose is of greater interest than its specific institutional arrangements. Basically, there are two parallel organizations, 'one consisting of business interests and the other of executive officials of the government department, both working together for common objects'.[14] The intention is to enlist the co-operation of the 'people' not merely in the implementation of the plan but in its formulation. In this respect Visvesvarayya anticipates the rather abortive efforts at popular participation made in the 1950s; but the emphasis that he places on the businessman is almost unique. As we shall see, private business has rarely been the darling of Indian planners, and it could be argued that Visvesvarayya, in emphasizing the need to enlist its active and willing co-operation, was wiser than some of his successors.

It is not surprising, however, that the NPC failed to echo its author's

[12] For further information about these plans, see below, pp. 41 ff. [13] pp. 180–4. [14] p. 183.

enthusiasm for private business enterprise as the main agency of economic development. Most of the businessmen on the Committee appeared to be lukewarm about planning itself; the Gandhians were hostile to large-scale industry and commerce; and Nehru, who provided most of the leadership and inspiration, was at this period a Marxian socialist. Nehru's role in the NPC, indeed, was similar to his role in the wider Congress organization. He wanted as much socialism as possible but was always prepared to compromise in the interests of unity.[15] Looking back at the Committee's vast and many-sided schemes, he subsequently wrote:

> All this was to be attempted in the context of democratic freedom and with a large measure of cooperation of some at least of the groups who were normally opposed to socialistic doctrine. The cooperation seemed to me worthwhile even if it involved toning down or weakening the plan in some respects. . . . So long as a big step in the right direction was taken, I felt that the very dynamism involved in the process of change would facilitate further adaptation and progress. If conflict was inevitable, it had to be faced; but if it could be avoided or minimized that was an obvious gain.[16]

Agreement was easily obtained on the nationalization of defence industries and the ownership of public utilities by some 'organ of the state', but a minority of the Committee—representing an important body of opinion in Congress and in the country—stood out against proposals for state ownership, as distinct from state control, of other key industries and of banking and insurance, in spite of Nehru's attempts to show that the relevant Congress resolutions indicated 'an approval of socialistic theories'.[17]

Nevertheless, advocates of *laissez-faire* could hardly feel encouraged by the reports of the twenty-nine sub-committees into which the NPC divided itself or by the resolutions founded thereon. All businesses were to be licensed by public authority, banking was to be both licensed and regulated, insurance was to be supervised by a National Insurance Board, strict state control was to be exercised over the coal industry, and the sizes of manufacturing units were to be decided 'in case of each industry by qualified authority'.[18] As for agriculture, individual enterprise

[15] It takes two to make a compromise, and the Congress 'old guard' was not so completely wedded to *immobilisme* as some have imagined. For Vallabhbhai Patel's and Nehru's views on the role of socialists in the Congress, see Sitaramayya, *Hist. INC*, pp. 32, 33–34.
[16] *Discovery of India*, p. 406.
[17] Note of Congress Policy, 21 Dec. 1938, in Shah, *Rep. NPC*, p. 35. Nehru apparently always held, despite massive evidence to the contrary, that Congress, *de facto*, went socialist in 1929. In a recent Lok Sabha debate, he said: 'Ever since 1929, the Congress has had two objectives in view, democracy and socialism. Socialism was not put in its objective and creed and all that but in its resolutions it appeared. Gradually, the idea has developed, but the basic concept has been there in the Congress since 1929' (21 Aug. 1961, lvii, 3671).
[18] Shah, *Rep. NPC*, pp. 139, 142, 158–61, 165, 169.

was regarded as merely temporary—to be 'subordinated to the needs of the community', while the transition to collective or co-operative farming was being made.[19] In many of these recommendations the general shape of post-independence planning was foreshadowed.

But considerable ambiguity remained, for no final comprehensive report was ever presented and even the NPC's resolutions on the reports of its sub-committees contained many inconsistencies. It was not clear, for instance, whether the resolutions on engineering and on fuel and power advocated state ownership or state control or a bit of both. After the Public Finance Sub-Committee had submitted its report the issue became even less clear, as this body proposed that, as a means of accumulating revenue 'for the nation-building activities of the State', all key industries 'should be progressively nationalized and administered by a statutory corporation [*sic*] created for the purpose'. Of this proposal the NPC could only say that it raised a matter of 'fundamental principle' on which there should be further discussion.[20] Already, as in a glass darkly, one can see the controversies that raged around the two Industrial Policy Resolutions of 1948 and 1956.

Another major problem, unsolved by the NPC and still in the field of controversy, was that of the respective roles of cottage and large-scale industries. This overlapped the capitalism v. socialism dispute, in that Nehru and the businessmen agreed that large-scale industries were essential to India's economic development, whereas the Gandhians (including the socialists among them) put their faith in small-scale, decentralized enterprise. Nehru, as Chairman, undertook at the outset the task of proving that Congress policy, as expressed in the resolutions of the All-India Congress Committee (AICC), was compatible with large-scale industrialization. His major obstacle was the 1934 resolution of the Working Committee on Swadeshi, which reaffirmed in 'unequivocal terms' the impermissibility of 'competition . . . on Congress platforms and in Congress exhibitions between mill-made cloth and hand-spun and hand-woven Khadi', and stated that for articles other than cloth Congress activity should be 'restricted to useful articles manufactured in India through cottage and other small industries which are in need of popular education for their support'. He circumvented this apparently sizeable road-block in the following way:

> It is clear that the Congress considered it unnecessary to push large-scale industries through its organisation and left this to the State as well as to their own resources. It did not decide in any way against such large-scale industry. Now that the Congress is, to some extent, identifying itself with the State, it cannot ignore the question of establishing and encouraging large-scale industries. . . . It is clear therefore that not only is it open to this Committee

[19] Ibid. pp. 223–4. [20] Ibid. pp. 188–9.

and to the Planning Commission to consider the whole question of large-scale industries in India, in all its aspects, but that the Committee will be failing in its duty if it did not do so. There can be no planning if such Planning does not include big industries. But in making our plans we have to remember the basic Congress policy of encouraging cottage industries.[21]

This was on 21 December 1938. On 4 June 1939 he found it necessary to return to the point, this time asserting that there was no conflict between cottage and large-scale industries.[22]

With guidance so ambiguous and opinion so divided, the NPC's conclusions on this subject could not reach a high level of consistency. The resolution on the Engineering Sub-Committee's report emphasized both the importance of heavy industry and the need to protect cottage industry from its competition. The resolution on the Manufacturing Industries Sub-Committee report called for a 'judicious adjustment' between the two. The view of the Rural and Cottage Industries Sub-Committees, that the large-scale competitors of cottage industries should be owned or controlled by the state in order to achieve 'proper coordination', was accepted; but its recommendation that the cottage industries should be 'organized and developed', as distinct from supported by the state, was sent back for reconsideration. When the NPC resumed work in 1945, after its wartime hibernation, a new element was injected into the discussion by the 'Revised Instructions and Directions to Sub-Committees', which suggested that support and protection of cottage industries was necessary only until the country reached 'the ideal of self-sufficiency'.[23] Once again issues of fundamental importance had been raised only to be left in confusion. Nehru's 'step by step' policy was producing some muddy compromises.

Only in its agricultural recommendations did the NPC express 'clear-cut social objectives',[24] and even then it avoided detailed proposals. All agricultural land, mines, quarries, rivers, and forests were to 'vest absolutely in the people of India collectively'. Intermediaries were to be abolished, and the introduction of various forms of 'restricted cooperation' (i.e. credit, marketing, and purchasing societies) was to lead the agriculturalist towards collectivization and 'other forms of cooperative farming.'[25] These recommendations vaguely prefigure the government's agricultural policies of the 1950s.

The modesty of the NPC's accomplishments was partly due to the inadequate financial support which it received from the provincial governments, partly to the lack of sustained interest in its work by more than a handful of its members, among whom Jawaharlal Nehru, its inspirer

[21] Ibid. pp. 28, 36–37. [22] Ibid. p. 41. [23] Ibid. p. 63.

[24] In the reports of the sub-committees, writes Dr N. Das, 'one misses . . . the clear-cut social objectives which, later, formed the basis of the Report of the Planning Commission' (*The Public Sector* (Bombay, 1961), p. 5).

[25] Shah, *Rep. NPC*, p. 222–3.

and Chairman, and K. T. Shah, its faithful Secretary, were the most prominent. These difficulties prevented it from completing its work in six to twelve months, as was originally and rather optimistically planned, with the result that the outbreak of war caught it in mid-stream. From then on, as Nehru said, it 'languished'.[26] Nehru's arrest gave it what was virtually the death-blow. The others were not prepared to carry on without his co-operation, and he himself, while in prison, was prevented by the government from studying papers and reports.[27] From August 1940 to September 1945 the NPC had formal existence only. After the end of the war three further sessions were held, but these, in the absence of sub-committee meetings and of any response from the provinces to an appeal for funds, accomplished practically nothing. Shah himself had to revise the sub-committee reports and bring them up to date, and their publication was made possible only as a result of a loan obtained from J. R. D. Tata & Sons. At the final session, held on 26 March 1949, and attended by only five members, including the Chairman and Secretary, a decision was taken not to scrutinize the sub-committee reports, but 'to place the result of their labours before the National Congress, the Central and Provincial Government [*sic*] and the people generally for such use as they deem fit to make of it'.[28]

(ii)

In the meantime, planning had been taken up by the Indian government itself, as a response to the exigencies of war and the anticipated needs of post-war reconstruction.

Although this 'conversion of the bureaucracy' had all the appearance of suddenness, precedents for an official interest in planning are not entirely lacking. As a response to the circumstances of the World Economic Crisis two official advisory bodies on planning had been established in the United Provinces during the 1930s, and both had produced reports of considerable interest. The first committee, under the chairmanship of Khan Bahadur Maulvi Muhammad Obaidur Rahman Khan, was the product of a resolution passed by the Legislative Council on 8 December 1933, on the initiative of the leader of the opposition, C. Y. Chintamani: 'That this council recommends to the Government to set up a Committee to draw up a five-years' plan of economic development for these provinces, with instructions to report also on the financial measures necessary to give effect to their recommendations.'

Established late in 1934, the committee, which did not bring any great sense of urgency to its task, reported in 1937. In presenting a modest programme designed to cost 17 lakhs of rupees, it argued that planning, although a 'delicate and difficult art', succeeded better than 'piecemeal

[26] See ibid. pp. 126–7. [27] Nehru, *Discovery of India*, p. 409.
[28] Shah, *Rep. NPC*, pp. 16–19, 244–5, 257.

and isolated developmental activities', and had the advantages of giving zest to the routine of administration, eliminating the 'personal factor' and making possible 'the apportionment of praise and blame for officials while at the same time engendering a spirit of emulation among the people themselves'.[29]

The programme placed main emphasis on agriculture, rural uplift, sanitation, and education, and, anticipating 'democratic decentralization', proposed that the panchayats, assisted by 'resident organisers', should become the basic developmental agencies.

> Economic planning superimposed from without [said the report] would be a waste of money, personnel and energy. A multiplicity of advisers and inspectors would not only lead to confusion but also strengthen the present belief among the masses, baffling all initiative and progress, that nothing substantial could come in the village except from outside. In the revival of the corporate life of the village through its traditional organ, the *panchayat*, lies the hope of economic planning.[30]

The other committee had 'Industries Reorganisation' as its subject. Established in November 1932, it reported in 1934, recommending that the Industries Department of the U.P. government should have 'a definite programme of work for say a period of five years' aiming at 'a systematic co-relation of the various branches of the work in order to achieve certain definite objects'. Its 159 recommendations included the development of the sugar, oil, and glass industries and the organization of the marketing of the products of selected minor and cottage industries; and it emphasized the importance of 'helping educated young men of the middle classes to set up in industry or business or failing that to find employment therein'.[31]

Although historically interesting, these plans did not amount to much. They aroused no enthusiasm among educated Indians, who were even more distrustful of a government bearing gifts than of one wielding *lathis*. The wartime plans, however, were in a very different category. The distrust, of course, remained and even deepened, but no one could now doubt the seriousness of the government's intentions or fail to notice that a big planning effort was being made. The whole attitude of the bureaucracy towards the role of the state in economic development had been transformed by the war, and it was obvious that any independent or semi-independent post-war Indian government would have to adopt an attitude towards detailed and comprehensive plans which, although not primarily Indian in inspiration, deserved respect as the product of hard work and deep thought.

[29] *Rep. on Econ. Planning in the UP* (1937), p. 4. [30] Ibid. p. 84.
[31] U.P., Industries Reorg. Ctee, *Rep.* (1934), p. 94.

The first step, taken—ironically enough—at about the same time as the Congress's own Planning Committee went into hibernation, was the creation of an official Board of Industrial and Scientific Research. This was followed by the establishment, under the Viceroy's chairmanship, of a Reconstruction Committee of the Council, equipped with a separate secretariat and associated with a number of expert committees representing provincial governments, state governments, and non-official organizations. In June 1944 a Planning and Development Department, under Sir Ardeshir Dalal, was brought into existence, and simultaneously the provincial governments and state governments were requested to establish their own planning organizations. Both they and the central departments were to draw up five-year plans. To provide general guidance the Reconstruction Committee formulated and published its *Second Report on Reconstruction Planning* (1945), which provided 'a summary of the views of the Departments of the Government of India on the issues that arise in so far as it has been possible to formulate them with the material and in the time at their disposal'.

This document was surprisingly bold and even socialistic in character. It proposed a fifteen-year 'perspective' plan embodying 'a more detailed plan for the first five years'. Among its aims was the removal of 'the existing glaring anomaly of immense wealth side by side with abject poverty'. Means included the provision of various amenities for the poorer classes, e.g. education, medical relief, and water supply; 'positive measures to secure a fairer deal for labour', e.g. reasonable wages, maternity and sickness benefit, holidays with pay, &c.; and the extension of small-scale and cottage industries. It not only recognized the need for large-scale industry but envisaged ownership by the state of those 'new and necessary' enterprises 'for which private capital may not be forthcoming'. It gave priority to the development of power resources and of 'important capital goods' industries'. It envisaged a balanced regional development in which industry would not be confined to a few provinces but 'extended in a rational manner over the whole of India', and endorsed at least one of the principles of Gandhian economics by insisting that industries should be 'located in rural areas or small towns when expansion is easy and labour can be obtained in close proximity to the village of its origin', and by proclaiming that 'the creation of a large industrial population divorced from its village of origin and living in squalor in large cities' should 'at all costs be avoided'. In matters of rural development it emphasized the importance of building up an infrastructure (e.g. irrigation, anti-erosion, and land-reclamation measures), pointed to the need for popular participation through co-operative societies and panchayats, and anticipated the 'block' system which was subsequently to provide the administrative foundation of the Community

Development (CD) Programme.[32] On administration, even then recognized as the potential Achilles' heel of any Indian development programme, its words deserve to be quoted in full:

> It must be recognized that present administration methods which have developed over a long period of years may not be suited to modern times nor be adequate for carrying out comprehensive development schemes. This is true not only of government departments at the Centre and in the Provinces, but even in the work of the Patwari in the villages. It is perhaps most marked in the districts.
>
> A comprehensive review of office methods and routine, of reports and returns, in fact of the whole system, is required. A better paid, and better qualified subordinate staff should be provided and when this is done it should be possible to secure a reduction in numbers. To carry out this work specially selected officers are required who have made a study of the subject; they should be capable of analysing the work done by every individual and be able to distinguish between what is and what is not essential and what simplifications of method are possible.[33]

In short, one may look in vain for any fundamental objective or method of the five-year plans of the 1950s which is not foreshadowed in this remarkable documentary product of the latter days of British rule.

Of the other central planning documents issued at this time, one of the most important was the Industrial Policy Statement of 1945,[34] which gave greater precision to the principles of industrial reconstruction embodied in the *Second Report on Reconstruction Planning*. Twenty major industries were to be brought under the control of the central government, while other 'basic industries of national importance' were to be nationalized if adequate private capital for their development was not forthcoming. Aircraft, automobiles, tractors, chemicals, dyes, iron and steel, prime movers, electrical machinery, machine tools, electro-chemicals, and non-ferrous metals were mentioned specifically as potential candidates for this treatment. All others were to be left to private enterprise, but subjected to licensing, investment controls, and measures to ensure a fair deal for labour, the elimination of excessive profits, and the improvement of the quality of products. The government was also to have 'primary responsibility' for the development of transport facilities, power production, scientific and industrial research, and technical education.

There is really very little to distinguish this statement of intentions from the Industrial Policy Resolutions of 1948 and 1956; and it might equally well have guided the actual practice, in matters of industrial development, of the government of independent India.

[32] Ibid. pp. 3–9. [33] Ibid. pp. 14–15.
[34] Summarized in Advisory Planning Board (APB), *Rep., Dec. 1946* (1947).

In the meantime, detailed plans were being produced by the Planning Department, by the other departments of the central government, by 'industrial panels', by the provinces and states, and by a number of specially constituted committees. The provincial plans, as the Advisory Planning Board of 1946 subsequently reported, varied in merit. Some were 'fairly integrated wholes', but others 'little more than collections of departmental schemes hastily thrown together'.[35] Their deficiencies were not entirely the fault of the provinces, for although the centre promised Rs1,000 crores worth of assistance (which subsequently failed to materialize) it gave little guidance, and the absence of adequate statistics was crippling. Hence most of them were similar to the U.P. plan, which had to admit the 'impracticability' of laying down 'definite quantitative or numerical targets in the elucidation of the general objective of the plan'.[36] Of the princely states Mysore did best, as might have been expected.[37]

Work of more importance was done by the industrial panels (of which twenty-two out of a total of thirty-one had reported by the end of 1946) and by the specialized committees. The years 1944–6 saw the publication of the 'Kharegat' report on agricultural development, the' Burns' report on the technological possibilities of agricultural development, the 'Gadgil' report on agricultural credit, the 'Saraiyya' report on co-operation, the 'Krishnamachari' report on agricultural prices, the report on the reorganization and expansion of the railways, the 'Nagpur' report on roads, the 'Adarkar' report on sickness insurance for industrial workers, the 'Bhore' report on public health, the 'Sargent' report on education, and the series of reports on irrigation projects. Some of these made extremely radical proposals. The 'Burns' report, for instance, did not hesitate to recommend 'some type of collective organization' for agriculture, and even drew favourable attention to 'the great Soviet experiment';[38] while the 'Saraiyya' report canvassed the possibilities of co-operative farming.[39] At the same time, they often displayed an understandable timidity when confronted by the need for socio-political, as distinct from purely economic, reforms. Thus the 'Burns' report envisaged

[35] Ibid. p. 68.
[36] U.P., *Post-War Reconstruction and Development Schemes* (*2nd Draft*) (1945), p. iv.
[37] See P. H. Krishna Rao, *A Plan for the Economic Development of Mysore* (*Draft*) (1946); Commissioner of Econ. Dev. & Planning, Mysore, *Introd. to Dev. Schemes.*
[38] W. Burns, *Technological Possibilities of Agricultural Development in India* (Lahore, 1944), p. 127.
[39] Cooperative Planning Committee appointed by the government of India on the recommendation of the 14th Registrars' Conference, *Rep.* (1945), pp. 27–34. It advocated the 'selection of centrally placed villages as cultural centres for a group of say four or five villages'. Here, it said, 'in a small settlement could live under reasonable conditions, the doctors, nurses, school teachers and subordinate officials responsible for providing the necessary services for the group'. The district officer should be assisted by a social development officer, with supervisory responsibilities for health, education, and agricultural and veterinary services, and each province should be equipped with a Land Development Service to look after soil conservation and irrigation.

reliance for reforming initiative on 'that kind of man who is in control of anything from a single village to a small state, the man variously called inamdar, jagirdar, sardar, taluqdar or zamindar'.[40] From the standpoint of the immediate future, the most important of this series were the reports on the irrigation projects. One need only mention the names Tungabhadra, Mahanadi, Damodar, Kosi, and Rihand to appreciate their significance.

It cannot be said that all this planning activity convinced Indian nationalists of the goodwill of the alien government. Few, perhaps, took much interest in it, as at this time all eyes were concentrated on Simla and the other places where Congress, Muslim League, and the Viceroy were conducting their abortive tripartite negotiations about India's political future. Of those that did give ear, few troubled to listen very carefully before passing unfavourable judgement. The reaction of S. N. Agarwal, a young Gandhian currently attempting to give coherent expression to the Mahatma's economic doctrines, was probably typical: 'I am convinced that Delhi is hastily planning for Britain and not for India .... Such economic plans drawn up by the Government of India are only meant to by-pass and side-track the fundamental issue of Indian independence.'[41]

Today, as might be expected, those Indians who have troubled to study them are far less hostile. Dr Ambirajan, an historian of Indian planning, writes:

> It was no doubt piecemeal planning, it was bureaucracy-bred and red-tape governed, but all the same these plans and proposals were the first attempts at national planning at Government level, and even though they lacked correlation and the necessary statistical background, they certainly helped to create an atmosphere for planning along the right lines.[42]

Indeed, they did much more; for many of the projects of this period were started during the later 1940s and eventually incorporated in the First Five-Year Plan. It can be fairly claimed, moreover, that they laid down fundamental principles that eventually became part—although, of course, without acknowledgement—of India's planning ideology.

Of the criticisms that can be directed at them, the most valid are those made by Professor C. N. Vakil and Dr P. R. Brahmanand, viz. that they 'lacked the necessary integration and coordination' and that they misconceived the nature of the post-war economic situation. The

[40] *Technological Possibilities*, p. 120.

[41] S. N. Agarwal, *The Gandhian Plan* (Bombay, 1944). This document is now reproduced in Shriman Narayan, *Principles of Gandhian Planning* (Allahabad, 1960). (Agarwal, who subsequently dropped his caste name, became a member of the Planning Commission with special responsibility for agriculture.)

[42] A. Ambirajan, *A Grammar of Indian Planning* (Bombay, 1959), pp. 60–61.

assumptions behind them were those of deflation, falling prices, and free availability of sterling balances. None of these came to pass, nor did the government 'visualise that the post-war period would be characterised by an acute imbalance between food needs and internal agricultural production, and that a large portion of its resources would have to be necessarily devoted for purposes of importing food grains'.[43] But what government anywhere in the world, it may be asked, *did* correctly envisage the post-war economic situation, and how many governments succeeded in producing 'integrated and coordinated' plans to deal with it?

(iii)

The most immediate, and in some ways most valuable, result of this official planning activity was that it stimulated Indians to try to do better than the imperialists. Of the three 'private' plans that all appeared in 1944, the best known—or at least the most publicized abroad—was the so-called 'Bombay' plan,[44] sponsored by some of India's most distinguished industrialists: Sir Purshotamdas Thakurdas, J. D. Tata, Sir Ardeshir Dalal, A. D. Shroff, Dr John Matthai, D. G. Birla, Sir Shri Ram, and Kasturbhai Lalbhai. Like Sir M. Visvesvarayya's plan, this emphasized industrialization, proposing a quintupling of industrial production in fifteen years. In some respects the methods envisaged anticipated those of the three Five-Year Plans. 'Production of power and capital goods' was to have priority, but to avoid hardship, prevent inflation, provide employment, and economize capital resources, 'the fullest possible use' was to be made of small-scale and cottage industries in the production of consumer goods.[45]

This realistic approach to an ideology-bedevilled subject was, however, counterbalanced by a great deal of utopianism in other parts of the plan. Of agricultural organization, for instance, it was said that 'cooperative farming appears to present less difficulties than any other method', while finance was held to offer serious problems only to those 'whose minds were still dominated by orthodox financial concepts'. Of a proposed total of Rs10,000 crores capital investment, no less than Rs3,400 crores was to come from 'created money'. To offset the inflationary effects of this deficit financing, 'practically every aspect of economic life will have to be so rigorously controlled by government that individual liberty and freedom of enterprise will suffer a temporary eclipse'. Coming from

[43] C. N. Vakil and P. R. Brahamanda, *Planning for a Shortage Economy: the Indian Experiment* (Bombay, 1952), p. 12. As a secondary source of information on the official plans described above, there is nothing superior to N. K. Sovani, *Planning of Post-War Economic Development in India* (Poona, Gokhale Inst. Pol. & Econ., 1951). This is particularly good on the provincial plans.

[44] Purshotamdas Thakurdas & others, *A Plan of Economic Development for India* (1944).

[45] Ibid. pp. 7, 27.

industrialists, these were strong words; but their authors paid no attention to the enormous administrative problems involved. Even their suggestions about planning machinery were tantalizingly brief: a National Planning Committee 'in which the various interests concerned will be represented and to which the responsibility for drawing up plans will be delegated', and a Supreme Economic Council for executive duties.[46]

The 'People's' plan,[47] promoted by M. N. Roy and the Indian Federation of Labour, was a very different kind of document. Whereas the 'Bombay' plan had an empirical approach and said little about the kind of society at which it was aiming, the 'People's' plan assumed the desirability (and necessity) of socialism and was much concerned with the expansion of the public sector of the economy at the expense of the private. In this respect it anticipated the 'socialist pattern' of the Avadi resolution and the Second Five-Year Plan. But it adopted a healthily sceptical attitude towards the famous and much-publicized Russian example. For instance, in arguing for giving consumer goods some priority over producer goods, it pointed out that India, unlike the USSR, had no need for a great defence effort. Moreover, it insisted that collectivization, which it presented as the long-term solution for agricultural problems, should be strictly voluntary. It was also distinguished from both the 'Bombay' plan and the Russian plans by the emphasis that it placed on agricultural development. Such emphasis was needed, in so far as the planning-equals-industrialization equation had been too easily accepted by most would-be developers; unfortunately the justification was in terms of economic arguments that were patently unsound.[48]

On finance, it was even more utopian than the 'Bombay' plan, for it believed that with the extension of public ownership to industry and collective ownership to agriculture, development could become 'self-financing' within six years. It also proposed a control of private industry and commerce, during the 'transitional' period, so rigorous that complete stultification could have been the only result.[49]

Another distinctive feature was its complete lack of enthusiasm for cottage industries, any 'considerable use' of which it held to be 'precluded by the very spirit of the plan which is to open up for the people a prospect of a continually improving standard of living'.[50] This *non sequitur*, no doubt, reflected the Marxian socialist's contempt for 'petty production'.

No such prejudices inspired the author of the 'Gandhian' plan. On the contrary, he was full of a typically Gandhian dislike of the large-scale and the centralized in all fields of human endeavour. Essentially, this

[46] Ibid. pp. 6, 8, 30, 45.

[47] B. N. Banerjee & others, *People's Plan for Economic Development of India, being the Report of the Post-War Reconstruction Committee of the Indian Federation of Labour* (Delhi, 1944).

[48] See M. N. Roy's Foreword, pp. ii & 4. [49] Ibid. p. 42.

[50] See G. D. Parikh's Foreword to the 2nd ed., p. vii.

was no plan at all, but an essay in economic morality, preaching the virtues of simplicity, manual labour, local self-sufficiency, decentralization, and the independent village community. Where strictly economic arguments were used, they merely provided additional support for proposals based on moral principles. Thus for instance:

> In Europe and America mechanization was a necessity because those countries had abundant capital and suffered from the scarcity of labour. To exploit and develop their natural resources fully, they were compelled to invoke the assistance of machinery, but in India, conditions are just the reverse of those obtaining in the Western countries; there is paucity of capital and abundance of labour.

This, of course, was quite a reputable argument. Few but the most ardent Gandhians, however, could have followed the logic of Mr Agarwal's case for natural as distinct from artificial fertilizers, or for the location of key industries in villages.[51]

Even so, reality breaks through. Despite his predilection for simplicity and decentralization, Mr Agarwal was constrained to produce a long list of 'basic' industries and to allocate to them a sum of Rs1,000 crores out of a capital budget of Rs3,500 crores. Similarly, in spite of his apparent belief that the panchayat could do most of the necessary administration, he proposed many new functions for the central government. It was to run public utilities, to acquire all private industrial enterprises, and during the 'transition' to exercise 'rigid control and supervision' over them. But his lack of interest in how all this could be done was almost complete.[52]

This plan revealed the impossibility of reducing Mahatma Gandhi's scattered and sometimes ambiguous *dicta* on economic organization to a logical and coherent system. Yet it was not without a more positive importance. In its emphasis on popular participation and its insistence that the willing co-operation of the ordinary villager must be won, it anticipated *panchayati raj*. Also of value was its attempt—however unrealistic—to define the objectives of planning in terms of a *way of life*, as well as in terms of percentage increases in per capita income. Whereas the authors of the 'People's' plan simply assumed that their variety of socialism was good, Mr Agarwal tried to *demonstrate* the goodness of his. The planners of the 1950s, in presenting their case for the 'socialist pattern', were following in his footsteps.

Despite their obvious faults and inadequacies, all these plans, both official and unofficial, had useful ideas to offer. Professor A. K. Das Gupta thus ably summarizes their long-term significance:

> Structurally the First Five-Year Plan may be said to be an offspring of the Bombay Plan. The formulation of a growth target, the application of the

[51] Agarwal, *Gandhian Plan*, pp. 38, 68, 95. [52] Ibid. pp. 79–83, 103 *passim*.

concept of investment by 'created money' which is another name for 'deficit-financing'—all these are apparently derived from the Bombay Plan. If, however, the structure is based on the Bombay Plan, its inspiration is derived from the National Planning Committee and its contents largely from the official Reconstruction Programmes. The later emphasis on Socialism may perhaps be traced to the framework of the People's Plan.[53]

(iv)

The immediate utility of these plans, however, was very limited. Any government with serious intentions about economic development would need a clearer definition of objectives, a more detailed assessment of financial and administrative resources, a more precise allocation of these resources among competing claims, and above all, a planning *machine*. Embryonically, such a machine had existed in the form of the Planning and Development Department, but this had been disbanded in 1946, despite Congress protests. The question of what should replace it was referred by the interim government to an Advisory Planning Board, with K. C. Neogy as Chairman and K. T. Shah and Penderel Moon as joint Secretaries. Its terms of reference were 'to do a rapid survey of the field and to make recommendations regarding the coordination and improvement of planning, and as regards objectives and priorities and the future machinery of planning'. It was given only two months to produce its report,[54] which saw the light on 18 December 1946.

As to objectives and priorities, it expressed general approval of the proposals contained in the government of India's *Second Report on Reconstruction Planning*. On public ownership, it quoted the Statement of Industrial Policy of 1945, but issued the following warning: 'We would give it . . . as our opinion that if the present juncture of the State attempted to take into its own hands the ownership and management of a large range of industries, the industrial development of the country might not be very rapid.' The Board also pointed out that 'the enlargement of State enterprise' would demand 'considerable alteration in the present methods of governmental administration'. It went on to express its hostility to 'foreign vested interests' in Indian industry and to give its approval to the development of cottage industries.[55]

None of this was very important, particularly as it was accompanied by notes of dissent from the Chairman, the Secretary (G. L. Mehta)

[53] Foreword to Radharani Choudhury, *The Plans for Economic Development of India* (Calcutta, 1959), p. vii.

[54] APB *Rep., Dec. 1946.* There is a brief account of its work in EC, 1957–8: *21*, pp. 1–2. Nehru, who was responsible for its appointment, subsequently admitted that 'it worked necessarily with some superficiality' (*Speeches*, 2nd ed. (1958), i. 100).

[55] APB *Rep.*, pp. 2–19.

and Sir Pheroze Kharegat.[56] Nor was anything new to be learnt from the appendices, which summarized, for greater convenience, the existing plans of the central departments, the provincial governments, and the industrial panels. The only vital part of the Board's report concerned the machinery of planning.[57]

First, it defined as follows the 'legitimate functions of any planning machinery established under the Central Government': (1) scrutinizing and co-ordinating provincial plans and the plans of the central departments; (2) advising on the allocation of central funds for development purposes; (3) formulating plans for the development of major industries and important minerals; (4) advising on state aid to and state control of industries; (5) advising on internal and foreign trade; (6) advising on monetary and financial policy; (7) watching and stimulating progress, compiling and publishing statistics, suggesting adjustments and modifications, and initiating new plans; (8) allocating material resources in short supply; and (9) examining the implications of scientific research and discovery for social welfare. Despite the lack of specific mention of agriculture, this was the clearest definition of the planning function that had emerged from any deliberations. Indeed, it listed more or less precisely what the present Planning Commission in fact does.

Some of these functions, the Board pointed out, were already being performed by the Co-ordinating Committee of the Cabinet, the Commerce Department, the Tariff Board, and the Planning Branch of the Department of Industries and Supplies. But there was no specific provision for no. 7 and none at all for nos 8 and 9. More importantly, there was 'no agency for taking a comprehensive view of planning as a whole and for tracing the interactions and repercussions of all the various plans, projected or in operation'. For this purpose, 'a single, compact, authoritative organization is required, which should be responsible directly to the Cabinet . . . and which should devote its attention continuously to the whole field of development'. In short, India required a Planning Commission.

Such a Commission, the Board considered, must be non-political and non-ministerial. It might consist of either five or three members. A five-member Commission should include, in addition to a Chairman 'with general experience of public affairs', two non-officials with knowledge

[56] K. C. Neogy and C. L. Mehta wanted even greater emphasis on private enterprise; Sir Pheroze Kharegat criticized the report's cavalier attitude, typical of this period, towards finance, and made the very far-seeing demands that 'the system of financial control should be suitably modified so as to do away with meticulous financial examination', and that 'powers of financial sanction should be entrusted to administrative departments so long as they are within the scope of certain recognised principles' (p. 29). K. T. Shah's very lengthy note criticized almost everything in the report and demanded, among other things, the 'liquidation' of private interests working for personal profit (pp. 30–64).

[57] Ibid. p. 23 *passim.*

and experience of agriculture and/or labour, one official versed in finance and general administration, and one scientist or technologist. Whatever its size and composition the Commission should be primarily advisory in character, except to the extent that it would act as a 'Priorities Board' for the allocation of material resources. It should be associated with the Scientific Consultative Committee (founded 1944), with a reconstituted Tariff Board, with a Central Statistical Office, the creation of which was recommended, and with a Consultative Body containing representatives of the provinces, states, agriculture, industry, commerce, labour, science, and 'other interests'. There should also be planning machinery of a similar but simpler kind in the provinces and in the districts.

The influence that these recommendations have had is obvious. The only major departure from them is in respect of the character and status of the Planning Commission, which is a much higher-powered and more political body than the one envisaged by the Board. This departure may have been—and in my own view was—a necessary one, but it still meets with criticism. For instance, the 21st report (1957–8) of the Estimates Committee of the Lok Sabha raised the question whether it was necessary 'to continue the formal association of the Finance Minister and other Ministers of the Central Government with the Commission' and whether the Prime Minister himself should retain his membership.[58] Yet this controversy was itself foreshadowed in the pages of the Advisory Planning Board report; for K. T. Shah, in his note of dissent, vaguely envisaged an even 'stronger' Commission than the one to be created in the 1950s. According to him the Commission was to be a kind of supreme executive, supervising the activities of a large number of boards, councils, and statutory corporations at the central and provincial levels. Fortunately, the creators of the present body refused to go to this opposite extreme.

Important support for the creation of a Planning Commission came from the Economic Programme Committee of the Congress,[59] whose distinguished membership included Nehru, Azad, Ranga, Shankarreo Deo, and John Matthai. Appointed by the AICC on 17 November 1947, it reported, unanimously, on 25 January 1948.

No immediate action was taken on these recommendations. Before India could make a planned assault on her economic problems she had to go through the transition to full independence, the hell of partition, the first and most serious phase of the conflict with Pakistan, and the infinitely complex processes of making a constitution, integrating the princely states, and defeating the Communist rebellion.[60] Even during

[58] EC 1957–8: *21*, p. 8. See below, pp. 70 ff. [59] AICC, Econ. Programme Ctee, *Rep.* (1948).

[60] Nehru himself emphasized partition as the main inhibiting factor. After the report of the Advisory Planning Board, he said, 'immediately we got caught up in the business of approaching Partition. After Partition we again got caught up with the business of the after-effects of Partition. So all these vital problems could not be solved. There they remained' (*Speeches*, i. 100).

the crucial period 1947–50, however, the government's economic policy was not merely one of drift. Grave mistakes, such as the de-control of foodgrains, were certainly made; business confidence was at low ebb, labour relations bad, and a spirit of cynical self-seeking abroad. But partial plans were attempted, such as the Ministry of Agriculture's five-year plan for increasing food production and the five-year plan of the Central Cotton Committee; and by the end of 1948 no fewer than 160 irrigation projects (many of a multi-purpose character) were being considered, investigated, or executed. The first Industrial Policy Resolution had been passed, with positive effects on business confidence; several important economic development agencies, such as the Industrial Finance Corporation and the Cottage Industries Board, were established; and negotiations with foreign firms were in progress for the creation of industries destined to figure prominently in the First Five-Year Plan, e.g. dry cables, machine tools, heavy chemicals, steel, penicillin, fertilizers, telephones, and locomotives.[61]

Even so, this central effort, like the feebler efforts being made in the provinces, lacked direction.

> I am afraid [said Nehru in 1950] that in spite of a good deal of talk about planning we have not done much. . . . We have tried to make good in many directions but there has not been that amount of coordination even within the Government or between the State Governments and the Central Government. I am frank to confess that in the Central Government there has not been a careful attempt to see the overall picture.[62]

This was a disappointment to those who had hoped for a 'great leap forward' with the achievement of independence, and some came to the conclusion that Congress's interest in planning had evaporated.[63] One of the severest critics, Professor Gadgil, was not pacified even by the eventual establishment of the National Planning Commission on 15 March 1950. By 18 December he was already of the opinion that it had 'failed'.[64] It is true, as he pointed out, that there was strong opposition to planning. Speaking in 1955, the Prime Minister said: 'About five years ago, planning was not acceptable to many people in high places.'[65] Sardar

[61] See Sovani, *Planning of Post-War Econ. Dev.*, pp. 13–22.

[62] *Times of India*, 26 Apr. 1950.

[63] See, for instance, D. Thorner, 'Problems of Economic Development in India', in *Annals of American Acad. of Polit. and Soc. Science*, Mar. 1950; D. R. Gadgil, 'The Economic Prospect for India', in *Pacific Affairs*, June 1949 (reprinted in his *Economic Policy and Development* (Poona, 1955)); D. F. Karaka, *Betrayal in India* (1950).

[64] See Preface to Sovani, *Planning of Post-War Econ. Dev.*

[65] *Speeches, 1953–57* (1958), p. 17. This quotation is from his well-known address to the 60th Session of the INC at Avadi, 22 Jan. 1955.

Patel, who shared power with Nehru during the immediate post-independence years, was at best lukewarm on the subject. But such foot-dragging was not universal, and, above all, Jawaharlal Nehru's own faith remained undimmed.[66] If he had faltered, the National Planning Commission might never have been created. When all is said, the really surprising thing is not that the advent of the Planning Commission was delayed but that it came as early as 1950.

(v)

The 'prehistory'of Indian planning illuminates the process by which a great nation felt its way towards the making of a major innovation. These early Indian planners deserve respect, despite all their mistakes, for they were pushing into still uncharted territory. Moreover, in so far as the objectives as distinct from the techniques of planning always have to be thought out anew, their discussions still have a contemporary relevance.

What emerges with the greatest clarity from this 'prehistory', however, is the decisive role played by one man: Jawaharlal Nehru. It was he who converted Congress to the idea of planning, and he who continued to insist on its importance at times when other, superficially more immediate, questions were tending to push it into the background.

This inspiration and leadership continued throughout the 1950s and into the 1960s, up to the very end of Nehru's life. He became responsible, as we shall see, for a number of serious mistakes in the Indian approach to planning; for his socialism and 'populism' sometimes clouded his vision and led him to put his trust in people who did little more than minister to his prejudices and in schemes based more upon ideological 'correctness' than upon real needs and possibilities. It should be added that his besetting sin of vagueness and his lack of capacity as an administrator also led him into avoidable error. Nevertheless, without the drive that he imparted to the planning process it would have faltered even more seriously than it actually did, and without his inspiration its long-term objectives might have completely disappeared from view. Moreover, he showed an extraordinary capacity, reminiscent of that for which his *guru*, Mahatma Gandhi, was famous, to express objectives in terms which a majority of educated and politically-vocal Indians could understand and accept.

These invaluable qualities were first revealed during the 'prehistory' which we have been outlining. As the remainder of this book will be predominantly concerned with the mechanics of the planning process, little more will be said about Nehru's personal influence. But throughout

[66] That does not mean, of course, that his ideas remained unchanged. The erstwhile Marxist, now Prime Minister, crossed swords several times in the Constituent Assembly with vehement and impatient nationalizers. 'Perhaps I have been affected by recent events,' he said on one occasion, 'but more and more I have felt that it is wrong to destroy something that is productive or capable of doing good' (*Speeches*, i. 123).

the account of the plans that follows, the fact that *he* was there, with his enormous prestige, actually guiding the efforts of the planners, stimulating the pioneers and exhorting the laggards, must never be forgotten. Up to 1964, India's plans were Nehru's plans. For both their successes and their failures, therefore, he and the men whom he personally selected must be held largely responsible.

III

THE MACHINERY OF PLANNING

(i)

THE government of India's intention to create a Planning Commission was announced to the Lok Sabha on 28 February 1950 by the Minister of Finance in his budget speech. The Commission was established on 15 March, by Cabinet resolution. Some have criticized the adoption of this method of bringing it into existence and have argued that the passing of a law would have been preferable. The Commission was originally conceived, however, as an 'arm' of the Cabinet, with purely advisory status, and its creators evidently thought that the less formal method of creation would afford greater flexibility and possibility of experiment.

The resolution[1] began by briefly recounting the history of economic planning in India and explaining the circumstances which demanded a better co-ordination of development programmes: 'The need for comprehensive planning based on a careful appraisal of resources and on an objective analysis of all the relevant economic factors has become imperative. These purposes can best be achieved through an organization free from the burden of the day-to-day administration, but in constant touch with the Government at the highest level.' The Commission, created to meet this need, was to take as its basic terms of reference the following Directive Principles of State Policy embodied in the constitution:

(*a*) that the citizens, men and women equally, have the right to an adequate means of livelihood;

(*b*) that the ownership and control of the material resources of the community are so distributed as best to subserve the common good; and

(*c*) that the operation of the economic system does not result in the concentration of wealth and means of production to the common detriment.

Bearing these principles in mind, it was to perform the following seven duties:

1. Make an assessment of the material, capital and human resources of the country, including technical personnel, and investigate the possibilities of augmenting such of these resources as are found to be deficient in relation to the nation's requirements;

2. Formulate a Plan for the most effective and balanced utilisation of the country's resources;

[1] No. 1-P(C)50, *Gazette of India*, 15 Mar. 1950.

3. On a determination of priorities, define the stages in which the Plan should be carried out and propose the allocation of resources for the due completion of each stage;

4. Indicate the factors which are tending to retard economic development, and determine the conditions which, in view of the current social and political situation, should be established for the successful execution of the Plan;

5. Determine the nature of the machinery which will be necessary for securing the successful implementation of each stage of the Plan in all its aspects;

6. Appraise from time to time the progress achieved in the execution of each stage of the Plan and recommend the adjustments of policy and measures that such appraisal may show to be necessary;

7. Make such interim or ancillary recommendations as appear to it to be appropriate either for facilitating the discharge of the duties assigned to it or on a consideration of the prevailing economic conditions, current policies, measures and development programmes; or on an examination of such specific problems as may be referred to it for advice by the Central or State Governments.

The resolution also specified, clearly and briefly, the Commission's role in the system of government: 'The Planning Commission will make recommendations to the Cabinet. In framing its recommendations, the Commission will act in close understanding and consultation with the Ministries of the Central Government and the Governments of the States. The responsibility of taking and implementing decisions will rest with the Central and the States Governments'.

Named as the original members of the Commission were the following:

Chairman: Shri Jawaharlal Nehru
Deputy Chairman: Shri Gulzarilal Nanda
Members:
Shri V. T. Krishnamachari,
Shri Chintaman Deshmukh,
Shri G. L. Mehta,
Shri R. K. Patil

Of these, Nanda was a prominent Congressman with special knowledge of labour questions, Krishnamachari an administrator with long and varied experience, Deshmukh a retired ICS man who had served as Governor of the Reserve Bank, Mehta a businessman who had been President of the Indian Tariff Board, and Patil an administrator and politician who, at the time of his appointment, was working as Food Commissioner. N. R. Pillai, the Secretary of the Cabinet, was appointed Secretary, with Tarlok Singh as his Deputy Secretary.

(ii)

During the thirteen years that have elapsed since the passing of this Cabinet resolution, the Commission's terms of reference have remained unchanged. Its membership, however, has not only increased in number but changed in character. Notably, the Commission has become a much more ministerial body. Originally, Nehru himself was the only minister member, but as early as May 1950 C. D. Deshmukh, on succeeding Dr John Matthai as Finance Minister, became another. Then, in 1951, the Deputy Chairman was appointed both Minister of Irrigation and Power and Minister of Planning. In the latter capacity his main duty was to act as liaison between the Commission and the Houses of Parliament. (In 1953, while remaining both member of the Commission and Minister of Planning, he was replaced as Deputy Chairman by V. T. Krishnamachari; in 1960, on Krishnamachari's resignation, he became Deputy Chairman once more.) C. D. Deshmukh's successors as Finance Minister, T. T. Krishnamachari (not to be confused with V. T. Krishnamachari) and Morarji Desai, were also appointed members of the Commission, and the inclusion of the Finance Minister may now perhaps be regarded as an established convention. Further ministerial appointments occurred in 1956, when V. K. Krishna Menon, Minister without portfolio and later Minister of Defence, became a member, and in 1962, when the former Finance Minister, T. T. Krishnamachari, came back to the Commission in his capacity of Minister without portfolio. (He was very shortly afterwards appointed Minister of Economic Co-ordination.) By late 1962 the Commission contained no fewer than five minister members, all of high status in the political hierarchy, viz. Nehru, Nanda, Desai, Krishna Menon, and T. T. Krishnamachari. Since then, the number of minister members has remained the same, although the personalities have changed. Menon ceased to be a member after his relinquishment of the Ministry of Defence, and Desai resigned on handing over the Finance Ministry to T. T. Krishnamachari. Nanda, although now (1964) Home Minister and no longer the Commission's Deputy Chairman, continues to hold office, and has been joined by Swaran Singh, the Minister of Food and Agriculture, and by a new Minister of Planning, B. R. Bhagat. On the death of Nehru, the new Prime Minister, Lal Bahadur Shastri, automatically took his place as Chairman. In view of such a large and distinguished ministerial membership, critics of the Commission may well claim that it has become much more than an advisory body.

Admittedly, non-ministerial membership has also increased. C. M. Trivedi's, Shriman Narayan's, and T. N. Singh's appointments in 1957 and 1958, combined with K. C. Neogy's resignation, raised it from 3 to 5. In 1959 P. C. Mahalanobis, previously a *de facto* member (in his capacity of statistical adviser), was given *de jure* status, A. N. Khosla was appointed, and J. C. Ghosh departed. There were now 6 non-ministerialists. With the resignation of V. T. Krishnamachari in 1960, the number was reduced to 5, but raised again to 6 in 1962, with the brief appointment of Vishnu Sahay. The latter's resignation was shortly preceded by that of Khosla, but 4 further non-ministerial appointments, those of Tarlok Singh, M. S. Thacker, V. K. R. V. Rao, and Asoka Mehta followed in rapid succession, bringing the total to 7. Over the years, however, non-ministerial membership has increased by only 2, while ministerial membership has increased by 4. Total membership has doubled. A full attendance, nowadays, would produce a meeting of 13, since there is a Deputy Minister of Planning with the right to be present. At one time there were two such Deputy Ministers.

Of the Commission's non-ministerial members, all but one, P. C. Mahalanobis, hold full-time appointments; and almost from the beginning each member has had specific 'functional' responsibilities. These have undergone fairly frequent changes, as might be expected in view of the expansion of the Commission's total membership and the changing balance between ministerial and non-ministerial members. Minister members, too, have their 'lines of country'. Indeed, Nanda, when Deputy Chairman and Minister of Planning, shared with his Deputy Minister a long list of responsibilities which included Plan Co-ordination, Economic Policy and Growth, Foreign Aid, Parliamentary Business, Housing, Social Welfare, Land Reforms, Labour and Employment, and Public Co-operation. Today (1964), as an ordinary member, he is 'functionally' concerned only with Public Co-operation. Of the other three ministers (apart from the Prime Minister), Krishnamachari deals with Financial Resources and Bhagat with Parliamentary Business. Swaran Singh, the Minister of Food and Agriculture, has apparently been given no functional responsibilities, but one may assume that he is expected to exercise general oversight of the agricultural aspects of the plan.

It is difficult to discover more than a few firm principles that have governed appointments. Nehru, of course, was indispensable, and his successor, Shastri, is likely to continue to use the chairmanship to give the Commission status and authority. Ministerial membership, as we shall see, is not universally regarded as necessary or desirable, but so long as there are ministers on the Commission, those of Finance and Planning select themselves, by virtue of their offices. T. T. Krishnamachari, when Minister of Economic and Defence Co-ordination, could lay claim to membership by virtue of his broad responsibilities for mobilizing resources for the defence effort. Swaran Singh's comparatively recent appointment reflects the fact that the role of agriculture in the plans, always vital, has become critical. Of all ministerial members, past and present, only Krishna Menon appears to have owed his membership to his individual qualities rather than to the duties of his office. Although Minister of Defence, he assumed functional responsibility for International Trade and Development. Essentially, he was there because of his political closeness to and personal friendship with Jawaharlal Nehru, who had a very high opinion of his abilities.

The original non-ministerial members seem to have represented a combination of political, administrative, and business experience. The first real 'expert' to be appointed was J. C. Ghosh, a scientist, and this seems to have set a precedent in so far as he was followed first by Khosla, an engineer, and then by another engineer, Thacker. In 1963 the expert element on the Commission was strengthened by the appointment of V. K. R. V. Rao, the eminent economist. Tarlok Singh, although not an expert in the same sense, must be regarded as belonging to this group, since he owed his appointment to his long experience of the techniques of planning, as Additional Secretary (and *de facto* Secretary) to the Commission. Mahalanobis, of course, has also held membership at least partly by virtue of his qualifications as a statistician. As for the remainder of the present non-ministerial members, T. N. Singh and Shriman Narayan represent a continuing 'political and public services' element, while Asoka Mehta, appointed Deputy Chairman in 1963, is an experienced if somewhat wayward politician of considerable intellectual depth and with strongly held views about economic and social problems. With the increase in non-ministerial membership, there seems to be a tendency to give greater weight to expertise and less to political acceptability and administrative experience. The original 'business' representation, it is interesting to note, has been entirely eliminated.

(iii)

The organization of the National Planning Commission has developed—its enemies would say 'proliferated'—over the years in a way that would be tiresome to follow. The best method of dealing with it is to describe it at the time of writing, with such references as may be necessary to explain the more important changes over the period 1950–64.[2]

The Secretary to the Cabinet remained Secretary to the Commission until January 1964, when the two posts were separated. Up to the time of separation, most of the actual secretarial work was performed by an Additional Secretary, a full-time officer of the Commission. Next in the hierarchy is a group of officials designated as Joint Secretaries, Chiefs, or Advisers. All but three of these are in charge of the various 'groups' into

[2] The descriptive material that follows is considerably, although by no means entirely, derived from S. R. Sen, 'Planning Machinery in India', *IJPA*, vol. vii, 1961; EC, 1957–8: *21*; EC, 1962–3: *15*; V. T. Krishnamachari, *Fundamentals of Planning in India* (Calcutta, Orient Longmans, 1962), pp. 49–68; H. K. Paranjape, *The Planning Commission* (IIPA, 1964). I am particularly indebted to this last work. The most careful and scholarly account of the Planning Commission as yet published, it is intended as the first volume of a full study of planning organization and process in India.

which the work is divided, e.g. Co-ordination; Irrigation and Power; Natural Resources; Agriculture; Industry, &c. The other three (who have the *ex-officio* status Additional Secretaries) are known as Programme Advisers, and their main job is one of liaison between the Planning Commission and the state governments. Each group is composed of one or more divisions, which fall into three classes, viz. 'General', 'Subject', and 'Housekeeping'. Each 'General' Division deals with an 'across-the-board' matter, e.g. perspective planning, statistics and surveys, plan co-ordination, programme administration, scientific research, natural resources, foreign exchange and international trade, labour and employment, public co-operation, information and publicity. Each 'Subject' Division is responsible for a 'sector' of the economy, e.g. agriculture, irrigation and power, industry and minerals, village and small-scale industries, transport and communications, education, health, housing, social welfare. As their name implies, the 'Housekeeping Divisions' are concerned with the smooth and efficient functioning of the Commission itself.

The top man of a 'General' or 'Subject' Division (whose rank depends upon his seniority and the scope of his responsibilities) usually has technical qualifications, often in economics or statistics. He is assisted by variously-designated officers, hierarchically arranged. The bulk of the detailed work of the division is performed by senior research officers and research officers (gazetted), by economic investigators, Grades I and II, and by assistants (non-gazetted). There is a rather inadequate staff of stenotypists and stenographers, a perhaps more than adequate one of upper and lower division clerks, and the usual crowd of (to use British terminology) 'minor and manipulative' personnel, including as many semi-occupied or entirely redundant 'peons' as one finds in any other Indian government establishment.

The divisions are the core of the Planning Commission. Their function is to get to know everything that is happening in their various fields of interest, to collate and interpret the massive quantity of statistical and other data they receive, and to transmit, upwards and sideways, well-digested information, considered criticisms of proposals, and new ideas. They are not expected to engage in technical research (which is the responsibility of ministries, other operational agencies, and specialized institutions), and hence are quite lightly staffed.[3] As of December 1963, the largest divisions were Economic, with a staff (economic investigator Grade II and above) of 36, and Perspective Planning, with one of 24. Both of these, it will be noted, were concerned with 'overall' planning of a kind that no individual ministry could undertake. Of the 'Subject'

[3] For a statement showing the approved strength of the Commission, according to information given to the EC and published in Feb. 1963, see App. I, p. 539.

Divisions (where overlapping with research work in the ministries is most likely) the largest, Industry and Minerals, had a staff of no more than 21, while the two smallest, Housing and Rural Works, were equipped with 5 each. During the process of formulating a five-year plan, each division is associated with one or more working groups, on which the appropriate ministries are represented. The *modus operandi* of these very important bodies and the nature of their relationships with the Planning Commission are briefly examined in our account of the making of the Third Five-Year Plan.

The key role played by the divisions in the planning process does not imply that the members of the Commission are somewhat remote personalities who occasionally meet to consider and approve proposals put up to them by the 'official' element. On the contrary, they are very active. The Commission meets at least twice a week, usually between the hours of 9 and 11.30 a.m., and when there is an emergency or when the pressure of business is considerable it meets daily. Although the attendance of minister members is of necessity irregular and that of the Prime Minister confined to those meetings where important decisions are to be taken, the non-ministerial members spend considerable time in formal discussions. Normally the Deputy Chairman presides, and only in the event of his being absent from Delhi or otherwise unavailable during an emergency would a meeting be held without him.

That the Commission assembles so frequently and deals with so much detailed business would seem to point to a weakness in its organization. One would expect to find a committee on the official level, consisting of group and divisional heads, which did all the preliminary sorting out and presented the members with well-prepared, mutually-agreed memoranda, setting forth the pros and cons of the various courses of action between which they had to decide. As far as can be discovered, no such committee exists. Such co-ordination as there is at the official level appears to be effected in an unorganized, informal way, through unminuted meetings between various senior officers, called sometimes on their own initiative and sometimes at the request of members. 'Sorting out', otherwise than by the Commission itself, seems to be the responsibility of the Additional Secretary, on whose shoulders a positively inhuman burden of work has been placed. Even the agendas of the Commission's meetings are not always systematically prepared. Items come in from divisions, groups, programme advisers, members of the Commission, ministers, &c., and priorities are rather hastily drawn up by the Additional Secretary in consultation with such members and senior officials as happen to be available. The role of the General Co-ordination Division is purely secretarial. It sends out notices of meetings, duplicates agendas, keeps the minutes, reminds people of their commitments, and tries to keep them to agreed deadlines. The only regular meetings, apart from those of the Commission itself, are the Deputy Chairman's meetings with divisional heads. At these, which are held twice a week, the divisional heads appear *in rotation*, each one attending, on the average, once every fourteen days. Such a pattern of contact between members and officials would suggest that the Commission does not actively encourage the official element to present collective recommendations.

Over-centralization and the under-utilization of technically qualified personnel would therefore seem to be among the Commission's organizational vices. One of the consequences is that a few key people, recruited to the Commission from the higher ranks of the civil service, are wearing themselves out with long hours of toil in the effort to keep the ship afloat and sailing in approximately the right direction. No more dedicated public servants than these are to be found anywhere in the world; but one's admiration for them is tempered by the thought that if they gave more of their attention to organization and less to trouble-shooting there would be fewer troubles for them to shoot, with the result that they could live more human lives and devote more time to the fundamental thinking for which they are admirably equipped. One should not exaggerate this problem, however. It has to be seen within an Indian administrative context where over-centralization often reaches pathological proportions and where the technician often suffers severely at the hands of the 'pooh-bah'. From the grosser of these defects the Planning Commission is relatively free. That it displays *some* of them is inevitable.

As we have seen, the divisions are the workshops of the Commission, while the working groups are the most essential of the advisory committees in which it participates. The latter, however, are no more than *ad hoc* bodies, which disband as soon as they have made their contribution to plan formulation. For more regular consultation, at any stage of the planning process, the Commission has set up a network of advisory bodies, most of which meet two or three times a year. There are advisory panels of economists and of scientists, and on agriculture, land reforms, *ayurveda* (the 'native' system of medicine), health, education, and housing and regional development. There are two advisory committees on public co-operation and one on irrigation, flood control, and power projects. The most important of these bodies is the Panel of Economists, but none of them appears to play a vital role. The future of the Economists' Panel itself would seem to be hazardous since the establishment in 1962 of a small, 'high-powered' advisory group of five eminent professors of economics.

To facilitate consultation with Parliament, there is a series of joint committees of the Lok Sabha and Rajya Sabha, which up to now have met either immediately before or immediately after the presentation of the Draft Five-Year Plan to the legislature (see pp. 142 and 199 f.). More informal consultation takes place through the Prime Minister's Consultative Committee, an all-party body meeting irregularly. Dr Sen exaggerates when he says that this committee 'gives an opportunity to the opposition leaders to take an intimate part in the work of planning' and that it earns for the plan 'the cooperation of all important political parties'; nevertheless it does provide the Planning Commission with a useful political sounding-board.

Within the ministries themselves there are planning 'cells', supposed to work in close association with the corresponding divisions of the Commission. For instance, the Planning Cell (Mining), is responsible for working out correlations between potential supply, potential demand, and potential transport facilities over a five-year period, using the 'rolling-plan' technique. All ministerial planning cells are involved in the formulation of the Five-Year Plans through the provision of information to the Commission's working groups, on which they will normally be represented.[4]

Of the bodies 'associated' with the Planning Commission, as distinct from those under its own control or supervision, the most important are the central ministries themselves, with which relationships are close and continuous. The Planning Commission is represented on various ministerial research institutes and advisory committees, and there is now a general rule that before a ministry presents to the Cabinet a new policy proposal of economic significance, it shall first be brought before the Commission, so that the latter may tender its advice. To facilitate interchange of views, ministerial representatives are often invited to attend the meetings of the Commission and members of the Commission (other than minister members) called to meetings of the Cabinet. By convention, the Deputy Chairman of the Commission attends all the meetings of the Cabinet's Economic Committee. With the Ministry of Finance relations are especially intimate—and almost impossible for the outside observer to describe. The Minister of Finance is *ex officio* a member of the Commission, and until January 1964 the two bodies shared an Economic Adviser. Often there is tension between the Ministry, which is oriented towards 'economy', and the Commission, which is oriented

[4] Information obtained through interviews at the Ministries of Mines & Fuel and of Food & Agriculture. It was suggested to me, by a high official of the Reserve Bank who has been intimately associated with the planning process, that there is considerable and wasteful duplication between the functions of the Commission's divisions and those of the ministries' 'cells'. The Commission, he considered, was largely engaged in repeating, rather inexpertly, the technical work already performed in the ministries. Members and officials of the Commission, of course, deny this with some vigour. Detailed investigation, impossible for an outsider, would be necessary to discover the truth. My general knowledge of Indian administration, however, would incline me to the opinion that a great deal of duplication—and misunderstanding—does occur.

towards 'development'. This is not necessarily unhealthy; nor is it true to say—as has often been said by those who misrepresent the Commission as a mere peripheral body of 'brains-trusters'—that the Ministry of Finance invariably wins the contest.[5]

Other important 'associated' bodies are the Industrial Licensing Committee, the Capital Goods Committee, the Foreign Agreements Committee, and the Development Councils. On all of these, which play key roles in the control of industrial development, the Commission is represented. With the Reserve Bank it also has intimate relations, sometimes marked by deep disagreements.[6] The Bank's well-staffed Economic Department often undertakes work for the Commission, and this department's research studies provide material of essential importance to the planners. With the Central Statistical Organization (CSO) there is a liaison symbolized by the fact that the organization occupies the upper floors of the Commission's own building. The Commission's Statistics and Surveys Division is in fact a 'cell' of the CSO financed from the CSO's own budget, and the CSO's Director is therefore the division's *ex officio* head.

Organizationally, relations between the Commission and the state governments are the concern of (*a*) the Programme Advisers, (*b*) the Programme Administration Division, and (*c*) the National Development Council.

The Programme Advisers, to whom reference has already been made, are essentially peripatetic 'trouble-shooters'. Senior ICS or IAS men of wide and distinguished administrative experience, their functions, as described by the Estimates Committee, are to

help to effect coordination between the States and the Planning Commission in regard to (i) preparation of the Five-Year Plan, (ii) preparation of the annual Plan, (iii) provision of adjustments in the Plan, (iv) watching the progress of the plan and attending to the problems of implementation which they come across during their visits to the States.

[5] It is alleged by some, however, that ministries are less respectful towards the Commission than they used to be. I was told, for instance, by one sufficiently highly placed to have plenty of inside knowledge, that ministers no longer go to the Commission for discussion but send their officials—'sometimes not even their highest officials'—and openly state that they will only comply with those of the Commission's proposals with which they agree. This is not to be taken too seriously. Abusing and challenging the Commission is a popular sport, and its very popularity is evidence that the Commission is something much more than the collection of powerless intellectuals that some of its detractors consider, and perhaps would like, it to be.

[6] In so far as it gives independent advice to the Finance Ministry on subjects such as mobilization of resources, priorities for investment, foreign exchange, deficit financing, savings, and taxation, the Reserve Bank may be regarded as a competitor of the Planning Commission. Generally speaking, its advice is 'conservative', and officials of the bank tend to regard the whole planning process with a certain scepticism. I received the impression that they were glad to be located in Bombay, away from the baleful influences of 'theorists' such as P. C. Mahalanobis and Pitamber Pant.

More specifically, they

> look into those projects which are assisted by loans and grants from the Central Ministries, and also note the States' efforts to raise resources. In the course of . . . discussions and field inspections, problems relating to bottlenecks due to non-availability of steel, technical personnel, allocation of foreign exchange, procedural delays in the approval of schemes and the sanctions for financial assistance by the Ministries of the Government and other such matters come to [their] notice . . . and are dealt with in their reports. The Planning Commission draws attention of the Ministries concerned to these problems through personal discussion and suggests that an immediate solution is necessary . . . . Advisers sometimes lead teams of experts from different Ministries to examine particular problems and make recommendations to the Government of India. They check the estimates of projects and assess the expenditure incurred on the projects in terms of the Plan. They also offer advice to the State Governments for improving the implementation of the projects and the Plan in different fields of development.[7]

These are very important and hard-worked men, whose chief business is to keep the rather clumsy machinery of centre-state planning relationships in working order. The surprising thing is that the Planning Commission has been able to get along with so few of them. Since the reorganization of the states in 1956 the distribution of work among them has not conformed to any logical pattern. As of March 1964, when there were—temporarily—four of them, the allocation of states and territories to Advisers was as follows:

S. R. Sen: Uttar Pradesh, Madhya Pradesh, Rajasthan.
P. P. I. Vaidyanathan: Bihar, West Bengal, Orissa, Assam, Nagaland, Manipur and Tripura, NEFA, Andaman Islands and Nicobar Islands.
Raja Surendra Singh: Mysore, Madras, Maharashtra, Gujarat, Goa, Daman and Diu.
M. S. Sivaraman: Kerala, Andhra Pradesh, Punjab, Jammu and Kashmir, Delhi, Himachal Pradesh, Pondicherry, Laccadive Islands, Minicoy Islands, and Amandive Islands.

Although—if we disregard some of the outlying territories—only Sivaraman had a geographically absurd parish, it is to be noted that the Commission had made no effort to relate its programme advisory organization to the comparatively compact and continuous areas covered by the Zonal Councils (see p. 392-3).

The Estimates Committee criticized the very similar allocation prevailing in 1959 as 'not conducive to efficient functioning', and recommended 'that each adviser should have a compact area preferably comprising of [*sic*] all the States in an administrative zone'. The

[7] EC, 1957–8: *21*, pp. 21–22.

Commission, however, replied that the existing arrangement had 'worked satisfactorily' and that 'no modification of it' was 'felt to be necessary'.[8]

The Programme Administration Division, in essence, is a technical bureau working under the Programme Advisers. During both the formulation and the implementation of the plan, it maintains continuous contact with the relevant authorities in the states. Its major responsibility is to ensure that the states' programmes, both five-yearly and annual, conform with overall plan outlays. It also advises the Planning Commission on those delicate and politically-loaded questions involved in the concept of 'balanced regional development'.

The National Development Council (NDC) is an advisory body which could be said to rival the Planning Commission itself in importance. Its creation was suggested by the Commission in the Draft Outline of the First Five-Year Plan, where it said that the need had arisen for a 'forum... at which, from time to time, the Prime Minister of India and the Chief Ministers of the States can review the working of the Plan and of its various aspects'. Its establishment (6 August 1952), like that of the Commission itself, was effected by Cabinet resolution, which defined its functions as follows:

(1) to review the working of the National Plan from time to time;
(2) to consider important questions of social and economic policy affecting national development; and
(3) to recommend measures for the achievement of the aims and targets set out in the National Plan, including measures to secure the active participation and cooperation of the people, improve the efficiency of the administrative services, ensure the fullest development of the less advanced regions and sections of the community and through sacrifices borne equally by all citizens, build up resources for national development.[9]

It consists of the Prime Minister, the Chief Ministers of the states, and the members of the Planning Commission, but its meetings are usually attended by others as well. Ministers of the central government with an interest in the items included on its agenda invariably attend; states sometimes send one or two ministers in addition to their Chief Ministers; and 'outsiders', such as eminent economists or the Governor of the Reserve Bank, are often called in to give advice.

From its creation to June 1962 the NDC held eighteen meetings. To these should be added the six meetings of a Standing Committee of the Council, established in 1955 and discontinued in 1958. The printed—and largely verbatim—minutes of these gatherings record a steady increase in its influence. During the period when the Third Five-Year Plan was being formulated and the Second Five-Year Plan repeatedly

[8] EC, 1962–3: *15*, pp. 44–45. [9] Krishnamachari, *Fundamentals of Planning*, pp. 65–66.

'adjusted', the Commission presented the Council with lengthy and carefully drafted memoranda, which usually asked it to decide between alternative lines of policy. Admittedly, the Commission had on these occasions come to its own conclusions, which it pressed vigorously and for the most part successfully. But the show of respect with which it approached the Council was more than a façade; for the Commission realized that in the Council it had the most important of its many sounding-boards. Discussions might be disorderly and inconclusive, but they did reveal just how much, when it came to the crunch, the states were prepared to stand for, and how far they were prepared to go in carrying out centrally-determined priorities. In this way the Council exercised an influence on the planning process which is imperfectly revealed in the planning documents.[10]

If the Commission has usually got its way, this is due partly to the prestige of its Chairman and partly to the fact that the states, which are all rival clients for the centre's favours, can rarely present a united front. It must be remembered, however, that the very proposals which the Commission presents to the NDC are influenced by the *anticipated* reactions of the states' Chief Ministers, and it may also be noted that at least on one occasion the states *did* get together to resist—successfully—a proposal from the Commission which would have involved a considerable reduction of the aggregate sum earmarked in a draft plan for central financial support of their projects.[11] The NDC, therefore, is equipped with collective teeth, even though most of the fang-baring that takes place during its discussions is by individual ministers trying to protect their individual states. On the other hand, it would be going much too far to claim that the NDC has replaced the Commission as the effective policy-maker. The NDC is, *de facto*, more than an advisory body; but it is also less than an executive one. It may best be described, rather lengthily, as the most important organized gathering where plans undergo adjustment in the light of the needs, pressures, prejudices, and capacities of the states.

Two other quasi-advisory bodies with which the Planning Commission is associated are the Central Committee for Community Development (established 1952), and the Central Committee for Land Reforms (established 1953). Flexible in membership, both include all the members of the Commission, of which they can be regarded as offshoots. Up to the establishment of the Ministry of Community Development, the first body had overall responsibility for the important programme from which it takes its name. Since then, it has been mainly concerned with the

[10] Relations between the Commission and the Council are illustrated in the chapters on the Second and Third Five-Year Plans.
[11] See below, pp. 202-3.

establishment of basic community development policies. The Land Reforms Committee advises the states on land reform legislation, watches progress, and attempts, within the limits imposed by the immense variety of local conditions, to establish common standards. It works in close association with the Land Reforms Divisions of the Commission and of the Ministry of Agriculture, which are under the direction of a common Joint Secretary.

To be realistic and effective, planning must be based on adequate research and subjected to regular evaluation. Much of the research, as we have seen, is done in the Commission itself, the ministries, the Reserve Bank, and the CSO. A great deal, however, is necessarily contracted out to university bodies and to non-official organizations such as the Indian Statistical Institute, the National Council of Applied Economic Research, and the Institute of Economic Growth. To guide and co-ordinate all these official and non-official efforts, and to ensure that research funds are employed as effectively as possible, the Commission has established a Research Programmes Committee, consisting of 'eminent social scientists' under the leadership of the Deputy Chairman. Even so, there seems to be some unnecessary and uneconomic duplication both of facilities and of projects.

Evaluation is organized in a rather complex way. Overall and current evaluation is the responsibility of the Commission as a whole. Through the Progress Unit of the Plan Co-ordination Section it receives quarterly reports from the ministries and from the states. These are often fragmentary and usually late. On the whole, better information is collected by the technical divisions, which have their own independent sources; but this is not always adequately diffused. Information flow, in fact, is not one of the stronger aspects of Planning Commission organization, and for a great deal of current evaluation it has to rely on the ministers' monthly reports to the Cabinet. The Plan Co-ordination Section is much concerned with deficiencies in this field, and is making efforts—which appear to be hampered by its own lack of status—to remedy them.

For the evaluation of specific projects there are two organizations. Although both are connected with the Commission, they act with a considerable degree of independence. The first, chronologically, is the Programme Evaluation Organization (PEO) established in October 1952 to assess the progress of the community projects and of other intensive development schemes in the rural areas. Its functions are now defined (unofficially but reliably) as:

(i) to study the progress of a programme and to measure its impact on the socio-economic life of the rural people;
(ii) to ascertain the reasons for the success or failure in respect of different items of the programme; and
(iii) to indicate the directions in which improvements may be sought.

Its staff has grown and its organization become more complex with the increasing coverage of rural projects and schemes.[12] In 1963–4 it had a staff of 434 persons, organized in a headquarters, five regional offices, and forty-two Field Evaluation Units. In May 1962 its work was brought under the 'guidance' of an Evaluation Advisory Board, consisting of the Director of the Institute of Economic Growth, a former official of the Ministry of Food and Agriculture, a Professor of Agricultural Economics, a Professor of Sociology, and the Director of the PEO itself.

Originally, the PEO was concerned mainly with questions of organization and administration; but from 1954–5 it began to turn its attention to an 'assessment of the achievement and impact' of the CD Programme, through the publication of the so-called 'Bench Mark' survey reports and of an annual *Evaluation Report on the Working of Community Projects and National Extension Service Blocks.* These, which revealed that results were incommensurate with effort and expenditure, made the PEO unpopular with those politicians and officials who had acquired a vested interest in 'CD', and particularly with the Minister at the centre and the Development Commissioners in the states. Their criticism of the PEO reached its height at the Development Commissioners' Conferences at Srinagar in 1960 and Hyderabad in 1961.[13] S. K. Dey, the Minister, won the battle. The PEO, under its new Director, has ceased to publish annual evaluation reports or indeed general surveys of any kind. Instead, it now selects 'a few of the important plan programmes for rural development for intensive and comprehensive study'. Its recent publications include case studies of successful panchayats, successful co-operatives, and pilot projects for the utilization of rural manpower, and surveys of the problems of minor irrigation, soil conservation, primary education in rural areas, rural electrification, and the utilization of short- and medium-term co-operative loans.

One result of this new orientation of the PEO is that its work is now similar to that of the other evaluation organization, the Committee on Plan Projects (COPP). The establishment of this body was recommended by the Planning Commission, and it owes its creation to a resolution of the NDC of May 1956. Its functions were then defined as follows:

(1) to organize investigations, including inspection in the field, of important projects, both at the Centre and in the States, through specially selected teams;
(2) to initiate studies with the object of evolving suitable forms of organization,

[12] For a good general description of the history and organization of the PEO, see PEO, *Structure, Functions and Activities* (Oct. 1962, mimeo.).
[13] See Ann. Conf. on CD, Srinagar, 6–11 June 1960, *Main Recommendations & Conclusions*; Ann. Conf. on CD & Conf. of State Ministers of CD & Panchayati Raj, Hyderabad, July 1961, *Main Recommendations, Proc. & Agenda Notes.*

methods, standards and techniques for achieving economy, avoiding waste and ensuring efficient execution of projects;

(3) to promote the development of suitable machinery for continuous efficiency audit in individual projects and in agencies responsible for their execution;

(4) to secure the implementation of suggestions made in reports submitted to the Committee on Plan Projects and to make the results of studies and investigations generally available; and

(5) to undertake such other tasks as the National Development Council may propose for the promotion of economy and efficiency in the execution of the . . . Five-Year Plan.[14]

The COPP consists of the Minister of Home Affairs, the Deputy Chairman of the Planning Commission, and the Ministers of Finance and Planning. To these are added, when a particular class of project is being investigated, two 'interested' Chief Ministers of states and the 'interested' central minister. The Committee's central staff, however, is on the strength of the Planning Commission, and some of the members of this staff have played important parts in the investigations which the COPP has conducted.

For such investigations, *ad hoc* teams of specialists are constituted. These have included an Irrigation and Power Team, a Study Team on Social Welfare and Welfare of Backward classes, a Team for Selected Building Projects (with 'panels' for National Water Supply and Sanitation Schemes and for Delhi School Buildings), a Seed Multiplication Team, an Industrial and Mining Team, a Minor Irrigation Team, and a Team for the Study of Community Projects and National Extension Service. The reports of the teams are first circulated for discussion to the states and the ministries concerned, then finalized in the light of their comments, and then submitted by the Planning Commission to the appropriate authorities with a request that progress reports on implementation shall be made at stated intervals.

Perhaps the most technical task as yet undertaken by COPP is the series of full-scale investigations of several of the great multi-purpose river valley projects (e.g. Koyna, Chambal, Nagarjunasagar, and Lakkavalli), under the leadership of N. V. Gadgil. But the most influential investigation was that conducted into the community projects by the team led by Balvantray Mehta. Commended by the central government and approved by most of the states, its main recommendations were the *fons et origo* of that great experiment in democratic decentralization known as *panchayati raj*.

The investigations of PEO now overlap those of COPP at many points. Both, for instance, have concerned themselves with community projects,

[14] Krishnamachari, *Fundamentals of Planning*, pp. 99–100.

minor irrigation, and seed multiplication. The administrative unification of all project evaluation work might therefore be of advantage.

(iv)

The Planning Commission's organization is complicated, and one may well ask whether it is not unnecessarily and inhibitingly so. More generally, is the Commission well adapted to the performance of its functions, and has it found its correct place in the structure of India's parliamentary democracy?[15]

Although the members of the Commission appear to be fairly satisfied with the position which they occupy and the methods which they employ, they have to face a barrage of criticism which is by no means confined to members or supporters of the opposition parties. Broadly, the attack takes the form of three interlinked allegations, viz. (1) that the Commission has undertaken responsibilities of too varied a kind, to the detriment of its main purpose, i.e. the making and adjusting of plans; (2) that it has become an *imperium in imperio*, thereby reducing the ministries, the states, and the Union Cabinet itself to mere 'agency' bodies and undermining the very foundations of parliamentary democracy; and (3) that it is too much of a political, and too little of a technical body, with the result that its proposals are devoid of any genuinely 'scientific' character and are simply the product of a complicated discussion between politicians, administrators, and economists, of which the public is kept in almost complete ignorance. These allegations must be examined before we pass on to a description of planning machinery at the state level.

In theory, it would be possible for the Commission to stand apart from the executive agencies. The latter would send in reports, on the basis of which it would assess their performance and tender the necessary advice. Whether such advice was accepted would be none of its business. One does not need much imagination or more than a slight knowledge of Indian administration to recognize that, in many cases, this would be a clumsy procedure, providing the maximum opportunity for bureaucratic delay. In such cases, it is obviously better that the Commission should be represented on the decision-taking body, to ensure that its decision is taken with full cognizance of planning needs and hence less likely to require correction later. This is the justification for Planning Commission representation on such bodies as the Industrial Licensing Committee, the Capital Goods Committee, the Foreign Agreements Committee, and the Development Councils. There might even be a case for wider representation of this sort, so long as it did not become so extensive and

[15] For a recent discussion of the constitutional position of the Commission, see S. P. Jagota, 'Some Constitutional Aspects of Planning', in Ralph Braibanti & Joseph J. Spengler, eds., *Administration and Economic Development in India* (1963).

time-consuming as to distract the members and officials of the Commission from their more central tasks.

The same considerations apply to the rule whereby ministers have to submit to the Planning Commission their proposed changes of policy. The need to do so ensures that, before presenting such changes to the Cabinet, the ministers concerned will at least have considered their likely effect on the progress of the current plan. It also ensures, of course, that the Cabinet itself will be fully apprised of this issue.

More serious is the allegation that the states have fallen victims to the Commission's arrogance and megalomania, and that the ministries themselves have become its humble servants. The Estimates Committee of the Lok Sabha, in its report on the Planning Commission, was distinctly uneasy about the practice whereby states and central ministries were subjected to what it called the Commission's 'annual and periodical allotment of finances', and suggested that consideration should be given 'to what extent this function should be performed by the Planning Commission and whether it should not be left to the Governments themselves, leaving the Planning Commission to concentrate on the evaluation of the current Plan and formulation of the future Plan'.[16] Professor D. R. Gadgil was even more critical, saying that the relation of the Planning Commission with states and ministries should be that of an expert body engaged in bringing out the implications of total policy in relation to the activities of particular organizations or authorities rather than an authority engaged in bargaining with, or bullying, or being bullied by another government organization.[17]

This sidesteps the real problem. The Commission, by delegation from the central government, is responsible for drawing up five-yearly and annual plans. Into these, as approved in general outline by the Cabinet, it must attempt to fit the individual plans of the ministries and the states. This inevitably involves bargaining of a kind that only the Commission can effectively undertake; for the Commission understands the shape of the provisional plan better than anyone else and is charged with the task of putting together all the bits and pieces into a coherent pattern. How could it do this if it were empowered only to 'bring out the implications of total policy in relation to the activities of organisations or authorities'?

Its decisions in these matters, moreover, are not final. Gadgil himself refers to its being 'bullied by' as well as 'bullying' other authorities. There are 'appeals' both to the NDC and to the Cabinet. If the Commission usually wins them, this only shows that in the process of planning there can be no rigid distinction between the making of policy and the giving of advice. A plan either does or does not cohere. If it does, then

[16] EC, 1957–8: *21*, p. 5.

[17] D. R. Gadgil, *Planning and Economic Policy in India* (Poona, 1961), p. 109.

modifications simply at the request of interested parties can make nonsense of it. One can argue, indeed, that one of the defects of Indian planning is that such modifications are made not too seldom but too often.

The evaluatory functions of the Planning Commission are often attacked on similar grounds. Some have suggested that evaluation should be confined to a separate agency, since the necessary objectivity is impossible for people with policy-making responsibilities. In considering this suggestion, one must distinguish current from long-term evaluation. Current evaluation is so intimately bound up with the making and adjustment of plans that no one but the planners themselves could do it. Long-term evaluation, however, is another matter. A planning body may be reluctant to admit to serious faults. It has been suggested, in fact, that the Commission's failure to publish a comprehensive evaluation report on the Second Five-Year Plan was due to this reluctance. This does not necessarily imply that serious evaluation has been neglected—for no Planning Commission can afford to deceive itself, however much it may try to deceive others. The really damaging consequences of such lack of candour is that there is no honest publicity. Some safeguard against such a possibility would therefore seem to be required. The best one is not necessarily the establishment of yet another evaluation body, with its own widely-ramified investigatory apparatus. In Indian conditions this might only aggravate what I have called, in another context, the 'Blight of Perpetual Inspection'. A better method might be the periodical setting up of what the Indians always describe as a 'high-powered' committee, completely independent of the Planning Commission, charged with the duty of presenting to the government and the public, after thorough inquiry, a comprehensive view of the way the plans are going.

As for the existing evaluation bodies, the PEO and the COPP, there would seem to be little cause to criticize the association of these with the Commission. It is essential that they possess freedom both of investigation and of criticism, but there is no evidence that the Commission has ever attempted to deprive them of it. On the basis of recent experience, it would seem that the danger to their independence comes from other sources.

What of the Central Committees for Community Development and for Land Reforms? Both take decisions and make recommendations which are of the highest importance for the realization of plan objectives. It would seem, therefore, of advantage to have the Commission represented on them, as the alternative would be the comparatively clumsy one of sending their minutes to the Commission for its comments. On the other hand, it is difficult to see the justification for appointing *all* the members of the Commission to membership of these two committees, and thereby making them in effect its offshoots. That it has acquired a special responsibility for community development and land reforms can be readily explained by reference to the history of Indian planning over the last twelve or thirteen years; but over-close involvement in these fields of policy and administration is likely to distract members of the Commission from their main task, excessively involve them in matters of detail, and lay them open to the accusation of 'empire-building'.[18]

With this exception, there is not much to justify the 'too varied responsibilities' allegation. One could certainly argue that the Commission's own *internal* organization has become over-complex; but this is a different matter.

Some of the sting in the second allegation, that the Commission functions as an *imperium in imperio*, has already been removed by the above discussion; but not all of it. The gravamen of this charge is that the Commission, which ought to be an advisory body, has become very much more. When presented to the Cabinet and the NDC, its recommendations already have the support of the Prime Minister and several leading members of the Cabinet; hence their acceptance is more or less a foregone conclusion. *De facto*, therefore, the Commission is not just advising on plan policy; it is making it.[19] Whether this is a true picture of the actual relationships of the Commission with Cabinet and NDC need not be investigated now; the immediate question is whether the Commission should possess the power that it derives from its influential ministerial membership.

The most fierce criticism of the Commission's constitutional status has come, not surprisingly, from the Swatantra Party. Minoo Masani, describing it as 'a non-responsible super-government', has demanded its abolition in order to 'free Cabinet Ministers and members of the Union and State Governments' from its 'extra-constitutional intervention'.[20] As the Swatantra Party makes no secret of its opposition to planning as such, these views need not be treated seriously by planners; but attention must be paid to similar, if more moderately-worded, charges, made by people whose belief in planning is not open to doubt.

[18] The EC considered that it was 'not necessary for the Planning Commission to examine as a matter of routine all pieces of legislation or proposals received from States relating to Land Reforms', and proposed that the Commission's Land Reforms Division 'should focus its attention on the difficulties experienced by the States in effecting land reform and offer suggestions for overcoming them'. The Commission replied, in effect, that this was precisely what was being done. The status and composition of the Central Land Reforms Committee were not raised in this dialogue (EC, 1962–3: *15*, pp. 22–24).

[19] Criticized for its empire-building tendencies by the EC, the Commission jettisoned some of its more peripheral and less useful sections in 1959. The Public Management Studies Section and the Prohibition Section were then discontinued. But the Commission successfully resisted the suggestion that its public co-operation responsibilities, for which it had established a 'small' section, 'should be transferred to an appropriate Ministry of the Government of India' (ibid. pp. 5, 7, 21–22).

[20] LSD, 14th sess., 2nd ser., lviii, 4651–2.

Ministerial membership of the Commission was one of the questions considered by the Estimates Committee of the Lok Sabha in its twenty-first report of 1957–8 (pp. 7–8). There the case against such membership was put as follows:

One view that could be taken is that the Planning Commission should be a body of experts, both in the technical and administrative fields, who would make an independent survey of the problems and formulate plans, without being influenced by day-to-day expedients. The Commission would, of course, have to work in close coordination with Central Ministries and State Governments, but would give independent advice. This would require also that the independence should be vouchsafed to it, both by its composition and the procedure of its functioning. According to this view, the purely advisory character of the Commission is lost if Cabinet Ministers, including the Prime Minister, are members of the Commission. A decision, to which they are a party, taken in the Planning Commission and transmitted to the Ministries, to be considered by them or in the Cabinet is . . . more than advice and is very nearly a final decision. Further . . . under this arrangement the very basis for the constitution of a separate Planning Commission, as 'an organisation free from the burden of day to day administration but in constant touch with the Government at the highest policy level' is affected.

The opposite case, for ministerial membership, was then stated in words which would appear to be extracted from evidence presented by the Planning Commission itself:

For the first time an experiment is being carried out of planning for social and economic development in a large underdeveloped country, with a democratic and a federal constitution. It is not possible to draw a parallel with other countries and we have to rely on our own experience. Planning in such a situation cannot be rigid and should have a degree of elasticity. If there was a Planning Commission consisting of whole time experts, it would be like a panel of economists and not really a Planning Commission. An expert body like that will think in a vacuum and may not take into account the social, political and other implications. Totally detached from Government, it will be an ineffective body. In this matter, the essential need is to have pragmatic advice. The Planning Commission started as a body with full-time members, without any minister, except the Prime Minister, who was Chairman, but the present system is found to be more advantageous. It brings an essential link between the Planning Commission and the Cabinet. The presence of Ministers does not prevent the Commission from bringing independent judgement to bear upon the problems under consideration. The Ministers in their personal capacity contribute their valuable experience to the Planning Commission. Even though they are members of the Cabinet, they function purely as members of the Commission within the Planning Commission. Even though a Minister may be in the Planning Commission, he may disagree with the view taken in the Commission when the matter is considered later on by the Cabinet and that has happened in actual practice.

The Estimates Committee was evidently more impressed by the former argument than by the latter, for it recommended that the membership both of the Prime Minister and of other ministers ought to be 'considered', and indicated its unwillingness to be persuaded that 'closer consultation and co-ordination' required their presence.

This can . . . be effected by the Minister being invited to attend the meetings of the Commission when a subject with which he is concerned is discussed. The coordination with the Cabinet can also be maintained by a representative of the Commission attending the meeting of the Cabinet when a matter of interest to the Commission is being considered. This practice is said to be followed even at present.

Support for this point of view came from Professor Gadgil. He held that the Commission had 'failed', and that the root of its failure lay 'in the process by which the Planning Commission, essentially only an advisory body', had 'come to mix itself with the actual process of the formulation of public policies even in matters other than that of development'. This was not the fault of the Commission's experts, who displayed 'competence . . . of high order'. It was the result of appointing ministers and other non-experts. Their natural desire 'to exercise power and patronage' was responsible 'for the neglect by the Commission of its main functions and for a needless extension of its activities over many irrelevant fields'. Moreover, the membership of the Prime Minister and Finance Minister had 'vested the Planning Commission and its decisions with an unnatural kind of prestige and importance'. The remedy was radically to reconstruct the Commission, by making it predominantly a body of experts, without political commitments.

Obviously the Prime Minister, and the Finance Minister, should cease to be members of the Commission. No minister of the Cabinet should be a member of the Commission except the Minister for Planning, if such a post is continued in the Cabinet, and he should be the Chairman of the Commission. The Deputy Chairman of the Commission should be, by preference, an administrator of wide experience. This is necessary, as the Planning Commission operates essentially through contacts with ministries and governments and their senior officers, and somebody acquainted with their ways should be the administrative head of the organisation. For the rest, the members should be experts, all of whom, however, have some experience of the handling of practical problems. The expertise chiefly required will be that of natural scientists, technicians, social scientists, statisticians and economists.[21]

Clearly, the Estimates Committee and Professor Gadgil have the better logic on their side. The defence of the present dispensation, as presented by the Commission, seems a little disingenuous. But there are problems

[21] Gadgil, *Planning*, p. 110.

here which do not yield to the straightforward application of logical principles. What the experience of many underdeveloped countries would seem to show is that a planning commission is more likely to be too weak than too strong. A mere advisory committee of experts can wield but feeble weapons against central ministries and state governments which are chafing at the restrictions imposed upon them by a plan, and all trying to go their own ways, often in the genuine conviction that their sectional interests coincide with the national interest. Unless there is a strong countervailing force, these centrifugal pulls can disintegrate a plan very quickly. Admittedly, such a force can be provided by a strong Prime Minister, committed to planning and equipped with a powerfully organized office designed to exhort the laggards, restrain the runaways, and generally to ensure that everyone treats his commitments seriously. But this is difficult to organize, and in any case likely to be less effective than a system by which some of the most powerful ministers in the government, including the Prime Minister himself, actually participate in the planning process and thus develop a sense of commitment to plan objectives. Under such an arrangement, people are more likely to sit up and take notice when the commission raises its warning finger. 'Experts' can easily be disregarded, but a chorus of the Prime Minister, the Finance Minister, and the Planning Minister has to be listened to. Moreover it can be argued that the experts themselves will then enjoy *more* influence, not less; for they will have direct and continuous relations with the policy-makers, with whom they carry on a running dialogue. Their advice may be disregarded; often it *ought* to be disregarded, for the expert has a narrower horizon than the politician; but at least the latter will know *what* he is disregarding and will have been duly warned of the probable consequences.

Such considerations provide support for the Commission's own view, expressed in its reply to the Estimates Committee, that 'the idea of the Planning Commission functioning as a completely detached body, consultations being secured with individual Ministers when necessary, is not likely to be very useful in practice'.[22]

What the Indian system, with all its faults, avoids is the situation, so dismal to the serious planner, in which the experts sit isolated and neglected in small back rooms, drawing up projections of economic development and making policy recommendations which few of the politicians read and none feel committed to. This used to be the situation in the Philippines, where the Office of National Planning was unable to compete in political influence with such powerful bodies as the Central Bank and the Ministry of Finance. It still is the situation in Greece, while in Pakistan and in Egypt efforts to overcome it have achieved only limited success. If India has leaned over backwards to avoid it, the error

[22] EC, 1957–8: *21*, p. 16.

would seem to be in the right direction. The cardinal virtue of the Indian system is that it has put political teeth into planning. The danger of the kind of reformation advocated by the Estimates Committee and by Professor Gadgil is that, in striving for an unattainable constitutional purism, it would extract them.

This does not mean that the Indians have achieved perfection in their central planning machinery and that all criticisms of it are misconceived. Indeed, it can be argued that, whereas the two allegations we have so far examined lack substantial foundation, the third, which remains to be examined, contains much truth. At first sight this might seem self-contradictory, for the substance of the third allegation (which is often confused with the second) is that the Planning Commission is too much of a political and too little of a technical body. The question now requiring answer, however, is not whether there ought to be political representation on the Commission or whether it should immerse itself in day-to-day decision-taking, but whether the balance between politician and expert which has been established *within* the Commission is correct.

One of the essentials of good planning is that the experts (i.e. the economists, statisticians, sociologists, technicians, &c.) should be enabled—and indeed encouraged or even compelled—to get together and, after hammering out their own problems in their own way, present the political decision-takers with common and coherent advice. In consultation with the experts, the politicians have to decide on broad objectives, which they then give back to the experts as terms of reference. The task of the latter, collectively, is to discover the most rational means by which these may be pursued. Having done so, they report to the politicians, who thereupon tell them which of their recommendations are politically inconvenient, dangerous, or impossible. The experts then return to their task with modified terms of reference, and this to-and-fro process continues until agreement or compromise is reached. This is a gross over-simplification of what actually happens. The interchange is inevitably much less formal, and one cannot pretend that there is so neat a distinction between politician and expert—as if the former lived in a state of complete technical ignorance while the latter never had an idea that could be labelled 'political'. Nevertheless, it is an ideal which, although unattainable, must be pursued; for if it is not, the planning process can get into a muddle where no one knows the precise reason for taking a particular decision and the outcome is a compromise which satisfies the demands neither of internal consistency nor of political acceptability. As we shall see, India's plans—and particularly the Second Plan—have been disfigured by these birth-marks.

The reason, as far as one can judge, is that the technical work has never been clearly separated from the political assessment of its results.

The planning is done by the members of the Planning Commission, who tend to regard the divisions under their command mainly as sources of statistics and ideas. With four exceptions, these members are politicians or politically-oriented administrators. None of them are 'experts' in the full sense. The real experts, in the divisions, would appear to lack both adequate status and the means of collective expression. It is hardly an exaggeration to say, of most of them, that they are highly skilled servants whose influence in the planning process largely depends on how successful they are in gaining the ears of their masters. It is their individual dependence rather than their collective independence that receives emphasis. This is aggravated by the fact that many of them, as Gadgil rightly points out, are birds of passage, posted from the government departments to the Planning Commission and from the Commission back to the government departments. Thus it is not only that they receive little encouragement to develop 'a special point of view, and a particular attitude of mind'; only a few, constituting the hard core of the Commission's staff, ever live with the Commission long enough to do so. It is mainly to these characteristics of the Commission that Gadgil attributes its dismal list of 'failures'.

> It failed to put together detailed and meaningful plans after due technical and other examination; it did not produce objective criteria relating to composition of programme allocations, etc.; it failed to produce annual plans with appropriate breakdowns, and failed to watch the progress of the plan even in its broadest elements; it failed to give advice insistently on right policies being followed, and at times even participated in the adoption of wrong and inappropriate ones.[23]

This, although exaggerated, contains sufficient truth to be alarming.

The problem is how to give the collective views of the experts their means of expression and their proper weight without reducing the Commission to a virtually powerless, 'non-political' body. One part of the solution might be to have a different type of non-ministerial member. By now, it should be possible to appoint as members the best and most experienced officials from the secretarial staff, from the groups and the divisions, and from the ranks of the Programme Advisers. Indeed, this has already been done in the case of Tarlok Singh. The second part of the solution would be to give organizational expression to the distinction between those members who are non-ministerial experts and those who are non-expert ministers. This might take the form of having two kinds of Planning Commission meetings. Ordinary meetings, at which the technical work was done, would be attended only by the non-ministerial

[23] Gadgil, *Planning*, p. 107.

members, together with such officials as they chose to call in for advice. Full sessions, at which the results of the technical work would be assessed and important policy decisions taken, would be attended by all members, ministerial and non-ministerial. Something of this sort already takes place in practice; but much would be gained by formalizing it. The third part of the solution would be to review the organization and the personnel policies of the Commission, to ensure that there is adequate machinery for regular and planned consultation between heads of divisions and greater stability of personnel. The object of this would be not only to raise the status and enhance the influence of the expert official, but to make possible a greater decentralization of the Commission's work, without loss of coherence, so that the members of the Commission could confine their attention to the major issues.

(v)

An Indian plan consists not of one document but of over twenty. In addition to the national plan produced by the Planning Commission there are separate plans for the states, for Delhi, and for the 'territories'. These are made simultaneously with the national plan and by very similar methods. It is one of the major tasks of the Commission to ensure that all these plans are mutually consistent, compatible with the projected total investment, and in conformity with centrally established priorities. The states and the other units, therefore, are essentially *subordinate* planning authorities, even though 'Economic and Social Planning' figures in the concurrent list of powers granted to the Union and the states by the Indian constitution.

The Commission, however, does not attempt to do a state's planning work for it. The state has to produce its own draft plan for submission both to the Planning Commission and to its own legislature. The final state plan, as we shall see, is inevitably the product of a compromise between state and centre, worked out through discussion with the Commission; but it is the state's own planning handiwork that provides the basis for this discussion. States also produce annual as well as five-yearly plans, and these have to go through a similar if rather simpler form of final processing.

Every state, therefore, needs to establish some kind of planning machinery whereby, at the very least, proposals emanating from the various state ministries may be gathered together, co-ordinated, and kept within the total resources likely to be available. No attempt has been made by the Planning Commission to ensure that this machinery is everywhere the same, and constitutionally, of course, the states are free to do their planning just how they like. The result is a considerable variety of pattern and procedure.

V. T. Krishnamachari attempts the following general description of planning machinery in the states:

In every State, there is a Cabinet Committee which is in close touch with the preparation of the plans and the manner in which they are carried out. This Committee is assisted by a committee of officials working under it for co-ordinating plans made by different Ministries and supervising implementation. In many States there are Advisory Committees of non-officials consisting of Members of Legislative Assemblies and others whose advice is likely to be useful.[24]

This is broadly true, but not very enlightening. The only way of bringing to life the variety that exists within this general framework is to select several states for examination. Those chosen are Uttar Pradesh, Maharashtra, Andhra Pradesh, and Madras.[25]

In Uttar Pradesh,[26] as elsewhere, the ultimate responsibility for the formulation and execution of plans lies with the Chief Minister, who heads a team of 7 Cabinet Ministers, 3 Ministers of State, and 11 Deputy Ministers. This means that at the official level responsibility is in the hands of the Chief Secretary. The actual work is performed by a Planning Secretary who also holds the posts of Development Commissioner and State Manpower Officer. To provide him with the status required for the exercise of his co-ordinative functions he has been given the rank of Additional Chief Secretary. Under his charge are the Planning Department and the Department of Economics and Statistics.[27]

There appears to be no Planning Committee of the Cabinet, but all ministers are *ex officio* members of a State Planning Board, which contains also 28 non-official representatives (including 15 MPs, MLAs, and MLCs) nominated by the government, and all of the government Secretaries. This board, which meets once a year under the chairmanship of the Chief Minister, is said to be 'the chief consultative body to advise the Government on the broader questions of planning such as the lines on which a long-term plan for the State should be drawn up, its content, the phases in which it should be executed and the role which non-official agencies can play in the execution of its programmes'.[28] It is obvious that such a body

[24] Krishnamachari, *Fundamentals of Planning*, pp. 63–64.

[25] The following account of planning machinery in these four states is based on an investigation made by the author in the autumn of 1962. Where possible, the information there collected has been brought up to date, as of 1964.

[26] For Uttar Pradesh I have relied considerably on Prof. P. N. Masaldan's useful little study entitled *Planning in Uttar Pradesh* (Bombay, Vora, 1962).

[27] In 1964, as part of an organizational shake-up, responsibility for planning was separated from that for rural development. Administratively, each is now under the direction of a district Commissioner and Secretary. The Commissioner and Secretary, whose post is designated 'Planning, Evaluation, and Economics and Statistics', heads a department which deals with the formulation and implementation of five-year plans and annual plans (*PANL*, June 1964, p. 8).

[28] Masaldan, *Planning*, p. 4.

is not a substitute for a Cabinet committee. The board has no great importance, and seems to owe its existence to the government's desire to make a gesture towards 'public participation' in the planning process.

At the official level, the most important body is the State Planning Committee. This bears no resemblance (such as might be suggested by its name) to the National Planning Commission. It is an interdepartmental committee consisting of Secretaries, with the Chief Secretary as Chairman and the Planning Secretary as Committee Secretary. Its function is to 'prepare and check material for the drawing up of a composite plan for the State and lay it before the Board and Government for consideration'. To enable it to achieve this purpose, the Secretaries of the various departments are enjoined to 'put up the departmental plans after proper scrutiny before the Committee to judge whether they are in conformity with the declared objectives and policy of the Central and State Government and the Board'. It is said by Professor Masaldan, in his study of planning in Uttar Pradesh, to command 'great power and prestige'. Like similar bodies in other states, however, it suffers from a defect peculiar to the Indian administrative system. This arises from the 'position occupied by its members, namely, Secretaries'.

> Secretaries to the Government are not responsible for execution of programmes in the field, this being the responsibility of Heads of Departments. The Secretaries, therefore, are not likely to be aware of practical details of Plans or of difficulties met with in the field. Nor are they authorised to take final policy decisions with respect to their particular departments; for the consent of the Minister would be necessary. Thus, the need for consultation with both Heads of the Departments and Ministers so circumscribes Secretaries that instead of taking decisions on the spot, they can mostly only indicate broad policy, assign matters for mutual consultation between departments and put the seal of the Committee on decisions already taken.[29]

For the making of sectoral plans, working groups are constituted, as at the centre. For the Third Five-Year Plan there were fourteen of these. Each is chaired by the Secretary of the department most immediately concerned with its subject-matter, and composed of other senior officials and of selected non-officials, including persons 'experienced in the fields of industry and management'. Its main duty is to prepare projects 'with the utmost precision possible', for which purpose it establishes as many sub-groups as may be required. Co-ordination between working groups is the responsibility of the Planning Department and the State Planning Committee, which in this respect appears to operate in the same way as the National Planning Commission. But co-ordination is necessarily weaker, for the Planning Department does not possess the status,

[29] Ibid. pp. 5–6.

expertise, or experience of the Commission, while the State Planning Committee is often a hurried meeting of very busy men.

For plan implementation there is a plethora of interdepartmental committees. These, unlike the working groups, are standing bodies. They include a State Development Co-ordination Committee, a Campaign Co-ordination Committee (for cereal production), a State Implementation Committee (working under the direction of the State Co-ordination Committee), a Manpower Officers' Committee, a State Committee on Employment, and a State Co-ordinating Committee (for the supply and demand of labour). Of these, the most important from the point of view of planning is the State Development Co-ordination Committee, which contains heads of departments as well as Secretaries and meets under the chairmanship of the Planning Secretary.

This co-ordinating apparatus does not work very well. The committees often fail to achieve their purposes, because there are too many of them, with overlapping jurisdictions, making demands on the time of the same hard-worked personnel. Moreover, all the people concerned have other—and usually more urgent—responsibilities, to which planning tends to take second place. This applies even to the Planning Secretary himself, who, as Development Commissioner, is responsible for the oversight and direction of the CD Programme.[30] The problem is aggravated by the fact that the Planning Department, where fundamental thought and research ought to be taking place, is small and rather poorly staffed, while the Department of Economics and Statistics, as in most other states, lacks well-trained personnel. Most serious, however, is the doubt that exists about the location of responsibility; for the Planning Department not only lacks the power and prestige that the National Planning Commission has: it confronts a formidable rival in the shape of the Finance Ministry. How serious is the conflict between the two, and how little this is allayed by the system of committees clearly emerges from the following passage in Professor Masaldan's study:

The Finance Department and the Planning Department both deal with financial allocation. As one Head of Department remarked, 'There are now two bottlenecks instead.' Information is often divided between the two agencies. What is worse, instead of exchanging information among themselves, they often require executive departments to secure it. For example, in connection with certain special schemes (1959) for the development of backward areas of Bundelkhand to be implemented with a loan from the Government of India, the Finance Department asked the Industries Department to obtain from the Planning Department the terms of the loan granted by the Government of India. The Industries Department replied that this information should be available in the Finance Department itself. The Finance Department denied

[30] No longer; see above p. 76 n. 27.

having the information. The Industries Department maintained that it was not likely that the Planning Department had corresponded with the Government of India in this connection since the conditions of the 'Block Loan for Miscellaneous Development Schemes of the State Government' applied to this loan also. All this and further correspondence and delay might have been avoided if the Planning and Finance Departments were better coordinated. Such lack of coordination can result in delaying even urgent schemes. In the case cited above, an advance from the State Contingency Fund was granted in the meanwhile in view of the urgency of schemes but where this is not possible delay would be the result.[31]

It may be objected that this is just a case study in administrative pathology and that the whole trouble could have been avoided if the bureaucrats in the two departments had been a little more sensible and co-operative. One must remember, however, that bureaucrats in India (apart from a few outstanding men at the top) tend to administer 'by the book' rather than by reference to a series of objectives. Indeed, the very conception of an 'objective' is alien to many of those who occupy the subordinate ranks. Furthermore—and this is a more serious point—the objectives of the Finance Department and of the Planning Department are different ones. Broadly, Finance thinks in terms of economy, Planning in terms of development. Sometimes this conflict of purpose means that, when the Planning Department is criticizing operational departments for shortfalls in expenditure, the Finance Department is delaying the issue of the necessary expenditure sanctions.

Other states have encountered the same problem, and some have decided to cut the Gordian knot by giving responsibility for planning to the Finance Department itself, in the hope that Finance will thereby become 'planning-minded'. One such is Maharashtra. *Prima facie* evidence that this state has one of the best planning machines in India is provided by the Maharashtrian Third Five-Year Plan, which *reads* more like a plan and less like a mere collection of schemes than the corresponding plans of any of the other states.

Like Uttar Pradesh, Maharashtra has a broadly-based committee to give general advice on planning problems. Unlike Uttar Pradesh, however, it does not organize this as a kind of extended Cabinet meeting, to which junior ministers, Secretaries, parliamentarians, industrialists, professors, &c. are all invited. Specifically called a *Consultative* Committee for Planning, the body is composed of 'outsiders' and parliamentarians (including the leaders of the opposition), meeting under the chairmanship of the Chief Minister, with the Planning Secretary in attendance.

Up to 1956 there was a Minister for Planning. The job was then taken over by the Chief Minister, with the assistance of a Deputy Minister for

[31] Masaldan, *Planning*, pp. 19–20.

Planning. This lasted until 1960, when planning duties were transferred to the Minister of Finance. To give general direction to plan preparation, there is a sub-committee of the Cabinet, consisting of the Ministers of Finance, Agriculture, and Planning. This is *ad hoc*; it guided the formulation of the Third Five-Year Plan and then dissolved.[32]

At the official level, there have been changes to correspond with the transfer of planning to the Finance Ministry. Originally, the Chief Secretary acted both as Planning Secretary and as Development Commissioner—a formidable combination of duties. Then a separate post of Development Commissioner was created, with planning 'attached' to it. When the Finance Ministry took over the planning function, the Development Commissioner relinquished his planning responsibilities, which were transferred to the Finance Secretary. However, as the Chief Minister retained his overall interest in the subject, the Chief Secretary continued to play an important role as co-ordinator. He is chairman of the planning committee of departmental secretaries, and he accompanies the Finance Secretary on the latter's visits to New Delhi to discuss the state's annual plans with the Planning Commission.

At first sight, this suggests the possibility of another built-in conflict situation; but it appears that relations between the Chief Secretary and the Finance Secretary (and presumably also between their respective ministers) are such that little inconvenience is experienced. All the officials whom the author consulted were united in the view that the location of day-to-day planning responsibilities in the Finance Ministry was an improvement. The specific advantages they claimed for it were (*a*) that it avoided the need for time-consuming cross-references between two departments, and (*b*) that the presence of the planners within the Finance Ministry had a salutary effect on the attitudes towards planning of that ministry's more orthodox minded officials. The Finance Minister himself spoke of the greater coherence achieved by bringing together Planning and Finance in the same department, and of the consequently improved mutual understanding between the people who formulated the plans and those who had to find the resources.

The technical planning machinery within the Ministry of Finance was, at the time observed, very small and somewhat rudimentary. One Deputy Secretary, an IAS man, was in general charge, and beneath him there were two Under-Secretaries, both from the state Administrative Service, one responsible for 'programme and progress', the other for financial aspects. An academic economist from the University of Bombay

[32] Another such committee has been set up in connexion with the Fourth Plan. As this has the additional duties of determining intersectoral priorities in annual plans, of watching progress, and of evaluating achievements, it is presumably intended to be permanent (*PANL*, Sept. 1963, p. 6).

was employed in a part-time advisory capacity. That such good planning work had been accomplished was a tribute to the quality of these people.

It was recognized, however, that if planning was to be improved a larger and more sophisticated organization had become essential, and preparations were in hand to reorganize this division of the Ministry into five 'wings'. An Economic Wing, with a Chief, two Assistant Chiefs, and an adequate complement of research officers, was to concern itself with 'perspective planning'; a Manpower Wing was to deal with manpower problems, including the provision of training facilities; a Programme Wing would take responsibility for drafting the five-yearly and annual plans; an Evaluation Wing would organize the appraisal of projects; and a Resources Wing would investigate the raising of finance. Recruitment of personnel for this extended apparatus was recognized as difficult, owing to the shortage of people with the requisite qualifications. It was proposed that both the recruitment and training of research officers and research assistants should be undertaken by the state Bureau of Economics and Statistics, and it was hoped that specially hand-picked superintendents from the Finance Department would form the nucleus of a new cadre of 'supervisors'.[33]

Madras provides another example of a state which has given planning responsibilities to its Ministry of Finance, and which holds that this is the right way of discharging them. Formally, its planning set-up is very similar to Maharashtra's; but the planning-finance merger is longer-established and there is strong resistance to the setting up of anything more elaborate and sophisticated than the present rather rudimentary machinery. This appears to be due to the key position held by the Finance Secretary, a man of strong personality and long administrative experience who has a profound knowledge of the problems of the state and is convinced that he can do all the planning that is necessary without much assistance. As is normal, ultimate planning responsibility rests with the Chief Minister. In practice, his influence is confined to ensuring that due emphasis is placed on his favourite priorities, such as the expansion of electric power supplies.

Within the Finance Ministry, there is virtually no specialized planning organization. The Finance Secretary believes that planning and budgeting are essentially the same process and that both ought to be done by the same person—himself. He has no very high regard for the services of economists or statisticians, and is of the opinion that the state's existing statistical service can provide him with all the data that he needs. Nor has he much use for the working groups which, in Madras as elsewhere, are given the responsibility for drafting the state's plan sector-wise. His fundamental position is that 'real' planning is done by the Planning

[33] See ibid. Feb. 1963, p. 5.

Commission, and that what is miscalled 'planning' at the state level means no more than the establishment of common-sense priorities and the tuning up of the administrative machine to a high level of efficiency. The state knows what it wants, i.e. higher agricultural production and more industrialization. It also knows that the first means more water, more fertilizers, better soil conservation, and the extension of the Japanese method of paddy cultivation; and that the second means encouraging the private industrialist through building up the infrastructure, providing finance, establishing trading estates, and pressing for a more generous allocation of industrial licences. Planning simply involves deciding how much of these can be done over a given period of years; ensuring, by a process of rough calculation, fructified by experience, that they all march together; and finding the necessary resources. For this, no elaborate apparatus is needed.

The formulation of the plan, therefore, is essentially an exercise whereby the projects of the various departments, devised to give expression to the broad policies and priorities established by the Cabinet, are gathered together in the Finance Ministry and cut down to correspond with the resources likely to be available. Its co-ordinated execution depends on regular reporting and firm centralized control. Every quarter, progress reports are submitted by the Heads of Departments to the Finance Secretary, who gathers them together for submission to the Cabinet. The Cabinet then holds a two-day meeting, with the Finance Secretary and departmental heads in attendance, where decisions are taken to speed progress and improve co-ordination.

If Madras is convinced that planning and finance are the same and ought to be united, its neighbour, Andhra Pradesh, is equally convinced that they are different and ought to be divided. In Andhra, as in Uttar Pradesh, planning is closely associated with community development.[34] There is a Minister for Panchayati Raj and Planning, and under him a Secretary for Planning and Local Government, who has the status of Additional Development Commissioner. (The Chief Secretary acts as Development Commissioner, for a constitutional reason which it would be tedious to explain.)

Overall responsibility is in the hands of a Cabinet Committee on Planning, identical in membership with the Cabinet itself. This meets on the same day as the Cabinet, either before or after the main meeting. Advice, as in Maharashtra, is provided by a Planning Advisory Committee, representative of industry, banking, universities, and voluntary organizations and containing MPs, MLAs, and MCLs. Sectoral preparation, as

[34] Also, as in Uttar Pradesh, a decision has recently been taken to separate the two. As from Sept. 1963 the Planning Dept was divested of its *panchayati raj* responsibilities, which are now discharged by a separate department (ibid. Sept. 1963, p. 5).

usual, is in the hands of working groups. Co-ordination of implementation is effected through a Co-ordinating Committee, which meets every two months and consists of the Chief Minister, all 'development' ministers, their secretaries, and the heads of the corresponding departments. This would appear to perform much the same functions as the quarterly 'extended Cabinet' meeting in Madras.

The Secretary for Planning and Local Government has the help of a Deputy Secretary, who is an IAS man with experience as a Collector, and an Assistant Secretary from the state Administrative Service. Preparation of planning data is largely in the hands of a Bureau of Economics and Statistics, which has personnel in the blocks and districts as well as in the capital. The Bureau contains a Planning Cell, which periodically assesses the progress of plan schemes and assists the heads of departments in the preparation of their progress reports. It also contains an Economic Research Section, a National Income Unit, and an Administrative Intelligence Unit. During the course of the Third Plan, Andhra, like Maharashtra, is proposing to strengthen this technical apparatus. The existing units of the bureau are to be given additional duties and more staff, and two new units, an Official Statistics Unit and a Labour Statistics Wing, are to be created. As Andhra Pradesh is a poorer state than Maharashtra, with a smaller reservoir of trained and experienced personnel, this expansion is likely to prove difficult.[35]

From the fragmentary information that exists about planning machinery and planning methods in the states, certain tentative conclusions can be drawn. First, there is a fundamental difference between planning at the centre and planning in the states. The centre has to draw up a viable plan for the whole of India; the state need do no more than produce a collection of projects which it hopes may be fitted into the all-Indian plan. The centre has to give careful consideration to priorities in relation to resources; the state, being heavily dependent upon the centre for financing nearly everything it undertakes, can simply 'unload' on the centre a list of all things it wants to do, and leave to the Planning Commission the unenviable task of sorting them out and relating them to financial availabilities. The centre needs to prepare the all-Indian plan with the utmost realism; the state may even acquire a vested interest in *un*realism, in so far as it may think that an unrealistically inflated state plan gives it more room for bargaining with the Commission. These features of the centre-state relationship (which are further analysed in Chapters IX and X) have their effects on the degree of seriousness with which the state

[35] These intentions were expressed in Andhra's Third Five-Year Plan report. Subsequently they were modified. The Govt. of Andhra decided to create, with effect from 1 Sept. 1963, a separate Planning Department in the Secretariat. This will consist of 4 'wings', viz. (1) Economic; (2) Resources; (3) Planning; and (4) Evaluation (see ibid.).

approaches its task of constructing a planning machine. No state would willingly go to the trouble and expense of establishing a cut-down version of the National Planning Commission. Most states, so far, have tended to regard planning as a slightly peripheral function, to be discharged by an official who has no special qualifications for it, possesses no special status, and sometimes combines planning responsibilities with other and extremely onerous duties.[36] The usual set-up consists of a Department (or Bureau) of Statistics, a Planning Department, and a Planning Secretary. The first rarely does much more than collect and present such data as are fairly readily obtainable; the second is a normal secretariat department, staffed with officials who may or may not have any interest or expertise in planning; the third is an administrator who is as often as not a bird of passage—and a heavily burdened one. Admittedly, there are improvements on the way. In Maharashtra and Andhra Pradesh, as we have seen, more attention is being paid to the technical planning apparatus and to the organization of statistical services; in Uttar Pradesh the Planning Secretary, although still 'doubling' as Development Commissioner (and indeed 'trebling' as Manpower Officer)[37] has been given the status of Additional Chief Secretary; while in many states some attempt is being made to develop special 'cadres' of planning technicians. But what has been done so far by no means amounts to a revolution; and the reason for the almost universal foot-dragging is simply that few state governments see the need for fundamental change.

Secondly, the state administrative machines are not devised for the co-ordination of development programmes, which is the essence of planning. Although vast new responsibilities have been undertaken and many new departments brought into existence for their discharge, organization and rules of procedure have changed little since British days, when, as Professor Masaldan rightly says, 'the coordinating agencies were used as a means of controlling and restricting the spending departments and not for stimulating them to new efforts and gearing their activities to a plan'. Difficulties springing from the same source, the extraordinarily long life of 'old father antique', the law of the British Raj, are also experienced at the centre, but there skillful and prestigious top-level administrators can often push a way through the jungle of ancient regulations, while the Planning Commission itself constitutes a powerful countervailing force. In the states, where administrators are, on the average, of lower quality, where their political masters keep them on rather short strings, and where

[36] Planning departments in the states, writes K. Santhanam, are 'never top level bodies' (*Union-State Relations in India* (1960), p. 50). The separation of responsibility for planning from that for rural development, however, has been made in a number of states during the course of the Third Plan (see above, p. 76 n. 27).

[37] No longer so (see p. 82 n. 34).

there is no equivalent of a Planning Commission, progress towards administrative rationalization and co-ordation is necessarily slower.

Thirdly, there is the problem of overcoming built-in departmental antagonisms, of which the most serious is usually that between planning and finance. If planning and finance are given to separate departments, there is inevitably a tussle between the two, in which the more bureaucratically-minded administrators will use all the weapons with which literally-interpreted regulations can equip them. Usually, the Finance Department wins, because it is more prestigious and possesses the ultimate sanction of the purse. But if planning and finance are united the danger is that the combined department will be dominated by either the one function or the other. If, by exception, planning comes out on top, then one of the most important purposes of a Finance Department, to enforce due economy in expenditure, may be neglected. If finance triumphs, planning may be pushed to the periphery and unduly subordinated to the alleged requirements of the annual budget. Maharashtra claims that it has effected a happy marriage between the two, but more evidence is needed before it can be provided with a certificate of conjugal compatibility. Madras also informs the inquirer that no difficulties are experienced; but in both states the apparent smoothness with which the machine runs would appear to depend on the presence of certain personalities.

That planning in many states displays a low level of efficiency is, of course, to be deplored; but the variety of approach which the states bring to their planning tasks is offensive only to dogmatists. In so experimental a field, no one can as yet be certain of having found the right answers, and it is clear that what works well in one context may work very badly in another. When the author began his tour of the Indian states, he held that to make the Finance Minister responsible for planning was invariably a mistake. By the time he had finished his discussions with state officials, he had become much less certain. Admittedly, there are some very poor variations. Many states have given little thought to their planning problems and have tended to adopt the 'easiest' solution. But if the laggards are sufficiently stimulated by the pioneers, India may well become an important laboratory for testing different kinds of planning machinery.

All states need to make improvements. At present, as a result of the defectiveness of their apparatus for formulating and co-ordinating projects, for collecting and collating statistical and other data, and for evaluating results, an enormous burden is placed on the National Planning Commission. If this body tends to proliferate and to become over-complex, part of the reason is that it now has to do a tremendous amount of work that could be done more effectively if it were geographically decentralized. Moreover, the states cannot reasonably complain that the Commission 'dictates' unless they themselves come forward with plans which are demonstrably well adapted to their individual needs and based upon realistic appraisals of their own capacities for resource-mobilization. It is true that part of the plan, e.g. that concerned with heavy industry, power production, and long-distance transport, is ineluctably 'national' in character, and that every other part has to conform with nationally determined limits, priorities, and proportions. But within this general framework the scope for effective regional and area planning is immense; and it is difficult to see how any national plan can approach optimum economic and political viability if the authorities at these levels adopt a 'leave-it-to-the Commission' attitude.

Better planning machinery is also necessary if the states are to cease living 'hand to mouth' and fully participate in the drawing up of long-distance plans. Otherwise there is a danger that perspective planning, as far as they are concerned, will be no more than an interesting arithmetical exercise. It is also important that they, no less than the centre, should feel themselves committed to the longer-term objectives. This point has been well made by the Planning Commission itself.

> During the next three years States will . . . participate in the drawing up of a long-term plan of development for the country . . . . This plan is intended to present the general design of development for the country as a whole over the next 15 years or so. It will be based on a study of the resources and possibilities of different parts of the country and will seek to bring them together into a common frame. This is a task of great complexity, as it is of great promise, and there will be need for close and continuous collaboration between various agencies at the Centre and in the States, especially those responsible for planning, as well as leading institutions in the country engaged in scientific, economic and social research. From this aspect as well as the implementation of the Third Plan and the preparation of the Fourth, it will be necessary for States to consider the lines along which the existing arrangements and machinery for planning at the State level should be further strengthened.[38]

Accordingly,[39] the Commission has urged the states to establish Planning Boards by adapting its own pattern to their more modest needs.

> Following the parallel at the Centre, it might be helpful if the Chief Minister could be Chairman of the Planning Board and the Finance Minister . . . a member . . . . In addition, it might be possible to secure for the State Planning Board the assistance of two or three persons with special experience and knowledge who may preferably serve full-time as members. The State Planning Board could gradually build up a nucleus organisation which could not only assess the proposals of the Departments and bring them together into a plan of Development, but could also help the Departments to plan more systematically

[38] *FYP(3)*, p. 289.

[39] D.O. letter no. 4(G)/62 Plan, 20 Mar. 1962, to Chief Ministers of all states from Deputy Chairman, Plan. Com. (mimeo.).

in a longer perspective and on the basis of further statistical and technical data. The State Statistical Bureau would of course need to work in very close association with the Planning Board. Over a period the State Planning Board would be able to build up its own expertise in planning.

Responses to this suggestion have been various. Some states have agreed to it, but without any conspicuous degree of enthusiasm.[40] Others, such as Madras, see no point in it. Many, while conceding that the establishment of a board might improve the quality of their planning, cannot see any likely source from which the necessary expert personnel could be obtained, and argue, quite rightly, that an inexpert Planning Board would be worse than none at all.

The Commission clearly hopes that the 'core' of the Planning Board will consist of whole-time planning experts, enjoying an adequate status in the administrative hierarchy. These might be associated, as in the Planning Commission itself, with a number of leading ministers, or might sit on their own under the chairmanship of the Chief Minister, Planning Minister, or Finance Minister. They would certainly need an apparatus under their own control, of the kind that is currently being constructed in Maharashtra and Andhra Pradesh. Their relationships with 'line' departments would have to be carefully worked out and clearly established.

That all states will eventually adopt some such form of planning organization seems probable, if the centre brings sufficient pressure to bear. The problems involved in rephasing the Third Five-Year Plan, in order to make greatly increased provision for defence, are adding urgency to the centre's arguments. But whether any real improvement in planning procedures is effected depends on several factors. One is the sense of commitment to planning on the part of the Chief Ministers. Some of these, it may be predicted, will continue to subordinate the need for long-range planning to that for winning the next election, and will therefore simply go through the motions of establishing Planning Boards in order to satisfy the whims of a remote and theory-bedevilled Commission. Another factor, as already indicated, is the availability of suitable personnel. States such as Maharashtra or West Bengal or Madras are obviously much better off in this respect than, for instance, Rajasthan, Orissa, Assam, or Andhra Pradesh; but none have a superfluity, and the only way of making good the shortage, as far as one can see, would be the establishment of a National School of Planning, perhaps attached to the Commission. A third factor is the ability and willingness of ministers,

[40] The Chief Minister of Mysore appears to be one of the more enthusiastic advocates of improved state planning machinery. In his Introduction to Mysore's Third Five-Year Plan, he writes: 'Since planning now is . . . a continuous process and constitutes a specialist job, it would lead to the conclusion that the question of establishing an expert machinery for planning at the State level needs to be seriously considered' (Mysore, *FYP(3)*, i: *Policy and Programme* (1961)).

secretariat officials, and heads of departments to adapt themselves to the new system, which will demand of them a flexibility of outlook and a capacity for mutual co-operation which few of them as yet have attained. Finally, much will depend on the evolution of the relationships between the Planning Commission and the states. If state planning is to have that extra significance necessary to provide adequate compensation for taking more time and trouble over it, the process of negotiation whereby state plans are geared to the national plan will need to be reconsidered.

IV

THE FIRST FIVE-YEAR PLAN, 1951–6

THE MAKING OF THE PLAN

(i)

THE Cabinet resolution of 1950 which established the Planning Commission neither specified a planning period, nor confronted the Commission with a deadline. If the members, however, imagined that they would have much opportunity to conduct econometric investigations or to pursue empirical inquires, they were soon to be disillusioned; for in July 1950 they found themselves called upon to produce a six-year programme to be placed before the Commonwealth Consultative Committee by September. This programme, later to be incorporated in the Colombo Plan for Co-operative Economic Development in South and South East Asia, they succeeded in completing by the end of August.[1]

In the nature of things, it was little more than a collection of projects, accompanied by a few attempts to estimate the resources likely to become available for capital formation. Of Rs3,219 crores worth of projects already in hand or seriously under consideration, the government, on the advice of the Commission, selected the Rs1,840 crores worth which it held to represent the essential minimum. Overwhelming emphasis was placed on agriculture, which accounted for 33 per cent of the proposed investment, and on transport and communications, which were to absorb 38 per cent. Only 13 per cent was allocated to fuel, power, industry, and mining. Public infrastructural investment, particularly in multi-purpose projects, transport, and communications, was expected to make possible a private investment of Rs160 crores per annum in the early stages of the plan, rising to Rs260 crores per annum in the later stages. Total investment, over six years, was to achieve a modest rise from an existing calculated level of 4 per cent of the national income to one of 5½–6 per cent. Domestically-financed investment was to rise from 2½ per cent to 4–4½ per cent.

With an optimism which now seems positively breathtaking, the government expressed the opinion that towards the end of the six-year period the need for public investment 'on the large scale projected for earlier years' would decline, and that after the end of the programme 'increased

[1] *DO(1)*, p. 2.

government revenues and domestic saving' should be sufficient to meet investment needs.[2]

The actual scale of the 'Colombo' programme did not differ greatly from that of the first published draft of the Five-Year Plan, issued in July, 1951. The former envisaged a public investment of 1,840 crores over the six-year period, the latter one of 1,493 crores over a five-year period.[3] The main difference—and it was a major one—was in the distribution of the proposed investment, the Draft Outline giving much more to agriculture (including the major irrigation projects) and much less to transport and communications.

A five-year planning period had been decided upon before the Planning Commission's work was interrupted by the demand for reasonable-looking figures for the benefit of the Commonwealth Consultative Committee. On 1 August 1950 the Prime Minister announced in Parliament that the Commission was drawing up a five-year plan in two stages, the first covering 1951–2 and 1952–3 and the second the subsequent three years. 'Preliminary work on the preparation of the plan', he added three days later, had 'reached an advanced stage'.[4]

From September 1950 the Commission became engaged, with the help of the central ministries and state governments, in 'examining in detail the schemes under execution as well as those proposed to be taken up in the First Five Year Plan'. It was also holding 'consultations with representatives of the principal industries for determining the main lines of development to be recommended for industries in the private sector'.[5] In accordance with the general method of work that had been adopted, both central ministries and state governments were asked to prepare detailed proposals for 1951–3 and broader outlines for 1953–6. By February 1951 these had been received and the Commission was almost ready 'to suggest detailed priorities to the Central Government and the States, and also to indicate the levels to which financial resources might be raised during the next few years'. Discussions with the state governments for the purpose of gearing their proposed development programmes to their anticipated financial resources began in the same month and extended over several weeks. According to Nehru's statement on 10 August 1951, the Planning Commission's extensive consultations produced 'general agreement'.[6]

(ii)

The Draft Outline, issued for public discussion in July 1961, was a cautious document. Circumstances did not seem to warrant any great optimism. Inflation had not been brought under control, industry was

[2] Cmd. 8080 (1950). [3] *DO(1)*, pp. 36–37. [4] PD, 1950, pt 1, iv, 37 & 273.
[5] *DO(1)*, p. 2. [6] PD, 1951, pt 1, vi, 1539–40.

stagnant, and agriculture stricken with a disastrous drought. Even the building up of a sizeable and unexpected surplus on the current balance of payments account, as a result of the Korean War, was of doubtful value, as the first Annual Report of the 'Colombo' Committee pointed out. The Commission, furthermore, was perhaps excessively aware of its own inexperience, of the inadequacy of the data at its disposal and of the difficulties of planning an economy such as the Indian.[7] Nevertheless, the Draft Outline of the First Five-Year Plan, despite the modesty of its proposals, is in an important sense the seminal document of Indian planning. In the chapter entitled 'The Approach to Planning' there are to be found most, if not all, of the basic ideas which still guide the work of the Planning Commission.

First, there is the emphasis on 'a large measure of agreement in the community as to the ends of policy'. The importance of unity of purpose, says the Draft Outline,

> is illustrated by the records of achievement a country sets up under the stress of emergency, such as war. The pressure of circumstances creates a unanimity as to the ends of policy which permits of no deviation from the pursuit of the objective in view. This unanimity produces a coherence of policies and of practical measures so essential to planning. It follows that a major task for a Government which embarks upon planning in peace-time and for a constructive end is to create in the community similar earnestness of purpose on the basis of which resources can be mobilised to the full extent. It is this earnestness of purpose which enables a community to make whatever sacrifices are necessary for the attainment of defined goals.

Some of the merits and, as we shall see, many of the demerits of the Indian approach to planning arise from successive attempts to give practical expression to this principle of unanimity.

Secondly, planning is conceived of as a democratic process, not merely in the sense that the governments doing it are responsible to an electorate as wide as the whole adult population, but in the sense that the people themselves participate actively both in the formulation of the plans and in their implementation. Thus:

> Democratic planning presupposes an overall unity of policy combined with proper diffusion of power and responsibility. In such planning, not only the Governments of States but also local self-governing bodies, such as municipalities, district and *taluka* boards and *panchayats*, and various functional organisations have to play a vital part. Measures to promote a healthy growth of such institutions, are, therefore, an integral part of democratic planning. We visualise that in due course it will be possible for the *panchayats* and other local, regional and functional bodies to participate actively in the preparation of plans. The role of the central planning authority will be to prepare a general

[7] *DO(1)*, p. 3.

framework for the Plan, to invite the appropriate local and functional bodies to send in the plans affecting their respective fields, and, when these are received, to amend and adapt them, in the light of overall needs and resources, and finally to work out, in consultation with the bodies concerned, a comprehensive National Plan. In the implementation of the Plan, again, the principle of diffusion of power and responsibility must be followed. The function of the Central Government is thus to evolve a coordinated policy and to act as an ultimate source of reference in case of conflict between local or sectional interests.

Thirdly, planning is to be directed towards the achievement of the 'Directive Principles of State Policy', as embodied in the constitution. Three of these had been written into the Planning Commission's terms of reference, viz.

(*a*) that the citizens, men and women equally, have the right to an adequate means of livelihood;
(*b*) that the ownership and control of the material resources of the community are so distributed as best to subserve the common good; and
(*c*) that the operation of the economic system does not result in the concentration of wealth and means of production to the common detriment.

The Draft Outline, however, indicates that it considers all the Directive Principles, from clause 36 to clause 51, as relevant to the Planning Commission's task. These include some rather more specific policy pointers of great importance, viz. (1) the organization of village panchayats, to be endowed with 'such powers and authority as may be necessary to enable them to function as units of self-government'; (2) the promotion of cottage industries 'on an individual or co-operative basis in rural areas'; (3) the provision, within ten years from the commencement of the constitution, of free and compulsory education up to the age of 14; (4) the promotion of the 'educational and economic interests of the weaker sections of the people, and, in particular, of the Scheduled Castes and the Scheduled Tribes' and the protection of these sections 'from social injustice and all forms of exploitation'; (5) the prohibition of intoxicating drinks, except for medicinal purposes; and (6) the prohibition of 'the slaughter of cows, calves and other milch and draught cattle'.

Fourthly, the Draft Outline attempts to lay down the principles to be followed in determining the choice between the competing objectives stated in or implied by its terms of reference, e.g. 'maximum production, full employment, lower prices, greater equality of incomes'. Here it begins to display the schizophrenia which still to some extent remains characteristic of the Commission's attempts to formulate its tasks in general terms. 'On the one hand we must concentrate on this, but on the other hand we must not neglect that' is the familiar formula which now makes its appearance. Although 'an increase in the output of essential consumption goods in the immediate future must have a high priority', the need to step up capital formation demands 'some sacrifice of current consumption'. Although it is 'necessary that the Plan provides for fuller employment', there are 'difficulties in the way of an acceptance of full employment as an immediate objective of policy'. Cottage industries 'have an important part to play', but if their promotion 'requires sacrificing indefinitely the fruits of technical progress, the loss to the community may be much greater than the gain'. Equality is 'indispensable for the survival of democracy, and a carefully worked out policy for reduction of disparities in income and wealth is the *sine qua non* of planning', but 'the rate at which progress may be made in the direction of equality has inevitably to be adjusted to the requirements of the present economic situation' and to those of 'democratic methods'.

Fifthly, the Draft Outline indicates the general approach, subsequently to be followed, to the techniques of planning. It mentions but rejects as a 'possible approach' the 'more or less complete nationalisation of the means of production and an extensive system of governmental controls on the allocation of resources and on the distribution of the national product'. Public ownership of the means of production, it concedes, 'may be necessary in certain cases; public regulation and control in certain others'; but the private sector has 'to continue to play an important part in production as well as in distribution', and the resources available to the public sector must be used for 'investment along new lines' rather than for 'the acquisition of existing productive capacity'. Hence 'planning, under present conditions . . . means . . . an economy guided and directed by the State and operated partly through direct State action and partly through private initiative and effort'. In respect of trade, to which the Industrial Policy Resolution had made no direct reference, the Draft Outline suggests that there are 'special considerations', the most important being the 'tendency in countries operating on small commodity margins for resources to go into the distribution of goods rather than their production'. To deal with this tendency, which could become inimical to development, it proposes that co-operative trading organizations should be encouraged and also that the State itself might 'enter the field and divert to itself the profits that might otherwise have gone into more or less unproductive investments'. State trading might have the additional advantage of helping to 'regulate the prices of certain commodities subject to wide fluctuations'. The export trade is specifically mentioned as the most likely starting-point.

The need for 'increasing coordination' and 'harmonious working' between the two sectors, public and private, is heavily underlined. In the field of 'organized' (i.e. large-scale) industry, this will be effected by regular consultation with the representatives of capital and labour. In that of the 'unorganized' sector (i.e. agriculture and small-scale production) 'it will be necessary to build up local and regional bodies as well as functional associations which can play an effective role in the formulation and implementation of the Plan'.

At the same time it will be necessary to operate a system of controls. These will comprise '(*a*) capital issues control, (*b*) licensing of new enterprises and of large extensions of existing ones, (*c*) foreign exchange allocations, and import and export controls, and (*d*) price and physical controls'. The Draft Outline gives only the most general indications of the manner in which these controls should be operated. Its very reasonable intention is to leave this to the government, advised by the Planning Commission, as each specific situation requiring control arises.

The only ideological element missing from this approach—as indeed from the final plan itself—is the 'socialist pattern of society', which did not become accepted policy until 1954. It is not easy to discover what 'pattern' the authors of the Draft Outline had in mind, and it may be that they were not very interested in any particular pattern, except to the extent that one was implied by the Directive Principles of the constitution. There are suggestions that the extent of public ownership should be determined solely by necessity and convenience, and one passage seems to imply that controls themselves may be dispensed with as soon as more abundant production (providing the 'conditions for a smooth functioning of an unregulated economy') has been attained.[8] But these isolated and rather ambiguous implications should not be taken too seriously; nor, indeed, should the impact of the subsequent 'socialist pattern'.

Of the instruments of planning, the Community Project is the only absentee; for the decision to embark on the Community Development and National Extension Movement was not taken until 1952, long after the publication of the Draft Outline. Here again, however, the absence is more apparent than real, as the chapter on 'Machinery for Rural Development' envisages an administrative set-up which is in no way fundamentally different from that subsequently adopted.

In general, the 'philosophy', methods, and techniques of Indian planning during the last fourteen years are all to be found (although sometimes only in embryo) in the Draft Outline of July 1951. By reading it carefully and critically, an observer with superhuman powers of prediction could have foreseen both the strengths and the weaknesses that the planning process was to display.

As we have already said, both the general aims and the specific proposals were modest. There was no bold econometric calculation; indeed, if any mathematics other than simple arithmetic had been done the fact was carefully concealed. There was no 'perspective' other than the

[8] Ibid. p. 31.

obvious and short-term one of rectifying the 'disequilibrium in the economy caused by the War and Partition' and developing 'certain basic resources so as to lay the foundation of more rapid economic growth in the future'.[9] If the proposed outlay looked rather more generous than that proposed for the Colombo Plan, the main reason was simply that a number of schemes financed out of current revenue, excluded from the Colombo Plan, were now included.[10] Dominated by the fear of continuing inflation, reluctant to exert more than a little extra pressure on an already hard-pressed economy, and perhaps fearful lest over-ambition might play into the hands of the anti-planners, the Commission limited its proposed outlay to cover little more than projects which were already in execution or due to begin. This amounted to Rs1, 493 crores, representing 'the outlay on development which seems manageable with the resources now in sight', and calculated to do no more for the ordinary man than 'restore the pre-war availability of essential consumer goods by the end of 1955–56'. If more were required, such as a solution to the food problem by a doubling of the irrigated area over the next fifteen years or a guarantee of 'a balanced and sustained utilization of the technical organization built up in connection with the various projects', another Rs300 crores would have to be found. This money could only come from foreign sources.[11]

For the determination of priorities no very esoteric calculations were required. It was as obvious to the Commission as to everyone else that in a predominantly agricultural economy the tempo of development would depend, 'in the initial stages, largely on the volume of agricultural production and the surpluses that are available from it'. As agriculture was both stagnant and hard hit by Partition, the main purpose of the plan had necessarily to be 'to meet the more glaring deficiencies' in production. A series of subsidiary or instrumental objectives also more-or-less determined themselves; to extend irrigation facilities, to increase the supply of fertilizers, to bring technical knowledge to the farmer, and to relieve the pressure of population on land (itself a cause of low productivity) by developing alternative employment opportunities in rural areas. Only second in importance was the development of transport and communications, on which depended 'to a great extent a more effective utilization of available resources and the necessary stimulus to further economic expansion'.[12] The railways, urgently in need of rehabilitation, were scheduled to absorb no less than three-quarters of the total transport investment. Social services came third in order of priority, not because the Commission thought that heavy expenditure on education, health, housing, &c. was immediately justifiable, but because, for political and

p. 109

[9] Ibid. p. 16. [10] Colombo Plan 1st Ann. Rep., Cmd. 8529 (1952). [11] *DO(I)*, pp. 36–37.
[12] Ibid. p. 39.

humanitarian reasons, a serious effort had to be made to rehabilitate the millions of refugees from Pakistan. Industry (other than power, which, being the product of multi-purpose schemes, is included in the agricultural figure for purposes of this rough analysis) came a very bad fourth in the priorities list. About one-third of the 6·7 per cent of total industrial investment was to take the form of assistance to 'private agencies', while most of the remainder was to be devoted to state-owned industrial projects which were already under execution. The most important of these, in respect of size of investment, were the Sindri Fertilizer Factory, the Bangalore Machine Tools Factory, and the Visakhapatnam Shipyard. Despite their potential importance as providers of employment in rural areas, cottage and small-scale industries could be spared an investment of only 16 crores out of the 100 crores allocated to industry as a whole. In the private sector, main emphasis was placed on 'raising the output of existing industries to their installed capacities'[13] rather than on the creation of new capacity. Only aluminium and cement (which had already undertaken large expansion projects) were scheduled to increase production at all spectacularly (aluminium from 3,600 to 20,000 tons, cement from 2,613,000 to 4,600,000 tons).

Expenditure was to be shared about equally between centre and states, the latter being responsible for 'agriculture and rural development, social services and the expansion of transport and communications falling within their jurisdiction', and enjoying central assistance, in the form of loans and grants, estimated at Rs211 crores.[14] The importance of correcting regional disparities was recognized, but 'limitation of resources and the need to complete projects already in hand' left little scope for the initiation of new schemes with this end in view.[15]

The estimate of resources available for the public sector rested on the assumptions (*a*) that the central government would maintain a surplus of Rs26 crores per annum on its revenue account; (*b*) that additional resources of Rs213 crores would accrue to the states, over the five years, through the widening of the coverage of existing taxes and the imposition of certain new ones; (*c*) that long-term borrowing would yield a total of Rs115 crores and small-scale savings and unfunded debt one of Rs250 crores; and (*c*) that non-developmental expenditure would not rise significantly. Totalling Rs1,121 crores, these resources left an expenditure gap of Rs672 crores, the covering of which would depend (except for Rs290 crores to be realized by running down sterling balances) on foreign assistance, of which some would be provided by the United States Food Loan and the aid offered by Canada and Australia under the Colombo Plan.

For large-scale industries in the private sector the estimated outlay was Rs250–300 crores. Total annual outlay, public and private, was

[13] Ibid. pp. 148–55. [14] Ibid. pp. 40–41. [15] Ibid. pp. 42–43.

expected to average Rs400 crores per annum. The Commission considered that this order of investment was 'feasible', but admitted that 'for an adequate analysis of the implications of the rate of development envisaged over the next five years' the data were not available.[16] Hence it refrained from making any attempt to quantify the overall economic improvement at which it aimed, contenting itself, for the moment, with specifying the absolute increases in production expected for each individual commodity. Production of foodgrains was to rise by 7,200,000 tons and their consumption from 13·67 oz. per adult per day to 14·50 oz.

(iii)

The publication of the Draft Outline provoked considerable public discussion, as it was intended to do. Between July 1951 and December 1952, when the final version of the First Five-Year Plan was submitted by the Commission to the government, the Outline was examined in detail by the central ministries and the state governments, debated in Parliament, in most of the state legislatures and in many district boards and municipal committees, studied by university seminars and *ad hoc* groups of officials and non-officials, subjected to criticism by a multitude of voluntary organizations, and widely commented upon by the press and other organs of opinion. There were those who held that the plan was too small; that it was too big; that its priorities were wrong; that it was a businessman's plan, useless to the common people; that it was a bureaucrat's plan, useless to the businessman; that it was fundamentally un-Indian (and specifically anti-Gandhian) in conception; and that it was no plan at all. Most if not all of these views were expressed in the parliamentary debate on the Draft Outline held on 15 October 1951,[17] but most of the significant discussion took place outside the walls of the Parliament building.

Apart from the Communists, Professor D. R. Gadgil offered the most radical criticism.[18] Indeed, virtually nothing in the Draft Outline met with his approval. Its targets were based on calculations devoid of real significance, its attempts at inter-sectoral co-ordination ludicrously inadequate and hopelessly wrong, its proposed methods of controlling the economy too feeble to be effective, its fiscal policies inflationary and its social implications grossly inegalitarian. Indeed, he seriously questioned whether it 'could be at all properly called a plan'.

His reaction is in many ways typical of that most articulate section of the Indian community, the intellectuals. Indeed, it goes a long way to

[16] Ibid. pp. 49–52. [17] PD, 1951, pt 2, xvi, 5039–228.

[18] Submitted to the Planning Commission in Sept. 1951, published in (a) *Econ. Dev. & Cult. Change*, Mar. 1952; and (b) D. R. Gadgil, *Economic Policy and Development* (Poona, 1955), pp. 122–44.

explain why, apart from a few outstanding exceptions, they have played no more than a peripheral role in the planning process. The framers of the Draft Outline were confronted with a certain constellation of economic, social, political, and administrative circumstances which severely limited their room for manoeuvre. They were not free to produce a 'socialist' plan, and had to devote their energies to devising the essential minimum of measures necessary to get some movement into a badly stagnant economy. Deficiencies of data restricted their capacity to make reliable forecasts; lack of any previous experience inhibited them from attempting to specify the techniques best adapted to deal with contingencies which, at best, they could only vaguely envisage. Their motto—a very sensible one under the circumstances—was *on s'engage et puis on verra.* Gadgil, on the other hand, wanted everything to be cut and dried, and demanded the employment of planning techniques most of which were then beyond the administrative capacity of the state and many of which still are. His criticisms, therefore, although entirely disinterested, were essentially unproductive. Between this type of criticism from the intellectuals and the crudely self-interested type from the various pressure groups, there was not much middle ground. Hence, although public discussion was undoubtedly valuable, it did not provide the Commission with a great deal of positive help in its task of working up the Draft Outline into a final plan, except to the extent that it suggested what might be the more profitable lines to follow from the standpoint of obtaining the maximum public co-operation.

Much more useful indications were provided by the important changes in the economic situation that took place between July 1951 and December 1952. As a result partly of government policies but mainly of external influences, inflation was being brought under control. Agricultural production was recovering, but investment in industry was sluggish, many industries were operating well below capacity,[19] and unemployment appeared to be increasing. Everything seemed to point in the direction of 'a more liberal policy in financing investment expenditures',[20] i.e. a bigger plan. It is not surprising, therefore, that the final plan increased total outlay from Rs1,493 to Rs2,069 crores.

[19] Between Apr. and Dec. 1952 there was 'appreciable improvement', over the corresponding period in 1951, in the production of cotton, cement, iron and steel, paper, paper board, ammonium sulphate, sewing machines, bicycles, rayon and jute goods, salt, ball and roller bearings, but falls in the production of aluminium, pumps, diesel engines, machine tools, looms, hurricane lanterns, dry and storage batteries, superphosphate, sulphuric acid, soda ash, paints and enamels, leather, glass, woollen manufactures and handloom cloth. Some of these falls were spectacular, e.g. pumps from 29,000 to 18,000, diesel engines from 5,000 to 2,000, and sheet glass from 4,158, to 2,450 tons (*PR 1951–2 & 1952–3*).

[20] For information about the economic situation up to Dec. 1952, see the First and Second Colombo Plan Reps (Cmds 8529 & 9016) and *PR 1951–2 & 1952–3.*

THE PLAN

(i)

By the time of publication of the final planning document,[21] on 7 December 1952, the plan which it purported to describe had been in operation for some twenty months. During that period, very slow progress towards the attainment of the Draft Outline's targets had been registered; consequently the increase in the size of the plan made the developmental backlog look even more formidable and threatened to throw very heavy burdens on an already overburdened administration. The manner in which the increase was effected, moreover, demanded some effort of adjustment on the part of those charged with implementation; for the proportions laid down by the Draft Outline had been considerably changed.

The biggest change was in the first item, 'Agriculture and Community Development', outlay on which went up from 12·8 per cent of the total (Rs191·69 crores) to 17·4 per cent (Rs345·84 crores). Rs90 crores of this increase were accounted for by the new CD Programme, another Rs30 crores by extra provision for minor irrigation, while most of the remainder was distributed between agricultural extension, soil conservation, resettlement schemes and 'training and experiments in co-operative organization'. The other big change was in the programme for industry, which now accounted for 8·4 per cent of total outlay (Rs172·87 crores) as against 6·7 per cent (Rs100·99 crores) in the Draft Outline. Alarmed by the sluggishness of the private sector and by mounting unemployment, the Commission had decided that 'the provision made for the development of industry in the public sector was insufficient'. It therefore stepped up the outlay on large-scale industry from Rs79·54 crores to Rs140·33 crores, and that on cottage and small-scale industries from Rs15·77 to Rs27·04 crores. Pride of place in this increase was taken by the proposed new iron and steel works, estimated to cost a total of Rs80 crores, of which Rs30 crores were included in the First Five-Year Plan provision. Other projects benefiting by the increase were machine tools, penicillin, scientific instruments, DDT, and shipbuilding. Village industries, some of which (e.g. handloom) had actually suffered further decline during the first twenty months of the plan, were to receive 'greater emphasis'. It should be noted that these changes of emphasis, significant as they were, did not affect the broad order of priorities laid down by the Draft Outline, which remained unchanged.[22]

Internal resources (i.e. the revenue and capital receipts of public authorities available for development expenditure) were now put at

[21] *FYP(1)*. [22] See Introd. & ch. 9, 'The First Five Year Plan in Outline'.

Rs1,414 crores, as against the Rs1,121 crores of the Draft Outline. The revenue surplus of the central government was to go up from Rs26 crores per annum, the 'additional revenue' raised by the states from a total of Rs213 crores to one of Rs232 crores. These two increases did not amount to much, and the Commission considered that 'any radical changes in the machinery of taxation or in the techniques of borrowing' were not to be looked for. It held, however, that the trend of the market for loans and small savings justified it in postulating a figure of Rs520 crores for capital receipts—Rs145 more than that forecast by the Draft Outline. It was from borrowing, in fact, that the 'main improvement . . . in the resources position' was to be expected. A resources gap of Rs655 was to be filled, to the extent of Rs290 crores, by deficit financing, now mentioned as such for the first time. This figure was determined by what the Commission regarded as the 'safe upper limit' of releases from India's sterling balances. Precisely the same as the figure mentioned in the Draft Outline (p. 52), it showed that the planners were still very nervous about inflation, in spite of the change in the economic climate that had taken place. The remaining Rs365 crores, they said, could be 'met only from external resources or, in the absence of it [*sic*], by additional measures of internal taxation and borrowing or by further deficit financing'. (External assistance of Rs156 crores was already in sight.) For the remainder of the plan a foreign exchange gap of Rs180–200 crores per annum was forecast. Of this about Rs50 crores was to be financed by sterling releases; ability to meet the balance would 'depend to a great extent on the availability of external assistance'.[23]

Four features of this statement of the resources position are worthy of note. The first, as already mentioned, is the Commission's continuing fear of inflation, particularly now that the size of the plan had been increased. The fact that the index of wholesale prices had risen somewhat above its 'low' of May 1952 appeared to indicate the need to persist with 'a disinflationary price policy', while the obstinate shortage of foodgrains suggested 'that the assumption of a continuance of the condition of relative scarcity'[24] was the only realistic one to make. Only later, when the great harvests of 1953–4 and 1954–5 produced relative abundance, was it realized that the Five-Year Plan's approach to deficit financing had proved unnecessarily cautious. Unfortunately, over-optimism about the possibilities of deficit financing then replaced the over-pessimism of 1952.

The second noteworthy feature is the reluctance of the Commission significantly to step up the rates of taxation. This was partly due to its awareness of the administrative difficulties of tax-collection in an under-developed country, and partly, no doubt, to its fear of political repercussions, particularly if the tax base were considerably widened. Mainly,

[23] See *FYP*(*1*), ch. 3, 'Assessment of Resources'. [24] Ibid. p. 177.

however, it would seem to reflect the extent of the Commission's reliance on private enterprise for the achievement of plan targets. While admitting that India's total tax revenue, as a proportion of national income, was one of the lowest in the world (7 per cent), the planners feared that direct taxation of the rich was more 'likely to impinge on their savings than on their consumption' and doubted whether 'alternative institutional arrangements' could be made quickly enough to compensate for the resultant 'loss of incentive in certain strata of society'.[25]

The third feature—a very ominous one—is the studied vagueness of the proposals for bridging the resources gap. The Commission hoped for more foreign assistance than was actually in sight and, if this did not materialize, suggested that recourse might be made to higher taxation, which it had already virtually ruled out, or to increased deficit financing, which it had already pronounced dangerous.[26] As it happened, the 'gap' presented no problem in the First Five-Year Plan, which drew neither on foreign assistance nor on deficit financing to the utmost practicable limit. The attitude adopted was none the less irresponsible, and the fact that the gamble came off on this occasion led to its repetition under circumstances where its irresponsibility all too quickly became apparent.

The last feature is the Commission's failure to bring together, in any meaningful way, the financial targets and the physical targets. Although it held that 'a programme which aims at using the resources of the country to the maximum advantage extent possible should be conceived of and translated back at every stage in terms of the various types of physical resources needed for its implementation',[27] it did not itself attempt any calculations of this sort, except in the form of a projected 3:1 capital-output ratio which was little more than an expression of hope. Undoubtedly, it would have liked to do so, but had neither the time nor the statistical data at its disposal. Later, when it had both, it allowed itself the luxury of a great deal of optimism in relating its financial with its physical targets. Once again, the 'success' of the First Five-Year Plan went to its head.

Apart from the changes in targets and the recalculation of resources, most of the plan was an expansion of the contents of the very much shorter Draft Outline. Two early chapters, however, presented material of fresh interest, which showed that the Commission was lifting its sights and developing its techniques. The basic political and administrative assumptions remained the same as those in the Draft Outline, except for the new emphasis placed on the 'readaptation of social institutions and social relationships'. After underlining the prevailing ignorance of 'human motivation and of social processes' and the consequential difficulty of predicting in advance the 'responses of individuals or of groups of individuals

[25] Ibid. p. 40. [26] Ibid. p. 46. [27] Ibid. p. 66.

or of classes', the Commission drew the conclusion that a 'considerable part' of its task was 'to assess the significance of some of these indeterminate or partially known factors at work in the life of the community and to recommend policies on the best judgement available'.[28] This was promising. Unfortunately it was never adequately followed up, either in the First Five-Year Plan or in subsequent plans. Lack of realism about both individual and group motivations has been, as we shall see, one of the basic weaknesses of the Indian planning process.[29]

But if the political and social assumptions behind the plan, to the extent that they were spelled out in the document, remained cloudy, the economic assumptions had been made much more precise. The main obstacle to a high rate of economic growth was identified as the inadequacy of India's 'stock of capital'. 'Other factors', such as 'certain forms of economic and social organization', were admitted to be important, but the achievement of rapid economic advance was essentially 'conditional upon additions to and improvements in the technological framework implicit in a high rate of capital formation'.[30] This was fully in line with most of the best thinking about economic development in the early 1950s, but coming as it did immediately after the paragraph about social factors, strongly suggested that the Commission was only too glad to push the latter into the background in favour of something more readily quantifiable.

International comparisons suggested to the Commission that the rate of capital formation would need to be raised from 5 to 20 per cent of the national income to enable the achievement of a 'rate of growth commensurate with the needs of an underdeveloped country with a low standard of living'. Most of the increase would have to come from savings, as, in the earlier stages of development, possibilities of utilizing India's abundant unemployed and underemployed manpower resources were restricted by 'lack of technical skill' and 'shortages of specific commodities and services'. During this critical initial period, two alternative methods of resource mobilization were available. In thus stating them, the Commission also made its choice between them:

> One is to impose on the community a high rate of saving through taxation, loans, price inflation, or by any other means and to utilise the resources thus made available for a sharp increase in the rate of capital formation. This certainly has its merits, as, in this way, not only would development be rapid but there would be immediately a large increase in employment. But this

[28] Ibid. p. 7.
[29] See Samaja Shastrajna's letter to *EW*, 4 Oct. 1952: 'When will economists and the Government realise that economic reforms need to take into account the social constitutions within which economic factors operate? Only in India could the Government launch on a five year plan without consulting a single sociologist who has a first-hand acquaintance with the social institutions of the people.'
[30] *FYP(1)*, pp. 13–14.

increase in employment will not lead to a corresponding increase in spendable incomes; the community as a whole will have very little more to consume than before and there would be set up severe inflationary pressures. The other alternative is to step up the rate of capital formation more gradually, but this would mean that progress would be correspondingly less rapid. Since the objective of planning is, in fact, to promote rapid development, the problem is one of stepping up the rate of investment by defined stages, so as to minimise the hardships in the initial period, but taking care at the same time that the community does put forth within a relatively brief period the big effort needed.

By ensuring, in fact, that increasing proportions of the national income were ploughed back as the national income itself increased, the Commission hoped to avoid imposing on the community 'any excessive degree of privation and suffering'.

In determining the possible rate of development, two further factors had to be taken into account, viz. '(*a*) the rate of growth of population, and (*b*) the increase in national output and income likely to follow from a given increase in the capital stock'. Population increase—apt, said the Commission with masterly understatement, 'to become more a source of embarrassment than of help to a programme for raising standards of living'—was put at 1¼ per cent per annum, which was the rate recorded during the last decennial period; the capital-output ratio was estimated, on the basis of international comparisons, as 3:1, with the increased output materializing 'in the third year from the date of investment'.

Using these assumptions, the Commission calculated that the national income of India (approximately Rs9,000 crores in 1950–1) could be raised by over 160 per cent in 22 years, and per capita incomes doubled, if capital formation were stepped up from the beginning by two-thirds of the additional income generated in each year. Such a rate, however, would cause organizational difficulties and require an actual 'reduction in per capita consumption standards for a period of from 10 to 15 years'. A smaller rate would, therefore, have to be adopted. In the First Five-Year Plan 20 per cent of the annual additional income would go to capital formation; this, supplemented by external resources, would generate, in 1955–6, a national income 11–12 per cent above the 1950–1 level. From 1957–8 the rate might be raised to 50 per cent. If this were done, saving as a proportion of total national income, having risen from 5 per cent in 1950–1 to 6¾ per cent in 1955–6, would thereafter rise steeply to 11 per cent in 1960–1 and to 20 per cent in 1967–8. From that time onwards, although resources devoted to investment would go up in absolute terms, capital formation as a proportion of total national income would remain steady. The result would be a doubling of per capita income by 1977 and a raising of consumption standards by a little over 70 per cent of the 1950–1 level.

Although the Commission described these calculations as 'illustrative', it clearly regarded a rate of development based on them as feasible. It even suggested that the rate might be exceeded. 'A fair proportion of the investment required', it held, 'could be drawn from the beginning from unutilized manpower and other resources'; comparatively low investment in such services as education, technical training, and agricultural extension could produce a comparatively high yield; the proportion of the national income devoted to defence could be reduced if the international situation remained favourable; and, 'with family planning on a nation-wide scale', the rate of population growth might be brought down to 1 per cent per annum 'or even lower'.

'In view of all these considerations', the planners courageously concluded, 'we regard the rate of development indicated . . . as not only the minimum that the community will have to aim at over the next few quinquenniums but as something which must be exceeded'. Thus ended the Commission's first essay in 'perspective planning'.[31]

In addition to the above, which was a major addition to the Draft Outline, one important change of emphasis should be noted. Although continuing to assert that the public and private sectors could 'well supplement each other and need not necessarily expand at the expense of one another', the Commission now envisaged a situation 'in which the public sector takes over progressively the promotional and managerial functions necessary for development'. This would render unnecessary 'large inequalities of income' and 'higher consumption standards for particular classes' and hence enable one of the most important items in the Directive Principles of the constitution to be put into effect. A necessary corollary was that 'the State itself must raise, to the extent possible, through taxation, through loans and through surpluses earned on State enterprises a considerable proportion of the savings needed'.[32] This point was neither emphasized nor worked out in detail, but its inclusion provided evidence of the way the planners' minds were moving. They were influenced, no doubt, by the sluggishness of private enterprise's response to the various incentives offered, but it is not unreasonable to suppose that, at Nehru's instigation, they were also firing the first few shots in the ideological battle which culminated in the adoption, by Congress, Parliament, and government, of the 'socialist pattern of society'.

(ii)

The plan was debated by Parliament on 15 December 1952,[33] when the government introduced a motion calling upon the Lok Sabha to give it 'general approval'.

[31] Ibid. pp. 13–23. [32] Ibid. pp. 30, 40–41. [33] LSD, 1952, pt 2, vi, 2367–834.

That the overwhelming majority of the Lok Sabha would vote for the plan was, of course, a foregone conclusion. Nevertheless, the number of amendments proposed to the government's resolution was considerable, and some of them were almost undisguisedly hostile to planning as such. One criticized the Commission for 'over-expectation' and 'unwarranted optimism' and predicted that its misconceived efforts would result in the 'disorganization of the entire economic system'. Another complained of 'regimentation' and forecast a 'lowering of the standard of living for the bulk of the population'. Others, by contrast, criticized the timidity of the plan, expressing disappointment at the 'low targets', calling attention to the lack of emphasis on manpower mobilization, and claiming that the problems of distribution and employment had been neglected. Socialist-inspired amendments pointed to the Commission's 'failure' to give expression to the Directive Principles of the constitution, inveighed against the plan's 'reactionary' industrial policy, which would intensify class domination, and demanded that the means of production, including the land, should be nationalized. One or two amendments, as might have been expected, had a Gandhian emphasis. Several, inevitably, drew attention to the injustices suffered by regions of the country which the plan was alleged to have neglected. The most important amendment, however, was that proposed by the Communist Party, asking the House to record its regret that the proposals 'fell far short of a real effort to achieve a social order for the promotion of the welfare of the people even as directed by Articles 38 and 39 of the Constitution'.[34] This amendment sounded mild enough, but the speeches of its supporters were very fierce. Of the less radical critics, only Krishnaswami made really telling points. He called for a bolder use of deficit financing, and claimed that the policy of relieving unemployment by developing the handloom industry made very little sense, as any increased production would come from the existing 3 million handloom workers, who did not 'have work for more than eight or ten days'.[35] For the rest, little was added to what had already been said during the public discussion of the Draft Outline.

IMPLEMENTATION

In his contribution to the Lok Sabha Debate, Nehru emphasized the flexibility of the First Five-Year Plan. 'The method of planning', he said, 'is ultimately the method of trial and error'.[36] Flexibility was indeed the keynote of plan implementation during the course of the remaining three and a quarter years. No major changes were made in the proportions of the plan but the process of upward revision, which had characterized the

[34] Ibid. cols 2382–8. [35] Ibid. col. 2498. [36] Ibid. col. 2375.

period from the publication of the Draft Outline in July 1951 to that of the final planning document in December 1952, was continued. Eventually, the projected total outlay rose to Rs2377·67 crores, which was Rs308·90 crores more than the figure which the planners had contemplated on the latter date.

The main reasons for this upward revision were the continued growth of unemployment and the greater scope given to the planners by the successful harvests of 1953–4 and 1954–5. It was the first that made further investment desirable, the second that made it possible.

During 1953 unemployment was causing widespread concern and criticism, which found ample reflection in a parliamentary debate, initiated by the Communists, which dragged on, through adjournment after adjournment, from 24 August to 18 December.[37] On 21 November the Finance Minister, C.D. Deshmukh, announced that he had come to the 'inescapable' conclusion that 'if the problem of unemployment is to be handled, the rate of investment must be brought up to such a level that it enables full utilization of the foreign exchange resources available either out of past savings or by way of current external assistance'. It would be 'quite ironical', he added, 'if a country, which has a big development programme, ends up with a surplus on external account'. The Commission, he informed the House, had therefore 'recently' decided to increase the size of the plan by Rs175 crores.[38]

On 4 December the Minister of Planning, Gulzarilal Nanda, gave details. The central ministries could devote an extra Rs45 crores to rehabilitation, Rs10 crores to a new road programme, and Rs15 crores to 'other schemes'. As for the states, a 'special programme' of repairs to tanks and roads and of other permanent improvements, designed especially for the benefit of the scarcity areas, had been produced.[39]

These additions, which were later added up to a total of Rs180 crores and which raised outlay on the plan to Rs2,248·77 crores, appeared to give satisfaction to the Lok Sabha.[40] It might, perhaps, have felt rather less satisfied if it had known what was subsequently revealed: that the so-called additions 'were in part at least substitutions for schemes in respect of which progress was slow for various reasons'.

Later additions, made in 1954–5, involved the allocation of extra funds for flood-control projects, for the rehabilitation and improvement of the railways, for loans to shipping companies, for the relief of unemployment among the educated, for local development works, for rural and urban water-supply and sanitation, for work among the backward classes, and for power projects designed to relieve unemployment by 'expanding power facilities in small towns and rural areas'. Together with the previous additions, these brought the total planned outlay up to the final 'adjusted'

[37] LSD, 1953, vii–x. [38] Ibid. ix, 448. [39] Ibid. cols 1517–21. [40] Ibid. x, 2531.

figure of Rs2,377·67 crores. They too, however, contained a large element of 'substitution'.[41]

The economic situation which made the policy of additions not only possible but necessary was characterized by the Commission's *Progress Report* for 1953–4 as one of 'strength and stability'. The strength arose from a harvest of foodgrains which reached no less than 150 per cent of the target for the final plan year. Stability was reflected in the balance of payments situation and in the price and cost-of-living indices.

Price and Cost of Living Indices, 1950–3 (1949 = 100)

Year	*1950*	*1951*	*1952*	*1953*
Prices	105	115	101	103
Cost of living	101	105	103	106

From this situation the Commission drew the following conclusion: 'So long as inflation, manifest or latent, was a major problem, a cautious attitude towards investment expenditure was unavoidable. But since excess money supply has now been completely liquidated and production is making steady strides, an acceleration of the rate of expenditure is not only harmless but also desirable'.[42]

At the same time the Commission detected certain ominous signs, suggesting that, in spite of the apparent buoyancy of the economy, no 'marked advance' could be recorded towards the attainment of the plan's 'long-range objectives'. Although business was now booming in the private sector, after the setback of 1952–3, only 40 per cent of the total outlay for the public sector had been spent during the first three years, and such vital fields of development as Community Projects, Railways, Industries, Education, Housing, and Rehabilitation were all markedly behind schedule. This could be attributed to delays in finalization, the late commencement of some schemes, 'insufficient working out of schemes in advance', the lack of certain types of equipment, the shortage of personnel with the requisite qualifications, and the 'time needed for setting up the necessary administrative machinery'—all remediable defects. More serious was the fact that no evidence was at hand to suggest that the rate of investment was increasing as a proportion of the national income. Equally disturbing was the lack of any firm evidence that the increase in agricultural production was in any way the result of planned

[41] See *PR 1953–4*, p. 5; ibid. *1954–5*, pp. 169, 172, 173, 186, 190, 230; *RFYP(1)*, pp. 18, 142–3, 231, 249–50, 273, 290.
[42] *PR 1953–4*, p. 5.

effort. But for the good luck of the monsoons, it seems that agriculture would have shown virtually no improvement on previous years.[43]

During the year 1954–5, however, the good luck held. There was another excellent harvest, and private industrial investment moved rapidly upwards. No financial difficulties were encountered, and public sector projects, having overcome some of their early problems, greatly increased their rates of expenditure. But high unemployment persisted and capital formation, particularly in the public sector, made little progress.[44] Particularly worrying to the Commission was the poor financial performance of the states. This had already been noted in the *Progress Report* for 1953–4.

TABLE 1

Agricultural Prices, 1949–56
(base year ended August 1939 = 100)

	1949	*1950*	*1951*	*1952*	*1953*	*1954*	*1955*	*1956*
Rice	495	514	544	527	514	417	442	549
Wheat	635	531	549	533	566	492	433	528
Jowar	274	340	297	216	212	185	119	249
Bajra	265	245	245	245	283	233	212	281
Gram	358	364	384	403	417	277	205	301
Food articles	390	410	410	360	381	358	304	373

Source: RFYP(1), p. 101.

In the 1954–5 *Report* the Commission again had to criticize the states for their 'inability to realize in full or even substantially the targets of revenues from additional taxation' and for their 'increases in developmental expenditures outside the plan'.[45]

Clearly, a rapid increase in outlay on development could not be indefinitely combined with virtual stagnation in public and private savings. It required only a bad or even average harvest to reveal the fundamental weakness of the economy. This came in 1955–6, the last year of the plan. The year was characterized 'by an increased rate of developmental activity in both the public and the private sectors', but

[43] Ibid. pp. 6, 8, 11, 59–60, 102–3, 118–19, 143–5. In the LSD on the *Progress Report* (22–24 Dec. 1954), Nanda admitted that the unemployment situation was serious and that little progress had been made in basic education, co-operation, land reform, and cottage and small-scale industries. He did claim, however, that 'certain calculations' had revealed that 'nearly half' of the agricultural achievements might be attributed to causes other than the good monsoon. Irrigation, for instance, had been responsible for an increase of 20 lakh tons, reclamation for 3, 'other improvements' for 10, fertilizers and manures for 8, improved seeds for 5, and community works for 4 (LSD, ix, 3944–5).

[44] *PR 1954–5*, p. 20. [45] Ibid. p. 14.

agricultural production was $2\frac{1}{2}$ per cent below the record figure for 1954–5, and consequently wholesale prices moved up by 11·6 per cent, thereby nearly wiping out the previous year's fall. This in itself did not worry the Commission very much, as falling prices, in a context of attempted rapid development, could hardly be regarded as a sign of economic health. But it did provide evidence that the economy was now under greater strain, a fact that was underlined, during the first six months of 1956–7, by a 'substantial fall in foreign exchange reserves'.[46] Although neither the government nor the Commission fully understood what was happening, the Indian economy, now that the slack had been largely taken up, was moving into that condition of extreme stringency in which it still remains. The planning 'honeymoon', in fact, was over. No repetition of the somewhat spurious achievements of 1954–6 was possible.

RESULTS

In attempting to assess the achievements of the First Five-Year Plan one is confronted with two difficulties; first, that the economic improvements registered during the period 1951–6 cannot all be attributed to the plan; secondly, and conversely, that much that was achieved during this period was in the nature of laying foundations for future advance and hence did not reflect itself in the overall figures of increased production, increased per capita income, &c. The Commission itself, of course, was acutely aware of these difficulties, and in its general *Review of the First Five-Year Plan*, published in 1957, did its best to make allowance for them. But as, in many of the fields of endeavour which it attempted to analyse, quantification was difficult and attribution of results to causes virtually impossible, it had to content itself in the end with a somewhat impressionistic statement.

In so far as results could be measured by public expenditure, they are given in Table 2 (p. 110) where realized outlay is compared with the outlay projected by the Draft Outline, by the original plan, and by the 'adjusted' plan. This shows, firstly, that the so-called upward adjustments of 1953–5, aimed principally at increasing employment, were fictitious, at least in respect of their effect on total outlay; for realized expenditure was in fact slightly smaller than the expenditure projected in 1952. How far the 'additions' affected substitution is as difficult to assess as is their effect on the employment situation itself. The other obvious thing to emerge from the expenditure table is the heavy shortfall under the heads of 'Agriculture and Community Development' and 'Industry and Mining'. Expenditure on the first was Rs46 crores less than the original plan

[46] Colombo Plan 5th Ann. Rep., Cmnd 50 (1956), p. 43. For agricultural prices 1949–56 see Table 1 (p. 108).

TABLE 2

First Five-Year Plan: Outlay—Allocations & Realizations

Heading	*Draft Outline*	%	*Plan*	%	*'Adjusted' Plan*	%	*Realized*	%
Agriculture & community development	191·69	12·8	345·84	17·4	354·32	14·9	299·61	14·8
Irrigation & power	450·36	30·2	561·13	27·2	647·46	27·2	584·96	29·1
Transport & communications	388·12	26·1	498·45	24·0	570·04	24·0	531·48	26·4
Industry & mining	100·99	6.7	172·87	8·4	188·24	7·9	99·84	5·0
Social services	254·22	17·0	341·32	16·4	395·86	16·1	325·57	16·2
Rehabilitation	79·00	5·3	85·00	4·1	135·70	5·7	97·29	4·8
Miscellaneous	28·54	1·9	64·23	2·5	86·02	3·6	74·31	3·7
TOTAL	1,492·92	100·0	2,068·77	100·0	2,377·67	100·0	2,012·63	100·0

Sources: *FYP(1)*: *Draft Outline*, p. 39; *RFYP(1)*, Annexure 1(1), pp. 333–5.

provision; on the second it hardly attained the provision made in the Draft Outline. However, if due allowance is made for early delays and difficulties, it was certainly an achievement to get within Rs56 crores of the original target for total outlay. In 1953 so near a miss had looked extremely unlikely. The hustle of the last two years had made up a remarkable amount of leeway.

So far as the achievement of physical targets is concerned, comparison can be only with the original plan (or with the Draft Outline), as only a few of the revisions of 1954–5 were expressed in other than financial terms. The most spectacular success of the period 1950–1 to 1955–6 was in the production of foodgrains, which went up from 540 to 649 lakh tons, representing an excess of 33 lakh tons over the targeted increase of 76 lakh tons and a percentage fulfilment of 143. Oilseeds also overfulfilled their target, by 156 per cent; but all other agricultural commodities showed shortfalls, serious in sugar-cane and jute. In other sectors, the only overfulfilments were in mill-made cloth (141 per cent), sugar (190 per cent), sewing machines (133 per cent), and locomotives (104 per cent). The construction of national highways just reached its targeted mileage and there were near misses in cement (90 per cent), ammonium sulphate (86 per cent), and bicycles (96 per cent). Electricity (installed capacity) came within 16 per cent of the targeted figure, but irrigation (acreage brought under) fell short by 29 per cent.[47]

In the private sector of industry 'investment targets . . . were fulfilled, and, through the more intensive utilisation of existing capacity, production was stepped up along the lines broadly envisaged by the Plan'; but in the public sector performance was very patchy.[48] For village and small-scale industries the aims were 'far from being fulfilled'. The railways, although reaching their revised financial provision, 'could not keep pace with the increase in traffic', while road transport in the states suffered severely from the fact that the state governments had displayed greater interest in the nationalization of existing facilities than in their improvement. In shipping, communications and broadcasting there were considerable shortfalls.[49]

Much more serious, from the standpoint of long-term development, was the shortfall in education. Although the number of children in primary schools or classes increased, over the plan period, by 61·3 lakhs, this represented only 60·6 per cent of the planned target. The percentage of schoolchildren in the age-group 6–11 was up by 9·9, as against a targeted 18·8. Secondary education fell even shorter of the target, partly because the new Ministry of Education programme, with its emphasis on multipurpose schools, came into effective operation only in the last year of the

[47] See below Table 3 (p. 112). [48] *RFYP*(*1*), p. 183; *FYP*(*2*), pp. 387–90.
[49] *RFYP*(*1*), pp. 212, 231, 236, 238–9, 244–6.

TABLE 3

First Five-Year Plan: Physical Targets & Achievements

	(*a*) *Prodn. Devel. Base 1950–1*	(*b*) *Plan Target (additional to (a))*	(*c*) *Achievement 1955–6*	(*d*) *Achievement as % of target*
1. *Agricultural Production*				
Foodgrains (in tons)	54·0	7·6	10·9	142
Cotton (lakh bales)	29·1	12·6	10·3	82
Jute (lakh bales)	32·8	20·9	9·0	43
Sugarcane (lakh tons of gur)	56·3	7·0	2·4	35
Oilseeds (lakh tons)	50·8	4·0	5·6	135
2. *Irrigation & Power*				
Area irrigated (m. acres)	51·0	19·7	14·0	71
Electrical energy (installed capacity m. kw.)	2·3	1·3	1·1	84
3. *Transport & Comms.*				
Shipping tonnage:				
(*a*) Coastal (lakh GRT)	2·2	1·05	0·2	19
(*b*) Overseas (lakh GRT)	1·7	1·15	0·7	61
Roads:				
(*a*) Nat. Highways (000 mls)	12·3	0·6	0·6	100
(*b*) States Roads (000 mls)				
Surfaced	97·5	—	24·1	—
Unsurfaced	151·0	—	44·1	—

4. *Industrial Production*				
1. Finished steel (lakh t.)	9·8	6·7	3·0	45
2. Pig iron (lakh t.)	15·7	12·6	2·2	17
3. Cement (lakh t.)	26·9	21·1	19·0	90
4. Aluminium (000 t.)	3·7	8·3	3·6	43
5. Fertilizer				
(a) Ammon. sulphate (000 t.)	46·3	404·0	347·7	86
(b) Superphosphate (000 t.)	55·0	125·0	16·0	13
6. Locomotives (nos)	3	170	176	104
7. Cotton manufactures				
(a) Yarn (m. lb)	1,179	461	454	99
(b) Mill cloth (m. yd.)	3,718	982	1,384	141
(c) Handloom cloth (m. yd.)	810	890	639	72
8. Jute manfs (000 t.)	824	376	230	61
9. Bicycles (000)	97	433	416	96
10. Sewing machines (000)	33·0	58·5	78·0	133
11. Power alcohol (m. gal.)	5·0	13·0	5·4	41
12. Sugar (000 t.)	1,100	400	760	190
5. *Social Services*				
Education:				
1. No. of pupils in primary schools (lakhs)	186·8	101·2	61·3	60·6
2. Percentage of school-going children aged 6–11	41·2	18·8	9·9	53·0
Health				
1. Hospital beds (000s)	113	12		
2. Dispensaries & Hospitals (nos)	8,600	1,400		

plan. In the production of teachers, too, there was 'much leeway to be made up'. University education, on the other hand, had undergone an expansion that was as ill considered as it was rapid. As for the other social services, water-supply and sanitation had made very little progress; even in the towns, at the end of the plan, about 45 million people lacked a protected water-supply, while 50 million were without sewerage facilities. The malaria programme, on the other hand, had succeeded, at a cost of only Rs11 crores, in reducing the number of reported cases from 60 million in 1953–4 to 20 million in 1955–6. However, this achievement, when placed side by side with the lack of any measurable results in the family planning campaign, could hardly be hailed with unrestrained joy by planners conscious of the fact that even in the most favourable of circumstances the race with population was going to be a severe one. Although an estimated total of 1·3 million houses, all of them urban, had been constructed by public and private agencies, the Low Income Group Housing Scheme had spent little more than half its allotted funds, and the Subsidized Industrial Housing Scheme had made a comparatively small impact. Rural housing had been 'scarcely touched'. Measures for the welfare of backward classes were said to have made rapid progress in the last three years of the plan, but their results could not be quantitatively assessed. Rehabilitation schemes had settled 4 lakhs of families on the land and another lakh in urban colonies and concentrations, but the Commission admitted that 'their rehabilitation was far from complete'. Land reform had progressed at variable rates from state to state; but there was little evidence to suggest that it had done much to achieve its proclaimed objective, viz. 'to bring about suitable changes in the structure of the rural economy which would, at the same time, promote rapid agricultural development'.[50] Community Development was still an act of faith, since no one could 'reconcile' none-too-reliable figures of achievement from the project areas with 'the overall progress in different fields made in a State or in the country as a whole'.[51]

On the basis of these summarized results, the verdict on the plan might have been 'good in parts'. Overall figures, however, were such as to give real satisfaction to the planners. National income (at constant prices) had increased by 18·4 per cent, from an estimated Rs8,850 crores in 1950–1 to an estimated Rs10,480 crores in 1955–6. Per capita income, also at constant prices, had risen by 10·8 per cent, from Rs246 to Rs274. Per capita consumption had increased by about 8 per cent. Four and a half million new jobs had been provided. Although inflationary trends had become evident in the last year of the plan, prices were still 13 per cent lower than they had been at the beginning. External accounts showed a slight surplus. From these facts the Planning Commission drew the

[50] Ibid. pp. 249–61, 273–82, 285–8, 290–1, 298–304, 314. [51] Ibid. p. 114.

conclusion that the 'overall picture' was one of 'stability and steady progress'. On the whole, it wrote in its introductory chapter to the Second Five-Year Plan (15 May 1956), 'the economic situation on the eve of the second plan is distinctly better than it was on the eve of the first plan; there is more confidence and greater readiness all round for a larger effort'.[52]

This, as we have already suggested, was an over-optimistic judgement. It failed to recognize the extent to which the economy had entered a phase of acute strain, and gave insufficient weight to the unfavourable long-term factors which the Commission itself had brought to light. The most important of these was the uncertain trend of investment. In 1951–2, total investment in the economy had been at the 'exceptionally high level' of 7 per cent of the national income. During the next two years it fell back to 5 per cent, then picked up to 6–6·5 per cent in 1954–5 and reached 7·3 per cent in the last year of the plan.[53] If the first year were disregarded, it could be held that investment had increased from about 5 to about 7 per cent; but this was obviously an impermissible (although frequently performed) procedure. The plain fact was that the period of the First Five-Year Plan displayed no discernible investment trend. The Planning Commission itself, moreover, admitted that the average figure of 6 per cent could not be regarded as 'impressive'. Particularly worrying was the trend of investment finance in the public sector. While the centre had found some Rs145 crores more than its planned target from taxation, the states had fallen behind by about the same amount. The railways, too, had failed to make their expected contribution, and this did not augur well for the extraction of surpluses, in the future, from less well-established public enterprises. The situation had been saved by the success of the public borrowings programme and by the fact that deficit financing to an extent of Rs428 crores, as against a planned limit of Rs290 crores, had proved possible;[54] but neither of these, and particularly the latter, was a source that could be counted on to flow as freely as in the past.

It could be argued, in fact, that the 'success' of the plan was due almost entirely to the good monsoons and to the existence of an economic climate (itself partly the result of the good monsoons) which encouraged industrialists to bring into production their unused capacity. (The extraordinarily favourable incremental capital-output ratio of 1·8:1 was clearly a product of both of these features.) The question therefore arose whether the plan itself had contributed anything to the achievements of the period 1951–6. As early as 9 October 1954 the *Economic Weekly*, in its comments on the recently-issued *Progress Report*, was arguing that the achievements recorded

[52] *FYP(2)*, p. 5. [53] Ibid. p. 3.
[54] *RFYP(1)*, pp. 27–29, 33–34. For sources of finance see Table 5 (p. 118).

TABLE 4

First Five-Year Plan: Sources of Finance

(Rs crores)

1. *Centre*

	Total 1951–6	*Planned*	
		Original	*Revised*
1. Outlay	1,114·9	1,233·7	1,389·5
Revenue acct	117·8	—	—
Capital acct	997·1	—	—
2. Budgetary resources	777·6	726·0	
Savings of public authorities			
—from current revenues	304·6	160·0	—
—from railways	115·4	170·0	—
Private savings absorbed through			
—loans from public	49·0	36·0	—
—small savings and unfunded debt	303·6	270·0	—
—deposits, funds and other miscellaneous sources	5·0	90·0	—
3. Transfer of funds from centre to states for development purposes (central assistance)	–349·7	–235·6	—
4. Gap in resources	687·0	743·3	—
5. External assistance	203·2	—	—
6. Deficit	483·8	—	—
—increase in floating debt	346·9	—	—
—sale of securities	25·2	—	—
—withdrawal from cash balances	111·7	—	—

2. *States*

	Total 1951–6	Planned	
		Original	Revised
1. Plan Expenditure	897·5	835·0	988·2
Revenue acct	424·1	—	—
Capital acct	473·4	—	—
2. Budgetary resources	499·7	531·5	—
Balance from revenue acct	269·7	409·7	—
Loans from public	155·4	79·0	—
Deposits & other misc. receipts on capital acct	74·6	42·8	—
3. Central assistance for Plan	349·7	235·6	—
4. Total resources (2 + 3)	849·4	767·1	—
5. Gap in resources	48·1	67·9	—
6. Gap covered by			
increase in floating debt	21·1	—	—
sale of securities held in reserve	10·2 }	67·9	—
withdrawals from cash balance	16·8 }		

Source: *RFYP(I)*, app. 2 & 3, pp. 42–43, 45–46.

TABLE 5

First Five-Year Plan: Public Revenues & Expenditures 1950/51–1955/56
(Rs crores)

	1950–1	*1951–2*	*1952–3*	*1953–4*	*1954–5*	*1955–6*
1. Revenue receipts	780	907	829	837	903	967
(*a*) Tax	632	746	677	674	723	760
(*b*) Non-Tax	148	161	152	163	180	207
2. Capital receipts	238	241	165	208	392	427
3. Total receipts	1,018	1,148	994	1,045	1,295	1,394
4. Total revenue receipts as percentage of national income	8·1	9·1	8·4	8·0	9·4	10·0
5. Expenditure, non-developmental	505	634	549	521	642	634
6. Expenditure, developmental	455	506	527	601	747	1,053
7. Expenditure, total	950	1,104	1,076	1,122	1,389	1,687

Source: RFYP(*1*), pp. 36–37.

in that document had little or anything to do with governmental policies. In fact, it wrote:

the financing aspect of the Plan has run so consistently counter to the essentials of development financing that one is almost tempted to conclude that the happy result has been achieved in spite of planning. Resources have been systematically withdrawn by the Exchequer and not fully utilised. Monetary policy has failed to create the conditions favourable for initiating development. If, in spite of all this, the economy has gone on expanding, all the credit goes to the resilience of the Indian economy and to its rural sector. The performance of the latter must be a pleasant surprise and an eye-opener.

This, perhaps, did rather more than justice to the rural sector and less than justice to C. D. Deshmukh, who, like most Finance Ministers, tended to err on the side of caution. It would be difficult to argue, however, that during those periods when prices were tumbling and a substantial surplus was being built up on foreign account, the government's financial policy did anything but hold back development. It might also not be easy to justify the fact that a high proportion of the total deficit financing was concentrated in the last year of the plan, when signs of strain were becoming apparent. One may agree with the Commission that the faults in the financing of the plan were largely due to the inadequacy of statistical and analytical techniques:[55] but it remains true that the Finance Ministry, presumably with the approval of the Commission, responded rather belatedly to movements in the economy instead of anticipating them.[56]

When the plan was over, a hostile but well-informed critic, Dr John Matthai, substantially confirmed the somewhat hasty judgement of the *Economic Weekly*. After writing off the plan as a mere 'programme of piecemeal development', he continued:

> With the exception perhaps of the Community Projects, every project included in the First Plan had been designed and partially erected before the National Government came into power. Two changes occurred since then. In consequence of the improvement in the food supply and the stabilisation of food prices due to the American Wheat Loan, to successive good monsoons and to the progress of irrigation, it became safer to supplement available resources by deficit finance. Secondly, the latter part of the first five-year period was marked in most countries by a revival of economic activity unprecedented since the cessation of the War. Partly aided by the Plan, India shared in this revival and was able to fulfil most of the moderate targets laid down in the First Plan.[57]

In some ways this contemptuous-sounding judgement may even be too kind. It attributes at least something to deficit financing and to irrigation; but the first, as we have seen, was not employed by the government with maximum effect, while the second does not appear to have been a major influence on agricultural production. In its *Review*, the Commission admitted gross under-utilization of the potential created by major irrigation schemes and refrained from attempting to estimate the impact of the minor ones.[58]

In the Second Five-Year Plan report (p. 258), the Commission had said that

> from the limited information available it appears that among programmes of development which have contributed to increase agricultural production during the first plan, minor irrigation works, increased use of fertilizers, land reclamation and development and the extension of the area under cultivation have been specially significant.

ECAFE, in its 1955 survey, had backed this up by stating that

> the popular impression that the increase in agricultural output in the past three years has been largely due to favorable weather . . . appears to be exaggerated when account is taken of large increases in irrigation facilities, larger

[55] Ibid. p. 18. [56] For details of the financing of the First Plan, see Tables 4 & 5.
[57] *The Times of India*, 16 May 1956. [58] *RFYP*(*1*), pp. 88–92, 144.

fertilizer supplies and improvement in agricultural practices, e.g. adoption of the Japanese method of paddy cultivation.[59]

By 1957, however, the Commission had obviously come to feel considerable scepticism about these attributions. Only fertilizer consumption, which had increased from 318,000 to 678,000 tons during the course of the plan, suggested a straightforward cause-and-effect relationship. On irrigation, the Commission's view had become very *nuancé*.[60] On the distribution of improved seeds, it reported 'poor' progress. On land reclamation, it gave some credit to the government-assisted effort of private farmers, but little to the operations of the government tractor organizations, and pointed out that 'at the end of the plan there were large areas awaiting recovery'. As for the Japanese method, although the area subjected to it was said to have increased from 400,000 acres in 1953–4 to 2·1 million acres in 1955–6, 'on the whole . . . programmes relating to the . . . adoption of improved agricultural practices did not receive adequate attention'. Moreover, other possible claimants of the credit for increased agricultural production were given equally short shrift.[61]

So far as agriculture is concerned, then, one can hardly accuse Dr Matthai of serious exaggeration. One might even go further and agree with the ever-critical D. R. Gadgil in saying that 'the major achievements of the First Five Year Plan' were 'not planned at all'.[62]

Nor can it be said that the years 1951–6 gave the Commission or the government much significant experience in the use of planning *techniques*. Administratively, of course, important lessons had been learnt from the attempt to organize various large-scale projects in the public sector, and considerable expertise has been gained in the use of budgetary and other financial weapons. But the employment of the specific controls envisaged both in the Draft Outline and in the plan itself had been rendered almost unnecessary by the peculiar nature of the economic circumstances. The ready availability of investment resources, in relation to demand from the private sector, meant that licences under the Industries (Development and Regulation) Act of 1951 could be freely granted, while the buoyancy

[59] UN, *Econ. Survey Asia & Far East, 1955*, p. 106.

[60] One of the reasons for the difficulty in assessing the impact of new irrigation potential was that 'while new minor irrigation works are constructed a proportion of the old works are falling into disuse' (*FYP*(*2*), p. 269).

[61] *RFYP*(*1*), pp. 93–97, 118 ff., 131. The *Review* concludes its section on Trends in Agricultural Production with the following words: 'While the general trend of food production would appear to be upward, it must be admitted that favourable seasons have played a notable part and there are substantial elements of instability despite the evidence of growth of agricultural production during the first five year plan. The experience of the first five year plan suggests the need for each State to undertake a critical assessment of the various factors which have operated in relation to its agricultural production trends during the past few years. From the overall production trends of the country as a whole only very cautious conclusions may be drawn' (pp. 100–1).

[62] Gadgil, *Planning*, p. 43.

of the balance of payments enabled the hand of the government to rest very lightly on the foreign exchange controls. In its *Review*, the Commission itself stated that the 'modest scale of investment', together with the overall improvement in the economic situation, obviated the need to exercise the regulation and control techniques which had been originally envisaged.[63] Throughout the plan, the only important application refused by the Industrial Licensing Committee was that of Birla to erect a pig-iron and steel plant at Durgapur; and the motivation in this case was political, not economic.[64]

As for the techniques of encouraging private industry, these had made only a modest beginning. The last two years of the plan, admittedly, saw a marked increase in the activities of the Industrial Finance Corporation and the State Finance Corporations, but their role was still peripheral. The 'gap-filling' Industrial Development Corporation had not been created until 1955, while the Industrial Credit and Investment Corporation (ICIC) was only just beginning to operate at the very end of the plan. Serious efforts to provide state credit for agriculture could not be made until the planners had at their disposal a thorough report on the whole agricultural credit situation, and that was not provided until the epoch-making All-India Rural Credit Survey appeared in December 1955. The gearing of taxation to developmental requirements had likewise to await the report of the Taxation Enquiry Commission.

From this distance it is, of course, easy to pour cold water on the First Five-Year Plan. Judged by economic results as recorded in 1956, it was not so much unsuccessful as irrelevant. But this form of judgement, in the context of a long-term programme of economic development, is itself an irrelevancy; for long-term development cannot be arbitrarily divided up into neat five-year periods. By 1956 certain foundations had been laid which, while having no immediate effect on output figures, could be of immense significance for the future: the major irrigation schemes, the power projects, railway rehabilitation, community development. Whether they were to fulfil their promise depended on the vigour with which they were to be continued and the intelligence with which they were to be utilized. Moreover, a number of interesting beginnings had been made, in industrial and agricultural finance, in co-operative organization, in

[63] *RFYP*(*2*), pp. 12–13. 'It must . . . be said that the modest scale of investment in the first plan and the improvement in the economic situation consequent on increases in both agricultural and industrial production obviated the needs on the part of the State to use the techniques of regulation and control with vigour. The improvement in the food situation in 1953–4 made it possible to abandon food controls and the satisfactory balance of payments situation almost continuously since the second year of the plan enabled the investment programmes to go through without causing any significant strain on the system. While this was a welcome development in itself, it has to be recognised that in a sense this situation prevented any testing out of the techniques or instruments for planned development in the report on the first plan.'

[64] *EW*, 4 Dec. 1954.

taxation policy, in education, in public health, and in the organization and management of public enterprises. Again, everything depended on the way in which they were to be followed up. Scientific and industrial research had also made significant progress and, thanks to the Planning Commission and its ancillary organizations, statistical and other data relating to the Indian economy were being improved. Perhaps most important of all, there was a feeling abroad that at last a decisive break had been made with the economic stagnation of former years, and that Indians, with the help of a fairly modest quantum of foreign assistance, could really 'do it themselves'. The value of planning may not have been proved by the 'results' of the First Five-Year Plan, but many *felt* that it had been proved, and the Planning Commission itself had acquired status and authority in their eyes. All this, admittedly, can be monstrously exaggerated; for there was little understanding of or enthusiasm for planning among the masses, whose horizons were still largely bounded by village, caste, and community. One has also to recognize that, during both the first and the second planning periods, the question of linguistic states produced far more popular excitement than did economic development. Nevertheless, among the educated and politically vocal planning had become an O.K. word. This, although intangible and unquantifiable, was sheer gain.

The danger, obviously, was *hubris*, and both government and Commission had begun to display it. The 'success' of the First Plan suggested that a much bigger plan was possible; the comparative ease with which the economy had been activated seemed to prove that a little extra effort could achieve miracles; the degree of enthusiasm which had been generated raised hopes that such effort could be readily stimulated. The result was an underestimation of the tasks that lay ahead.

V

THE SECOND FIVE-YEAR PLAN

FORMULATION

(i)

THE process of formulating the Second Five-Year Plan may be divided into two fairly distinct periods, viz. (1) from the early months of 1954 to 17 March 1955, and (2) from 17 March 1955 to 15 May 1956. The dividing line is provided by Professor Mahalanobis's 'Plan Frame'.

The first period saw the formulation, by the ministries and the Planning Commission, of some very general and tentative ideas about the total magnitude of the plan and the broad division of projected investment resources among the various sectors. These provided the basic data for the calculations carried out by the Indian Statistical Institute which, from the autumn of 1954 (when Mahalanobis, its chief, became Nehru's economic adviser), functioned as the Planning Commission's agency 'for the study of the technical and statistical problems relating to national planning'. It was during this period, too, that the states were attempting to implement—with varying degrees of enthusiasm and success—the Planning Commission's recommendations of April 1954 about the preparation of village and district plans, especially for agricultural production, rural industries, and co-operation.[1] But the most important feature of this period, for which Nehru and Mahalanobis were jointly responsible, was the development of a distinctively Indian planning ideology, to which the Avadi meeting of the National Congress gave expression in its resolution on the 'socialistic pattern of society'.

Few of the political élite were socialists in any meaningful sense of the word, but Nehru had by this time achieved that degree of eminence where his own public approval of socialism virtually became an act of policy. At the third meeting of the NDC on 9–10 November 1954, in a lengthy speech about his planning philosophy, he said:

> The picture I have in mind is definitely and absolutely a Socialistic picture of society. I am not using the word in a dogmatic sense at all, but in the sense of meaning largely that the means of production should be socially-owned and controlled for the benefit of society as a whole. There is plenty of room for private enterprise there, providing the main aim is kept clear.

[1] *FYP(2)*, pp. xi–xii. See below, pp. 350-1.

According to the record, no one chose to challenge him on the subject. Some, perhaps, thought that so vague a concept would make little real difference to the actual practice of economic planning; others may have felt that a plan described as 'socialistic' would win wider approval than one not so described. In any case, it was already becoming clear that the type of plan being envisaged would involve a great deal of public enterprise, whether or not any formal commitment to socialism was made. Nehru himself underlined this in the emphasis which he placed on heavy industry, particularly machine-building industry.[2]

This, of course, was to be one of the characteristic emphases of the Second Five-Year Plan. So, on the other hand, was the development of 'small and cottage and village industry', presented by Nehru in the same speech as a means of satisfying the demand for consumer goods, providing employment, and diversifying the rural economy.

As one of the means of achieving his objectives, the Prime Minister was already envisaging changes in the government's industrial policy. It was necessary, he said, that 'the whole industrial policy should be revised. The Government wanted to encourage private enterprise; but they wanted to encourage the State enterprise even more'.[3]

Thus the general character of the Second Plan may be regarded as having been decided by the third meeting of the NDC. Its size, however, was still very open to discussion. The Finance Minister, C. D. Deshmukh, told the meeting that whereas V. T. Krishnamachari (the Deputy Chairman of the Commission) 'was envisaging a plan involving an outlay of

[2] The adoption of the 'socialist pattern of society', by resolution of the Lok Sabha on 20 Dec. 1954, was surprisingly casual. The motion under discussion was 'that the present economic situation in India be taken into consideration'. In place of this, the government accepted the following substitute motion, prepared by N. M. Lingam (Coimbatore): 'This House having considered the economic situation in India and the policies of the Government in relation thereto, is of the opinion that (i) the policy of Government is in harmony with the policy statement of the 6th April, 1948, (ii) the objective of our economic policy should be a socialistic pattern of society; and (iii) towards this end the tempo of economic activity in general and industrial development in particular should be stepped up to the maximum possible extent' (LSD, pt. 2, ix, 3692).

[3] Whether this meant that Nehru was already considering the amendment of the 1948 Industrial Policy resolution is not certain. Such amendment would seem to be implied, but only a few weeks later Nehru expressed himself thus on the subject of the resolution: 'I see absolutely nothing in it which is wrong from our present point of view, and I think it is a good indication of how we should proceed' (ibid. 20 Dec. 1954, col. 3609). That there was tension within the government over the extent of the public sector is well known. Even ministers who were by no means 'rightists' sometimes expressed their disagreement with Nehru on the 'demarcation' question. Thus, for instance, T. T. Krishnamachari in parliamentary debate: 'It is not possible to demarcate any sector in a planned economy as belonging either to the private sector or the public sector. If anybody attempts it, he will be attempting folly, because in an underdeveloped economy, where our resources are inadequate, where everything that we have has to be put to some kind of use which will generate more production and therefore more wealth, we cannot afford these nuances of demarcating spheres and saying, 'I will have none of it: I won't enter that' (ibid. col. 3682).

the order of Rs2,500 crores–3,000 crores in the public sector and 2,500 crores in the private sector', these figures were intended only as a guide. It will be seen that in the autumn of 1954 the planners had comparatively modest ambitions. Deshmukh presented these figures as upper limits; but the plan as eventually approved envisaged an investment of Rs4,800 crores in the public sector alone.

During the latter part of 1954 and the early months of 1955 it was evident that the government was engaged in cranking up the machine in preparation for a big planning push. The Avadi resolution committed Congress to socialism, a large public sector and 'physical' planning; the Imperial Bank of India had been nationalized; the All-India Rural Credit Survey Committee was completing its massive report; and preparation was under way for the introduction of a new Companies Act which would give the government greater control over the private sector and provide more comfortable legal accommodation for state-owned companies.

Even more important was the appearance of the three-volume report of the Taxation Enquiry Commission,[4] which proposed fiscal reforms designed to 'increase the resources for investment available to the public sector with as small a diminution as practicable of investment in the private sector' and to impose 'the largest possible restraint on consumption by all classes'. It advocated a stiffening of the income tax and an increase in indirect taxation, simultaneously with the granting of 'tax holidays' to nationally important industries which needed such a stimulus.

In presenting India's first allegedly 'socialist' budget, C. D. Deshmukh gave effect to the first two of these recommendations. Reflecting the optimism which had now become general among the planners, he also justified a 'sizeable' budgetary deficit on the grounds that all the economic indicators showed that 'the country could go ahead more boldly'.[5]

By that time, this boldness had already found expression in the announcement by several ministries of their physical targets. The Minister of Commerce, for instance, offered 6 million tons as his Five-Year Plan target for iron and steel, while the Minister of Finance himself envisaged the creation of 24 million additional jobs during the course of the next ten years. By March 1955, therefore, both official and public opinion had been well prepared for the acceptance of the big plan that Mahalanobis, with the help of his foreign economic advisers, was preparing to propose.

(ii)

The Plan Frame,[6] which appeared on 17 March 1955, was based on a four-sector model of the Indian economy. Into it were built certain

[4] Taxation Enquiry Commission, 1953–4, *Rep.* [5] LSD, 28 Feb. 1955, pt 2, i, 658.

[6] P. C. Mahalanobis, *Draft Recommendations for the Formulation of the Second Five Year Plan, 1956–61* (17 Mar. 1955).

assumptions that were already accepted policy, such as a 5 per cent annual rate of growth and the production of 6 million tons of iron and steel in the last plan year. These gave it a much greater *de facto* rigidity than it was supposed to possess, and, significantly enough, after all the discussions which occupied the following year, the ultimately-accepted sectoral allocations differed very little from the Mahalanobis ones (see Table 7, p. 134).

At the head of his list of objectives Professor Mahalanobis put the promotion of rapid growth 'by increasing the scope and importance of the

TABLE 6

Second Five-Year Plan: Investment Allocations by Sector (per cent)

Sector	*Plan Frame*	*Second Plan*
1. Industry: basic investment goods	33·0	34·4
2. Industry: consumer goods	17·0	18·2
3. Agriculture	17·1	17·2
4. Household Enterprises	3·6	3·6
5. Services	29·3	26·6
Total (per cent)	100·0	100·0

(Adapted from Table 5 in Wilfred Malenbaum, *Prospects for Indian Development* (1962).)

public sector', and the development of heavy industries 'to strengthen the foundations of economic independence'. Production of the required supplies of consumers' goods would be mainly 'through household and hand industries', which were to be protected against competition from the factory-made article. Agricultural productivity came fifth in the list, followed by housing, health and education, the liquidation of unemployment (ten years) and an increase in the national income of 25 per cent.

The justification of this developmental pattern followed lines which have subsequently become very familiar. Heavy industry was to increase the country's capacity for capital formation and thus the general rate of industrialization, and to make India independent of foreign imports of producer goods. The labour-intensive household industries would offset inflationary tendencies by meeting the increased demand for consumer goods and create 'relatively more employment . . . among the poorer sections of the people so that a greater portion of the increase in income would go to them'. Factory-produced consumer goods had to be limited in quantity, in order to conserve resources and maximize welfare, until such time as unemployment had been liquidated; their expansion could be justified only when domestic supplies of certain items (e.g. antibiotics) could be increased in no other way, or when the factory product was an important earner of foreign exchange. As for agriculture, the necessary increases in production could be obtained by the more intensive application of the specifics already adopted: land reform, National Extension and Community Development, public credit, and co-operatives. As the prospects for total agricultural production looked deceptively good in 1955, considerable emphasis was placed on its diversification.

On the subject of 'balanced development and controls', the Plan Frame stressed the need for 'adequate increases' in basic services such as electricity, irrigation, transport and communications; for financial operations (e.g. public sector investments, expenditure on social services, &c.) to avoid both inflation and deflation; for the maintenance of adequate food-grain and raw material reserves; and for the use of physical controls, if need be, to deal with short-run shortages. Quite extraordinarily in the light of subsequent events, it suggested that deflation rather than inflation was likely to be the main problem.

The proposed emphasis on the public sector hardly needed specific justification, as this was already government policy. It was to expand 'relatively faster' than the private sector and its contribution to capital formation was to be enhanced by the government's entry into the fields of banking, insurance, foreign trade, and internal trade. The private sector was to be made to 'conform in a general way' with the overall production programme and to be offered various inducements to take up forms of investment given priority in the plan.

To provide resources, the rate of investment would have to rise from 7 to 11 per cent of national income over the plan period. Resources for the public sector would be obtained by increased taxation, the profits of public enterprises, and deficit financing (to a limit of Rs1,000–1,200 crores). No difficulty in the capital financing of the private sector (estimated at Rs2,200 crores) was anticipated; in fact it was held that 'conditions of easy credit' were 'likely to emerge'. Payment for increased imports of capital goods was to be met by foreign assistance, the withdrawal of sterling balances, the curtailment of non-essential imports, and the promotion of exports.

In the light of the experience of the Second and Third Five-Year Plans, it is now hardly necessary to emphasize the lack of realism in the assumptions upon which these proposals were based. The problem of inflation was grossly underestimated, the financial difficulties rather airily brushed aside, the balance of payments situation given little serious consideration, the prospects for agriculture exaggerated, and the capital-output ratio put far too low.

Nevertheless, as the Mahalanobis group was the only one to have done the necessary arithmetic, effective criticism of the Plan Frame, at least from the standpoint of its internal consistency, was difficult for the outsider. This became quite evident when the document was presented for comment to the Planning Commission's Panel of Economists. The report of this body,[7] made public on 10 April 1955, merely suggested a few changes of emphasis and issued a number of general warnings.

Vaguely phrased as they were, however, these had a certain importance. The complementarity of agriculture and industry was stressed and the 'importance of maintaining and expanding agricultural production in the Second Plan period' underlined. The proposed investment, it was predicted, would 'strain the economy a very great deal' and could not be met without measures of taxation which went considerably beyond the recommendations of the Taxation Enquiry Commission. Specifically criticized was Mahalanobis's allegedly excessive reliance on deficit financing. Whereas a 'limited measure' (e.g. Rs200 crores per annum) was feasible during the first year or two of the plan, continuous deficit financing on this scale would be dangerous. The permissible maximum over the five-year period was Rs1,000 crores, and even this projected total should be re-examined at the end of the second year or at mid-point. Some of these warnings had already appeared in the 'Tentative Framework' document, issued on 21 March by the Economic Divisions of the Ministry of Finance and of the Planning Commission.[8] This too had expressed the view that continued reliance on deficit financing might 'disrupt the price structure and create instability'. In many other respects, however, it was more optimistic than the 'Plan Frame' itself. Shortages of foodstuffs and raw materials were proclaimed to have 'disappeared', while the fall in agricultural prices had emphasized the inadequacy of the 'rate of investment in the economy'. The economists' warnings, therefore, were by no means pointless.

Only one economist, Professor Shenoy,[9] disagreed *in toto* with Mahalanobis's ideas about planning, and he appeared to be committed to *laissez-faire* methods in so doctrinaire a manner that no one, outside certain business circles, took much notice of his criticisms. But although Shenoy's was the only formal dissent, plenty of other reputable economists had their reservations and criticisms, some of which had been foreshadowed in the papers they had presented to the Planning Commission before the publication of the Plan Frame. B. K. Madan, for instance, expressed three disagreements on matters of principle. First, there was Mahalanobis's allegedly 'short-term' approach to the unemployment problem. Madan held that emphasis on the protection of village industry was misplaced. 'Decentralised industry', he wrote, 'has considerable advantages

[7] *FYP(2)*: *Basic Considerations Relating to the Plan Frame,* Memo. prepared by the Panel of Economists, Plan. Com. (10 Apr. 1955).

[8] *Working Paper prepared by the Economic Division, Ministry of Finance, Economic Division, Planning Commission, in consultation with the Central Statistical Organisation and Indian Statistical Institute.*

[9] 'A Note of Dissent on the Memo. of the Panel of Economists', in *FYP(2)*: *Basic Considerations.*

from the socio-economic point of view and can be successful in the economic race, if it is technically assisted with power and machine. But decentralisation with technical stagnation is a retrograde policy which will lead to economic reaction, not development'. Second, there was the question of balance. Madan held that the prevention of inflation required a larger expansion of consumer goods production than the Plan Frame provided for, that there was no point in aiming at 'practical self-sufficiency' in the production of capital goods, and that the strengthening of the infrastructure of the economy (i.e. irrigation, transport and communications, power, education, public health and housing) should continue to be given major emphasis. Thirdly, he considered—quite rightly, as it turned out—that the Frame's estimates of the increment in productivity obtainable from a given quantum of extra investment were unrealistic.[10] He was neither the first nor the last to criticize along these lines, but neither he nor anyone else succeeded in producing a viable alternative framework in quantitative terms. That the Plan Frame so quickly became 'the book of the plan' was unfortunate; for although Mahalanobis had performed a valuable service in raising the planners' sights, he had also done them the grave disservice of presenting them with a document which was based on unrealistic assumptions and which made no serious attempt to discuss priorities in terms of costs and benefits. Mahalanobis, in fact, must bear much of the blame for the subsequent planning muddles. He raised excessive hopes and created a planning 'orthodoxy' founded upon nothing much more solid than an enthusiasm for heavy industry and a preference for Soviet-type methods.

The deed, however, had been done, and from this time onwards the Commission, instead of treating the Plan Frame as a hypothesis to be tested, was mainly concerned with trying to accommodate within its four rather rigid walls the various demands that began to pour in for increases of outlay in almost every sector of the economy.

At the meeting of the Standing Committee of the NDC on 5 May, where the Plan Frame, the Tentative Framework, and the Economists' Memorandum were discussed, only two members offered any fundamental criticisms. B. C. Roy, the highly individualistic Chief Minister of West Bengal, considered that a plan of the proposed size was beyond the country's capacity and that any attempt to operate it would give rise to serious inflation; Sampurnanand, of Uttar Pradesh, also expressed scepticism about the mobilization of resources. They received some support from Ramakrishna Rao, of Hyderabad, and from Bhimsen Sachar, of the Punjab, both of whom had doubts about taxable capacity. The latter, however, hoped that 'if sufficient enthusiasm was created among the people for local works and other projects and their co-operation in

[10] 'Criticism of the Draft Plan Frame', *RBIB*, Sept. 1955.

the form of cash or labour contributions secured, it would indirectly have the same effect as an increase in the revenues of the Government'. Optimistic as this was, it seemed positively sober by comparison with Mahalanobis's contention that 'if hand industries could be activated, the fear of unemployment could disappear during a period of five years'.

At the full meeting of the Committee on the following day, some scepticism, normal at NDC meetings, was expressed about the ability of the states to raise further resources; but several ministers demanded an even 'bolder and bigger plan'. The acceptance of the Plan Frame's approach, however, was a foregone conclusion, as was the approval of its income and employment targets. The NDC also decided that 'the Second Five-Year Plan should be drawn up so as to give concrete expression to the policy decisions relating to the socialistic pattern of society', and sanctioned the government's proposed timetabling of the further stages of plan formulation, viz.

1. June–September 1955: discussion of detailed plan proposals with the central ministries and the state governments;
2. October–November 1955: publication of Draft Outline, to be followed by general and parliamentary discussion;
3. March 1956: publication of the final plan.

Immediately a Cabinet Committee was to be set up to discuss with the Planning Commission the question of available resources, while the states, for their part, were to undertake reviews of the recommendations of the Taxation Advisory Commission.

In the same month the AICC, meeting at Berhampore, drew favourable attention to the Plan Frame and its associated papers and called for the 'widest thinking and consultation'.

Thinking there was in plenty during the summer and autumn of 1955. The Central Advisory Council for Industries, for instance, criticized the textiles target for private factory enterprise as 'too conservative'. It was in response to this plea for a larger mill output that the Minister of Commerce and Industry, T. T. Krishnamachari, then declared himself 'a complete convert to the philosophy of the handloom'. At the same meeting, K. C. Neogy, talking of transport bottlenecks, gave a fillip to a developing controversy about railway investment by claiming that both the Railway Board and the Planning Commission had 'failed to grasp the magnitude of the problem'.[11]

(iii)

Not until July did the Planning Commission begin its discussions with the central ministries and the state governments, through the formation of

[11] *AR*, 1955, p. 324.

'working groups in which senior officials from the Central Ministries, State Governments and the Planning Commission collaborated'.[12] These discussions, scheduled to conclude in September, actually stretched out until the end of the year. This prolongation was partly due to the fact that proposals for expenditure totalling Rs12,000 crores had to be cut down to fit the public investment target of 4,300 crores, of which the states' share had been fixed at Rs2,100–2,200 crores. Mainly, however, it was a product of the diversion of interest and confusion of counsels that rapidly developed during the autumn and winter of 1955. Interest, particularly in the states, was diverted by the publication of the report of the States Reorganization Commission, which 'virtually pushed everything, including the Second Plan, into the background'.[13] Confusion of counsels was evidenced by the endorsement, by the NDC of the Planning Commission's view that the Plan Frame proposals would generate 8–8½ million additional jobs, not 10–12 million, simultaneously with the publication of an AICC Sub-Committee report[14] which demanded that if the Plan Frame was insufficient to realize the employment target, total investment should be raised. Even more serious evidence was the attempt to satisfy part of the railways' demand for twice their Plan Frame allocation, by pushing up the total public sector outlay from Rs4,300 to Rs4,800 crores. A proposal to meet the cost, within the original total, by cutting down on the allocation for heavy industry was rejected, but the Finance Minister, C. D. Deshmukh, in announcing the increase, gave no indication of how the extra money was to be raised, and one may surmise that his hand had been forced.[15] Even the economists who had endorsed the Plan Frame were now becoming worried, and it was perhaps less surprising than the *Economic Weekly* thought to find, at the 38th Indian Economic Conference at Poona in January 1956, that those who had signed the Economists' Panel Report were 'openly repudiating it'.[16] The ablest of India's younger economists, K. N. Raj, was already envisaging circumstances in which the plan might break down:

> Already there is some reason to suspect that the output of food-grains in the coming year may be somewhat lower than in the current year, and no-one can say what will happen if the Finance Minister provides for a large deficit . . . , there is a failure of the monsoons, and the Government's spending machinery at the same time becomes suddenly efficient and incurs all the expenditure provided for in the budget. The point is that, even if all these terrible things do not happen next year, there is always the possibility of their happening, and rapid economic development over a period cannot be planned on that basis.[17]

Officially, however, optimism prevailed, particularly on the subject of resources. On 2 November C. D. Deshmukh thought that the question of

[12] *FYP(2)*, p. xiii. [13] *EW*, 22 Oct. 1955. [14] Summarized in *AR*, 1955, p. 403.
[15] *EW*, 19 Nov. 1955. [16] Ibid. 7 Jan. 1956. [17] Ibid. 26 Jan. 1956.

raising foreign loans might become of importance 'only during the course of the Second Plan', while T. T. Krishnamachari, addressing the annual general meeting of the Associated Chambers of Commerce on 12 December, expressed his strong personal opposition to 'asking for foreign aid'.[18]

By the end of the year the Commission had succeeded in producing a Draft Memorandum on the Second Plan, and on 6–7 January 1956 this was considered by the Standing Committee of the NDC. Instead of looking closely at the document, the Committee chose to have a very general and wide-ranging discussion in which central-state relations and the implications of 'socialism' were the main subjects. In the same month the Commission had consultations with 'a large number of Members of Parliament belonging to all parties'.

At its full meeting, the NDC received from the Commission a note embodying all the suggestions which had been made both by the members of the Standing Committee and by the MPs. Many of these were of a 'left' character, asking for such things as a clarification of the 'socialist pattern', more scope for public ownership, a ceiling on incomes, greater emphasis on co-operation in general and on co-operative farming in particular, the introduction of fiscal measures to ensure the mopping up by the state of 'a growing proportion' of private profits, and a speeding up of land reform. Less controversial demands were for additional taxation, greater specificity in annual planning, well-prepared regulatory measures to cope with unexpected difficulties, and balanced regional development 'within the resources available'. The most important suggestion was for the division of public sector investment into two parts, respectively totalling Rs4,400 and Rs800 crores, of which the latter represented the amount to be obtained by foreign assistance.

Opening the NDC's discussion, the Finance Minister indicated that the fiscal position was going to be 'very difficult indeed', as the total amount of tax income projected was Rs70–80 crores more than what the states had said they could raise. When all estimated sources of income had been taken into account, including a reasonable measure of deficit financing, 'a gap of Rs400 crores was still left uncovered'. Indeed, this figure was still optimistically low, for the estimate of foreign assistance, which had been raised from Rs400 crores to Rs800 crores, possessed 'no factual basis'. That he could express himself thus so shortly after both he and Krishnamachari had publicly proclaimed their indifference about foreign assistance is testimony to the extent to which confusion of counsel still prevailed.

In the discussion that followed, most of the Chief Ministers simultaneously opposed any reduction in the size of the plan and expressed scepticism about the capacity of their states to raise extra tax revenues. One

[18] *AR*, 1955, p. 476, 566.

Chief Minister suggested remitting the whole question of resources to 'a panel of financial experts'; another contented himself with the assertion that 'the necessary resources could be found if the responsibility for raising them was taken boldly'; while a third rather desperately commended the suggestion, of unspecified provenance, 'regarding raising money by raffles'. The only constructive proposals came from Subramaniam, Madras's able Finance Minister, who argued for the psychological value of earmarked taxes, and from Gopalan Reddy, Chief Minister of Andhra Pradesh, who favoured compulsory savings. Discussion of other suggestions before the Council was desultory, and no conclusions were recorded.

Nevertheless, the Draft Memorandum had now received the approval of the NDC and the way was open for the Planning Commission to issue the Draft Plan (10 February 1956). Comments and discussion were invited.

(iv)

The 'Approach' chapter of this document, while emphasizing the need for greater effort, gave expression to that self-confident, we-can-do-anything spirit which the ominous rumblings of approaching storms had not yet dissipated. Targets set by the First Five-Year Plan had been achieved, and in some cases exceeded, 'without excessive strains or imbalances developing in the economy'. This enabled the planners to move forward in an 'atmosphere of confidence and . . . of heightened expectations'.

The basic objective of the Second Five-Year Plan was 'to secure a more rapid growth of the national economy and to increase the country's productive potential in a way that will make possible accelerated development in the succeeding plan periods'. Specifically it was oriented towards

(*a*) a sizeable increase in national income so as to raise the level of living in the country;
(*b*) rapid industrialisation with particular emphasis on the development of basic and heavy industries;
(*c*) a large expansion of employment opportunities; and
(*d*) reduction in inequalities of income and wealth and a more even distribution of economic power.

Rapid industrialization in general, and in particular the production of 'machines to make machines', was presented as the 'core of development'. This was obviously a difficult developmental pattern, financially and administratively: highly absorptive of scarce capital, likely to cause inflation, not directly creative of much new employment, and demanding comparatively unfamiliar technical and managerial skills. To offset inflation and create employment, therefore, consumer goods industries would have to be developed even more vigorously on a predominantly

TABLE 7

Second Five Year Plan: Outlay

Head	*First Plan (revised)*		*Draft Outline 2nd Plan*		*Second Plan (orig.)*		*Second Plan (1st revision)*		*Second Plan (2nd revision)*		*Second Plan (Achievement)*	
	Rs crores	%	*Rs crores*	%	*Rs crores*	%	*Rs crores*	%	*Rs crores*	%	*Rs crores*	%
1. Agriculture & Community Development	372	16	565	12	568	11.8	568	11·8	510	11·3	530	11
2. Irrigation & Flood control	395	17	458	9	486	10·1	860	17·9	820	18·2	420	9
3. Power	266	11	440	9	427	8·9					445	10
4. Industries & Minerals	179	7	891	19	890	18·5	880	18·4	790	17·5	900	20
Village & Small-Scale Industries							200	4·2	160	3·6	175	4
5. Transport & Communications	556	24	1,384	29	1,385	28·9	1,345	28·0	1,340	29·8	1,300	28
6. Social services, Housing & Rehabilitation	547	23	946	20	945	19·7	863	18·0	810	18·0	830	18
7. Miscellaneous	41	2	116	2	99	2·1	84	1·7	70	1·6		
8. Total	2,356	100	4,800	100	4,800	100	4,800	100	4,500	100	4,600	100

Sources: Plan Reports and Plan Progress Reports.

labour-intensive basis, while in the field of social services there would have to be greater emphasis on technical education. It was nevertheless admitted that the creation of employment opportunities would have to take comparatively low priority. New jobs, calculated at 10 million (of which 8 million would be in sectors other than agriculture) would be no more than sufficient to match the increase in the labour force; there would be 'no significant impact on the carry-over of unemployment from an earlier period'.[19]

Industrialization would obviously demand much greater provision for transport and communications, both relatively and absolutely. Power production would also have to be stepped up, even though outlay on it was to fall slightly as a percentage of total expenditure. To compensate for percentage increases of 12 for industry and minerals and of 5 for transport and communications, agriculture and community development were to go down by 4 per cent, irrigation and flood control by 8 per cent, social services by 3 per cent, and power by 2 per cent. As, however, the new plan was more than twice the size of the old, actual outlay would increase considerably in all departments[20] (see Table 7).

That increases in outlay for agriculture and irrigation were comparatively modest (i.e. from Rs372 to Rs565 crores, and from Rs395 to Rs458 crores respectively) reflected the misplaced confidence of the planners that the food production problem was well on the way to solution. While warning that there could be no 'question of a relaxation of efforts to increase agricultural productivity', they nevertheless believed that 'the shortages of food and essential raw materials which presented a serious problem when the First Plan was formulated' had 'been overcome'.[21]

Another wildly optimistic judgement was that in Irrigation, Power, Railways and Community Development experience had already taught the basic administrative lessons and that 'the necessary personnel is either available or can be quickly trained'. Hence, given the financial resources, there should be comparatively little difficulty in irrigating an extra 21 million acres, in increasing the flow of electricity from 3·4 to 5·8 million kw., in burdening the railways with an extra 15 per cent of passenger miles and an extra 35 per cent of freight tons, and in extending the community development coverage from 80 to 325 million people—'almost the entire rural area'. It was in industrial and mineral development that the planners expected to encounter the major problem of 'strengthening the organization and administrative personnel available to the Government'.[22]

In the light of subsequent experience, these proved bad misjudgements; but equally ill conceived were the plan's financial provisions, which had become distorted as a result both of the optimism of the planners and of the

[19] *DO*(*2*), pp. 6–8. [20] Ibid. p. 22. [21] Ibid. p. 23. [22] Ibid. p. 12.

manifold pressures for increased expenditure to which they were subject. They themselves admitted that deficit financing to the extent of Rs1,200 crores was a 'risk', and they could justify the figure of Rs800 crores for external assistance only by vaguely referring to the 'surpluses available in more developed countries for investment abroad'. When these very hypothetical totals had been added to the targets for taxation, loans, and small savings, there was still that much-discussed 'uncovered gap' of Rs400 crores. 'It is not possible', said the planners, 'to indicate at this stage how this amount is to be raised. *Prima facie*, the task is exceedingly difficult'. The reality behind this apparently irresponsible statement seems to have been that, although the planners were of the opinion that their proposed taxation was 'by no means excessive either in relation to possibilities or to needs' and that it could be further stepped up without damage to the economy, they had met with a firm *non possumus* both from the Finance Ministry and from the states.

On the vital question of foreign exchange, the Draft Outline reported that the position was currently good, as indeed it was. At the same time, the Second Plan would 'necessarily involve a heavy strain on foreign exchange resources'. Net deficit on current account, over the five years, was estimated at Rs1,100 crores in the light of a whole series of assumptions some of which were to prove more realistic than others. Among the less realistic ones were (*a*) that the terms of trade were to remain as favourable as in 1954–5 (described by the Commission itself as 'somewhat optimistic'); (*b*) that imports of iron and steel would average 15–16 lakh tons over the first four years and 'virtually disappear' in the final year; (*c*) that imports of foodgrains would total 4 million tons ('more or less the same average annual rate as in the last two years'); and (*d*) that imports of intermediate products would not rise 'significantly beyond the present level'.[23]

Clearly, in relation both to total investment and to foreign exchange resources, the Planning Commission was giving itself the full benefit of every possible doubt. In favour of the biggest possible plan, and under constant pressure from those who wanted to have everything but pay for nothing, it took off from the firm ground of economics and entered the thin air of speculation. Propelled by the euphoria generated by the 'overfulfilment' of the First Plan and by Nehru's belief that with 'enthusiasm' and 'united effort' democratic India could perform Soviet-type miracles, it convinced itself and tried to convince others that two and two, when added together by an Indian planner, could make considerably more than four. The few who persistently pointed out that this was a mistake did not, unfortunately, have the ear of the Prime Minister.

The Draft Outline was also somewhat disfigured by various ambiguities of the type with which the student of Indian planning soon becomes

[23] Ibid. pp. 27–34.

familiar. Indeed, on the admittedly difficult subject of village and small-scale industries it displayed something approaching schizophrenia. In arguing the need to 'promote, modernise and reorganise' this crucial sector of the economy', the planners wrote:

> The problem is one of devising effective policies as well as making suitable organizational arrangements. Unregulated or haphazard application of modern techniques in all spheres of production is apt to create or aggravate technological unemployment. There is need for regulation here. This is not to suggest that a freezing of existing techniques or a preference for inefficient industries is at all indicated by considerations of economic or social policy.[24]

This statement is an almost classic example of the 'on-the-one-hand-but-on-the-other-hand' substitute for argument, in which a form of words is employed to conceal differences of opinion. Admittedly, it appears in the 'Approach' chapter, not in the chapter on 'Village and Small-Scale Industries'; but the latter by no means clarifies the issue. Indeed, it adds another ambiguity by deliberately avoiding all the crucial questions relating to 'common production programmes' embracing both large and small-scale industrial units.[25]

A similar schizophrenia is evident in its treatment of 'balanced regional development', a subject on which the planners were being pressed very vigorously by the representatives of the more backward states. While agreeing 'in principle' with the NDC 'that within the resources available for development every effort should be made to provide for balanced development in different parts of the country', it made little effort to translate this statement of objectives into concrete policies. It held out somewhat delusive hopes that 'decentralised industrial production' would itself help to iron out regional disparities, and referred, rather vaguely, to the need for 'organised schemes of migration and settlement from more to less densely populated areas' (without, it should be added, including in the plan any financial provision for such schemes). For the rest, it assured the aggrieved parties that in the location of new enterprises where there was a 'large field of choice', 'consideration should be given to the need for developing a balanced economy', and referred to the NDC's recommendation 'that there should be continuous study of the problems of diminishing regional disparities and a suitable set of indicators should be evolved'.[26]

The fact that the Draft failed to 'add up' was a consequence, as we have suggested, of the multitude of powerful pressures that the planners were attempting to satisfy, in order to produce a document which would receive the maximum of public support. Its faults, therefore, reflected the new opportunities which India's democratic system of government was now giving to pressure groups of all kinds, both official and unofficial. Thus,

[24] Ibid. pp. 14–15. [25] Ibid. p. 131. [26] Ibid. p. 20.

although the planners were in one sense more free than they had been in 1951 and 1952, when much of the plan they were supposed to be formulating had in fact already been made for them, in another sense they were much less free; for people had now become more conscious of the planning process, more aware of the possible benefits that the plan might bring them, and hence more determined to ensure that their own interests were adequately built into it. At the same time, resistance to such pressures was considerably weakened by the prevailing optimism and by the fact that the Commission itself was becoming more and more of a 'political body', where economists and econometricians tended to be on tap rather than on top, as we have already noted in Chapter 3.

One further feature of the Draft Outline demands special notice: its attempt to relate the plan to the long-term objective of a 'socialist pattern of society'. This, it said by way of definition, 'means that the basic criterion for determining lines of advance is not private profit but social gain'. More specifically, (*a*) major decisions were to be made by 'agencies informed by social purpose', (*b*) benefits were to accrue more and more to 'the relatively less privileged classes of society', (*c*) there was to be a 'progressive reduction of the concentration of incomes, wealth and economic power', (*d*) greater opportunities for 'vertical mobility of labour' were to be given to the small man, and (*e*) the public sector of the economy was to undergo rapid expansion.[27] This collection of aims might justifiably be called 'socialistic', and there could be no doubt that some of them, such as greater vertical labour mobility and more public enterprise, were actually embodied in the provisions of the plan. But those relating to economic equality were not, to say the least, given any very conspicuous expression; for the Commission was only too well aware of the potential contradiction between development and equalization in a 'mixed' economy where some 90 per cent of enterprise was still private, and likely to remain so for a long time to come. On taxation, for instance, it was careful to point out that each proposal had to be 'examined in the light of its revenue yield, its effect on incentives' and 'its administrative implications', as well as in the light of the 'net contribution it makes to . . . the reduction in inequalities'. The suggestion of the Taxation Enquiry Commission, that thirty times the prevailing per family income was a reasonable ceiling on net personal income after tax, was presented as an objective to be advanced towards 'by stages'. Fiscal measures could contribute towards its attainment, but 'more important than these' were 'positive measures to increase incomes at lower levels, to expand employment opportunities for disadvantaged classes, to expand training facilities all round and to eliminate exploitative credit and marketing arrangements'. The elimination of existing inequalities, in fact, was given low priority in favour of what was

[27] Ibid. p. 9.

described as the creation of 'conditions in which great disparities of income will not develop'. For this purpose, organizational changes, 'such as reform of land tenures, reorganisation of land management, encouragement of decentralised modes of production and the increasing role of the public sector' were said to be of 'vital importance'.[28] In brief, whereas advantages for the disadvantaged were items of policy, equality as such was little more than an article of faith.

The main 'socialistic' feature of the plan was undoubtedly the expansion of the public sector and the more positive use of the whole apparatus of controls at the disposal of the government. Public sector expansion, however, was justified by reference more to empirical than to ideological considerations.[29] As for controls, these had to form 'a fairly integrated system' if they were to succeed. More vigorous use of the instruments for the promotion of private enterprise, such as the various finance and development corporations, was also required. But, in the end, neither regulatory nor promotional devices would meet the needs of a developing economy.

> Progressively . . . the State—and the co-operative sector—has to enlarge its field of operation, and this carries with it increased capacity to gather the surpluses arising out of sales of the goods, services and amenities provided . . . . It is not only regulation within the existing structure that can answer the needs of development; the structure itself has to change.[30]

This sounded revolutionary enough, and indeed bore some relation to the content of the plan, which placed considerable emphasis on both the public and the co-operative sectors of the economy. But a predominantly public-and-co-operative economy was a very distant ideal, and in the meantime the selective stimulation and regulation of private enterprise was of the highest importance. Of this the planners were well aware, and they might have done better to emphasize it more heavily.

Immediately on publication of the Draft Outline the 61st Session of the Congress at Amritsar expressed approval of its 'the approach, policy and proposals' embodied in the Outline.[31] The Minister of Railways and Transport, however soon allowed his scepticism to show on the adequacy of the allocations he had received.[32] The states' Agricultural Ministers, too, were unhappy. At their conference of 24–25 February, they recommended that certain schemes 'such as production of fruits and vegetables, animal husbandry and supply of milk to big cities, and the question of different programmes in the agricultural sector, should be referred to the Planning Commission for further clarification'.[33] Even more unhappy, as might be expected, was the Federation of Indian Chambers of Commerce, which, at its 29th Annual Session on 4–5 March, expressed its opposition

[28] Ibid. p. 19. [29] Ibid. pp. 9–10. [30] Ibid. p. 18. [31] Summarized in *AR*, 1956, p. 673.
[32] LSD, 1956, pt 2, i, 718–22. [33] *AR*, 1956, p. 698.

to increased taxes, to 'undue' emphasis on the public sector, to the policy of 'ceilings' on incomes and landholdings, and to the proposals to create a State Trading Corporation and to nationalize life insurance.[34] There was also some criticism voiced in the Lok Sabha in connexion with the annual demands for grants.[35]

All this, however, was insignificant compared with the famous 'Neogy Dissent', which became public round about the beginning of May. K. C. Neogy, an experienced and respected member of the Planning Commission, had come to the conclusion that the Draft Plan was impracticable. In his note to the NDC, considered at its meeting of 1–2 May 1956, he wrote:

> If the plan is seriously attempted to be maintained at its present size, and the visible domestic resources cannot be stretched to provide more than half the outlay in the Public Sector, deficit financing of the order of Rs1,200 crores may no longer be the upper limit, as urged by the experts, but the inevitable minimum. Once inflationary conditions supervene as a concomitant of this order of deficit financing, all monetary calculations of the Plan expenditure will be upset, costs of projects will be increased and Plan fulfilment reduced in real terms.

Too much, he considered, was being attempted, and too little effort had been made to define priorities. Relative underinvestment in railways and shipping would create bottlenecks and progress would also be held up by lack of technical personnel. As a result, annual planning would have to diverge considerably from the Five-Year Plan provisions, with consequent disappointment, confusion, and demoralization—'too dear a price to pay for economic progress'. Basically, the trouble was that a 'massive superstructure had been raised on precarious foundations', consisting of 'abstract formulas borrowed from other lands'.

The reply to this onslaught was entrusted to V. T. Krishnamachari, the Planning Commission's Deputy Chairman. In a simultaneously presented note, he argued that 'with the issues placed before the country clearly, the necessary national effort should be forthcoming'. His solution to the problem of inflation, however, was no less astounding than the Neogy dissent, coming as it did right at the end of two long years of plan preparation—to step up agricultural production, without extra investment, by 40 per cent.

At the NDC the Neogy note received little discussion and no support. Morarji Desai, the Chief Minister of Bombay, opposed the reduction of the plan on the grounds that 'some risk had to be taken'. Ramakrishna Rao of Hyderabad agreed, and so did Subramaniam of Madras, although the latter pointed ominously to the 'increase in prices particularly during the last two or three months, particularly of articles of food and cloth'.

[34] Ibid. p. 710.
[35] LSD, 3 Apr. 1956, pt 2, iii, 4096–142, 4148–85, 4188–247, 4250–8, 4266–313.

On the 'Krishnamachari 40 per cent' there was serious dissent. Nehru and Desai supported it, the former referring optimistically to the results that could be expected from the extension of the Japanese method of paddy cultivation. Subramaniam also thought it feasible, but only on condition that more resources were made available. Deshmukh expressed sympathy, placing *his* reliance on a 'reorientation' of the work of the Gram Sevak (Village Level Worker), on the stabilization of agricultural prices, and on a reduction in the price of fertilizers. The Minister of Food and Agriculture, however, thought it too big, while B. C. Roy, of West Bengal, made no secret of the fact that he considered it ridiculous. The matter was eventually dropped after Nehru had said that 'the Minister of Food and Agriculture and the Planning Commission should now hold discussions with individual states and settle new targets of production'. A resolution approving the Draft Five-Year Plan was passed with one dissentient.

In an unusually perceptive comment on these proceedings the *Eastern Economist* (4 May 1956) editorialized:

> The national Development Council has dutifully endorsed the size of the Plan indicating that, whatever its sympathies with Mr Neogy's presentation, this is not a politic moment to suggest that the public sector has overreached itself. But anyone who can read between the lines of the Prime Minister's speech—and the adoption of a higher target for food grains in order to combat the inflationary pressures to which Mr Neogy refers—must admit in fact that Mr Neogy has won his case. It has been agreed that the investment of the order of Rs4800 crores in the public sector cannot be attained without inflation unless the Plan is substantially modified on the agricultural output side.

A week later (11 May) it added that the 40 per cent was in 'the realm of fantasy' and that only confusion could be the product of the introduction, at so late a stage in the planning process, of a figure which was 'clearly outside reach'.

It will help the clarity of our narrative if, at this juncture, the further history of the '40 per cent' is briefly told. On 28 June 1956, at a conference of states' Agricultural Ministers, held at Mussoorie, Ajit Prasad Jain, the Minister of Food and Agriculture, announced his 'broad conclusion' that the foodgrains target could be raised to 25 per cent as against the 15 per cent laid down in the plan. Nearly all the ministers present agreed with him that the 40 per cent target was completely impracticable, but most added that even the 25 per cent one would require the allocation of additional resources.[36]

Foodgrains became the main subject of the discussions between the Planning Commission and the states during the succeeding months. These were followed by an examination of the problem at the 'expert' level, and

[36] *AR*, 1956, p. 911; *EE*, 6 July 1956.

the experts' recommendations were remitted to another meeting between the Commission and the state Ministers of Agriculture. As a result of these consultations, the Commission was able to present revised targets to the NDC its meeting on 8–9 December, 1956: a 28 per cent increase for agricultural production as a whole, split up into 25 per cent for foodgrains and about 34 per cent for commercial crops—all to be achieved by more intensive cultivation, without the injection of new resources (see Table 8).

TABLE 8

Second Five Year Plan: Revised Targets of Agricultural Production

Commodity	*Unit*	*Est. prodn. 1955–6 (as given in Plan)*	*Taxation target of prodn. as in Draft Plan*	*Revised targets of prodn.*	*Percentage increases in index of prodn.*	
					As in Draft Plan	*As revised*
Foodgrains	million tons	65·8	75·0	80·5	15	23·8
Oilseeds	million tons	5·5	7·0	7·6	27	36·2
Sugarcane (Gur)	million tons	5·8	7·1	7·8	22	34·5
Cotton	million bales	4·2	5·5	6·5	31	54·8
Jute	million bales	4·0	5·0	5·5	25	37·5
Other crops	million tons	—	—	—	9	22·4

Source: FYP(2): PR, 1958–9, p. 30.

The NDC accepted this new dispensation; but by that time the crisis of the Second Five-Year Plan, which was to lead to a whole series of reappraisals, had begun.

To return to the events of the summer of 1956, on 15 May the Draft was presented to the Lok Sabha, which later gave it a three-day debate, on an 'approval motion'.[37] Between the presentation and the debate, the Draft was referred to four joint committees (A, B, C, and D) of the Lok Sabha and Rajya Sabha. Of these only the first,[38] whose terms of reference were 'Policy, Outlay, and Allocation' reported in time for the debate. Its discussions contained little of major interest, as the size of the Committee and the limitations on its time ensured that members could do no more than make the usual politically-oriented speeches.

[37] LSD, 1956, pt 2, vol. v.

[38] Committee 'A' on Second Five Year Plan (LS Secretariat, *Synopsis of Proceedings* 18–20 May 1956 (1956)).

Nehru's opening speech in the debate on the floor of the House was intended to take the wind out of most of the critical sails. In supporting the 'approval' motion, he attacked the regionalists, who wanted 'balanced' development at the expense of production, the childish equalitarians, who wanted to put ceilings on everything, the Luddites, who opposed technological progress in the name of employment, the enemies of the private sector, who wanted to nationalize everything, and other doctrinaires of every variety. He said: 'The whole philosophy lying behind this plan, is to take advantage of every possible way of growth and not by doing [*sic*] something which fits in some doctrinaire theory and imagine we have grown because we have satisfied some text-book maxim of a hundred years ago.' These remarks were provoked by amendments which, among other things, demanded (*a*) the prohibition of foreign capital investment; (*b*) comprehensive social security measures; (*c*) free and compulsory primary education; (*d*) a second shipbuilding yard; (*e*) stringent ceilings on wealth, salaries, dividends and landholdings; (*f*) more attention to 'the less developed States like Assam'; (*g*) more attention to the Harijans and Scheduled Castes; (*h*) the nationalization of all basic and heavy industries; and (*i*) heavier taxation of the rich.[39] The irresponsibility of most of these demands needs no underlining, but they present a fair picture of the kinds of pressures with which the Planning Commission had had to contend.

A. K. Gopalan, of the Communist Party, leading for the opposition, endeavoured to voice as many of these criticisms as could be accommodated within the four walls of the party's policy. He accused the government of 'tampering' with the sacred Plan Frame, of backsliding on nationalization, of excessive tenderness towards the private sector, of raising financial resources by methods which made the rich richer and the poor poorer, of lack of attention to the backward areas, of indifference to land reform, and of neglect of the panchayat as the basis of popular participation in plan formulation and implementation.[40] Asoka Mehta, of the Praja Socialist Party, then gave the House a lecture about economic development (*à la* Arthur Lewis), in which he emphasized the rather obvious point that the proposal to increase agricultural production from 15 per cent to 40 per cent made nonsense of the 'balance' that the plan was supposed to display.[41] The Finance Minister, C. D. Deshmukh, who intervened in the interests of 'clarification' after several back-benchers had spoken, dealt gently but effectively with one or two crackpot proposals, but was general to the point of vagueness on resources and 'balance'. Perhaps his most important remark was that which he addressed to those members who, he considered, attached too much 'sanctity' to the Plan Frame.

[39] LSD, 1956, pt 2, v, 9383–410, 9487–90. [40] Ibid. cols. 9420–35. [41] Ibid. cols. 9438–53.

Emphasizing the lack of adequate data when this document was drawn up, he said:

> The planners . . . did have certain contacts with some Ministeries of the Central Government. From some they got some idea of what their targets were and what the corresponding financial counterparts were. In other Ministeries they found that people were not prepared with their information. Their contacts with the State Governments were almost non-existing; that is a very important point—that is about the half the plan.[42]

It was not only an 'important point'; it was an important admission, for the Plan Frame had been presented to the public as a 'scientific' answer to planning problems and, indeed, for all the changes that had been made, the Draft followed very closely the proportions that it had laid down.

The implications of Deshmukh's admission were brutally underlined by an able back-bencher, Dr Krishnaswami (Kanchupuram), who devoted his speech to advocacy of planning via the price mechanism. After condemning the plan as 'the result of pressures which we have not had time to synthesise', and therefore 'a veritable hotch-potch', he continued: 'As it is resources do not tally with the proposals to increase production; proposals do not tally with the supply of transport that would be available in the coming five years. Targets for specific schemes do not tally with the allotments for them.' He did not think that adopting the plan as it stood would 'do much harm'; but neither would 'much good result', for 'realities have a way of shaping plans'.[43] The Draft Plan, of course, was approved.

The summer months of 1956 provided further evidence of disagreement among the top-level planners, exacerbated by the receipt of a World Bank Mission report which gave weighty support to those who claimed that the plan was too ambitious. On 20 June 1956 three official personalities addressed the Central Advisory Council for Industries. While T. T. Krishnamachari announced an upward revision in the target for consumer goods, and expressed his confidence that plan targets generally would be exceeded, K. C. Neogy forecast 'stresses and strains everywhere', and Lal Bahadur Shastri, the Railways Minister, bemoaned the inadequacy of the funds allocated to transport and expressed his sense of disturbance at the moves to revise upwards the targets for agriculture and industry.[44] At a press conference, Krishnamachari then announced the raising of the textile target by 1,700 million yards, to a total of 8,400 million. This would provide a per capita consumption of 18.5 yards, as against the 22 yards recommended by the Bombay and Ahmedabad millowners. The Commerce Minister added that the government was 'not unprepared' to accept a higher target, and mentioned 20 yards as a possibility.[45]

[42] Ibid. cols. 9589–604. [43] Ibid. cols. 9622–3. [44] *AR*, 1956, pp. 891–2.
[45] *EE*, 22 June 1956.

Between 16 July and 1 August Committees B, C, and D of the Lok Sabha and Rajya[46] were discussing the details of the plan. Nothing emerged from their sittings which had not been already ventilated in the Lok Sabha debate. These months were bad ones for planning discussions, not merely because of the humid heat but because political interest was almost monopolized by the States Reorganization Bill, the Constitution (Ninth Amendment) Bill, and the imposition of presidential rule in Travancore-Cochin. Meanwhile the Planning Commission had prepared the final planning document,[47] running to 641 closely-printed pages.

THE PLAN

The first chapter of the Second Five-Year Plan was entitled 'Development of the Economy: Achievement and Perspective'. After discussing the results of the First Plan, it attempted to spell out in greater detail, and to justify, the long term projection thus laconically outlined in the 'Draft':

> It will be recalled that in the first plan contained an illustrative model of long term development which envisaged a doubling of the national income by 1971–72. The increase in national income over the first plan period has been about 18 per cent. If the rate of increase in national income in the third and subsequent plan periods is of the order of 25 per cent over five years as in the second plan, it will be possible to double the national income by 1967–68, that is, four years in advance of the time originally estimated.[48]

For purposes of these calculations, it was assumed that the First Plan's estimate of a 12·5 per cent population growth for the decade 1951–60 was about right. For 1961–70 the rate assumed was 13·3 per cent, and for 1971–80 14 per cent. These estimates, said the Commission with striking prevision, might 'well prove to be on the low side'.

The incremental capital-output ratio, which the First Plan had estimated at 3:1, had actually worked out at 1·8:1—a 'highly favourable outcome' which was partly the result of good monsoons and partly of the fact that 'considerable expansion in industrial output had been possible through utilisation of unutilised capacity'. For the Second Plan period, the estimated ratio was 2·3:1, reflecting 'a somewhat higher capital intensity than the one which prevailed in the first plan . . . in view of the shift in emphasis towards industrialisation'. For the Third, Fourth, and Fifth Plans, it was put at 2·6, 3·4, and 3·7 respectively. These ratios, cautioned the Commission, were only 'illustrative'; they contained a considerable 'element of conjecture'. Justifying its 2·3 ratio, which was

[46] *Proc.*, published in 3 vols. by LS Secretariat, July 1956. [47] *FYP(2)* (1956).
[48] *DO(2)*, p. 26.

very much lower than that prevailing in most other countries (said to lie between 3:1 and 4:1), it said that it was making allowance for non-monetized investment and for the 'direct utilisation of labour and raw materials' in the rural economy.

On the 'likely or feasible rate of investment', the planners now found their former estimations excessive. Instead of an investment coefficient rising to 20 per cent in 1957–8 and thereafter levelling out, as projected by the First Plan, they now assumed a rise to 16 per cent by 1970–1.

The simultaneous reduction in the envisaged increase in the proportion of national income invested and the bringing forward of the 'doubling of the national income' target by four years was, to say the least, surprising. It was based upon nothing more solid than a highly optimistic estimate of capital-output ratios, together with the fact that the rise in national income recorded in the First Plan had been 'above initial expectations'.

In discussing the changes in economic structure which would accompany this quantitative development of the economy—broadly the expansion of the secondary and tertiary sectors at the expense of the primary sector—the Commission made the point firmly for the first time in a public document that no significant new employment opportunities could be created in 'traditional small-scale industries' which were 'already burdened with excessive numbers'. 'The problem here is to prevent too rapid technological unemployment and to maintain and raise incomes through improvements in equipment, techniques and organisation. The bulk of the new employment opportunities have, therefore, to be found in mining and in modern industry, large-scale as well as small.' This was a hard saying for the Wardha school of economists, but refreshingly realistic. Equally realistic was the Commission's view that 'with the best effort that can be made', some increases in the agricultural workforce might be 'unavoidable for some years to come'.

Under the heading of 'Financial and Physical Planning' there was also something new and perhaps surprising, viz.

> A plan unfolds itself in first upsetting an existing balance and then establishing a new one at a higher level. One has to ask: will the supplies of machinery needed be forthcoming? Will the necessary labour . . . be available? Will it be necessary to secure some of the equipment from abroad and if so, will the community be in a position to export the additional amounts required to pay for the same? Will employment opportunities on the required scale be created and will the sum-total of all effort yield the results expected in terms of national income? To an extent, a plan worked out in terms of real resources can provide for the necessary balances through the pattern of investment . . . , and where this cannot be done, the bottlenecks to be faced and overcome can be concretely envisaged. The tasks of training the large number of technicians and other experts can hardly be conceived in any other terms.

This did not mean, of course, that the Commission had been converted to 'bottleneck' planning *à la* Hirschman. It did suggest, however, that the conception of 'flexibility' was becoming more clearly and concretely understood.

At the same time, the Commission issued a warning against any tendency to use 'flexibility' as an excuse for making a series of merely *ad hoc* adjustments. It must be expressed in terms of the annual plans, by way of giving consideration, when central and state budgets were being formulated, to 'the overall needs of the economy and the experience in respect of the fulfilment of tasks for the year about to end'. This, said the Commission, was not easy, as India's federal structure put difficulties 'in the way of forming an early or precise judgement as to the progress of performance as as to determine the size and content of the next year's programmes'. The time-lags in making necessary adjustments to the First Five-Year Plan, which we have already noted, were no doubt very much in the Commission's mind when it emphasized the need for 'expeditious processing and analysis of data'.

The following chapter, on the 'Approach to the Second Five Year Plan,' was essentially an expansion of the corresponding chapter in the Draft Outline. One or two additions and changes of emphasis are, however, worth noting. On labour-intensive methods for the production of consumer goods, the Commission stressed that their use might imply that a smaller proportion of the incomes generated was available for saving and investment, and demanded that steps should be taken to ensure that this did not 'happen on any significant scale'. As nothing more was said of this difficult subject in the remainder of the plan, one can only assume that the 'steps' which the Commission had in mind did not go beyond an intensification of the small savings drive.

Amid a great flood of words on 'Reduction of Inequalities', one change of emphasis and one new suggestion emerged. While repeating the point that raising incomes at the lowest levels was more important than reducing incomes at the top, the Commission nevertheless held that 'early and purposive action in regard to the second aspect is also called for'. Hence it was 'possible' that 'rather far-reaching changes in the tax system would be required', such as the introduction of an expenditure tax—a device which had been commended to the Indian government by several economists, including Nicholas Kaldor. The Commission's approach to this delicate subject, however, was very tentative. It repeatedly gave warning against undermining 'the incentive to work harder or to save more', and even suggested that excessive haste to reduce disparities of income might be incompatible with the maintenance of free institutions. On the subject of property taxes it was somewhat bolder. It advocated a 'moderate tax on wealth', and held that the estate duty (the yield from which was 'negligible') should be supplemented by gift taxes, which had the advantage of yielding considerable revenues without impairing incentives'. It hastened to say, however, that these observations were 'not meant to indicate that any or all of the measures mentioned' could be 'adopted immediately'.

Much of the 'Approach' consisted, *de facto*, of argument with the various critics of the Commission's planning 'philosophy'. Its remarks about taxation were clearly aimed at the left-wing opposition. Those about controls, on the other hand, had the 'right' as their main target. There had been of late, wrote the Commission, 'a good deal of discussion' whether planning should confine itself to overall fiscal and monetary regulation or adopt, in addition, 'devices like export and import controls, licensing of industries or trades, price controls and allocations which influence and regulate economic activity in particular sectors or sub-sectors of the economy'. The answer was that the latter type of control had become a regrettable necessity; since a 'comprehensive plan which aims at raising the investment in the economy substantially and has a definite order of priorities in view' could not be 'seen through on the basis merely of overall fiscal and monetary control'. Even controls on essential consumption (e.g. foodgrains) could not be ruled out in 'particular situations'. These, however, would become less necessary to the extent that the government succeeded in building up buffer stocks.

The table of Plan Investment and Allocations (see Table 6) showed only very minor differences from that presented in the Draft Outline. Total outlay, of course, remained at Rs4,800 crores. The distribution of outlay as between the centre and the states had been changed only fractionally. Some of the physical targets, however, had been significantly raised (see Table 9, p. 149). In industry, these increases partly reflected higher expectations of private investment: but the public sector was also expected to play its part. The railways, for instance, were required to carry 181 million freight tons by 1960–1, instead of 162, without any additional investment allocation, while the mileage of surfaced roads had been raised from 111,000 to 125,000. In education, higher physical achievements were expected of an investment allocation reduced from Rs320 crores to Rs307.[49] It is significant that nearly all the revisions were upwards, and we shall see that the practice of pushing up the physical targets continued even after the plan had been approved. The only important target that underwent a slight decrease between the Draft Outline and the plan was that for fertilizers. In view of the talks currently being held about the 'Krishnamachari 40 per cent', this was surprising.

The finance and foreign exchange estimates remained exactly the same as in the Draft Outline, but there was some crystallization of ideas

[49] *FYP(2)*, pp. 51–61.

TABLE 9

Second Five-Year Plan: Changes in Physical Targets as between the Draft Outline and the Plan (selected)

Commodity or Service	*Anticipated production in 1960–1 according to:*	
	Draft Outline	*Plan*
Industry		
Railway locos (nos)	300	400
Tractors (nos)	1,600	3,000
Cement (m.t.)	10	13
Fertilizers		
(*a*) Nitrogenous (000 t.)	1,600	1,450
(*b*) Phosphatic (000 t.)	600	720
(*c*) Total (000 t.)	2,200	2,170
Electric transformers (000 KVA)	880	1360
Electric cables (t.)	15,000	18,000
Electric fans (000s)	450	600
Transport & Communications		
Railways (freight carried—m.t.)	162	181
Surfaced roads (000 miles)	111	125
Social Services		
Education		
(*a*) Primary (% of eligible children attending)	60·0	63·0
(*b*) Middle (% of eligible children attending)	19	22·5
(*c*) Higher secondary (% of eligible children attending)	10	12
(*d*) Teacher training institutions (no.)	1,080	1,412
(*e*) Enrolment in teacher training institutions (000s)	111·4	134·2

Sources: FYP(2): Draft Outline, pp. 37–39; *FYP(2)*, pp. 58–61.

about the bridging of the Rs400 crores gap. Although, in the 'scheme of financing envisaged for seeing through the development programme', the Commission kept the target for additional taxation at 450 crores, it later stated, as an 'inescapable' conclusion, that this should be raised to Rs850 crores. However, as to methods it was still extremely vague. It referred to a wealth tax and a gifts tax (both of which it had previously suggested were not ripe for immediate adoption), and to a 'widening of the concept of income so as to include in it capital gains'. It repeated the 'suggestion' of an expenditure tax, and held out hopes of the closing of 'some of the loopholes in the present system which offer scope for tax evasion'. But it immediately reminded the reader of its previous warning that 'taxation has its limits', and said that supplementation of the tax effort should be sought through 'institutional arrangements which bring directly into the public exchequer the surpluses which accrue from the sale of goods and services to the public'. The Commission also called for 'the greatest degree of economy in both plan and non-plan expenditures'; but as all this was not accompanied by any attempt to quantify the expected yield of the proposed measures, one can only conclude that the Commission still relied on faith rather than on works.

As for the foreign exchange gap of Rs1,100 crores, the planners admitted that it was 'sizable, both absolutely and in relation to the funds that have so far been forthcoming'. In the nature of things, they could not guarantee that it would be covered; but there was hardly any excuse for their complacent assertion that 'any shortfall in resources to be raised externally' might be 'made good by a greater effort at augmenting domestic resources'. They had already stated, in the context of an assumed gap of Rs1,100 crores, that taxation would need to be raised some Rs400 crores above plan target. They were now suggesting that an even greater effort might compensate for any shortfall in anticipated foreign assistance; and they were additionally assuming, by implication, that locally-raised resources were fully substitutable, in terms of physical requirements, for those that the government might have failed to raise from abroad. The alarming irresponsibility of the Second Five-Year Plan's chapter on 'Finance and Foreign Exchange'[50] represents the lowest point ever reached by Indian planning during the whole decade.

The Lok Sabha debate on the plan, which took place in September, produced few new ideas or arguments.[51] Among the effective points made by Renu Chakravati in her statement of the Communist case was the plan's vagueness on the subject of taxation policy.[52] Shri Mohiuddin (Hyderabad City) also made a palpable hit when he pointed out that although the target for agriculture had been revised upwards, the Planning Commission had left the target for ammonium sulphate unchanged at 375,000 tons.[53] Feroze Gandhi, in an able speech packed with facts and figures, provided distinguished support to those who claimed that transport was being dangerously neglected.[54]

The ministerial spokesmen, as might be expected, expressed that optimism which is *de rigueur* on the publication of a plan, but there was a

[50] Ibid. Ch. 4. [51] LSD, 1956, pt 2, viii, 6254–396, 6620–8780. [52] Ibid. col. 6663.

[53] Ibid. col. 6713. He was presumably referring to the figure of 380,000 tons for the year 1955–6 (*DO*(*2*), p. 38; *FYP*(*2*), p. 59). Actually, the 1960–1 production target had been reduced from 16 to 14·5 lakh tons.

[54] Ibid. cols. 6803–26.

painful embarrassment in some of their pronouncements about agriculture. Nanda essayed another explanation of the '40 per cent', by claiming that the original estimates were the product of a period of falling prices.

> Later, when the Plan was being finalised, it was on the background of rising prices and fears about deficit financing. Then, it occurred to us that we should try to look at the possibility of increasing agricultural production. Even before, we had a feeling that more could be done than was being done. There was not enough time to go minutely into these estimates. The National Development Council took the view that we should try to increase.[55]

The main characteristic of the debate, however, was a series of ministerial statements positively alarming in their irresponsibility. The Deputy Minister of Planning, S. N. Mishra, in a superficial, elegant, euphoristic speech, full of good debating points, dismissed the criticisms of the plan as mostly of a 'peripheral' nature, predicted that India's rate of growth would not be inferior to China's, and made the following extraordinary pronouncement on transport:

> All this traffic of 180·8 million tons . . . can only occur if the development in other spheres takes place. We do not pray for shortfalls in this respect. But if developments take place in other spheres, we can also be optimistic that there would be enough of stimuli working upon the economy which can give some resources that may be required for the purpose.[56]

In other words, the fulfilment of targets would generate resources which had not been planned for, and some of these, diverted in some unspecified way to the railways, could be used, again in some unspecified way, to remove what one only could conclude was a planned transport bottleneck!

Even more extraordinary was Krishnamachari's contribution. On the one hand he expressed the view that plan outlay might increase from Rs4,800 to Rs5,600 crores. On the other he drew attention to the deteriorating foreign exchange position and to the fact that there were 'vital points in the economy' which were 'under pressure because of technical demand-and-supply considerations and the rising tempo of developmental expenditure' and said that in spite of these disturbing trends a downward revision was 'ruled out'. Even this more cautious pronouncement was based on a juggling with resource figures which the kindest of critics could not have described as less than optimistic.[57]

Concluding, Nehru said that he was not going to deal with criticisms of the plan 'because that would lead me in all kinds of directions', and invited members with 'constructive' criticisms, such as Feroze Gandhi, to discuss them with the Ministers and the Planning Commission. On the resources gap he was at his very worst: 'All these gaps that you see,

[55] Ibid. col. 6276. [56] Ibid. col. 6773. [57] Ibid. cols. 6903–932.

the gaps that people lay stress on, the difference of Rs800 crores or whatever the gap is supposed to be in our foreign exchange and other matters, all these gaps can be very largely covered if we can increase our agricultural production. In fact that is the surest and easiest way of covering.'[58] Thus, unconsciously, he pronounced the epitaph on the Second Five-Year Plan as it was then conceived.

IMPLEMENTATION

(i)

How serious an impact the critics made on the Planning Commission is not easy to say. Coming from a member of the Commission itself, the 'Neogy Dissent' compelled some last-minute rethinking but was finally brushed under the table with the remark that there was 'always room for differences of emphasis.'[59] The report of the McKitterick Mission of the World Bank, released on 14 August, which condemned the plan as over-ambitious in relation to India's administrative, technical and financial resources,[60] undoubtedly came as a shock, if only because it was likely to influence the view of the agency upon which the country depended considerably for external loan-finance. But its impact on the Commission and on the government was probably diminished by the fact that it appeared to reject some of the basic political presuppositions of Indian planning and to be inspired by a typically American hostility towards the public sector of the economy.[61] In any case, by the end of the year the bank had swallowed its objections to the extent of agreeing to 'process for external financing' the projects for steel, railways, ports, shipping, and hydro-electricity.[62] By that time, moreover, the very facts of the situation had made it clear that the plan would have to be revised in one way or another.

What does seem extremely odd, and provides evidence of the strength of the pressures to which the Commission had become subject, is that even under these circumstances the process of target-raising continued. Admittedly, the new agricultural targets involved, at least in theory, no significant extra expenditure, but this could not be said of the new textile targets, fixed in June 1956.[63] Other post-plan additions to outlay were in respect of steel (from Rs350 to Rs510 crores),[64] private sector industries (from 685 to 840 crores),[65] minerals (from Rs73 to Rs143 crores),[66] oil (from Rs11·5 to Rs30 crores).[67] shipping (from Rs45 to Rs54 crores).[68] It is probably impermissible to add these to a total of

[58] Ibid. cols. 7126, 7132–3. [59] *FYP(2)*, p. 617. [60] *AR*, 1956, p. 1074.
[61] Ibid. p. 1073. [62] Ibid. p. 1178.
[63] Plan. Com., *Appraisal and Prospects of the Second Five Year Plan* (May 1958), p. 58.
[64] Ibid. p. 61. [65] Ibid. p. 64. [66] *PR 1958–9* (Apr. 1960), p. 93. [67] Ibid. p. 94.
[68] Ibid. p. 123.

Rs413.5 crores, as there may be some overlapping; but the post-plan increase was clearly substantial, and it made heavy additions to foreign exchange requirements. Even as late as May 1957, when the Finance Minister was presenting a sombre picture of the resources situation and attempting to save the 'core' of the plan by cutting down on inessentials,[69] the Railway Minister, in presenting his budget, was claiming that his allotment of Rs1,125 crores was 'quite inadequate'. Later in the year he announced that railway schemes under the Five-Year Plan were 'now estimated' to cost Rs1,425 crores.[70]

An early indication that, even within the original outlay of Rs4,800, the financial squeeze could be severe was provided by the new taxation measures introduced by T. T. Krishnamachari in September and November 1956.[71] Their purpose, explained Krishnamachari, was 'to buttress the finances of the Plan, limit the need for deficit financing, save foreign exchange, restrain non-priority spending and act as a corrective to inequalities of income and wealth'. As a yield of no more than Rs4 crores was expected of these measures, they aroused the opposition of business interests without making any significant contribution to the solution of the growing financial crisis. Just over a week later Nehru warned the NDC, at its eighth meeting (8–9 December) that foreign exchange reserves had been 'rapidly depleted' and that 'a stage had been reached when brakes had to be applied even at the cost of certain activities'. At the same time, and without any apparent sense of contradiction, he informed the Council that 'because of the rise in prices and of certain very important additional items, the size of the plan might go up by Rs400 or Rs500 crores from the figure of Rs4,800'. The Council agreed that, in view of raised targets, higher costs, and the increasing danger of deficit financing, still further taxation would be necessary, and suggested that the centre and the states should undertake, in 1957–8, a tax effort calculated to yield a further outlay of Rs900 crores for the plan.

The immediate problem, however, was the drain on foreign exchange, largely due to the heavy import requirements of the private sector and to the generosity of the government in granting it licences. Action was taken at the beginning of 1957, when new and much more stringent foreign exchange regulations were issued. From this time onwards neither public authorities nor private undertakings could enter into fresh foreign exchange commitments of a capital nature unless these (*a*) were covered by fresh foreign aid or foreign investment or by suitable deferred payments arrangements, or (*b*) were in respect of projects within the following

[69] *Budget 1957–8*, Fin. Minister's speech, p. 250. [70] *AR*, 1957, pp. 1463, 1671.

[71] LSD, 31 Aug. & 3 Sept. 1956, viii, 5152–3, 5344–482; 30 Nov., 5 Dec., 11 & 12 Dec. 1956, 1987–92, 2079–132, 2574–603, 2648–781.

categories: (1) 'core' projects (i.e. steel, coal, railways, ports, and certain power projects), (2) projects in a comparatively advanced stage on which the bulk of the foreign exchange expenditure had already been incurred, and (3) projects which would earn or save foreign exchange within a short period of time. At the same time, monetary policy was redirected with the aim of 'securing selective control over bank credit so as to discourage speculative hoarding of stocks'.[72]

These measures were obviously right, indeed considerably overdue; but their immediate efficacy was slight. No existing foreign exchange commitments were cancelled, and 'selective credit' had to be worked out by the monetary authorities and assimilated by the traders. Hence the situation continued to worsen. The White Paper of 1957–8, presented to Parliament in May 1957 as background information to the Finance Minister's budget speech, spoke of 'growing strain and imbalance'. The index of agricultural production had fallen to 113·7 in 1955–6, while that of industrial production had gone up, by over 10 points, to 132·7. Increases in outlay, both in the public and private sectors, had greatly outstripped the expansion of public and private savings. Hence deficit financing had risen from Rs160 crores in 1955–6 to Rs216 crores in 1956–7, while the indebtedness of the private sector to the banks had increased by Rs117 crores. Not unnaturally, prices had registered a 'significant rise', particularly for agricultural commodities. Deficit on current account, estimated at Rs148 crores for 1956–7, had almost reached that figure during the first half of the year. Hence the foreign exchange gap would be 'substantially larger than the original estimate of Rs1100 crores', and far more external resources than 'the Rs900 crores envisaged by the Plan' would be needed. The country, in fact, had 'entered a crucial phase of development'.[73]

In his budget speech, the Finance Minister underlined these warnings. There was no longer any question of carrying out the plan as originally formulated; the question was now whether what had become known as the 'core', i.e. steel, coal, transport, and power could be saved.[74] During 1957–8 the crisis became still more intense. While the foodgrains production index slumped, the consumer price index continued to rise. Deficit finance, which the Finance Minister had put at Rs275 crores, 'a level somewhat higher than I would consider safe',[75] reached a record figure of Rs497 crores, while foreign exchange assets fell from Rs681 to Rs421 crores. Additional central taxes, which had been calculated to yield Rs93 crores during the financial year, yielded no more than Rs73 crores, while additional state taxes yielded only about Rs30 crores, of

[72] *Budget 1957–8*, White Paper, p. 157; *Budget 1958–9*, White Paper, p. 122.
[73] Ibid. White Paper. [74] Ibid. Fin. Minister's speech, p. 250. [75] Ibid. p. 261.

which Rs14 crores accrued from tax measures which had been adopted in the previous year, 1956–7.[76]

(ii)

Clearly, an even more fundamental reappraisal of the plan was needed. Material for this, under the title of 'Resources for the Plan: a Review', was prepared by the Commission's Economic Division and presented to the NDC in September 1957. This admitted that serious miscalculations had been made and came to the conclusion that only two-thirds of the plan was likely to be completed, and then only if a further Rs44 crores worth of foreign exchange became available. The NDC's reaction to this document, however, was rather less than decisive. It agreed that a greater tax effort was necessary, particularly in the states, and that the small-savings campaign should be reinvigorated; but it chose to occupy most of its time in a discussion of land reform and co-operative farming.

Reappraisal on a scale more commensurate with the requirements of the situation had to wait until May 1958, when the Commission presented to the NDC its famous *Appraisal and Prospects of the Second Five Year Plan.* In preparing this document the Commission had worked in close consultation with the Ministry of Finance, which had already indicated to Parliament that two major decisions had been taken, viz. (1) not to allow total financial outlay to exceed the original plan target of Rs4,800 (which, of course, was itself eroded, in physical terms, by the rise in prices), and (2) to permit further foreign exchange commitments only for 'core' projects and for those which were in an advanced stage of execution.[77]

The *Appraisal and Prospects* began with an attempt to reallocate outlay as between the major heads of development, on the assumption of a 'final ceiling' of Rs4,800 (see Table 6). This was done by treating 'Industry and Minerals' as sacrosanct (its allocation was actually *raised* from Rs690 to Rs880) and cutting down on Irrigation and Power, Social Services, Transport and Communications (very slightly) and Miscellaneous.[78] In the thorough examination of the resources situation which then followed, the Commission found (*a*) that the tax effort had not been sufficient to provide significant resources for the plan, still less to cover anything of the Rs400 crores gap; (*b*) the government loans had not been able to compete effectively with the 'demand for funds in the private sector' and that the small savings drive had as yet failed 'to reach down to the semiurban and rural areas sufficiently to mobilise savings on the scale envisaged in the Plan'; (*c*) that further foreign assistance, over and above the amounts authorized but still unutilized, was unlikely to exceed Rs600 crores; and (*d*) that deficit financing would have to be limited to Rs283 crores

[76] *PR 1958–9* (Apr. 1960), p. 22. [77] *Budget 1958–9*, White Paper, p. 125.
[78] *Appraisal & Prospects*, pp. 5–6.

during the remaining two years of the plan. Even on the most generous assumptions, total budgetary resources for the plan, over the five years, could not be made to total more than Rs2,262. If, therefore, external assistance did not rise above the expected figure of Rs1,038 crores (i.e. the Rs438 crores already 'in hand' *plus* the Rs600 crores estimated as likely to be available during 1959–60 and 1960–1), and deficit financing had to be kept down to Rs1,200 crores (i.e. the Rs917 crores of the first three years *plus* the Rs283 crores projected for the last two), total outlay would have to be cut to Rs4,500 crores. This rather suspiciously round figure was therefore proposed as the outlay 'to correspond with the resources position'. A 'pruning of outlays all along the line' followed. Even expenditure on Industry and Minerals was reduced from Rs880 crores to Rs790 crores, and a further small cut made in the admittedly inadequate allocation to Transport and Communications.

These financial cuts were considered to imply no lowering of the physical targets in agriculture, although the CD Programme would have to be rephased, by way of postponing by two and a half years the date set for complete coverage of the rural area. Additional irrigation facilities, however, would total only 10·4 instead of 12 million acres, and then only 'if the requisite funds were available'. The target for installed electrical generating capacity was lowered from 3·5 million kw. to 'nearly' 3 million; that for coal from 60 million to 56–57 million tons. In large and medium industries, a number of public sector projects would have to be 'deferred or substantially slowed down', while private sector shortfalls were predicted for aluminium, ferro-manganese, caustic soda, cement, dyestuffs, refractories, most types of machinery, automobiles, cables, paper and newsprint, rayon filament and sugar. These and other industries, moreover, would not be able to carry out their modernization and replacement programmes in full. There would probably also be shortfalls in the programmes for handloom, small-scale industries, and industrial estates. Railways, while keeping their original targets for passenger and freight transport, would have to postpone certain constructional and manufacturing projects; ports would be unable to carry out their 'original programmes in full'; roads were likely to experience 'some shortfall in the total programme'; shipping became subject to some 'uncertainty'. In Communications and Broadcasting, only the two air corporations would escape cuts. In the Social Services, there would be general shortfalls except in education, the only service expected to achieve or even exceed its Second Five-Year Plan targets in spite of reduced allocations. Absolute priority was to be given only to the 'core' projects.

When presented to the NDC on 3–4 May 1958, the *Appraisal and Prospects* caused considerable controversy. Morarji Desai, the new Finance Minister, argued the Planning Commission's case, but many Chief

Ministers strongly opposed the cuts, which they considered psychologically damaging. Although sceptical, as usual, about the potentialities of taxation, they expressed some hope of an increase in loans and small savings. Nehru, as on many other occasions, produced a compromise formula. The total outlay was to be kept at Rs4,800 crores, but programmes were to be divided into two groups, a high-priority one totalling Rs4,500 crores and a lower-priority one totalling Rs300 crores. The division of projects between the two was to be effected in consultation with the states. As to the methods of raising new resources to fill the 'gap', now estimated at Rs240 crores, the resolution passed by the NDC had nothing much of value to offer; for the Council had displayed something less than unanimity on this subject.

The crisis in the plan naturally aroused wide discussion and controversy, both before and after the issue of the *Appraisal and Prospects* document and its consideration by the NDC. Meeting at Pragjyotishpur on 18–19 January, the 63rd Annual Session of the Indian National Congress had demanded an intensification and reorientation of the agricultural programme, with particular reference to the production of green manures, the utilization of irrigation potential and enlistment of popular support through village panchayats and co-operatives.[79] The Economists' Panel concluded a three-day meeting ending on 25 January by emphasizing the importance of organizational difficulties and recommending that, in order to fulfil the 'core', all 'postponable expenditure should be abandoned and a strictly utilitarian approach adopted in matters of all construction work and the provision of amenities'. It also registered another dissent from Professor Shenoy.[80] The Communist Party Congress meeting at Amritsar on 6–18 April expressed its support for the 'progressive features' of the plan and attributed the difficulties which had arisen to 'unwarranted and harmful concessions, to Big Business', 'excessive reliance on foreign capital', 'iniquitous taxation' of the common people, deficit financing, and 'dependence on the bureaucratic machinery'.[81] With the last point the Praja Socialist Party apparently agreed. At its Fourth Annual Conference at Poona on 25 May, it accused Congress of weaknesses in organization, maladministration, corruption, and an 'inability to comprehend and communicate to the people the stubborn difficulties inherent in the rapid social and economic transformation of society'.[82] In the Lok Sabha, between 10 February and 9 May, there were no fewer than 63 questions about the plan, only 18 of them being of the usual 'constituency' type. During the budget debates, the plan was the subject of twelve 'cut' motions of the most varied kind.[83]

[79] *AR*, 1958, pp. 1859–60. [80] Ibid. p. 1871. [81] Ibid. p. 2010. [82] Ibid. pp. 2079–80.
[83] LSD, xv, 10007–84, 10091, 10098–126, 10208–901, 10296–332, 10333, 10341, 10342, 10343–50, 10432–546; xiii, 5891–92, 5894–957, 5969–86, 6070–140; xiv, 6519–20, 6521–87, 6593, 6597–658, 6748–92, 7914–79, 7980, 7992–8026, 8115–203, 8569–613, 8616, 8617–87.

Weightiest criticism came from the report, published in May, of the two-man team from the International Bank,[84] whose views were transmitted to the important five-power 'Aid-to-India' Conference in Washington. This reiterated many of the points made by the McKitterick Mission. It urged that future plans should be based on a more realistic assessment of resources, both domestic and foreign, that investment in industry, power, and transport should be 'on a less ambitious scale', that higher priority should be given to agriculture, and that the Community Development Movement should concentrate more single-mindedly on the improvement of productivity. Like the report of the Panel of Economists, it also stressed organizational weaknesses. To relieve 'overstrain' on the central administrative machine, it made the suggestion that the state should limit its industrial responsibilities.

Amid this babel of voices, the Planning Commission, guided by the resolution of the NDC, undertook, in collaboration with the central ministries and the state governments, its 'further examination' of the distribution of outlay and the raising of resources.

(iii)

By September it had something to show—a brief document entitled *Reappraisal of the Second Five Year Plan: a Résumé*. This proved that what the International Bank called 'undue pressure' had indeed been brought to bear, both by the state governments and by the central ministries, with the result that the good resolutions of May 1958 had been considerably diluted. The Commission reported that 'special concern' had been expressed by Chief Ministers about the impact of the proposed new allocations for social services and for village and small-scale industries. It was clearly the result of such 'concern' that the level of expenditure in the states was now 'set at an appreciably higher level than in the first three years of the Plan'. As for the central ministries, they had persuaded the Commission that they needed another Rs150 crores, with the result that total proposed outlay was now raised to Rs4,650 crores. The ministries responsible for industries and minerals must have been particularly persuasive, as their plan outlay went up from Rs790 to Rs882 crores. Yet although the Commission had apparently accepted these demands, its proposals for raising the necessary additional resources were vague in the extreme.

Together with the *Appraisal and Prospects* document, the *Résumé* was debated by both Houses of Parliament in September 1958. In the Lok Sabha[85] Nanda made a series of statements which revealed the sharpness

[84] *Current Economic Position and Prospects of India*. As I was unable to obtain a copy of this document quotations are from the summary published in *AR*, 1958, p. 2267.
[85] 17, 18, 19, & 22 Sept., xx, 7069–94, 7225–394, 7502–63; xxi, 7745–926.

of the unresolved disagreements about the size of the plan. On the first day of the debate, 17 September, he said that the Commission had come to the conclusion that a larger effort than that which it had envisaged during the discussions of the previous May had become 'imperative'. On the following day, however, he denied that the extra Rs150 crores represented anything more than an indication 'of pressing demands which should be thought of', and stated that the plan 'stood at Rs4500 crores, unless more resources could be raised'. He himself seemed bankrupt of ideas on further resource mobilization, and the government had to call upon one of its father-figures, G. B. Pant, the Minister of Home Affairs, to reassure an anxious House with the following comfortable words: 'There has been considerable recovery even in the course of the last few months. The money market, which was tight some days ago, is now in a flourishing condition. We can develop industries. We can get large loans, and I do not think that Rs4800 crores or Rs4500 crores is the limit of our aspirations.' No one else had anything significantly more constructive to offer.

This debate marked the nadir of the Planning Commission's parliamentary reputation. Many harsh things were said of it, and there was considerable sympathy for a substitute motion which demanded that it should be reconstituted as a body of 'experts, not belonging to any political party'.[86]

The government, of course, retained its majority and the 'consideration' motion was duly passed. The *Résumé* then became part of the documentation of a series of further discussions with the state governments and the central Ministry of Finance during the months of September and October.

(iv)

Precisely what took place in these discussions is not known, but one may surmise that there was some extremely plain speaking, particularly on the part of the Finance Minister. The outcome was yet another document, entitled *Plan Resources and Outlay: A Review*, which was presented to the NDC on 8–9 November. This abandoned not only the Rs4,650 of the *Résumé* but the Rs4,500 crores of the *Appraisal and Prospects* and came to the conclusion that the plan would have to be limited to Rs4,200–4,300 crores. The cutting down of outlay to this figure, it said, could be avoided only if more resources for the plan could be raised in non-inflationary ways. Whether and how far such resources were realizable it referred for consideration by the NDC 'in the light of the fairly detailed assessment of the position' given in the *Review* itself.

This assessment sharply underlined the deterioration of the resources position at the centre, of which a massive increase in deficit financing as

[86] Ibid. cols. 7247–8.

between the years 1956–7 and 1957–8 provided alarming evidence. While plan outlay and central assistance to the states had increased by Rs158 and Rs32 crores respectively in 1957–8, the centre's domestic budgetary resources showed a fall of Rs142 crores. On the basis of a Rs4,500 plan, the gap in resources at the centre would work out at Rs438 crores during the last two years of the plan. This obviously could not be met by deficit financing, which had to be limited to a maximum of Rs100 crores a year. Even on the assumption that the centre could raise for the plan another Rs40 crores by way of fresh taxation, the gap would still amount to Rs198 crores.

In the states the resources position was also bad, despite the shot in the arm they had received (at the expense of the centre) from the Finance Commission. An improvement of Rs44 in the states' revenue resources and of Rs46 crores under 'loans from the public and small savings' had been 'offset substantially by outflows under miscellaneous receipts on capital account'. The Rs12 crores worth of extra taxation which they had agreed to raise over the next two years was obviously inadequate to fill their resources gap. When every possible source of finance had been accounted for, this stood at an estimated figure of Rs82 crores.

When this gloomy document was brought before the NDC on 8–9 November, both Nehru and Desai underlined the warnings that it contained. Nehru said that 'they had now to pull themselves out from the maze of schemes and think afresh as to where they were and what they could do because there was a certain danger in being overwhelmed by events and by multiplicity of detail'. Desai confronted the assembled Chief Ministers with the plain facts of the financial situation. The Chief Ministers, however, expressed firm opposition to any further cuts in their own state plans and decided to pin their hopes on price control through state trading in foodgrains. During the discussion of this Nehru introduced his currently-favoured panacea for rural backwardness: multi-purpose village co-operatives. 'They were facing difficulties', he said, 'because they had not attached enough importance to such cooperatives . . . . They had already lost irretrievably four or five years of the nation's life.' Eventually agreement was reached, or at least recorded, on four points, viz.

(1) The State should take over wholesale trade in food grains and a scheme for State trading in foodgrains should be worked out;
(2) For increasing agricultural production, mobilising local manpower and other resources and generally for rebuilding the rural economy, co-operatives should be organised on the basis of the village as the primary unit; and responsibility and initiative for social and economic development at the village level should be placed fully on the village cooperatives and the village panchayats . . . ;
(3) With a view to achieving economy in construction costs, fewer buildings

should be constructed than originally contemplated and such buildings as have to be constructed should be at a cheaper basis [*sic*] . . . ;

(4) The question of introducing schemes of compulsory savings should be examined carefully.

These statements of intention were the justification for the NDC's decision to maintain the Second Five-Year Plan's level of outlay at the previously-agreed figure of Rs4,500 crores. The idea of dividing the plan into two parts, it will be noted, had been dropped.

For the states' annual plans for 1959–60, the NDC agreed to a total outlay of Rs450–55 crores, of which Rs230 crores would represent central assistance and Rs220–225 crores the states' own contribution. This required the raising by the states of Rs25–30 crores over and above their previous estimates. 'To the extent that state resources fell short of the level indicated their total outlay would be smaller.'

(v)

This was the darkest hour of the Second Five-Year Plan. During the first half of 1958–9 every conceivable thing seemed to go wrong and, as we have seen, there was great confusion of counsel. Towards the end of the calendar year, however, a few chinks of light began to appear. The slowing down of industrial growth itself somewhat reduced inflationary pressures, with the result that, in spite of the poor harvest of 1958 (the worst since 1953–4), the all-India cost-of-living index, which had soared from 110 in March to 123 in October, dropped to 119 in December. As a result of the new import licensing policies and the stepping up of foreign assistance, the strain on the balance of payments was easing. Foreign exchange reserves, which had fallen to the alarmingly low figure of Rs178 crores in October, were beginning to recover, and the out-turn for 1958–9 was eventually to show a decline of only 42 crores, as against one of 260 crores for the previous financial year. Measures for the mobilization of internal resources were also beginning to take effect. The sharp jump in receipts from loans (from Rs70 crores in 1957–8 to Rs230 crores in 1958–9) no doubt mainly reflected the investment of PL480 rupee funds in government securities by the State Bank of India, but simultaneously the yield of additional taxation increased from Rs178 crores to Rs218 crores, that of small savings from Rs69 crores to Rs80 crores, while the 'Unfunded Debt and Miscellaneous Capital Receipts' item moved from a negative figure of Rs53 crores to a positive one of Rs107 crores.

The 1959 Economic Survey was therefore able to report more cheerfully,[87] and the Planning Commission itself was put in better heart by the results of the discussions which it held with the states, during the months of

[87] *Budget, 1959–60*, White Paper, O. 130.

December 1958 and January 1959, about allocations for 1959–60. These indicated that the resources available to the states, during the fourth year of the plan, were likely to exceed previous estimates. Hopes for a significantly greater financial effort from the states had often been belied, but this time something was forthcoming. The states' budgets for 1959–60, although departing in detail from the 'allocation suggested by the Planning Commission', were at least 'in terms of the estimates agreed on at the . . . annual plan discussions'.[88] These budgets proved the beginning of a financial effort on the part of the states during the last two years of the plan that was as considerable as it was unexpected.

By the middle of 1959 it appeared that the corner had been turned. Encouraged by the record harvest of 1958–9 and a substantial increase in external assistance, the Commission was able to predict, with some confidence, that outlay for the five years would 'reach, if not exceed, the total of Rs4,500 crores envisaged by the National Development Council in November 1958'.[89] In the end, total outlay amounted to some Rs4,600 crores. Deflating this figure to allow for the rise in wholesale prices, one arrives at a total of about Rs3,700 crores in terms of the price-level for 1955–6, the year in which the plan was originally formulated. The shortfall from Rs4,800 crores was, of course, very considerable, but during the crisis of 1957 and 1958 it had seemed that the gap between intentions and achievements would be much greater.

That the last two years of the plan were a success story in comparison with the crisis-laden first three years clearly emerges from the Commission's *Progress Reports for 1958–9* and *1959–60*. 'The general outlook', said the latter document,[90] 'had greatly improved as the economy moved into the fifth and final year of the second plan.' Although it registered an appreciable decline in foodgrains production from the 'bumper' year, 1958–9, it expressed the opinion that output, estimated at 75 million tons in 1958–9 and 73·5 million tons in 1959–60, 'compared not too unfavourably with the plan target of 80 million tons'. It placed particular emphasis on the strengthening of the infrastructure of the economy that had taken place, found encouragement in the 'growth of basic capital and producer goods industries', refuted the 'general impression' that consumer goods industries had 'lagged behind', recorded 'all-round progress in the implementation of the various agricultural development programmes', gave the nation credit for 'an intensification of the internal resources mobilisation effort', and pointed hopefully to the fact that the rate of decline of India's foreign exchange reserves had been 'arrested'. Among major weaknesses it listed the inadequate expansion of employment opportunities, the continued rise in the price level, the stagnation of exports, and the serious condition

[88] Plan. Com., *Plan Resources and Outlay, a Review* (July 1959), pp. 77–78. [89] Ibid. p. 81.
[90] Still in mimeo. form at the time of writing.

of the balance of payments. The original target for employment outside agriculture had been reduced, during the reappraisal, from 8 million persons to 6·5 million; but only 4·5 million were likely to have been absorbed by the end of the year 1959–60. Despite several checks in the upward movement of the price index, a net rise of about 21 per cent had been registered during the first four years of the plan. Export receipts had declined during the second and third years, and had not recovered much of the lost ground during the fourth—although 'an encouraging feature was that non-traditional items such as sewing machines, bicycles, electric fans and other engineering goods had begun to figure in the export trade'. The adverse trade balance, although reduced from Rs639 crores in 1957–9 to Rs300 crores in 1959–60, showed an aggregate figure of Rs1,858 crores, while Rs540 crores had been lost by the foreign exchange reserves.

What the report failed to emphasize was the continued heavy dependence of agricultural production on the monsoon, the serious shortfall in steel production, the development of transport bottlenecks, and the sluggishness of domestic capital formation. These were to bedevil the early years of the Third Five-Year Plan.

(vi)

At the time of writing, no general *Review of the Second Five-Year Plan* has been published. For the evaluation of its results, therefore, one has to rely on scattered information and on the chapter entitled 'Ten Years of Planning' in the Third Five-Year Plan document. The latter, unfortunately, provides only rather sketchy statistical data and does not always distinguish with sufficient clarity the results of the 1956–61 exercise from those of the previous one. The figures given in the last column of Table 10 (p. 164), therefore, must be treated with some reserve. They have been derived from various sources, mainly on the principle that the later are more likely to be accurate than the earlier ones.

As during the last years of the First Plan, the weather became the planners' ally, and it is quite impossible to estimate how much of the 79·5 million tons of foodgrains, representing a shortfall of only half a million tons on the revised target, was to be attributed to the favourable monsoon and how much to improved techniques. That the total was only 4 million tons higher than that of the previous 'good' year, 1958–9, suggests that, for all the resources which had been poured into agricultural extension, community projects, and irrigation, progress in productivity was still extremely slow. In respect of minor irrigation, the shortfall—12 million acres—was enormous; and the wide gap, revealed by cropping statistics, between irrigation potential and utilization was, in the words of one of the Commission's Programme Advisers, 'a matter of great concern'. In spite of the near-attainment of the production target, no one could disguise the fact

TABLE 10

Second Five-Year Plan: Targets & Achievements

Note: Approximate correctness only can be guaranteed for these figures. Each figure for actual production (1955–6) and achievement (1960–61) is taken from the *latest* available planning document, the last to be consulted being the *Third Five Year Plan Mid-Term Appraisal* (Nov. 1963). Unfortunately successive documents do not always use the same units or contain the same list of items. Hence the construction of a series is made rather difficult.

1 *Item*	2 *Unit*	3 *Actual prodn. 1955–6*	4 *Plan Target (original)*	5 *Plan Target (as later adjusted)*	6 *Achievement 1960–1*
1. AGRICULTURAL PRODUCTION					
(*a*) Foodgrains	m. tons	64·8	75·0	80·5	79·6
(*b*) Cotton	Lakh bales	40·0	55	65	54
(*c*) Jute	Lakh bales	42·0	50	78	40
(*d*) Sugar cane	Lakh tons of gur	58·6	71	78	104
(*e*) Oilseeds	Lakh tons	56·6	70	76	65·2
(*f*) CD Blocks & NES Blocks	Nos.	1,075	3,800	3,087	3,110
(*g*) Population served by CD & NES Blocks	Millions	68	325	204	204

2. IRRIGATION & POWER (*a*) Area irrigated	m. acres	63·3	88		73
(*b*) Electrical energy	Installed capacity, m. kw.	3·4 (calendar year)	6·9		5·58
3. TRANSPORT & COMMUNICATIONS (*a*) Railways	m. passenger train miles	38,774			48,600
	Freight, m. tons	114	181	168	154
(*b*) Roads National highways	000 miles	12·9 } 122·0*	13·8		} 144·0
Surfaced roads	000 miles	121·6 }	125·0	144·9	}
(*c*) Shipping: Coastal	Lakh GRT	2·4	4·3	4·9	2·92 } 8·57†
Overseas	Lakh GRT	2·4	4·7	4·1	6·13 }
(*d*) Ports, Major	Handling capacity, million tons	25	32·5		37
(*e*) Posts & Telegraphs Post Offices Telegraph Offices Telephones	 000 000 000	 55 5·1 280	 75 6·3 450		 77 7·0 463

* Figure given in *FYP(3)*. † Figure given in *MTA*.

TABLE 10 (cont.)

1 *Item*	2 *Unit*	3 *Actual prodn. 1955–6*	4 *Plan Target (original)*	5 *Plan Target (as later adjusted)*	6 *Achievement 1960–1*
4. INDUSTRIAL PRODUCTION (*a*) Finished steel	m. tons	1·3	4·3		2·4
(*b*) Pig iron (for sale to foundries)	m.t.	0·38	0·75		1·1
(*c*) Cement	m. t.	4·6	13	10–11	7·8
(*d*) Aluminium	m. t.	7·5	25·0		18·2
(*e*) Fertilizers: Ammonium sulphate	000 t.	394	1,450		402
phosphatic	000 t.	71.0	720		316
(*f*) Locomotives	Nos	179	400		295
(*g*) Cotton textiles	m. yards	6,552	8,500		6,978
(*h*) Jute mfrs	000 t.	1,054			1,071
(*i*) Bicycles	000	513	1,000		1,063
(*j*) Sewing machines	000	111	220		297

(*k*) Power alcohol	m. litres	47·5			49·0
(*l*) Sugar	000 t.	1,860	2,300		3,000
(*m*) Machine tools	Value in Rs. lakhs	78	300		724 (calendar year)
(*n*) Cement machinery	Value in Rs. lakhs	34	200		60
(*o*) Sugar machinery	Value in Rs. lakhs	19	250		330
(*p*) Textile machinery	Value in Rs. lakhs	412	1,950	1,700	900
(*q*) Paper machinery	Value in Rs. lakhs	neg.	400		650–700
(*r*) Power driven pumps, centrifugal	000	37	86		107
(*s*) Diesel engines	000 H.P.	103·6	205		442·64
(*t*) Automobiles	Nos.	25,300	57,000		54,789
(*u*) Tractors	Nos.	—	3,000		2,000
(*v*) Sulphuric acid	000 t.	164	470		354
(*w*) Soda ash.	000 t.	81	230		145
(*x*) Caustic soda	000 t.	36	135		197
(*y*) Crude processed petroleum	m. t.	3·6	4·3		5·7

TABLE 10 (cont.)

1 *Item*	2 *Unit*	3 *Actual prodn. 1955–6*	4 *Plan Target (original)*	5 *Plan Target (as later adjusted)*	6 *Achievement 1960–1*
(*z*) Electric transformers (33 kw & below)	000 kw	625	1,360		1,200
(*aa*) Electric cables	Tons	9,000	18,000		22,000
(*bb*) Electric motors	000 h.p.	272	600		700
(*cc*) Paper & paper board	000 t.	187	350		343
(*dd*) Electric fans	000	275	600		106
5. SOCIAL SERVICES (*a*) Education—school-going children aged (i) 6–11	% of age-group	52·9	63·0		61·1
(ii) 11–14	% of age-group	16·5	22·5		22·8
(iii) 14–17	% of age-group	7·8	12·0		11·5
(*b*) Health (i) Hospital beds	000	125	155		186
(ii) Medical institutions (dispensaries & hospitals)	000	10	12·6		12·6

that, at the end of the Second Five-Year Plan, India's progress towards the solution of the most basic of her problems, agricultural production, was inadequate.

In industry, the picture was much brighter. The general index of industrial production had risen from 139 in 1955–6 (base year 1950–1) to 194 in 1960–1, while that of machine production had soared from 194 to 503. Throughout the period of the first two plans, industrial production had grown at an average rate of 7 per cent. To observers conditioned to believe that private enterprise was being throttled by socialistic policies, the expansion achieved by the private sector was particularly surprising. 'The best news in India's first decade of planned growth', wrote Miss Barbara Ward, 'is . . . that enterprise exists irresistably and unquestionably, that it is growing at a speed to create a whole new climate of opinion favourable to development and to provide interlocking expansion and external economies by which enterprise in one field assists it everywhere else.'[91] As evidence for this perhaps over-optimistic judgement there were the facts that in the organized private sector investment had outpaced all the official forecasts and that there was a widespread proliferation of small-scale enterprises, causing considerable pressure on the resources of the states' industrial finance agencies. On the other hand the steel industry, to which so much had been sacrificed, registered a production of 2·4 million tons as against its target of 4·3 million.

Much of the progress achieved in industry reflected the strengthening of the infrastructure of the economy. In this department, however, there were some serious shortfalls, already causing strain and certain to cause much more. Power production, held back mainly by the shortage of foreign exchange, had missed its target of 6·9 million kw. by 1·2 million. Underinvestment in the railways system, a consistent feature of both plans, was responsible for increasingly serious bottlenecks as the tempo of development picked up after the crisis years of 1957 and 1958. Although the road programme was reasonably well up to schedule, road transport was not yet capable of taking the whole of the extra burden, while coastal shipping had fallen far short of its not-too-ambitious target. Posts and telegraphs, by contrast, had done rather better than planned, and education, measured by the percentage of children in the various age-groups attending school and by the expansion of the various kinds of technical colleges, had performed creditably.

The Third Five-Year Plan document put the increase in the national income, over the five years of the Second Plan, at 20 per cent. Assuming, rather rashly, that this figure is reliable, the shortfall was only 5 per cent, but the planners were bound to contrast it rather ruefully with the excess of 6 per cent over target achieved by the First Plan.

[91] Barbara Ward Jackson, 'India on the Eve of its Third Plan', *Foreign Affairs*, Jan. 1961, p. 261.

Much had been achieved—much more than had seemed possible in 1958; but the Indian economy was still a very long way from 'take-off', and ominous signs abounded. Prices continued to rise alarmingly. During the last year of the plan the wholesale index (1950–1 = 100) went up from 104·7 to 111·6. The pressure on foreign reserves had been no more than temporarily eased, and, given the size of the Third Five-Year Plan, another foreign exchange crisis could be confidently predicted. Domestic capital formation had risen, over the plan period, by no more than 1·2 per cent of national income—from 7·3 per cent in the first year to 8·5 per cent in the last. 'Bailed out from crisis to crisis', as Barbara Ward rather rudely puts it, the planners had used up Rs1,090 crores worth of foreign assistance as against an admittedly over-optimistic estimate of Rs800 crores and had become dependent, for the realization of their Third Plan targets, on even greater injections of external funds. Population increase had proved far more rapid than even the most pessimistic prophet had dared forecast. The provisional census data of 1961 revealed that by 1976 India would have a population of 625 million, instead of the 578 million estimated by the CSO in 1959. The newly calculated rate of natural increase meant that, for all India's efforts, the per capita national income had risen by an average of only about 1·6 per cent per annum. Various inquiries, moreover, suggested that the distribution of the national income might have become more rather than less unequal; indeed, the second agricultural labour inquiry claimed it had evidence that the landless were actually sinking deeper into an already horrifying poverty.[92] For full measure, one has to record the very general opinion that the administrative apparatus was barely capable of coping with the immense number of new and unfamiliar tasks which it was now called upon to perform, and that among the population at large, communalism, casteism, linguism, and other disintegrative tendencies were making alarming headway.

These were some of the problems that confronted India on the eve of her Third Five-Year Plan. It remained to be seen whether the planners, in implementing it, would be able to avoid some of the mistakes which had marred their performance during the years 1956–61.

[92] The accuracy of its figures and the validity of its conclusions were, however, strongly disputed.

VI

THE THIRD FIVE-YEAR PLAN

FORMULATION

(i)

THE circumstances in which the preparation of the Third Five-Year Plan began were very different from those which had attended the birth of the Second. There was a financial crisis, a foreign exchange crisis, and a food crisis. The Second Plan had been cut down to a 'core' of Rs4,500 crores, and there was considerable doubt whether even this reduced outlay could be met. Foreign opinion was critical, and the Americans, in particular, were insisting that India's plans were over-ambitious. 'Over-ambition' had also been the main theme of International Bank's two-man team that reported in May 1958. In addition it emphasized the dangers of pursuing welfare at the expense of efficiency, and the difficulty of reconciling a policy of reducing inequalities with one of rapid economic development. Nehru himself was in one of his 'back-to-the-wall' moods. The planners, he told the NDC, would have to 'pull themselves out from the maze of schemes and think afresh as to where and what they could do, because there was a certain danger in being overwhelmed by events and by multiplicity of detail'. It was against this gloomy background that the Planning Commission, round about November 1958, began to consider the general pattern of resources and outlay for the Third Plan.

Some work relevant to the Third Plan period had, of course, already been done; indeed, it is clear that by the middle 1950s the whole process of plan preparation had become a continuous one. As early as August 1957 the Deputy Minister of Planning, S. N. Mishra, informed the Lok Sabha, in a written answer, that 'preliminary steps for studies and investigations in selected fields' where very long-term planning was required, e.g. technical manpower, irrigation and power, steel and other heavy industries, and agriculture, had been taken by the Planning Commission and by the relevant central ministries.[1] Just over a year later he announced that 'preliminary work' was being done in the states as well as at the centre, that working groups for agriculture, irrigation, power, and education had already been set up, that 'special attention' was being paid to the mobilization of more adequate statistical and technical data, and that

[1] LSD, iv, 6985, Written Answer.

estimates of foreign exchange requirements were being attempted for those Second Plan projects that would have to be carried over into the Third Plan.[2] By November 1958 the Planning Commission had requested the state governments to establish their own working groups for the formulation of Third Plan targets.

The immediate question now confronting the Planning Commission was whether the total Third Plan outlay of Rs9,900 crores, as envisaged in the 'perspective' part of the Second Plan document, represented an attainable objective. Material to enable it to come to a decision was prepared in the Commission's Economic and Perspective Planning Divisions, and the thinking there done crystallized, during the months of November and December, into three basis papers: 'Approach to the Problems of Resources for the Third Plan' (27 November 1958) and 'Problems of Resource Mobilisation' (15 December 1958), both by J. J. Anjaria, the Commission's Economic Adviser, and 'Dimensional Hypotheses concerning the Third Five Year Plan', by Pitamber Pant, Mahalanobis's disciple and head of the Perspective Planning Division.[3]

Anjaria's papers sounded an ominous note. He did not state, in so many words, that the outlay target of Rs9,900 crores was unattainable, but held that its attainment involved radical organizational changes which would be very difficult to make.

'The limitations of a purely financial approach', he wrote,

> have always been recognised; the question is how effectively physical resources actual or potential, can be pressed into service in a system which operates mainly in terms of financial incentives and disincentives. An imbalance between financial outlay and resources can be avoided or held in check only to the extent that real resources come into the system effectively. This latter depends on how far the community is organised for more work and greater austerity.

Achievements in this respect, he suggested, had so far been extremely feeble.

> Neither hard work . . . nor austerity are conspicuous in the Indian environment today. The Plan has meant so many projects undertaken by the Centre and the States; the community has watched the progress of these projects with interest and admiration, but it has not yet been called upon to be active or full participants. If some sections of the community have made sacrifices . . . this has been the result of an economic policy . . . which is remote to them. Only marginally have they been called upon to offer their labour for works of local interest: roads, school buildings and the like.

The objectives of planning as already defined could not, in Anjaria's view, be achieved 'without the type, if not the actual degree, of effort which

[2] Ibid. xx, 6102–04, Written Answer.
[3] These three papers have not been published and remain in mimeo. form.

the authoritarian regimes had shown themselves capable of putting forth'. The essential question, therefore, was whether India, while remaining a democratic country, could put itself on such a 'war economy footing' for several quinquennia.

The answer, one might have thought, was obvious; but Anjaria refrained from giving it. He did, however, suggest that even if the necessary organizational changes were made, 'it should not be assumed that they would add to the resources available in the near future'. He also pointed out the 'obvious dangers in cluttering up the system with too many checks and counter-checks'. Thus, although he confined himself to asking questions, he appeared to be leading the unprejudiced reader to the conclusion that an effort on the 'Chinese' scale was not feasible and that therefore the investment target would have to be reduced.

This paper was presented to the Planning Commission at an 'informal meeting' on 28 November. There is no record of how the Commission reacted to it, but evidently at some stage during the course of the next fortnight agreement was reached on the necessity for an effort on the heroic scale; for the first paragraph of Anjaria's second paper, 'Problems of Resource Mobilisation', which is dated 15 December, reads as follows:

> The discussions of the last few weeks point clearly to the conclusion that the Third Five Year Plan must not only maintain, but, to the limit of practicality, accelerate the tempo of development attained in the Second Plan. There is no doubt that the basic objectives and priorities of the Second Plan were right. If difficulties have arisen, as they undoubtedly have, in implementing the Plan, that only calls for far more effort and far better organisation of it than has so far been attempted.

The question was where the 'limit of practicality' lay. Anjaria made no attempt to define it, but mentioned two figures which, in his view, represented the maximum effort and the minimum. The first, Rs9,900 crores, would produce 'satisfactory results in terms of increases in national income and employment'. The second, Rs7,500 crores, would permit the maintenance of the existing rate of investment, viz. 11 per cent of the national income. The issue to be decided was 'where precisely between this minimum level of Rs7,500 crores and the desirable level of Rs9,900 crores the balance should be struck'.

Taking the lower aggregate figure for purposes of calculation, he found that investment in the public sector would have to absorb at least Rs4,800 crores. But likely resources, computed on the basis of current trends in the yield of taxation, small savings, borrowings, profits of public enterprises and foreign assistance, were no more than Rs3,400 crores. The balance of Rs1,400 crores could not be met, even in part, by deficit financing, nor could it be covered by 'direct utilisation of unutilised manpower', necessary and important though that might be. It would therefore have to come from 'additional taxation and/or profits from industrial enterprises and State trading'. Thus, in order to hit even the minimum investment target, the government would have to impose 'more taxation of the agricultural sector, more excises, more sales taxes, more import duties, and higher direct taxes in certain income brackets', as well as increasing the profits of public enterprises and promptly 'mopping up—by suitable extensions of State trading—the surpluses that arise from time to time in the economy at various points'. The actual size of the plan would depend on 'how far and how quickly public savings could be increased' along these lines.

Anjaria's two papers may be regarded as preliminary explorations. The document which give a firm basis to subsequent discussions was Pitamber Pant's *Dimensional Hypotheses concerning the Third Five Year Plan*, which appeared on 21 December 1958. Essentially, this was the Plan Frame for the Third Plan—with the vital difference that it was never published or offered for general discussion. Like the Plan Frame, it was a laconic document, revealing nothing of the processes that had gone into its making. One may be reasonably certain, however, that the methods of computation and projection on which it was based were roughly the same as those set out in W. B. Reddaway's *The Development of the Indian Economy* (1962)[4]—although probably rather less sophisticated.

As his basic assumption, Pant took the high target of Rs10,000 crores net investment at 1957–8 prices (which was supposed to correspond with the Rs9,900 mentioned in the Second Five-Year Plan document). Other assumptions included (*a*) a population increase of 2 per cent per annum; (*b*) an increase in national income of 6 per cent per annum; (*c*) an increase in agricultural output of 5 per cent per annum; (*d*) the absorption of all additional employment-seekers; and (*e*) a balance between the public and private sectors which would 'broadly conform to the industrial development policy of the government and reflect the growing importance of the public sector in the economy as envisaged in the objective of achieving in due course a socialist pattern of society'.

Tables provided projections of investment allocations, of the balance of investment between the public and private sectors, of the financing of government investment, and of national income (see Table 11). Net investment as a percentage of domestic product was to reach 14·1 per cent by 1965–6, of which 4–5 per cent was to be provided by foreign assistance.

Essentially, the Third Five-Year Plan was to be a continuation and intensification of the Second. The balance of investment would not be substantially different—30 per cent of the aggregate being accounted for

[4] No. 1 of Studies in the Economic Development of India.

TABLE 11

Third Five-Year Plan: Projections in Pant's 'Dimensional Hypotheses'
(a) Investment Allocation

Sector	*Percentage of Total*	*Rs crores (1961–6)*
Mining & oil	3	300
Power	7	700
Basic & other organized large-scale industries	20	2,000
Small-scale industries	3	300
Transport & communications	17	1,700
Total	50	5,000
Grand Total	100	10,000

(b) Investment, Public and Private
(Rs crores)

Sector	*Base yr 1960–1*	*1961–2*	*1962–3*	*1963–4*	*1964–5*	*1965–6*	*Total*
Public	900	1,050	1,200	1,340	1,500	1,650	6,700
Private	500	550	600	660	700	750	3,300

(c) Financing of Government Investment

Major Sources with Approx. Yield	*Rs crores (5 yrs)*
1. Revenue receipts	8,300
2. Surpluses of public enterprises	1,200
3. Additional indirect taxes & profits of state trading	1,500
4. Additional corporate, wealth, income taxes &c.	500
5. Taxes on agricultural production or additional land tax	1,000
6. Domestic savings & borrowings (net)	1,800
	14,300
7. *Less* total revenue expenditure	8,600
	5,700
8. *Plus* borrowings from abroad net of repayments	1,000
9. Net investment in public sector	6,700

TABLE 11 (cont.)

(*d*) *National Income*
(*Rs crores*)

Source	*1960–1*	*1965–6*
Agriculture	5,950	7,650
Mining & manufacture	1,350	2,500
Small industries & construction	1,100	1,400
Railways & communications	350	550
Trade & commerce	1,950	2,600
Professions & services	750	950
Government administration	550	750
Rentals	500	600
Domestic product	12,500	17,000
Estimated population (m.)	424	473
Per capita domestic product (Rs)	295	359

by industry and half by industry, mining, power, transport, and commerce taken together. The 'heavy industry' pattern, said Pant, could not be interrupted or reversed; indeed, it seemed to him even more vital in view of the strain on the balance of payments. The model as a whole was offered as presenting the quickest possible method of making the transition to a 'self-generating economy', without recourse to totalitarian methods.

Even if one disregards the size of the effort demanded, *Dimensional Hypotheses* provides evidence of a certain utopianism, comparable with that formerly displayed by the Plan Frame. Like Mahalanobis, Pant looked forward to a 'massive mobilisation of surplus manpower for carrying out projects of permanent improvement'. 'If this can be done on a sufficiently large scale all over the country, in the main without recourse to normal wage-payments, not only the main difficulty of employment but that of investable funds would be substantially eased.' No doubt he was right in his supposition, but he had no suggestion as to *how* it could be done without using methods comparable to those employed by the totalitarian Chinese.

One more important document was presented before the next meeting of the NDC on 3–4 April 1959: 'Certain Policy Implications of a Plan for a Self-Generating Economy', by S. R. Sen,[5] an economist from the Ministry of Agriculture who was shortly to become a leading official of the Planning Commission. This well-argued paper posed most of the problems involved in the transition to self-sustaining growth. Were

[5] Published in S. R. Sen, *Strategy for Agricultural Development and other Essays in Economic Policy and Planning* (Bombay, Asia Publishing House, 1963), pp. 81–98.

machine-building, steel, fuel and power really the essentials? he asked. If so, how did one decide on their relative priorities, and how did one reconcile the concentration of investment in these capital-intensive and slow-yielding projects with the provision of adequate wage-goods and employment opportunities, so as to minimize the strains inevitably arising from this type of investment? Among his suggested solutions was the balancing of long-gestation projects against short-gestation ones, particularly in agriculture. This would involve a sharp reorientation of community development towards enhanced productivity, and the giving of relatively low priority to large-scale irrigation projects as compared with small-scale works and with the more intensive utilization of existing facilities.

As for resources, the tightness of foreign exchange might indicate the need for a two-part plan, involving the separating out of the 'less essential' projects which were realizable only if assistance from abroad reached sufficient proportions. On the domestic front, in addition to stepping up the yield of indirect taxes, loans, and public enterprise profits, it was necessary to cream off the rural surplus by devices which made 'the agriculturalists interested in taxing themselves'.

But if all this was to be accomplished without arousing popular discontent which would not only jeopardize planning but undermine the stability of the government itself, a *serious* advance towards economic equality was needed. 'Conspicuous destitution' no less than 'conspicuous consumption' would have to be attacked; for

> the common man has to be given a feeling that extreme disparities of income are being gradually eliminated and something visible is happening in his neighbourhood and there is a reasonable promise of his own standard of living and employment opportunities improving during the next decade or so although immediately he is being called upon to bear some strain.

Sen's view of the relationship between the maximization of growth and the reduction of inequalities was, in fact, just the opposite of the International Bank's.

(ii)

From the above account, it will be seen that there was considerable caution, and even misgiving, in the initial approach to the Third Five-Year Plan. There was no shouting of target figures from the housetops, no general circulation of 'framework' papers, no public consultation of the Panel of Economists. As late as 18 December 1959 there had still been no announcement of an overall investment figure; S. N. Mishra, the Deputy Minister of Planning, in answer to an M.P. who asked him whether the Rs10,000 crores mentioned in the newspapers was correct, replied that no target had been fixed.[6] He was by no means deceiving the House, for it was not until March 1960 that the Planning Commission placed even 'tentative magnitudes' before the NDC for its consideration. The formulation of the Third Plan, in fact, seems to have much more of a back-room exercise than the formulation of the Second. This, no doubt, was partly deliberate—a product of the planners' realization that the bandying around of figures encouraged pressure-group politics rather than popular participation. But it may also have reflected a certain slackening of public interest in the process of planning, due, no doubt, to the impact of more immediate economic and political problems.

On the basis of its discussion of the papers we have summarized and of other documents, the Planning Commission succeeded in producing a 'Main Issues' paper for the benefit of the NDC's meeting on 3–4 April 1959. This followed fairly closely the line of argument of the two Anjaria papers, and spelled out at some length the consequences of the proposed concentration on heavy industry.

There has to be special emphasis on planning development in a manner that would make the economy 'self-sustaining' as early as possible. This involves the setting up and expansion of industries that will produce the machinery and equipment needed to manufacture machines and capital goods required for further industrialisation. In this connection there are two sets of considerations. Under this pattern adequate restrictions on consumption will have to be faced and consumption standards will have to be relatively kept down. Progress depends on the extent to which this can be achieved under democratic conditions, for the larger the investments in the more 'remote' stages or production, the larger and more varied is the ancillary investment required to support and make full use of these processes, and the greater, therefore, is the sacrifice involved in consumption 'for the time being'. In the second place, until the base has been built up, industrial development remains largely dependent on foreign exchange being made available from outside for setting up the industries required. Quicker progress towards the 'self-sustaining economy' in the sense of its being technically equipped to make capital goods and equipment it needs will raise the foreign exchange component of the Third Plan and will necessitate a larger measure of external assistance. On the other hand, if this obstacle to economic development is not got over as early as possible, the period of dependence on external resources tends to be prolonged.

This has been quoted *in extenso* not for the originality of its thought or the impeccability of its analysis, but because it shows (*a*) that the minds of the planners were now dominated by the conception of 'self-sustaining economic growth'; (*b*) that they considered the rapid development of machine-building to be the essential means to this end; and (*c*) that they were well aware of the problems involved in a quick transition to so

[6] LSD, xxxviii, 5830–37.

'round-about' a mode of production. The attempt to give concrete shape to this basic objective and to circumvent the obstacles that littered the path towards its attainment had a determining influence on the process of formulating the Third Five-Year Plan.

On the question of resources, the Commission was brutally realistic. Existing taxation would yield no current surpluses available for financing investment; indeed, the gulf between taxation and expenditure would widen as revenue account expenditures in the Second Plan became 'committed' expenditures in the Third Plan period. New taxation would be required, therefore, even to balance current budgets. Foreign exchange expenditure would have to be met entirely from fresh external assistance, and for the first two years, at least, even repayment obligations would have to be discharged from the proceeds of new borrowings from abroad. The phasing of the plan, therefore, would depend on how much and what kind of foreign aid could be mobilized; and it was obviously desirable that most of it should be of a kind which did not 'increase the servicing burden on the balance of payments for a considerable period in the future'. Finally, the 'utmost care' would have to be taken to avoid inflationary pressures. These fairly obvious but none-the-less ominous thoughts were the product of the Commission's 'preliminary examination' of resources.

On organizational problems, the Commission underlined the need to utilize manpower reserves through communal projects, and expressed the hope that 'the idea of customary obligations' might be 'extended to activities vital for meeting the new needs of rural development'. The problem of increasing agricultural production, it held, was 'primarily one of administration and organization and enthusing the people'. *Panchayati raj* was now the new rural panacea, and confidence was expressed in its 'rapid progress'.

It cannot be said that the NDC gave this document the consideration that it deserved. The only member to offer constructive ideas about raising resources was Subramaniam. Discussion of his proposals was cut short by B. C. Roy's claim that the National Sample Survey's target of 110 million tons of foodgrains (which had not been mentioned in the 'Issues' paper) was 'unnecessarily high'. After Mahalanobis had revealed a disagreement on this subject between the Survey and the Ministry of Agriculture (whose independently collected data indicated a target of 95 million tons), the Council decided to defer discussing it, pending an investigation of per capita food consumption. General agreement was reached (or at least was recorded in the appended 'Conclusions') on the importance of aiming at the provision of certain minimum amenities (e.g. clean water, schools, and feeder roads) in the rural areas; on the necessity of raising resources locally, on a 'matching' basis, through the panchayats; and on the desirability of ensuring that projects which

13

involved the use of unskilled and semi-skilled labour should be 'carried out to the extent possible in each village by the community concerned so that the employment provided and its benefits should accrue to the rural population'.

These ideas were somewhat marginal to the central issues of resource mobilization put by the Commission. The latter were only briefly considered by the Council, whose recorded conclusion on them were somewhat hesitant. But although the state ministers, as usual, forbore to commit themselves unambiguously to a greater tax effort, they agreed that an increase in land revenue was one of the 'possibilities' that 'ought to be investigated by the Planning Commission and the States'.

Despite this inconclusiveness, the NDC had in fact given the Commission its 'Go Ahead' signal.

(iii)

Its task was now to continue the 'macro' planning, along the agreed lines, to give more sustained attention to the 'micro' planning, which had already become the responsibility of numerous working groups, and to bring the two together in fruitful conjunction.

At the macro level, it had the assistance of the CSO, the Indian Statistical Institute, the Panel of Economists (which met for its first Third Plan discussion in March 1959), and the Research Section of the Reserve Bank of India—to name but a few participating organizations. It also had the advice of S. R. Sen, who contributed another important paper entitled 'Criteria for Investment Priorities'.[7]

Sen's concern was to emphasize the importance of cost-and-benefit calculations, particularly when, in a given constellation of projects, the element of substitutability was greater than that of complimentary. Only through such calculations could the authorities get to know 'which projects would help maximize the benefits to be derived from a certain quantum of investment although the latter might have been decided on the basis of non-economic considerations'. To illustrate this point he defined certain coefficients to guide investment choices and applied them to (*a*) two steel projects, (*b*) a few selected industries, (*c*) certain groups of industries, and (*d*) the major sectors of the economy. He claimed that these examples represented something more than a mere theoretical exercise, as they were based on 'certain data collected from diverse sources and the judgement of a few knowledgeable people', and suggested that it would be useful if the 'parties' making specific economic development proposals were required to provide the type of information needed for quantitative judgements.

[7] Published in Sen, *Strategy for Agric. Dev.*, pp. 99–122.

This was an attempt to carry the techniques of plan formulation to a further point of sophistication; but although it mapped out the path ahead, it was not followed up to any significant extent, because few of the 'parties' concerned had the necessary information at their disposal and even fewer were properly equipped to collect it. At this level of macro planning, most decisions were still the product of guesswork, inspired or uninspired.

During the first half of 1959, the working groups were seriously getting down to their assignments. No fewer than twenty-two had been established, and the bigger and more important of them, such as the Agricultural Working Group, divided themselves into numerous sub-committees. Each group consisted of from 10 to 15 members, drawn from the ministries and other central government agencies concerned and from the Planning Commission itself. The Secretary of the 'leading' ministry was usually in the chair, while a representative of the Planning Commission functioned as Secretary. For industry, transport, and power there was a special 'Steering Committee', under the chairmanship of the Secretary of the Planning Commission. All working groups operated under the rather vague general direction 'that they should take a long-term view of development in their respective fields and that the targets suggested for the Third Five Year Plan should fit into this perspective'.[8] With the obvious exception of the Working Group on Resources, all were instructed to treat physical requirements and physical possibilities rather than financial resources as the limiting factors. Nevertheless, each group had to estimate the cost, including the foreign exchange component, of the projects which it suggested for inclusion in the plan. It was also asked to estimate its requirements for extra technical personnel.

Working group discussions were the means of translating general objectives into concrete proposals. The object was to draw on the knowledge and experience of all concerned, to co-ordinate the schemes of the various ministries and agencies, and to create a sense of commitment among those who would have the operational responsibilities. Co-ordination between groups was attempted by interlocking membership and by the ubiquitous presence of Planning Commission personnel, which came to working group discussions with tentative proposals formulated in the Commission's various divisions. A vital feature of the whole process was the constant re-working of reports in the light of the proposals made by other working groups and of the series of commodity balance calculations periodically made by the Commission.

To illustrate this 'micro-planning' process we will take the three key sectors of Industry, Agriculture, and Resources.

[8] See LSD, xxxii, 877–8 & app. 1 (8th sess., 1959), pp. 98–99; xxxviii, 5830–37.

The working groups for the Heavy Industry Division, dealing respectively with fuel, fertilizers, machinery, and steel, were instructed to operate under the guidance of the Steering Committee for Industry, Transport, and Power.[9] First, the Steering Committee formulated certain very general and tentative targets. These were submitted to the groups, which used them as a guide in attempting provisional quantifications of requirements for investment, foreign exchange, and ancillary services. Preliminary proposals were also made with regard to the balance of production increments as between new enterprises and expanded old ones, and to the allocation of the various products as between different potential consumers. Particular attention was paid to the most limiting of all physical bottlenecks, viz. rail transport.

On the completion of their studies, the working groups in this division reported to the Steering Committee, which then gave them a broad indication of the financial resources likely to be available and of the allocation of these resources to the various sectors. Its ability to provide such guidance, at this stage, was due to the fact that it had been briefed by the Resources Working Group, which now had approximations of the totals likely to be raised from domestic and foreign sources and tentative proposals for the distribution of investable funds among the various sectoral claimants. In the light of these financial limitations, now brought fully into the picture for the first time, the industrial working groups were required to revise their original proposals.

Only those industries regarded as of key importance were given the formal 'Working Group' treatment. Simultaneously the Ministry of Commerce and Industry and the Planning Commission itself were dealing with the others. Towards the end of 1958 the Ministry, having been alerted by the Commission, proceeded to consult the nineteen or twenty Industrial Development Councils, each of which had a mixed membership of employers, trade unionists, technicians, government officials, and Planning Commission personnel. In theory, these were to formulate the development plans for their various industries, which were then to be scrutinized by the Ministry and passed to the Planning Commission for final 'processing'. In practice, the formulation of targets for the 'organised private sector' was taken in hand by the powerful and well-staffed Development Wing of the Ministry of Commerce and Industry, which maintained close contact with the employers and their representative organizations.

Although the Development Wing and the Planning Commission's Industrial Division were supposed to work together on these problems, it is not quite clear how far they did so. Some tension exists between the two organizations, and each is rather inclined to take exclusive credit for

[9] The formation of this body was announced to the Lok Sabha on 13 Feb. 1959 (ibid. xxv, 840–3).

industrial planning. But in the end, as an official of the Industrial Division put it, 'certain ideas emerged'. These, of course, had to be transmitted to the interested working groups, including the Resources Working Group, so that the familiar 'doing and re-doing' exercises could be performed. Industries which had no Development Councils were made subject to schemes drawn up by the Development Wing, in informal consultation with the Committee of the Federation of Indian Chambers of Commerce and Industry.[10]

Village and small-scale industries constituted another distinct problem. The detailed formulation of their plan programmes was undertaken by the various national boards which had been constituted to supervise and/or organize them, e.g. the Handloom Board, Small-Scale Industries Board, Handicrafts Board, Sericulture Board, Khadi Board, and Village Industries Board. The proposals of these bodies were then processed and co-ordinated by a special group set up by the Minister of Commerce and Industry.

One of the major questions which had to be asked throughout this complex decision-making process was what balance of responsibility should be established as between the public and private sectors. Ideology and government policy provided part of the answer. For the rest, it was necessary to estimate, with reference to past performance, present trends, and expressed intentions, just how much the private sector was capable of doing, financially, technically, and inclinationally. This involved, of course, an attempt to predict what effect the projected pattern of resource mobilization for the public sector, by way of taxes and loans, would have on business incentives and business behaviour. It also involved the even more complex estimation of how far the disincentives imposed on private business by the effort to raise massive resources for the public sector would be offset by the incentives accruing from the expansion of the infrastructure and the general stepping up of the level of monetarized economic activity. Linked with this was the question of the directions in which the private sector should be encouraged to expand, and of the means (e.g. financial and fiscal incentives, exchange controls, licensing, raw material allocations &c.) which should be used to induce it to fulfil the planned priorities. Issues of this kind arose at every stage of the industrial discussions, both within and without the working groups. Their resolution certainly owed as much to informed guesswork as to rational calculation.

Even more complex were the problems confronting the Working Group on Agriculture and its twenty-three sub-committees. While industry was predominantly a 'central' subject, agriculture was a shared one. Guidance and financial support might be provided by the centre, but policy and performance were in the hands of the fifteen states. Others with very large fingers in the pie were the Central Water and Power

[10] See Krishnamachari, *Fundamentals of Planning*, p. 83.

Commission (irrigation), the Community Development Administration (agricultural extension and village uplift), the Commodity Boards, the various bodies concerned with the development of co-operation (with the Reserve Bank as their financial apex), and the central Warehousing and Marketing Board with its corresponding organizations in the states. Possibilities of increasing agricultural production, moreover, were limited by the output of certain industries (e.g. fertilizers), by the speed with which irrigation facilities could be brought into operation, by the progress and character of land reform, and by the availability of technical and administrative personnel. Above all, the ultimate result would be the product of the efforts of tens of millions of individual producers who could not be effectively ordered around and whose reactions to incentives, encouragements, and appeals were highly problematical.

In agriculture, it was essential that planning at the two levels, centre and states, should proceed simultaneously. In the spring of 1958 the Minister of Agriculture set the ball rolling by requesting the states to prepare plans on the basis of physical potentialities. Thus, by the time that the Agricultural Working Group was established, in the autumn of 1958, the state governments had at least begun to think in general terms about what they might be able to do, in readiness for the consultations which, in due course, their representatives would be required to engage in at the centre. The group itself was given very broad terms of reference.[11] In the longest forseeable run (i.e. by the end of the Fifth Five-Year Plan) the per capita income of the agricultural population was to be doubled and food consumption considerably diversified and raised from a level of 2,000 calories *per diem* to one of 2,600. In the short run, the annual rate of increase in agricultural production was to be raised from 4 to 5–6 per cent.

The group first threw this sizeable ball to its twenty-three sub-committees. These, in working out their requirements for e.g. fertilizers, transport, tractors, irrigation machinery, and agricultural and veterinary graduates, had to enter into consultation with the working groups simultaneously engaged in calculating the targets for these items. There was, indeed, no working group whose activities did not impinge, directly or indirectly, on the matters that the sub-committees of the Agricultural Working Group were considering, and the process of cross-referencing, balancing, and rebalancing must have presented considerable complexities.

By July 1959, however, each sub-committee had produced a preliminary report. The group then organized a series of conferences with what one participant described as a 'huge official army' of states' representatives.[12] Each conference lasted two or three days, and the whole process of

[11] See Min. of Food & Agric., *Approach to Agricultural Development in the Third Five Year Plan* (Sept. 1959, mimeo.), pp. 2–4.

[12] See LSD, xxxii, 877–8 & app. 1 (8th sess., 1959), pp. 98–99.

consultation occupied two months. Simultaneously discussions were taking place with the Ministry of Irrigation and Power, the Ministry of Community Development, the Reserve Bank's Department of Co-operation, the officials of the Ministry of Commerce responsible for fertilizer production, the manufacturers of insecticides, and many others.

As a result of all this work, the group as a whole was able to present the Planning Commission, by the late summer of 1959, with a series of overall physical and financial targets.[13] Annual production of foodgrains was to rise to 100 million tons; minor irrigation was to cover 15 million acres, contour bunding 12·5 million, reclamation schemes 2 million. An additional 50 million acres would become subject to green manuring; the consumption of nitrogenous fertilizers would rise to 1·25 million tons; and no fewer than 233 million acres would receive improved seeds for foodgrains, produced by 1,000 seed-multiplication farms. The cost of all this and much else, computed at Rs1,351 crores on the completion of discussions with the states, was subsequently put at Rs1,000 crores. This nice round figure was Rs200 higher than that originally suggested by Pitamber Pant and represented more than three times the amount considered likely to be spent on agriculture during the 1956–61 period under the latest 're-appraised' version of the Second Five-Year Plan.

The Commission, which now had preliminary reports from all the groups, including the Resources Group, inevitably came to the conclusion that such an objective was beyond the bounds of possibility. Holding that all the essential needs of agricultural development could be met by an investment of about two-thirds of the proposed size, it accordingly cut the total to Rs640 crores. This figure then became the quantitative financial limit within which the Agricultural Group had to work, and the group accordingly proceeded to revise its investment allocations, once again in consultation with the states, the other working groups, and the ministries and agencies of the central government.

All groups, of course, had to adjust their plans to the availabilities as indicated by the Resources Working Group. Meeting under the chairmanship of the Secretary of the Ministry of Finance, this group contained two senior officers from the same ministry, representatives of the Ministry of Commerce and Industry, representatives of the Reserve Bank, and Planning Commission personnel. Its size fluctuated considerably, representatives of other ministries being called in from time to time for consultation.

It did its work in two stages. During the first stage, the assumption was one of no extra taxation and no extra effort by way of internal and external loans, small savings, &c. The already projected rate of expansion of the national income was taken as given, and a calculation made of the resources for investment that would become available. This was mainly

[13] Min. Food & Agric., *Approach to Agric. Dev.*

an exercise in arithmetic. The second stage demanded imagination as well as arithmetic, for it involved computing the likely yields of various increases in taxation and estimating the additional amounts which might be obtained from domestic savings and foreign loans. Although similar working groups had been established in the states, the central Resources Working Group at first operated independently of them (without, of course, confining its attention to centrally-raised resources), and the first approximation which it produced was the result of its own exclusive work. Most of the data on which it relied was prepared by the Ministry of Finance and the Reserve Bank.

Not until the final resources estimates were being worked out for incorporation in the Draft Plan did financial consultations with the states take place. These were conducted in the Planning Commission itself, through its Economic Division.

In December 1959 the Deputy Minister of Planning, answering a parliamentary question about preparations for the Third Five-Year Plan, said that during the months of September and October the Commission had reviewed the tentative proposals of all the working groups, in consultation with them. Three new working groups had subsequently been established: (1) on price policy; (2) on exports and imports in relation to production programmes; and (3) on programmes for co-operative development. 'Preliminary informal consultations' were taking place, during the discussions of the 1960–1 annual plan, with the representatives of the state governments; and the Commission was engaged 'in considering the more important issues of the Third Five Year Plan with a view to drawing up a Draft Outline in the course of the next two or three months'.[14] By this time it was clear that total outlay would be about the figure originally envisaged.[15]

Meanwhile in the states the process of planning had been proceeding at varied rates. Some, such as Andhra Pradesh, had started comparatively early and worked comparatively fast. By October 1959 all Andhra's working groups had reported,[16] Mysore, which had started even earlier, succeeded in placing a draft plan before its Council of Ministers by August 1959.[17] Rajasthan, on the other hand, although also starting early, finished comparatively late, as a result of its decision to consult the newly-formed representative organizations under the 'democratic decentralization' scheme of which it was the pioneer.[18] Bombay, having begun

[14] LSD, xxxviii, 5830–7 (18 Dec. 1959).

[15] Rs 10,000 crores was the figure more or less taken for granted in two reports published in the autumn of 1959, viz. Congress Planning Sub-Committee, *Rep.* (Sept. 1959), and Fed. of Indian Chrs of Comm. & Ind., *The Third Five Year Plan*; *a Tentative Outline* (New Delhi, n.d.).

[16] Andhra Pradesh, Plan. & Local Admin. Dept, *FYP*(*3*), pp. 14–15.

[17] Mysore, Plan., Housing & Soc. Welfare Dept, *FYP*(*3*), i: *Policy and Programmes* (1961), p. i.

[18] Rajasthan, Plan. Dept, *FYP*(*3*) (1961), pp. 20–21.

consideration of its plan in May 1958, was badly held up in late 1959 and early 1960 first by the prospect and then by the reality of bifurcation into Maharashtra and Gujarat (1 May 1960), with the result that no draft outlines for the two new states could be presented before September 1960.[19]

These variations, which could easily be multiplied by reference to the performance of other states, meant that the Planning Commission, when formulating its first outline of the Third Five-Year Plan for presentation to the Cabinet, could not present even a tentative state-wise allocation of objectives and resources. At this stage, however, this mattered comparatively little. For one thing, state-wise allocation was in the last resort dependent on the overall magnitudes of the Draft Plan; for another, the broad distribution of outlay as between centre and states could be calculated with reference to past experience of the states' performance as developmental agencies, the established pattern of central assistance, and the constitutional division of responsibilities within the federal system.

(iv)

The Planning Commission's Memorandum on the Third Plan was presented to the Cabinet in March 1960, and approved. The proposed overall investment target was Rs9,950, of which the public sector accounted for Rs7,000 crores. The states' share was fixed at Rs3,650 crores. The specific aims of the plan were stated as: (1) a 5 per cent per annum increase in the national income; (2) self-sufficiency in foodgrains and increased agricultural production to meet the needs of industry and of the export market; (3) the development of basic industries in such a way that India could meet from her own resources, within a period of ten years, the further requirements for industrialization; (4) a substantial expansion of employment opportunities; (5) a reduction in inequalities of wealth and a more equal distribution of economic power. The most significant feature of this list is the degree of priority given to agriculture. During the latter stages of plan preparation the country, as we have seen, was in the midst of a food crisis. This was the sole subject of the discussion at the thirteenth meeting of the NDC on 5–6 September 1959. Although the new Minister of Food and Agriculture, S. K. Patil insisted that the situation was 'not alarming', two highly expert committees of inquiry, one under the chairmanship of Asoka Mehta,[20] the other organized by the Ford Foundation,[21] had shown how very critical it had become.

[19] Gujarat, Gen. Admin. Dept (Planning), *FYP(3) (1961–6) Gujarat State*, pp. 7–8; Maharashtra, Fin. Dept (Planning), *FYP(3) Maharashtra State* (Nov. 1961), p. 1.

[20] Foodgrains Enquiry Ctee, *Rep.* (1957).

[21] Ford Found. Prodn Team, *Rep. on India's Food Crisis and Steps to Meet it* (Apr. 1959).

Immediately after receiving the Cabinet's approval, the Memorandum was presented to the NDC, which considered it on 19–20 March 1960. The Council, while expressing agreement with all the main proposals, suggested various modifications for consideration. It hoped, for instance, that greater investment allocations might be given to roads, village and small-scale industries, rehabilitation, and technical education. It also thought that the idea of balanced regional development might be explored more fully, and favoured 'measures by which as large a proportion as possible of the benefits of the Plan would reach out to rural areas and to small towns'. These suggestions, of course, reflected some of the main preoccupations of the state governments. On two specific matters it directed that there should be further investigations, viz. (1) price policy, and (2) the division of resource-raising responsibilities between the centre and the states. The first of these was to come before a special meeting of Chief Ministers, the second to be the subject of discussion between the Planning Commission and the states.

Having received the go-ahead signal from the Cabinet and the NDC, the Planning Commission began to work on the Draft Outline. This appeared towards the end of June 1960.[22] In the meantime, discussions with the states had pushed up the total proposed outlay by Rs250 crores, with the result that the 'Draft' figure for total outlay became Rs10,250 crores, of which the public sector component accounted for Rs7,250.

(v)

The Draft's introductory chapter, 'Approach and Perspective', laid early stress on the CSO's new estimates of population growth—estimates which, although considerably higher than those used for the Second Plan, were soon to prove far too conservative (see Table 12). Giving itself, as usual, the benefit of the doubt, the Commission assumed 'widespread changes in attitudes and a high degree of success in spread of family planning practices'.[23] Later it tried to justify this assumption by making provision for increasing the number of family-planning clinics from 1,800 to 8,200.

National income, as already projected in the Second Plan, was to rise by 5 per cent per annum during the Third Plan period, with the result that over the fifteen years, 1951–66, the total increase would be of the order of 80 per cent. To achieve this, investment would have to be stepped up from about 11 per cent of national income at the end of the Second Plan to about 14 per cent by the end of the Third.

That in the distribution of investable resources much greater attention would have to be given to agriculture was several times emphasized. The actual list of aims gave it, in fact, pride of place.[24] In essence, this

[22] *DO(3)* (June 1960). [23] Ibid. p. 5. [24] Ibid. p. 23.

was a partial return to the pattern of priorities characteristic of the First Plan.

Another distinguishing feature was its frank recognition of the importance of external assistance. This, too, had been heavily underlined by the experience of the crisis years, 1958 and 1959. For the first time, the planners now specifically admitted that the very effort to achieve self-sustaining growth at a comparatively early date actually increased the

TABLE 12

Perspective Plans

1. *National Income*

(*Rs crores*)

	1951	*1956*	*1961*	*1966*	*1971*	***1976***
First Plan	9,000*	10,000	11,200	13,300	17,000	23,000 (1950–1 prices)
Second Plan		10,800*	13,480	17,260	21,680	27,270 (1955–6 prices)
Third Plan			14,500*	19,000	25,000	33–34,000 (1960–1 prices)

2. *National Income per Capita*

(*Rs crores*)

First Plan — No figures given. Doubling of 1950–1 per capita income by 1977 projected.

Second Plan		281*	331	396	466	546 (1955–6 prices)
Third Plan			330*	385	450	530 (1960–1 prices)

3. *Net Investment as Proportion of Total National Income*

Rs crores

First Plan	5*	6¾	11	20(1967–8)	20	20
Second Plan		7*	11	14	16	17
Third Plan			11*	14–15	17–18	19–20

* Actuals

TABLE 12 (cont.)

4. *Population Projections (millions)*

	1951	*1956*	*1961*	*1966*	*1971*	*1976*
First Plan	356	379	403	429	456	485†
Second Plan	362	384	408	434	465	499
Revised (CSO) estimates 1959	362	391	431	480	528	578
Third Plan (Provis. est. Census 1961)			438	492	555	625

† Figures not given in 1st Five-Year Plan, but calculated on basis of given percentage of $1\frac{1}{4}$% p.a.

dependence of the country on external resources during the intervening period. Ten years were envisaged as necessary for 'securing viability on external account', and the Third Five-Year Plan's scale and pattern of investment would have to be directed towards this end.[25]

Although paying lip-service to the 'reduction in inequalities', the Draft Outline placed this fifth and last in its list of objectives and contrived to suggest, without actually saying as much, that if and when equality and growth came into conflict, it was the former that would have to be sacrificed. A lengthy section[26] on this subject expressed the opinion, unsupported by quantifiable evidence, that various measures already taken had had a significant 'total effect in reducing economic and social disparities'. Rather surprisingly, it emphasized the role of the private rather than that of the public sector in diffusing prosperity. Assistance to small-scale enterprises through financial and licensing policies was, of course, a well-established objective; the novelty lay in restating these policies in the context of the 'reduction in inequalities'. It was interesting, too, that the Commission here appeared prepared to give 'equality' some limited priority over growth. While admitting that large and well-established firms had 'certain advantages in organisation and expertise, better access to the capital market and to sources of foreign collaboration and availability of funds on a larger scale from business or industries which are within their control or influence', it nevertheless held that from the 'broader social angle there should be a wide diffusion of enterprises in the private sector and new entrants should be encouraged'. This slightly ambiguous formulation reflected controversies about licensing policies which were to become much more acute during the course of the next few years.

[25] Ibid. pp. 8, 10–11. [26] Ibid. pp. 12–14.

In tabulating public sector outlay, the Draft broke new ground for a published plan document, by distinguishing between current outlay and investment (Table 13). Rough and ready as this distinction undoubtedly was, it did at least enable the plan-implementing authorities (and particularly the states) to form some idea of the magnitude of that part of the plan outlay which would become 'committed expenditure' on the completion of the plan. Private sector investment during the plan period

TABLE 13

Third Five-Year Plan, Draft Outline: Outlay
(*Rs crores*)

Group	*Plan Outlay*	*Current Outlay*	*Investment*
1. Agriculture, minor irrigation & community development	1,025	350	675
2. Major & medium irrigation	650	10	640
3. Power	925	—	925
4. Village & small industries	250	90	160
5. Industry & minerals	1,500	—	1,500
6. Transport & Communications	1,450	—	1,450
7. Social Services	1,250	600	650
8. Inventories	200	—	200
9. Total	7,250	1,050	6,200

was estimated at Rs4,000 crores. Total investment, therefore, would be Rs10,200 crores.

Having thus fixed a total, by a process of calculation which presumably covered all prospective resources (and probably, in a manner that was becoming unhappily familiar, exaggerated their likely magnitudes), the Draft immediately proceeded to suggest that somewhere in India there was a magic wand which, if appropriately waved, could conjure up resources for an even greater outlay. In the relevant sections of the Draft, said the planners,

attention has been drawn to certain fields in which, in the interest of rapid development, the present targets may have to be stepped up and the allocations relating to them suitably adjusted. Thus, it is envisaged that for approved programmes and targets, under agriculture, village and small industries, primary education, technical education, special works programmes for utilising manpower resources etc., for which additional domestic resources are found to be necessary as a result of examination by States and Ministries, resources needed will be made available. In respect of approved projects for which substantial external finance is required, once the necessary foreign exchange is found, every effort will be made to find the requisite internal resources.[27]

This had both a reminiscent and an ominous sound. Working, as usual, amid powerful pressures for the stepping up of expenditures beyond any reasonable estimation of prospective resources, the Commission was finding great difficulty in drawing the appropriate practical lessons from its previous mistakes.

More realistic, and very necessary, was the emphasis which it put on the correct phasing of projects. To enable this to be accomplished more effectively than in the past, it proposed the application of four 'broad criteria' and 'five categories of priority', none of them very esoteric and most of them much easier to state than to apply.[28]

Although a series of physical targets for the various sectors of development was tabulated, the Commission warned that these were still 'preliminary in character'. Before they could be finalized, further consultations with the representations of private industry had to take place, central ministries had to work out in detail the projects for which they were responsible, and the states had to amend their own outline plans 'in the light of the local plans which will be drawn up in the districts and on the basis of further study'. The most important target remaining to be fixed was that for foodgrains, which the Draft Outline put, in terms of additional production, at '25 to 30' million tons.

Outstanding among the industrial targets was the increase in the number of industrial trading estates from 60 to 360.[29] This represented a lesson drawn from experience; for one of the successes of the Second Plan had been the proliferation of small industries, and demand for accommodation in the existing estates was outstripping the supply. Village industries, on the other hand, received relatively less emphasis, the tentative allocation for handlooms exceeding anticipated Second Plan expenditure (Rs32·1 crores) by only Rs3·9 crores, and that for khadi and the others exceeding the corresponding expenditure (Rs80·5 crores) by only Rs8·5 crores.[30] Unwelcome as it may have been to the Gandhians, this too was a decision based on experience. Heavy industry, of course, continued to receive the major emphasis. One could argue, as Wilfred Malenbaum and others have done, that the emphasis placed upon it was altogether excessive, in the light of India's relative factor endowments and foreign exchange difficulties; but the 'heavy industry pattern' represented a firm political commitment undertaken at the beginning of the Second Plan and could not be seriously modified except at the cost of jettisoning the Indian government's long-term economic perspectives.

The chapter on 'Resources for the Plan' began by giving an assurance that although the mobilization of resources on an adequate scale would

[27] Ibid. p. 28. [28] Ibid. pp. 29–30, 32. [29] Ibid. p. 35. [30] Ibid. p. 198.

involve 'restraint in consumption', there was no question of 'depressing the current levels of consumption'. Indeed, given the projected annual increase in the national income and in the rate of domestic savings, it would be possible to permit consumption to rise at over 4 per cent per annum—a 'significant increase'.[31]

The plan for the financing of the public sector,[32] with comparative figures for the expected contribution of each source during the Second Plan period, is given in Table 14.

TABLE 14

Third Five-Year Plan, Draft Outline: Sources of Finance
(Rs crores)

	Second Plan	*Third Plan*
1. Balance from revenues on the basis of existing taxation	−100	350
2. Contribution of the railways on the existing basis	150	150
3. Surpluses of other public enterprises on the existing basis		440
4. Loans from the public	800	850
5. Small savings	380	550
6. Provident funds, betterment levies, steel equalization fund & misc. capital receipts	213	510
7. Additional taxation, incl. measures to increase the surpluses of public enterprises	1,000	1,650
8. Budgetary receipts corresponding to external assistance	982	2,200
9. Deficit financing	1,175	550
10. Total	4,600	7,250

In the light of the experience of raising resources during the period of the Second Plan, some of these figures looked optimistic. Admittedly, an increase of Rs650 over and above the Second Plan yield from additional taxation was not beyond the bounds of possibility, although the Commission recognized that it would involve 'considerable effort on the part of the Central and State Governments to broaden their tax structure'. But the projected increase of Rs450 crores from existing taxation appeared to be based on an underestimation of the rise in current governmental expenditure (including, of course, 'committed" expenditure from the Second Five-Year Plan). Experience suggested, moreover, that there was little justification for expecting surpluses from public enterprises 'on the

[31] Ibid. pp. 44–45. [32] Ibid. pp. 46–51.

existing basis' to rise to a total of Rs440 crores, while the Commission itself admitted that a small savings target of Rs110 crores a year was 'high relatively to the collections during the second plan'. As for deficit financing, the figure of Rs550 crores had little meaning, since, as the Commission stated, there was no precise way of 'estimating the safe limits' of this financial device.

Even less meaningful was the large figure of Rs2,200 crores for 'budgetary receipts corresponding to external assistance', except as a statement of what was likely to be needed to implement a plan of the projected size. This sum, it should be remembered, represented the external deficit considered likely to be incurred in respect of plan projects only; the total deficit, obviously much higher, was estimated in the Draft Outline at Rs3,200 crores.[33] Essentially, this was an advance bill presented to the 'consortium' and other foreign powers presumed to be interested in the Third Plan's success. The planners recognized that uncertainty about prospects of external assistance meant that commitments to foreign exchange expenditure would have to be made 'only on the basis of external resources that are clearly in sight'. They also indicated the need to pursue a flexible policy based on the advance preparation of 'a sufficient number of projects that can be executed as soon as the necessary foreign exchange has been secured'.[34]

Calculations of the resource-raising potentialities of the private sector[35] were, of necessity, even more approximate. They were based, mainly, on the extrapolation of past trends. Of a total projected investment of Rs4,200 crores, a sum of Rs200 crores was to be provided by way of transfer of resources from the public sector and an estimated Rs300 crores from foreign assistance. Finding the balance would not, in the planners' estimation, present the private sector with any 'insuperable difficulties'.

One of the most important parts of the Draft Outline was the lengthy chapter entitled 'Policy and Organisation'. In this, considerable attention was paid to the much-discussed subject of utilizing rural manpower.[36] It was proposed that there should be 'comprehensive works programmes' in all rural areas, and that these should be divided into five categories, viz.

I. Works projects included in the plans of States and local bodies which involve the use of unskilled and semi-skilled labour.
II. Works undertaken by the community or by the beneficiaries in accordance with the obligations laid down by law.
III. Local development works towards which local people contribute labour while some measure of assistance is given by Government.
IV. Schemes to enable village communities to build up remunerative assets.
V. Supplementary works programmes to be organised in areas in which there is a high incidence of unemployment.

[33] Ibid. p. 55. [34] Ibid. p. 55. [35] Ibid. pp. 51–52. [36] Ibid. pp. 66–71.

This categorization perhaps enabled those concerned with rural development to look at the problem more systematically; but it is curious that manpower utilization should have been introduced, by implication, as something 'extra' to the main body of the plan; still more curious that little attempt should have been made, after several years of discussing this subject, to quantify its potentialities or to estimate its cost. At least two of the categories (viz. I and V) involved the use of paid labour, and all except II gave rise to some financial outlay on the part of governmental authorities. Yet no clear indication was given whether such costs had been taken into consideration when estimating plan outlay on agriculture and community development. The only reference to the financial aspects of such schemes appeared later, in the section on 'Employment',[37] where it was stated that the activities could be organized 'at a low cost on wages at subsistence rather than the market level', and where the 'additional cost' of organizing half a million new workers was estimated at some Rs12·5 crores per year. That manpower-utilization projects should have been relegated to the category of 'physical programmes' for which resources *might* be made available, given favourable circumstances, is testimony to a central weakness in Indian planning.

Similar vagueness characterized the section on 'employment' itself. The plan provided for the employment of 14 million of the anticipated 15 million new entrants into the labour market, 10·5 of them outside agriculture and 3·5 of them inside. This obviously meant that, over the five years, unemployment would increase by at least 1 million. 'Thus', said the planners, 'the objective of not allowing the unemployment situation to worsen during the plan period will require about 1 million extra employment opportunities.' They then listed seven ways of increasing employment which would not 'call for the use of scarce materials, specialised skills, or foreign exchange'. One can only wonder why these had not been embodied in the plan calculations themselves. On examination, one finds that some of them must have been thus embodied, that others would not in fact increase total employment, and that a third group fell outside the scope of the general proviso. The planners could hardly have failed to notice, in making their calculations about the quantum of private investment, that the electrification of small towns and villages would offer opportunities 'for the expansion of small scale enterprises with the use of power', which was the first method suggested for the absorption of the extra million. They could scarcely have been serious in their argument that the location of suitable processing industries in rural areas could be effected without the use of 'scarce materials' and 'specialised skills', or that the mere *location* of an industry in a particular place could significantly affect *total* employment opportunities, unless such an industry

[37] Ibid. pp. 83–88.

was additional to the industries for which resources had been provided in the plan. And they surely should have made provision, within the scope of their total planned outlay, for the very considerable *cost* of training 'out of the available labour force, a number of workers who can be moved to other places where there is need to supplement local labour for the purpose of doing special jobs or for which local skills are not immediately available'. The whole section on employment, in fact, may be not unfairly described as one in which the planners were whistling to keep their courage up.

In general, although a more skilful exercise than its predecessors, the Draft Outline evaded rather than faced a number of serious problems, attempted to be precise in certain areas where precision was virtually impossible, and succeeded only in being woolly in many where greater precision was vitally needed.

With its publication, wider discussion of the Third Plan became possible. Up to this time it had been fairly muted, partly because very little information had been put out by the Planning Commission and partly because the politically interested public had more immediate matters to occupy their attention. Even in the Lok Sabha there was little to record apart from Mishra's periodical answers to 'progress' questions. Nor was controversy stimulated, as it had been during the later stages of the formulation of the Second Plan, by critical foreign reactions: for all friendly governments were now agreed that help was the important thing. On 19 April there had appeared the very enlightened report of the World Bank Mission[38] which, after indicating that India would need Rs3,400 crores worth of foreign assistance for her Third Plan, suggested, among other things, that most of it should take the form of grants and low-interest loans on a government-to-government basis (in default of sufficient multilateral aid) and that the donor governments should get together in order to co-ordinate their donations. As far as planning techniques were concerned, it went no further than to emphasize the need for flexibility, as 'no foreign government can give any advance assurance of the quantum of aid it can offer'. It is not surprising, therefore, that even after the publication of the Draft Outline provided ample material for the controversialists, they did not take as vigorous advantage of the opportunity as they had taken in 1955–6, following the appearance of Mahalanobis's Plan Frame.

There was a change, too, in the nature of the controversy and in the *dramatis personae*. In the Lok Sabha debates of 1956, the Communists had made the running. It was now the turn of the right-wing Swatantra Party, recently formed and following the able parliamentary leadership of N. G. Ranga and Minoo Masani. As the Swatantrists appeared implacably hostile to planning in general and to the Planning Commission in

[38] H. Abs, Sir Oliver Franks, & Allan Sproul, *Letter to the President, International Bank for Reconstruction and Development* (New Delhi, Mar. 1960, mimeo.).

particular, there was a natural tendency for the forces of the left, including the Communists, to 'rally round the Plan'.

In the Lok Sabha's four-day debate of the Draft (22–26 August 1960),[39] the Swantantra Party presented an amendment which indicted the document in a most comprehensive fashion, denouncing it as 'unrealistic, misleading and improvident'. Specifically, the amendment claimed that it overestimated resources and underestimated outlay; that it was inherently and irremediably inflationary; that, in emphasizing heavy industry, it would cause hardship and limit employment opportunities; that it placed excessive and unnecessary stress on the public sector; that it relied too much on foreign aid; that it attenuated states' rights, undermined civil liberties, and eroded the institutions of parliamentary democracy; that it was deliberately partisan in conception and would increase waste and corruption; and that its total effect would be to 'reduce the real incomes and standard of life of this generation'.[40]

Opposition so trenchant had not been heard in the debates on the Second Plan—although it had perhaps been foreshadowed in the speech by Krishnaswami. The Swatantra's attack on the Third Plan, in fact, was much more fundamental than the Communists' attack on the Second;[41] for although the Communists had bitterly criticized the government for its alleged abandonment of the principles of the Plan Frame, they had not attacked—and obviously could not attack—planning as such. It was just this, of course, that the Swatantrists were doing.

Masani and his colleagues received a good deal of *de facto* support, during the course of the debate, from Gandhians of the type of Acharya Kripalani, who bitterly attacked the Draft's allegedly inadequate emphasis on the 'decentralized sector', i.e. cottage industry and agriculture. At one point, during the Planning Minister's winding-up speech, an extraordinary discussion broke out on the subject of whether Gandhi himself would have approved or disapproved of the Draft Plan. This was somewhat reminiscent of disputes among Marxists.[42] Had it continued, and had this been the real issue, there can be little doubt that the plan's opponents would have won the argument.

In order to dissociate themselves from this Swatantra–Gandhian coalition, the Communists had to 'play it soft'. They did not, on this occasion, claim that heavy industry was being neglected. Their main criticisms, voiced by A. K. Gopalan and Hiren Mukerjee, were that the government was reluctant to soak the rich, unenthusiastic about state trading, dilatory and half-hearted on land reform, and unprepared to divert foreign trade 'towards the socialist economies'.[43] Many of the back-bench speakers

[39] LSD, 22–26 Aug., xlv, 3974–4082, 4256–382, 4571–728, 4849–5014, 5125–60, 5198–205.
[40] Ibid. cols 4001–3. [41] Ibid. cols 4651–9. [42] Ibid. cols 5137–41.
[43] Ibid. cols 4018–31, 4280–90.

concentrated on 'balanced regional development', invariably claiming that their particular states were being neglected. Even Gopalan had to put in a word for his own Kerala.

On 26 August, after every conceivable criticism had been ventilated and a great variety of grievances expressed, the Swatantra amendment met its inevitable defeat by 221 votes to 9.

(vi)

The way was now open for further negotiations between the Planning Commission and the states. Discussions, on the official level, about financial resources began soon after the Lok Sabha debate and finished about the middle of September. There followed two months of meetings in which the states were represented by their Chief Ministers and at which attention was focused on 'the major physical targets to be realised and the determination of the principal magnitudes for outlays and resources to be adopted by States for presenting their own revised plans which would eventually be embodied in the Plan'.

To smooth the path for these a meeting of the NDC was held on 12–13 September. The Council had before it a Memorandum from the Commission underlining some of the politico-administrative implications of the Draft Plan for the states. Its main emphasis was on reorientation of the community development schemes towards increased productivity, the adaptation of projects to the requirements of each area, the elimination of overlap between the agricultural ministries and the Community Development Administration, and the rectification of the under-utilization of irrigation facilities. All minor irrigation, soil conservation, contour bunding, and dry farming schemes, it considered, should be operated as community projects, 'with local contributions in money and labour'. In general, the utilization of rural manpower was to be 'one of the most important features of the Third Plan'. This raised three 'broad questions of policy' on which the NDC was invited to give its opinion, viz. (1) the placing of obligations on the beneficiaries of community schemes; (2) the organization of 'days of free labour' by the village panchayats; and (3) the building up by village communities of 'remunerative community assets'.

Nehru, in his opening remarks, asked that these and the many other issues defined in the Memorandum should be seriously discussed. Individual states' problems, he suggested, should be avoided. In the past, he said, the NDC had got 'into the habit of hearing a long story of the States' difficulties and this succession of such stories had often produced a very depressing effect on him, possibly on others too . . . .' Dealing in advance with an expected complaint, he poured scorn on the idea that India was over-taxed. 'Never had there been so much riches being flaunted about in

India by certain circles as today. Never so much money thrown about. Never shops so full of goods. Never so many purchases of these goods from the shops in the cities.'

According to the record, taxation received little discussion; but despite Nehru's warning the Chief Ministers occupied a very large part of the meeting with allegations of the neglect of their various states by the Planning Commission. The Deputy Chairman of the Commission, replying to their complaints, indicated the impossibility of not reducing the outlays contained in the various state draft plans, for the simple reason, known to every state representative present, that they totalled three times the amount allocated to the states by the Draft Outline. He concluded by saying that 'there was broad acceptance of the Draft Outline' and that the suggestions made 'were mainly regarding adjustments with regard to allocations between different sectors'—which was true but misleading. The Council then devoted the remainder of its time to a discussion of the co-operative movement. Little had been accomplished apart from a vigorous blowing off of steam.

During the month of November 1960, five joint committees of the Lok Sabha and Rajya Sabha met to give further parliamentary consideration to the Draft Plan. To the four (Policy, Industry, Agriculture, and Social Services) that had dealt with the Second Five-Year Plan, there was now added a Committee on Technical Manpower and Scientific Research.

As before, Committee 'A' (Policy, Resources, and Allocation)[44] was the most important, being concerned with the general shape of the plan rather than with the detail of its various parts. On 'policy' it made some palpable hits. It complained of lack of clarity about the 'socialist pattern'; alleged that inequalities had increased and ought to be diminished; expressed dissatisfaction with the proposals for reducing unemployment and utilizing rural manpower; demanded more information about the effect of planning on rural-urban migration; and grumbled about 'the inefficiency and lack of vigour and sense of responsibility on the part of the vast bureaucratic machinery that has been set up to implement the Plan'.

On 'resources', it doubted the realism of the Draft's estimates of the yields of taxation and public enterprise surpluses, and warned against any attempt to make up for shortfalls by deficit financing. Only 'some members', however, advocated higher direct taxes, and all appeared to agree on the need for 'care' in extending indirect taxation.

In the 'allocation' part of the discussion, some unease about the priority given to large-scale industry made itself evident. Members not only demanded larger allocations for small-scale industry, but expressed the view that where there was competition for resources between industry and

[44] See LS Secretariat, *Synopsis of Proc. 10–13 Nov. 1960* (Dec. 1960).

transport-plus-power, the latter should receive priority, and held that 'absolute priority' should be given to clean drinking-water, drainage, and universal elementary education.

Committee 'B' (Industry, Power, Transport)[45] spent much time, as might have been expected, in the discussion of regional disparities. It also gave many members, both from the Congress and from other parties, the opportunity to express their suspicions of private business and their hostility to the profit motive—so much so that T. N. Singh, the member of the Planning Commission for Industry, found it desirable to put up a mild defence of the private sector, saying: 'The assistance of the private sector, which had certain advantages of tapping certain (e.g. foreign) sources that were not open to the Government, came in handy, and wisdom and prudence required that the way should not be blocked. After all, the needs of the country for industrial development were very great.'

Committee 'C' (Agriculture and Rural Economy) produced the mutually contradictory criticisms that the target for agriculture was too low (i.e. 105 million tons as against the 110 million tons recommended by the Ford Foundation) and too high (i.e. a 40 per cent increase in the next five years as against a 29 per cent increase in the last ten). Members from rural constituencies also alleged that agriculture was being neglected by planners who were predominantly urban-oriented.

The other two committees produced little of specific interest; but it is worth noting that there were general complaints of the committees' powerlessness to have much influence on a Draft Plan that had already been approved by the Planning Commission. The Chairman of Committee 'B' suggested that in future it should be submitted to them at an earlier stage and that in addition, the committees should be called together for discussion when a current plan had been in operation for one or two years.

'All the suggestions of the Members', writes V. T. Krishnamachari, 'were considered by the Planning Commission and changes made whenever needed.'[46] This is no doubt true, but the process of consideration has left no discoverable record, as it might have done if the Commission had 'reported back' to the Committees or to the Lok Sabha as a whole. Hence one can only mention the Committees among the many influences responsible for the changes made in the Draft Plan. No quantification of their impact on the planning process is possible.

By January 1961 the final stage in the planning process had been reached. Both the central ministries and the state governments had prepared detailed proposals, within the limits set by the Draft Outline, and had discussed them with the Commission. Negotiations between the Commission and the Chief Ministers of the states had finished, with the

[45] See ibid. [46] *Fundamentals of Planning*, p. 85.

result that the allocation of financial responsibility was known. Most of the states had completed their Draft Plans and had presented—or were presenting—them to their legislatures; and the first set of annual plans for the 1961–6 period was in an advanced stage of preparation. Hence the Commission could now take an 'overall view' and present its revised proposals. These, entitled 'Outlay in the Third Five Year Plan: Centre and States', it placed first before the Cabinet and then before the NDC at its seventeenth meeting on 13–14 January 1961.

Even now, many of the figures in this document are difficult to interpret. Their ambiguities must have been extremely perplexing to the states' ministers present at the NDC. The general picture, however, was clear enough. Since the publication of the Draft Outline the targets both for resources and for outlay had been pushed considerably upwards, but the latter much faster than the former. The Council was, in fact, confronted with an estimated outlay of about Rs8,000 crores as against estimated resources of Rs7,500. This would have been serious enough if the latter figure could have been regarded as reasonably firm; but it was highly optimistic, as the Commission itself admitted. Not only was there a possibility that increased defence expenditure would encroach on it; the estimates of the yields of taxation, loans, and public enterprise profits on which it was based were 'on the high side'. Furthermore, all possibility of further raiding of foreign exchange reserves had disappeared, and deficit financing (in view of the 25 per cent price increase during the Second Plan period) had to be confined to the prescribed minimum.

How was the gap to be bridged? For the states, it was suggested that some reduction outlays might be possible and that economies in construction costs might be effected. For the centre, the Commission recommended 'flexibility' in the industrialization programme and rather obscurely remarked that 'it should be possible to suggest reasonable financial limits within which the Ministries concerned could formulate concrete programmes of development on the assurance that every effort would be made to provide the resources needed through annual budgets'. These solutions, it might have been thought, were not particularly convincing, but they appeared to satisfy the NDC, which resolved that 'in physical terms, the plans drawn up for the Third Five Year Plan should be somewhat larger in size than the present estimate of financial resources', and 'noted' that the estimate of resources for the public sector had been raised from Rs7,250 to Rs7,500 crores. It then appointed a committee to look further into the raising of resources, particularly through stepping up the rate of domestic savings.

In another paper, the Commission indicated, in a 'preliminary and provisional' way, the big changes that had been made in certain agricultural programmes, as a result of a 'third round' of talks with the states

(December–January). The Draft Outline's allocation of Rs625 crores for agricultural programmes (based on the final recommendations of the Agricultural Working Group) had been reduced to Rs557 crores and somewhat radically redistributed. The 'dry farming' target had been cut down from 40 to 22 million acres, while the target for organic and green manures had been stepped up from 74 (or 72 according to the Memorandum) to 148 million acres. This was clearly due to the growing faith in the benefits of green manuring and to the patent fact that the production of inorganic fertilizers was falling well behind demand.

In a further paper on 'Employment Aspects of the Third Five Year Plan', the Commission came up with a new approach to the perennial problem of utilizing unemployed and underemployed rural manpower: the establishment of thirty-two 'pilot projects' for irrigation, afforestation and soil conservation. (These, it should be added, had been proposed by the Ford Foundation, which was also prepared to finance them.)

Discussion by the NDC of this mass of material appeared, on the surface, to follow the usual pattern, with each state attempting to put in its last-minute claims for special treatment. Beneath this familiar froth, however, there seems to have been a deep division of opinion. The Prime Minister, the Planning Commission, and the states were for a 'bold' plan, while the Finance Minister, according to the usually well-informed *Economic Weekly*, 'clung doggedly to an investment programme of Rs6,000 crores and a current outlay of Rs1,050 crores as the target of public sector expenditure'.[47] If this is so, then it appears that the decision to fix a physical target of Rs8,000 crores and a financial one of Rs7,500 represented a compromise formula heavily biased towards the majority view.

This reading of the situation is confirmed by the record of the eighteenth meeting of the NDC (31 May–1 June 1961), the last to which the present writer had access. The 'Savings Committee', presenting its report, placed its 'main hope' in the surpluses which public enterprises might be expected to yield. Subramaniam, who had been a member of this Committee, even argued that the outlay target might be raised to Rs8,300 for the public sector—although mainly on the grounds that this 'would create an atmosphere of greater effort'. Rajasthan and Uttar Pradesh (the one distinguished for its backwardness and the other for its stagnation) supported him, but the Finance Minister, Morarji Desai, immediately said that even Rs7,500 crores was optimistic and that 'he needed to be convinced that resources beyond Rs7,500 crores could be raised'. Nehru, for his part, blew hot and cold: 'As regards the internal resources he did not think that it was a question of statistical estimation. It was essentially the kind of approach to be conveyed to the people in order to create an atmosphere of optimism and an urge for achieving and over-fulfilling Plan targets.'

[47] Ann. no., 4 Feb. 1961, pp. 119–20.

But, alas, not much was being done in this direction. Although 'they were at the turning point in a historical epoch in India's history . . . he did not think that it was reflected in the public mind at all'. Even the public undertakings, the very core of the 'socialist pattern', 'were motivated by a sense of public service which was of the average kind and devoid of the spirit of dynamism'.

THE PLAN

Running to 758 pages, the Third Five-Year Plan was released on 3 August 1961. One of its more important yet most disappointing chapters was that entitled 'Ten Years of Planning'. The opportunity here provided for serious self-criticism was not seized, and the tenor of the Commission's remarks under this heading was rather complacent and self-congratulatory, reminding the reader that the plan was a *political* document in more than one sense. Little attempt, moreover, was made to provide statistical and other material which would enable an assessment to be made of the Second Five-Year Plan as such; hence the planners could hardly complain of the criticism, unfair as it may have been, that they were more interested in concealing than in revealing the errors and shortcomings of the period 1956–61. To talk of the 'stresses and strains' experienced during the ten years of planning as though they were nothing more than 'the growth pains of an economy struggling to find its way out of deep-rooted poverty and the economic stagnation of decades' was a little disingenuous; to refer, in general, to 'failures and errors that might have been avoided' was not helpful; while to present the ten years as 'a story of continuous endeavour reaching into the far corners of the land and drawing within its fold all sections of the people'[48] was to exaggerate.

Apart from the raising of total financial outlay by Rs250 crores, the Third Plan followed the Draft Outline very closely. The extra money was distributed among all heads of development, 'Power' and 'Social Services and Miscellaneous' being the major beneficiaries. Percentage provision was changed hardly at all (see Tables 8–10). However, the gap between financial outlay and physical targets, vaguely hinted at in the Draft Outline, was now quantified at Rs500 crores, in accordance with the decision of the NDC. Justifying the decision to combine a 'financial' plan of Rs7,500 crores with a 'physical' one of 'over Rs8,000 crores', the Commission said that 'if a Plan for a five-year period was prepared only in terms of the financial resources in sight at the time of the preparation of the Plan, the fullest use could not be made of all the opportunities which presented themselves in the course of the implementation of the Plan'. This sounded reasonable, but left one wondering why the same purpose might not be better and more realistically achieved by the formulation of

[48] *FYP*(*3*) p. 47.

alternative projects within the anticipated resources limit (itself optimistically calculated) rather than of *extra* ones outside it. Such a procedure, indeed, would have covered, in a way much more logical than the raising of the 'physical' target, certain contingencies specifically envisaged by the Commission, viz. that 'as the Plan proceeds, it may be found that some of the projects approved for implementation may not be completed within

TABLE 15

Second & Third Plans: Public Sector Outlay, Total
(Rs crores)

Head	*Second Plan*		*Third Plan Draft Outline*		*Third Plan*	
	Total Expend.	*Percentage*	*Provision*	*Percentage*	*Provision*	*Percentage*
Agriculture & Community Development	530	11	1,675	23·1	1,068	14
Major & Minor Irrigation	420	9			650	9
Power	445	10	925	12·8	1,012	13
Village & Small-scale Industries	175	4	250	3·4	264	4
Organized Industry & Minerals	900	20	1,500	20·7	1,520	20
Transport & Communications	1,300	28	1,450	20·0	1,486	20
Social Services & Miscellaneous	830	18	1,250	17·2	1,300	17
Inventories	—	—	200	2·8	200	3
Total	4,600	100	7,250	100	7,500	100

the Third Plan period, and a part of the investment may in fact be deferred to the early phase of the Fourth Plan'.[49] Always optimistic, however, it suggested the possibility that resources to cover the whole 'physical' programme might actually be raised.

In the opinion of the Commission, the effect of the financial-physical gap would be felt mainly at the centre. Financial provision for the states' programmes (Rs3,725 crores) did not fall far short of physical targets

[49] Ibid. p. 57.

TABLE 16

Third Five-Year Plan: Public Sector Outlay, Centre & States
(Rs crores)

Head	*Draft Outline States (& Union Terrs.)*	*Centre*	*Total*	*Plan States (& Union Terrs.)*	*Centre*	*Total*
Agriculture & Community Development	850	175	1,025	943	125	1,068
Major & Minor Irrigation	645	5	650	632	18	650
Power	800	125	925	903	109	1,012
Village & small Industries	150	100	250	141	123	264
Organized industry & Minerals	30	1,470	1,500	70	1,450	1,520
Transport & Communications	225	1,225	1,450	261	1,225	1,486
Social Services & Miscellaneous	950	300	1,250	950	350	1,300
Inventories	—	200	200	—	200	200
Total	3,650	3,600	7,250	3,900	3,600	7,500

Note: The above table does *not* indicate the *source* of the outlay, but only responsibilities for expenditure. It is based on the assumption, as stated in the Draft Outline, 'that as a general principle all development schemes *executed* by State Governments will form part of the plans of the States and that only certain limited categories of schemes will be shown in the plans of Ministries as being "sponsored" by the Centre'.

requiring an expenditure of Rs3,874 crores, and it was considered that 'given the necessary additional taxation, States should find it possible to finance fully the physical programmes'. The much more considerable gap at the centre appeared to be related (though to what extent was not made entirely clear) to shortage of foreign exchange resources. 'As foreign exchange becomes available', wrote the Commission, with an obscurity

TABLE 17

Second & Third Plans: Investment in Public & Private Sectors
(Rs crores)

Head	*Second Plan*		*Total*	*Per-centage*	*Third Plan Draft Outline*		*Total*	*Per-centage*	*Third Plan*		*Total*	*Per-centage*
	Public Sector	*Private Sector*			*Public Sector*	*Private Sector*			*Public Sector*	*Private Sector*		
Agriculture & Community Development	210	625	835	12	675	800	1,475	14	660	800	1,460	14
Major & Minor Irrigation	420	*	420	6	640	*	640	6	650	*	650	6
Power	445	40	485	7	925	50	975	10	1,012	50	1,062	10
Village & Small Industries	90	175	265	4	160	275	435	4	150	275	425	4
Organized Industry & Minerals	870	675	1,545	23	1,500	1,000	2,500	25	1,520	1,050	2,570	25
Transport & Communications	1,275	135	1,410	21	1,450	200	1,650	16	1,486	250	1,736	17
Social Services & Miscellaneous	340	950	1,290	19	650	1,075	1,725	17	622	1,075	1,697	16
Inventories	—	500	500	8	200	600	800	8	200	600	800	8
Total	3,650	3,100†	6,750	100	6,200	4,000†	10,200	100	6,300	4,100†	10,400	100

* Included under agriculture and community development.
† Excludes transfers from public to private sector.
Sources: Draft Outline, table 2, p. 26; table 3, p. 59; *FYP(3)*, table 3, p. 59.

typifying its whole approach to 'gap' questions, 'necessary steps will have to be taken to raise the requisite rupee resources.'[50]

More alarming than this vagueness was the fact that, on the size of the gap, the Commission appeared to be deceiving those of its readers who were prepared to take its own arithmetical exercises on trust. From figures given at various places in the 'Outline' chapter, the following contrasts between financial and physical targets emerge (Rs crores):

Sector	*Financial target*	*Physical target*
Public sector industry	1,520	1,882
Transport	1,486	1,655
Social Services	1,300	1,526

Thus, even on the supposition that these sectors alone accounted for the total discrepancy between the financial and the physical, there was a shortfall of Rs757 crores. Hence the Commission's statement that 'the total cost of completing all . . . programmes' *exceeded* 'Rs8,000 crores for the public sector' assumed the appearance of a white lie of considerable size; for the actual total could not possibly have been less than Rs8,257 crores. One can only conclude that the Commission, having failed once again to prevent the appearance of a resources gap, was now attempting a somewhat transparent concealment of its actual size.

Targets as expressed in terms of actual physical production were for the most part either the same as or somewhat higher than those given in the Draft Outline (see Table 18). The outstanding exceptions were the targets for (*a*) foodgrains, which was put at the lower of the two Draft Outline figures, and (*b*) ammonium sulphate, which was reduced from 1 million to 800,000 tons (in terms of nitrogen). The latter reduction reflected the fact that, as a result of a serious shortfall of fertilizer production under the Second Five-Year Plan, the starting-point for the Third was much lower than had been anticipated. Even so, the plan contemplated a fivefold increase in the consumption of nitrogenous fertilizers and a sixfold increase in that of phosphatic. The most notable increases in target figures were those for electrical energy, ports, aluminium, sewing machines, sugar, sulphuric acid, petroleum products, and hospital beds. In respect of education, the Commission balanced greater optimism in one direction against greater pessimism in another. The target for intakes of engineering, technological and agricultural colleges was stepped up, but that for the percentage of school-going children in the age-group 6–11 was reduced from 80 to 76·4. The latter reduction, however, reflected no falling off of enthusiasm for primary education, but a realistic appraisal of the impact of the CSO's new and alarming population projections (see Table 12, p. 190) on educational provision.

[50] Ibid. pp. 58–59. See also p. 102.

TABLE 18

Third Five-Year Plan: Selected Physical Targets

(Rs crores)

	1960–1 (realized)	*Draft Outline 1965–6*	*Plan 1965–6*
1. *Agricultural Production*			
Foodgrains (*m.* tons)	79·6	100–105	100
Cotton (lakh bales)	54	72	70
Jute (lakh bales)	40	65	62
Sugar cane (lakh tons of gur)	104	90–92	100
Oilseeds (lakh tons)	65·2	92–95	98
CD & NE Blocks (nos)	3,110	5,217	5,223
Population served by CD & NE Blocks (m.)	204	374	359
2. *Irrigation & Power*			
Area irrigated (m. acres) net	70	90	90
Electrical energy (installed capacity, m. kw.)	5·7	11·8	12·7
3. *Transport & Communications*			
(*a*) Railways—freight (m. tons)	154	245	245
(*b*) Roads (surfaced, including nat. highways) (000 miles)	144	164	169
(*c*) Shipping (coastal & overseas, lakh tons)	9·05	11	10·9
(*d*) Ports (major) Handling capacity (m. tons)	33	—	49
(*e*) Post & Telegraph			
(i) Post Offices (000s)	77	95	100
(ii) Telegraph Offices (000s)	6·5	8·3	8·5
(iii) Telephones (000s)	460	675	660
4. *Industrial Production*			
(*a*) Finished steel (m. tons)	2·4	6·9	6·8
(*b*) Pig iron (m. tons) for sale to foundries	0·90	1·50	1·50
(*c*) Cement (m. tons)	7·9	13·0	13·0
(*d*) Aluminium (000 tons)	18·5	75·0	80·0
(*e*) Fertilizers			
(i) Ammonium sulphate (000 tons) (in terms of nitrogen)	110·0	1,000	800
(ii) Phosphate (000 tons) (in terms of P_2O_5)	55	400–500	400
(*f*) Locomotives (nos) (steam)	295	1609* (steam and diesel)	1,175* (steam)
Locomotives (diesel)	—	(see above)	434*
Locomotives (electric)	—	232*	232*
(*g*) Cotton textiles (m. yds) (mill made)	5.127	5,800	5,800
(*h*) Jute manufactures (000 tons)	1,071	not stated	not stated
(*i*) Bicycles (000s)	1,063	2,000	2,000
(*j*) Sewing machines (000s)	303	450	700

* Relates to five-year period.

TABLE 18 (cont.)

	1960–1 (realized)	*Draft Outline 1965–6*	*Plan 1965–6*
Power alcohol (m. litres)	490	not stated	not stated
Sugar (000 tons)	2,700	3,000	3,500
Machine tools (value in Rs lakhs)	550	3,000	3,000
Cement machinery (value in Rs lakhs)	60	450	450
Sugar machinery (value in Rs lakhs)	330	1,000	1,000
Textile machinery (value in Rs lakhs)	900	not stated	not stated
Paper machinery (value in Rs lakhs)	650–700	not stated	not stated
Power-driven pumps, centrifugal (000s)	107	not stated	not stated
Diesel engines (000s)	40·0	66·0	66·0
Automobiles (nos)	54,789	100,000	100,000
Tractors (nos)	2,000	10,000	10,000
Sulphuric acid (000 tons)	359	1,250	1,500
Soda ash (000 tons)	152	450	450
Caustic soda (000 tons)	101	340	340
Petroleum products (m. tons)	5·7	7·4	9·9
Electric transformers (33 KV & below)	1,200	3,500	3,500
Electric cables (000 tons)	22	44	44
Electric motors of 200 b.h.p. & below (000 h.p.)	700	2,500*	2,500*
Paper & paper board (000 tons)	350	700	700
5. *Social Services*			
Education			
Schoolgoing children as percentage of children in respective age-groups			
(*a*) 6–11	61·1	80	76·4
(*b*) 11–14	22·8	30	28·6
(*c*) 14–17	11·5	15	15·6
Technical institutions (intake)			
Engineering & technology			
degree	13,858	18,500	19,137
diploma	25,570	34,000	37,390
Agriculture	4,600	6,000	6,200
Vetinary	1,300	1,550	1,460
Health			
(*a*) Hospital beds (000s)	186	190	240
(*b*) Medical institutions (dispensaries & hospitals)	12·6	14·6	14·6

* 300 b.h.p. and below.

The agricultural targets presupposed a doubling of the rate of growth, and those for industry a general percentage increase of 70 over 1960–1 and much higher percentage increases in the vital sectors of iron and steel, machinery, and chemicals (see Table 19).

Transport needs continued to be underestimated, even on the basis of physical targets. This seems to have been deliberate, and suggests that the Commission was still working on the 'principle' that the railways could always continue to operate under an annually increasing strain.

TABLE 19

Third Five-Year Plan: Index Nos of Industrial Production (1950–51 = 100)

Group	*1960–1*	*1965–6*	*Percentage increase*
General index	194	329	70
Cotton textiles	133	157	18
Iron and Steel	238	637	168
Machinery	503	1,224	143
Chemicals	288	720	150

Although it was fully conscious of the mounting pressures on their capacity, it nevertheless allocated only 20 per cent of total outlay to transport and communications, as against 28 in the Second Plan. Aware of this discrepancy, the Commission promised that the Third Plan's transport programmes would be 'reviewed' as soon as the currently sitting 'Neogy' Committee on Transport Policy and Co-ordination had produced its final report.[51] It should have been obvious, however, that by the time policy decisions had been formulated in the light of the Committee's recommendations, the transport situation would have become critical.

On the much discussed subject of utilizing rural manpower, the Commission was now able to be more specific than it had been in the Draft Outline. It announced that the thirty-four pilot projects had been commenced, with the object of providing 'experience in organising works programmes which will make some impact on the problem of unemployment and under-employment'. These programmes it hoped 'to extend . . . on a mass scale to other areas, specially [*sic*] to those with heavy pressure of population and chronic under-employment'.

Tentatively, it is envisaged that employment through the works programmes should be found for about 100,000 persons in the first year, about 400,000 to 500,000 persons in the second year, about a million in the third year, rising to about 2.5 million in the last year of the Plan. Limited financial provision for the early phases of the programme has been made in the Third Plan. It

[51] Ibid. pp. 539–40.

is reckoned that the programme as a whole might entail a total outlay of the order of Rs 150 crores over the Plan period.[52]

This, although sounding like a serious expression of intention, raised questions that the Commission made no attempt to answer. Was the 'limited financial provision' to be equated with the provision of Rs2 lakhs 'suggested for each [pilot] project for the period ending March, 1962'? Was the Rs150 crores to be raised by reducing outlay in other sectors, or did this sum represent yet another addition to the financially uncovered 'physical' target? As 'works programmes' nowhere figured separately in the tables of outlay, the reader of the plan had no means of telling to what extent, if any, they had been financially provided for. Hence, in spite of the emphasis which the Commission placed, in several different contexts, on this aspect of the plan, it continued to look almost as peripheral as it had looked in the Draft Outline. Apart from a rather ambiguous quantification, the plan was quite as vague as the Draft Outline—although more wordily so—on the means of providing 'extra' employment.

New estimates of likely financial resources had, not surprisingly, brought them into correspondence with the new figure for total financial outlay. A comparison between the Draft Outline's estimates and the plan's estimates is presented in Table 20 (p. 212).

These figures reflected the Commission's conclusion, born of fourteen months' continuous study and negotiation since the publication of the Draft Outline, that a considerably greater financial effort might be expected from the states. This conclusion had actually been reached in two stages. First, as a result of various discussions with the states during the latter half of 1960, the Commission had raised the original estimate of the states' contribution from Rs1,200 to Rs1,346 crores—the figure presented to and accepted by the NDC in January 1961. Then, as a result of studies of the states' 1961–2 budgets, it found further cause for optimism, and accordingly raised the figure to Rs1,462. The greater part of the excess of the plan total over the total of January 1961 was to be found under item 1, 'Balance from Current Revenues at 1960–61 Rates of Taxation', which went up from minus 12 to plus 140. To some extent this increase reflected the Commission's confidence that the states were now becoming more efficient tax-collecting machines, but its main justification was to be found in two other factors, viz. (*a*) the impact of the rising tide of economic activity, during the last two years of the Second Plan, on the states' revenue yields, and (*b*) the increase in transfers of resources from the centre to the states via 'shared' taxes (i.e. income-tax and excises).

[52] Ibid. p. 165.

In respect of centrally-raised resources, on the other hand, re-examination during the first half of 1961 had made the Commission slightly more cautious. 'Balance from current revenues' was down by Rs23 crores on the January figures, 'Loans from the public' by Rs25 crores, 'Steel equalization fund' by Rs55 crores, and 'Balance of Miscellaneous Capital Receipts' by Rs13 crores. The net result was a decline in central contributions of Rs69 crores from the January total of Rs6,107 crores.

TABLE 20

Resources for the Third Plan

(Rs crores)

Item	*Draft Outline Estimates*			*Plan Estimates*		
	Centre	*States*	*Total*	*Centre*	*States*	*Total*
1. Balance from current revenues at 1960–61 rates of taxation	385	—35	350	410	140	550
2. Contribution of railways	150	—	150	100	—	100
3. Surpluses of other public enterprises	300	140	440	300	150	450
4. Loans from the public (net)	520	330	850	475	325	800
5. Small savings (net)	190	360	550	213	387	600
6. Provident funds (net)	170	60	230	183	82	265
7. Steel equalization fund (net)	160		160	105	—	105
8. Balance of misc. capital receipts over non-plan disbursements	325	—205	120	428	—258	170
9. Total of 1 to 8	2,200	650	2,850	2,214	826	3,040
10. Additional taxation, incl. measures to increase the surpluses of public enterprises	1,100	550	1,650	1,100	610	1,710
11. Budgetary receipts corresp. to external assistance	2,200	—	2,200	2,200	—	2,200
12. Deficit financing	550	—	550	524	26	550
Total	6,050	1,200	7,250	6,038	1,462	7,500

Source: FYP(3), pp. 94, 100.

On the whole, the Commission was optimistic about domestically-raised resources, although it stressed the impossibility of indicating precisely 'the lines along which the gap between the requirements of the physical programmes and the financial provisions could be bridged. What must have given the careful reader of the 'Financial Resources' chapter cause for alarm was the following obscure statement:

The experience of the Second Plan highlights the fact that despite all the care that may be taken in estimating the contribution likely to be secured from each of the sources indicated in the table, the outturn on individual items is, in practice, liable to diverge from the estimates. For the five-year period ahead, it is, therefore, essential to focus attention on the adequacy of the financing scheme as a whole rather than on estimates in respect of each item taken by itself.[53]

The explanation of this which followed was hardly more reassuring, as it appeared to be based on the assumption that a shortfall in one source of finance could always be compensated by a surplus in another. The falsity of such an assumption need hardly be stressed, nor does one need to be an econometrician to know that a 'financing scheme as a whole' can be no more meaningful than the individual items that compose it.

The plan gave no figures for the distribution of the fiscal burden among the various kinds of tax. 'The details of tax measures to be adopted during the Third Plan', it said, 'will have to be decided upon in the light of the economic situation as it emerges from year to year'. While stating that there was 'scope in a developing economy for increasing the receipts both from direct as well as from indirect taxation', it warned that the possibilities of raising the rates of direct taxation were 'generally . . . limited'. Loopholes for evasion would have to be stopped up and tax concessions to industry would have to be kept under 'continuous review'; but the greater part of the extra strain would be borne by indirect taxation. Saying that this was 'a sacrifice that had to be accepted as part of the Plan', it offered the following consolation to the consumer:

It should not be forgotton that if [indirect] taxation is insufficient, the benefit is likely to accrue to middlemen and traders in the shape of undue profits. Some of these indirect taxes affect the poorer classes but a great many fall on those who have comparatively high incomes. There is, in other words, an element of progression even in indirect taxes.[54]

Estimates of private capital formation differed by only Rs100 crores from those in the Draft Outline (see Table 21, p. 214). Although emphasizing that their estimates, of necessity, were 'exceedingly rough', the planners thought that the new total of Rs4,300 crores could 'probably be financed, consistently with the public sector claims on savings'. They

[53] Ibid. pp. 90, 94–96. [54] Ibid. p. 104.

admitted, however, that as total requirements for the private industrial sector (including replacement and modernization as well as new investment) came to Rs1,350–1,400 crores, the resources estimated to be available (Rs1,250 crores) 'would appear to be somewhat short relatively

TABLE 21

Second & Third Plans: Investment in the Private Sector
(Rs crores)

	Second Plan		*Third Plan*	
	Original estimates	*Revised estimates*	*Estimates*	
			D.O.	*Plan*
1. Agriculture (incl. irrigation)	275	675	850	850
2. Power	40	40	50	50
3. Transport	85	135	200	250
4. Village & small-scale industries	100	225	325	325
5. Large & medium industry & mines	575	725	1,050	1,100
6. Housing & other construction	925	1,000	1,125	1,125
7. Inventories	400	500	600	600
8. Total	2,400	3,300	4,200	4,300

Sources: Draft Outline, p. 51, table 2; *FYP*(*3*), p. 105, table 5.

to needs'. Moreover, the achievement of the 'replacement and modernization' component of this total (Rs150 crores) was a matter of 'hope' rather than of calculation.[55] The physical-financial gap, therefore, extended itself to the private sector. Perhaps this was of no great concern, for the experience of the Second Plan suggested that the private sector would tend to overshoot rather than fall short of its targets.

'Budgetary receipts corresponding to external assistance' were kept at Rs2,200 crores, the Draft Outline figure, and the figure of Rs2,600 crores

[55] Ibid. p. 461.

for 'total external assistance' (exclusive of PL480 imports) was also retained. Recalculations of the balance of payments position, however, assumed that receipts from exports would total Rs3,700 crores as against the Draft Outline's Rs3,450 crores. This new target was said to have been worked out 'on the basis of a study of the export possibility in respect of all major commodities', and presented as 'the minimum to be aimed at' if the future progress of the economy were not to be 'seriously jeopardized'. The import requirements for plan projects alone were put at Rs3,650 crores, a figure which was admitted to be some Rs150 crores short of needs and therefore to imply the toleration of 'some under-utilization of capacity'. Clearly, even if the total for external assistance were realized and export possibilities correctly estimated, the external financing of the plan was going to be a very tight squeeze. Admitting this, the planners wrote:

What emerges on the whole is that the balance of payments position will continue under strain and that the external account will barely balance even with exports of the order of Rs3,700 crores. This target of exports is by no means easy of achievement. It postulates fairly favourable conditions abroad, and an overriding priority to exports in domestic policy decisions. It must be stressed in this connection that the import requirements of machinery and equipment for the Plan are higher by Rs130 crores–Rs2,030 crores as compared with the earlier estimate of Rs1,900 crores. In presenting the estimates . . . it has been assumed that payments out of external assistance for such imports will be limited to the total of Rs1,900 crores. This means that effort will have to be made to finance the balance by increased export earnings even beyond the level indicated . . . .[56]

Without in any way minimizing the difficulties confronting the Commission or the uncertainties inevitably involved in projecting the development of the economy over a period of five years, one is bound to say that all this was far too reminiscent of the Second Plan. (For actual and projected Second Plan expenditures, and projected Third Plan expenditures, in terms of 1952–3 prices, see graph p. 216.) Calculations based on optimistic assumptions had again ended in a series of 'uncovered gaps' which the planners proceeded to paper over with exhortations.

In general, the plan could not but raise doubts about feasibility among those who disregarded its verbiage and concentrated on its calculations. The planners, of course, could argue that it represented the minimum that a country with India's overwhelming developmental needs dare attempt. To this there were two replies, viz. (*a*) that minima have no meaning except in relation to prospective resources, and (*b*) that a global minimum is a complex target, achievable in different ways, of which the

[56] Ibid. pp. 113–14.

one chosen by the Commission, involving a high degree of concentration on heavy industry, was not necessarily the best. It could also be argued that to set the sights high and deliberately to choose one of the more difficult development patterns stimulated that 'effort' and 'enthusiasm' which made economic miracles possible. To this the reply was that, as Nehru himself had admitted, effort and enthusiasm of the non-self-regarding

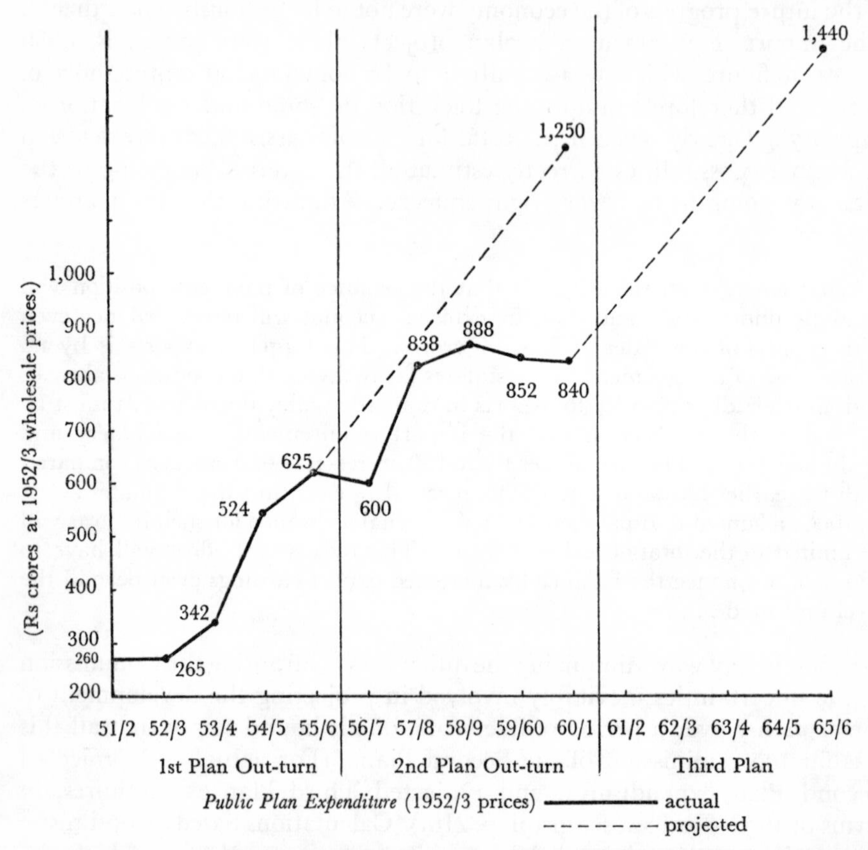

Public Plan Expenditure (1952/3 prices) ———— actual
- - - - - - - projected

Source: I. M. D. Little, 'India's Third Five Plan', *Oxford Economic Papers*, Feb. 1962.

kind that was being demanded hardly existed in India and was not likely to be brought forth by the planners' brave words. A third argument, not used in public but sometimes whispered in private, was to the effect that, although the plan was over-ambitious in relation to prospective resources, this very fact would stimulate foreign countries to effect a massive rescue operation, similar to the one they had already effected in 1957–8. Thus India would get more foreign assistance than she was ever likely to get by being modest. This argument, indeed, had a great deal to commend it; nevertheless it rested on certain rather dangerous assumptions about the willingness of foreigners, for self-interested or philanthropic reasons or a combination of the two, to continue to underwrite plans which manifestly failed to add up.

The brightest gleam of hope on the horizon was, in fact, the amount of assistance already in sight. The Consortium had promised Rs1,089 crores, the USSR Rs238 crores, and other friendly countries Rs67 crores. These totalled Rs1,403 crores towards the Rs2,600 crores, and there was a carry-over from the Second Plan of Rs365 crores.[57] Internationally, therefore, the Third Plan was getting off to what the Commission described as a 'good start'.

TABLE 22

Percentage Increase in Real National Income

	First Plan (actual)	*Second Plan (actual)*	*Third Plan (planned)*
National income	18·5	19·5	30·0
—per annum	3·5	3·6	5·4
Per capita income	7·2	7·8	17·0
—per annum	1·4	1·5	3·2

Source: FYP(3), pp. 35, 55.

The most serious obstacle to the realization of its objectives, both long- and short-term, was the rate of population growth, recently revealed by the CSO as far greater than anyone had previously imagined. The CSO's new projections had come too late to affect the Third Plan's financial targets, but it was certainly more responsible than any other factor for the pushing up of physical targets during the last few months of plan formulation. Indeed, in the many passages where the planners insisted on the need for heroic efforts to fulfil these targets, one can detect a note of suppressed hysteria generated by the thought that at least 8 million, and possibly as many as 10 million, new Indians were being born every year.[58] This situation, one may reliably surmise, was also responsible for planners' frequent insistence that growth itself must be given priority over even the most desirable of 'social' aims, such as the reduction of inequalities and the ironing out of regional disparities. Although frequent mention was made of these ideals, there was an increasing tendency to regard them as comparatively distant objectives. Only in respect of the 'diffusion of

[57] Ibid. pp. 114–15. [58] Ibid. e.g. p. 27.

enterprise', to prevent the rise of a degree of concentration of industrial power that might endanger the government's basic political purposes, did the Commission recommend anything in the nature of drastic action in the pursuit of equality.

Also of note, because of its rarity in planning documents, was the planners' overt recognition of the existence of important social obstacles to economic progress:

> On account of the rigidities of the caste system as well as economic differences, India's social structure already presented numerous inherent conflicts and barriers to economic advance. While some of the old distinctions are passing—a process which is being speeded up—urbanization and the growth of modern industry tend to introduce new disparities in levels of income and opportunity. In turn, these are reflected in modes of living, social behaviour and a general increase in the spirit of acquisitiveness. It is the aim of public policy to check undesirable tendencies and to ensure that these do not come in the way of building up a society which is fundamentally integrated from within and derives its strength from common rules and a sense of shared citizenship.[59]

Unfortunately, this passage displayed a great confusion of mind between obstacles to economic progress and obstacles to socialism, which it tended to identify. Moreover the references to 'caste' and to 'acquisitiveness' were not in any way followed up, and the implications of these extremely important things for 'public policy' were left to the reader's imagination. Indeed, the Third Plan was as devoid as the First or the Second of any serious sociological inquiry. Yet it should have been obvious, long before 1961, that the 'cake of custom' was an even more serious obstacle than the shortage of resources.

An increased awareness of the social obstacles to economic progress, together with some criticism of the Commission for failing to pay sufficient attention to them, found expression in the Lok Sabha's debate on the Third Five-Year Plan, which took place between 21 and 24 August.[60] Nehru, an increasingly frustrated man, engaged in one of his familiar outbursts against casteism, communalism, linguism, &c., saying that people's minds were so 'engrossed in narrow sectional loyalties' that they had 'no concept of India, no concept of the progress of India' and 'no concept of what the modern world is'.

Asoka Mehta, who made his usual intelligent contribution, appealed for greater realism on the subject of social tensions; but how little he himself understood the problems of planning in a 'transitional' society, equipped with democratic institutions, was made evident in his concluding appeal for a 'politics of responsiveness' to replace the existing politics of partisanship.

[59] Ibid. p. 10. [60] LSD, 14th sess., lvii, 3670–4620.

Another pertinent criticism of the planners came from Acharya Kripalani, who claimed that the Commission displayed a reluctance to admit to or profit by its own mistakes. Among these he listed the mishandling of foreign exchange resources, the failure to utilize irrigation facilities, the miscalculation of coal and transport needs, poor administration, and rising prices. In all these matters he believed that there was no prospect of improvement. The so-called 'socialist pattern', moreover, was a fraud, as the gap between the rich and the poor continued to widen. As a remedy he demanded 'the revival and extension of decentralized industry'. As in the Draft Outline debate, he found himself in curious and probably undesired alliance with the Swatantrist leader, Minoo Masani, who said that the object of the plan was 'to foist on the people of this country the Soviet pattern of State capitalism', and accused the government of conspiring with 'licensed monopolists' to exploit the public.

In his reply to the debate, Nanda concentrated most of his fire on the Swantantrists. He could not neglect, however, those who had criticized the plan on 'socialist' grounds, or those who had claimed that their particular regions were being unfairly neglected. In answering the first, he admitted that there might be a conflict between the promotion of socialist ideals and the stimulation of the maximum rate of economic growth, and stated, without equivocation, that in such an event priority must be given to the latter. On regional disparities, he produced figures designed to suggest that, proportionately, the Third Five-Year Plan would give more attention than the Second to the 'backward' states. For this purpose, he divided the states into three groups, viz. A: Bihar, Orissa, Madhya Pradesh, and West Bengal; B: Maharashtra, Gujarat, Andhra Pradesh, Madras, Mysore, and Punjab; C: Assam, Kerala, Rajasthan, and Uttar Pradesh. As between the three groups, public and private investment projected for the Third Plan was said to compare thus with that achieved in the Second Plan, in terms of percentages of total investment:

Group	*Second Plan*		*Third Plan*	
	Private	*Public*	*Private*	*Public*
A	73·2	86·9	55	73
B	23·4	12	29·4	18
C	3·4	1·1	15·6	19

This looked rather impressive, but as the grouping of states was a very arbitrary one and as no information was given about relative rates of development and standards of prosperity already achieved, it did not really shed much new light on one of the Commission's most difficult politico-economic problems. The debate concluded with the defeat of the Swatantra amendment by 132 votes to 10.

IMPLEMENTATION

The fact that this chapter was being completed early in 1964, when the Third Plan was less than three years old, means that any account of its implementation must be provisional and inconclusive. Useful material for an assessment, however, is provided by the Commission in its *Mid-Term Appraisal*, published in November 1963. This shows, beyond all possible doubt, that the plan is in a critical condition. Our purpose, therefore, must be to discover why it has become so seriously distorted and to consider what might be done to save it.

It would have been all too easy for the Planning Commission to place major responsibility on the Chinese aggression of October-November 1962. To its credit, it has made no attempt to do so. China's massive invasion over the North East Frontier has undoubtedly increased India's economic difficulties, in so far as it has induced her to double her defence budget. But the increase in defence expenditure has done no more than intensify certain problems which had already become painfully evident by the summer of 1962.

During the first year of the Third Plan, the rate of increase in the national income had slumped from a record figure of 7·5 per cent in 1960–1 to one of 2·1 per cent—only just over half the average annual increase for the Second Plan period and less than sufficient to keep pace with population growth. Much of this decline was attributable to the disappointing harvest; but industry had also put up a poor performance, registering a 6·8 per cent growth as against 10·4 per cent for 1960–1 and an 11 per cent target. Although some of the falling off could be set down to the Indian tendency to make the five-yearly period operational rather than conceptual (resulting in a 'maelstrom of official activity about two years before the end of one plan, which is too late for the early years of the next'),[61] much more obvious causes were the acute shortage of power and transport, the inadequate increase in coal production, the continuing decline in India's foreign exchange reserves, and the failure

[61] I. M. D. Little, 'A Critical Examination of India's Third Five Year Plan', in *Oxford Economic Papers*, Feb. 1962, pp. 2–3. The situation is exacerbated when an annual 'hiccup' is superimposed on a quinquennial one. This often occurs as a result of obsolete budgetary procedures. It was pointed out in 1957, for instance, that dilatory sanctioning of Grow More Food schemes meant that in many cases the money did not start flowing until towards the end of the year. This resulted in 'confusion, injudicious expenditure, and either the sacrifice of quality for quantity, or a partial or total lapse of the sums allotted' (Foodgrains Enquiry Committee, 1957, *Rep.*, pp. 117–18).

of the government to secure from the Consortium the essential minimum of foreign aid commitments. As a result of these bottlenecks, most industries were working well below capacity and providing very few new opportunities for the swelling hordes of job-seekers.[62] An illustration of how plan implementation in the states was affected is provided by Uttar Pradesh's *Progress Report* for 1961–2, which attributes the following shortfalls to the non-arrival of essential supplies:

	Target	*Achievement*
Masonry wells	45,000	21,587
Primary school buildings	7,000	1,827
PWD buildings	Rs417 lakhs	Rs232 lakhs

The report specifies the coal shortage as the main villain of the piece, stating that during the calendar year 1961 only 20,725 wagons of an allotment of 50,000 had been received.[63] Although one suspects it of using this as a convenient overall alibi, there can be no doubt that so sizeable a deficiency in the supply of an essential commodity must have seriously held up the progress of a great variety of schemes.

The only cause for satisfaction in the economic record of 1961–2 was the decline in the general price level, and even this was all too clearly a temporary phenomenon. Mainly attributable to the fact that 'unusually large outputs of agriculture and industry realized during the previous year' had 'helped to narrow down the gap between total availabilities and total demand in respect of a variety of commodities',[64] it obviously could not long outlast the current year's stagnation in agricultural and decline in industrial production.

Very few crumbs of comfort, therefore, could be scattered by Gulzarilal Nanda when he presented to the Lok Sabha, on 25 August 1962, what amounted to an interim report on plan progress.[65]

He implicitly admitted that the transport bottleneck, which by holding up the movement of coal had a major share of the responsibility for the decline in the rate of economic growth, was due to a planners' miscalculation. 'Demands for transport', he said, 'tend to rise faster than our estimates may always allow for.' Hence the government had approved an additional Rs145 crores for the railways—'Rs120 crores for works and

[62] *PR, 1961–2,* Ch. I; R. E. Kaufman, 'India's Five Year Plans: the First of the Third', *Asian Survey*, Aug. 1962, p. 41.
[63] Uttar Pradesh, Plan. Dept, *FYP(3)*, *The First Year, PR 1961–2* (Jan. 1963), p. 11.
[64] *PR, 1961–2,* p. 1.
[65] Quotations from this speech are extracted from a mimeo. version issued by the Planning Commission.

rolling stock related to the movement of coal, Rs10 crores for line capacity works required to meet the increase in the target of movement of general goods, and Rs15 crores for works for facilitating coal movements in the early period of the Fourth Plan'. These measures, together with improvements in efficiency, would 'progressively ease the transport situation'.

As for the power shortage, Nanda claimed that this had been foreseen. During the Second Plan the brunt of the foreign exchange cuts had fallen on electricity-generating capacity, and the planners had recognized that 'this would bring problems in the future'. He nevertheless admitted that the Third Plan's targets for power development had proved insufficient, and indicated that since the finalization of the plan the government had agreed to their stepping up by 500,000 kw. and had already sanctioned the installation of additional capacity. These measures, he added, would 'undoubtedly prove helpful', although their immediate effects might be small.

Among the measures to speed the growth of industry, he laid emphasis on a new scheme of priorities for licensing, and stated that it had 'also been laid down that new licensing priorities for the setting up of industrial units should be granted on the basis of utilizing capacity at least to the extent of two shifts'. As shortages of supplies were already compelling many vital industries to work considerably below capacity, this was not, one might have thought, a particularly powerful stimulus.

In the 'most crucial sector', agriculture, there was need, he said, 'for still greater intensification of our various activities'—in short, the mixture as before, only stronger. Special attention was being given to increasing the production of cotton and oilseeds and to stepping up the programmes for minor irrigation and soil conservation. For these purposes an additional allotment of Rs50 crores was being made. He also stated that the rural works programme would be accelerated and that a 'programme of rural industries projects' would be launched, without, however, specifying how much extra outlay would be needed.

These proposals were made against a background of a shortfall in resources which was serious enough even in relation to the original constellation of plan objectives. They therefore implied a considerable rephasing of the plan as a whole. This, however, he did not admit; but he did concede that, as a result of the increased allotments for transport and power, there would be a further aggravation of the balance of payments problem.

As for external aid, this would have to be larger than the Rs2,600 crores mentioned in the plan. Available assistance, authorized or promised, amounted to Rs1,890 crores; another Rs1,100 crores would be needed. The internal resources situation was rather better as a result of an improved tax effort, but experience showed that it would be necessary 'to strive even harder to achieve the targets under loans, small savings and surpluses from public enterprises'.

Altogether, Nanda gave the impression that the planners, unable to devise remedies strong enough to cure the infant plan's diseases, were rather desperately hoping that something would turn up. Within three months, something did—the Chinese. National defence now became the first priority, and there was much talk of 'reorienting' the plan towards this objective. Both the Planning Commission and the NDC produced their preliminary ideas on the subject, and a circular on 'Reorientation of Development in the States in view of the Emergency' was sent out. Many people hoped that, in spite of Chinese intentions—real or alleged—to disrupt the plan, the effect of their assault would be to rally the nation for the task of economic development in the manner so persistently anticipated for and so seldom realized.

If the armed struggle had continued, such hopes might conceivably have been fulfilled—always assuming, of course, that India would not have faced complete military collapse. But the Chinese, having broken through the Himalayan barrier, organized a 'unilateral' cease-fire and withdrawal, thereby confronting the Indians with the difficult and confusing 'no-peace-no-war' situation which remains to this day (1965). In such a situation, the maintenance of patriotic fervour is impossible, the sacrifices made in the heat of the moment begin to look rather unnecessary, a feeling of being militarily 'all dressed up and nowhere to go' gains ground, and the violence of the politicians' anti-Chinese diatribes has a diminishing effect on public opinion. Yet the 'defence effort' has to continue—or so India's leaders believe. Hence, from the standpoint of the plan—as indeed from every other standpoint—the total effect of the Chinese aggression has been sheer loss. It has merely aggravated the difficulties which were being experienced long before the Chinese mounted their assault.

Precisely what impact all this has had on the shape of the plan is curiously difficult to discover. If statements by the government and the Commission are to be taken literally, the effect has been marginal. When the NDC met on 18 January 1963 to consider plan outlay and mobilization of resources for 1963–4 Nehru said that of the plan as it stood, some 85 per cent was essential for defence and the remaining 15 per cent 'largely concerned with the defence effort'. Hence, although 'some parts of it might be slowed down or adjusted otherwise, . . . in effect by far the greater part of the Plan was itself essentially for defence'[66]. This 'business as usual' attitude might appear to be contradicted by the budget for 1963–4, which nearly doubled defence provision and proposed the raising of additional resources to the tune of Rs305·90 crores, Rs275·50 crores of

[66] *IN*, 23 Jan. 1963.

it through additional taxation;[67] but the effect of these proposals was to increase total defence outlay from a mere 2½ per cent to no more than 5 per cent of the national income, and, in the event, some of the more unpopular additions to taxation were abandoned.

Documents produced by the Planning Commission confirm that the policy has been one of 'adjustment' rather than wholesale revision. The *Progress of the Third Five Year Plan* (July 1963), however, warns against any underestimation of 'the strains that may develop in the economy, if larger increases in production are not achieved'. 'The requirements of defence and development', it continues, 'are bound to gather momentum in the coming year and the increased defence commitments and the rising tempo of plan expenditures necessitate diversion of resources from non-investment and civilian consumption uses to investment and defence uses on an unprecedented scale'.[68]

Fragmentary indications of the extent of such 'diversion of resources' specifically to defence are contained both in this pamphlet and in the *Mid-Term Appraisal*. The social services necessarily suffer. For instance, the outlay on housing proposed for 1963–4 was 35 per cent less than that proposed for the previous year, which meant that expenditure on this item, which in 1962–3 ran at 18 per cent of the quinquennial provision, was reduced to14 per cent. 'Drastic economies' were also effected in expenditure on social welfare, which, moreover, was 'reorientated' to 'cater for the needs of the families of jawans [Indian soldiers] and their children'. Estimates for health programes were reduced from Rs71·45 crores (1962–3) to Rs64·74 crores (1963–4).[69]

Other heads of development to suffer economy cuts were Major and Medium Irrigation and Village and Small Industries. The former, covering mainly slow-yielding projects of little immediate economic benefit, had its estimates reduced from Rs120 crores (1962–3, revised) to Rs117 crores (1963–4, budget); the latter's estimates were maintained at Rs44 crores (see Table 23).

By contrast, the rate of increase of expenditure on Agriculture and Community Development was sustained, while that on Power and on Industry and Minerals was considerably stepped up. Transport and Communications, which had been receiving urgent attention since the beginning of the Third Plan, received rather less additional provision in the 1963–4 budget than in the 1962–3 budget, but this item was calculated to absorb by the end of the financial year no less than 71 per cent of its total plan provision (see Table 23). Moreover, 'with the onset of the emergency' a substantial increase in road programmes' had been adopted, 'besides certain additions in the Railway programme and in the programme of the Posts and Telegraphs Department'. Of an increase of Rs125 crores

[67] Ibid. 9 Mar. 1963. [68] pp. 2, 5. [69] *PR 1961–2*, pp. 22–23; *MTA*, pp. 167, 171, 161.

in the total plan outlay for roads maintained by the central government, about Rs75 crores was 'accounted for by new schemes connected with the emergency'. Scientific research and technical education were also affected. To step up the number of trained persons, 'admissions both for diploma and degree courses were increased in selected institutions' and the plan targets for admissions to degree and diploma courses in engineering were raised from 56,000 to 72,000.[70]

TABLE 23

Third Five-Year Plan: Outlay by Head of Development, 1961–4
(Rs crores)

1 *Major Head*	2 *1961–6 financial provision*	3 *1961–2 (actual)*	4 *1962–3 (revised)*	5 *1963–4 (budget)*	6 *1961–4 total*	7 *as % of col. 2*
Agriculture & CD	1,068	147	187	227	561	53
Major & Medium Irrigation incl. Flood Control	650	104	120	117	341	52
Power	1,012	139	183	247	569	56
Industry & Minerals	1,520	186	258	365	809	53
Village & Small Industries	264	38	44	44	126	48
Transport & Communications	1,486	302	361	389	1,052	71
Social Services & Miscellaneous	1,300	214	261	265	740	57
Inventories*	200	—	—	—	—	—
Total	7,500	1,130	1,414	1,654	4,198	56

* Expenditure in respect of inventories is distributed under various heads.
Source: FYP (3), MTA.

The information contained in the above paragraphs is as much as the planners seem prepared to vouchsafe about the impact of the accelerated defence effort on the Third Five-Year Plan. One suspects that this impact is much more considerable than they, faithfully following their Chairman's 'business as usual' approach, are as yet ready to admit. There would be no contradiction in arguing, however, that it *ought* to be much greater than it is, if India is seriously intending to throw the Chinese out of her

[70] *MTA*, pp. 17, 138–9, 142 f., 149, 153.

TABLE 24

Third Five-Year Plan: Utilization of Capacity, 1960–3

Industry	Unit	*1960–1*		*1961–2*		*1962–3*		Notes
		Installed capacity	*Production*	*Installed capacity*	*Production*	*Installed capacity*	*Production*	
Iron & Steel								
(*a*) Steel ingots	m. tons	6·0	3·3	6·0	4·27	6·0	5·39	
(*b*) Saleable steel	m. tons	4·5	2·4	4·5	2·9	4·5	4·0	
(*c*) Pig iron for sale	m. tons	1·1	1·1	1·1	0·97	1·1	1·06	
Ferro-manganese	000 tons	157·8	89·3	157·8	103·5*	157·8	108·0	*Calendar yr.
Aluminium	000 tons	18·1	18·2	27·5	19·4	53·35	41·97	
Non-ferrous metals								
(*a*) Copper	000 tons	8·8	8·8	9·0	9·0	9·0	9·48	
(*b*) Lead	000 tons	6·0	3·7	6·0	3·15	6·0	3·37	
Steel wire ropes	000 tons	6·1	3·3*	6·27	2·55	15·0	4·8†	*Calendar yr. †Est.
Cast iron pipes	000 tons	270	209*	270	229·5*	270	230†	*Calendar yr. † Est.
Castings & Forgings								
(*a*) Steel castings	000 tons	39·0	34·0	43·5	40·0	52·2	43·57	
(*b*) Steel forgings	000 tons	43·0	35·0	48·0†	48·0	56·6	53·0	†Est.
Industrial machinery								
(*a*) Sugar mill	Rs crores	11·6	4·2*	11·6	4·6*	15	6·42	*Calendar yr.
(*b*) Cotton textile	Rs crores	12·0	10·4*	12·5	12·5	13·0	13·0†	*Calendar yr. †Est.
(*c*) Cement	Rs crores	1·1	0·6*	4·5	0·9	5·25	0·7†	*Calendar yr. †Est.
Machine tools	Rs crores	8·0	7·24	8·92	8·5	11·3	11·48	
Automobile & ancillary industries								
(*a*) Passenger cars	000s	20·2	19·1*	20·2	27·78	20·2	20·84	*Calendar yr.
(*b*) Commercial vehicles	000s	28·0	27·5*	28·0	25·50	28·0	25·7	*Calendar yr.
(*c*) Jeeps & station wagons	000s	5·5	5·5*	5·5	7·30	5·5	7·44	*Calendar yr.
Motor cycles & Scooters	000s	23·0	17·6	24·0	19·13	30·0	23·62	
Ball & roller bearings	m.	1·7	3·2	3·5	3·3	3·5	4·0	

Agricultural machinery & implements								
(*a*) power-driven pumps	000s	128·0	105·0	137·0	128·0	146·45	131·1	
(*b*) diesel engines (stationary)	000s	47·7	43·2	49·0	43·02	55·44	45·28	
(*c*) tractors	000s	Neg.	Neg.	5·5	0·88	7·5	1·6†	†Est.
Electric transformers (33 kv and below)	m. kva	1·40	1·39	1·50	1·98	1·96	2·40	
Electric motors (200 h.p. & below)	m. h.p.	1·13	0·73	1·13	0·86	1·13	1·03	
Electric cables & wires								
(*a*) ACSR conductors	000 tons	19·3	23·6	31·4	24·8	31·4	30·47	
(*b*) VIR & PVC cables	m. yd.	463·0	214·2	487·2	243·0	529·2	306·7	
(*c*) Winding wires	000 tons	6·8	4·6	7·4	5·64	7·49	6·71	
(*d*) Paper insulated wires	Miles	884·0	620·0	884·0	884·0	884·0	884·0	
Fertilizers								
(*a*) Nitrogenous (in terms of N)	000 tons	158·3	97·2	238·36	140·0	386·6	175·2	
(*b*) Phosphatic (in terms of P_2O_5)	000 tons	57·3	53·0*	89·7	61·9	129·6	78·9	*Calendar yr.
Heavy chemicals								
(*a*) Sulphuric acid	000 tons	483·12	354·0	563·87	428·2	777·0	474·0	
(*b*) Soda ash	000 tons	268·0	145·0	268·0	177·9	268·0	229·9	
(*c*) Caustic soda	000 tons	124·0	97·0	126·0	120·8	126·6	125·5	
Drugs & pharmaceuticals								
(*a*) Sulpha drugs	tons	366	145*	399	156·0	399·0	196·3*	*Calendar yr.
(*b*) Penicillin	m. Mega units	55·0	39·7*	65·0	50·18	65·0	62·3*	*Calendar yr.
(*c*) DDT	Tons	2,800	2,786*	2,800	2,768	2,800	2,568	*Calendar yr.
Paints & varnishes	000 tons	85·0	52·0	85·0	60·6	100·0	61·65	
Soap	000 tons	250·0	140*	242·7	144·5	227·2	147·5	*Calendar yr.
Starch	000 tons	148·6	68·5	148·6	70·6*	148·6	75·3†	*Calendar yr. †Est.
Automobile tyres	m.	1·61	1·49	1·87	1·59	2·4	1·76	
Cement	m. tons	9·2	7·8	9·7	8·2	9·7	8·8	
Refractories	m. tons	0·82	0·55	0·83	0·6	0·84	0·66	
Power & industrial alcohol	m. gals.	40·1	20·4	45·2	39·9	45·8	37·5	
Woollen cloth	m. yd	48·0	15·3*	48·00	16·02	48·0	20·6	*Calendar yr.
Sugar	m. tons	2·25	3·0	2·25	2·7	2·67	2·3	

Source: MTA—extracted from Annexure, Selected Physical Targets and Achievements, pp. 129–33.

'sacred' but barren Himalayan soil and not just thinking in terms of a further intensification of the conflict with Pakistan. As it is, political double-talk in India has obscured her real objectives so thoroughly that it is difficult to say whether assessed defence needs are provided for adequately—or as adequately as possible—in the various adjustments to the plan that have been made.

So far as the general progress of the plan is concerned, the *Mid-Term Appraisal* tried—in places slightly desperately—to make the best of an extremely patchy record. There were certainly some improvements on the first year to provide at least an excuse for talk of 'rising tempo'. The intense pressure on resources of transport, power, coal, and steel had relaxed—although, as Subramaniam admitted, 'to a certain extent, improvement in these basic sectors reflected the lack of adequate development in other sectors'.[71] Industrial production for 1962–3 registered an increase of 8·0 per cent as against one of 6·5 per cent for 1961–2. Although this was still well below the 11 per cent annual average postulated by the plan, and although the utilization of capacity in some sectors was still deplorably low (see Table 18), the Commission could still take heart from the fact that production trends were much more favourable in the industries producing 'capital goods and basic intermediate goods' than in those producing consumer goods. Thus the 'structural changes' in industry which the planners regarded as essential for the 'attainment of a self-reliant economy' were still being made.[72]

In agriculture, the situation was bad. The production index, which went up marginally from 139·6 in 1960–1 to 141·4 in 1961–2, fell back to an estimated 136·8 in 1962–3. Even so, the Commission presented 'some ground for thinking that over the years the amplitude of fluctuation in the downward direction' had been somewhat reduced, and thought it 'reasonable to expect that, with favourable monsoons, there could well be a sizeable increase in total agricultural output during the remaining period of the Third Plan'. But as the production of foodgrains had risen to only 77 million tons in 1962–3 from 66 million tons in 1955–6, the Commission could hardly claim that there was any likelihood of reaching the target of 100 million tons by 1965–6.[73] Even its trust that the weather would 'average out' during the quinquennial period seemed doomed to disappointment, for the almost unprecedented cold spell in northern India from mid-January to mid-February 1964, combined with an unusual delay in the onset of the winter rains, gave rise to 'serious anxiety' about harvest prospects.[74]

How seriously the plan as a whole is running behind schedule emerges from the stark fact that during the first half of the plan period the national

[71] Speech to Assoc. Chrs of Comm., Calcutta, *IN*, 21 Dec. 1963.
[72] *MTA*, pp. 8–9. [73] Ibid. pp. 7–8, 70. [74] *The Times*, 19 Feb. 1964.

income increased by no more than 5 per cent. It is now obvious that, even if there is an acceleration comparable with that achieved during the last two years of the Second Plan, the possibility of raising the national income by the planned 30 per cent over the quinquennial period has disappeared. The planners have recognized this to the extent that their 'likely achievement' figures for 1965–6 are now, in several vital sectors, considerably below the plan targets (see Table 25, p. 230). These figures, however, are themselves highly optimistic. Many of them imply a considerable, and in some cases positively fantastic, stepping up of the rate of progress during the last two and a half years of the plan, to be achieved by an injection of resources smaller than that hitherto made. Total availability of resources for investment in the public sector was estimated by the *Mid-Term Appraisal* at 8,000 crores—for a programme which, without the various additions made during the first half of the plan, had been calculated to cost 8,300 crores of rupees which at the time of calculation were at least 10 per cent more valuable than they are now (February 1964). Of this Rs8,000 crores, Rs4,200 will have been spent by the end of the financial year 1963–4. Hence, to achieve even the Commission's scaled-down targets, the investment of the remaining Rs3,800 crores will have to stimulate a very much faster rate of progress than that so far recorded.[75] One need not don the mantle of Cassandra to predict that it cannot be done.

If one looks, not at resources as a whole, but at their vital foreign exchange component, the position is equally serious. India's export earnings have shown only a very moderate increase, and those from non-traditional exports (such as new manufactures), on which considerable reliance was placed, underwent a serious decline between 1960–1 and 1962–3.[76] The gap between available foreign exchange resources (excluding external assistance) and foreign exchange requirements to finance 'imports required for the maintenance of the economy' was estimated at Rs700 crores by the *Mid-Term Appraisal*. This is the extent of India's need for 'non-project assistance' from the Consortium and other countries. The Consortium meeting held on 7 August 1963 stated that of a total pledged assistance of Rs501 crores for the year 1963–4, Rs200 crores would 'probably' be in the form of non-project assistance. Taking into consideration an estimated 'spill-over' of Rs50 crores worth of non-project assistance into the Fourth Plan, this meant that India would require another Rs450 crores for 1964–5 and 1965–6.[77] The trouble is that India simply does not know how much foreign money she is likely to get in this form, as donor countries, in general, prefer to earmark the greater part of their assistance for specific projects, and tend to recognize more in theory than in practice the undoubted fact that 'non-project assistance has

[75] *MTA*, p. 21. [76] Ibid. p. 45, table 3. [77] Ibid. pp. 48–49.

TABLE 25

The Third Plan: Progress during 1961–4, Selected Targets

Item	*Unit*	*1960–1*	*1961–2*	*1962–3*	*1963–4 (target)*	*1961–6*	
						Plan target/est.	*Likely achievement*
1	2	3	4	5	6	7	8
Nitrogenous fertilizers (consumption)	000 tons of N	200	280	350	450	1,000	800
Irrigation: Major & Medium							
Potential	m. acres (gross)	12·09	12·81	14·27	16·34	29·47	23·16
Utilization	m. acres (gross)	8·59	9·40	10·60	13·08	22·77	18·60
Power: installed capacity	m. kw	5·58	6·03	6·72	7·75	12·69	12·50
Prodn of:							
Steel ingots	m. tons	3·3	4·27	5·39	5·74	9·2	7·8
Aluminium	000 tons	18·2	19·4	41·97	50·0	80·0	68·0
Machine tools	value in Rs crores	7·24	8·50	11·48	14·50	30·0	25·0
Sulphuric acid	000 tons	354·0	428·0	474·0	539·0	1,500·0	1,200·0
Cloth:							
mill-made	m. yd	5,048	5,100	4,921	5,200	5,800	5,550
handloom & khadi	m. yd	1,995	2,320	—	—	2,960	2,750 to 2,810
Minerals							
Iron ore	m. tons	10·7	12·6	—	—	30	25
Coal	m. tons	55·5	55·2	63·8	69·04	98·6	89·9
Index no. of indust. prodn	1950–51 = 100	195	206	222	—	329	—
Railways:							
Freight carried	m. tons	153·8	158·0	174·7	191·5	245·0	241·3
Road transport:							
Commercial vehicles on roads	000s	210	—	270	—	365	330
Shipping tonnage	lakh GRT	8·6	9·1	10·6	—	10·9	15·0
General education:							
Students in schools	m.	44·7	49·9	54·4	58·8	64·4	68·2
Technical education:							
Engineering & technology—							
degree level (annual admission)	000s	13·8	15·9	17·2	20·4	19·1	23·1
diploma level (annual admission)	000s	25·8	27·7	30·9	36·3	37·4	47·5
Health:							
Hospital beds	000s	185·6	193·3	202·0	214·0	240·1	240·1
Doctors (in practice or in service)	000s	70·0	74·5	77·8	80·0	81·0	85·0

a crucial role to play' in the present phase of India's economic development. To this should be added the likelihood that the planners, with their customary optimism, are underestimating India's total foreign aid requirements. So far, aid has been running at the rate of slightly more than Rs500 crores (approx. $1 million) per year. At the Consortium meeting of June 1963, the Indians asked for only a little more, i.e. for $1,285.[78] But *The Economist* (23 Feb. 1963) has calculated that 'if one adds together the Third Plan's imports uncovered by present aid or export earnings, the need for extra arms and for defence support India may require in assistance not a billion dollars a year, but nearer two billion for some time to come'.

The plan is indeed in a critical condition. So, of course, was the Second Plan in 1957–8, yet eventually it came within striking distance of reaching its goal, to the extent that this can be adequately measured by the percentage increase in the national income. There is evidence, however, which suggests that the crisis of the Third Plan is deeper than that of the Second.

India is therefore likely to be confronted with the need for a 'reappraisal' more fundamental than any hitherto attempted. Despite the formidable amount of intelligence and experience of which the Commission disposes, Indian planning seems to have got into a rut. Approaches and methods are persisted with, even when their results are disappointing, and there is some reluctance to admit, even privately, that anything can be fundamentally wrong. It is time, therefore, for the planners to ask themselves whether the things they are trying to do are really the right things. Every aspect of planning, from the distribution of industrial investment to the organization of the Community Projects, bears looking at again with fresh, unprejudiced eyes.

It may be, of course, that India's planning problems are unsolvable within the framework of the existing social and political institutions. But so much has already been accomplished that it would be a tragedy if the world's outstanding example of democratic planning were allowed to run into the sands, for want of taking fresh thought and changing direction.

It would be presumptuous to suggest precisely what should be done. All we can attempt to do here is to define the problems. Some of these have been clarified, *en passant*, during the course of these narrative chapters. Further clarification will be attempted in Part II.

[78] *IN*, 15 June 1963.

PART 2

ASPECTS OF INDIAN PLANNING

VII

THE SOCIO-POLITICAL BACKGROUND

In the foregoing chapters, we have to some extent isolated the planning process from its social and political context. The general emphasis has been on formal machinery and procedures. We must now attempt some estimation of the significance of planning in the evolution of Indian social and political life during the post-independence period. Only when this has been done will it be possible to discuss realistically the various problems of plan implementation with which the remainder of this book will be chiefly concerned.

(i)

Marxists of all shades, including those in the Indian Communist Party, have posed questions about the 'class basis' of the present regime and attempted answers which would provide the 'key' to its future. During the immediate post-independence period, the answers appeared reasonably precise. India was a country of landlords, peasants, capitalists, proletarians, and artizans, in which the 'big bourgeoisie' played the leading political role, using the Congress Party as its agent. The ultimate power holders were the Birlas, Tatas, Mundhras, Thakurdases, Shri Rams, &c. During the independence struggle these had concealed the pursuit of their class aims behind nationalist and anti-imperialist slogans, but with the achievement of independence this disguise was beginning to wear thin. As the tool of big business interests, Congress was losing its 'national front' character and being compelled to pursue policies hostile to the interests of the masses and incompatible with planned and balanced economic development.[1]

The situation between 1947 and—say—1952 seemed to provide some justification for this type of analysis, grossly oversimplified as it was.[2] We need not, of course, pay much attention to what the Communists were saying at this time; for their 'analysis' only reflected the orders they had received to wage a revolutionary stuggle against a government stigmatized as the neo-colonialist agent of 'Anglo-American imperialism'. When Russia began to see virtues in neutralist regimes and to discern 'progressive' features in the Congress Party's policy, they began to sing a different

[1] See, for instance, R. Palme Dutt, *India Today and Tomorrow* (1955). Kremlinologists will find interest in comparing this edition with the previous one.

[2] See references in n. 47 p. 63.

tune. But they were by no means alone in their belief that Congress had sold the pass. The failure of the government to take firm control of the country's economic life suggested that 'vested interests' held all the important strings; in particular, its precipitate de-control of foodgrains, in defiance of the advice of the Commodity Prices Board, seemed evidence enough that the 'tough' Patel, generally considered the chief representative of business interests in the counsels of the party, had triumphed over Nehru, the democratic socialist. Even the staid *Statesman* joined the critics, while D. R. Gadgil, the eminent economist, saw the situation as one in which 'business' was taking control of the government and pushing into the background the more socialistic aspects of the Congress Party's programme.

> The Government of the Indian Union [he wrote] has failed most notably in the sphere of economic affairs. It has showed neither understanding nor firmness in controlling the turn of economic events, and India has made little progress in the direction of either short-term recovery or the planning of long-term development. In part, this has been due to a conflict of forces within the Congress Party; this is being resolved gradually. The attitude and affiliations of most of the top leaders of the party have always favoured Indian business interests; however the economic programme put forward by it in all its campaigns was egalitarian and socialistic. This programme proved a considerable handicap to the party when confronted with the budget of Mr Liaqat Ali Khan in the days of the Interim Government, but its influence persisted for a considerable time after the party's assumption of office. For example, as late as January 1948 a party committee presided over by the Prime Minister reported in favour of early nationalization of most of the major industries in the country. The old socialistic programme has, however, receded more and more into the background during the last twelve months and a new pattern of economic policy, especially industrial policy, has begun clearly to emerge.

Whether this new policy would be compatible with economic progress depended on 'the extent to which the decision to develop the resources of the country through private enterprise' could be 'reconciled with the aims and expectations placed before and entertained by the mass of the people'. Gadgil thought that such a reconciliation, which depended on the government's 'intelligence and firmness' in controlling private enterprise, was extremely unlikely; for the Indian industrialist was 'somewhat exacting in his demands', requiring 'profits such as those enjoyed in 1948' to 'spur him to productive effort', and the government appeared 'to have no means other than the profit incentive of regulating his production'. The new approach meant not only abandoning nationalization and relaxing controls but 'permitting and encouraging the concentration of wealth and income'. The result would be an intensification of social tensions leading—possibly—to a revolutionary situation.[3]

[3] *Econ. Policy & Development*, pp. 113, 116 f., 121.

There are still elements of truth in this analysis. In spite of the adoption of the 'socialist pattern' as the goal of economic and social policy, big business remains influential in Congress circles and provides the party with a substantial proportion of its funds. There is evidence, moreover, that even before the Chinese aggression strengthened the forces of the 'right', business was infiltrating Congress more systematically and pressurizing the politicians and administrators more effectively than ever. For D. R. Gadgil, these facts justified a restatement, with variations, of his original point of view. In the Foreword (p. xvi) to his *Planning and Economic Policy in India*,[4] dated 5 November 1960, he wrote:

> The intelligentsia, including the professionals and the top salariat, who formerly commanded wide respect are . . . fast losing it because of their exorbitant claims on the national product and increasing association with private business. The rot has progressively spread to political leadership. The full situation in this respect is to a certain extent masked today by the fact that political power is overtly in the hands of certain national leaders with a historical background. The most prominent of these were leaders of national political struggle in which their capacity for sacrifice and for objective national leadership was tested and proved. This fact has been helping the Indian government to a large extent during the last ten years. However, it is obvious that neither this leadership nor the hangover from the previous epoch can last for ever. In the not-too-distant future, there is bound to be definite confrontation of the actual possessors of politico-economic power in the country, the large business interests, the top administrative and professional groups and the political parties supported by them with the mass of the common people, and such a confrontation would have very serious results for the plan and for stability and order in the country. Such a situation could be avoided only if political leadership becomes more intelligent and more perceptive.

This analysis, indeed, summarizes the views of those who interpret the Indian situation in fairly straightforward Marxian terms. The fact that Gadgil combines it with a Gandhian-type appeal to those in power to 'regain moral authority' by 'showing some convincing overt signs of their sincerity' is an inconsistency which is also typical.

For Gadgil and his fellow thinkers, the 'large business interests' not only run Indian society; they batten on it. Business has replaced imperialism as the villain of the piece. Just as, in pre-independence days, the issue was one of imperialism versus the masses, so nowadays it is business versus the masses. This 'confrontation', it would appear, is of two kinds, viz. (1) of employers with employees, consequent upon the exploitative behaviour of the former, and (2) of the 'bourgeoisie' in general with the broad masses of the people, consequent upon the incompatibility of bourgeois class interests with rapid economic development and the wide diffusion of its benefits.

[4] Poona 1961.

The first confrontation is, at least for the moment, of minor importance. That employers and employees are conscious of having different interests is, of course, an established fact, in India as elsewhere. But this divergence of outlook and purpose is no more characteristic of the private sector than of the public sector; it is built into any employer-employee relationship. Moreover, one must remember that, whatever views are held about the justice of this relationship, the conditions of the factory worker who finds regular employment, although very poor by European standards, compare very favourably with those of the non-factory worker. In India, as in many other underdeveloped countries, the true industrial proletarian, exploited as he may be, is something of an aristocrat of labour, and his status as such is reinforced by the labour laws, which include provisions for compulsory arbitration of disputes which often produce concessions far more substantial than any obtainable by the ordinary process of collective bargaining.[5] The class struggle *within* industry, therefore, is not likely to play an important political role, even when industry becomes a more significant sector of the economy than it is at present.

More important is the allegation that the dominance of private business holds back economic development, or distorts it in such a way as to deprive the majority of its fruits. At first sight this appears incompatible with the fact that the private sector in industry not only fulfilled but in many fields considerably and embarrassingly over-fulfilled its planned targets during the Second Plan. But one can still argue that, in the main, private business has concentrated on seeking quick profits in comparatively easy fields of economic activity, leaving the more difficult ones to the state; that the businessman's high propensity to consume and reluctance to be taxed has lowered the rate of capital formation and slowed up the absorption of the unemployed and underemployed into productive occupations; and that the inequalities which inevitably characterize a private enterprise system, together with the corruption of politicians and officials which disfigure its present phase of development in India, have created a general atmosphere of self-seeking which makes nonsense of the government's efforts to raise the enthusiasm and win the co-operation of the masses.

The actual situation, however, is extremely complex. Indian businessmen do not all behave in the same way. Whereas some choose the easier

[5] A Code of Conduct and Discipline was drawn up in 1958 and has been voluntarily accepted by the three major management associations and the four major trade union federations. 'As a result partly of the code and partly of the pragmatic and realistic approach of the government to labour problems, and partly because of the growing maturity of both trade union leadership and of the workers themselves, labour-management relations have greatly improved in the past few years. The number of man-days lost because of strikes has been falling since the Code of Discipline was created' (P. S. Lokanathan, 'The Indian Economic System', in C. B. Hoover, ed., *Economic Systems of the Commonwealth* (1962), p. 312).

paths, others are pioneering 'difficult' industries in collaboration with foreign partners. Whereas some are only interested in getting rich quickly, others take the longer view and perhaps contribute more to capital formation through savings than they would ever contribute through taxation, even if corporate and individual taxes were considerably higher and honestly paid. In other words, Indian business displays all the characteristics of a period of transition from the merely exploitative to the genuinely capitalist mentality. Rather than issue a general condemnation or a general certificate of approval, one has to ask in each case whether the state is likely to do better or worse. Upon one's answer, if honestly given, depends the optimum balance between the public and the private sectors of the mixed economy.

The honesty of the answer, of course, may constitute the crux of the problem. Is big business using its political influence to ensure that a *wrong* answer, unduly favourable to itself, is being consistently given? Support for such an allegation might appear to be afforded by the present tendency to tip the public-private balance outlined by the Industrial Policy Resolution of 1956 in favour of the private sector, particularly in heavy and extractive industries.[6] But this is essentially ambiguous evidence; for it can be argued that, given the administrative capacity of the state, the public sector is already relatively overextended. Hence, in the actual circumstances, 'softness' toward the private sector may be justified on grounds of public policy. At least, 'undue influence' is not the only possible explanation.

As for 'undue influence' at the lower levels, such as the use of contact men to expedite the progress of applications through the Development Wing of the Ministry of Commerce and Industry, this undoubtedly exists. Equally so, it gives advantages to the richer businessman over his poorer competitor for the state's favours. But, given the fact that all applications cannot be accepted and the prevalence of low standards of public honesty, one can hardly see how it can be avoided. In the present situation, it may even possess certain merits. As Myron Weiner writes:

> the bakshish system is not as disruptive as might at first appear. It lends to the administrative system discretion and flexibility . . . without which many businesses would find it difficult to function. Indeed, some businessmen have argued that if the government enforced all the regulations provided for in industrial relations acts, industrial regulations acts, import and export controls, and the like, economic growth would come to a grinding halt.[7]

[6] Sri Bharat Ram, the President of the Indian Chambers of Commerce and Industry, writes: 'It is encouraging that in actual practice Government policy has . . . been flexible. We have instances of industries like aluminium and fertilizers, supposedly reserved for the public sector, which have been thrown open recently to the private sector as well' ('Government and the Private Sector', *IJPA*, July-Sept. 1963, pp. 421–2).

[7] M. Weiner, *The Politics of Scarcity* (1962), p. 121.

It is true that the large fortunes that many businessmen make—and often make without much effort, because the licensing system has virtually killed competition among the larger enterprises—offend against the principle of equality, to which the Congress Party continues to pay lip-service. More seriously, the conspicuous flaunting of wealth against a background of Asian poverty creates plenty of that envy and class hatred which Congress says it aims at avoiding. With fortunes too easily made and too openly displayed by the fortunate few, talk of 'enthusing' the masses and enlisting their spirit of self-sacrifice in the cause of economic development can sound hollow. One may doubt, however, whether the conspicuous consumption of the *jeunesse dorée* of the great cities, which is seen only by city dwellers, really has much effect on the attitudes of the peasant masses, who need 'enthusing' most urgently if India is to solve her critical food problem.[8] In any case, it should by now be obvious that no country can base a long-term development programme on sustained idealism and self-sacrifice. Material incentives are needed, in the public no less than in the private sector.

It is the provision of such incentives to the private businessman that raises the cry of 'bourgeois dictatorship'. This can easily arouse anger in a country where the prestige of business is traditionally low and where business initiative has been largely in the hands of exclusive and unpopular groups, such as the Marwaris, Gujaratis, and Parsis. The contradiction that India faces in the private sector is simply this: that the government cannot succesfully run a mixed economy by treating the businessman as a pariah, yet as soon as it treats him as something more respectable it is accused of toadying to capitalists, neglecting the masses, abandoning socialism, &c. Nor can it escape these accusations by concentrating its efforts on building up the public sector in power, transport, heavy industry, and irrigation; for these increase the opportunities available to the private businessman, by the expansion of the 'external economies' at his disposal, and hence can be represented, like Bismarck's 'socialism', as essential to the promotion of capitalism by a capitalist-dominated government. Without a revolution, or at least a change of heart on the part of the politicians and the bureaucrats, the masses can never win. The Marxist circle is complete.

It is not to be supposed, of course, that the private sector *never* succeeds in harmfully deflecting government policies; or that there is no danger of 'capitalist dictatorship'. The very existence of a well-defined and powerful

[8] Inconclusive but suggestive evidence on this subject has been provided by the Indian Institute of Public Opinion, which conducted a survey of 'popular attitudes towards the private sector'. In Calcutta, 46 per cent were hostile; in the rural areas of West Bengal only 38 per cent. As against 24 per cent 'don't knows' in Calcutta there were 39 per cent in the rural areas (IIPO, *Monthly Public Opinion Surveys*, I, nos 10, 11, & 12, May, June, July 1956). These figures are quoted in Weiner, p. 125.

'right wing' in the Congress Party, together with the fact that business provides Congress with a substantial part of its funds, indicates that at any time the constituents of the mixed economy may be changed for reasons that have nothing to do with economic development. But this is quite different from suggesting that there is a natural and necessary antagonism between the claims of the private profit-maker and those of the masses, and that every concession made by the ruling party to the former can be only at the expense of the latter. If this were so, the only right policy for any serious economic developer would be to bring the whole experiment with the mixed economy precipitately to an end. The real-life situation is much more complicated. A government, consisting predominantly of middle-class intellectuals, has conceived certain economic policies which it holds to be in the national interest, and is constantly adjusting them both in the light of experience and in response to the different pressures to which it is subject. Of these, the pressures that come from the private sector of industry are very important; but they are not the only ones nor invariably the most effective.[9]

One might, indeed, extend the 'class' type of political analysis of which Gadgil is an exponent by pointing to the existence of a class which, in many respects, may possess more effective power than the business class. This is the substantial peasantry, the men who have done well out of land reform and government assistance to agriculture. These kulaks, as the Russians would call them, often dominate the economic and political life of the villages and are likely, at least in the short run, to be the main beneficiaries of the new system of democratic decentralization known as *panchayati raj*. It is well known, if only from the reports of the PEO, that they have already absorbed the lion's share of the benefits accruing to the countryside from the Community Projects and National Extension Service (NES); it is equally well known that they form the core of the opposition to all proposals to raise the rate of agricultural taxation. Their power derives from the inability of the administration to do anything effective in the countryside without their co-operation and from the fact that they possess an electoral influence which can make and unmake governments, particularly at the state level.

Like the businessmen, they play an ambiguous role in the process of economic development. In so far as they are content merely to establish themselves as local élites, they contribute to the ossification of rural society, thereby restricting the initiatives and throttling the responses of others. In so far as they succeed in resisting efforts to tax them, they hold back the

[9] Weiner (ch. 5) argues that these pressures are more effective at the state than at the Union level and at the administrative than at the political level. This is a hypothesis that deserves further investigation. It may be that Weiner is arguing too exclusively from the evidence he has so assiduously collected in West Bengal.

process of capital formation in other sectors of the economy. As yet, Indian governments have failed to adopt a consistent attitude towards this class. The local administrator, who often despises it for its lack of culture and combination of rural cunning with rural stupidity, has nevertheless to try to find ways and means of enlisting its support for policies of agricultural development—particularly now that *panchayati raj* is in vogue. The central government alternately threatens it and cajoles it, and occasionally frightens it by producing paper schemes for co-operative farming. In general, it is treated by the authorities with a curious mixture of patronage, deference, and hostility. This combination of incompatible attitudes is, as we shall see, one of the major causes of the contradictions in the rural policies of the Indian government.

If the interests of the business class and the kulak class coincided, we could conceivably provide the Indian government with a dual 'class basis'. According to such an analysis, policy would be the product of two dominant pressure groups, urban and rural, the first consisting of the industrialists, the financiers, and the traders, great and small, the second of the 'bourgeoisified' peasants and associated rural elements. In many ways this would be a realistic view of the situation. Both groups wield considerable political influence, broadly in the same direction. Both, for instance, are committed to an essentially individualist way of life.[10] The urban bourgeoisie resists nationalization; the rural resists co-operative farming. Both are highly resistant to taxation. Both, oddly enough, accept the 'socialist pattern', the former because it extends the infra-structure of the economy, opens up new markets, and limits competition; the latter because it provides seeds, water, fertilizers, credit, and other valuable services. In many respects, indeed, the urban and the rural bourgeoisie would seem to be the main beneficiaries of 'socialism'; and it is at least possible that these classes, rather than the professional classes, will provide India with its new political leadership. Nor would a leader-ship of 'progressive industrialists' and 'progressive farmers' necessarily be a bad one. Much would depend on whether these classes were able to take a sufficiently long-term view of their own interests. But it would not, of course, be a socialist leadership in any meaningful sense.

Such a picture of the Indian socio-economic situation, although more realistic than Gadgil's, would still, however, be over-simple, even in purely 'class' terms. The village poor, for instance, are by no means a negligible factor, even if such influence on policy as they at present exert is only a function of their revolutionary potential. In the towns, the

[10] 'Individualist', that is, in the sense that they are instinctively opposed to state-promoted collectivist policies that limit their economic freedom. This is quite compatible with the traditional caste or joint-family collectivism of which we shall have something to say later in this chapter.

professional classes exert effective pressures through their family connexions with the politicians and the higher members of the bureaucracy, while the 'mob', particularly in Calcutta, can often bring about important changes of policy through mass action. In sum, India has an exceptionally complicated and highly fluid class structure, in which it would be futile to search for any unique social source of political power. In time, the picture may become clearer, but at present its lines are not precisely drawn. The roles of the various classes in the process of economic development are also ill defined. That certain private vested interests which appear to be in the ascendant are necessarily incompatible with economic development is an assumption which lacks proof, either from Indian experience or from that of other underdeveloped countries. They may, indeed, be incompatible with a particular (i.e. socialist) type of economic development, and hence the object of a *guerre à l'outrance* on the part of those who believe that no other type is worth having. But this is an entirely different issue. It is as impermissible to equate socialism with economic development as to equate capitalism with economic stagnation.

(ii)

The above 'class analysis' is a useful exercise up to a point, but the enlightenment that it offers is limited; for there is perhaps no country in the world where the Marxian hypotheses about class and state make less immediate sense, whatever 'ultimate' validity they may possess. Unfortunately, few writings about Indian politics by Indians attempt to transcend these hypotheses, which have great fascination for the radical intellectual. Many authors, indeed, fall short even of this level of analytical sophistication, and content themselves with purely formal presentations of constitutional arrangements, governmental institutions, political parties, &c. If Indian political studies are now being rescued from sterility, the credit must go to the anthropologists, whose techniques of investigation compel them to take into account the very things that most students of politics would prefer to avoid: the phenomena of caste, faction, status, community, language, &c., together with the interpenetrative coexistence of several different styles or idioms of political life. We can now, in fact, learn far more about Indian politics from a competent and politically aware anthropologist, such as M. N. Srinivas,[11] than we can from even the most brilliant of politico-economic analysts, such as Gadgil.

No observer of the Indian political scene, however, need sit at the feet of the anthropologists to discover that the 'class' interpretation is insufficient. The greatest political struggles of the post-independence period have had community and language, not class, as their focus. It was the controversy about linguistic states, not antagonism between capitalists and

[11] See particularly his *Caste in Modern India and Other Essays* (1962).

workers or landlords and peasants, that nearly pulled India apart. In that hive of small-scale capitalism, the Punjab, the major cause of political excitement is the demand of the Sikhs for a separate state. In Assam, the enemy is the Bengali; in Bengal, it was the proposal for union with Bihar which brought people out on the streets of Calcutta and threatened paralysis of economic life; in the south of India, it is the alleged domination of the country's political life by the north that rouses the deepest political emotions. If any major group feels that, at any moment, its life is liable to become considerably less than secure, it is the 40-million strong Muslim community, not the bourgeoisie. When the central government, in 1961, appointed a committee on 'Emotional Integration', it was expressing its concern, not with any exacerbation of the class struggle, but with the growth of communal, caste, and regional antagonisms. It is certainly possible, if one possesses sufficient intellectual agility, to present all these controversies and antagonisms as epiphenomena of class; but only the most convinced Communist could regard such an exercise as anything but talmudic.

India, it is true, possesses a modern-looking collection of political parties, which seem to behave in much the same way as 'western' political parties. They have 'platforms', individual members, hierarchies of committees, paid officials, voluntary workers, and representatives in the central and state legislatures. Their leaders use the familiar political language[12] and present themselves as exponents of policies which ought to command the support of a majority of public-spirited citizens. It is even possible to give each party a 'class basis' by examining and interpreting its programme and identifying its most influential members and supporters. Congress would thus appear as the party of the bourgeoisie, the Praja Socialist Party as that of the radical (but 'confused') petty-bourgeoisie, the Communists as that of the workers and poor peasants, the Jan Sangh and Ram Rajya Parishad (and to some extent the Swatantra) as those of the 'reactionary feudal elements', &c. But all this is superficial and schematic. The parties are quite different from what they appear to be because they are operating not in a modern society but in a transitional one, where people's views about politics and their conceptions of political interest are profoundly affected by their involvement in traditional forms of social organization. This might be of no more than temporary importance if these traditional forms were in a state of dissolution and decay, under the impact of the growth of market relationships, the improvement in opportunities for social mobility, the expansion of communications, and the spread of modern education. There was a time, not very long ago, when almost every informed observer imagined that the traditional would rapidly give

[12] On India's political 'languages', see W. H. Morris-Jones's extremely perceptive essay, 'India's Political Idioms', in C. H. Philips, ed., *Politics and Society in India* (1963).

way to the modern as soon as economic development was seriously undertaken. That economic development *has* profoundly affected the traditional forms of social organization is clear for all to see;[13] but its effect on them has belied expectations. In many ways, far from undermining them, it has provided them with new and wider fields of action.

The fullest explanation of why and how this has happened is presented in Dr Selig Harrison's *India, the Most Dangerous Decades* (1960). Harrison is mainly concerned with the phenomenon of caste, and his general thesis is succinctly summarized by Professor Morris-Jones in a single sentence: 'From the traditional society, itself changing, caste moves out into politics.'[14]

Caste, instead of being seriously weakened, has changed its significance—or rather developed new significances in addition to its older ones. In former days it was predominantly a local phenomenon, providing a principle of social organization, a means of status determination, a basis for the division of labour, a prescription for interpersonal relationships, and a pattern of ritualistic observances for village and town alike. It still performs these functions, although less consistently, less efficiently, and—at least in those areas where the impact of economic development has been most marked—with less self-confidence. With the growth of communications and the spread of education, however, the brotherhood of the caste (or, more correctly, the sub-caste) has widened geographically and assumed essentially political forms. The result is the creation of caste associations over considerable areas, sometimes coinciding with the area of the state itself.

Part of the function of a caste association is to provide its members with social services. This aspect is naturally more developed when the caste is both wealthy and educated. In 1956 it was reported that the Association of the Chitrapur Saraswat Brahmans of Bombay operated 22 educational institutions, 13 fraternal and social agencies, and 12 housing co-operatives—all for a membership of 18,900. But primarily the association functions as a political pressure group, acting on behalf of its caste at all levels where pressures may be profitably or hopefully applied. Hence in each state there exists what Dr Harrison, using the American analogy, aptly terms a 'caste lobby'.

The importance of these caste pressure groups, which were already present in pre-independence India, has been enhanced by the greater 'pressureability' of politicians dependent on votes for office, and by the fact that, since economic planning and economic controls were introduced,

[13] This point, which has recently suffered from some neglect owing to the 'rediscovery' of caste, is usefully re-emphasized by Prof. Robert O. Tilman in his essay on 'The Influence of Caste on Indian Economic Development', in Braibanti & Spengler, *Admin. & Econ. Dev. in India.*
[14] In Philips, *Politics & Society*, p. 139.

the governments have more favours to dispense than ever before: jobs, licences, contracts, special privileges, permits, &c. Moreover, with the raising of expectations on the part of the populace, an inevitable consequence of economic development, competition for these favours has become extremely intense. But why, it may be asked, should the participants in this competition be *castes*, as well as individuals? Harrison offers the following answer:

> Caught in a never-never world of frustration, somewhere between newly aroused desires for equality and the scant spoils of progress that are actually available, it is inevitable for a man to turn to a loyalty he knows and understands to fortify his quest for equality with those above him and to assure that he is 'more equal' than those below. While in time some dissolution of Hindu values and social ties will follow industrialisation and urbanisation, while in time successful members of rising castes will forsake their group allegiances for a broad new middle class consciousness, in the decades immediately ahead most Hindus will pursue equality as members of caste lobbies.

Generalizing, he states that 'in an economy of plenty social lines are eroded by the change to urban life, but in an economy of scarcity the lines harden'.[15]

Whether so broad a generalization can be sustained is answerable only by the mobilization of evidence from a large number of developing countries. Much would seem to depend on the original hardness of the lines. In India they were very firmly drawn, and the effect of economic development has been to move them up and down rather than to dissolve them. Caste, in fact, seems to have become an agency of collective competition. Formerly low-placed castes take advantage of new economic opportunities to improve their standards of living. As they move upwards in the economic scale they try to adopt the ritual prerogatives of higher castes and eventually begin to demand a correspondingly higher status. This process, widely observed, has been christened 'sanscritisation' by M. N. Srinivas. The more successful of them become the 'dominant' castes of their state or region.

The very conception of 'dominance' indicates how far caste has travelled away from its original role. The idea of mutual obligation is replaced by the idea of political power. The old caste hierarchy was a ritualistic, not a political one; any coincidence between ritual status and political influence was accidental to—rather than inherent in—the system. The new hierarchy, which now exists side by side with the old in uneasy juxtaposition, is essentially political in character, and those at the top or on the way up make constant efforts to achieve a ritual status to correspond with their political position. The new hierarchy, moreover, is less pyramidical, less symmetrical, and more flexible. The new dominant

[15] *India*, pp. 102, 104–5.

castes are generally more numerous than those (such as the Brahmans) who are still ritualistically at the top of the tree; they sometimes face challenges from equally numerous rivals; and the perpetuation of their dominance is by no means guaranteed. They dominate, at least for the time being, in the localities or regions where they have established their status; they run the village panchayats and control the *panchayat samitis*, the *zila parishads*, and the municipal boards; they have their representatives in the legislative assembly of the state; but it is by no means the rule that one caste eventually achieves state-wise dominance. It may be that at present there is little effective challenge to the Marathas in Maharashtra or to the Patidars in Gujarat; but in Mysore Lingayat faces Okkaliga, in Andhra Pradesh Reddi faces Kamma, in Rajasthan there is an uneasy balance between Rajput, Jat, Gujar, and Ahir, while in Kerala the dominance of the Nayar is anything but secure.

One of the consequences of this situation is that in many states—not in all, as is sometimes alleged—politics are predominantly caste politics, and the politicians, however sophisticated and westernized they may be, have to make the necessary adaptations. When candidates are being picked, caste appeal becomes one of the first considerations; when policies are being framed, the likely reactions of dominant castes must be carefully assessed. Caste-brothers must be supported as fully as may be compatible with a proper respect for the claims of other electorally-significant caste groups, and in the distribution of jobs, contracts, and state aid to agriculture a nice balance must be maintained between the more important collective competitors. Congress, perhaps, understands these requirements most fully. It has the necessary experience; it is less dominated by ideology than most of the other national parties, particularly at the state and local levels; and, as the ruling party, it can trade in past favours as well as in the expectation of future ones. Yet all the other parties, even the most ideology-dominated of them, are compelled to behave similarly. The result is sometimes a radical contradiction between behaviour and profession, most strikingly illustrated by the record of the Communist Party in the state of Andhra Pradesh, whose political life is dominated by the antagonism between Reddis and Kammas.

The involvement of the Communists in Andhra's caste politics is all the more extraordinary because the struggle is not one between a comparatively high-ranking and prosperous caste and a comparatively low-ranking and depressed one. Both Reddis and Kammas are, by Indian standards, prosperous farmers, and the Kammas, from whom the Communists have drawn support and who indeed supply the leadership of the state's Communist Party, own more than three-quarters of the land in the fertile Krishna–Godivari delta. The facts of the situation, which are not in dispute, have been presented by Dr Harrison in his *Caste and the Andhra*

Communists (1956), and are summarized by Professor C. von Fürer-Haimendorf in his essay on 'Caste and Politics in South Asia'.[16] Briefly, the Communists gained Kamma support by appealing to their anti-Brahman sentiments and by leading the agitation, which for various reasons captured the Kamma imagination, on behalf of a Telugu-speaking state. They maintained that support, even during the Telengana revolt of 1948–50, by the simple expedient of restraining their poor peasant followers from attacking the estates of the Kamma landlords (thus contriving, with extraordinary dexterity, to combine all-out class war with limited and specific class collaboration). During the following years they retained their Kamma base and even spread their influence to other sections of the 'exploiting' classes, by promoting the claims of delta-located Kurnool as the capital of the new Andhra state. Subsequently they lost ground, because the Congress Party, recognizing that exclusive identification with the Reddis had become a serious weakness, succeeded in putting up its own Kamma candidates (or the Kamma candidates of allied parties) against those of the Communists. In the election of 1955, writes Dr Harrison, 'the Kammas responded to the general strength of the Congress cause, coupled with a successful appeal to the caste's economic stake in keeping the Communist Party out of power'. The Communists, for their part, complained that 'all quarrels of caste or community had been forgotten', and that the landlords had 'united to face the common people'.[17] The party situation, therefore, has become more fluid; but the basic caste antagonism, which gave the Communists their original opportunity, and which all parties have to take into account, appears to remain unchanged. A recent observer of Andhra's political life, Hugh Gray, is reported by Professor von Haimendorf as follows:

> In Andhra the evidence I have from two districts shows that there has been no change in traditional leadership . . . . In both these districts the struggle for office and power is overtly between the Kammas and the Reddis, and no attempt is made to disguise it . . . . At the state level alliances are fluid, the Reddi and Kamma networks are in opposition, but seek allies from each other's groups and from outside.[18]

According to Harrison, caste was also the basic force behind the agitation for the linguistic state. He quotes G. S. Ghurye, the leading Indian authority on caste organizations, to the effect that from the beginning of

[16] In Philips, *Politics & Society*. [17] *India*, p. 241.

[18] In Philips, *Politics & Society*, p. 61. In an interesting, if rather less than objective, study of Communism in Kerala, Dr Jitendra Singh develops the thesis that in this state the Communists are essentially the party of the Ezhavas, who occupy the bottom rung in the caste hierarchy. Although he makes his point, I have considered the Andhran example more immediately relevant than the Keralan, because in Kerala there seems to be closer coincidence, at least as far as the Nayars and Ezhavas are concerned, between caste status and economic status (see J. Singh, *Communist Rule in Kerala* (New Delhi, 1959)).

the nineteenth century 'linguistic boundaries fixed the caste limits'.[19] As the linguistic idea has now triumphed, the state becomes incomparably more important as a focus of political power, as a centre of political loyalties, and as a theatre of caste struggles. More and more effectively, as the Congress old guard is replaced by new men who have worked their way up through the local political machines, the power of the state challenges the power of the centre. Scarred by the caste battle, limited in their horizons, and dependent for electoral support on provincials whose provincialism has been exacerbated by their own political propaganda, these new leaders lack the degree of all-India loyalty possessed by the old. Their own community, their own state, and their own region (e.g. the South) come first, second, and third in order of political importance. Hence the very unity of India, so painfully achieved, is now in jeopardy. Dr Harrison specifically envisages a breakdown of the present regime and its replacement, during the post-Nehru era, by 'a shambles of feuding regional ministries held loosely together by a government in New Delhi whose writ in economic development clearly does not extend to much of the country', perhaps to be followed by the establishment of 'new authoritarian or quasi-authoritarian order'.[20]

One may doubt, however, whether he has proved his case. The sequence of dominant caste, linguistic state, and national disunity is too unilinear an explanation. Does linguism invariably strengthen the state as against the centre? It certainly gives political force to the sense of exclusiveness possessed by those who speak a common tongue, and thereby increases the difficulties of mutual comprehension. If, moreover, it is associated with the control of state politics by a single dominant caste, its effect may be strongly centrifugal. But, as Harrison himself shows, the state does not invariably fall under such exclusive domination. Often it becomes a battleground of contending caste interests, and for this reason may be no stronger *vis-a-vis* the centre than its predecessor, the non-linguistic state. Even in those states where a single caste does dominate, internal tensions may be no less pronounced. As Dr Hugh Tinker has pointed out, pressure of numbers tends to compel 'the middle castes who now control politics . . . to share power with the lowly'.[21]

Again, is it true that linguism exacerbates inter-state and inter-regional rivalries, as Harrison suggests? One would have thought that, to the extent that state boundaries now coincide with linguistic boundaries, a major cause of rivalry had been eliminated. The Punjab problem, of course, remains to be settled, and practically every state contains linguistic minorities which are a cause of tension. But the period when language functioned as a major divisive force would appear to have begun with the

[19] Harrison, *India*, pp. 10, 106. [20] S. Harrison, ed., *India and the United States* (1961), p. 6.
[21] H. Tinker, *India and Pakistan* (1962), p. 149.

'fast unto death' of the Andhran, Potti Sriramulu, in 1955, and ended with the bifurcation of the united Bombay state into Gujarat and Maharashtra in 1960. If language provokes further disasters, the linguistic state, as such, is unlikely to be the responsible agent. The most dangerous possibilities arise from the attempt to impose Hindi upon an unwilling South and from the possible loss of English as an effective *lingua franca* for political and administrative purposes. Rivalry between individual states and between groups of states for the favours bestowable by the centre will continue, as will rivalry between geographically contiguous states for the control of the waters of the important rivers which flow across their boundaries. But these rivalries have little to do with language or with caste; they are endemic in any federal system.

Is it even true that caste is the *fons et origo* of state exclusiveness? The fragmentary and sometimes ambiguous evidence suggests that it is true only in some cases. In West Bengal, for instance, 'caste seems to play only a minor role in politics. Many of the urban intellectuals including Brahmans have largely broken away from the ties of caste, and some of the younger members of leftist groups have found within their political party new group loyalties and an exclusive new set of values.'[22] Broadly, the internal political struggles of this state are dominated by class rather than by caste. Nevertheless, it is no less conscious of its statehood than—say—Maharashtra, with its dominant Maratha castes, or than Andhra, the home of the Reddis. Even where caste-dominated politics are the rule, it is not always possible to locate a caste which enjoys state-wide dominance, or even a small group of castes competing for such dominance. In Orissa, for instance, state-wide caste organizations are only embryonic, and 'lines of cleavage both between parties and within parties are not illuminated by looking at caste membership'. This makes it 'difficult and dangerous for a candidate to rely too greatly or too openly on caste loyalties to get his votes for him'.

In all except tribal constituencies, no one caste comes anywhere near constituting a majority of the electorate, so that their support alone cannot win an election. Secondly, as with the village, too close an identification with one caste will automatically line up other castes against a candidate. Thirdly, castes, like villages, are commonly split into factions, and to gain one faction is to lose the other.[23]

Yet despite the primitiveness of its caste organization as compared with that of many other states, and despite the fact that the two castes that could be described as 'dominant', the Karan and the Brahman, lack the

[22] C. von Fürer-Haimendorf, in Philips, *Politics & Society*, p. 65. See also Tinker, p. 150.
[23] F. G. Bailey, 'Politics and Society in Contemporary Orissa', in Philips, *Politics & Society*, pp. 105–6.

means of expressing themselves politically *qua* castes, it could hardly be said that Oriya 'nationalism' was a feeble force.

Lastly, one must beware of overplaying the divisive forces in the Indian polity and underplaying the unifying ones. The divisive forces have always been there, but so far the Congress Party has succeeded in keeping them in check, partly by compromise, partly by discipline, and partly by the use of Nehru's *charisma.* The new leaders, admittedly, are different from the old: coarser, less idealistic, less intellectual, more caste-bound, more provincial. But, as Professor Morris-Jones has put it, 'they do much more than simply express region-caste claims. They are also the men, the only men perhaps, who can and do tame and instruct the wild forces beneath them; they lead then into the ways of the Plan and the all-India polity; they are the great intermediaries between the two styles of politics.'[24] Indeed, they have the grossest of material interest in so behaving. Without a national plan, India cannot develop at the rate which *all* politically-conscious Indians demand. Left economically to themselves, or as sovereign units making economic bargains with other sovereign units, the states could hardly achieve even their present modest rate of economic growth. Reluctant to tax, they are dependent on the centre for money; short of talent, they look to it for administrative and technical assistance; limited in their horizons, they wait for it to produce the new ideas. All want more than they get, but all get something. They bargain with vigour, but in the last resort accept the discipline of the plan, not only because they have to but because it is in their long-term interest to do so. To imagine that the state politicians are not conscious of these facts of political life, or that they would not do their utmost, when it came to the point, to preserve the unity upon which their success in the last resort depends, is to give them less credit than they deserve. Kamaraj was certainly first and foremost a Madrassi, unskilled in English and ignorant of Hindi; but he sent the able and cultured Subramaniam to attend the meetings of the NDC and to bargain with the Planning Commission, permitted him to express an all-India point of view, and eventually 'gave' him to the centre as Minister of Steel and Heavy Industry.[25] Chavan achieved fame as a Maharashtrian political boss and Chief Minister: but when the call came he went off to Delhi to take up the post of Minister of Defence and to cause speculation whether Nehru's successor had at last been found. Such men, moreover, know that their political future in their own states depends, at least in part, on their success in putting the case in New Delhi, where the important decisions are taken. They press hard, but when the bargain is completed they know that to violate its terms too

[24] From a review of Harrison, *India*, in *Parliamentary Affairs*, Spring 1961, p. 271.

[25] Subsequently Kamaraj himself gave up the Chief Ministership of Madras to become Congress President.

outrageously will bring retribution; and if they themselves eventually go to the centre as ministers, they know that merely to act as agents for their states will not, to say the least, endear them to their colleagues from elsewhere or win them the national reputation that they all desire. Hence, although the Congress Party may be ramshackle and corrupt, and the central government less able than formerly to avoid decision by compromise, the prospect of India's becoming divided into 'feuding principalities' is not perhaps an immediate one; nor will a solution to political problems necessarily be sought along authoritarian lines. Vitally important as caste is in Indian political life, it provides neither the key to its nature nor the clue to its development. Nor, as we have seen, does class. Together they may be helpful, but the difficulty is to know how to conjoin them.

If we use the concept of caste *status* as a measure of socio-economic power and influence (rather than as one of traditional standing in the ritual hierarchy), caste and class would appear to be automatically identified, at least over a broad area. Furthermore, there is a tendency, as we have seen, for ritual status itself to move in the direction of correspondence with socio-economic status. More and more castes which are on their way up the socio-economic ladder claim a ritual status of the Vaisya kind. Conversely, those on the way down, for whatever reason, find that their traditional ritual pretensions are of declining significance. This appears to be happening, although very unevenly, to both Brahman and Ksatriya. 'In a society like that of India today, where the Vaisya is supreme, the Brahman and the Ksatriya seem likely to lose more and more of their old status, to be increasingly assimilated to the Vaisya and the Sudra, and to live more and more by their wits rather than by their position.'[26] It is also true of many areas that 'castes which are in the lower strata of the social hierarchy invariably constitute the labour force'. In Orissa, for instance, Dr F. G. Bailey found a 'high degree of coincidence between politico-economic rank and the ritual ranking of caste'.[27]

Later, however, he discovered that this coincidence was subject to so many exceptions that its value as a generalization became doubtful. Thus, in Bisipara village, the 'dominant' Warrior caste owned less than 30 per cent of the land, while the Pans, 'who as a dependent caste should have no land at all', owned over 20 per cent of it. Furthermore, the Warriors' income per head was smaller than that of several other castes; and although they dominated the village council, they were unable to make use either of the economic sanction or the sanction of force to control the other castes. Did this mean that the 'dominance' of the Warriors was mythical, or that the formerly-dominant Warriors were facing a challenge?

[26] W. N. Brown, 'Class and Cultural Traditions in India', in M. Singer, ed., *Traditional India* (1959), p. 38.

[27] *Caste and the Economic Frontier* (1957). See also his *Tribe, Caste and Nation* (1960), p. 258.

Dr Bailey chooses the latter solution to his problem, and identifies the Distillers, formerly of low status in the ritual hierarchy, as the challengers. This situation could be reconciled with the original model by supposing that 'the system is moving all the time towards an equilibrium structure of one dominant and several dependent castes'. But it seemed 'to have got stuck at a point short of the abstract model'.[28]

A similar situation may be observed at the regional and state levels in many parts of India. A caste may dominate a particular area, but face a challenge, within the region, from a caste exercising dominance over another area; similarly, a regionally-dominant caste may have to compete with another regionally-dominant one for control of the state. If these rival castes enjoy, *ex hypothesi*, equality of socio-economic status, the caste-class equation no longer holds good, at least to the extent that it implies an element of class *solidarity*, which alone would make it politically significant. One might argue, of course, that the long-term dynamism of the process of economic development will create such solidarity and that as a consequence the equal but rival castes will liquidate their rivalries and come together in a solid middle-class block to face the growing challenge of the depressed and dependent. By analogy with other societies, this would appear to be likely; but the mere existence of such a possibility does little to help explain the balance of political forces either now or in the immediate future.

There are also other complexities. One is the existence of significant political cleavages within the dominant caste itself. Another, which may in some cases be the cause of this phenomenon, is that fact that members of a particular caste do not all enjoy the same socio-economic status. Hence, when a caste moves upwards, the richer members of it have to carry their poorer fellows with them. Sometimes, as Dr Bailey says, 'the wealthy within a caste group can . . . lighten their upward passage by jettisoning poorer caste-fellows', through the formation of a sub-caste. But this, for traditional reasons which are still persuasive, is not easy. Moreover, the poor, aware that 'mobility adheres to groups and not individuals', attempt to safeguard their position by supporting 'their own "middle classes" in the struggle against higher castes'.[29]

(iii)

In brief, the social and economic situation in India, which provides the basis of the country's political life, is not susceptible to any single, simple, or unilinear explanation. This negative finding could be reinforced if we chose to bring in factors other than class and caste, such as religion, community, and region, to say nothing of the all-pervading cultural dichotomy of town and countryside. What emerges is the intense particularism

[28] *Caste & Econ. Frontier*, pp. 258–63. [29] Ibid. p. 270.

of the Indian political scene. The picture is one of an immense number and variety of groups, traditional and non-traditional, caste-based, community-based, and occupation-based, all jostling for position and all attempting to use the democratic political system for their own 'selfish' ends. These provide the unacknowledged foundations of that system; the political parties are merely the superstructure. Each, within the limits of its own ideology—and even outside those limits—attempts to gain the support of as many groups as possible, particularly the more powerful ones. To the extent that it succeeds, it is able to impose some coherence by compromise upon their rival demands. The Congress Party, being the oldest, the most experienced, the best organized, and the most prestigious, has been more successful in this task, both at the Union and at the state levels, than any of the others. It is still the great 'fixer', as it was in the days when it held together so many disparate elements in the struggle for national liberation. Rather tarnished, split by rival factions, and containing its fair measure of hypocrites and time-servers, it yet manages to hammer out reasonably coherent policies, capable of winning the active support of the few and the passive acceptance of the many, and to hold together as a political unit a nation which, without it, would rapidly degenerate into a mere assemblage of rival communities and regions. It manages to work a constitution which no one likes very much but which no one, except Jayaprakash Narayan, thinks he knows how to improve on. It wields the powerful, unpopular, but essential weapon of the IAS, that 'steel frame' which was Britain's most valuable legacy to independent India. Although it can command no more than a minority of votes, it retains its electoral strength more or less unimpaired, and retains office thanks to a hopelessly divided opposition, whose divisions are themselves, in the last resort, a reflexion of the prevalent socio-economic fragmentation and particularism.

There is nothing 'heroic' about this political situation—nothing to capture the imagination. To the idealists and ideologues it is a matter for beating the breast. A regime of almost universal self-seeking and group-seeking seems a poor reward for the independence-fighters, that diminishing band who look back nostalgically to the great days of 'all for one and one for all'. This is not the 'community of service' as conceived by Mahatma Gandhi, nor yet the social democracy of the dreams of Jawaharlal Nehru. It is certainly a political democracy of some sort; for it has all the necessary trappings of free elections, rival political parties, and comprehensive civil liberties. But the question inevitably arises whether political democracy itself will for long remain a viable system, in conditions where rival groups are battling for scarce supplies of politico-economic goods.

Some, such as Selig Harrison, incline to the view that it will not; and the experience of other underdeveloped countries which have attempted to work democratic systems certainly provides no encouragement to those who hold the contrary view. Others, such as Barbara Ward[30] and Thomas Balogh, make the preservation of democracy dependent on the rate of economic development, and hence call for the stepping up of aid to 'save India for the West'. Both, I believe, try to prove too much.

Harrison, as we have seen, tends to overestimate the divisive forces and to disregard the unifying ones. He also misses some of the significance of the traditional forces in Indian society, by presenting them as wholly inimical to the preservation of a democratic polity. This is curious in an American, who ought to be familiar enough with group politics and with 'fixer-type' parties. There are, of course, basic differences between the respective groups, Indian and American, even though the parties themselves may bear resemblances close enough to be significant. Many of the Indian groups, as we have seen, have their roots in a social order which is qualitatively different from the new social order struggling so desperately to be born. So far as caste and community groups are concerned, their psychology, so to speak, is pre-democratic. They do not share common assumptions about the nature of the political process and are, indeed, ignorant of the conventions and compromises which are essential to give any democratic system stability and vitality; and even if they were less ignorant of these things in theory, sheer pressure of demand would compel them to ignore them in practice. All this is broadly true, but it is not the whole truth. For one can argue that, from a democratic standpoint, even traditional-type groups are better than no effective groups at all, particularly if such groups, as with those in India, are undergoing a subtle process of adaptation. For one of the most frequent causes of the collapse of democratic regimes would seem to be the lack of any middle-level, voluntary organizations to mediate between the government and the individual. 'Individualist' democracy has always been a myth and is today, in developed and underdeveloped countries alike, more mythical than ever. Could it be, therefore, that these much-maligned groups which appear to press so hard against the democratic frontier are in fact one of the forces that preserve it from violation? Could it be that they have a positive role to counterbalance the negative one that Harrison and others have expounded so learnedly and eloquently? These questions, while admitting of no definite answers, are at least worth exploring, and are indeed already being explored. In other underdeveloped countries, write Lloyd and Suzanne Rudolph:

> it is precisely the eclipse of traditional associations without the emergence of new ones to replace them which has led to disillusionment concerning the

[30] See her 'An Accident of History', in Harrison, *India & the United States*, pp. 16–26; also her *India and the West* (1961).

possibilities of democratic government. Through the familiar, traditional channel, caste organisation and its leadership provide the means whereby the bulk of the population, which in other areas remains mutely outside the political system, is able to be integrated into democratic political processes.[31]

This certainly suggests that Harrison's pioneering trip through the jungle has revealed no more than part of the landscape.

On the other hand, it is unrealistic to imagine that economic development will, of itself, reduce the intensity of group demands and thus cause them to relax their pressures on the democratic frontier. On the contrary, economic development has itself stimulated these pressures and demands—not only of the traditional groups, but of the more modern ones, such as business associations, trade unions, professional associations, and student federations, which will become more significant, perhaps at the expense of the traditional groups, as economic development proceeds. As Myron Weiner says:

Economic progress is . . . likely to be accompanied by a rise in organized demands. Within a few decades, there may very well be substantial increases in unionisation. Existing caste, tribal and other community and regional groups may be better organized. With a rise in educated unemployment, student militancy may increase, and urban areas may become even greater centers of discontent than they are today. Peasant agitations, especially of the landless, may be expected; and peasant proprietors may demand greater expenditures. As the economic supply grows, 'consumer' political demands may increase even faster. Thus, economic growth is not likely to diminish the political repercussions of scarcity. The argument that economic growth provides government with greater revenue, thus enabling it to satisfy more of the demands made on it, assumes a constancy of demand for which there is neither historical precedent nor theoretical justification.[32]

This analysis is implicitly critical of Balogh's view that the preservation of democracy in India depends on the ability of the government to increase national investment 'towards 20 per cent of the national income within a measurable time, say by 1970', and to accelerate national real output to 'at least 8 per cent per annum'—if necessary by 'ruthless' methods.[33] As a

[31] 'Towards Political Stability in Underdeveloped Countries', in Harvard Univ. Graduate School of Business Admin., *Yearbook, 1959*. For a development of this view see their 'The Political Role of India's Caste Associations', *Pacific Affairs*, Mar. 1960. The politically 'mediating' role of caste, at the local level, is suggested also by Adrian Mayer. In the central Indian village which he was studying, he found that the headmen on various occasions 'moved as much as possible with the approval of the leaders of . . . caste groups' other than their own. 'In this way the caste divisions in the village . . . served to temper and "democratize" the situation' (*Caste and Kinship in Central India* (1960), p. 112).

[32] *Politics of Scarcity*, pp. 238–9.

[33] Balogh, 'Thoughts on the Third Plan', *Capital* (Calcutta), 30 Mar. 1962, pp. 491–2.

prescription for the achievement of economic 'break-through' this may be correct; as one for preserving democracy it is more doubtful. The heroic effort that Balogh envisages could certainly be undertaken by a totalitarian or at least highly-authoritarian government, backed by a disciplined élite and equipped with a regime in which some groups had been liquidated and the remainder brought under strict control. If tried by a democratic government, it might either produce a political explosion or grind to a halt in the sands of group resistance and general inertia. In 'democratic' planning, there is conflict between the economic and the political optimum. If this conflict were absolute one might as well dispense with democracy as soon as possible; because it would be doomed anyway. If, however, the conflict is less than absolute, it *may* be feasible to produce a plan which, while economically less than optimum, is sufficiently radical to effect a break-through, and which, while politically less than optimum, can be successfully steered, by a government which has acquired the requisite driving skill, through the shouting and gesticulating crowds of interest groups. On the assumption that Indian democracy is worth preserving, it is obviously at this sort of plan that the Indian government should be aiming. There is grave danger in urging it to drive faster, regardless of the consequences, and in assuring it that extra pressure on the accelerator will hold the democratic bodywork together and not shatter it to pieces.

We must ask, therefore, whether such a plan, with combined political and economic viability, is feasible; whether India is seeking it with sufficient persistence and intelligence; and whether, having found it, the government has the political *nous* and administrative capacity to carry it through.

(iv)

We are now, indeed, at the crux of this discussion. The political features we have emphasized possess a double significance for planning: they enter into the formulation of the plan, and they influence the manner in which it is implemented. Unless they are regarded by the plan formulators and plan implementers alike as imposing certain limitations and opening up certain possibilities, and not just as constituting inconvenient and perhaps impermanent obstacles which may be hopefully disregarded, then the plan is likely to go seriously astray. That they are eventually taken into account is inevitable; but whether they are taken into account at the right stage and with full understanding is another matter.

The plan begins with a series of political and technical assumptions, the joint products of the party, the government, and the Commission. How realistic are these? So far as the technical assumptions are concerned, we have seen that they are based on considerable intellectual effort devoted to the study of statistical and other data. But with the political assumptions one is on different ground.[34]

No one reading the plans can fail to be impressed by the frequent unrealism of these assumptions. So much appears to be contingent upon the realization of the unrealizable. *If* people work harder, *if* they save more, *if* they are less selfish, and *if* they make the plan 'theirs', *if* the administration is less corrupt and more efficient, *if* the peasants make full use of the irrigation waters, *if* the Community Projects create the desired response, *if* the business community becomes public spirited, *if* the trade unions behave themselves, *if* the prejudices and antagonisms associated with region, community, and caste are significantly diminished, *if* there is more wholehearted co-operation between the states and the centre: the list of unrealistic or exaggeratedly hopeful presuppositions is almost endless. They are sometimes explicit, sometimes implicit, but always present.

The sources of this unrealism are complex. It may be explained, partly, by the fact that many of the plan formulators are ideologues in whose minds a variety of western-derived theories, all too often divorced from Indian reality, jostle for predominance.[35] Nehru himself provided both the worst and the most distinguished example. Theory was always his strong point; but it was a little difficult to say whether he was a liberal contaminated by Marxism, or a Marxist contaminated by liberalism. Famous for his almost mystical powers of contact with the peasant masses, he never displayed, even in his overtly Marxist days, any firm grasp of the problems of the Indian countryside. He did not know whether to encourage or scold the businessman, and his fulminations against casteism, communalism, and factionalism, Jericho walls which are always about to fall at the sound of his trumpet, contributed little to the solution of India's most important socio-economic problem.[36] Always he was hopeful that the Indian people were about to 'rally round', at last persuaded to see the light of liberal-Marxist reason; always he was disillusioned and angry;

[34] As Prof. Wilfred Malenbaum says: 'Indian planning has progressed from the relatively simple one-sector formulation of the first plan through the plan-frame's four-sector model for the second to the much more complicated models underlying the third. It is not certain that there has been parallel progress in the degree to which the models are meaningful approximations to the changing Indian economy and society' (*Prospects for Indian Development* (1962), p. 202).

[35] Prof. Edward Shils terms this 'xenophilia' and associates it with 'a severely deficient sympathy for the states of mind of one's fellow countrymen', a 'lack of intimacy with the material environment' and a 'social blindness to the capacities and incapacities of one's fellow countrymen and their problems' (*Econ. Dev. & Cult. Change*, Oct. 1957, pp. 55–62).

[36] '. . . few people seem to realise that the caste system is entirely opposed to both democracy and socialism. If we want a socialist structure of society, we have to put an end to the caste system as we know it. Only then can the beginning of democratic socialism come to our society' (from an article by Nehru contributed to a souvenir issued on the occasion of the 68th INC, Bhubaneshwar, quoted in *IN*, 11 Jan. 1964).

and always he turned towards some new panacea, whether it was community development, co-operative farming or *panchayati raj*. Increasingly intolerant of those who failed to see the light as he currently saw it, yet as anxious as any other politician to conciliate those with the power to make trouble for him, he often took refuge in vagueness and ambiguity. Of his greatness there is no doubt, and his services to India were incalculable; but he set some bad intellectual fashions.

Minds of this quality often try to solve practical difficulties by the simple process of the imaginative leap. They are encouraged to do so, in India, by historical experiences that are still recent enough to be remembered. At the end of the First World War Gandhi, perhaps the most unpromising political figure since Joan of Arc, waved his magic wand, brought the masses to life, and gave India a degree of unity and a sense of purpose she had never experienced before, throughout the whole course of her curiously cyclic history. The power of his word and the force of his example conferred dignity on the undignified, spirituality on the materially-minded, and a capacity for self-sacrifice on the self-interested. It was an astounding achievement.

It is tempting to argue that what was done once can be done again, and to imagine that the powerful word from the charismatic personality can unite the people for the task of economic reconstruction, as it once united them for that of national liberation. No Indian, of course, literally believes this—for in the Indian mind naïveté is subtly blended with sophistication; but Indians often behave as though they believed it. Unity of thought and community of purpose are their *ignis fatuus*, and much of their planning is based on the assumption that although today it may be elusive, tomorrow it will be caught. While recognizing the existence of a multitude of divisive forces in Indian society, they tend to think in terms not of manipulating these forces but of eliminating them. Their implicit political theory, although perhaps derived from eastern rather than western sources, is Rousseauan. The purpose of democratic institutions is not to achieve a limited consensus but to discover a unique general will which must then become the 'real self' of every individual participant. Thinking thus, they give inadequate attention, at least during the plan-formulation stage, to the problems of interest-adjustment which are of the essence of democratic statesmanship;[37] indeed, the only interests which engage their continuous attention are those of the states, which the federal nature of the constitution

[37] 'Snap judgements' about motivation are a corollary of this neglect. S. K. Dey, the Minister of CD & Co-operation, provides frequent and rather frightening examples. Thus, in a circular on the subject of holidays in connexion with CD projects, he expresses himself as follows: 'Whereas in many other countries people could be inspired to rise to an effort on material incentives, in India the people could be moved only on the incentive of spiritual appeals or around events connected with history or religion' ('Personal and confidential' letter, Administration, CPA, New Delhi, no. 7/45, 15 July 1954).

compels them to take seriously. What seems to happen is that plans are formulated on the assumption that a degree of unity in action which is normally obtainable only under non-democratic conditions—where groups are liquidated and silenced, where organized opposition is forbidden, and where a single party has a monopoly of political propaganda—can be achieved under democratic conditions, where groups are active and vocal, organized opposition is not only permitted but constitutionally encouraged, and the public's ears are assailed with the sound of many voices. In a sense, the Indians are trying, or at least hoping, to combine the advantages of democracy and totalitarianism. The danger is that they will get only the disadvantages of both.

It is not that appeals for unity are futile. As all governments make them, one may assume that something is gained by their utterance. The trouble is that, in India, they tend to be regarded as a substitute for creative democratic politics. There is too little advance examination of group demands, in order to decide which of them can be accommodated, which must be resisted, and how the greatest possible number of them may be either mobilized or neutralized. A frequent result of this failure, as Myron Weiner has pointed out, is that group demands receive satisfaction only when they reach a level of disorderly expression sufficiently menacing to compel the government's attention.[38] Once the immediate crisis has subsided, the search for the will-o'-the-wispish 'general will' continues.

Other factors which help to explain this lack of realism are the influence of the Gandhian concept of selfless and 'non-political' community service; the prevalence, among some of the better people at the top, of an aristocratic-intellectual contempt for 'mere politics'; the political insensitivity of the IAS; and the sheer remoteness of the politicians, administrators, and planners of New Delhi from what is happening in the field.

The first, of course, is one of India's most valuable assets. It inspires a handful of the sub-continent's greatest men, such as Vinoba Bhave and Jayaprakash Narayan; it helped Nehru himself to bear a crushing burden of work and to maintain his reputation for incorruptibility and integrity; and it sustains the morale of many key administrators whose work has become their life. But it also induces, particularly in those who are criticizing from the side-lines, a certain pharisaism and inflexibility, an unwillingness to come to terms with the real facts of socio-political life, and a perfectionism which functions as a standard of judgement for others more frequently than for themselves.

As for the contempt for 'mere politics', this is both a cause and a result of political failure, and usually allied with the perfectionism we have just been discussing. Even the Communists—or at least the right-wingers

[38] *Politics of Scarcity*, chs 8 & 9.

among them, who tend to be Indians first and Communists second—occasionally inveigh against the 'dirtiness' of politics and envisage the emergence of some kind of general will.[39] Carried to an extreme and combined with a Gandhi-inspired enthusiasm for social service, this attitude can lead to complete withdrawal from ordinary political life and to the devotion of a great man's intellectual talents to the formulation of utopian proposals for the 'reconstruction of the Indian polity', such as those advanced by Jayaprakash Narayan, who appears to think that the faction-ridden village can provide the foundation of a pyramidical democracy without parties, in which decisions are taken by unanimous consent.

The IAS also makes its contribution to the prevalance of utopian values and anti-political attitudes. The successor to an ICS which was essentially a ruling caste, it tends to hold in quasi-aristocratic contempt most politicians, most businessmen, and most of the interest groups which constitute the grass roots of Indian political life. Its function is to administer 'objectively', to discover the 'right' policies and the 'right' methods of policy-enforcement, to provide a standard of rectitude by which lesser mortals may be measured. When rightness is deflected by the impact of group pressures, it becomes uneasy and begins to feel that something is seriously amiss. It is too remote, too cut off by educational background and manner of living from the great majority of the community, to be fully effective either as a means of group-consultation or as a listening post. Admittedly, it is gradually changing as the area of its recruitment gradually widens; it has become far more development-minded and, particularly since the introduction of *panchayati raj*, more flexible in its approach. But the old traditions die hard, and are constantly being reinforced by the prevalence of casteism, which endows the administration itself with 'caste' characteristics. As a high proportion of the personnel of the Planning Commission itself has been recruited from the IAS (and much of its senior personnel from the old ICS), the influence of these characteristics and attitudes cannot fail to be of importance.

This remoteness of the upper policy-makers is reinforced by their physical isolation in New Delhi. The capital is totally different in atmosphere from the rest of India. Administrators in the field, faced with the duty of giving effect to inoperable directives, commonly refer to Yojana Bhavan, the home of the Planning Commission, as the 'ivory tower'. To some extent this is unavoidable. The remoteness of the planner is a common cause of complaint in all countries, and misunderstanding between the central policy-maker and the peripheral policy-enforcer is in the last resort uneliminable. But in India the malady is aggravated by the sheer size and variety of the country. It is somewhat alleviated by the

[39] *Future of Asian Democracy* (Indian Bureau of Parl. Studies, New Delhi, 1959), p. 87.

fact that most of New Delhi's top-level administrators have had field experience during the course of their careers. But such experience, unless periodically renewed, tends to fade rather quickly, and to become of doubtful relevance as conditions change and new tasks or new methods replace old ones. Hence physical isolation continues to contribute its quota to the various unrealisms which are built into the planning process.

It would be foolish to suggest that Indian planning takes place in a rarefied atmosphere of which ideology and econometrics are the sole constituents. Clearly, the real political situation exerts continuous influence on the process of plan formulation. But the Commission's approach, as revealed in the three plan reports, suggests a tendency to regard political factors as tangential rather than central. The planners come up with certain ideologically-inspired or economically-calculated proposals which are then modified or deflected by a variety of group pressures. The result is compromise, inconsistency, and lack of realism. Much of this could be avoided if the whole constellation of socio-political circumstances were treated as basic data. 'Politics' could then be built into the plan itself, rather than being left to impinge upon it. Admittedly there are politicians on the Planning Commission—and on the NDC—who can tell the experts what the various sections of the Indian public will, and will not, tolerate; but this is not good enough. Nor is it sufficient that there are plenty of experts around who, some time or other, have had experience in the field. What is required is that adequately verified and 'processed' social and political data should enter into the very substance of the plans. At present, these data tend to be disregarded, with the result that the planner's reflection of reality is a distorted one. The rural planner, for instance, who disregards caste, class, and faction, gets a distorted picture of village life, by virtue of which he conceives expectations which are doomed to frustration. A realistic analysis and appreciation of the socio-political situation ought therefore to take place at the beginning of the planning process, before anyone starts playing around with sectoral calculations, capital-output coefficients, and all the rest. Unfortunately it does not take place at the beginning, in the middle, or at the end. The plan reports themselves are witnesses to its absence.

Instead, the Indians have developed what might be described as a 'planning orthodoxy', consisting of a series of assumptions about Indian society on which the approach to planning is based. The assumptions involve the necessity of unanimity and the irrelevance of 'politics'; the approach necessitates over-reliance on collective effort. In practice, this means that within the Planning Commission itself a whole number of sacred cows graze undisturbed. No one dares touch them, and few but irreverent foreigners question the need for their continued existence. One wonders what would happen to the bright young Indian economist, sociologist, or political scientist, employed by the Commission, who argued that from the standpoint of achieving the most rapid economic development, the Community Projects were misconceived, *panchayati raj* was premature, heavy industry given exaggerated emphasis, or the 'socialist pattern' irrelevant? One suspects that his career would receive a setback. Yet it is the duty of Planning Commission personnel to say such things, if they believe them to be true. A planning agency cannot and should not make political policy but, in its single-minded devotion to the cause of economic growth, it must subject all political and ideological presuppositions to rigorous examination. This the Indian Planning Commission, so far, has failed to do with sufficient vigour.

One might put the matter another way by saying that, in the process of plan formulation, the basic question is incorrectly formulated. The Commission tends to start by assuming a given rate and kind of growth and then asks how prevalent attitudes and modes of behaviour must be transformed to make this feasible. The alternative and more realistic approach would be to assume the relative persistence of attitude and behaviour-patterns, and to ask what rate and kind of economic growth can be achieved with their help or through their manipulation. It is only by the latter approach that the 'cans' and 'musts' of economic planning may be fruitfully conjoined. The former tends to separate them without hope of reconciliation. The defects of Indian planning, which have become increasingly evident since 1957, are therefore largely attributable to the selection of unrealistic 'input factors'.

To go on to suggest, however, that the very intelligent men in the Planning Commission are wholly unaware of this situation would be absurd. They are aware of it with varying degrees of clarity, and their reactions to that awareness are equally various. Among them, there are attitudes ranging from the apologetic to the cynical. A brief glance at the two extreme types will help to explain why socio-political blindness is not a self-curing disease.

The apologist has two key words in his vocabulary—'flexibility' and 'enthusiasm'. He recognizes that the plan is more or less unrealistic, but argues that this is a virtue. Idealistically conceived, it has to be tailored, year by year, to fit the actual circumstances. That its targets should be too high to be attainable, and that it should demand of people more than they are prepared and able to give: these are praiseworthy rather than blameworthy features. The object is a psychological one: to draw from the community that extra bit of effort that would not be forthcoming for a less 'bold' plan. If the plan were more modest, or more carefully calculated to appeal to selfish interests rather than to patriotic spirit, achievements might fall even farther short of objectives. Only when the screw is being applied will results—even inadequate ones—be squeezed out.

In totalitarian conditions, where the party possesses a political monopoly, controls communications, and plays an unchallenged 'leading role' in every sector of political and social life, arguments of this kind, as we have seen, possess considerable validity. They are even valid, up to a point, in democratic conditions where a high degree of consensus has been stimulated by the emergency of military or economic disaster, as in Churchill's Britain of the 1940s or Roosevelt's America of the 1930s. But India is no totalitarian country, and her democracy is a fragile one, embodying the minimum rather than the maximum of consensus attainable in a free political system. The 'emergency', of course, is plain for all to see: the persistent and degrading poverty that the plans aim at alleviating; but mere poverty, as is well known, tends to be a divisive rather than an integrating force. Hence the recommended type of appeal falls, in the main, on deaf ears. Even worse, the persistent gap between objectives and achievements is one of the major causes of public cynicism, and a welcome gift to all those who are attempting, as they are fully entitled to do under democratic conditions, to discredit the government, the Commission, and the very idea of planning. The 'apologist' therefore, is involved in one of those mental confusions rather characteristic of the 'soft' democratically-minded ideologue, as distinct from his 'hard' totalitarian-minded counterpart. If he comes to realize this, he may feel that the only alternatives are to 'go totalitarian' himself or to relapse into cynicism and despair.

The transition from the apologist to the cynic may, therefore, be very abrupt. But not every cynic has travelled this road. There are many officials who have become cynical not as a result of ideological disillusion but because they, who understand something of the realities of the socio-political situation, despair of exercising any real influence over the policies which they are supposed to be helping to formulate. The cynic of this type tends to become alienated from Indian society, contemptuous of Indian politics, and sceptical of the efficacy of all development plans. Having become convinced of the futility of trying to make the planning process more realistic, he finds refuge in the performance of routine duties and perhaps intellectual excitement in the making of econometrical calculations. He knows that, even if a dissident view makes itself heard at the higher levels, it tends to become 'absorbed'. The atmosphere of the Commission is at present hostile to the clear confrontation of ideas, particularly when they have political implications. The frequently employed formula, 'Although we must concentrate on *this*, on the other hand we must not neglect *that*', ensures that unanimity prevails—or at least appears to do so. This being the case, why bother to rack one's brain with hard thinking about fundamentals?

We are here attempting to isolate observable *tendencies* and to define certain types of thinking which are extreme rather than typical. The actual situation is far better than the foregoing paragraphs would suggest. One must nevertheless emphasize the wide—and perhaps widening—gap that exists between the political thinking of the planners and the political situation in the country. Although its existence is readily explicable, it is hard to bridge, being no artificial or accidental creation but the product of a dichotomy in Indian society itself.

The essence of the problem is that India's intellectual élite, whose members dominate the Planning Commission and occupy the highest positions in the government service, have not yet learnt either to look clearly and unflinchingly at the facts of the social order of which they form a part, or fully to accept the political implications of the federal-democratic system they have brought into existence. Hence the comparative failure of their attempts to translate radical aspirations into terms of effective policy. Faced with certain traditional institutions and attitudes which, *prima facie* inimical to economic development, display an unexpected and unwelcome resilience and persistence, the radical intellectual either pretends that they are not there, or attempts to conjure them out of existence by verbal magic. If the rational and the real do not coincide, they must be made to do so. This is essentially a totalitarian approach—but our intellectual does not possess the totalitarian mentality, nor does he have at his disposal the totalitarian apparatus. Hence the flight from reality.

If India is to remain a democracy and Indian planners are to achieve the modest yet encouraging successes which are the most that can be expected of democratic planning under conditions of extreme economic backwardness, social fragmentation, and incipient disorder, they must become more oriented *towards* their own society. Only thus can they become better aware of the real limitations under which they labour and the real opportunities with which they are presented. In Professor Apter's *schema*, summarized in the introductory chapter, India is characterized by her 'reconciliation' approach to political problems. The outstanding feature of her chosen system is 'the high value it places on compromises between groups which express prevailing political objectives and views'. In such a system rapid economic growth is possible 'only if there are extensive self-discipline, popular participation, and great civic devotion'. It is obvious that weakness of such pre-conditions in India both limits the rate and affects the kind of economic growth that can be achieved. It is possible, therefore, that quantitatively and qualitatively satisfactory growth presupposes a change-over to a 'mobilization' system, attainable only through a political revolution. If this is so, the sooner it is recognized the better. If, on the other hand, the existing system is to be retained, the planners must learn to understand its distinctive characteristics and to work *with* them rather than *against* them. 'Self-discipline, popular participation and great civic devotion' cannot be conjured into existence, and plans which presuppose their presence (or the possibility of significantly stimulating their growth by the arts of democratic persuasion) will come unstuck. It is useless, while retaining a 'reconciliation' system, to hope for results attainable only under a 'mobilization' (i.e. totalitarian or authoritarian) system. It is equally useless to imagine that a 'reconciliation' structure can be combined with 'mobilization' measures. Yet such hopes and imaginings have persistently haunted the Indian Planning Commission from its earliest days, and have been responsible for a great deal of the unrealism that has characterized the planning process, particularly in the rural sector. The tendency, as we have seen, has been to produce one panacea after another, none of them based on serious grass-roots investigation and each embodying unrealistic presuppositions about the social and political situation.

We have now investigated, in general terms, both the political realities of the Indian situation and the political ideologies of the planners. Between the two there is tension and contradiction, expressing itself in a widening gap between theory and practice, between aim and achievement. It is in the light of this situation that, during the course of the remaining chapters, we will attempt to analyse a few of the more specific, and characteristically Indian, aspects of the planning process.

VIII

ADMINISTRATION

(i)

ASSUMING that a plan is sufficiently realistic to be implementable, effective implementation is largely a function of administrative efficiency. One does not need to be a trained sociologist, however, to realize that the word 'efficiency', in this context, is ambiguous almost to the point of meaninglessness. Normally, 'efficiency' is presented as an overall characteristic of a bureaucracy which conforms with the Weberian model. According to this slightly naïve view, 'the administration' is a passive and neutral instrument engaged in the implementation of political decisions, and its success may be judged by the degree to which it has economized scarce resources in the expeditious attainment of the ends prescribed for it by the political process. As a formal characterization of bureaucracy and a criterion for the measurement of its achievements in a state predominantly concerned with 'law and order' and tax-gathering, this is not altogether inappropriate; but as a starting-point for the understanding of bureaucratic functions and measurement of bureaucratic success in a more developed type of politico-administrative system, where the state is concerned with the promotion and regulation of economic activity and with the provision of a variety of services, 'social' and otherwise, it is not very useful. Even in a night-watchman state, the bureaucracy possesses views both about the ends of its activities and about the methods most appropriate for attaining them. It also functions as a distinct and sometimes extremely powerful vested interest. In the new type of state, these characteristics become stronger and more important, because the points of contact between bureaucracy and society become more numerous, the impact of bureaucracy on society becomes more continuous, and its role as the mere 'carrier out' of policies less distinct, in so far as it is now being called upon, not merely to implement the rules and regulations, but to exercise initiative and generally to behave in a 'creative' fashion.

The transition from the one kind of bureaucracy to the other has taken place comparatively smoothly and slowly in the more advanced countries. In the less developed ones it must take place quickly, and at a time when the acquisition of independence tends simultaneously to disrupt the old administrative machine and to confront the administrator with the traditional type of 'law-and-order' problem in a particularly acute form.

In such circumstances, it is exceedingly difficult for a bureaucracy—particularly if it consists predominantly of new men, themselves deeply involved in the political struggle—to develop the distinctive characteristics responsible for the success of its counterparts in the West. Unfortunately, underdeveloped societies tend, almost by definition, to have underdeveloped administrations. As it is to the administrations that a major share of the practical tasks of development is confided, we have here another of the notorious vicious circles that whirl around in developers' nightmares.

Fortunately, there are degrees of viciousness. India, for all the administrative deficiencies which she displays, is exceptionally fortunate. The British left her with a well-articulated, smoothly-functioning administrative machine, headed by an élite corps which could stand comparison with any analogous body of senior administrators anywhere in the world. Admittedly, it was well laced with 'expatriates' at the top, and still largely geared to the traditional functions of government (hence the use of 'collector' as synonym for District Officer). But, during the later years, indianization had proceeded apace and the bureaucrat had become increasingly concerned with economic regulation and the provision of services. The disappearance of the 'expatriates' and the withdrawal to Pakistan of the majority of Muslim civil servants were blows, but by no means disabling ones; for the educated middle class was of a sufficient size to make practicable an 'emergency recruitment' to replace the losses, and the administrative *ethos* sufficiently well established to enable the new recruits to be absorbed into the system with comparative ease. In these circumstances, the main problems were (*a*) to prevent degeneration, (*b*) to adapt and diversify, and (*c*) to establish new and more fruitful relationships between bureaucrats, their political masters, and their 'clients'. The last was—and remains—the most difficult task; for the bureaucrats had themselves been the masters under the British raj, and hence tended to be regarded with suspicion by the new democratic representatives and with indifference or hostility by the new democratic electorate. Nevertheless, India at least began with advantages denied to many other underdeveloped countries.

(ii)

While by no means unaware of this comparative good fortune, the government and the Planning Commission have recognized administrative deficiencies as a serious obstacle to planned economic development. They have also looked at the problems very frankly, making no attempt to gloss them over. Part 2 of the First Five-Year Plan, on 'Administration and Public Cooperation', began with a recognition of the 'decline in the standards of administration' since the acquisition of independence. This it ascribed mainly to a combination of increased work with a shortage of experienced personnel. As a result, key administrators were working 'under considerable strain and pressure'. The need for administrative reform, therefore, was 'urgent'.

Broadly, the problems fell into three groups, viz. (1) those 'bearing on the entire field of public administration, such as . . . the achievement of high levels of integrity, efficiency and economy'; (2) those bearing upon 'the adminstration of development programmes in the district', where the official was in most immediate and intimate contact with the ordinary man; and (3) those relating to the enlistment of popular co-operation in 'formulating and implementing various programmes'. The solution of all three, and particularly the last two, required not merely organizational and procedural changes, but a 'reorientation in outlook on the part of officials as well as non-official representatives'.[1]

That these promising prefatory remarks were followed by a rather vague and fragmentary chapter on 'Reform of Public Administration' was not entirely the fault of the Commission, which had to do its work in a hurry with the aid of such materials as lay readily to hand. These were by no means plentiful, and the Commission's main reliance was placed on the very short and generalized, if thought-provoking *Report on Public Administration* (1951),[2] prepared at its behest by a distinguished but impatient ICS officer, A. D. Gorwala.

After a few remarks about administrative leadership, the question of integrity received pride of place. Stimulated by the shortage of essential supplies, corrupt practices had made alarming headway. The Commission thought that various improvements in disciplinary procedures, together with the strengthening of the Prevention of Corruption Act, 1947, could help to root them out, particularly if public opinion were roused, but rightly pointed to administrative delays as 'one of the most important sources of corruption'. Their eradication, therefore, was bound up with the improvement of efficiency.

On the latter question the Commission had little to say. Gorwala had not gone into any detail, and it was clear that concrete proposals would have to emerge from further inquiries. That efficiency had reached a dangerously low ebb was stressed by quoting the words of 'an experienced observer':

> The impressions of a recent tour through the larger portion of the country, combined with many years of official and non-official experience, lead to the

[1] *FYP(1)*, pp. 113–14.

[2] Other material of comparatively recent origin included the 'Tottenham' report (1945–6), the report of the 'Bajpai' Committee on Secretariat Reorganization (1947), N. Gopalaswami Ayyangar's review of the machinery of government (1949), and the reports of the 'Lalbhai' Economy Committee (1949) and of R. A. Gopalaswami on the Improvement of Efficiency (1950).

conclusion that the machine, though sound in essentials and capable of improvement in undertaking arduous tasks, is at the present moment run-down. The work allotted to it has increased, the quality of its output has deteriorated. The parts removed from it have, in many instances, been replaced by those of inferior workmanship. The edge has been taken off through strain and, occasionally rough treatment, of many of those that remain. The tenter [*sic*] too is new, often impatient and inefficient. Coordination is frequently wanting. For reasons, some within and many beyond the machine's control, efficiency is undoubtedly impaired. All in all, there is considerable room for improvement.

The aspect of this situation which the Commission chose to emphasize was the tendency to push upwards the level of effective decision-taking, with the result that a very few highly-placed civil servants had become loaded with an unreasonably heavy burden of work. No explanation of this phenomenon was volunteered, but the reasons for it were made explicit in a Planning Commission paper of 1961, which found it still characteristic of Indian administration. Two of these were political in character, viz. (1) the 'increase in the number of representations to the top levels of administration'—one of the inevitable consequences of the introduction of democracy, and (2) the liability of ministers, in a parliamentary democratic regime, to public accountability for 'the details of their activities'. To these were added two factors derived from the multiplication of administrative responsibilities, viz. (1) the greater proportion of new activities, demanding more attention than 'continuing activities' from ministers and senior officials, and (2) the dilution of the quality of administrative personnel in the field, 'particularly as experienced personnel [are] drawn increasingly to the Secretariat to assist in the formulation of policy and its implementation'. A fifth reason, commented on at length by the Commission, was the failure to discover, or even to seek with sufficient persistence, adequate motivations for the acceptance of responsibility by civil servants at the lower levels of the hierarchy.[3]

During the ten years of planning there has been wide agreement on the appropriateness of the remedies suggested by the First Plan. Time and again it has been said that the departments must be strengthened in organization and personnel; that there must be clear lines of responsibility,

[3] Cabinet Secretariat, *Papers on Measures for the Strengthening of Administration* (1961), Paper no. 3, prepared by O & M Division, on 'Administrative Capacity', pp. 25 ff.; espec. pp. 32–33. In Indian discussions of administrative reform, questions of motivation, although constantly raised, are equally constantly pushed into the background by questions of organization. So far, there has been little more than frequent repetition of the truism thus expressed by Dr Ajit M. Banerjee: '. . . behavioural aspects are no less important than mechanistic concepts of unity of command, span of control, precedents and rules; and unless they are paid due attention, it is doubtful if any administrative reforms or reorganisation based largely on the scientific management approach will effectively and comprehensively improve the operations of government' ('Fifteen Years of Administrative Reform', *IJPA*, July–Sept. 1963, p. 456).

with authority commensurate with responsibility, from the top to the bottom of the hierarchy; and that the Secretariats must confine themselves to the policy-making and policy-reviewing functions for which they were designed. Progress in these directions, however, has been slow, barely keeping pace with the increase in the number of administrative agencies and in the volume of their work.

Personnel is the key problem, and it was to this that the 'Reform of Public Administration' chapter of the First Plan next turned. Personnel requirements, it considered, could be divided into three categories: '(*a*) administrative (including economic), (*b*) scientific and technical, and (*c*) subordinate and clerical'. The first two were short in both numbers and qualifications, the third in qualifications but not in numbers. This was clear enough; but indicative of the hurry in which the plan had been drawn up and of the insufficient information upon which it had been based was the lack of any attempt to quantify needs. Equally notable, and more serious, was the failure to recognize and provide for the vastly increased demands that successive plans would make for qualified scientific and technical manpower. The 'Public Administration' chapter did no more than note that there was a shortage; the chapter on 'Education', after mentioning that there had been an 'extensive development in the provision of courses leading to degrees and diplomas' in technology, suggested that, until the Technical Manpower Committee of the All-India Council for Technical Education had assessed the country's needs, 'it would be advisable to consolidate the work of existing institutions and not to embark upon new ventures', except in certain specialized fields.[4] Such caution had much to recommend it, but the fact that not even an interim assessment of needs was attempted shows how far the Commission, at this stage, underestimated the importance of manpower planning. Not until the process of formulating the Second Plan, with its emphasis on heavy industry and large-scale projects, revealed the width of the gap between supply and demand, was this matter treated with the seriousness that it merited; and by then much valuable time had been lost. Unfortunately, it has never been recovered. Tarlok Singh himself admits that, throughout the period of planning, the approach to personnel problems 'has been cautious and conservative, especially in relation to technical personnel', and that 'invariably, the requirements have been either underestimated or reckoned for too short a period'.[5]

On another aspect of personnel policy, too, the planners revealed some rather ominous mental limitations. One of the characteristics of Indian administration is the concentration of decision-making ability at the top levels, where a few highly educated and carefully selected 'generalists'

[4] *FYP(1)*, p. 549.
[5] 'Administrative Assumptions in the Five Year Plan', *IJPA*, July–Sept. 1963, p. 341.

direct the work of large clerical staffs, trained to do little more than to obey instructions and conform with regulations. This has become one of the most potent causes of that over-centralization which the planners so frequently deplore. Clearly the remedy is to strengthen the middle- and lower-level administrative cadres, so that they can be trusted with greater discretionary authority. At the time of the preparation of the First Plan, however, the minds of the planners were working very largely within the confines of the old system. The plan report provides no evidence that much serious thought was at this time being given to the recruitment and training of subordinates. Attention was over-concentrated on the IAS and on comparable services in the states. This limitation of outlook has tended to persist; even today most discussions of Indian administrative problems are excessively IAS oriented.

The main proposals under 'Personnel', in fact, did little more than emphasize the need to 'supplement' the existing administrative services by recruiting people with special qualifications for (*a*) 'economic' work, (*b*) managing industrial enterprises, and (*c*) work in development, land reform, and food administration. For economic work it was suggested that efforts should be made to recruit qualified and experienced people who had exceeded the normal age-limit for entry into the civil service;[6] that junior officers should be specially selected for 'economic' training; and that there should be an extension of the existing practice of 'obtaining for responsible senior positions individuals with special experience and knowledge from other fields such as universities, banking and finance and industry'. These proposals were sound enough in themselves, but they tended to assume that the prestige of the government service would remain high enough to attract people for whom the very development of the economy might offer tempting opportunities elsewhere. This may have seemed a reasonable assumption in 1952, but it has been progressively falsified by subsequent experience.

For the two other categories no specific proposals were made. The formation of an industrial management cadre was said to be 'under consideration', as indeed it was. As far as people capable of undertaking developmental, land reform, and food administration work were concerned, the Commission could hardly avoid admitting that it was still ignorant of the extent of the need. The strengthening of this third category, it said, *might* 'call for supplementary recruitment, depending upon the situation in individual states'.

On methods of recruitment, the Commission was justly critical of the

[6] There was nothing very revolutionary about this suggestion, as 'emergency' and 'special' recruitment had already been used to make good the loss of 600 ICS officers through repatriation and 100 through partition. For details see V. S. Hejmadi and V. A. Pai Panandikar, 'The Public Services; Recruitment and Selection', ibid. pp. 355–7.

archaic and dilatory procedures employed by the Union and state Public Service Commissions. It demanded, among other things, that there should be closer contact between the Commissions and the departments, particularly for the purpose of expediting recruitment and reducing the large number of temporary and *ad hoc* appointments (for which the slowness of the normal recruiting methods was largely responsible). It also suggested, very reasonably, that 'methods and procedures adopted for selection to different kinds of posts—administrative, technical, scientific, etc.,—should be continually reassessed and adapted to meet new requirements'.[7]

Among a collection of rather vague remarks about training was the proposal to develop the IAS Training School at New Delhi into 'a kind of staff college for higher grades of administrative persons serving both at the Centre and in the States'. This proposal foreshadowed the creation of the present National Academy of Administration at Mussoorie.

From personnel the planners turned to methods. The traditional ones, they said, were adapted to a former situation in which 'the magnitude of the government's business was small and personnel for exercising supervision was available in adequate measure'. To devise more up-to-date ones required continuous study, for which the central government should equip itself with an Organization and Methods Division. This recommendation was put into effect some fifteen months later, in March 1954. Whether the Commission's faith in 'O & M' was justified has subsequently become a matter for considerable controversy. The experience of the more developed countries indicates that 'O & M' offers the solution to many administrative problems, provided that suitable people can be found to staff the investigatory units and co-operative relationships can be established between these and the 'line' authorities. In the less developed countries, neither of these provisos is easy to realize, as India has discovered.[8]

The remainder of the Commission's suggestions about methods concerned 'the arrangements in government offices for supervision and

[7] Some improvements were subsequently made (for instance, see below pp. 288, 298–9), but rather slowly and haltingly. Uttar Pradesh, in its Third Plan report, admitted that during the Second Plan, 'procedural delays in recruitment . . . affected timely availability of personnel even in those categories in which apparently there are no shortages' (Uttar Pradesh, *FYP(3)*, i: *Rep.*, Nov. 1961, p. 27). Among the 'bottlenecks' listed by Punjab was 'recruitment of personnel through the Public Service Commisssion or the Subordinate Services Selection Board' (Punjab, *FYP(2): Review of Progress for 1956–7 & Plan for 1957–8* (1957)). The Union Public Service Commission, no doubt, is more competent than most of the state Commissions, but like them its staff suffers from 'lack of professionalization'. Perhaps it is due to the innate conservatism of the unspecialized administrators who serve it that 'despite a certain amount of public and academic criticism, the methods employed in the recruitment and selection to the public service have not materially changed' (Hejmadi & Panandikar, *IJPA*, July–Sept. 1963, p. 364).

[8] A balanced survey of the achievements and shortcomings of 'O & M' in India is provided by R. N. Vasudeva, 'Organisation and Management: the Centre', and A. Avasthi, 'Organisation and Management: the States', ibid.

inspection', which it found inadequate. It particularly stressed the importance of improving human relations between superiors and subordinates. It deplored the fact that 'reports on the work of individual officials' had become 'less specific and less objective than before', and that 'the easy course of neither blaming nor praising' was frequently adopted. It also condemned the prevalent use of seniority as the main criterion for promotion. The Commission was here in the field of well-known abuses and deficiencies and its treatment of them rarely rose above the level of the hortatory. On the important subject of evaluation, however, it could do little more than demand that this 'should become a normal administrative practice in all branches of public activity'; for it could point to its own recently-formed PEO as an example of the systematic organization of this activity.

More definite, if unduly timid, proposals were made for strengthening administration in the states. Perhaps out of deference to the states' well-known prejudices, it avoided recommending the creation of any new all-India services, but suggested that the central government 'should investigate the possibility of establishing Central development cadres in fields of technical development, such as agriculture, engineering, forests and public health'. No action, however, was taken on this *pis-aller* recommendation, and no new all-India services were even agreed to in principle until 1961, when the Council of States passed a resolution by the necessary two-thirds majority in favour of constituting an Indian Service of Engineers, an Indian Forest Service, and an Indian Medical and Health Service. Since then, the necessary legislation has been passed, and consideration is now (1964) being given to the constitution of all-Indian Agricultural and Education Services. On the much-discussed 'deputation' system, the Commission agreed that this should continue and should be used for technical as well as for administrative personnel.[9]

On the administration of public enterprises, which the expansion of the public sector of the economy was making a vital subject, it rather wisely refrained from expressing any opinion, on the grounds that sufficient experience had not been gained 'to permit any conclusions regarding the working of different undertakings or the results of the present pattern of organisation and management'. It considered, however, that there was need for 'a central board which could give detailed attention and advise the government in respect of questions of general importance for the public sector as a whole, such as personnel for industrial management, financial and accounting problems, price policies, investment programmes

[9] For very different views of the 'deputation' system, see (*a*) Bombay Admin. Enquiry Ctee, *Rep.* (1948), and (*b*) Bengal, Admin. Enquiry Ctee, *Rep.* (1944–5). These are conveniently summarized by Jitendra Singh in 'The Administrative Reform Reports of the States: a Content-Analysis', in *IJPA*, July–Sept. 1963, pp. 509–11.

etc'. This somewhat ambiguous proposal, which bore all the hall-marks of a verbal compromise between conflicting opinions, seems to have been a pale reflection of Gorwala's dangerous demand for 'one big board' to supervise and co-ordinate all the state enterprises.

Perhaps the most important proposal in this chapter was that the Union and state governments should get together with the Commission to study the whole subject of financial control. No specific justification of it was offered, except the suggestion that existing methods fell somewhat short of certain broadly specified *desiderata*. To see how urgent it had become, if the schemes in the Five-Year Plans were to achieve any *élan*, we have to turn to the Estimates Committee's report on 'Administrative, Financial and other Reforms',[10] published some eighteen months later. Criticizing the system whereby all items of expenditure were subject to multifarious checks and sanctions by the Ministry of Finance, the Committee stressed that this had gone so deep into the minds of administrators that 'even where there are delegations of powers and the administrative Ministry could normally take decision itself, it has often resorted to consultation with the Ministry of Finance in order to escape any criticism later on'.[11] Of the procedure for budgetary sanction of schemes, the Committee presented the following rather horrifying picture:

At present, the Budget Estimates for the following financial year are prepared towards the middle of the current financial year and are broadly stated. The Budget Division of the Ministry of Finance receives the various proposals from the Ministries in one lump during one or two months towards the close of the financial year. Consequently, the Budget Division does not have sufficient time to examine the proposals in greater detail and to scrutinise each and every item carefully. The practice has, therefore, been that the Budget Division applies broad checks and determines certain gross amounts for the various schemes without committing itself or the Ministry of Finance to their spending during the next financial year. The system is that whatever has been included in the estimates is merely with a view to get the vote of the House thereon and does not entitle the administrative Ministry to incur expenditure unless a detailed expenditure sanction has been issued by the Ministry of Finance. This means that after the Budget is voted by Parliament and the Financial year has set in the Ministry concerned begins to think about the proposals and to prepare detailed estimates and other justification for its execution. In this process, considerable time elapses before the Ministry of Finance and the administrative Ministry agree to proceed with the scheme. After the administrative Ministry has got the concurrence of the Ministry of Finance, it then sets about to get the necessary manpower, the sites, the buildings or other equipment which in turn

[10] EC, 1953–4: *9*.

[11] Ibid. p. 3. This is apparently still the case. The Secretary of the Expenditure Dept, Min. of Finance—himself a strong advocate of more rational forms of expenditure control—assured me in October 1962, that ministries did not demand delegations of financial power and were reluctant to accept them.

take their own time under the complicated rules of the machinery of Government. The result is that by the time the Ministry prepares to start a scheme or to go ahead with it, a good part of the year is already over and it is suddenly found at the end of the year that the non-utilised funds may lapse or that they may have to approach again the Ministry of Finance for including the amounts in the Budget and according fresh expenditure sanction. It appears to the Committee that this procedure is, to say the least, irksome, wasteful of time and money, and hampers initiative.[12]

Since this report was issued, many improvements in financial procedure have been made, as we shall see; but the essential problem, of ensuring proper public accountability without hamstringing the whole developmental process, has not been solved. The Planning Commission's *Papers on Measures for Strengthening of Administration*, prepared in connexion with the Third Five-Year Plan, said that the new procedures introduced in 1958 and 1959 had not 'worked as intended mainly because Ministries [had] not found it possible as a rule to furnish adequate details of their schemes before the framing of the Budget'. It also noted that these procedures had 'not materially reduced the need for consultation with the Finance Ministry especially in establishment matters', and maintained that there was 'need for a much larger delegation of powers to individual Ministries in the use of funds provided in their budgets'.[13] All of which goes to show that there is nothing more difficult, or more necessary, in a country which largely relies for its economic development on massive programmes in the public sector, than to loosen the stranglehold of the Finance Ministry over departmental expenditure. In theory, the need is everywhere recognized; in practice, it is well-nigh impossible to persuade administrators or parliamentarians that 'liberalization' will result in anything but an orgy of extravagance and peculation.

The fault, of course, does not lie exclusively with the Ministry of Finance. It also lies, as the authors of the First Five-Year Plan said, in the failure of the ministries and other executive agencies 'to plan carefully and in detail in advance of execution'. Basing their judgement on the experience of the First Plan's first eighteen months, the planners held that far too many projects had received acceptance in principle or in respect of their preliminary stages before they were ripe for implementation, with the result that unceasing control over the 'minutiae of expenditure' became the uneconomic substitute for proper planning.[14] Criticism on this score has been an ever-recurring theme, and sufficient improvements have been introduced to prevent the whole governmental machine from breaking

[12] Ibid. pp. 4–5.
[13] Cabinet Secretariat, *Papers on Measures*, p. 11. Such 'larger delegation' was actually made in 1961 and 1962, as we shall see (pp. 294–5 below).
[14] *FYP*(*I*), p. 124.

down. Nevertheless, the already-quoted *Papers on Measures* document of 1961, and the Third Five-Year Plan itself, found it necessary substantially to reiterate what the First Plan had said on the subject. 'Without advance planning and accurate estimate of costs', wrote the planners, 'the success of a project cannot be assured. It is also essential that programming techniques should be improved continuously so as to secure at each stage the maximum benefits from the outlays incurred and to achieve the targets within the budgetting time and resources.'[15] To this the statement laid before the Lok Sabha on 10 August 1961 added ominously: 'Arrangements for technical preparation of projects and scheduling of work relating to them require to be strengthened, particularly as information relating to a large proportion of projects included in the Third Plan is still unsatisfactory.'[16]

So far as these broad administrative problems are concerned, the First Plan report did little more than define them and suggest the general lines along which solutions might be sought. But on district administration the planners presented a series of much more specific suggestions, based upon a fairly detailed analysis of the impact on the district of the community programmes.[17]

The need for a reorientation of district administration arose partly from the breakdown of the old arrangements in many areas, and partly from the attempt to convert a regime mainly geared to the maintenance of law and order and the collection of revenues into one capable of coping with the tasks of economic and social development. The traditional relationship between the district administrator and 'influential persons such as *zamindars*, *zaildars*, village headmen and the like' had been disintegrating in the latter days of British rule; land reform gave it the *coup de grâce*, at least in the *zamindari* and *jagirdari* areas. Here it was necessary 'to create a new system of village administration', and even a 'new system of village records'—an immense administrative task. Elsewhere, the imposition of restrictions on the rights of large landholders and the conferment of new rights on tenants and agricultural labourers

[15] *FYP(3)*, p. 282.
[16] Cabinet Secretariat, *Papers on Measures*, p. 3. The necessity for such 'strengthening' is underlined by the following quotation from Andhra Pradesh's *FYP(3)*, which is dated 10 Dec. 1960—less than six months before the Third Plan's date of commencement: 'Unless the implementing agencies . . . start now . . . finalising the details of the schemes and getting the plans and estimates ready, fixing the responsibilities of officers at district and lower levels, making advance arrangements for the procurement of scarce materials like iron, steel, cement, coal and imported equipment, initiating land acquisition proceedings etc., it would not be possible to better our past performance . . . .' Andhra, of course, is one of the more backward states administratively, and its *cri de coeur* may be contrasted with the self-confidence of Maharashtra, which reported that better preliminary surveys and investigations were being organized and referred to the activities of its Water Resources Investigation Circle, Central Designs Organization, Engineering Research Institute, and Irrigation Commission (Maharashtra, *FYP(3)*, p. 144).
[17] *FYP(1)*, ch. 7.

called for 'sustained administrative action at various levels reaching down to the village'. Simultaneously, in all areas, there was the problem of staffing, guiding, enthusing, and co-ordinating the various technical services, each of which was trying to reach the cultivator through its own thinly spread, inadequately trained, and departmentally-minded personnel. These things had to be done, moreover, by a machine which had been considerably disorganized as a result of excessively frequent changes in the administration of food controls, which had 'sometimes been instituted without sufficient regard to administrative implications'.

The basic solution to these problems, the planners considered, was to place primary emphasis on 'the implementation of development programmes in close co-operation and with the active support of the people'. More specifically, the reorganization of district administration had to provide for:

(1) strengthening and improvement of the machinery of general administration;
(2) establishment of an appropriate agency for development at the village level which derives its authority from the village community;
(3) integration of activities of various developmental departments in the district and the provision of a common extension organisation;
(4) linking up, in relation to all development work, of local self-governing institutions with the administrative agencies of the State Government; and
(5) regional coordination and supervision of district development programmes.

With the second and fourth of these recommendations, which represented the first tentative steps towards that 'democratisation' of district and local administration which culminated in the adoption of *panchayati raj*, we shall be concerned in a later chapter. It is worth mentioning here, however, that the Commission already showed some awareness of the various dichotomies that made this policy so difficult to pursue. There was the contradiction between the desire to develop democracy at the grass roots and the obviously decadent condition of most of the existing self-governing bodies. There was the evident danger of relying 'only upon those who are chosen by popular vote', which the Commission, with little sociological insight, hoped to offset by introducing the co-optive principle. There was the equally evident danger of entrusting bodies which had 'little understanding of social needs and of their own obligations' with the administration of sizeable resources. These problems, however, received hardly more than interstitial mention, and such awareness of them as the Commission may have had did not prevent it from suggesting the conferment, by legislation, of an extraordinarily large number of difficult responsibilities on the village panchayats.[18] As we shall see, the contradictions thus vaguely foreshadowed in the First Plan have become intensified, as a result of the decision to force the pace of democratic decentralization, to such an extent that the Prime Minister himself, in a rather desperate defence of *panchayati raj*, said: 'We must give power to the people even though it leads us to hell.'[19]

On the more 'straight-line' needs of district administration (nos 1, 3, and 5) the First Plan had some useful suggestions to make. The provision of a senior assistant to the grossly overworked District Officer, the elimination of unnecessary bureaucratic formalities, the recruitment and training of village revenue officials in the permanently settled and *jagirdari* areas, and the training of all revenue officials in rural development work were among obvious ones. The Commission also thought that attention should be paid to the excessive size of some districts and to the creation of an adequate number of subdivisional administrative units. These proposals for 'filling in' the district hierarchy (which still tended to suffer from the traditional disease of being all top and bottom) were accompanied by an attempt to persuade state governments of the advantages of interposing between the state capital and the district a regional unit, headed by 'an officer who is not himself involved in detailed administration and development in his area'. This was justified on two grounds, viz. (1) that district plans 'would gain in value' if they were 'also part of well-considered regional plans', and (2) that many District Officers were new and raw and needed guidance of a kind that they could hardly obtain from a comparatively distant state administrative headquarters. The planning point was well made, but the suggestion of a new supervisory level was rather a desperate remedy for what the Commission described as a 'fairly general decline in standards of training, supervision and performance' in the district. The Commission did not, apparently, consider the compatability, in Indian administrative conditions, between the creation of this additional step in the hierarchy and the satisfaction of its demand that district officers should not have their time taken up 'in matters such as formal attendance on higher authorities and submission of reports'.

It did recognize, however, that no improvements in administrative arrangements could take the place of the development of more adequate cadres. Its suggestions on this subject, although rather vague, contained the important point that the growth of efficient administration would be

[18] The academic exercise of listing the functions that panchayats might be called upon to perform was excessively popular at one time. It culminated in the list of 41 functions produced by the Development Commissioners' Conference at Mysore City in 1959 (Nat. Conf. on CD at Mysore City, *Main Recommendations and Conclusions*, pp. 1–29).

[19] *IN*, 10 Aug. 1963. It is only fair to add that his next sentence was: 'We will certainly come out of hell if we get there.'

assisted if 'there were liberal opportunities for the best among the personnel of the State services to enter the all-India services'. Today this requirement is satisfied (although whether adequately so is still a matter of controversy) by the earmarking of 25 per cent of the posts in the IAS for recruits from the state Administrative Services.

By and large, the Commission's proposals on district administration were well-conceived, providing the inspiration of many subsequent improvements. As in most aspects of Indian administration, however, one has the strong impression that reforms have hardly kept pace with growing requirements, with the result that the old problems persist and even become aggravated. In respect of district administration, this impression is confirmed by the latest report on the subject, produced for the Planning Commission by Sir V. T. Krishnamachari.[20] This emphasizes the continued inadequacy of arrangements for training members of the state Administrative Services, and lays down once again the desideratum that 'the network of administrative and technical services in the State should . . . function as a well-knit structure at all levels with their duties clearly defined and enforced' and with 'an uninterrupted chain of responsibility in administrative and technical matters reaching down to the village units'. These principles, says the author, are embodied in laws and rules and the state authorities recognize them as valid. It only remains that 'they should be embodied in administrative practice'.[21] The gap between theory and practice is at its widest in district administration, which not only faces the most difficult of all developmental assignments but has had to adapt itself to a veritable political revolution, the introduction of *panchayati raj*, towards the end of one planning period and at the beginning of another.

Assessment of the administrative progress achieved during the First Plan and some analysis of the new problems that had arisen were presented in the Second Plan report, and in the subsequently-published *Review of the First Five Year Plan*. In the meantime, however, two further critiques of Indian administration had appeared: the Estimates Committee's report on 'Administrative, Financial and other Reforms'[22] and the document known as the First Appleby Report.[23]

That informed Indians were well aware of the deficiencies of the administrative machine and of the reforms required for their rectification emerges from a comparison between these two documents, the one produced by an all-party committee of MPs, the other by an American expert of international repute. But neither said very much by way of

[20] Plan. Com., *Rep. on Indian and State Administrative Services and Problems of District Administration*, by V. T. Krishnamachari (Aug. 1962).

[21] Ibid. p. 51. [22] See above, n. 10.

[23] P. H. Appleby, *Public Administration in India: Rep. of a Survey* (Cab. Sec., 1953).

criticism and suggestion that had not already appeared, in embryo, in the Gorwala report and the report on the First Five-Year Plan. Their importance lies less in their originality than in the stimulus they gave to the cause of administrative reform by provoking a widespread and sometimes acrimonious discussion of the subject. This is particularly true of the Appleby report, the first survey by an outsider of Indian administration since independence.

Most of Paul Appleby's criticisms, very general in character, had a familiar ring, but were expressed with a trenchancy that compelled attention. He discussed the slowness and unimaginativeness of administrative procedures, the 'didactic and confining' Rules of Business, the diseconomies of meticulous financial control, the lack of 'programme consciousness', the inadequacy of checks on performance, the 'feudalistic heritage' in personnel policies, and the 'astonishing' absence of effective administrative delegation. All of these had at least been referred to in the First Plan report, and many of them also figured prominently in the Estimates Committee's 'Administrative, Financial and other Reforms'. More useful, because less emphasized in previous studies, was his attribution, in part, of over-centralization to a lack of adequately qualified intermediate personnel, for which he proposed the remedies—in language rather typical of American public administration specialists—of 'more . . . lateral proliferation . . . at lower levels' and 'a substantial increase in hierarchical depth'. Even more apposite was his reference to an 'unconscious' and highly deleterious form of delegation, whereby 'the view of the man at the bottom of the hierarchy who writes the first 'note' on a file is all-important in most instances'.[24]

Like the Estimates Committee, he was particularly concerned with the clumsy and time-wasting administrative and financial relationships that were developing between the centre and the states in connexion with the formulation and implementation of developmental projects. Most developmental matters, he wrote,

> are likely to wend their laborious ways through . . . different organisations (e.g. Food and Agriculture, Health, Education, Commerce and Industry, Natural Resources, Rehabilitation, States and Finance, Planning Commission, Railway Board). They move . . . in three stages—first, and properly, as broad programs, second as particular projects under the programs, and third, as particular problems arising under the projects, when such detailed and widespread review is almost inexcusable. When foreign exchange or rationed material are involved, they will have to travel additional paths.

As a result,

> the influence that is associated with Central financial assistance is so cumbered

[24] Ibid. pp. 20, 23.

by an intricate system of multiple reviews both in the States and in the Centre that the Centre often may be said to rescue the States from trouble rather than stimulating [*sic*] the States to bold, big, new action. And responsibility for all this is so diffused that almost no one knows who can be held accountable for what.[25]

This was plainly put, and might well have stimulated immediate action. Unfortunately, interest in these matters was soon to be pushed aside by the politically explosive issue of state boundaries, and little could be done until the reorganization of the states had been completed. As we shall see in Chapter X, it was not until the later stages of the Second Five-Year Plan, by which time the whole problem had become exceedingly acute, that simplification and rationalization were seriously attempted.

On the more general questions of centre-states relationships, Appleby was less helpful, displaying a degree of political obtuseness surprising in one who had lived under a federal form of government. To him, the constitutional powers of the states seemed little more than an arbitrary obstacle to rational developmental administration. Of power and irrigation projects, he said that 'such undertakings should be exclusively carried on by the Centre, without control being shared by the states'; and he raised the question whether there was any 'consistent theoretical reason' for putting public health, agriculture and fisheries *exclusively* in the jurisdiction of the states', while leaving 'the regulation of mines and mineral resources in the national jurisdiction'.[26] Of course there was no consistent theoretical reason, any more than there is for the division of powers between the federal and state governments in the United States constitution; but there were plenty of highly persuasive reasons of a practical political kind. The proposal to concentrate responsibility for power and irrigation in central hands simply showed how little he was aware of these. His fellow countryman, Professor Henry Hart, in *New India's Rivers*,[27] displayed much more political horse-sense.

The Appleby report was influential partly because of the shock tactics which it employed. No serious-minded Indian could fail to sit up and take notice when a great foreign expert said of the Community Projects Administration, as Appleby did: 'I can recall having encountered no equally self-defeating organisational lay-out'.[28] More importantly, however, it was known that Appleby had the ear of Nehru, who reposed that degree of confidence in him that the Prime Minister reserved for a small

[25] Ibid. p. 45. During the First and Second Plans, some of the most notorious delays in obtaining technical clearance were the responsibility of the Central Water and Power Commission. An extreme case of three years was quoted to me by the Planning Secretary of Andhra Pradesh. An improvement was later effected by the application of the rules (*a*) that schemes of less than Rs10 lakhs should be exempt from technical clearance, and (*b*) that there should be no technical clearance in respect of annual financial allotments for approved schemes.

[26] Ibid. pp. 43, 17. [27] Calcutta, 1956. See particularly ch. IX.

[28] *Public Admin. in India*, p. 49.

circle of chosen advisers, among whom Solomon Trone, P. C. Mahalanobis, and Krishna Menon are perhaps the best-known names. It is for this reason, perhaps, that the more easily operable of Appleby's recommendations, such as the creation of an Organization and Management or Public Administration Office, the establishment of a government-sponsored Institute of Public Administration, and the development of academic graduate programmes in public administration, were fairly rapidly put into effect.

In 1956 Appleby returned to India and produced a second report, clumsily entitled *Re-examination of India's Administrative System with Special Reference to Administration of Government's Industrial and Commercial Enterprises*.[29] With the part of this document which deals with public enterprise we shall be later concerned. The general re-examination repeated the previous criticisms with variations, and gave special attention to the role of the 'reviewing agencies', i.e. the Ministry of Finance, the Ministry of Home Affairs, the Comptroller and Auditor-General, and the Central Purchasing and Central Construction Units. This report pointed to Parliament itself as one of the main sources of over-centralization, in as much as parliamentarians subjected civil servants to continuous pettyfogging criticism and tried to keep the administration on too tight a string. Moreover, Parliament's prestigious watch-dog, the Comptroller and Auditor-General, was singled out as 'a primary cause of a widespread and paralysing unwillingness to decide and to act.'[30] This attack, although justified, was decidedly tactless, and provoked hostile reactions in the Lok Sabha,[31] to which the somewhat aggressive Americanism of the language of the report added fuel. It offers, indeed, a classic example of the attempt by a foreign adviser to step beyond a line which can rarely be usefully crossed.

(iii)

By the time that the Second Five-Year Plan was ready to go into operation, therefore, the central government was far better equipped with advice on matters administrative than it had been in 1952. Experience in implementing the First Plan, moreover, had underlined certain old lessons and taught a few new ones.

However, neither the Second Five-Year Plan report nor the *Review of the First Five Year Plan*, published about a year later, undertook any systematic assessment of progress in public administration. Only with regard to state and district administration was there any attempt to answer the question how far the First Plan recommendations had been put into effect. Here the planners could record some progress in strengthening

[29] Cabinet Secretariat, O & M Division, 1956. [30] Ibid. pp. 28, 45.
[31] LSD, pt 2, viii, 6555–605, 10 Sept. 1956.

and rationalizing the administrative machine, but little in developing those organs of local democratic participation in which they had come to place such great faith.

The shortage of administrative cadres, particularly in the newly integrated states, had been 'largely made good', while some of the burden on the top people in the administrative hierarchy had been eased by the appointment of additional District Officers and of District Development or Planning Officers, and by greater delegation of authority.[32] The Commission offered no examples of these improvements, but there is plenty of evidence, from 1955 and 1956, that some of the states were at least trying to modernize their administrative machines. The Punjab, for instance, reported that new sub-divisions were being created and greater authority was being given to sub-divisional officers. At the district level, a newly-appointed 'General Assistant' was to act as 'Principal Administrative Officer to the Deputy Commissioner' (i.e. to the District Officer), with special responsibilities for control of the office and for the investigation of complaints from the public.[33] Travancore-Cochin (at this time under President's Rule) announced its discovery that

> for the effective implementation of the Five Year Plan it was essential to decentralise power and delegate it on the one hand to Heads of Departments and their district representatives as the agency primarily responsible for the execution of the Plan, and on the other to Collectors and the Revenue Divisional Officials as the agency responsible for securing coordination of the departments at district and taluk levels.[34]

Accordingly, considerably enhanced financial authority was given to the administrative departments, while Collectors (i.e. District Officers) were declared heads of district administrations.[35] The Rajasthan Administrative Enquiry Committee recommended,[36] *inter alia*, the limitation of the secretariat departments to their true functions of policy formation and general administrative supervision, the creation of a Planning and Development Department with special responsibility for the Community Projects, the strengthening of the staff of the collectorates, the separation of revenue from development work, and the up-grading of Block Development Officers (BDOs). To discourage 'elaborate noting by the subordinate staff' of the Secretariat, orders went out that a case should not normally be seen by more than two officers (including the minister) after the Dealing Clerk had taken initial action. It was also said that 'the levels at which decisions were taken on cases of varying importance had . . . been clearly defined to reduce any vagueness'.[37] Many other examples might be quoted.

[32] *FYP(2)*, pp. 149–50. [33] *IJPA*, ii (1956), p. 177.
[34] President's Rule in Travancore-Cochin, *A Review of the Progress of Execution of the Second Five Year Plan Schemes* (1956), p. 1.
[35] *IJPA*, ii (1956), p. 272. [36] *Rep.* (1956). [37] *IJPA*, ii (1956), p. 377.

It cannot be said, however, that even in the best governed states reform was rapid or radical enough to keep pace with the ever increasing demands on the administration. As late as 1958, a study group of the Indian Institute of Public Administration reported that in the comparatively advanced state of Bombay an increase in administrative activity had not been offset by any greater delegation of financial authority, and that rapid promotions had combined with a fall in educational standards to reduce administrative efficiency.[38] One of the most serious problems, throughout the period of the plans, arose from the indiscriminate proliferation of administrative agencies, itself often the product of a series of *ad hoc* 'reforms'. In Mysore, for instance, responsibility for rural industrialization had by 1957 become divided between the Industries Department, the Rural Industrialization Department, the Community Projects Administration, the Agriculture Department, the Revenue Department, and the Electricity Department. Of general rural development in the same state, P. R. Dubashi wrote:

> There are the traditional rural water supply and rural communications schemes; there is the local development works scheme; there is the National Extension Service works programme; there are departmental development schemes, e.g. cheap design scheme for rural schools. The extent of the people's participation in these several schemes varies; powers of sanction of the appropriate officers differ, as also the methods of financing and powers to check measurements [*sic*]. No wonder one scheme tends to jeopardise the success of another.[39]

The framers of the Second Plan were, of course, fully aware of these problems. 'The existence of a larger number of agencies whose work has to be co-ordinated through a district plan', they wrote, 'suggests certain possibilities of reorganisation of development machinery in the districts'. But the kind of reorganization claiming most of their attention was that designed to evoke a higher level of popular participation. In respect of the development of democratic institutions in the district, they said, with great restraint, 'a certain hiatus had continued which it was necessary to remove'. The suggestions made in the First Plan about the association of representative bodies with the process of plan implementation had not been 'carried out to any great extent'. Almost all states had set up district development or planning committees, partly appointed and partly representative, but these had 'not secured the degree of participation and cooperation from the public which is implicit in the concept of district planning'. As for the panchayats, a little reading between the lines of pages 150–5 of the plan report was sufficient to indicate that their performance was rarely satisfactory and indeed frequently non-existent. To

[38] *The Problem of Financial Control in the Bombay State*, summarized in *IJPA*, iv (1958), pp. 435–50.
[39] 'Further Thoughts on Coordination', *IJPA*, iii (1957), pp. 16–21.

bring these various 'popular' bodies to life, the government and the Commission had come to the conclusion that real responsibility would have to be thrust upon them. Indeed, a general picture of the system of 'democratized' administration subsequently to be called *panchayati raj* had already formed in their minds, as the following important passage from the plan report clearly shows:

The need for creating a well-organised democratic structure of administration within the district is now being widely felt. In this structure village panchayats will have to be organically linked with popular organisations at a higher level. In some States it may be convenient to have a democratic body at the district level, in others at the level of sub-divisions. In either case there are two essential conditions to be aimed at. In the first place, the functions of the popular body should come to include, if necessary by stages determined in advance, the entire general development and administration of the area other than such functions as law and order, administration of justice and certain functions pertaining to revenue administration. The second condition is that for smaller areas within the district or sub-division such as development blocks or talukas, sub-committees of the popular body should be assigned clear functions in the implementation of local programmes.[40]

For the detailed working out of these proposals it was recommended that the NDC should set up a special investigatory body. (This, of course, was the origin of the Balvantray Mehta Committee.) In the meantime, district Development Councils and block (or taluka) Development Committees should be established, predominantly representative in composition and with wide advisory powers. Progress along these lines, thought the Commission, would emphasize 'two specially valuable features of district and area planning'.

Local programmes represent an area of common action significant for the welfare of the mass of the people in which differences in view and affiliation are of relatively small consequence. Secondly, working with one another and with the people and their representatives will go a long way to bring the outlook and attitudes of local officials in line with the requirements of the socialist pattern of society and to break down barriers between different grades which are themselves an impediment to success in the common effort.[41]

This, perhaps, was the Grand Illusion of the Second Plan period. What 'progress along these lines' actually meant will be considered in the chapter on 'Grass Roots'.

In respect of the more general administrative needs, the Commission was able to report progress on several fronts. The COPP had been brought into existence; an Organization and Methods Directorate had been

[40] *FYP(2)*, pp. 159–60. [41] Ibid. p. 163.

functioning for two years, and 'O & M' units had been established in many ministries and in some of the states; further arrangements had been made for the recruitment of experienced people to the IAS; the establishment of an Industrial Management Service (for public enterprises) had been decided on; and there was to be an Administrative Staff College, on the Henley model.[42] The plan itself, moreover, showed that the Commission, with the help of the Engineering Personnel Committee, was now able to present fairly precisely-calculated requirements for technical cadres.[43] Among the other features of the document that pointed towards improved administrative rationality was the proposal—unfortunately not to be fulfilled—for the drawing up of 'specific and detailed plans for each year', after the annual budget. The Commission had also become very much concerned with the 'expansion and strengthening' of the rather rudimentary planning apparatus to be found in most of the states.[44]

Its general view of the conditions of Indian administration, however, remained sombre. The basic deficiencies emphasized by the First Plan report not only persisted but had become more serious—so serious that the Commission even allowed itself to express doubts whether 'in its range and quality administrative action would prove equal to the responsibilities assumed by the Central and State Governments in the second five year plan'. As a result of experience in implementing the First Plan, much of the stress formerly placed on the resources bottleneck was now transferred to the administrative bottleneck. Indeed, this shift of emphasis may have gone too far; for hindsight suggests that the planners were guilty of exaggeration when they suggested that if the administration did its work 'with efficiency, integrity and a sense of urgency and concern for the community, the success of the second Plan would be fully assured'.[45] It was just not true that the plan resolved itself 'into a series of well-defined administrative tasks'. The difficulties subsequently experienced were as much the result of economic miscalculations as of administrative failures. At the comparatively remote level of the Planning Commission, it was all too easy to use the administration as a whipping-boy, to be alternately exhorted and abused.

Nevertheless, it cannot be gainsaid that some serious efforts at administrative reform were made during the period of the Second Plan, both at the centre and in the states. At the centre, the years 1958 and 1959 saw the changes in financial procedure to which reference has already been made.[46] Ministries were equipped with 'internal' financial advisers, in consultation with whom expenditure of up to Rs50 lakhs, within the approved budget,

[42] Ibid. pp. 132–7.
[43] See Ch. 8, 'Personnel Requirements and Training Programmes'.
[44] Ibid. pp. 138–40. [45] Ibid. p. 126. [46] See above, p. 276.

could be undertaken.[47] About the same time, the procedures whereby states obtained central approval for their plan expenditures were drastically simplified. Manpower planning was improved by the constitution of a Cabinet Committee on this subject and of a Directorate of Manpower in the Ministry of Home Affairs. The National Register of Scientific and Technical Personnel was reorganized and expanded, and the reports of the Engineering Personnel Committee (1956) and the Agricultural Personnel Committee (1958) gave the government, for the first time, a clear account of anticipated needs for technical cadres. Several new functional services were created (e.g. Statistics, Supply, Health, Information) and 'pooling' arrangements were made for specialists in economic administration, industrial management, and science and technology. In training, the tendency was towards broader syllabuses and the provision of refresher courses. The Administrative Staff College at Hyderabad opened its doors, and the newly established National Academy of Administration at Mussoorie (which replaced the old IAS training establishment in New Delhi) pioneered the breaking down of over-rigid service barriers by providing a 'foundation' course for all recruits to All-India and Class I central (non-technical) services.[48] The field of recruitment was widened by the government's acceptance of the Mudaliar Committee's[49] recommendation that a university degree should no longer be the minimum qualification for clerks and certain categories of junior officer, and prospects for the clerical employee (and therefore, presumably, his incentives) were improved by the decision to recruit upper division clerks exclusively by promotion from the lower division.[50] 'O & M' became quite the rage in the central government. It was laid down that the 'O & M' Division should be consulted before any staff was appointed to a new office or branch. To make the administration more economy-minded, the efforts of the Economy Unit in the Ministry of Finance were now supplemented by those of economy boards or committees in individual ministries and of economy 'cells' in individual departments. 'Outstanding issues' regarding economy and efficiency were to be referred to a top-level committee of secretaries.[51]

A few of the states, as soon as 'linguistic' reorganization was completed, appointed variously named committees to examine their administrative

[47] This reform did not prove very useful, as the powers given to the 'internal' advisers to refer matters to the Finance Ministry reduced it, in the words of the high official responsible for its *modus operandi*, to 'a farce'. Later, during the first year of the Third Plan, a scheme was introduced whereby a minister could either appoint his own financial adviser or use the services of one provided by the Ministry of Finance. In neither case could there be any 'reference' of expenditure covered by delegation. In respect of such items the financial adviser was a consultant only (see A. K. Chanda, 'A Profile of Financial Administration', *IJPA*, July-Sept. 1963).

[48] See S. P. Jagota, 'Training of Public Servants in India', in Braibanti & Spengler, *Admin. & Econ. Dev.*

[49] Public Services (Qualifications for Recruitment) Committee, *Rep.* (1956).

[50] *IJPA*, vi (1960), p. 298. [51] Ibid. iii (1957), pp. 392–5.

machines and to suggest reforms. Mysore went to the extent of calling in the redoubtable A. D. Gorwala, whose report, *The Mysore Administration: Some Observations and Recommendations* (1958), is a positive encyclopaedia of administrative malpractice. Everywhere, even in the most administratively backward states, such as Assam, some action was taken, particularly to bring under control the 'mounting administrative expenditures' which were eating so rapidly into resources earmarked for plan projects.[52] Andhra, for instance, attempted to economize on personnel by reorganizing its Secretariat, while Rajasthan announced a cut of 5 per cent in its ministerial staff. Attempts to simplify procedures and delegate responsibilities were also made.[53] Bombay introduced a greater delegation of financial powers to heads of departments and regional administrators;[54] Punjab produced the rather original idea of 'flying squads' to eliminate delays in the Secretariat and other government offices;[55] most state governments, following the example of the centre, set up 'economy committees';[56] and most were persuaded to inaugurate manpower studies in preparation for the Third Five-Year Plan.[57]

It is difficult to say what all this amounted to. There must have been some genuine improvement, in the absence of which no amount of foreign assistance could have rescued the Second Plan. But no fundamental changes occurred, either in organization or in attitudes. Painstaking subordinates, working slowly and unimaginatively within a framework of rather obsolete routines, continued to carry out the orders of a handful of highly intelligent but fantastically overworked top-level 'generalists', inadequately advised by an insufficient number of technical specialists. New approaches to training made only the slightest dent in this situation. The barriers to inter-service promotion remained high and the 'Pooh Bah' status of the IAS, obliquely criticized in the Second Plan report,[58] remained unshaken. Morale, particularly at the middle and lower levels of the services, was undermined by favouritism in promotion (in which caste politics often played a part), and by the continued erosion of inadequate salaries by inflation. Corruption certainly did not diminish, although the IAS and services of equivalent status seem to have remained—and indeed still do remain—relatively immune from it.

Independent India, in fact, had taken over an 'imperialist' administrative machine, with all its old virtues and vices, to which she had added a few new ones. The new virtues were mainly at the top, in the shape of a fresh generation of administrators who, although inferior to their predecessors in educational background and general 'culture', surpassed

[52] Ibid. vi (1960), p. 189. [53] Ibid. iv (1958), pp. 218–19.
[54] Ibid. v (1959), p. 100. [55] Ibid. iii (1957), p. 64. [56] Ibid. pp. 392–5.
[57] Ibid. iv (1958), pp. 95–96. The appointment of 'administrative reform' committees of various kinds in the states still continues (1964) (see *MTA*, pp. 58–59).
[58] *FYP(2)*, p. 134.

them in development-mindedness. The many vices clustered around the lower levels of the hierarchy, where literal-mindedness and petty corruption continued almost unchecked.

Perhaps the most extraordinary thing, to the observer unfamiliar with Indian conditions, was the retention, with only peripheral changes, of the old codes of civil service regulations, reasonably well adapted to the needs of a night-watchman state run by an expatriate administrative aristocracy, but ill adapted to those of a planned and economically developing society. Of administration in Uttar Pradesh, Professor Masaldan has written:

> Much of the difficulty and distress felt by the development departments under British rule was due to the complicated rules and their interpretation according to precedent. In this light, it is unfortunate that many of the rules have . . . continued unchanged. Budget rules are contained in the Budget Manual whose latest edition was published in 1941 under the Act of 1935, but which did not differ in substance from the one issued under the Act of 1919; Account rules as contained in the Financial Handbook have been in effect since 1925; the Fundamental Rules which deal with the financial aspect of personnel management were made in 1935; the Civil Services (Classification, Control and Appeal) Rules, which govern personnel management, were made in 1930. Amendments have been made from time to time but they refer mostly to details. The rules continue to remain complicated. A sub-committee of the U.P. Economy Committee suggested 'substantial simplification' of the rules contained in the Financial Handbook.[59]

All the reorganizations, the exhortations, and the 'O & M' studies of the Second Plan period made only a minor impact on this type of situation. The reason would appear to lie partly in a failure of nerve, partly in 'politics', and partly in sheer administrative inertia. Nervousness finds expression in a reluctance to tamper with a going concern—even though it may be going far too slowly—for fear that the result may be a complete breakdown. 'Politics' come into the matter in three ways. Firstly, the Indian bureaucracy itself constitutes a politically influential segment of society, with certain habits and expectations which it is reluctant to see disturbed. From its point of view, radical reform would at least involve the learning of new tricks by old dogs and might conceivably mean the wholesale dismissal of a mass of superfluous personnel which could not find alternative employment. For these reasons, there is a strong vested interest in retaining the familiar and employment-creating complexities of the system. Secondly, few politicians are interested in administrative reform as such, and are dependent on the bureaucrats themselves for such

[59] *Planning in Uttar Pradesh*, p. 25. It would, of course, be quite wrong to suggest that no effort has been made to bring the codes up to date. The centre, particularly, has given continuous attention to this matter (see *MTA*, p. 59). But even at the centre progress has been slow, while in many of the states it has been almost imperceptible.

advice on the subject as they receive. Thirdly, the attitudes of the politicians are in many cases *positively* unhelpful. Politicians are no less interested than the bureaucrats themselves in 'making work'; they persistently interfere, for self-interested reasons, with administrative processes which should be insulated from their direct influence; they seldom realize that their power over the administrator is one to be used with tact and discretion; they resent advice from the administrator which cuts across their prejudices and predilections; and they are a major source of the prevalent corruption. These political factors, which obviously favour the maintenance of the *status quo*, are reinforced by an inertia which comes from the genuine respect which the less imaginative of the bureaucrats feel for the established system, and the difficulty they experience in conceiving of any alternative set of arrangements which would be workable. In view of these obstacles, and of the fact that India is a democracy, it is not very surprising that the administrative *desiderata* laid down by the Second Plan report remained unrealized. It is their realization that would have been surprising.

Even so, there is still a balance of avoidable mistakes to put on record. Perhaps the most serious is the self-defeating character of some of the methods by which administrative reform was attempted. It seems to be *de rigueur*, in India, to try to cope with an administrative problem either by referring to it a 'high-powered' committee or by establishing a new *ad hoc* agency. (Usually it is the committee, in its report, which recommends the establishment of the agency.) This practice not only wastes time; it increases the complexity of the administrative apparatus and exacerbates the problem of co-ordination. 'High-powered committees' have become something of a joke among the more sophisticated Indian civil servants, and the proliferation of agencies reduces them to despair. The latter proclivity was the subject of a warning by Appleby[60] in 1956, when he pointed out the danger of 'special organisations within the government of such numbers and variety as to be unmanageable by government', and laid down the sound principle that 'in every marginal judgement, choice of expansion should be in favour of expanding a going organisation'.

In some respects his advice was followed, as in the bringing together under common managements of the steel plants and the fertilizer plans. But in general the Second Plan saw a positive riot of organization-creating, and if some of the 'high-powered committees' had had their way, still more would have littered the administrative field. The Agricultural Administration Committee,[61] for instance, wanted (1) a Food Production and Development Commissioner, who would 'coordinate the activities

[60] *Re-examination*, p. 13. [61] *Rep.* (1958).

of the various departments . . . so as to open up bottlenecks' and 'ensure the orderly execution of programmes'; (2) special agricultural officers in the Irrigation Department 'to serve as liaison between the agriculturalists and the State Departments of Agriculture'; (3) a Farm Advisory Service, 'to form an effective link between the research institutions and the field level extension agency'; and (4) an Agricultural Information Service, 'consisting of a trained staff of Information Officers specializing in mass communication methods'. The Foodgrains Enquiry (Asoka Mehta) Committee recommended, *inter alia*, the establishment of an inter-departmental Price Stabilization Board, a Foodgrains Stabilization Organization under the Ministry of Food and Agriculture, a Central Food Advisory Council, and a Price Intelligence Division.

Even in the field of 'O & M' there are *two* central agencies, the Organization and Methods Division and the Special Reorganization Unit. (Not surprisingly, the Estimates Committee, which has displayed much common sense on administrative matters, recommended that they should be united in 'a compact single organization which should be a model of efficiency based on considerations of maximum of economy'.)[62] Even the Planning Commission insists on retaining, for evaluatory purposes, a PEO *and* a COPP.[63]

Such proliferation not only makes co-ordination more difficult; it has the effect of inducing existing organizations to 'contract out' responsibilities which they alone can effectively discharge, particularly when the new organizations are of a supervisory or inspectoral kind. This effect was noticed by the acute A. D. Gorwala in his remarks about the establishment of an 'efficiency audit' in Mysore: 'Enquiries from those competent to know and judge invariably elicit the reply that because of the Efficiency Audit, no departments and offices are more efficient than they were; rather that many today are less efficient, on account of the absence of interest in this matter of those most immediately concerned.'[64] Even more scathing was the judgement of the Estimates Committee on the functioning of the central 'O & M' Division and the Special Reorganization Unit:

> After many years of working both had to be reorganized, and even then it cannot be said that they have performed functions commensurate with the expenditure incurred on them. Rather, the Committee regret to note, considerable time and money have been spent on futile work and, as the impression goes, the O and M Units have perhaps considerably added to the useless procedures and overburdened the already slow system of Secretariat working.[65]

[62] EC 1958–9: *55*, p. 17.

[63] It should be noted, however, that R. N. Vasuveda combines (1963) the posts of Joint Secretary, Reorganization Unit, Director, O & M Division, and Secretary, COPP.

[64] *Mysore Administration*, p. 56. [65] EC, 1958–9: *55*, p. 16.

(iv)

The framers of the Third Five-Year Plan, therefore, were not confronted with fewer administrative problems than their predecessors of 1952 and 1956. Most of the old problems remained and a series of new ones had arisen, particularly as a result of the transition to *panchayati raj* in the rural areas, which confronted officers at the district and block levels with difficult and unprecedented tasks.

The chapter on 'Administration and Plan Implementation' began with a statement which, if it had been meant literally, would have condemned the Third Plan to complete frustration: 'In the last analysis the Plan rests on the belief that the requisite effort will be forthcoming and that, at each level in the national life, within the limits of human endeavour, an attempt will be made to implement it with the utmost efficiency'.[66] If the plan had indeed rested on this belief, it would have been entirely utopian. As, therefore, it is insulting to the intelligence of the Commission to suppose that efforts up to or indeed anywhere near to 'the limits of human endeavour' were considered by them to be within the realms of the practicable, the statement must be interpreted as purely exhortatory. This is confirmed by the fact that their general presentation of the administrative problem was admirably realistic:

The past decade has been a period of considerable change and adaptation in the field of administration. Innovations have been introduced and new institutions established, although perhaps many of them have yet to be integrated with one another and with the structure as a whole. With the increase in the range of Government's responsibilities and in the tempo of development, the volume and complexity of administrative work has also grown. The administrative machinery has been strained and, at many points in the structure, the available personnel are not adequate in quantity and numbers. The administrative burden of carrying out plans of development, large as it is at present, will increase manifold under the Third Five Year Plan, and doubtless new problems in public relations will also come up. In the recent past, certain aspects of administration have attracted pointed attention. These include the slow pace of execution in many fields, problems involved in the planning, construction and operation of large projects, especially increase in costs and non-adherence to time-schedules, difficulties in training men on a large enough scale and securing personnel with the requisite calibre and experience, achieving coordination in detail in related sectors of the economy and—above all, enlisting widespread support and co-operation from the community as a whole. In the larger setting of the Third Plan, these problems are accentuated and gain greater urgency. It is widely realised that the benefits that may accrue from the Third Plan will depend, in particular in its early stages, upon the manner in which these problems are resolved. As large burdens are thrown on the administrative structure, it grows in size; as its size increases, it becomes slower

[66] *FYP(3)*, p. 276.

in its functioning. Delays occur and affect operations at every stage and the expected outputs are further deferred. New tasks become difficult to accomplish if the management of those in hand is open to just criticism. In these circumstances, there is need for far-reaching changes in procedures and approach and for re-examination of prevalent methods and attitudes.[67]

Although this was well said, the actual proposals which followed might be described as the mixture as before. Indeed, in the absence of any intention of completely recasting the administrative machine (which, politics apart, is an exceedingly hazardous operation to undertake in the middle of a series of development plans), they could hardly be anything else. Stress was laid on (*a*) the clearer definition of responsibility at the various levels, the elimination of unnecessary and time-wasting consultation on matters of detail, and the bolder delegation of financial powers; (*b*) the confining of the duties of the secretariats to those of 'policy, general supervision and the enforcement of standards'; (*c*) the judgement of administrative performance by results; (*d*) the breaking down of general targets into 'smaller units in terms of time-schedules and responsibility for execution'; and (*d*) the introduction of morale-building and performance-stimulating incentives, both material and non-material.[68]

Some of these proposals were spelled out in greater detail by the Commission in its *Papers on Measures for the Strengthening of Administration* and several became the subject of specific undertakings made by the government in the statement it laid before the Lok Sabha on 10 August 1961. This statement announced that, in future, 'ministries need not conform to a standard pattern of organisation', and indicated that further devolutions of responsibility for financial management would be made. A scheme about to be tried out in four ministries was to include:

(*a*) formulation of a programme for intensive pre-budget scrutiny between the Ministry of Finance and administrative ministry necessitating the preparation of budget estimates earlier than usual in cases in which actuals of the last year are not an important consideration, (*b*) further liberalisation of financial powers to the Ministries in order to avoid reference to Finance Ministry in the post-budget period except on vital matters and (*c*) the exercise of control of important financial aspects by the Finance Ministry through an adequate reporting system and test checks.[69]

[67] Ibid. p. 277. [68] Ibid. p. 279.

[69] Cabinet Secretariat, *Papers on Measures*, pp. 2–3. This scheme was later (1962) extended to all ministries. The 'pre-budget scrutiny', however, was not successful and in 1962–3 the Finance Ministry was constrained to permit the submission of 'lump-sum' appropriations at any time during the financial year. As soon as clearance had been given, by the prescribed 'pre-budget' process, to any project included in one of these appropriations, it became subject to the scheme of financial delegation (interview with Mr Boothalingam, then Secretary, Dept of Expenditure, Min. Fin., Oct. 1962).

To facilitate judgement by results, it was promised that officials in key posts should be kept in their jobs for at least five years. As a means of improving personnel management, control of staff up to and including Section Officers was to be transferred from the Ministry of Home Affairs to the individual ministries. To improve 'arrangements for technical preparation of projects and scheduling of work relating to them', it was proposed that work on the Fourth Plan should begin 'almost immediately' and that studies for Fourth Plan projects should be completed during the ensuing three years.

On 'Projects in the Public Sector',[70] the Third Plan report considered that experience had proved that the following 'lines of action . . . should help increase the speed and efficiency of implementation . . . and secure greater economies in . . . construction and operation': (1) the use, for larger projects, of a planning period in excess of the normal five years; (2) the improved organization of technical services, through the setting up of planning cells and panels of technical advisers in the appropriate ministries; (3) more adequate arrangements for scrutiny of cost estimates and examination of economic aspects; (4) better phasing, to reduce the gestation period and ensure a 'continuous flow of benefits from projects under execution at each stage of the Plan'; (5) the provision of 'suitable units for evaluation and review . . . which will function under the control of the top management authorities without . . . being involved in day-to-day operations'. Under the heading 'Economy in Construction',[71] these suggestions were supplemented by some solid management-textbook maxims that hardly require repetition here.

One of the problems causing the Commission particular disquiet was the excessively rapid turnover and general mal-utilization of India's scarcest resource, technical personnel. 'Work in projects as well as in important programmes,' wrote the planners, 'has frequently suffered because of rapid transfers of officials'.[72] For the more important assignments, they considered, five to ten years was 'rarely sufficient for producing large results'. Krishnamachari considered that instability of technical personnel at the level of district administration was 'fatal to efficiency,' and demanded 'urgent action' to put an end to it.[73] The government, as we have seen, gave its approval to assignments for a minimum of five years.

Another personnel problem stressed in the plan report was the 'considerable under-estimation of the management implications of large projects as well as of programmes of development in different fields'.[74] At last it was beginning to be realized that the quality of top-level management depended on that of middle-level management, since the former would have to be recruited mainly by promotion from the latter. An

[70] *FYP(3)*, pp. 280–2. [71] Ibid. pp. 285–7. [72] *Papers on Measures*, pp. 14–15.
[73] *Rep. on Ind. & State Admin. Services*, p. 52. [74] *FYP(3)*, p. 283.

ordinary government department could at least 'get by' with an organization based on the direction of the activities of a mass of semi-skilled subordinates by a handful of administrative aristocrats; but a development project with this pattern of organization was surely heading for disaster. The development of the 'middle grades of personnel', comparatively neglected in the previous literature of planning, was now recognized as important, although the Third Plan report still failed to deal with it at any length and the government's statement did no more than promise that the 'managerial skills of the public servants' would be increased 'through a sustained programme of executive development by training and counselling'.[75]

Little was said in the plan report about the methods of fulfilling the Commission's demand for 'a more positive approach' to the training of personnel, as the chapter on 'Personnel Requirements and Training Programmes' was largely devoted to estimating needs in the various categories and planning to meet them through the creation of new institutions and the expansion of existing ones. The government statement, however, was a little more specific, in that it announced that training arrangements would be undertaken 'to develop individual and group responsibility'. This was an implicit recognition of the failure—or at least the insufficiency—of the comparatively (and sometimes extremely) formal training methods hitherto employed. The problem was to use training schemes not merely to impart instruction but to make the administrator more 'action-oriented', and thereby correct what Appleby had recognized as the most 'general fault' in Indian administration, viz. 'the practice of seeking agreement on everything by everybody before anything is done'.[76] Some progress in this direction had already been achieved by the National Academy of Administration and the Administrative Staff College, but these institutions could only directly influence the attitudes of the very few at the top. Urgently needed, all down the line, was the type of training which, in the words of the statement, fostered initiative and a sense of individual responsibility.[77]

In the last section of the chapter on 'Administration and Plan Implementation', the planners turned again to some of the administrative problems presented by the planning process itself. Here they stressed the need for a better and speedier flow of information from the periphery to the centre. Had more attention been given to this, they considered, many of the mistakes made in the Second Five-Year Plan might have been avoided or mitigated. Thus:

In the first phase of the Plan, the decline in foreign exchange reserves might have been spread over a longer period and the consequent reductions in foreign

[75] *Papers on Measures*, p. 2. [76] Ibid. p. 13. [77] Ibid. p. 5.

exchange allocations might have been less drastic in relation to power development and the production of fertilisers. The considerable lags which occurred in the utilisation of irrigation from large and medium irrigation projects could have been reduced. The shortages and imbalances recently reflected in the difficulties of coal transport could have been countered in advance to a greater extent. Finally, the intensity of fluctuations and the rise in prices during the past two years might have been moderated.[78]

One may perhaps detect in this passage a tendency to use deficiencies in information-flow as an alibi. The 'imbalances' of the Second Plan were not simply the product of slow, inaccurate, and insufficient reporting. Many of them were inherent in the plan itself, as informed critics had frequently pointed out during the process of its formulation. Others arose, not from a lack of knowledge of what was happening but from a determination to persist, up to the eleventh hour, with policies which, although clearly mistaken, were thought to involve the government's prestige or had enlisted the support of powerful interest-groups. Nevertheless, the Commission was right in drawing attention to the problem of information flow, which was becoming more serious as 'large projects in industry, transport, power and other fields', involving 'complex technical and economic problems and vast amounts of expenditure', assumed 'an increasingly important place in national planning'. It was also right, and speaking from bitter experience, in criticizing former progress reports for lacking 'focus' and failing to bring to light current weaknesses or to anticipate problems requiring action.

What it did not recognize, or at least record, was one of the major reasons for these deficiencies. This lay deep in the nature of Indian administration. The Commission could issue a multitude of forms to make the task of reporting, at the lower levels, relatively simple and almost automatic; but it could not ensure that the information thus provided, to be added up and eventually transmitted to New Delhi in generalized form, was of real evidential value. Particularly in the countryside, officials were under pressure to show 'results'. Fear of reprimand, anxieties about promotion, and desire to please superiors entered into combination with low morale and lack of 'action-orientation' to produce reports which exaggerated or even invented achievements. Every district officer knew that this was taking place, but he himself was frequently under pressure and in any case short of means for checking and inspecting on the spot. No formal improvements in the methods of reporting, such as the Commission seemed to have in mind, could put this matter right. It required fundamental changes in the attitudes adopted and methods employed by administrators—and indeed by politicians. The Commission's

[78] *FYP(3)*, p. 288. In the *MTA* (p. 61) the Commission returns to this point, saying that 'while arrangements for reporting within each State have improved, these relating to reporting as between the States and the Centre are not quite satisfactory'.

announcement that it would be holding consultations on the subject with central ministries and state governments did not, therefore, hold out the prospect of radical change; but it is difficult to envisage what other action the Commission could have taken.[79]

The report's approach to the question of personnel[80] displayed one major strength and a number of weaknesses. The strength was in the field of manpower planning, where the Third Plan showed as notable an advance over the Second as the latter did over the First. Calculations had been greatly improved in precision, and estimates for the types of personnel requiring long periods of training (e.g. in engineering, technology, and science) were presented for the Fourth Plan as well as for the Third. The main weakness was the lack of a coherent view of personnel needs in the administrative services. In spite of the emphasis placed upon the improvement in the quality of middle-level personnel, the report's two paragraphs devoted to 'Administrative Services' were almost exclusively IAS-oriented.[81] Although never explicitly stated, the assumption that the administrative aristocracy could continue to play its omnicompetent role suffered little disturbance. Here, perhaps, we confront one of the deepest unconscious prejudices of the planners. More surprising was the further implicit assumption that, in spite of the vast new responsibilities that government was assuming, the size of this tiny aristocracy need undergo no more than a very moderate increase. Over the decade of planning, the strength of the IAS had increased from about 1,200 to over 2,000. For the Third Plan, additional requirements were put at 400. This would have brought it up to about half the strength of the British Administrative Class, with which, in respect of purpose and function, it may be most closely compared. Krishnamachari, it is true, pointed to the need for a more vigorous recruitment policy, but only for the purpose of ensuring that, by the end of the Third Plan the total strength of the cadre should reach the figure of 2,400, at which he expected it to be stabilized.[82] No one, apparently, asked the question whether a developing country as vast as India could afford to have an administrative pyramid so wide at the base and so narrow at the top. Many good men, of course, were doing highly responsible work in the state administrative services, which the

[79] The Commission, of course, is very dependent upon the quality of statistical services in the states. These vary from the fairly good to the very bad. All states made proposals, in their Third Plans, for the improvement of their statistical services. It was notable, however, that those with the more adequate services made the best proposals. Maharashtra, for instance, identified the following 'gaps' to be filled during the course of the Third Plan: (1) growth indicators, (2) information about the tertiary sector (e.g. the professions), (3) information on small-scale industries, (4) the socio-economic conditions of labour, (5) crop production, (6) demographic information, (7) distribution of incomes, (8) incidence of taxation (Maharashtra, *FYP(3)*, p. 145).

[80] *FYP(3)*, ch. 9 & pp. 283–4. [81] Ibid. pp. 179–80.

[82] *Rep. on Ind. & State Admin. Services*, pp. 7–13.

planners thought would have to undergo 'much larger increases' than those projected for the IAS. But the states themselves were desperately short of personnel of the quality that only the IAS could provide. A rapid increase in IAS strength might dilute that quality, of which India was justly proud; but it was difficult to believe that a country of 450 million people could not, with proper attention to higher education and post-entry training, produce more than 2,400 individuals qualified to occupy the top-level administrative posts.

District administration did not receive a separate chapter, as in the two previous plan reports; but much was said about it in the chapter on Community Development.[83] Here the planners had to walk somewhat warily, for the biggest problem confronting district administration, adaptation to *panchayati raj*, was an entirely new one. Democratic decentralization had only just been introduced, and several states had not even decided on how best to apply it. The 'suggestions . . . offered for ensuring the effective and successful working of Panchayati Raj institutions', therefore, were necessarily of a general, tentative, and hortatory kind. What emerged from them most clearly was the immense complexity and delicacy of the tasks now confronting the officials at all levels of the district administration.[84]

The introduction of the new system clearly offered an opportunity for overhauling a machine which, as the planners stated, had developed over the decade in a somewhat haphazard and uncoordinated manner. When the CD Programme had been introduced, from 1952 onwards, it was 'super-imposed on the traditional district administration without adequate connecting links'. Consequently many districts, even before the recent super-imposition of *panchayati raj*, were attempting to promote development policies through no fewer than four types of organization, three of them with separate and imperfectly co-ordinated hierarchies, viz.

(i) the revenue administration which looks after certain specified development functions, such as taccavi (i.e. loan) advances, recoveries, etc.;
(ii) the established Development Departments at the district, taluka and other levels;
(iii) the community development organisation with block officers and village level workers, linked at the village level with panchayats and co-operatives; and
(iv) Local Boards (where these have not yet been abolished).[85]

To put an end to this 'considerable overlapping', the Commission called for 'some measure of rationalization in district administration and fresh definition of functions and relationships'. As yet, however, nothing very radical has been attempted and most of the work remains to be done.

[83] Ch. 20. [84] *FYP(3)*, p. 340. [85] Ibid. p. 341.

Only on one administrative subject, the 'Organisation of Public Enterprises',[86] did the plan report break new ground. This subject had been raised rather tentatively in the two previous reports. The Commission now felt that, with many public enterprises already in operation and a new crop promised during the Third Plan, the time had come 'to give close attention to the question of how best to manage these enterprises'. The most interesting feature of this chapter was its revelation that the Commission had given up the search for an 'ideal' form of public enterprise. In the Second Plan report[87] it had recorded that the joint-stock company form was being 'increasingly adopted', expressed the opinion that the 'normal' government department failed to provide a suitable framework for industrial and commercial management, and stated that greater experience was necessary before 'a clear view as to the relative advantages of different forms of organisation could emerge'. At that time the Commission was more immediately interested in building up a cadre of managers to replace the civil servants and other unsuitably qualified people who had had to be used, as a temporary expedient, to staff the public enterprises.[88] In the Third Plan report, after referring to the three organizational forms currently in vogue—the department, the statutory corporation, and the joint-stock company—it assumed that the company would be the norm, particularly for manufacturing industry in the public sector. The Commission then went on, very sensibly, to discuss the practices and conventions which were required for the successful operation of any public enterprise, whatever its organizational framework might be.

For the most part, the Commission followed—although without specific acknowledgement—the proposals made in the second 'Appleby' report. It stressed the need for greater delegation of responsibility from the ministries to the boards, from the boards to the general managers, and from the general managers to subordinate managerial personnel. It demanded that the Financial Adviser attached to each enterprise should be an aid to management rather than a spy in the service of the Ministry of Finance. It advised on the composition and functioning of the board of directors and emphasized the key role of the managing director. It commended the policy of bringing together similar public enterprises in what Appleby had called 'coherent missions', through the creation of large companies such as Hindustan Steel Ltd, the Heavy Engineering Corporation, Heavy Electricals Ltd, Hindustan Insecticides Ltd, and the

[86] Ch. 16. [87] *FYP(2)*, pp. 136–8.

[88] Its main proposal was for the creation of an Industrial Management Service. During the course of this Second Plan, an industrial management 'pool' was actually created; but its functioning gave little cause for satisfaction. For an illuminating critique of this experiment, see H. K. Paranjape, 'The Industrial Management Pool: an Indian Administrative Experiment', IIPA, 1962.

Fertilizer Corporation. It gave great attention—as in the Second Plan report—to the development of more competent managerial cadres.

All this, like so much else, was soundly based on experience, both Indian and international. The difficulty was to find ways and means of rapidly developing the new managerial personnel without which no enterprise could function efficiently, to keep such personnel in the public sector (when opportunities for employment in the private sector, frequently on more favourable terms, were increasing), and to persuade the central government departments to refrain from interfering with managerial responsibilities and to confine their role to one of co-ordination and the general direction of policy. These *desiderata* are difficult to achieve even in highly developed countries. In less developed ones, such as India, where politicians are anxious to have their fingers in every pie, bureaucrats believe in their own omnicompetence and managers are held in comparatively low esteem, the path towards their attainment is strewn with obstacles.

(v)

What general features of the chapters on administration in the three plan reports should be stressed? On the credit side, there is increasing precision in the definition of administrative needs and tasks, particularly in the field of manpower planning. On the debit side, there is the extreme vagueness of many of the recommendations, accompanied by a tiresome *penchant* for exhortation. One sometimes gets the feeling that the Commission considers that the discussion of administrative ways and means is an irksome extra task which the government has imposed on it, and that the authorities ought to be able to put their house in order without the benefit of its constant help and advice. This is an attitude easily adopted by a body staffed mainly by people with qualifications in economics and statistics. It may even be a reasonable attitude; for one could argue that advising on administration is no part of a Planning Commission's job, and that the responsibility for thinking about the implementation of development programmes should be placed firmly and unambiguously where it belongs: with the central ministries and the state governments. Certainly, a situation where the Commission is constantly nagging about administration, and the administrative authorities are treating its representations with a kind of indulgent nonchalance, is not a very desirable one.

On the other hand, there is also a case for the Commission's saying, as it does say, to the administration: 'The plan that we have formulated has the following general administrative implications: please do something about them.' Except in estimating manpower requirements and providing for their realization, which are integral parts of the planning process itself, this approach is characteristic of the Third Plan report. The Third Plan, in fact, displays—at least on paper—a fairly logical approach to the defining and breaking down of administrative tasks. The Commission says, in general, what is required, and the 'O & M' Division of the Cabinet Secretariat produces a paper which puts the requirements into sharper focus. The government then lays before Parliament a statement expressing, with some precision, its intentions in matters administrative; and the ball is finally thrown to a Cabinet Committee on Administration charged with giving practical shape to these intentions. This seems a real advance on previous procedures.

If, however, this type of relationship between the Commission and the administrative authorities is to be retained, it would seem that the Commission's conception of its advice-giving responsibilities is too restricted. There are, of course, certain fields on which it cannot trespass. It cannot, for example, question the provisions of the Indian constitution, even when these appear to stand in the way of rational planning; it cannot criticize appointments to ministerial office, however foolish they may be; it must show due deference to Parliament, the NDC, and the state legislatures, whatever idiocies these august bodies choose to perpetrate; and it must steer clear of any overt political commitment. But as far as the machinery of government is concerned, there seems to be no reason why it should stop short of the highest levels and leave to others the task of critically reviewing the overall pattern. The division of functions between central ministries, for example, or the relationships between these ministries and their numerous subordinate or attached agencies, are matters of the highest importance for planning; yet the Commission, if it has ever considered them, has left no published evidence of its deliberations. One may concede that these matters have political overtones, in that the layout of ministerial responsibilities, for instance, will affect the distribution of power and influence within the Cabinet and assist or inhibit the realization of the political ambitions of the members of the Congress Party's top leadership; but there is little that the Commission touches that is not, in the last resort, 'political', and on questions of this sort it is surely vital that the government should receive objective advice from some expert agency, cognizant of the requirements of a planned economy.

The extraordinary thing is that, as far as one can discover, there is no provision for the systematic study of the machinery of government at the top level. Although the Commission's terms of reference (i.e. to 'determine the nature of the machinery which will be necessary for securing the successful implementation of each stage of the Plan in all its aspects')[89] would appear to include it, the planners so far have refused to grasp this nettle. So have the 'O & M' Division of the Cabinet Secretariat and

[89] See above, p. 292.

the Special Reorganization Unit of the Ministry of Finance.[90] Nor does there appear to be a Cabinet committee which regularly considers it. It has never been dealt with, except interstitially, by any of the published reports on administrative reform. Gorwala does not discuss it; Appleby, while approaching it from several angles, tactfully avoids any direct confrontation; and there is nothing about it in the Estimates Committee's reports on 'Administrative, Financial and Other Reforms' (1953–4), on the 'Planning Commission' (1958), and on the 'Ministry of Finance' (1958–9).[91] Even more significantly, it is totally excluded from the government's *Papers on Measures for the Strengthening of Administration* (1961) and therefore, presumably, from the new Committee on Administration's terms of reference.

As far as one knows, the only occasion since independence when the machinery of government has been systematically reviewed was in 1950, when Gopalaswami Ayyanger, as Minister without portfolio, was assigned this responsibility.[92] Since then, although ministries have been frequently created, abolished, amalgamated, and divided,[93] functions persistently redistributed, and many new *ad hoc* agencies brought into being, no one has been asked to take a fresh look at the whole set-up. In fact, the only reasonably comprehensive critical account of the development of the Indian machinery of government, since 1948, is the long chapter on 'The Executive' in Asok Chanda's *Indian Administration*. This provides a detailed account of departmental reorganizations between 1948 and 1957, and concludes that they have been made, not in accordance with any rational plan, but 'to suit the convenience of ministerial changes or to widen the avenues of advancement of secretariat personnel'.[94] That, as a result,

[90] See the accounts of their work in EC, 1960–1: *118*, pp. 50–95. Vasudeva considers that O & M's work 'should not be restricted merely to matters of office procedures and methods'. It should be 'suitably equipped to consider analytically questions of organizations and structures of Departments and Ministries and be permitted to offer advice at the highest levels of Government' (*IJPA*, July–Sept. 1963, p. 382).

[91] The Committee, however, has occasionally made recommendations about redistribution of ministerial functions in its reports on particular branches of administration. Thus, for instance, EC 1955–6:*19* suggested the bifurcation of the Ministry of Railways into two Ministries, of Railways and of Transport.

[92] See the account of his proposals in Asok Chanda, *Indian Administration* (1958), pp. 66–69.

[93] Up to 1963 the most important reorganization of central ministries was that which followed the second General Election. The Ministries of Production and of Natural Resources and Scientific Research were abolished; a Ministry of Steel, Mines, and Fuel was created; the Ministry of Transport was combined with the Ministry of Communications, and Food with Agriculture; the Ministry of Education acquired scientific research; responsibility for oil was transferred from the Ministry of Works, Housing and Supply to the Ministry of Steel, Mines, and Fuel: and the Ministry of Labour was redesignated 'Labour and Employment' (see *IJPA*, iii (1957), p. 254).

[94] pp. 82–93. Prof. N. Srinavasan, who carries the story up to 1962 in his 'Changes in Central Ministries and Departments since Independence' (*IJPA*, July–Sept. 1963) expresses himself more cautiously than Chanda, but adopts substantially the same view.

top-level co-ordination of policies has become more difficult was underlined by S. K. Patil, then Minister of Irrigation and Power, in a speech to the Lok Sabha on 26 March 1958, where he complained that 'there was little coordination even in such a vital matter as food production'.

He said that if he had his way, he would like a thorough streamlining of the entire administrative structure. There was, at present, the Planning Commission which went far beyond mere planning. There was his ministry responsible for the construction of irrigation projects to increase food production. Then came the Food and Agriculture Ministry and a host of departments in different states dealing with the same subject. On top of all this, there was the Community Projects Department, also concerned with food production. He was aghast to find how many departments were dealing with the same subject. But when it came to a question of fixing responsibility, everyone wanted to get out of it.[95]

The demand for better 'coordination' receives constant expression, both in official and in unofficial circles. The trouble is that, when it is attempted, those who take it in hand are so anxious not to disturb the working of existing organizations (which have strong vested interests in their own perpetuation) that they tend to make confusion worse confounded by the superimposition of a new series of 'co-ordinating' bodies, which have the effect of further dispersing responsibility and intensifying inter-agency competition.

The Planning Commission's recent proposals for 'intensive development of small industries in rural areas' provide an example of this tendency. The Third Plan deplored the overlapping and duplication of effort which appeared to be holding back the existing small industries programme; proclaimed that, for the larger programme that it was proposing, there would have to be closer 'cooperation of the various institutions and agencies working at the regional or block level'; and announced its intention of examining 'the various aspects of this question further in consultation with State Governments and Boards'. To formulate and supervise the programme a Rural Industries Planning Committee was appointed, as an associated body of the Planning Commission (by government of India resolution no. VSI/8/(6)/61 on April 18 1962). This body proposed (*a*) that it should itself 'undertake the necessary coordination and assist State Governments in carrying out the programme'; (*b*) that it should constitute 'a Standing Committee for continuous guidance of the programme'; (*c*) that the Planning Commission should 'set up the necessary establishment for implementing the programme which will function under the supervision of the Standing Committee'; and (*d*) that each state should establish a 'high-level Advisory Committee for Rural Industries', whose Secretary, 'a senior State official connected with village and small scale industries', should 'ensure coordination between various

[95] Quoted in Chanda, *Indian Administration*, p. 168.

agencies under the State Government as well as non-official organisations'. The responsibilities of the Ministry of Commerce and Industry, the Ministry of Community Development, the corresponding ministries at the state level, the Khadi and Village Industries Commission, the Community Project authorities, the co-operative organizations and the numerous other agencies with fingers in the village and small-scale industries pie (many of which, such as the Indian Handicrafts Development Corporation and the National Small Industries Corporation, were not even mentioned in the report) were to remain undisturbed. Even finance was to continue to flow from these different sources, viz. '(*a*) funds from the State Plan and all-India Boards according to their respective programmes and allotment for the area; (*b*) loans and credits from financial and cooperative institutions and under the State Aid to Industries Act; and (*c*) additional funds to be given to the project as its own nucleus.' But all this was to be 'coordinated' by yet another set of authorities. It is difficult to imagine a more perfect recipe for administrative failure.[96]

'Reorganization', of course, continues to occur periodically, at the higher as well as at the lower levels. Since the beginning of the Third Plan, for instance, there have been several reshufflings of ministerial offices, some of which may conceivably be justified on ground of administrative rationality. One of the more important took place in September and November 1963, as a result of the decision to transfer a number of leading central ministers to posts in the party organization.[97] There is no indication, however, that administrative considerations have been uppermost in the minds of those responsible for any of these reorganizations. Perhaps one is naïve to expect anything else, for the general rule is that the higher the level at which reorganization is effected, the larger loom the factors of party and personality. But a society which is serious about planning its development cannot afford to allow a complete triumph of prejudice over rationality at these levels. These, indeed, are the levels where administrative planning is most important, even although its dictates may sometimes have to be overruled or modified by 'reasons of state'. For arrangements at the top will determine, or at least influence, arrangements all down the line.

The systematic improvement of the top-level machinery of government has, therefore, been the most serious *lacuna* in India's plans for administrative reform. It is no one's major duty or regular responsibility. Since 1950 it has never been the subject of serious scientific thought. Whether this neglected task should be given to the Planning Commission is disputable; but it should be given to *someone*, preferably with high authority and real understanding of the administrative needs of a planned economy.

[96] See Plan. Com., *Projects for Intensive Development of Small Industries in Rural Areas* (July 1962).
[97] See *PANL*, Sept. 1963 & Dec. 1963.

Only through such an overall review, as distinct from the normal type of 'O & M' investigation of individual units, can a path be opened to the radical simplification of administrative procedures. How urgent simplification has become is well illustrated by some of the 'cases' recently collected by the Indian Institute of Public Administration.[98] To these it may be useful, for illustrative purposes, to add one of the many examples collected by the author during the course of conversations with officials in many parts of India.

The agency concerned is the Andhra Pradesh Mining Corporation, a state-owned public enterprise of very recent vintage. The subject-matter is foreign exchange. When the Managing Director requires further supplies of this scarce commodity to purchase equipment, he first has to apply to the Bureau of Mines for an 'essentiality certificate'. Before rendering it, the Bureau may have to consult with the Export Promotion Department (Ministry of Commerce and Industry), which is naturally anxious that imported equipment should be used, as far as possible, in industries with good export potentialities. Clearance is also needed from the Development Wing of the Ministry, which is concerned with plan priorities, and which will certainly inquire whether there is any possibility of obtaining the equipment from an indigenous source. Another application goes to the 'sponsoring' ministry, the Ministry of Mines and Fuel, which will refer the matter to the Department of Economic Affairs (Ministry of Finance) for foreign exchange clearance. If problems arise at this stage, there will be correspondence with the Bureau of Mines and the Development Wing. When these have been settled, the Ministry of Mines and Fuel issues a clearance letter, of which one copy goes to the Chief Comptroller of Imports and another to the Andhra government. The Corporation then prepares its application for an import licence and sends it to the Chief Comptroller, who will require another copy, for confirmation, from the Ministry of Mines and Fuel. When the Comptroller has issued the licence, together with a letter of authority, the Corporation is at last free to place its order with the overseas supplier.

This, said the Director, is the normal procedure in a 'straightforward' case. Even so, progress has to be expedited by 'persistent reminders', and an 'immense file of papers' is accumulated. If, as often happens, the Bureau of Mines considers that the information initially supplied is inadequate, or if 'inadequacies' are detected at any later stage, a 'tremendous correspondence' is built up. In such a case, the delay in obtaining the necessary permits may be one of years rather than of months.

This type of procedure is not exceptional but normal. Much of the delay involved is obviously due to the existence of obsolete routines and

[98] See B. S. Narula, ed., *Cases in Indian Public Administration* (New Delhi, 1963); S. S. Khera, *The Establishment of the Heavy Electrical Plant at Bhopal* (New Delhi, 1963).

to the lack of a sufficient sense of urgency in governmental offices. Better internal organization and more highly trained personnel, therefore, could expedite the process. But over and above this, and ultimately more important, is the question of the distribution of functions between the agencies involved. Given the shortage of foreign exchange, no agency is performing a superfluous function. But whether each function is being performed by the right agency at the right time and in the right place, and whether adequate provision has been made to ensure that they are all working to a common policy, are matters which have never been properly examined by anyone sufficiently aware of the need for speed and coherence. The whole arrangement is one of checks and balances, apparently designed to ensure that everyone is consulted and no one has the chance to make a 'mistake'. The result is a diffusion of responsibility and a massive built-in tendency towards the commission of the most serious of all mistakes in a would-be developing economy—procrastination.

The Planning Commission, as we have said, has not yet got to grips with this crucial administrative problem, which is perhaps beyond its capacities. If this is so, then other machinery to cope with it is urgently needed.

(vi)

But although the restructuring of the administrative system is very important, we should be wrong to place the final emphasis on it; for this would be to share the once prevalent but now fast-fading illusions about the efficacy of reorganization as a panacea. In India the current emphasis is on the improvement of personnel, and there can be no doubt that this represents an advance in realism. Unfortunately, in spite of the widening of the area of recruitment and the devotion of considerable resources to the education and training of administrators, most informed observers seem to be of the opinion that, at all levels, the quality of personnel is deteriorating. There may possibly be an element of illusion in this view. Perhaps the administrator is neither better nor worse than before and the appearance of deterioration is simply due to the fact that he is trying to do more difficult things. That Indian maid-of-all-work, the District Officer, for instance, must now, in addition to seeing to the collection of revenue and the maintenance of order, co-ordinate the activities of a large number of economic and social agencies, impart developmental drive to district administration, and keep on good terms simultaneously with his hierarchical superiors and with the local leaders on whom 'democratic decentralization' has conferred authority. At the lower levels, the BDO and the Village Level Worker are confronted with similar problems. Even a moderately conscientious administrator, in fact, finds himself burdened with an appalling work-load, particularly if he has the bad luck to be posted to a rural area. Nevertheless, it would not be surprising if the Cassandras were right and the quality of personnel was, on the average, declining. That there has been a moral decline is hardly open to doubt. Everyone agrees that corruption is more widespread than it ever was in British days, and no one believes that the numerous Anti-Corruption Committees and Vigilance Units can do anything effective about it. There is some evidence, too, that, with the development of career opportunities in the private sector, the civil service is proving less attractive to the bright young man; and it is certain that the bright young man's education, particularly at the university level, has undergone deterioration, except in a few nationally-famous institutions. On the other hand, anyone who moves in Indian administrative circles quickly becomes aware that, among the best of the younger civil servants, there is a capacity for initiative and a flexibility of mind rarely found among their elders.

The question of personnel, however, cannot be considered in isolation, any more than that of administrative structure. In general, the characteristics of the administrative corps will reflect rather than transcend those of their social and political environment, which is certainly not conducive either to the development of administrative rationality or to the improvement of administrative morality.

The average administrator has little incentive except to stick like a limpet to his job—which he can best achieve by acting 'correctly' according to the rules and regulations—and to try to raise himself in the hierarchy through blameless service and ministrations to the self-esteem of his superiors. In spite of almost universal lip-service to administrative reform, there are powerful vested interests which inhibit its realization; for reform inevitably means a reduction in numbers at the lower and middle levels, a disturbance of established expectations, and a radical alteration of bureaucratic habits. Although such interests exist in all countries, developed and underdeveloped, they are particularly powerful in a status-oriented society where educated unemployment is very high and government jobs are greatly prized.

There are, of course, countervailing forces, such as the fine traditions and immense work-capacity of the IAS, the genuine 'development-mindedness' of its best members, and the pride of craft and enthusiasm for the job to be found among many of the technical specialists. But these men are suffering from so much frustration that it is uncertain whether their traditions, enthusiasm, and capacity for work can be indefinitely maintained.

Hence there is a perpetual and perhaps widening gap between the tasks set by the planners and the capacity and even willingness of the administrators to discharge them. Among the best-informed observers of the Indian administrative scene, some pessimism prevails about this situation.

H. M. Patel, formerly Principal Secretary to the Ministry of Finance, has written: 'An honest and frank and objective appraisal of public administration during the years since Independence leads me to only one conclusion as to the future: the outlook is bleak.'[99] Language of the same sort has also been used by other distinguished retired ICS men, such as A. D. Gorwala, as well as by radical publicists like D. R. Gadgil.

Nevertheless, one should not accept uncritically the views of these prophets of woe; for their jeremiads are as much an expression of the perfectionism of the Indian intellectual as of the imperfections of the actual situation. Their 'exposures' of Indian administration have some of the features of a self-purifying exercise in the Hindu tradition. They cannot be satisfied with mere improvements, but only with a complete moral revolution. Patel, for instance, proclaims that 'the outlook will remain bleak until such time as moral standards begin again to be respected and there is a radical change in our attitude towards administration.'[100] Sovani, generalizing more widely, assures us that 'the ruling and the dominant persons and groups have to show greater foresight and vision and have to stand ready to shed with good grace positions of prestige, privilege, and advantage—social, economic and political—if young and vigorous leadership is to rise to take their place'.[101] This type of sentiment contributes little to reform.

In general, Indian critics of Indian administration may be divided into two camps, viz. (1) those who place their faith in changes in organization, education, and training, pioneered by 'high-powered' committees, and (2) those who, convinced that such changes will achieve little, demand a 'change of heart'. Between the two, the matter that requires the most careful study—the motivations and social relationships of the bureaucracy—tends to become lost from view.

Given the existing socio-political set-up, a moral revolution is inconceivable and an organizational revolution of uncertain benefit. The way forward, if there is one, can only be through 'piecemeal social engineering', unlikely to produce spectacular results over a short period. Such engineering should become easier as India modifies her traditional social institutions. The present difficulty is that a fast enough rate of modernization cannot be achieved by spontaneous processes. It depends on the success of an economic development which is itself largely the product of administrative action.

Whether this vicious circle can be broken without also shattering India's framework of political democracy is still uncertain. If it cannot, then the prospect may be one of descent into chaos (of the kind envisaged

[99] 'The Outlook for the Future', *IJPA*, July–Sept. 1963, p. 514. [100] Ibid.
[101] N. V. Sovani, 'Non-Economic Aspects of Economic Development', in Braibanti & Spengler, *Admin. & Econ. Dev.*, p. 280.

by Selig Harrison), out of which there might conceivably emerge a totalitarian or authoritarian regime (or collection of regimes) with the will and the power to impose organizational change and transform administrative behaviour by the familiar strong-arm methods. The alternative to the democratically-controlled, self-disciplined administration which seems to evade India's grasp is a dictatorially-controlled, party-disciplined, and ideologically-strait-jacketed one. The latter kind, however brutal and wasteful its methods, can cope with the tasks of economic development. We do not know, as yet, whether the former can do so, particularly in the harsh conditions of India. Nor do we know how near breaking-point the present administrative set-up has reached. It appears to be very near indeed, but Indian appearances are notoriously deceptive.

IX

CENTRE AND STATES, 1: THE SHARING OF BENEFITS AND BURDENS

(i)

THIS chapter is concerned with one of the most difficult and delicate tasks confronting the Indian planners. The fact that the government and the Commission has to find a *modus vivendi* with fifteen states,[1] each armed with its own powers under the constitution and equipped with representative institutions, is bound to inject an element of irrationality into the process of planning. We are not suggesting that completely centralized planning is the only rational kind; on the contrary, it is usually outstandingly irrational, particularly in a country of great size and conspicuous diversity. In India, regionalization of the planning process is inevitable, and the Commission, given a free hand, would doubtless divide the country into a number of planning regions, demarcated by economic and geographical characteristics, and equip each one with a subordinate planning unit endowed with a considerable degree of autonomy. But it has never had this opportunity, as constitutional and political considerations have ensured that plans shall be partly formulated and implemented by states whose boundaries are linguistic, rather than geographical or economic, and whose natural tendency is to assert themselves against, rather than subordinate themselves to, the centre.[2]

Federalism is invariably a headache to the central economic planner. Whether India has a 'genuine' federal constitution, in view of the fact that the constituent states of the Union can be abolished or divided by fiat of the central legislature and made subject to 'presidential rule' in an emergency, is a question on which pedants will continue to spill ink. The facts are that in normal times the states possess and exercise certain autonomous powers and—what is more important—are politically self-assertive units whose interests and views the central government cannot

[1] Now sixteen, with the creation of a separate Nagaland state. Only the previous fifteen, however, are taken into consideration in this and the following chapter.

[2] The States Reorganization Commission of 1955 referred to the view that 'only a unitary form of government and division of the country into pure administrative units can provide a corrective to separation tendencies'. Declaring this to be 'unrealistic', it said that other methods of creating the necessary unity would have to be found. Unfortunately, most of the 'correctives' which it proposed were rejected by the states (see *EW*, 21 Jan. 1961, p. 75).

afford to ignore. Some of the juridical essentials and much of the vital spirit of federalism are therefore present.

According to the constitution, planning is a 'concurrent' subject, which means that responsibility for it adheres to both centre and states, with the proviso that in the event of conflict the will of the centre shall prevail. Most of the things that have to be planned, however, appear either on the Union list or the state list, but not on both. In practice, this means that the centre is responsible for the planning of major industries, railways, national highways, civil aviation, communications, major ports, shipping and, of course, overall monetary and fiscal policies; while the states have responsibility for agriculture, irrigation, power, education, health, welfare, small industries, roads and road transport, and minor ports. This division of powers, however, is complicated by the central Parliament's constitutional authority to provide for the regulation and control of certain subjects on the states' list, such as roads, inland waterways, industries, mines, and inter-state rivers, if it considers this to be expedient in the public interest. The Union is also given the power to co-ordinate and to lay down standards for institutions engaged in higher education and research, and it possesses even greater authority over those that are partly financed from central funds and declared by Parliament to be of 'national importance'. In addition, there is the 'reservation' of certain categories of legislation for consideration by the President (i.e. the central government), and the power of the Union Parliament, with the approval of not less than two-thirds of the members of the Council of States (Rajya Sabha) present and voting, to legislate for a period of a year in respect of matters on the states' list.

Commenting on these provisions of the constitution, V. T. Krishnamachari says that their object is 'to promote cooperation on a voluntary basis between the Union and States and among States and groups of States in investigation of matters of common interest, in legislative procedures and in administration, thus avoiding rigidities inherent in federal constitutions and ensuring flexibility in working'.[3] One may agree that the constitution has been subtly devised to promote unity in diversity, and has shown a remarkable capacity to withstand political strain. Nevertheless, the task of constitution-building was undertaken before the days of planning, and it cannot be said that any of the architects had the needs of planning conspicuously in mind. If they had been thinking of these needs, a very different structure might have emerged. Krishnamachari, it is true, offers a justification, from the planner's point of view, for the existing division of powers. After listing the subjects within the competence of the states, he says: 'Programmes under these heads have their impact on the lives of many millions of families; and obviously plans for them will have to be prepared by the States'.[4] But Paul Appleby

[3] *Fundamentals of Planning*, p. 21. [4] Ibid. p. 13.

could find no rational principle behind the division of competences, and saw danger in the fact that the nation was 'crucially dependent on the states for actual achievement of the chief programmatic objectives'.[5]

There is plenty of room for controversy here, but the discussion is not likely to be fruitful. Particularly since linguistic reorganization, the states have become powers in their own right, unwilling to countenance any erosion of their prerogatives for the benefit of the centre, even while competing vigorously for the benefits of central assistance. Any 'streamlining' of the planning machinery to the detriment of state powers is therefore politically impracticable. The states were not created for planning purposes; they do not plan with any great competence; their competitive self-assertion makes rational planning on an all-Indian scale immensely more difficult. But their existence is the most important fact of Indian political life. The Planning Commission and the central government have no alternative but to accept it and to make the best of a difficult job.

The greatest difficulty is to balance the requirements of development against the demands of equity. Its appearance coincided with the advent of planning itself, if only because people do not complain about maldistribution of resources until distribution has become a deliberately-organized process as distinct from a 'spontaneous' one. As the *Eastern Economist* has written:

> Industry has tended to concentrate in the States of Bombay and Bengal. Irrigation had developed mainly in Madras, Uttar Pradesh and Punjab. This was the result of the operation of free enterprise and provincial autonomy. So long as the Government of India did not embark upon a planned economy, there was no particular feeling of injustice and bitterness. Now the position has been reversed. There is a strong feeling that somehow or other industries should be set up in all States, that irrigation should be developed irrespective of cost and that social services should be brought to a common level.[6]

Unfortunately, this 'strong feeling' is bound to affront the Planning Commission's all-India conception of economic rationality. To conserve resources and to achieve the most rapid rate of long-run development, investment needs initially to be concentrated at those points where the highest returns (i.e. the maximum rate of growth for the minimum quantum of investment) will be yielded. The location of these points is determined partly by geographical factors (e.g. the distribution of natural resources), and partly by the pre-existence of man-made 'external economies'. Neither

[5] *Public Administration*, p. 9.

[6] *EE*, 7 May 1958, Spec. Plan Suppl., p. ix. The *EE*'s rival, the *EW*, published on 24 Dec. 1960 an article in which 'Industrial Economist' demanded not only that expensive differential encouragement should be offered to small industries in the 'mofussil' areas but that each of the *very* backward areas should be presented with 'some large-scale unit in the public sector which will not be dependent for its working on local resources or market'.

is compatible with an even spread of new investment over the whole area subject to planning. Inevitably, the tendency will be to 'bunch' investments at the points where considerable economic development has already occurred. Consequently, the pre-existing gap between the comparatively advanced and the comparatively backward areas will tend to become wider. In theory, the gap will eventually be filled as a result of 'spread effect' from the new *pôles de croissance*. Unfortunately, as Gunnar Myrdal has pointed out, this effect is counterbalanced, in an underdeveloped economy, as in the world economy as a whole, by a 'backwash effect'.[7] Hence the danger is that the more backward areas will *never* catch up and that the gap between them and the more advanced ones will continue to increase. Moreover the inhabitants of the backward areas are not likely to wait patiently until the fullness of time and the operation of alleged economic laws bring them—or their grandchildren—the benefits already accruing to their more fortunately located fellow citizens; and if they possess, as they do in India, a sense of regional solidarity and the means of political self-expression, their impatience becomes a factor which the central economic planner disregards at his peril.[8]

All this is a matter of elementary knowledge, but to find the 'right' point of balance between the concentration and dispersal of investments is a problem for which the textbooks provide no neat solutions. In some cases, of course, the choice of the planners is more or less predetermined. A steel plant, for instance, must be located as near as possible to its sources of raw material and with some regard to the adequacy of the existing transport network. An irrigation-cum-hydro-electric project is obviously tied to a river valley—though *which* river valley to choose for its location, when there are several alternatives in several different states, may be a question which cannot be answered by 'costs-and-benefits' calculations alone. In almost every other field, the choice between maximum economic returns and 'balanced regional development' is one of political judgement. The planners will naturally argue for maximum economic returns, on the grounds that the most rapid growth has first priority and that 'balance' can wait until the more immediate pressures on the economy have become eased. But if the result of such single-minded concentration is a degree of political tension between the advanced and the backward regions which endangers the very unity of the country, then the pursuit of growth becomes self-defeating. Thus, even from the most severely practical point

[7] See *Econ. Theory & Underdev. Regions*, particularly ch. 3.

[8] 'During the course of our investigations', wrote the States Reorganization Commission, 'we found that most of the demands for constituting new States were based primarily on alleged unfair and unequal distribution of development expenditure'. Its proposed remedy for this situation, viz. to 'ensure that Central Government expenditure is, as far as possible, spread uniformly all over the country', simply reflected the fact that the Commission was not composed of economists and knew very little about planning (*Rep.* (New Delhi, 1955), pp. 266–9).

of view, which disregards all considerations of equity and humanity, some compromise has to be found.

It is perhaps not surprising that, on so delicate a question, the Planning Commission has expressed itself with less than its usual clarity and has refrained from enunciating unambiguous principles. It is in this field, indeed, that the Commission's 'on-the-one-hand-but-on-the-other' approach has received most anguished expression. In the Third Plan report it produced the following cloudy formulation of the problem:

> Development of regions and of the national economy as a whole have to be viewed as parts of a single process. The programmes of the national economy will be reflected in the rate of growth realised by different regions and, in turn, greater development of resources in the regions must contribute towards accelerating the rate of progress for the country as a whole. Excessive emphasis on the problems of particular regions and attempts to plan for their development without relating their needs to the requirements of the national economy have to be guarded against, for, in the final analysis, it is as integral parts of the country that different regions can best hope to realise their full potential for growth. Balanced regional growth emerges eventually from a whole series of connected developments, many of which are of a long-term character. Over a short period, advance towards the goal will frequently seem small and incomplete. This is true for individual regions and, equally, for the national economy as a whole. Whatever the present shortcomings, the aim must be that over a reasonable period all regions in the country should realise their potential for economic development and should attain levels of living not far removed from those of the nation as a whole.[9]

Just what this means in practical terms is not easy to discover; but it is clarity itself compared with the NDC's observations on the narrower but allied problem of the 'determination of outlays for States in the Third Five Year Plan'—observations which were supposed to provide 'a basis for more detailed planning in the states':

> Outlays for the Third Plan for each State will have to be arrived at after study of its needs and problems, past progress and lags in development, likely contribution to the achievement of major national targets, potential for growth and the contribution in resources which the State is able to make towards its development plan. In assessing needs and problems, such factors as population, area, pressure on cultivated land, extent of commitments carried over from the Second Plan, commitments on account of large projects and the state of technical and administrative services available, will have to be taken into account. Due attention will have to be given both to national and to State priorities. It will, of course, be necessary to guard against those States whose resources are unavoidably small being required to undertake development on a scale which may be altogether insufficient. At the same time, States which are able and willing to make a bigger effort in mobilising their own resources can legitimately

[9] *FYP*(*3*), p. 153.

expect this factor to be taken into account in determining their outlays for the Third Plan.[10]

But while it is easy to criticize these vague and muddled formulations, it is difficult to devise alternative ones which would simultaneously effect a reconciliation between the contradictory *desiderata*, provide satisfaction to the demands of the states, and present clear guide-lines for detailed policy-making.

The problem is further complicated by lack of definition of what constitutes a region. For the individual state 'balanced regional development' means that the state itself, as a political unit with defined boundaries, should get its 'fair' share of available resources. But for the Planning Commission 'region' and 'state' do not coincide. In its pamphlet, *Economic Development in Different Regions in India* (p. 1), it divides the states 'into five regions on the basis of Zones laid down in the States Reorganization Act, 1956, except that the southern region is taken to include four States, namely, Andhra Pradesh, Madras, Mysore and Kerala, and the western zone to include only two States, namely, Maharashtra and Gujarat.' It then produces a mass of figures showing the progress achieved by each of these regions during the course of the two plans, and the division of regional outlay (state sector only) as between state resources and central assistance. Although the ostensible purpose of this publication is simply to provide information hitherto unavailable and although no conclusions are drawn, there is a fairly strong implication that no region has been unfairly neglected. Indeed, in respect of the Southern Region, from which the most anguished complaints of neglect have come, the point is well made. This region, the second most populous of the five, comes second for cultivated area irrigated, first for surfaced road mileage, third for installed generating capacity, first for towns and villages electrified, first for percentage of 6–11 age-group at school, and third for doctors per million of population. In respect of central assistance to state plans (per capita—Third Plan), it is slightly better off than the Central, Eastern, or Western Regions although considerably behind the Northern. Comparison between regions in respect of benefits from central government industrial projects is not attempted, and indeed, owing to the heavy weightage of the steel projects, which are necessarily located in the North and Centre, would not mean very much; but there is a long list of important southern-located projects in the Third Plan, as against only one or two northern-located ones.[11] However, if this publication is intended to prove to the states that balanced regional development, as they understand it, is being achieved, it will surely fail in its purpose; for

[10] Plan. Com., *Economic Development in Different Regions of India* (1962), p. 3.

[11] See ibid. tables, diagrams, & annexures.

they think in terms not of north, south, east, west, and centre, but of sixteen separate political units.[12] Each of the Commission's regions, as its own figures show, contains states with widely differing levels of development; and other figures, not quoted by the Commission, suggest that, whatever may be happening to the gap between regions, that between the more advanced and the less advanced states has not been narrowed as a result of ten years of planning.

When the economist, Dr P. N. Radakrishnan, says that 'a decade of planning has not even touched a fringe of the problem of regional disparity', it is to the states that he is referring, not to the Planning Commission's five regions. Figures produced by the Indian Institute of Public Opinion, which he quotes, tend to confirm his judgement. In respect, of percentage increase in per capita income from 1955–6 to 1960–1, the states appear in the following order: (1) Punjab (25·63); (2) West Bengal (20·24); (3) Orissa (19·14); (4) Gujarat (18·00); (5) Kerala (9·84); (6) Madhya Pradesh (9·58); (7) Bihar (8·37); (8) Madras (8·29); (9) Maharashtra (5·97); (10) Uttar Pradesh (5.69); (11) Andhra Pradesh (4.96); (12) Assam (4.85); (13) Rajasthan (4.67); (14) Mysore (4.66); (15) Jammu and Kashmir—not available. The all-India average is 10·64.[13]

These figures should be used with caution. They are based on calculations that differ both in their methods and in their degree of sophistication. Moreover they prove very little about economic planning as such. The increases in per capita incomes are the joint product of efforts in the public sector and in the private sector, and we know far too little about the mutual relationships of the two sectors to be able to apportion attributability. How far, for instance, was private sector investment in a particular state stimulated by publicly provided improvements in the infrastructure? *Per contra*, to what extent was it held back by the time-consuming procedures involved in obtaining multifarious permits and licences? Nevertheless, the fact that only four states achieved per capita increases

[12] Thus, although the Southern Region as a whole cannot be said to have suffered from adverse discrimination, the state of Kerala is strongly of the opinion that it has received far less than its entitlement in view of the well-known special problems which it has to face. 'It is a matter of some disappointment', wrote the Kerala planners, 'that in spite of the crying need for industrialisation in the State, not much progress could be made in this sphere in the First and Second Plans. While the country has made notable progress by the setting up of several important projects and factories like the Iron and Steel Plants at Durgapur, Bhilai, Rourkela and several others like the Hindustan Machine Tools Factory, the Penicillin Factory etc. there has been no industry set up by the Government of India in Kerala. As against the total investment of a sum of Rs657·9 crores by the Government of India in the Central Sector, the investment made in Kerala . . . is only Rs0·79 crores, representing not even 0·1 per cent of the total investment in the Central Sector.' They also complained of inadequate grant assistance for food production schemes, in comparison with states such as Orissa, Assam, and Kashmir (Kerala, Plan. Dept, *FYP(3): Policy & Programmes* (1961), pp. 15–21).

[13] P. N. Radakrishnan, 'Regional Balance in Economic Development', *Economic Affairs*, Sept. 1962, pp. 432–8.

greater—and in every case *much* greater—than the national average suggests that the planners' efforts to disperse the benefits of economic development have not been very successful. Of these four, two, Gujarat and West Bengal, entered the period of planning already comparatively well developed. One of the other two, Punjab has seen a remarkable efflorescence of small private enterprise, which has perhaps surprised the planners as much as anyone else. The remaining state showing a high per capita increase in income, Orissa, is an odd-man-out; a poor state, it has been presented with an inflated figure as a result of its good fortune in providing the site for the Rourkela Steel Plant & Fertilizer Factory. The impact of this development on the per capita income for a population of

TABLE 26

Second Plan: Share of Central Contribution to State Plans

	%		%
Orissa	89·5	Bihar	59·6
Madhya Pradesh	75·0	Andhra Pradesh	59·4
Rajasthan	74·0	Uttar Pradesh	54·9
Punjab	71·3	West Bengal	54·5
Assam	70·1	Madras	48·4
Mysore	65·5	Kerala	45·3
		Bombay	40·8
Average 61·3			

Source: *EW*, Spec. no., June 1960.

17 million is naturally greater than that of a similar development (i.e. the Bhilai Steel Plant in Madhya Pradesh) on the per capita income for a population of 32 million. As steel plants are not deliberately located to benefit poor states rather than rich ones (Durgapur is in West Bengal), and as the Punjab's high development rate was not consciously planned, the Commission cannot take much credit for such dispersal of benefits as the Orissa and Punjab figures may appear to show. In general, with the outstanding exception of Maharashtra, the richer states have enjoyed a more rapid rate of economic growth than the poorer ones.

A contributor to the *Economic Weekly* goes further than this and comes very near to accusing the Planning Commission of deliberately increasing rather than reducing the disparities.[14] After listing the percentage central contributions to the plans of the states and the state-wise location of major industrial projects in the central sector (both for the Second Plan—see Tables 26 and 27), he comments: 'It may be noticed . . . that many a

[14] 'Planning at State Level', *EW*, June 1960, pp. 901–6.

State which receives a high percentage contribution ... also gets important central sector investments in industries, while those States which get a relatively small share of Central contribution are also deprived of any substantial Central Sector investment.' This, however, is not borne out by the figures. Assam, which appears high in the 'central contribution' list, does not figure at all in the 'major industrial projects' list. The same applies to Rajasthan. Bombay, on the other hand, has less than average central assistance and only a small collection of projects. There is no correlation here, nor should there be. Central projects are normally

TABLE 27

Second Plan: Major Industrial Projects in the Central Sector in the Different States

	Rs crores
Orissa (Rourkela steel & fertilizers)	186·00
Madhya Pradesh (Bhilai, heavy electrical)	147·65
West Bengal (Durgapur, cables, National Instruments Factory, Chittaranjan)	143·25
Madras (lignite, integral coach, sugar & cotton mills)	72·00
Punjab (Nangal fertilizers)	27·11
Andhra Pradesh (Hindustan Shipyard, Hyderabad Tools)	10·55
Bombay (anti-biotics, paper, penicillin, salt)	9·50
Mysore (iron & steel, machine tools, telephones)	8·86
Bihar (Sindhri fertilizers)	8·40
Kerala (DDT)	0·79

Source: as for table above.

located where they are likely to be most successful, and a backward state is given preference in this respect over an advanced one only where the choice between the two is economically indifferent. Central assistance to state plans follows—or is supposed to follow—the complicated collection of criteria listed above in the quotation from the NDC's resolution. The location of a project in a particular state provides no reason for reducing that state's share of centrally disposable funds; on the contrary, the arrival of the project may well involve the state in additional expenditures which will not be offset by increased revenues for many years. Therefore, although it is arguable that the Commission has not made sufficient effort to promote 'balanced regional development', it cannot be argued, at least on the evidence provided, that it has deliberately aggravated the existing imbalance. But although the Planning Commission may be acquitted of using 'balanced regional development' in a merely deceitful manner, it can hardly be commended for the clarity with which it has

TABLE 28

Comparisons between Infrastructural Expenditure by States (2nd and 3rd Five-year Plans)

State	1	2	3	4	5	6	7	8	9	10	11	12	13	14	15	16	17	18
			Transport & Communications				*Irrigation & Power*				*Education & Culture (including Tech. Education)*							
	Population 1961 (to nearest m.)	*Per capita income 1960–1 (Rs)*	*Expenditure per capita*		*Expenditure per capita as a percent. of per cap. income*		*Expenditure per capita*		*Expenditure per capita as a percent. of per cap. income*		*Expenditure per capita*		*Expenditure per capita as a percent. of per cap. income*		*Total 'infra-structural' expenditure per cap. as a percent. of per capita income*		*States above (+) & below (−) the av. of figs in cols 15, 16.*	
			2 FYP (est).	*3 FYP (proposed)*	*2 FYP*	*3 FYP*	*2 FYP (est.)*	*3 FYP (proposed)*	*2 FYP*	*3 FYP*	*2 FYP (est.)*	*3 FYP (proposed)*	*2 FYP*	*3 FYP*	*2 FYP*	*3 FYP*	*2 FYP*	*3 FYP*
West Bengal	35	436	4·8	5·5	1·1	1·3	9	17	2·1	3·9	8·5	8·6	1·9	1·9	5·1	7·1	−	−
Punjab	20	358	5·2	6·4	1·5	1·8	39	52	10·9	14·5	5·1	12·1	1·4	3·3	13·8	19·6	+	−
Maharashtra	39	335	4·9	9·7	1·5	2·9	18	38	5·3	11·3	4·0	8·0	1·2	2·3	8·0	16·5	−	−
Gujarat	21	323	11·4	10·0	3·5	3·0	24	47	7·4	14·6	5·1	8·2	1·5	2·5	12·4	20·1	+	−
Kerala	17	282	3·7	6·4	1·3	2·3	18	35	6·3	12·4	6·6	10·8	2·3	3·8	9·9	18·5	−	−
Madras	34	263	1·5	3·3	0·5	1·2	28	37	10·6	14·0	4·3	9·4	1·6	3·5	12·7	18·7	+	−
Assam	12	253	6·6	8·5	2·6	3·4	9	29	3·5	11·4	7·0	14·0	2·8	5·5	8·9	20·3	−	−
Madhya Pradesh	32	250	2·7	5·9	1·1	2·3	17	36	6·8	14·4	4·5	10·0	1·8	4·0	9·7	20·7	−	+
Andhra Pradesh	36	231	1·5	3·2	0·6	1·4	26	40	11·2	17·3	3·3	6·5	1·4	2·8	13·2	21·5	+	+
Rajasthan	20	230	5·1	6·6	2·2	2·9	19	60	8·3	26·0	5·5	10·5	2·4	4·6	12·9	33·5	+	+
Uttar Pradesh	74	222	2·1	4·1	0·9	1·8	11	22	5·0	9·9	2·3	8·1	1·0	3·6	6·9	15·3	−	−
Orissa	18	201	3·2	4·7	1·6	2·3	23	30	11·4	14·9	3·7	9·6	1·8	4·8	14·8	22·0	+	+
Mysore	24	197	5·7	5·5	2·9	2·8	22	46	11·2	23·3	4·5	8·5	2·3	4·3	16·4	30·4	+	+
Bihar	46	169	2·9	4·7	1·7	2·7	12	30	7·1	17·8	4·1	6·7	2·4	4·0	11·2	24·5	+	+
														Average	11·1	20·6		

explained its policies. As far as the location of central projects is concerned, it can put up a good case—a much better one than the states deprived of the benefits of having such projects within their borders are prepared to allow.[15] But the principles on which central assistance to state plans is allocated have never been made clear. What balance is struck between population, needs, administrative capacity, willingness to contribute from own resources, pre-existing level of development, &c. &c? When criteria conflict, as they usually do, how is a decision reached? At present no one knows, and even if the Commission has this all worked out, no one is likely to be told, at least just yet. For if the whole complex process were laid bare, existing complaints of inequity, serious enough already, would be redoubled. The Commission's silences and ambiguities have, in fact, a political purpose; and one may well conclude that, even though the method may be slightly disreputable, the end is justified: to keep within manageable bounds the fissiparous tendencies which threaten national unity and with it national planning.

There is, however, one reasonably precise statement of the Planning Commission's by which its performance in this field might be judged, if sufficient statistical evidence existed. While admitting that regional equalization is a long-term goal, it has said that the advance towards it involves, primarily, building up in the poorer states an infrastructure which will enable them, in the course of time, to realize their full development potential. This point, indeed, was made by the government's own Industrial Policy resolution of 1956, which, after pointing out that the concentration of industries in certain areas was partly due to the 'ready availability of power, water supply and transport facilities', said: 'It is one of the aims of national planning to ensure that these facilities are steadily made available to areas which are at present lagging behind industrially or where there is greater need for providing opportunities for employment, provided the location is otherwise suitable.'[16] This would seem to imply that the policy was to make a proportionately greater infrastructural effort in those areas, even though such effort might yield few tangible results in the short run. Is such an effort being made?

Information to provide a conclusive answer is not available. However, some light may be shed on it by comparing the 'infrastructural' expenditures of the various states (whether centrally or locally financed) with their levels of development, as measured by income. If greater attention

[15] That is, if the fundamental nature of the plan, with its degree of concentration on heavy industry and other large-scale projects, is accepted. A different *kind* of plan, undoubtedly, would facilitate regional balance. The states, recognizing this, occasionally suggest that there should be more concentration on small-scale industry and small-sized hydro-electricity plants, 'since in these fields the conditioning factors which limit large-scale industrial development do not apply' (see NDC, 14th mtg, 19–20 Nov. 1960: Conclusions and Recommendations).

[16] Quoted in Plan. Com., *Econ. Dev. in Diff. Regions*, p. 13.

is being paid to the more backward states, then infrastructural expenditure per capita as a percentage of per capita income should be higher in states with a small per capita income than in those with a large one. An attempt at a calculation along these lines is presented in Table 28 (p. 320). It is necessarily a crude one. Infrastructural expenditure is rather arbitrarily confined to expenditure on (*a*) transport and communications, (*b*) irrigation and power, and (*c*) education, and the income figures are of doubtful reliability and comparability. The picture presented, therefore, is suggestive rather than conclusive. What it suggests (see columns 17 and 18) is that there was *some* bias towards the backward states in the Second Plan and that there is rather more in the Third. The 'superiority' of the Third over the Second in this respect is more clearly illustrated if the states are divided into two groups: (1) the 'top four', West Bengal, Punjab, Maharashtra, and Gujarat, all with per capita incomes exceeding Rs320, and (2) the remainder, with per capita incomes ranging from Rs282 to 169. If the average infrastructural expenditure per capita as a percentage of per capita income is worked out for each group separately, the result is as follows:

	2nd Five-year Plan	*3rd Five-year Plan*
Group 1	9·8	15·8
Group 2	11·4	22·5

The Second Plan, according to these slightly suspect numerical indicators, had an infrastructural bias of 1·6 per cent towards the backward states, and the Third Plan has one of 6·7.

The only other provisional conclusion to emerge from the table is the neglect of India's most populous state, Uttar Pradesh, the cradle of so many Congress politicians. This great stagnant heartland of India has far more cause for complaint than any state of the south. Uttar Pradesh is indeed justified in its fear, expressed in its Third Plan report, that failure to devote sufficient resources to 'social overheads' within its boundaries will perpetuate its backwardness. While admitting the absurdity of the claim that 'every region should have its own steel plant, jute mills, sugar factories etc.', the Uttar Pradesh planners agree with Dr Radakrishnan's view that it is 'perfectly legitimate to agitate for the uniform growth of educational facilities, transport and communications facilities, health and social welfare etc.',[17] and express their alarm lest the state's inability to get its fair share of these good things may discourage the more directly productive forms of investment, both public and private.[18]

We can conclude that there has been *some* element of 'balanced'

[17] *Economic Affairs*, Sept. 1962, p. 434. [18] Uttar Pradesh, *FYP* (*3*): *Rep.*, p. 14

regional development in the Second and Third Plans. We cannot be sure, however, that the Planning Commission aimed at precisely this much, for it is obvious that all kinds of accidental and adventitious factors may have contributed to the result. Nor are we justified in saying that the Commission either overstressed or understressed this element; for 'balance' was only one of the many criteria affecting its decisions about the distribution of central aid, and we cannot say what exact weight the Commission chose to give it. Even when the elimination of backwardness receives high priority, intractable circumstances often triumph over good resolutions. An economically backward state, for instance, is usually administratively backward as well, and consequently unfitted to have large funds placed at its disposal. Such a state, moreover, may well display a reluctance as well as an inability to 'match' central contributions. A comparatively advanced state, on the other hand, may require large infrastructural investments in order to maintain a given developmental momentum. Again, the location of a great deal of infrastructural investment is predetermined by previous decisions about industrial investments, some of the most important of which cannot conform to the principle of regional balance. Finally, there is always the agonizing problem of how much weight to give to short-term considerations, which generally point towards concentration, and to long-term ones, which *may* point towards dispersal.

All we can say with confidence, therefore, is (*a*) that the Commission has 'regional balance' constantly in mind, (*b*) that its long-term policies are directed towards the achievement of this ideal, and (*c*) that its short-term policies have shown *some* tendency towards the correction of regional imbalances, particularly by way of infrastructural investment. But one must add that thirteen years of planning have not yet reduced the gap between the more advanced and the more backward states, and may even have increased it.[19] Hence many states continue to express dissatisfaction both with what they have already received, and with what they are likely to receive in the foreseeable future, by way of benefits from the planning process.

(ii)

It is not easy to judge how far the points of view expressed, and the pressures brought to bear by the various states, influence the shape of the quinquennial and annual national plans. Most politicians and administrators in the states proclaim that they are largely at the mercy of a dictatorial Planning Commission. This, as we have seen, is an exaggeration,

[19] The Commission itself, in default of adequate statistical information and possibly for reasons of prudence, has expressed itself very cautiously on this issue. Asked whether the differences between the states were becoming wider, it replied, 'It is not altogether easy to answer this question' (NDC, 16th mtg, 12–13 Sept. 1960).

reflecting the fact that a compromise between the claims of sixteen separate authorities, rivals for scarce resources, cannot satisfy any one of them. Nevertheless, the subordination of the states to the national plan is as obvious a feature of India's political economy as the comparative feebleness of the states' own planning efforts. The reasons for this are complex. The constitution, which by making social and economic planning a 'concurrent' subject gives the centre the last word, clearly has some influence; so have the ubiquity and solidarity of the IAS, the inexperience and parochialism of politicians at the state level, the superior technical knowledge available to the centre, and the fact that the Congress Party holds office in nearly all the state capitals as well as in New Delhi. But there can be no doubt that, of all the influences contributing strength to the central planners, the financial dependence of the states is the most important. Without an understanding of financial relationships between centre and states, therefore, planning relationships between them are unintelligible.

The states' financial dependence on central subventions, which has been the subject of so much discussion, was certainly not foreseen by the makers of India's constitution, who, in providing for the division of revenues between centre and states, had no conception of the 'scope and magnitude' of the successive Five-Year Plans.[20] Like the allocation of powers, the division of revenues fairly closely followed the pattern of the 1935 constitution, which in its turn reflected the varied experience of central-provincial financial relations during the forty-five years that had elapsed since Lord Mayo's famous Financial Resolution of 1890, which effected the first decentralization of financial powers to the provinces of British India. Moreover, when it came to taking decisions about the 'devolution' of centrally-levied taxation and the making of grants and loans by the centre to the states, the government of independent India was heavily dependent on the studies produced by a series of British-appointed advisory bodies, such as the 'Meston' Committee of 1920, the First 'Peel' Committee of 1931, the 'Percy' Committee of 1932, the Second 'Peel' Committee of the same year, and the 'Niemayer' Mission of 1935.[21] Although these had done a thorough job, they were even less conscious than the constitution-makers of 1948–50 of the financial implications of a planned economy.

The Seventh Schedule to the constitution divided taxation powers between a Union list and a state list. To the Union it assigned (1) taxes on income other than agricultural income; (2) customs and excise (apart from excise on alcoholic liquors and narcotic drugs); (3) the corporation tax; (4) capital taxes; (5) taxes on property, other than

[20] *FC(3)*, 1961, p. 34. [21] See B. R. Misra, *Indian Federal Finance* (Bombay, 1960), chs 2–5.

agricultural property; (6) taxes on succession, other than succession to agricultural land; (7) terminal taxes and taxes on railway freights and fares; (8) taxes on stock exchange transactions; (9) stamp duties (on listed items); (10) newspaper and advertisement taxes. To the states it assigned (1) land revenue; (2) taxes on agricultural income; (3) succession duties on agricultural land; (4) estate duties on agricultural land; (5) taxes on lands and buildings; (6) taxes on mineral rights; (7) taxes on the entry of goods into the local area for consumption; (8) taxes on the consumption or sale of electricity; (9) sales taxes; (10) advertisement taxes, other than advertisements in newspapers; (11) vehicle taxes; (12) taxes on animals and boats; (13) tolls; (14) taxes on professions, trades, callings, and employments; (15) capitation taxes; (16) luxury taxes; (17) stamp duties other than those specified in the Union list.

Responsibility for fixing the rate of a Union tax and for collecting it did not necessarily give the central government the right to monopolize its proceeds. Items 5, 6, 7, 8, and 10 on the Union list were to be assigned to the states; the income-tax was to be shared with them according to 'such percentage as may be prescribed . . . in such manner and from such time as may be prescribed' by the President, 'after considering the recommendations of the Finance Commission'; the excise was to go to the states in whole or in part 'in accordance with such principles of distribution as may be formulated . . . by law'.

The constitution also provided that grants-in-aid might be made by the Union to 'such States as Parliament may determine to be in need of assistance', after consideration of the recommendations of the Finance Commission (Art 275). Of equal and ultimately greater importance was the first of the 'Miscellaneous Financial Provisions' (Art. 282), which authorized the Union or a state to 'make any grants for any public purpose, notwithstanding that the purpose is not one with respect to which Parliament or the Legislature of the States, as the case may be, may make laws'. It is by virtue of this clause that the Union has extended to the states that massive 'non-statutory' assistance essential to the implementation of the plans.

A key role in the devolution of tax proceeds and the making of statutory grants-in-aid was to be played by the Finance Commission, a quasi-judicial body responsible for advising Parliament or the President (as the case might be) on (*a*) the distribution and allocation of 'shared' taxes, (*b*) the principles governing grants-in-aid, and (*c*) 'any other matter referred to the Commission by the President in the interests of sound finance'. The Commission was to consist of a chairman and four other members and had to be appointed by the President 'within two years from the commencement of this Constitution and thereafter at the expiration of every fifth year or at such earlier time as the President considers necessary'. Until the first Commission could be appointed, the sharing of income-tax and the payments of grants-in-aid were to be regulated by Presidential Order (Arts 280 & 281).

Borrowing powers were given to both the Union and the states, and the Union was authorized to make loans to the states. As long, however, as a state was indebted to the Union or dependent on the Union for a loan guarantee, it required Union permission for the further exercise of its loan-raising powers (Art. 293).

Although these provisions were based upon past experience rather than on anticipation of future needs, they had certain obvious merits. Overlapping powers of taxation were, for the most part, avoided. The division of the proceeds of central taxation was not rigidly prescribed but made subject to periodical amendment on the recommendations of a quasi-judicial body. The statutory grant-in-aid was given a similar flexibility, while Article 282 opened up the possibility of non-statutory grants on a scale which few of the Founding Fathers could have envisaged. Furthermore, the states found themselves endowed with exclusive jurisdiction over taxes which appeared to possess a degree of elasticity sufficient to meet their foreseeable financial needs. In making these provisions the framers of the constitution were influenced by the experience of the United States, Canada, and Australia as well as by that of pre-independence India.[22] The result was that, although the advent of planning gave rise to difficult problems, it proved possible to accommodate the requirements of a centrally-planned economy within the financial framework of a federal constitution. This considerable achievement can be too easily obscured by the subsequent accumulation of difficulties in the financial relations between centre and states.

An immediate problem, which had to be solved even before the constitution came into force, was to make interim arrangements for the allocation of the proceeds of the income tax (and also those of the jute export duty, in respect of which there were specific, although temporary, problems). This was done by the so-called 'Deshmukh Award' of 1950.[23] A more considered adjustment of financial relationships had to await the report of the First Finance Commission, which appeared in 1952 and contained recommendations for the quinquennium 1952–7.

By 1952 the First Five-Year Plan had—at least in theory—started; but the final report of the Planning Commission had not yet been issued. Consequently, even at this stage, the impact of planning on finance could be no more than dimly envisaged. As we have seen, the First Plan,

[22] See B. N. Ganguli, 'Federal-State Financial Relations in U.S.A., Canada and Australia and their Lesson for India, in N. V. Sovani & V. M. Dandekar, *Changing India; Essays in Honour of Professor D. R. Gadgil* (1961), particularly p. 92.

[23] See Misra, *Ind. Fed. Finance*, pp. 158–60.

particularly during its earlier years, did not generate severe financial strains at any point, and hence the idea continued to prevail that most of the states would be able to 'live of their own', if adequate delegations of central taxation were made, and that grants from the centre, whether statutory or non-statutory, would be fairly marginal, being devoted mainly to 'equalisation' and to the assistance of states which had a great deal of leeway to make up in the provision of certain services. In 1952 only Assam and Bihar depended upon Union subventions for more than a quarter of their revenue, and it was not expected that, in general, the need for assistance would change rapidly.

Accordingly, there was nothing very spectacular or unexpected about the Commission's recommendations. The states' share in the proceeds of the income-tax was to be increased from 50 to 55 per cent, and to be allocated to the extent of four-fifths on a basis of population, and one-fifth on a basis of collection. They were also to receive 40 per cent of the Union excise duties on tobacco, matches, and vegetable products, allocated on a formula which took both population and 'backwardness' into account. The effect of these proposals was that all the states, except Bombay, Mysore, Punjab, Saurashtra, and Travancore-Cochin, were to receive larger shares of central taxation than in the past. General grants-in-aid, under clause 275 of the constitution, were recommended for seven states only: Assam, Mysore, Orissa, Punjab, Saurashtra, Travancore-Cochin, and West Bengal. These were considered to have special needs, among which budgetary weakness, affectation by partition, and responsibility for scheduled tribes figured prominently. In no case was a general grant of more than Rs125 lakhs recommended; but the Commission established a precedent which was later to cause controversy by recommending that eight states, viz. Bihar, Madhya Pradesh, Hyderabad, Rajasthan, Orissa, Punjab, Madhya Bharat, and the Patiala and Eastern Punjab States Union (PEPSU), should receive special grants for the support of their primary education programmes. Assam, Bihar, West Bengal, and Orissa were to receive grants under Article 273 of the constitution in lieu of their share in the export duty on jute and jute products.[24]

These recommendations were accepted by the Union government. It has been calculated that their effect was to transfer to the state governments, via 'shares' and grants in a normal year, 'Rs21 crores more than the annual average of Rs65 crores transferred during the three-year period 1949–50 to 1951–52'.[25] The general principle behind them was that a state should meet its normal expenditure from the proceeds of its own taxes and of the shared taxes and should regard grants under Article 275 as marginal and justified only by special circumstances. The question,

[24] Ibid. pp. 160–6. [25] Ibid. p. 164.

already becoming vital, of how *plan* expenditure should be divided between the various sources of revenue, and particularly between general statutory grants and specific non-statutory grants, received no clear answer; but its importance was shown by the fact that in 1952–3 grants of the latter kind already amounted to 48·7 per cent of the total.[26]

How completely the expectations of 1952 were falsified is shown by the increase in the average of centre-borne state expenditure from 19 per cent in 1951–2 to 36 per cent in 1960–1. Figures for the individual states[27] (adjusted to take account of the reorganization of 1956) are as follows:

TABLE 29

Percentage of State Expenditures Borne by the Centre

State	*1951–2*	*1960–1*
Andhra Pradesh	17·45	35·42
Assam	28·34	52·95
Bihar	25·63	47·86
Bombay	22·80	31·12
Jammu and Kashmir	0·02	52·71
Kerala	20·27	32·15
Madhya Pradesh	10·97	36·93
Madras	17·21	33·57
Mysore	21·14	30·50
Orissa	24·33	47·91
Punjab	14·34	28·59
Rajasthan	22·57[1]	37·87
Uttar Pradesh	18·61	37·28
West Bengal	23·14	39·29

[1] In respect of the year 1952–3.

This increase had several components. Shared revenue played an important part. The Second Finance Commission (which reported in 1957) raised the states' share in the proceeds of income-tax from 55 to 60 per cent, and gave them more excise money (even while reducing their share of the centrally levied excises from 40 to 25 per cent) by widening the tax base to include sugar, tea, coffee, paper, and oils.[28] As a result of these and other improvements, the total share of the states in divisible taxes increased from Rs67 crores in 1956–7 to Rs120 crores in 1957–8.

[26] *FC(3)*, 1961, p. 40.

[27] Quoted from Ursula Hicks, *A Memorandum on the Financial Relations between the Union Government of India and the States* (mimeo. document presented to FC (3)).

[28] *FC(2)*, 1957; see also Misra, *Ind. Fed. Finance*, pp. 166–77.

The Commission also increased statutory grants-in-aid, on the grounds that those awarded by its predecessor had not taken 'the requirements of development' fully into account. Accordingly, the total jumped from Rs23 crores in 1956–7 to Rs46 crores in 1957–8.[29] These increases, however, were dwarfed by the spectacular rise in non-statutory, discretionary, conditional grants under Article 282 of the constitution. Already, by the end of the First Plan, the proportion of shared taxes and statutory grants to the total resources transferred from the centre to the states had fallen from 43 (1951–2) to 20 per cent (1956–7).[30] While, as a result of the increase in the states' share of central taxation, this proportion did not change very significantly during the Second Plan, the actual amount of assistance via non-statutory grants more than doubled (from Rs54 crores in 1957–8 to Rs114 crores in 1960–1). In the latter year the states received a total grant-aid of Rs163 crores, of which only Rs49 crores was accounted for by statutory grants.[31] This meant that the states were receiving the overwhelming proportion of their grant-aid direct from the central government for specific plan projects and that the greater part of grant policy had consequently fallen outside the purview of the Finance Commission.

During the Second Plan, too, Union-to-state loans came to play a role far larger than had originally been envisaged for them. The Second Finance Commission recorded their 'phenomenal growth' from a total of Rs194 crores in 1951 to one of Rs900 crores in 1956.[32] By the time the Third Commission reported (1961), the total indebtedness of the states to the centre had considerably exceeded this sum, and payments of interest (many of which were in respect of slow-yielding or non-yielding assets) were placing a heavy burden on state revenues.[33] Indeed, in order to relieve this burden where it had become unsupportable, the financially dangerous practice had been introduced of making new loans to enable states to pay the interest on old ones.[34]

The other side of this coin of increasing financial dependence is the decreasing role of the states' own contribution. During the First Plan, their tax-raising efforts were quite inadequate. The Second Finance

[29] Hicks, *Memo.* [30] *RBIB*, May 1956. [31] Hicks, *Memo.* [32] *FC(2)*, sec. 14.
[33] *FC(3)*, p. 41.
[34] This has now become established practice. In the financial year 1962–3 the estimates of total loans to the states were revised from Rs453 to Rs523 crores. The bulk of the excess, said the Finance Minister, 'was attributable to grant of *ad hoc* loans to seven State Governments to clear their overdrafts with the Reserve Bank'. 'Despite a grant of substantial assistance from the Centre for financing their Plan and non-Plan outlays, and a larger share of Central Taxes and grants accruing to them as a result of the Third Finance Commission's award', he continued, 'some of the States had overdrawn their accounts. While agreeing to clear their overdrafts, he had to stipulate that the States should impose tight financial discipline, raise additional resources, and keep expenditure within their means' (*IN*, 9 Mar. 1963).

Commission recorded[35] that the total sums collected represented the following percentages of the First Plan's taxation targets:

Assam	94	West Bengal	12
Bihar	41	Hyderabad	14
Bombay	102	Madhya Bharat	55
Madhya Pradesh	22	Mysore	33
Madras	20	PEPSU	10
Orissa	21	Rajasthan	79
Punjab	90	Saurashtra	45
Uttar Pradesh	22	Travancore-Cochin	55

Corresponding figures for the Second Plan are likely to be better than these, if only because the targets were set more realistically. But the absolute increase in taxation revenues between 1955–6 and 1960–1 was no more than Rs158 crores, and during the latter years of the plan the rate of increase was very slow, the total sums rising from Rs373 crores in 1958–9, to Rs404 crores in 1959–60, and Rs440 crores in 1960–1.[36] Much of this increase in yield, of course, was wiped out by inflation.[37] More importantly, the proportion of tax revenue raised by the states to their total revenue fell from 46·6 per cent in 1957–8 to 41·8 per cent in 1960–1.[38] Moreover the contribution which the states' tax revenues could make towards plan projects was being constantly eroded by the unexpectedly rapid increase in 'non-developmental' expenditures.

The story thus told in figures is a familiar one to the citizen of any modern federation. The Indian case, nevertheless, has its unique features. The change in the balance of financial power between centre and states has been unprecedentedly swift and associated with a planning system which involves the annual doling out of sums of money for specific centrally-determined purposes. Not surprisingly, critics of these developments have presented them as an uncontrolled slide towards a unitary

[35] *FC(2)*, p. 28. [36] *FC(3)*, pp. 104–7.

[37] Even states which exceeded their Second Plan taxation targets, such as Andhra Pradesh, registered no improvement in real terms. The following table gives Andhra's tax revenues for the last four years of the Second Plan (*a*) in money terms, (*b*) as 'deflated' by the application of the all-India wholesale price index (in the absence of any better index).

	1957–8	*1958–9*	*1959–60*	*1960–1*
(*a*) Tax revenue	36·00	35·77	42·37	43·61
(*b*) Price index	108	113	117	125
(*c*) 'Deflated' tax revenue	33·33	31·66	36·21	34·89

Source: Andhra Pradesh, Bureau of Econ. & Statist.

[38] *FC(3)*, pp. 104–7.

form of government, in which the states, in virtue of their rapidly-increasing dependence on the centre for financial resources, are being reduced to the status of mere administrative agencies of New Delhi.

There is plenty of material here for those who seek political support by banging the 'states' rights' drum. Thus Minoo Masani, the Swatantra leader, warns the states that they 'will lose their rights' and 'become mere glorified municipalities and district local boards if they do not look out'.[39] But many moderate and politically less committed people have also put up the danger sign. K. Santhanam speaks of the creation of a 'vertical federalism' whereby, under the aegis of the Planning Commission, each central department becomes a 'sort of empire', with the corresponding departments at the state level as its satrapies. This he links specifically with the growing number of central loans for capital expenditure, the effect of which, he considers, is effectively to tie up even those grants which are nominally free of strings.[40] P. R. Dubashi makes much the same point and also underlines the paradoxical nature of a situation in which a programme of 'democratic decentralisation' is 'being ushered in progressively in all the States, under vigorous Central direction'.[41] The *Economic Weekly* accuses the central and the state ministries of a form of 'collusion' whereby 'any objections coming from the [state] Planning Department are met . . . with the argument that the proposals have already been approved and have actually been suggested by the Centre'.[42] In an interview with the present writer, a member of the Rajasthan Secretariat ascribed the 'infructuousness' of much of the state's agricultural expenditure to the fact that assistance was much more easily obtainable for a scheme invented by the Union Ministry of Agriculture than for one of the state's own choice. This was also the view of A. D. Gorwala, who accused the government of Mysore of undue readiness to 'jump in for any scheme which the Central Government suggests, offering a grant or loan or either to meet part of the expenditure, without considering it from the point of view of the State and without pausing to compare it with other schemes that may be more useful but for which the Centre is making no offer.' As an example, he quoted the decision to go ahead with the establishment of new seed farms, despite the failure of the old ones:

Sanction has been accorded a few days ago to a further 35 farms for the same purpose. The total cost is estimated to be 30 lakhs, of which the State is to bear 17 lakhs and the Centre 13 lakhs. This is a hurrying up of the original plan proposal by one year, because of the insistence of the Government of India. Indeed the noting [i.e. on the files relating to this project] shows very clearly that the State, although feeling very doubtful about the results, is letting itself

[39] LSD, lvii, 4318, 23 Aug. 1961. [40] *Union-State Relations*, pp. 55–56.
[41] *IJPA*, vi (1960), p. 251. [42] Spec. no., Jan 1960.

be pushed into this because of the pressuring of the Planning Commission and the Government of India.[43]

An even more authoritative source, the Third Finance Commission, finds the 'ever-increasing' dependence of the states on the centre 'disturbing'. It is 'diluting, on the one hand, the accountability of the state Cabinets to their legislatures; on the other hand, it is coming in the way of the development of a greater sense of responsibility in their administration'.[44]

These lamentations should not be allowed to go unexamined. They mostly come from people who are committed to a particular conception of the federal relationship and sometimes to a somewhat static view of the constitution itself. There is, after all, no reason why the views which seem to have been held by the constitution-makers of 1948–50 should be given priority over the requirements of a centrally-planned economy. Such a priority may, indeed, be nonsensical when the success or failure of planning is in the balance. Furthermore, the real extent of 'dependence' can easily be exaggerated.

The states, as we have seen, are not without political influence at the centre. At the very least, they can make the Planning Commission and the ministries think twice simply by dragging their feet. Moreover, they still obtain a large proportion of their centrally-delegated resources in the form of tax-shares and unconditional grants. This money is not tied to any specific centrally-promoted projects, but is given, as of right, on the recommendations of a judicially-minded Finance Commission, for a period of five years. Admittedly, the central government, which is not bound to accept the Finance Commission's recommendations, could use the quinquennial re-examination as an occasion to 'discipline' the states, by way of using their collective behaviour as a criterion governing the size of the total sum to be transferred, and their individual behaviour as a criterion for its allocation; but there is no evidence that it has tried to do so. Indeed, it accepted the recommendations of the first two Finance Commissions *in toto*.

Nevertheless, as conditional grants steadily gain precedence over statutory grants and shared taxes, and as the indebtedness of the states to the centre mounts up, the sense of dependence is bound to grow, and with it a tendency either passively to accept what is offered, on any terms that may be suggested, or to kick vigorously against the pricks. Neither reaction facilitates the process of planning. By 1960–1 conditional grants financed about one-quarter of the states' total expenditure and about four-fifteenths of their *plan* expenditure.[45] In respect of the carrying out of plan projects, therefore, the dependence of the states is extreme. The question is whether anything can be done about it, compatibly with

[43] *Mysore Administration*, pp. 22, 60. [44] *FC(3)*, pp. 36–37. [45] Ibid. p. 103.

having a national plan for the whole of India—and, indeed whether any change in the existing relationship would be a change for the better, from the planners' point of view.

One possible change is that the states should use their own taxing powers more vigorously. They have not lacked encouragement to do so, either from the Planning Commission or from the central government; for these authorities are reluctant to dip ever deeper for the states' benefit into the central exchequer's rapidly emptying purse. Time and again, at the NDC, the states have been urged to make greater tax-collecting efforts, and time and again they have replied with a *non possumus*, while protesting with equal vigour against any proposed reduction in the size of the plan to correspond with the rather puny fiscal exertions which they claimed to be the limit of their capacity. This is not because they have been supplied by the constitution with comparatively 'inelastic' sources of revenue. Both the land tax and the excise provide autonomous tax-bases that are potentially strong; but neither has been exploited, while the agricultural income tax, which has the advantage of progressiveness over the other two, seems to be regarded—perhaps not without reason—as political dynamite.

There is a combination of technical and social inhibitions here at work. Methods of assessing land tax are complex, vary from state to state, and usually involve time-consuming cadastral re-surveys, very difficult to undertake at a time when land reform is in progress.[46] Agricultural income-tax also involves the assessor and collector in serious problems, while the excise, although comparatively easy to assess and collect, has suffered from the whittling away of its base by the complete or partial imposition of prohibition. But these are by no means the only reasons for the fiscal feebleness of the majority of the states. No politicians who were serious about the raising of resources would have passively accepted the decline in the burden of the land tax from 3·9 per cent of the gross value of agricultural output in 1938–9 to 1·0 per cent in 1950–1, without making some effort either to reverse the process or to find other ways of making the agriculturalist pay his share. At first sight, an increase in the total yield from Rs48 to Rs100 crores over the period 1951–61 would suggest that such an effort was actually made; but the figures are deceptive, for the increase is no more than a reflection of (*a*) increased coverage (as a result of the introduction of the tax for the first time in some of the former princely states) and (*b*) the abolition of intermediaries, such as the *zamindars*. Indeed, most of the extra resources which thus accrued were absorbed by compensation payments to the intermediaries and by the

[46] For a brief summary of methods of assessing land tax, see K. Balasubrahmaniam, 'Revenue Administration in India', in G. S. Halappa, *Studies in State Administration* (Dharwar, Karnatak Univ., 1963).

heavy costs of abolishing them and of establishing a public tax-collecting apparatus in the areas where they had acted as the government's fiscal agents.

Fundamentally, the reluctance of the states to impose new taxation is a product of their comparative proximity to a tax-shy electorate, reinforced by the fact that the taxes upon which they depend, such as the land tax and the sales tax, have a wider coverage and more immediate impact than those reserved for the central government, such as the income-tax and the 'non-alcoholic' excises.[47] These are the factors which, reinforced by the desire of each state government not to appear 'less generous' to the taxpayer than its neighbours, are responsible for the failure to increase even rates of land revenue which have remained stable, in money terms, for the last thirty to sixty years.[48] Unwilling, for political reasons, to impose either regressive taxes which would evoke popular protest or progressive ones which would affect the pockets of the 'notables' who run their party machines, the politicians prefer to pass the poisoned chalice to the central government. In a sense, the position of dependence suits them very well. It enables them both to avoid taking unpopular measures and to attribute failures to 'circumstances over which we have no control'—in fact to enjoy the fruits of political office without bearing the full burdens of political responsibility.

That this was the essence of the situation did not become fully evident during the First Plan, which, as we have seen, was not big enough to put a serious strain on resources. If few of the states, during this period, exerted themselves to increase the yield of taxation, to make their commercial undertakings pay, or to obtain the fullest possible value for every rupee spent, the consequences of their idleness, although less than helpful to the cause of economic development, were far short of disastrous. It was the extreme financial stringency generated by the attempt to carry out the much more ambitious Second Plan that revealed the full extent of their irresponsibility.

In 1957–8, when inflationary pressures were mounting and preparations being made for cutting down the plan to an irreducible 'core', a majority

[47] Hence fairly persistent proposals, towards which the states inevitably adopt a somewhat ambivalent attitude, to replace state-levied by centre-levied taxation and to extend the scope of 'sharing'. The NDC, at its 12th meeting on 3–4 Apr. 1959, was presented with a paper from the Planning Commission which, after expressing doubt whether the states would be able to impose adequate taxation in the rural areas, suggested that 'agricultural and non-agricultural incomes and wealth' might be treated 'on the same basis by direct taxation to be imposed by the Centre, the proceeds being shared with the States on an agreed basis'. An extension of centrally-levied excises in place of state sales taxes was also mooted. The NDC, after discussion, was reported as agreeing that 'in principle' the agricultural income-tax and the general income-tax should be placed on a uniform basis, and that the extension of centrally-levied excises 'should be studied further'. There is no record, however, of the NDC's having given further attention to either of these matters.

[48] *FC(3)*, pp. 38–39.

of them budgeted for a deficit on revenue account. Orissa, with an estimated shortfall of Rs4·56 crores, West Bengal, with one of Rs10·28 crores, Assam, with one of Rs4·60 crores, Bombay, with one of Rs3·17 crores, Andhra Pradesh, with one of Rs5·48 crores, and Madhya Pradesh, with one of Rs7·17 crores, all announced that they intended to impose no new taxation. Rajasthan, Punjab, Madras, and Uttar Pradesh, while increasing their taxation, failed to increase it sufficiently to wipe out more than a fraction of the deficit estimated on the basis of the old rates. Only Kerala and Jammu and Kashmir aimed at a balance or a surplus.[49] In most states natural reluctance to increase taxes was temporarily reinforced by expectations, soon to be realized, that the Second Finance Commission would act as fairy-godmother by increasing the share of divisible taxes and the volume of statutory grants.[50]

Once the new allocations had been made Finance Ministers could claim that the case for fresh taxation had disappeared. In his 1958–9 budget speech, the Finance Minister of Uttar Pradesh, announcing the narrowing of the deficit from Rs11·67 to Rs4·54 crores, 'took credit for imposing no new taxes', and praised the 'bounteous award' of the Finance Commission.[51] This, said the *Eastern Economist*—normally a champion of the states against the centre—was 'a disappointment to those who expected that a valiant attempt might be made this time by the State Government to balance its budget in response to Central exhortation'.[52] Andhra Pradesh, in announcing the prospect of a surplus for the first time since its creation as a state in 1953, was also full of praise for the Finance Commission. Assam and Mysore rejoiced in the transformation of the deficits of the previous years into small surpluses, West Bengal in the reduction of its deficit from Rs10·28 to Rs3·83 crores. None of these imposed new taxation. Kerala and Rajasthan were content with a very small improvement in their fiscal efforts. Only Bombay, Punjab, and Madras proposed to raise through taxation more than an extra crore of rupees (Bombay: Rs3 crores; Punjab: Rs2·3 crores; Madras: Rs1·7 crores).[53]

Hence, although the revenue budgets of the states were reported in May 1960 to be in a 'comfortable position', this was attributable much less to fiscal effort on their part than to 'the increasing scale of resources transferred from the Centre in the forms of shared taxes and grants'. The overall balance was by this time deteriorating rapidly. An overall surplus in 1958–9 was replaced, during the two following years, largely as a result of the stepping up of plan outlay, by overall deficits of Rs42 crores and Rs60 crores respectively. As the Reserve Bank said, the financial position of the states as a whole reflected 'growing strain'.[54]

[49] *AR*, 1957, pp. 1278, 1358, 1462, 1465, 1486, 1496, 1519, 1524, 1548, 1601, 1957.
[50] See *EE*, 13 Sept. 1957, pp. 395–6. [51] *AR*, 1958, pp. 1915–16. [52] 21 Feb. 1958, p. 420.
[53] *AR*, 1958, pp. 1915, 1916. 1931, 1958; *EE*, 14 Mar. 1958, p. 564. [54] *RBIB*, May 1960.

To the extent, therefore, that the states' financial dependence on the centre is a product of their own reluctance to raise money, their complaints about Planning Commission 'dictatorship' have rather a hollow ring. Well might the Commission reply with a 'tu l'as voulu'. To make their behaviour the subject of moral censure, however, is neither helpful nor sensible. Like the federal units of the United States, Canada, and Australia, they are run by democratic politicians who naturally prefer not to take any avoidable action that would forfeit or reduce electoral support. If these men appear to be less responsible than their counterparts in other countries, the reason is simply that they have to work to a much less well-informed public opinion in conditions of infinitely greater financial stringency. Hence it may as well be accepted that no exhortations from the centre, however vociferous and anguished, are likely to effect any radical change in their attitudes. In matters of taxation, it is safe to predict that the states will continue to drag their feet. The centre, therefore, is likely to have to continue to provide an increasing proportion of their expenditure.[55] All it can do is to try to ensure, by the use of appropriate incentives and controls, that the resources it releases are economically and efficiently used and distributed in a way that gives the maximum 'built-in' stimulus to self-help.

Satisfaction of both of these *desiderata* can be facilitated by the 'matching' grant, allocated on the principle that the more money the recipient raises for a particular project or series of projects the more he will receive from the donor. The actual effect of the grant depends, of course, partly on its size and partly on the kind of 'matching' principle which it embodies. If it represents a very high proportion of total expenditure, it will significantly stimulate neither efficiency nor self-help. If, on the other hand, its contribution to total expenditure is small, it may stimulate efficiency only at the expense of failing to achieve its major purpose (i.e. to ensure the provision of the service concerned at a certain level of adequacy), and its effect on self-help will be negligible. If it is allocated as a straightforward percentage, it may give rise to unnecessarily extravagant expenditure on the particular service for which it is earmarked to the detriment of necessary expenditure on other services. If, on the other hand, the 'unit grant' principle is adopted, economy may be achieved at the expense of adequacy. These contradictions are fully familiar to every student of Union-state or state-local financial relations. They cannot be resolved, but a proper understanding of them can enable the donor to distribute his

[55] The *MTA* (p. 5.) reports: 'While efforts to mobilise resources for the Plan have been on the whole encouraging, there are some States which are experiencing difficulties in raising resources on the scale envisaged in their plans. Additional taxation undertaken in these States has been low in comparison with their initial targets. These States will find it difficult to fulfil their plans without further steps to strengthen their financial position.'

gifts in a way that, on balance, seems likely to have the most beneficial and least detrimental effects.

A further complication, however, is introduced by the fact that 'matching' can never be used as an exclusive principle. If only for political reasons, no Union government can single-mindedly follow the Biblical injunction of giving to those that have. The matching grant, which favours not merely the more strenuous-minded states but also the wealthier ones, is obviously hostile to the increasingly powerful demand for equality. This demand can be satisfied, wholly or partially, in three ways: an 'equalization' element may be introduced into the matching grant itself; or a separate grant, based exclusively on the equalization principle, may be given as a supplement to the matching grant; or these two methods may be combined—usually at the cost of some confusion. In any case, the effect of the introduction of this principle will be to dilute the stimulatory effects of the grant system, unless some incentive to efficiency and self-help can be built into its equalization components.

Additional complexities arise when, as in India, grants are geared to the achievement of certain centrally-planned targets. A state may undertake to raise a given proportion of the cost of a project. The first instalment of the corresponding central grant is then issued, and work begins. The state, however, soon discovers that it has 'overestimated' the size of its promised contribution—perhaps deliberately. What happens then? Is the project to be slowed down or stopped? Or does the centre step up its financial assistance, so as to ensure that the creation of what may be an important national asset is not impeded or delayed?

Problems of this kind have greatly exercised both the Planning Commission and the Finance Commission, and the fact that there are two separate bodies involved in the allocation of central assistance has not facilitated the search for a solution. In general terms, it may be said that the Planning Commission works to the 'matching' principle while the Finance Commission is more concerned with equalization. Nevertheless, the former cannot disregard the claims of 'balanced regional development', while the latter's attempts at equalization (which use population as the main criterion) are somewhat crude. Moreover, the Finance Commission, like the Planning Commission, has frequently expressed its concern with the amount of 'effort' which the various states devote to the raising of resources. Lastly, both are very much dependent on the accuracy and honesty of the estimates presented to them by the states, and usually find themselves the recipients of totally different sets of figures, for reasons which must be explained.

As the Finance Commission, in its recommendations for the 'devolution' of centrally-levied taxes and statutory grants, is engaged in filling the 'revenue gap', the states are tempted to present it with figures which underestimate their resources. On the other hand, in their representations to the Planning Commission they consistently overestimate their resource-raising potentialities, because the more they promise to do, the more they are likely to get. As, hitherto, the process of plan formulation has not coincided with the deliberations of the Finance Commission, it is not very difficult for them to play the one body off against the other. Evidence of this practice may be found in some of the states' own Third Plan reports.

Bihar, for instance, told the Planning Commission in 1960 that its balance from current revenues for the Third Plan, at 1960–1 rates of taxation, was likely to be Rs22·3 crores and that it could raise an additional Rs41·00 crores from further taxation. But by the time its plan report appeared, the Third Finance Commission had been constituted and had reached an 'advanced state in its inquiries'. Not surprisingly, the Bihar planners had second thoughts: 'On a reassessment of both the estimates and receipts and also of expenditure it is apprehended that the balance from current revenues may not be as high as the figures reported to the Planning Commission.'[56] Mysore promised the Planning Commission to raise Rs42 crores by additional taxation—'more than two and a half times its previous effort'—and offered a total contribution to the plan of Rs110 crores. By the time the Finance Commission was considering its requests, however, it had discovered new difficulties. Revenue expenditure was increasing with unforeseen rapidity; the introduction of prohibition would virtually wipe out excise receipts; the promised provision from reserves (Rs15·00 crores) 'might not be available'; and the prospect of being able to impose additional taxation had become 'doubtful'. Thus, said the planners, '. . . it is seen that the State's resources, which were anticipated to be of the order of Rs110·00 crores, will have, on account of the effect of later events, to be reviewed on the basis of the award of the Finance Commission, and additional resources to be raised, and annual plans phased accordingly'.[57]

Kerala, which had originally estimated, for the benefit of the Planning Commission, a balance of Rs10·40 crores from current revenues, found that 'between the finalisation of discussions with the Planning Commission (September 1960) and the presentation of figures to the Finance Commission (October 1961) . . . several changes had occurred in the resources position of the State'. These it specified as:

the expansion of the administrative machinery at the headquarters and the districts consequent on the reorganisation of the States and the increase in the number of districts in the State to satisfy the felt needs of the people; the taking over by the Government of the educational and medical institutions under the control of the District Board and Local Bodies in the Malabar area; the unification and revision of the salary structure of the services necessitated

[56] Bihar, *FYP(3)*, i (1961), pp. 41–42. [57] *FYP(3)*, i. 82.

by the State's reorganisation; the increased commitments in servicing the public debt liability passed on from the Madras State; the introduction of the system of direct payment of salaries to teachers in aided schools; and the last, but not the least, the committed expenditure under the completed programmes of the Second Five Year Plan.

As a result, the new forecast showed a negative balance of Rs27·18 crores instead of a positive one of Rs10·40 crores. 'The State Government have placed all these facts before the Finance Commission and have requested it to allocate a larger share of Central taxes and duties to the States [*sic*] supplemented by liberal grants-in-aid to cover the revenue gap of the State.'[58]

This kind of sharp practice was not quite universal. West Bengal, for instance, reported that it estimated its total resources for Third Plan projects at Rs19·73 crores in August 1960, Rs73·08 crores in November 1960, and Rs132·81 crores in January 1961.[59] Although it did not state what figures it put before the Finance Commission, this rapid transition from pessimism to optimism about its own resource-raising potentialities may conceivably be explained by its comparative lack of interest in the Finance Commission, from which so comparatively wealthy a state could not expect very much.[60] This exception, however, looks rather like a rule-proving one, and certainly does nothing to disprove the contention that the operations of the Finance Commission incite the states to conceal their true resource-raising potentialities. Admittedly, those of the Planning Commission cause them to exaggerate such potentialities, which can have an equally deleterious effect. Nevertheless, as the states' contributions to the plan are reassessed annually, the Planning Commission has frequent opportunities to correct errors arising from this source; while the Finance Commission, which works to a five-yearly period, does not. Once the devolution has been made, it has statutory effect until revised on the basis of the next Finance Commission's report. The Finance Commission, therefore, as one of the custodians of the nation's purse, has been very anxious to discover means of ensuring that the 'revenue gaps' reported to it are genuine ones, representing irreducible minima after the states have done their utmost to raise resources and exercise economies.

It has not had much success. Among the criteria adopted by the First Commission and accepted by the Second for assessing the necessary extent of devolution were (*a*) 'clear cases' of a state's failure to maximize its tax effort, and (*b*) 'the State's endeavour to secure reasonable economies'.[61]

[58] Kerala, *FYP(3)*, pp. 32–35. [59] W. Bengal, Dev. Dept, *FYP(3)* (1961), pp. 6–8.
[60] It had been awarded no grant-in-aid by the Second Finance Commission, and in fact received from the Third no grant in respect of 'ordinary' revenue, as distinct from the 'revenue component' of the Third Plan.
[61] *FC(2)*, pp. 24–25.

These criteria, as the Second Commission itself recognized, were uncommonly difficult to apply, and there is no evidence that it made any serious attempt to apply them. The Third Commission decided that the whole job was too big for it and suggested that only a special 'high-powered' Commission could undertake so complicated an assignment:

> The comparative determination of the tax efforts of the States cannot be in absolute terms. It has to be related to their tax potential, and this calls for special study. Similarly, the assessment of the measure of economy effected and the degree of efficiency reached in a State's administration is a complicated exercise which, in any event, we could hardly undertake with the organisation and time at our disposal. Yet, without reliable and comparable information on these two essential ingredients of a grant-in-aid, it is difficult to determine the quantum of assistance that would be necessary and justified. This and other considerations lead us to the suggestion . . . that an independent Commission should be constituted to review, among other things, the financial relations which, in the new situation of planned development, should subsist between the Union and the States.

In default of this 'reliable and comparable information', the Third Commission, like its predecessors, was compelled 'to cover the annual budgetary gaps of all the States, whether caused by normal growth of expenditure, the maintenance cost of completed schemes and mounting interest charges or even by a measure of improvidence'. In doing so, it clearly recognized that, in contrast with the Planning Commission, it was completely at the mercy of the states.

> Secure in the knowledge that the annual budgetary gap would be fully covered by devolution of Union resources and grants in aid, the States are tending to develop . . . an allergy to tap resources in the rural sector on many considerations and also a disinclination to make up the leeway in others. They do not also attach the same importance to a proper and adequate control on expenditure in the matter of services and supplies as before. Cadres expand, pay-scales get revised upwards, negligence develops in the procurement of supplies and execution of projects in the absence of proper cost control. While there is a close scrutiny of, and consultation on, the contents of the Plan, there is hardly any on the contents of the annual estimates; there is no counterpart at the national level in regard to non-Plan expenditure which is progressively increasing as a result of planning itself.[62]

A possible method of circumventing these defects of the 'stringless' grant, based on alleged fiscal needs, is provided by the formula used by the Commonwealth Grants Commission in Australia. A few Indians, among whom the best-known is B. N. Ganguli,[63] have expressed interest in this rather successful institution, which works to a 'budget standard' with which the actual budgets of the claimant states are compared, and

[62] *FC(3)*, pp. 29, 38. [63] See above, n. 26.

has evolved methods of assessing tax effort and of making allowances for objective conditions that affect per capita expenditure. Professor Ganguli believes that these techniques can be and ought to be adapted to Indian requirements, although he recognizes that this would demand a considerable amplification of the statistical data at present available; and one may suppose that the Commission itself, in recommending the appointment of a high-level committee to investigate Union-state financial relations, was thinking in similar terms.

Certainly, this would seem to be the way to improve the Finance Commission's present unsatisfactory procedures, if they are to be improved at all. Before it is attempted, however, there is a question of basic importance that demands an answer: whether, in the context of a planned economy, the Finance Commission itself has any *raison d'être*. For there are many reasons for believing that, however sophisticated it may become in its methods of assessing needs and distributing resources, a situation in which control over central subventions is divided between two bodies cannot be satisfactory.

Some writers have already come to the conclusion that the Finance Commission has outlived its usefulness, because the development of a planned economy has made obsolete the distinction between the 'ordinary' expenditure and the 'plan' expenditure of the states. As D. N. Sharma says:

> Both receipt and expenditure sides of the Plan budget are determined in advance in course of discussion with the Planning Commission. The 'normal' budget is also determined simultaneously. Thus the budget that the State Finance Minister presents to the Assembly is basically nothing but what was drawn up earlier in discussions with the Planning Commission. The State Finance Minister can neither propose any new item of expenditure nor draw upon any new source of revenue from which to finance such expenditure. Almost everything is predetermined.

He therefore concludes that 'there is . . . no justification for dividing the transferable fund into two parts and giving them different names', and suggests that, as the work originally regarded as the prerogative of the Finance Commission has, *de facto*, been largely taken over by the Planning Commission, the former body might appropriately be made a department of the latter (or become a Committee of the Rajya Sabha or be superseded by the NDC).[64]

But although this suggestion would seem to be well supported, it naturally makes little appeal to the Finance Commission, which in its Third Report has attempted to extend its own jurisdiction at the expense of that of the Planning Commission. In view of the Finance Commission's

[64] 'Centre-State Financial Relations', *EW*, 17 Dec. 1960.

self-confessed inability to act as an effective custodian of the public purse, such an attempt appears, at first sight, to be nothing more than irresponsible empire-building. We must therefore look rather carefully at the Commission's reasoning.

In its chapter on 'Grants-in-Aid', it asked whether, in view of the instructions it had received to take note of the requirements of the Third Plan, it 'should give full coverage to the estimated revenue component of the Plan or should limit it on practical or other considerations'. On this question it was presented with 'two points of view', which it attempted to summarize thus:

The first is that the Plan itself is flexible and is subject to adjustments at the annual reviews undertaken and there is need to ensure that the States conform to the priorities and provisions laid down. If full financial allocation is made by us, these reviews would be rendered difficult. The other point of view is that the Plan having been endorsed by the National Development Council and approved by Parliament, it is only logical to guarantee the necessary resources to the States to enable them to forge ahead. It is suggested that devolution and grants-in-aid by the Finance Commission would be more in tune with the provisions of the Constitution and that it would inculcate a greater sense of responsibility in the States as the grants-in-aid would then become an integral part of their resources. It has further been urged that it is inconceivable that the scope and targets of the Plan, except in an emergency, could possibly be revised downwards. Further, that, in an emergency, the provisions we make would in any case come to be suspended; and that there should, thus, be no impediment or practical difficulties in the way of our providing for the fiscal needs of the Plan even in full.[65]

Clearly, it was the second point of view that represented the Commission's own preference. Not only did it feel that the states ought to be given more 'flexibility and room for adjustments' than they received at the hands of the Planning Commission; it explicitly agreed with the contention (of which Sharma has been quoted as an exponent) that to attempt to draw a line between plan and non-plan expenditure was 'not really sound'. But, unlike Sharma, it considered that a greater portion of the total expenditure should be met by its own devolutions and grants and a smaller portion by those forms of assistance dispensed by the Planning Commission. The dividing line between the two portions, it suggested, should be drawn as follows:

(*a*) assistance which is meant to fulfil what can rightly be described as national purposes, such as power, flood control, major irrigation works, agriculture, family planning, etc. should continue to be governed by strict conditions regarding their utilization; and
(*b*) grants, which are meant to strengthen the State sector in matters which must necessarily be decided with fullest regard to local rather than national

[65] *FC*(*3*), pp. 29–30.

needs, such as education, health, minor irrigation projects, etc., should be such that the States have the freedom to reappropriate from one head of such allocation to another while adhering to the broad objectives of the Plan.[66]

Oddly enough, this rather vague differentiation did not follow the division of powers as laid down in the constitution. Essentially, it was no more than a cock-shy at a distinction between the 'national and onerous' and the 'local and beneficial'—a distinction which an examination of the experience of other countries would have quickly proved to be illusory. Moreover, it was presented as a suggestion to the proposed Commission of Inquiry and not as the foundation for the Finance Commission's actual recommendation, which was based on an entirely different principle, viz. 'that the total amount of grants-in-aid should be of an order which would enable the States, along with any surplus out of the devolution, to cover 75 per cent of the revenue component of their Plans'.[67]

Precisely how the figure of 75 per cent was arrived at it did not explain, except by way of saying that it had been 'influenced, among other things, by the fact that the Plan contains repetitive schemes of a continuing character'. This, of course, introduced an entirely new consideration which, one would have thought, required a full and detailed explanation. The Commission's whole argument on this issue was so deficient in quantification and so full of loose ends that one can hardly credit it as the production of an 'expert' body.

But this was not all. Having given with one hand the Finance Commission proceeded to take away with the other. The grant-in-aid going to each state, it had said, would have the advantage, over the Planning Commission's grants, of 'inculcating a greater sense of responsibility', in so far as it was given as of right and not as of grace. Yet on the following page that part of the grant earmarked for the fulfilment of the purposes of the plan was characterized as 'specific' and therefore subject to yearly review, 'should the necessity arise, by Parliament under article 275(1) or by the President under article 275(2) as the case may be'.[68] It would seem, therefore, that the Finance Commission was less concerned with removing the 'demoralization which dependence inevitably breeds', than with taking away from the Planning Commission the responsibility for annually reassessing a considerable proportion of the states' financial needs in respect of plan expenditure. Rational explanation of the contradictions displayed by this section of the report is impossible. It would seem that the Finance Commission just did not like the Planning Commission.

Further evidence that this short-lived, *ad hoc* body was convinced of the superiority of its own hunches to the accumulated wisdom of the Planning

[66] Ibid. p. 31. [67] Ibid. pp. 31–32. [68] Ibid. p. 32.

Commission is provided by its last and most extraordinary proposal: that an earmarked grant should be made 'for the improvement of communications in the interests of national economy and national integration'.[69] One could only conclude that the Planning Commission, during the course of its long examination of transport and communications problems, had somehow failed to notice 'the pressing need to open up backward areas, to break down barriers of isolation and stagnation, to develop social services and social sense, to mobilise economic resources and above all, to bring about a feeling of oneness in the minds of the people of these regions with the rest of the community'. There could hardly be a clearer example of attempted usurpation of the planning function.

These views did not, of course, pass uncriticized. Indeed, the most effective attack on them came from the Commission's own member-secretary, G. R. Kamat, in a long Minute of Dissent appended to its report.[70] Kamat held that the Commission, in proposing to finance a part of the revenue component of the Third Plan, had gone beyond any reasonable interpretation of its terms of reference. If the Second Commission had made grants for this purpose, the reason was that there had been an uncovered gap in the revenue plans of the states. The position was now different, in that no such gap appeared in the Third Plan. As for the autonomy of the states, this would not be significantly enhanced, as they would still be dependent on the centre for their capital requirements as well as for that portion of the plan grants not covered by the proposed devolution. Moreover, as a result of the introduction of new procedures by the Planning Commission (which will be examined in the following chapter), considerable progress had been made 'towards greater flexibility in the making of these grants and in their reappropriation from one scheme to another'. These improvements had already given the states as much autonomy as was consistent with the accepted practice of centralized national planning. The proposed scheme would therefore have none of the advantages claimed for it. On the other hand, it would display very distinct disadvantages, from the standpoint of carrying out the plan in a coherent and flexible manner. It would introduce a harmful 'statutory rigidity' in respect of the transfer of revenue resources; it would tend to discourage the states from stepping up their tax efforts. If the attempt were made to avoid these disadvantages by the type of parliamentary or presidential 'annual review' suggested by the Commission, this would merely mean the replacement of the existing review procedure by a more 'onerous and rigid' one, from which not even the states themselves would derive any benefit. Such defects as remained in the existing system could be removed by 'adjusting procedural details after a joint

[69] Ibid. p. 32. [70] Ibid. pp. 51–60.

consultation between the Union and the State Governments'. To displace that system by one of statutory grants was 'like throwing the baby out with the bathwater'. As for the proposed earmarked grant for 'the improvement of communications', no such grant was necessary 'in the context of overall planning', as the Planning Commission had already provided the sums which it thought appropriate for this purpose.

Kamat was clearly on the side of those who would enhance the role of the Planning Commission and would confine that of the Finance Commission to the making of peripheral adjustments in the financial relationships between centre and states. He did not, however, suggest that the Finance Commission should cease to exist as a separate body, although this possibility had been referred to by the Commission itself.

The report had mentioned the proposal 'to transform the Planning Commission into a Finance Commission at the appropriate time' only to dismiss it, on the grounds that it would further 'dilute' the autonomy of the states and inhibit 'the development of a greater sense of responsibility in their administration'. Consistently with their recommendations on the financing of the Third Plan, the Commissioners favoured the enlarging of their own functions 'to embrace total financial assistance to be afforded to the States, whether by way of loans or devolution of revenues, to enable them both to balance their normal budgets and to fulfil the prescribed targets of the Plans'. This, they considered, would be 'in harmony with the spirit and even express provisions of our Constitution', and would also make the Commission's recommendations 'more realistic, as they would take account of the inter-dependence of capital and revenue expenditure in a planned programme'.[71]

Perhaps the strongest evidence that such a course would be mistaken and the clearest case for transferring the functions of the Finance Commission to the Planning Commission are provided by the confusions of the Third Finance Commission's own arguments, which gave Kamat so easy a target. The case is further strengthened by the existence of tensions and misunderstandings between the two bodies, which cannot but confuse and complicate the planning process. The only reputable argument for the separate existence of the Finance Commission is that it can act as an impartial arbiter between the financial claims of the states and those of the centre. If the essence of the planning process lay in the quasi-judicial adjustment of such rival claims, the preservation of the Finance Commission's independence would be important. But if it lies, as it obviously does, in the rational allocation of scarce resources, a 'quasi-judicial' approach is inappropriate and 'independence' comes perilously close to irresponsibility. Admittedly, political factors make strict economic rationality an unattainable ideal. The states have their politically-motivated claims,

[71] Ibid. pp. 35–37.

which they will continue to press both individually, in their negotiations with the Planning Commission and the central ministries, and collectively, through the NDC. But the adjustment of those claims, both to one another and to the claims of the centre, needs to be made in the context of the overall national plan, rather than in the light of what some detached body holds to be the 'proper' balance of power under the federal constitution. If national planning is to be taken seriously, this conclusion seems inescapable. If it is denied, the implication is that national planning for economic development has less than first priority; and not even the Finance Commission has gone as far as to say that.

As it is, the Planning Commission, about a year after the completion of its quinquennial exercise, has to adapt its operations to the financial arrangements recommended by a body over which it has no influence. Yet these arrangements are of the essence of planning, in a country where developmental responsibilities are divided in the federal pattern. It matters greatly what tax resources will be left to the centre, after the share-out of central revenues with the states has been completed; for this decision determines how much money, at a given level of taxation, will be available for financing the centre's own projects and how much will be available for transfer to the states in the form of grants, both statutory and discretionary. It is equally important to be able to decide, during the course of the planning process, what proportion of the grant-money is to be tied to particular projects and schemes and what proportion is to be 'free'; and to be able to adjust to specific requirements and, if necessary, to vary the terms on which the various categories of grants are made. This would seem obvious, and the meeting of such requirements will be facilitated now that it has been decided, rather belatedly, to make the Finance Commission's quinquennium coincide with the Planning Commission's. But, so long as there are two separate bodies with their fingers in the pie, an unnecessary mess can hardly be avoided.

This is not to say that the *functions* of the Finance Commission are obsolete. Although it is conceivable that all centre-to-states assistance should take the form of discretionary grants, annually reviewable, and that the present arrangements for tax-sharing and making statutory grants ought to be abolished, this is by no means self-evident; for one can argue that the effective use of economic resources, over an area as wide and varied as India, demands a measure of administrative decentralization which is incompatible with the tight centralized control that an exclusive use of conditional and variable financial assistance almost inevitably involves, whatever countervailing measures may be used. Moreover, even if it were economically and administratively rational, it would be politically impossible; for no central government could contemplate subjecting the political sensitivities of the states to so outright an affront. Tax-sharing and statutory grant-making are therefore likely to continue as long as India remains a federation, and therefore someone will have to conduct the necessary investigations into the extent to which they are desirable, and make the appropriate recommendations to the central government. What we are arguing is that these functions, being inseparable from the process of planning, ought to be confided to the Planning Commission.

In making financial subventions to the states, the central government is trying to ensure five things, viz. (1) that broad planning priorities are observed; (2) that these priorities are adapted to the states' individual needs; (3) that the states are given the strongest possible incentive to develop and tap their own resources; (4) that all resources, whatever their origin, are employed with the maximum economy and efficiency; and (5) that the states are encouraged to contribute creatively to the planning process. To do all these simultaneously is difficult, as they are not necessarily complementary. The planner is often confronted with the fact that the more of one means the less of another. He has to make a choice or effect a compromise, in the light of his comprehension of the short-term economic situation and the long-term economic perspectives. Such a crucial decision, if it is to be well made, must be based on the fullest possible information and experience. Such information and experience is possessed only by the Planning Commission. The financial relations between centre and states are only a part—albeit a vital one—of the whole process of planning for which the Commission has the penultimate responsibility. We have arrived at the point, therefore, where we must cease to treat them as a separate subject of study and consider them in the context of the formulation and implementation of both the national plan and the state plans.

X

CENTRE AND STATES, 2: MAKING AND IMPLEMENTING THE PLANS

(i)

CONCEPTUALLY, one may distinguish three phases in the planning relationship between the centre and the states. In the first, the state's five-year plan is formulated, amended, and adjusted to the national plan; in the second, the state's annual plan is similarly formulated, amended, and adjusted; in the third, state and centre collaborate in the process of implementation. For purposes of analysis it will be convenient to treat these phases separately; but the process from which they have been separated out is a continuous one, in which the phases interpenetrate. Quinquennial and annual plans are simply formal documents in which centre and states set themselves certain targets and enter into mutual undertakings for their achievement. The actual process of both formulation and implementation involves almost day-to-day communication, both formal and informal. There is a formidable flow of correspondence from Planning Commission to state governments, from central ministries to state ministries, from a variety of central *ad hoc* organizations, directly or indirectly, to their state counterparts, and vice versa. There are regular meetings of Finance Ministers, Development Commissioners, Ministers of Industry, Ministers of Agriculture, and the like. There are the visits to the state capitals of the Commission's peripatetic Programme Advisers. There are innumerable journeyings of official personalities from New Delhi to the states, and from the states to New Delhi. There are 'trouble-shooting' missions in both directions, and conferences in great abundance. It is during the course of all this complex activity that the *modus vivendi* which the various planning documents imperfectly reflect is somehow established. To *describe* the process without over-simplifying it would demand a series of case studies which no one, as yet, has had the temerity to attempt. Here we can do no more than make a broad analysis, on the basis of such factual information as is fairly readily available.

In respect of five-year-plan formulation, India has witnessed during the period under review some very important developments in centre-state relationships. These will now be examined.

In the preparation of the First Plan the states did little more, in reality, than provide the Commission with information. They attempted forecasts of revenue and expenditure over the five-year period and stated what projects they had in hand, in preparation, and in contemplation. For this they were given little enough time. On 6 September 1950 the Commission sent them a letter,[1] accompanied by a simple form, asking them to submit, by the end of the month, 'a rough forecast of the resources likely to be available during the five years, 1951–52 to 1955–56'. On 11 October it asked[2] them to prepare their first drafts of their two-year and five-year programmes by the end of November. To assist them it listed seven very general 'considerations' that they should bear in mind. It expressed the somewhat surprising confidence that they would ensure 'that the plans in different sectors and for the State as a whole are mutually consistent with one another, and that in each case the physical targets proposed are capable of being achieved through the schemes included in the plan'; but it quickly followed this up with an indication that rather less than this was really expected of them: 'It is realised that in view of the limited resources which are available, in a number of directions, it may not be practicable to do more than maintain the existing activity; in some even this may not be found possible.' Heads and sub-heads were provided as 'a convenient method of presenting different aspects of the Plan', together with another set of forms.

By 24 May 1951, the Commission was able to announce[3] that it had 'completed its discussions with most of the Part 'A' and Part 'B' State Governments regarding their development programmes for the two years 1951–52 and 1952–53 and for the period of five years ending 1955–56'. During these discussions, it added, 'the programmes for agriculture, industries and irrigation and power were finalised in considerable detail and for these and other heads certain financial allocations for the two-year and five-year periods were agreed upon'. The states were now called upon to provide, by 12 July 1951, 'five statements in their final form with a view to incorporation in the national plan'. Forms of some complexity were provided for this purpose, and one may imagine that, despite the Commission's insistence on the need for 'completeness and accuracy', the state governments had to exercise considerable statistical imagination in filling them up. These statements provided the basis for much of the Draft Outline, published in July 1951.

Three weeks later the Commission sent another letter[4] to the state governments. This gave the go-head for the 'various development schemes provided for in the State plans', many of which, it said, were already in operation. It also proposed the holding of further discussions with those 'few' states whose final statements 'differed somewhat from the figures reached during discussions with the Governments concerned'. For the preparation of the final plan report, it asked the governments to fill in a

[1] D.O. No. PC(C)99/50. [2] No. PC(C)/106/50. [3] No. PC(C)106/51. [4] No. PC(C)/26/51.

Schedule of Development Schemes and to give physical and financial details of schemes costing Rs10 lakhs or more. The rest of the letter was largely pep-talk, calling for action as recommended by the Draft Outline, particularly in the field of administration.

In brief, the states had some eleven months to draw up their plans, discuss them with the Commission, and present them in more or less final form. As the governments concerned were new, poorly equipped with statistical information, and without any planning machinery worthy of the name, very little could be expected of them in so short a time; and it is clear that the Commission did not in fact expect much. 'Decentralization' was affected only in the sense that the Commission gathered in from the states information about more or less isolated projects already in hand or in contemplation, and decided, in consultation with them, which of these should benefit from such central assistance as was likely to become available.

(ii)

For the preparation of the Second Plan, greater time was available. The states, moreover, had acquired some planning experience and had developed their own planning machinery, albeit of a rather rudimentary kind. It became possible, therefore, to call upon them to assume greater responsibilities.

The first of the Commission's letters to the states about the Second Plan[5] went out as early as 23 March 1954. Its subject, Irrigation and Power Projects, was one that required a long period of consideration, as both centre and states had learnt to their cost. On 20 February an Advisory Committee on Irrigation and Power Projects had been established. This now required from the state governments 'a brief description of the various schemes which they have in view'.

A further letter,[6] dated 28 April, dealt with a subject that had almost become an *idée fixe* with the Planning Commission: the preparation of plans at the district and lower levels. Its main purpose was 'to convey suggestions on . . . the manner in which, within the district, the work of planning may be organised and plans prepared for individual villages and groups of villages such as tehsils, talukas, National Extension development blocks, etc.' This might have seemed, and probably did seem, premature to most of the states; but the Commission was evidently assuming that work on the Second Plan had already commenced at the higher levels. Otherwise, the following passage would have had no point:

> In asking districts to prepare local and village plans, departments at the State level should indicate the general framework for district plans. Thus, at the district level, there should be information and guidance about the

[5] No. PC(V)IV(5)/54. [6] No. FY11/CDI/1/54.

programmes contemplated by the State Government, for instance, in respect of irrigation and power schemes, road system, reclamation programmes, industrial schemes, programmes for education, health etc.

During the following months the Commission attempted to ensure that the states went ahead with the good work and kept New Delhi regularly informed about its progress. Irrigation and power received the most immediate attention. On 13 May the states were sent a lengthy form on which they were asked to enter the 'full information and data' required by the Advisory Committee.[7] A fortnight later (31 May) they received a check-list to help their Engineering Departments to ensure that 'the project reports are complete in all respects'.[8] On 21 June they were requested to expedite the information asked for in the letter of 24 March, as this had become somewhat overdue.[9]

Other letters sent out during the early stages of the planning process (i.e. during the year 1954) were concerned with Industry and Transport. An 'industry' letter, dated 10 September 1954,[10] contained the warning that 'any proposals for new large-scale industrial projects to be taken up by State Governments, or even for expansion of existing undertakings, will require very special justification if they are to be approved for inclusion in the next Five Year Plan'. A 'transport' letter,[11] issued on 15 June by the Minister of Railways, indicated that, although no more than 1,500–2,000 extra miles of line could be built in the Second Plan, total requests from the states amounted to 15,000 miles. State governments, therefore, must decide what new constructions were urgent and arrange them in order of priority. They were also warned,[12] on 10 July, against failing to assess in advance the transport requirements of their big projects. Shortly afterwards they received from the Ministry of Transport a directive[13] about the preparation of their roads programmes. On 18 September the Commission informed them[14] that the nationalization of road transport did not have 'high priority' and urged them to abandon 'restrictive licensing policies'. Schemes for the nationalization of road freight services, they were told, would not be considered for inclusion in the Second Plan, but consideration would be given to 'phased programmes' of road passenger transport nationalization if certain conditions were accepted.

Attention was also given, towards the end of the year, to the expansion of the NES and CD Programme during the Second Plan period.[15] Each state was provided with a tentative statement showing the number of blocks allotted to it, together with the share of the total expenditure it would be asked to meet, and told that it might 'now proceed to adumbrate'

[7] No. PC(V)1/3(A)/54. [8] Ibid. [9] Ibid. [10] No. PC(III)19/4/54. [11] 54/W/150/5.
[12] No. PC(III)19/49/54. [13] PL-15(39)54. [14] No. PC(III)13/61/54.
[15] CPA/163/36/54P.

its Second Five-Year Plan for CD and NES on that basis, 'drawing up a phased programme from year to year and formulating requirements of key personnel for the implementation of the expansion programme'.

Financial resources for the Second Plan were the subject of a major request for information on 15 July.[16] The Commission stressed the anticipated tightness of the resources position, and hopefully incited the States to look again at land taxes, water rates, betterment contributions, district or local 'cesses', and agricultural income-taxes. It asked them to provide data to enable it 'to review the progress of resources and expenditure during the First Plan period and to assess in broad terms the financial resources which the State Governments themselves are likely to be able to find, at existing levels of taxation, for financing the new activities to be undertaken in the next Plan'. For the *additional* resources that they proposed to find through taxation a separate note was required. On the attached forms they were asked to provide estimates of receipts on revenue account, estimates of expenditure on revenue account, forecasts of developmental expenditure, estimates of receipts on capital account, estimates of disbursements on capital account, forecasts of capital outlay under development heads, and estimates of resources likely to be available for the Second Five-Year Plan, all up to the year 1961.

During the early months of 1955 the planning correspondence continued unabated. Further advice was given about the preparation of village and district plans,[17] states were asked to formulate their health programmes,[18] and much needed directives on the classification of expenditure[19] were issued. By 24 March the Commission was able to announce that work on the preparation of the Second Plan was 'well advanced in most States'. It therefore requested[20] that state plans should be submitted to New Delhi by the middle of July. To ensure uniformity and comparability it promised suggestions about 'suitable forms and indicators'. A few days later it specified that the plans should include 'to the maximum extent possible all programmes to be implemented by a State Government or by public authorities such as local bodies or special boards set up within a State', irrespective of the extent to which the central government participated in their financing. Although, as a result of frequent consultation with central ministries, the states were 'already sufficiently familiar with the thinking at the Centre', further information would be provided about the 'kind of development programmes' which they 'might specially consider including in their plans'. In the meantime, they were asked to 'proceed on the basis of their own appreciation of needs and practical possibilities and of the working of the First Five Year Plan', taking also into account

[16] No. PC(1)/VII/(1)/54. [17] No. PC(P)58/54; No. FYII/CD1/6/55.
[18] No. PC(VI)HL/1(1)55. [19] No. PC(I)VII(1)54; No. FYII/CD1/13/55.
[20] D.O. No. FYII/CD1/8/55.

'suggestions which may have been reached in any recent conference or exchange of views between the Central Government and the States'.[21]

The states, therefore, were not suddenly confronted, in March 1955, with a demand to deliver up their draft plans within four months. With varying degrees of efficiency and enthusiasm, they had been involved in the work of plan preparation for at least the previous twelve months. During that period they had received from the centre a great deal of advice, some of it not very realistic, and had provided the centre with a great deal of information, some of it not very accurate. Occasionally they found themselves treated like naughty children, to be warned and scolded; sometimes the Commission or a ministry decided that a little teeth-baring was necessary and sent out something that looked very much like a directive. Indeed, it was not unknown for a state, feeling discomfort in the policy vacuum which seemed to surround it, to *ask* for a directive, as Hyderabad did 'in respect of roads'. In general, however, the states were left reasonably free to discharge their plan-making functions to the best of their very variable abilities. Not until their plans had been drafted and sent up to the centre, in July 1955, did the attempt begin to adjust them to the magnitudes and priorities which the Commission had in the meantime roughed out for the national plan. This process lasted from July to December 1955, the period immediately preceding the issue of the Draft Memorandum (January 1956) and the Draft Outline (February 1956).[22]

The procedure outlined above did not work entirely smoothly. It is difficult, in fact, to envisage any procedure that would be wholly adequate; for a planning process which involves collaboration between a number of separate authorities tends to move in a series of vicious circles. The top-level planning authority would like to know, in advance, what the lower-level authorities intend to do, while the lower-level authorities feel that until they have been informed of the former's intentions, plan-making on their part is little more than an academic exercise. Hence they are inclined to do the job with rather less than the needed skill and enthusiasm, with the result that the top-level authority obtains from them rather second-rate information and is thereby hindered in its efforts to provide, for their guidance, a reasonably realistic general framework.

In the formulation of the Second Plan, it was the states that had the more serious cause for complaint. After the plan-making process had been in operation for some eight months, they were told, by Chintaman Deshmukh, that 'only certain broad figures could . . . be taken as a guide' and that 'if a Plan went beyond these limits, it would not be accepted'. These figures, said to be 'envisaged' by V. T. Krishnamachari, were for 'a plan involving an outlay of the order of Rs5,500 crores—3,000 crores in the public sector

[21] No. FY/CD1/14/55. [22] *FYP(2)*, p. xii.

and 2,500 crores in the private sector'.[23] Such information was of little use, even when supplemented, as it was to be during the following months, by ministerial announcements of provisional targets for various sectors. Indeed, it was not until *after* the states had been requested to send up their draft plans to New Delhi that the first firm estimates of magnitudes and priorities were issued, in the shape of the Mahalanobis Plan Frame and its accompanying documents.

Even more important to the states was some indication of the amount of central assistance that they might expect. This they did not obtain until very late in the day. They were informed, a week or two after the request for the submission of draft plans had gone forth, that the 'question of the form and quantum of Central assistance for individual development schemes' was 'not being considered at this stage', and that the whole subject would be dealt with 'later from a more general point of view'.[24] In fact, the centre delayed making any firm commitment until January 1956.

Well might the Development Minister of Assam complain that it was 'difficult for the States to prepare their schemes unless some indication was given about the size of the second plan and the likely central assistance', and demand that 'to enable the State Governments to prepare their plans in time, . . . the breakup of targets statewise should be indicated as urgently as possible'.[25]

To blame the Commission for this failure, however, would be unfair. Like the states themselves, it was caught in the vicious circle. In spite of the adoption of improved procedures for the formulation of the Third Plan, the same complaints were again voiced; and it is likely that they are being heard again today, during the process of formulating the Fourth Plan. Short of abolishing the federal constitution, there is little that can be done to eliminate them.

(iii)

Nevertheless, the improvement in centre-state relationships achieved during the preparation of the Third Plan was very real. From the 'perspective' part of the Second Plan report, the states had some general indication of what the Third Plan was intended to achieve. They knew that, as the principles and objectives of the whole planning process had been firmly laid down, the Third Plan would require of them no new departures but rather a continuation, *de plus belle*, of what they were already doing. They could even assume that the proportion of total expenditure met by central assistance would not be significantly changed. They also knew that, although the magnitude of the plan was still under discussion,

[23] NDC, 3rd mtg, 9–10 Nov. 1954. [24] No. FY11/CD1/14/55, dated 7 Apr. 1955.
[25] NDC, 4th mtg, 6 May 1955.

a total outlay of about Rs10,000 crores was highly likely. Most important of all, they had given their approval, through the NDC, to the proposals embodied in the Commission's 'Main Issues' paper. All this was much more satisfactory. So were the later stages of plan-making. Whereas, in the First and Second Plans, the states had been required to present their drafts before—and, in the case of the Second Plan, a long time before—the publication of the Draft Outline, in the Third Plan the Draft Outline came first. This change was not, perhaps, entirely voluntary, for the confusions attendant upon states reorganization would in any case have imposed delay; but it seems to have been advantageous.

The main interest in the third plan-making exercise, so far as the states are concerned, is to be found in the operation of the working groups which they established. Such groups had been a feature of the preparation of both the previous plans, but they were now employed much more consistently and systematically. On the initiative of the Planning Commission, they were set up at various times during the later months of 1958 and the early months of 1959. How far the states regarded them as useful instruments of planning and how far as a Planning Commission's 'gimmick' (which it was advisable to *appear* to take seriously), is uncertain. As we have seen, Madras treated them rather contemptuously. Bombay, on the other hand, went to the extent of printing their reports for official circulation.

Ideally, one should attempt a comparative study of the use of working groups in several states. This, however, would be difficult, as comparable information on this subject is hard to come by. We shall therefore have to be content with one example of working group procedure. For this purpose, we have chosen Bombay.

Each working group (or 'study group' as it was called in Bombay state) was given a broad area of developmental programming as its province. Groups were constituted for (1) Irrigation and Power; (2) Industry and Mining; (3) Transport and Communications; (4) Agricultural Production, including Development of Agricultural Co-operatives; (5) Land Development, including Development of Forests; (6) Animal Husbandry and Dairy Development; (7) Fisheries; (8) Education; (9) Health; (10) Social Welfare, including Backward Classes and Housing; (11) Town Planning; (12) Statistics and Intelligence. The nucleus of each group consisted of the senior officials directly or indirectly interested in the subject under consideration. For instance, to the Study Group on Irrigation and Power there were appointed the Secretary of the Public Works Department (Chairman and Convenor), the Chief Engineer of the Bombay State Electricity Board, the Chief Engineer of the Koyna Project, the Chief Engineer for Irrigation Projects in the Public Works Department, the Director of Agriculture, the Director of Industries, the Deputy

Secretary (Planning) of the Political and Services Department, a Deputy Secretary in the Finance Department, and the Deputy Secretary (Irrigation) of the Public Works Department.[26] At its first meeting the group set up two sub-groups, one for irrigation and the other for power, to which a total of eight further officials were co-opted.[27]

Terms of reference varied in their specificity. The Agriculture Group was simply asked to formulate proposals 'for the Third Five Year Plan after assessing (i) the progress made so far and (ii) the long term potentialities of development'.[28] The Industry and Mining Group had to '(*a*) examine problems involved in the sphere of the development of Industry and Mining from a long term point of view, (*b*) try to set out possible dimensions of various programmes, (*c*) examine the nature of physical and technological limitations of development and the manner of overcoming them and (*d*) formulate proposals to be taken up in the Third Plan period keeping in view the perspective of the 15 year development plan'.[29] The Irrigation and Power Group was given similar terms of reference but also asked to direct its attention specifically to the following:

(*a*) An assessment of the achievements during the First Five Year Plan and also the anticipated achievements during the Second Plan with a view to finding out the causes of lack of progress, if any;
(*b*) An appraisal of the likely achievements at the end of the Second Plan, taking into account the existing organisational, material and financial resources available for development and also the progress so far achieved in the respective spheres;
(*c*) Formulation of the broad requirements over the next three plan periods and specific requirements for the Third Five Year Plan;
(*d*) Formulation of the physical targets for the next three plan periods and more definitely for the Third Five Year Plan, keeping in view the technical and organisational resources;
(*e*) Determination of priorities, measures and machinery for achievement of both short-term and long-term objectives of development;
(*f*) Estimates of the financial cost involved, both internal and external, for implementing the programme required for the achievement of the target during the Third Five Year Plan period;
(*g*) An assessment of the requirements of scarce resources, such as cement, iron and steel for construction and foreign exchange required for execution of schemes.[30]

The reports of the groups tell us little about their methods of work. Data and proposals from the various departments of the state government

[26] Bombay, Pol. & Services Dept, *FYP(3): Bombay State, Rep. of Study Group on Irrigation & Power*, Feb. 1960, p. 1.
[27] Ibid. pp. 2–3.
[28] SG on Agric. Prod'n incl. Dev. of Agric. Cooperatives, Mar. 1960, *Rep.* (Poona, 1960), vol. i, p. iii.
[29] SG on Ind. & Mining, Dec. 1959, *Rep.* (1960), p. 1. [30] *Rep.*, p. 1.

provided the bulk of the material placed before them. Most of them formed sub-groups, variously named. The Irrigation and Power Group, as we have seen, formed two. The Industries Group appointed one 'Panel' to deal with Cottage and Small-Scale Industries and Industrial Co-operatives, and another to deal with Large and Medium Industries, Geology, and Mining. The Health Group had eight sub-committees.

Meetings began at various dates between January and April 1959, and most groups submitted their reports by the middle of the year. Those concerned with Agriculture and Animal Husbandry, however, had first to submit tentative proposals, through the central Ministry of Food and Agriculture, to the central Working Group on Agriculture, and then revise them in the light of discussions held in New Delhi during the month of July. The number of meetings varied widely from group to group and appeared to be uncorrelated with the importance of the subject-matter. The Industries Group, for instance, held only two full meetings (January and August); its Second Panel also met only twice, whereas its First Panel met five times.[31] The Irrigation and Power Group met three times (January, September, and October), the third meeting being entirely devoted to the subject of atomic energy; each of its sub-groups met twice.[32] Of the three meetings of the Health Group, the second, to which the eight sub-committees reported, was distinguished from all other group meetings by lasting for five days (25–29 May).[33] The Statistics and Intelligence Group held no fewer than ten meetings.[34] In general, the groups did not meet frequently enough to enable them to do much original or detailed work.

It may be, indeed, that most of them did not take themselves very seriously. How far the proposals contained in their reports represented a selection from rather than a collection of the various departmental schemes submitted to them is not entirely clear; but one has reason to suspect that the 'live-and-let-live' principle predominated. Departments are not usually prepared to compromise on their proposals until confronted by inescapable financial and/or physical limitations; and at this stage of the planning process no such limitations had been laid down. It is true that the centre had ruled that, for the social services, 'the Third Five Year Plan should not exceed three times the outlay of the Second Five Year Plan';[35] and that the state government had indicated that the Third Plan was likely to be about 60–65 per cent larger than the Second. The first limitation, however, was totally lacking in realism, while the second could easily be disregarded, since the Groups were asked to use their own

[31] *Rep.*, p. 2. [32] *Rep.*, pp. 2, 11, 29. [33] SG on Health, Dec. 1959, *Rep.* (1960), pp. 1–2.

[34] SG on Statist. & Intelligence, Dec. 1959, *Rep.* (1950), p. 1.

[35] SG on health, *Rep.*, p. 2. This was later revised and a more realistic formula adopted and communicated to the states. As the revision dated from July 1960, however, it did not affect the work of Bombay's study groups.

judgement whether, in view of past neglect, their particular sectors deserved a greater proportionate increase.[36]

That the groups should not have been very much concerned whether, collectively, their proposals made sense was inevitable. Ideally, they should have been working to a general Plan Frame for the state, showing the projected rate of income increase, the relations between the various sectors, the capital-output coefficients, the nature and distribution of final consumer demand, and so on. No such information was available to them; nor could it become available until a national plan had been roughed out and Bombay's expected contribution towards its realization indicated. As it was, they did not even know what central assistance would be available or what resources the state government would be prepared to raise. Long after the groups had completed their work, the government of Maharashtra (now responsible for the southern part of the former State of Bombay's territory) was still in the dark about the dimensions of its plan. In the document entitled *Approach to the Third Five Year Plan, Maharashtra State, (1961–62 to 1965–66)*, published in August 1960, it wrote:

> While there can be no two opinions about the Third Five Year Plan of the State having to be much larger than the Second Five Year Plan, it is difficult at this stage to indicate what its size should be. The size of the State's Plan will depend not only upon internal resources but also on the quantum of assistance available from the Centre. The internal resources of the State . . . are being assessed. There is as yet no indication from the Planning Commission as regards the size of the States' plan or the quantum of Central assistance that is likely to be made available to this State. All that is known at present is that the total size of the States' Plans will be of the order of Rs 3,650 crores and that the amount of Central assistance which is likely to be made available . . . to all the States taken together would be about Rs 2,500 crores. It is not known whether in the allocation of Central assistance the Planning Commission follow some objective standards as area, population, internal resources, the present state of development etc. and if so, what weight is attached to each of these factors. No indication has so far been given by the Government of India regarding the schemes that will be treated as Central Sponsored schemes. It is also not known what part of the financial outlays on such schemes will be provided in the Central Plan.[37]

There is some exaggeration in this *cri de coeur*. The state government could make—and was making—fairly shrewd guesses as to the size of these various unknowns. But so long as the final negotiations with the Commission were still ahead, there seemed no point in telling the groups to keep their proposals within realistic limits. The more they demanded, the more they might get. This policy was rationalized by the use of the 'physical practicability' concept. As the 'Approach' document put it: 'While

[36] Information supplied by S. G. Barve, Min. Finance, Maharashtra.

[37] Issued by the Finance Dept, Bombay, p. 3.

they have taken note of the limitation of resources, their approach has been based essentially on the principle that what is physically practicable in the sphere of economic development and what is the minimum necessary in the matter of social services should be made financially practicable.'[38] That such 'terms of reference' were nonsensical hardly requires demonstration. Obviously, no group could decide what was 'physically practicable', so long as it was laying claim to resources for which there were alternative uses. Nor, for the same reason, could it lay down what was the 'minimum necessary in the matter of the social services'. In fact, the groups simply seized on such rough-and-ready criteria as lay to hand and then argued that the very large programme said to be based on them represented the irreducible minimum.

The Irrigation and Power Group emphasized the need to liquidate the considerable back-log of irrigation projects, to 'keep a little ahead of load development' and to catch up with Mysore and Madras in the electrification of rural areas. In respect of power development it did not need to do any elaborate calculation, as it could use the Load Surveys of the Central Water and Power Commission and the interim report of the central working group.[39] The Transport and Communications Group was likewise helped by the Road Development Plan for India (1961–81), the successor to the 'Nagpur' plan. This provided it not merely with a long-term target but a series of formulae 'for arriving at, for any given unit of the area, the mileages required for National Highways, State Highways, Major District Roads, other District Roads and Classified Village Roads'. The Third Plan, said the group, should represent a 'suitable step' towards the realization of long-term needs; but it made no attempt to estimate the actual availability of physical resources for the programmes which it proposed.[40] The Industry and Mining Group's 'Cottage and Small Scale Industries' Panel contented itself with a general, non-quantitative statement of objectives, viz.:

> The Panel recommends that the various schemes for the development of Cottage and Small Scale Industries should be viewed from their ability—(*a*) to provide increased employment particularly in the rural areas, (*b*) to result in increased production, and (*c*) to achieve technological improvement and increased per capita productivity.

For Khadi it simply accepted the targets already recommended by the Boards; for the rest (e.g. small industries, industrial co-operatives, handlooms, &c.) it attempted no justification of the size of its recommended programmes.[41] The 'Medium and Large Scale Industries' Panel was

[38] Ibid. p. 3. [39] *Rep.*, pp. 7, 18–19.
[40] SG on Transport & Communications, Dec. 1959, *Rep.* (1960), pp. 3–5.
[41] *Rep.*, pp. 11, 13 f.

equally vague. After restating the accepted policy that the state was to act as catalyst and promoter rather than owner and manager, it framed proposals 'consistent with this thinking', and 'observed' that these would cost Rs898·30 lakhs as against Rs76·14 lakhs for the Second Plan.[42] The Town Planning Group proposed, without apparently making any investigation of physical resources, that 202 out of 371 towns should be provided with 'basic' amenities, and that, despite the almost complete lack of staff with training in town-planning, either at the state capital or in the municipalities themselves, 100 development plans should be prepared during the quinquennial period. The total cost, Rs6515·5 lakhs, was said to represent a 'not overgenerous' provision, in view of the 'fact' that the bulk of it 'would be for schemes which *may* have been included in the plans of other Departments, such as Public Health, Education, Industries and Co-operation, etc'.[43] The Health Group itself, having proposed schemes costing Rs124 crores (as against a provision of Rs36·69 crores in the Second Plan), found itself a little embarrassed at the thought that this slightly exceeded the 'three times' limit. It felt, however, that in view of 'the growing health consciousness among the public, the need to eradicate major diseases like Malaria, Cholera, and Smallpox, the increased cost of equipment and drugs, the need for greater research and modernization in the field of medicine', no reduction in the programme was possible 'without seriously affecting its usefulness'. It therefore divided its proposals into a 'Priority A' group, costing Rs116 crores, and a 'Priority B' group, costing Rs7·77 crores.[44] Slightly more moderate in its demands, the Education Group nevertheless proposed schemes costing exactly three times the Second Plan outlay; it did, however, produce a sensible and reasoned list of priorities.[45] This was more than could be said of the Social Welfare Group, which, after saying that progress had not been fast enough during the Second Plan, simply listed a number of schemes and estimated their cost. Why the money should have been distributed as recommended between work under the Children Act, work under the Beggars' Act, Welfare of Prisoners, Women's Welfare, Encouragement of Cultural Activities, Youth Welfare, Mental Hygiene, Rehabilitation of Burnt-Out Lepers, &c., was not explained. Each of these schemes was someone's baby, and the principle of distribution appears to have been 'a little for everything'.[46] On the subject of 'Slum Clearance Schemes' it produced the following curious reasoning:

The Slum Clearance projects sanctioned so far under the Second Five-Year Plan are of the value of Rs395 lakhs and some more projects to the extent of

[42] Ibid. pp. 31–33. [43] SG on Town Planning. Dec. 1959, *Rep.* (Bombay, 1960), pp. 2–3.
[44] *Rep.*, pp. 2–3. [45] SG on Education, Dec. 1959, *Rep.* (Bombay, 1960), pp. 3–4.
[46] SG on Social Welfare incl. Backward Classes & Housing, *Rep.* pt 1: *Social Welfare*, Feb. 1960 (Bombay, 1960), pp. 3 f.

Rs28·53 lakhs are under consideration. The total grant during the Second Five Year Plan period under the Scheme may, therefore, be of the extent of Rs450 lakhs. In this urbanised State there are several cities and industrial towns with big populations and naturally their slum clearance schemes are very large. Corporations of Bombay and Ahmedabad alone were in a position to prepare Schemes costing more than 10 crores during the Second Five-Year Plan but had to be discouraged owing to paucity of funds. It is, *therefore*, felt that the ceiling during the Third Plan should be Rs1,500 lakhs.[47]

In other words, three times the Second Plan figures with a bit more for luck!

The only attempts at serious calculation undertaken by the groups themselves are to be found in the reports on agriculture, animal husbandry, fisheries, and forests. The Agriculture Group, for instance, assumed the desirability or necessity of self-sufficiency in foodgrains by the end of the Third Plan, and used population projections and estimates of consumption per head to work out a rough-and-ready and undifferentiated production target.[48] For eggs, the Animal Husbandry and Dairy Development Group assumed a demand which could be met by increasing production by two and a half times, through improving feed and upgrading stock.[49] The Fisheries Group produced the most sophisticated calculations, using per capita availability, a projected annual increase in production, and a capital-output ratio.[50] As far as one can gather, this approach was unique.

It may be assumed that none of the other states did better than Bombay, which was probably the best administered state, with the highest quality personnel, in the Indian Union. In view of the fact, therefore, that its groups did so little to impose order and coherence on the schemes put up to them by the departments, the question arises whether the whole exercise was more than an elaborate pantomine, in which a large number of busy administrators dutifully went through motions prescribed for them by the Planning Commission.

This view has some substance. There is also evidence, from many sources, that the inherent weakness of the interdepartmental group, as at present organized, is aggravated by the kind of contact which it has with the central ministries. While the Planning Commission is doing its best to inculcate a feeling of corporate responsibility, both as between groups and as between their constituent departments, the central ministries are doing just the opposite. For the struggle over the share-out of scarce resources in the states is paralleled by a similar struggle in the centre; and as the states depend on the centre for assistance, the various groups

[47] Ibid. pt 2: *Housing*, Mar. 1960, p. 9. [48] SG on Agric. Prod'n, *Rep.*, App. 'A', pp. 19–21.
[49] SG on Animal Husbandry & Dairy Dev., Mar. 1960, *Rep.* (Bombay, 1960), p. 14.
[50] SG on Fisheries, Dec. 1959, *Rep.* (Baroda, 1960), p. 9.

and departments tend to adopt a 'client' relationship towards their central counterparts. As in all such relationships, mutual advantages are promised. Demands from the states can strengthen the central ministry's claims; 'suggestions' from the central ministry can be quoted by the states as evidence of the reasonableness of proposals which would otherwise appear monstrously inflated. Thus there is a vertical conspiracy to defeat horizontal co-ordination.

The existence of these close vertical contacts during the 'working group' phase of the states' plan-formulating process is sometimes denied. A Maharashtrian minister, for instance, said that the working groups in his state had held 'no consultations' with central ministries or with any other central agencies. This, no doubt, was strictly true; but he went on to speak of the maintenance of 'normal' contacts by departmental officials. A member of the Secretariat, more frank than his minister, said that each group not only tended to inflate its section of the plan to the maximum conceivable size, but was actively encouraged to do so by the relevant central ministries, all of which were anxious to increase their own bargaining powers. In Rajasthan the Secretary for Agriculture said that, during his period of office as Chairman of the state's Agricultural Working Group, he 'oscillated between Jaipur and New Delhi, maintaining continuous contact with the Central Ministry of Agriculture'. In some states, at least, there seem to have been regular exchanges of views and information not only with the central ministries but with the central working groups. This was so in Uttar Pradesh,[51] while in Andhra Pradesh the groups were actually instructed to draft their proposals in close consultation with their central counterparts.[52] This meant, said the Planning Secretary, that 'masses of paper came down and passed through my hands'. The same official accused the central ministries of encouraging 'unrealistic planning' for 'empire building' purposes.

Does this mean, then, that the whole 'working group' exercise is really useless? Such a conclusion would be unwarranted. If treated seriously, the group can at least ensure that before a set of departmental proposals is finalized it has been scrutinized and vetted by the representatives of other 'interested' departments. The very juxtaposition of proposals enables them to be seen in wider perspective. Some officials, moreover, are of the opinion that the freedom from 'restrictive' terms of reference enjoyed by the groups is a positive advantage, in so far as it enables them to think in terms of physical needs and administrative possibilities and thereby produce schemes which, even if financially impracticable during the quinquennial period immediately ahead, are useful as a guide to future

[51] Uttar Pradesh, *FYP(3)*, i: *Rep.*, p. 14.
[52] Interview with Mr Narashiman, Sec. for Planning & Local Govt, Andhra Pradesh.

planners, or as a 'scheme bank' to be drawn upon if financial possibilities unexpectedly improve.[53] This particular argument, perhaps, should be looked at sceptically, for it has the hall-marks of a rationalization; but whatever may be the virtues and vices of the 'working group' system as at present operated, one would be unwise to condemn it in general, before it has had a real opportunity to show its worth. If clearer and more precise terms of reference could be given to the groups their value might be greatly enhanced. To formulate such terms of reference is, of course, difficult, for reasons that have been explained. Nevertheless, it looks as though, in preparing for the Fourth Five-Year Plan, certain states are going to make the attempt. The goverment of Maharashtra, for instance, has decided to set up 'a Planning Committee, under the chairmanship of the Chief Minister, for providing effective and authoritative guidance in the formulation of the policies and programmes for planned economic and social development, and for exercising a close watch on the implementation of plan policies and programmes'. This body is to have the following functions:

(1) To determine the objectives and priorities for development within the broad framework of the National Plan.
(2) To formulate the designs for long-term development of the State with due regard to balanced development of its component regions and within the framework of such a long-term plan to draw up the Fourth Five Year Plan of the State.
(3) To determine inter-sectoral priorities and allocations in the State's annual plans within the financial resources that may be indicated by the Finance Minister.
(4) To identify the areas of coordination between the departments, the Zilla Parishads and other institutional framework and to ensure such coordination for proper implementation.
(5) To watch progress, evaluate achievements, and make periodical appraisal of the Plan and important projects in the Plan.[54]

This is a worth-while experiment, the results of which should be interesting. Will the new committee work out a fresh approach to the difficult problems of planning at the state level, or will it go the way of the many previous 'high-powered committees' which have promised so much and achieved so little? Much will depend on how well the committee is 'serviced' by the new planning organization which Maharashtra has established[55] and which is now being imitated by other states.[56]

[53] Ibid.
[54] *PANL*, Sept, 1963, p. 6. Similar bodies have been appointed in certain other states. Bihar, for instance, has set up a state Board for Planning and Development, and Gujarat a state Planning Advisory Board (see ibid. 1964, p. 4).
[55] See above, p. 81. [56] For instance, Andhra Pradesh (see ibid. p. 5).

(iv)

Sooner or later, the proposals of the various groups have to be brought together into a Draft Plan for the state. At this stage, the aims are (*a*) to produce something that at least looks like a coherent and co-ordinated statement of purposes, expressed in terms of both physical objectives and financial costs: (*b*) to reduce proposed total outlay to a figure which is usable for purposes of serious bargaining with the Planning Commission; and (3) to mobilize public opinion in support of the state's programme. Inevitably, it becomes the occasion for fierce horse-trading between departments and loud voicing of demands by interest-groups. Although the procedure varies from state to state, it has certain common features. The proposals of the working groups have to be considered individually by the departments of government and collectively by inter-departmental and inter-ministerial committees. Either simultaneously or later, the advice of members of the legislature and of representatives of interest-groups may be enlisted. Lastly, when the government has formulated its Draft Plan for submission to the Planning Commission, the approval of the legislature itself is generally sought.

Consultation is variously organized. Maharashtra, for instance appointed an *ad hoc* Consultative Committee of 'leading public men', to which it submitted its 'Approach' document—essentially a first attempt at a Draft Outline.[57] Assam seems to have sent its working group reports straight to a state Planning Advisory Board, consisting of ministers, MPs, officials, and non-officials.[58] In Andhra Pradesh, after inter-departmental meetings which scaled down the working groups' suggested total outlays from Rs588 crores to Rs475 crores—amid 'resistance on all sides'—the amended proposals were submitted to a state Advisory Committee, composed of legislators and various 'interest' representatives.[59] In Mysore, a draft emerging from rather complicated interchanges between the working groups, the Secretaries to government, and the Council of Ministers was first submitted to the state Development Council and then 'distributed to the members of the State Legislature, Members of Parliament for Mysore, members of the state Development Council and the public', with a request for suggestions and comments.[60] Madras used an all-party committee of the legislature.[61] Rajasthan submitted both the state's Plan Frame and the reports of the working groups to its Planning Board, a widely representative body which worked through standing committees.[62] All states made some effort to elicit opinion from district and local bodies. In most cases this perhaps amounted to little more than 'going through the motions', but Rajasthan, as befitted the pioneer of

[57] Maharashtra, *FYP(3)*, p. 2. [58] Assam, Plan. & Dev. Dept, *FYP(3)*, i.
[59] Andhra Pradesh, *FYP(3)*, pp. 14–15. [60] Mysore, *FYP(3)*, vol. i, p. i.
[61] Madras, *FYP(3)* (1961), pp. 11–12. [62] Rajasthan, *FYP(3)*, pp. 20–22.

panchayati raj, organized an elaborate scheme by which the 232 *panchayat samitis* were required to draw up their own programmes. 'To a substantial extent' (reported the planners with a degree of exaggeration which can be appreciated only by those familiar with the state's rural areas) 'the concept of planning from below . . . materialised in the formulation of the Third Plan of Rajasthan.'

Consultation, it should be noted, is not part of the process of cutting down the state's plan to size. On the contrary, it usually has an inflationary effect—one that is not always unwelcome to the state government, which likes to be able to assure the Planning Commission that it is restraining with the utmost difficulty the public's demand for a big plan. In Assam consultation produced such an inflated figure that the Assamese Government itself had almost to halve it. In Andhra Pradesh the Advisory Board raised the suggested total from Rs475 to Rs482 crores. In West Bengal, the government could claim that the *panchayati raj* bodies (to which the draft had been referred) were behind its 'irreducible minimum' of Rs341 crores.[63] The use of consultative machinery, therefore, may be regarded in one of its aspects as part of the state government's preparations for the hard bargaining with the Planning Commission in which it will shortly find itself engaged.

These Tweedledum-Tweedledee battles at the state level are brought to an end by the appearance of the Monstrous Crow, in the shape of the Commission itself. Each state in turn is summoned to New Delhi for the final reckoning, at which the adjustment of proposed outlay to potential resources is undertaken in all seriousness. By this time the Commission has a great deal of knowledge at its disposal. Through its Programme Advisers[64] and through a multitude of contacts, both formal and informal, it has followed the process of planning in the states. It has worked out, and published in the Draft Outline, the general size and shape of the national plan. It has considered the resource position in the states, estimated the availability of central assistance, and formed some judgement as to the size and nature of the plan that each state, with the total resources likely to be at its disposal, can reasonably be expected to undertake. When, therefore, the states send first their Draft Plans and then their representatives to New Delhi, the Commission is well prepared to receive them.

Discussions take place simultaneously with personnel from the 'interested' central ministries, and are organized in three stages. First, there is a general discussion at which the state representatives and the members of

[63] W. Bengal, *FYP(3)*, pp. 3–5.

[64] In its letter of 3 Oct. 1962 (PC(P)2/62) the Commission stated: 'The Planning Commission is arranging for its Programme Administration Advisers to visit the States with which they are concerned for preliminary discussions and exchange of views in advance of the discussions on the Annual Plan. On matters requiring special attention, State Planning Secretaries may communicate with the Programme Administration Advisers at an early date.'

the Commission reach a broad agreement on the size and proportions of that state's plan and on the quantum of central assistance that it is to receive. Here the views of the Programme Adviser, who is in attendance, are of great importance. Secondly, there are detailed discussions of the various aspects of the state's plan in a series of working groups, where the state's representatives sit together with representatives of the Commission and of the relevant central ministries, normally under the chairmanship of the secretary of the ministry most immediately concerned.[65] Thirdly, there is another general discussion with members of the Commission, for making the final adjustments and registering formal agreement.

No records of the first and last stages were available to the author, but the Madras government provided him with an example of the second stage in the form of a *Summary Record of Discussions held with the Planning Commission in New Delhi on 21st, 22nd and 23rd November, 1960* (1960). This begins with a tabular summary (Table 30, p. 367) of the 'cutting down' process. Madras, as will be seen, planned with fair realism and hence got off rather lightly. The slashing of social service expenditure, however, is typical. Most states put this up as high as they dare, partly because the human needs are obvious and pressing, partly because it is a good vote-winner. Inevitably, when the Planning Commission gets to work on it, nearly everything except education goes down with a bump; for national priorities, inhuman as they may sometimes seem to the man in the village, have to be enforced. The same applies to 'Large and Medium Industry'. This is primarily a matter for the central government, and the state governments cannot be allowed to jump the gun.

Madras's record of the discussions, although not verbatim, is detailed enough to show that the representatives of this state presented their case with vigour and were not in the least overawed by the array of talent on the other side of the table. In the 'Irrigation and Power' Group, for instance, T. A. Varghese strongly argued that certain extensions to the important Neyveli power station should not be included in the state plan. These extensions, he understood, were in the 'central sector' and consequently should be paid for by the central government. Madras, indeed, had prepared its plan on that basis. The representative of the Planning Commission then explained that the 'ceiling' of Rs100 crores for power projects, suggested by the Planning Adviser (see Table 30),

[65] In the Planning Commission's letter on 'State Plans for 1963–64' (No. PC(P)2/62 dated 3 Oct. 1962), the following information and advice is provided under the heading 'Procedure for Working Groups': 'In the working groups attention will be concentrated on a critical appreciation of the main factors affecting implementation and on the consideration of the more important proposals for 1963–64 and subsequent years. Information and proposals should be so presented that the more significant aspects can be isolated from the rest of the detail. It is also suggested that the team of officials who are requested to visit Delhi on behalf of the State Government should be fairly limited in number, particular attention being given to briefing and preparation at the State level prior to the discussions.'

TABLE 30 *Third Five-Year Plan: Madras (Rs crores)*

Head of Development	*Second Plan Anticipated Expenditure*	*Third Plan*			
		State's Proposals	*Tentative proposals of Adviser (PA)*	*Recommendations of Working Group*	*Provisions as Finally Approved*
(1)	(2)	(3)	(4)	(5)	(6)
Agricultural Production	4.84	10.34	—	11.07	10.82
Minor Irrigation	5.56	17.00	—	12.80	12.80
Animal Husbandry	1.95	4.95	—	3.52	3.52
Dairying & Milk Supply	1.62	3.81	—	2.75	2.75
Forests	0.73	3.20	—	2.12	2.12
Soil Conservation	1.43	3.83	—	2.75	2.50
Fisheries	0.85	3.62	—	2.22	2.22
Marketing & Warehousing	1.10	2.75	—	0.25	0.25
Total	18.08	49.50	35.48	37.48	36.89
Cooperation	0.72	2.54	3.75*	4.71*	4.71*
Community Development	12.75	26.00	20.00	20.47	20.47
Total	13.47	28.54	23.75	25.18	25.18
Irrigation	14.45	40.00	27.00	27.42	27.42
Power	78.13†	1,18.10	1,00.00	1,00.19	1,00.19
Total	92.58	1,58.10	1,27.00	1,27.61	1,27.61
Large & Medium Industry	0.98	10.00	4.00	3.35	3.35
Village & Small Industries	12.45	28.17	19.50	20.16	20.16‡
Total	13.43	38.17	23.50	23.51	23.51
Roads	5.34	13.77	10.00	11.00	11.00
Tourism	0.04	0.40		0.25	0.25
Total	5.38	14.17	10.00	11.25	11.25
General Education	11.28	35.03	24.00	25.43	25.43
Technical Education	2.08	9.17	6.00	6.73	6.73
Health	14.85	30.92	20.00	19.00	19.50
			3.00§	2.00	2.00§
Housing & Urban Development	4.66	13.56	7.00	7.00	7.00
Welfare of Backward Classes	4.32	15.85	4.00	2.76	3.26
Social Welfare	0.22	0.84	0.84	0.52	0.52
Labour & Labour Welfare	0.48	2.91	1.50	1.33	1.33
Total	37.89	1,08.28	66.34	64.77	65.77
Statistics	0.08	0.30	2.50	0.24	0.24
Publicity	0.16	0.56		0.35	0.35
Aid to Local Bodies	0.77	1.20		—	—
Total	1.01	2.06	2.50	0.59	0.59
Grand Total	1,81.84	3,98.82	2,88.34	2,90.39	2,90.89

– Not available. * Includes provision for Marketing and Warehousing.
† Includes Rs10·34 crores on account of equipment cost of Kundah Project.
‡ Plus Rs90 lakhs for Category 'B' Schemes.
§ For Water-supply Schemes of the Corporation of Madras.

'included the provisions necessary for the Neyveli extensions'. The working group accordingly decided that Rs20 crores, within the state's plan, should be allocated to the 'Neyveli Stage II'. This decision, however, was not an agreed one, and Varghese announced that the whole question would 'be discussed by the State Government with the Planning Commission separately'.[66]

A similar disagreement arose over the item 'Preliminary expenses for a nuclear power station' included in the state's draft plan. The representative of the Planning Commission 'pointed out that in general no State Plan provided for expenditure of this nature for a nuclear power station and that any amount required towards this would have to be provided only in the Plan of the Atomic Energy Commission'. Following his advice, the working group declined to recommend any provision for this item. Varghese then announced 'that the State Government would spend this amount all the same'.[67]

In the Working Group on Transport and Communications, the government of Madras was accused of actually having done for road transport what Varghese was threatening that it would do for nuclear power: make expenditure outside the plan. The representative of the Planning Commission said: 'They were taking new routes, some of them competing with the railways. It was not known how the State Government were providing funds for road transport in the State. No provision was made for road transport in the Second State Plan and the State Government had not proposed any provision for it under the Third Plan.' He proposed that such provision should be included and that the state government 'should set up a Corporation to manage their road transport services in accordance with the decision that all road transport undertakings should be managed through Corporations in which the Railways participated'. There is no record of any reply from the representative of the state government, nor of any recommendation on this subject by the working group, which proposed an allocation for transport and communications which took no account of the state's road transport responsibilities. Nor, as yet, is there any indication that the Madras government intends to comply with the Planning Commission's wishes in respect of either the organization or the financing of its road transport undertaking.[68]

There were other disagreements, however, which found settlement on the spot. One was about the state government's proposal to establish a coke-oven plant. The state's representative, T. K. Palaniappan, presented this as an attempt 'to solve the chronic shortage of coke for the foundry and engineering industries in the Madras State'.

Experience of the last few years had demonstrated that even when supplies of pig iron and coke were stated to be satisfactory in over-all terms, the

[66] *Summary Record*, pp. 25–26. [67] Ibid. p. 26. [68] Ibid. pp. 33–34.

despatches to Madras and other Southern States were highly disappointing. This was due to breakdowns in long-distance transportation of these vital products from the supply centres in the north. This situation made it imperative for the State Government to think in terms of establishing a coke oven plant in Madras and thus develop supplies of coke nearer the centres of consumption than would be the case otherwise. He urged for a fair and proper consideration of the proposal against the background detailed by him.

To this the Chairman, E. P. Moon of the Planning Commission, replied that there was such a shortage of metallurgical coal, even for the steel industry, that 'hardly any significant surplus could be reckoned to be available for an independent coke-oven plant'. Even Grade I coal (the use of which had been suggested) was in short supply, and the installation of the necessary facilities to wash it 'would call for release of additional foreign exchange'. To ease the situation he suggested examining the possibility of carrying the coal by sea. He also indicated that 'the line capacity works in progress on the south-eastern railway were likely to bear fruit in the coming years and facilitate movement of traffic from north to south'. It was finally agreed that provision for the coke-oven plant need not be made, but that the state government should accelerate its investigations into the coking of lignite.[69]

In another instance no final decision was taken, as further inquiries were thought desirable. The state government's proposals for the development of the handloom industry appeared, in some respects, to be out of line with national policies. After some discussion, in which the state representatives argued that Madras's special problems demanded special solutions, it was agreed that the state government should 'forward new schemes which were not covered by the existing pattern of assistance to the All-India Handloom Board for clearance'.[70]

The above examples are not quoted as typical of procedure for the final settlement of the details of a state's plan. Information such as Madras provides is not readily available for other states. Even if it were, to concentrate on areas of disagreement, as we have done, inevitably falsifies the general picture. Madras, moreover, as the home of southern separatism, is under certain political compulsions to treat the Planning Commission and the central ministries with a suspicion which sometimes verges on outright hostility. Nevertheless, one may be reasonably certain that, in the autumn of 1960, plenty of arguments of the type displayed in Madras's *Summary Record* took place. The state representatives come to New Delhi prepared for some hard bargaining and hoping that, on most of the issues that are politically important to them, they will be able to force the Planning Commission and the central ministries to a compromise. Sometimes they succeed and sometimes they fail. It depends on how much

[69] Ibid. p. 28. [70] Ibid. p. 30–31.

money is involved, how 'disruptive' the state's proposals seem to be, how ready the state is to contribute from its own resources, what the effect will be of granting to one state something that it is proposed to deny to others, how delicate is the balance of political forces within the state, and a whole number of other factors, most of them difficult or impossible to quantify. But no state is without hope or without bargaining power. We must, therefore, beware of accepting uncritically the exaggerated but frequently expressed view that the state representatives make their journeys to New Delhi cap in hand. Varghese of Madras never adopts that posture, and there are few states' representatives of comparable stature who find it either congenial or profitable.

On the other hand, one should not exaggerate the *solidarity* of a state's representatives on these occasions. Frequently, the interdepartmental arguments that attended the plan-making process in the state are continued in the presence of the Planning Commission and the central ministries. There may even be a continuation at this late hour of the 'ganging-up' of the state department with its corresponding central department.[71] In discussion with a group of officials in Maharashtra, the author was informed that the cuts imposed at the state level on departmental proposals continued to be resisted by departmental representatives during the 'working group' discussions in New Delhi. The Planning Section of Maharashtra's Finance Department was, in fact, very pleased with the new 'emergency' procedure introduced in connexion with the 1962 annual plan, as this eliminated the great trek of departmental officials to New Delhi, and consequently also eliminated these eleventh-hour internecine wrangles. At all stages, therefore, one finds the tension, already noted, between the 'horizontal' and the 'vertical' principles, although when New Delhi is finally reached the 'horizontal' principle necessarily tends to prevail.

As we have seen, the state never knows quite what it is going to get out of these discussions, although the Programme Adviser has presumably given it some preliminary idea. The criteria for judging state plans, which the Commission has publicly proclaimed, are at the best vague and at the worst ambiguous.[72] As an intelligent and experienced informant in Maharashtra put it, the extent to which the Planning Commission agrees to accept the state's own targets and to supplement the state's own resources depends on a process of 'haggling' in which a great deal of cunning but very little science is displayed on both sides.

(v)

When agreement has been reached, the state's representatives go home to put the final touches to their plan and to publish it, as a guide to their quinquennial exercise. Like the national plan, it has no legal force,

[71] See below, p. 379. [72] See above, pp. 315–16.

although of course it is discussed and approved by the state legislature. 'Flexibility' is as much a *desideratum* at the state level as at the national level.

State plans vary considerably in presentation, sophistication, and degree of detail, although all contain comparable sets of figures. Some look like mere assemblages of projects; others attempt to put the projects in some kind of perspective and to present a coherent argument in support of the chosen mode of economic development, with reference to the special features of the state's economy. The latter sort are obviously of greater interest to the student, and it is tempting to say that they are the better plans. This, however, is not necessarily so. Madras's Third Five-Year Plan, for instance, is a dull and pedestrian document, but everyone knows that Madras is in fact one of the better-planned states. Some of the more sophisticated-looking efforts, on the other hand, are rather obviously the product of an attempt by some bright official with a literary talent to make the best of bad job. Nevertheless, a 'good' planning document probably indicates that the state's Planning Department is taking its own job seriously; and there is even the possibility that a 'good' plan may be taken more seriously by others.

As state plan reports are not generally available in this country—some, indeed, are not easy to find even in New Delhi—it will be useful to present a brief summary of one of them. Maharashtra's has been chosen for this purpose, not because it is typical but because it is unusually good.

Proclaiming itself as the 'first plan of Mahrashtra State as a single homogeneous unit', the document begins with a brief description of the state's own planning process. This is followed by an unusually long and interesting 'Approach' chapter, in which the objectives of the plan are related to the special characteristics of the state. Some of the latter may be set out in tabular form, by way of comparison with all-India averages (Table 31, p. 372).

What emerges from these figures is the 'dual' nature of the Maharashtrian economy. Although, in comparison with the Indian average, highly urbanized, the state has a backward rural hinterland where the 'spread effect' of urban prosperity is very feeble. In this respect Maharashtra is a microcosm of India itself, just as India is a microcosm of the world. The concentration of industry in the Bombay–Poona area, together with its recent diversification, is the 'result largely of automatic economic forces and not of deliberate State planning'. These forces have left the rural areas almost completely unaffected. Hence, prominent among the objectives of the Third Plan is what is termed 'agro-industrial development', the achievement of which will 'involve the resolution of the apparent paradox of the coexistence of agricultural poverty and industrial prosperity'. Among the rural areas, Konkan, Vidarbha and Marathwada are particularly backward and therefore need special attention.

Like the national plan, Maharashtra's plan, in its 'Approach', defines an attitude towards public and private enterprise. Rather significantly, in a state where private business interests are powerful, there is no talk of 'socialism'. That, apparently, is left to the Union government. The task of the state planner is mainly to stimulate self-help.

In the economic sphere, the State Plan confines itself mainly to the economic development of those sections of society which cannot achieve it on their own. The economic categories whose problems the Plan seeks to solve are the agriculturalists, animal breeders, milk producers, fishermen, forest workers, artisans, persons engaged in traditional handicrafts and so on. The State Plan no doubt provides encouragement to prospective entrepreneurs to set up industries and to take to mining and existing entrepreneurs to expand their activities, but that is largely with a view to making available to the weaker sections of society the benefits of gainful employment, direct and indirect, associated with industrial and mineral growth.

TABLE 31

Features of the Maharashtra Economy

	Maharashtra	*India*
Urban residents (per cent)	27·9	17·8
Persons engaged in production other than cultivation (per cent)	13·1	10·6
Engaged in commerce (per cent)	7	6
Engaged in other services (per cent)	13·7	12·1
Cultivators (per cent)	47·2	55·8
Non-cultivating owners (per cent)	2	1·5
Dependent on agriculture (per cent)	60	70
Income generated by agriculture (per cent)	33	44·48
Gross production per acre of net sown area (rupees)	Rs. 140	Rs. 200
Irrigated land (percentage of net sown area)	6	17

The size of the state's own financial contribution to the plan is estimated at Rs390 crores, of which Rs220 crores will be raised within the state (through taxation, savings, profits of public enterprises, &c.), and Rs170 accrue from the devolution of central revenues, as fixed by the Second Finance Commission. This total includes an estimated contribution of Rs9·4 crores from the Maharashtra State Electricity Board and the Bombay State Road Transport Corporation, whose revenues are being mobilized for plan expenditure for the first time. In accordance with national policy, it excludes continuing current expenditure on Second Plan schemes ('committed expenditure'), which is estimated at Rs63·55 crores for the Third Plan period. The balance of financial resources (Rs125 crores) to cover a plan of Rs515 crores is provided by 'complementary outlays from other agencies'. Of these, the most important is the government of India, which puts up money for 'centrally-sponsored schemes' and 'partnership projects'. Also participating are the Reserve Bank (share capital in co-operative societies), the All-India Commodity Boards (agricultural schemes), the other All-India Boards (miscellaneous industrial schemes), the Land Development Banks (schemes for lift irrigation and horticulture), the Co-operative Banks (schemes for the 'propagation of improved implements'), and the Industrial Finance Corporations (schemes for industrial estate co-operatives, agricultural processing co-operatives, and other industrial co-operatives). Appendix II (p. 540) clearly and conveniently sets out, under appropriate heads, the magnitudes of outlays in the state plan and complementary outlays for other agencies.

The greater part of the document consists of a description and justification of the various schemes. In this respect the Maharashtra plan is like any other state plan. More distinctive—and characteristic of Maharashtra's very practical approach to the tasks of planning—is the unusually long and detailed section devoted to 'Implementation'. This places major emphasis on decentralization, as a means of ensuring speed and flexibility in execution, of adapting broad programmes to local requirements, and of enlisting active public participation. The plan attempts to meet the first of these requirements by giving important responsibilities to autonomous bodies, such as the Electricity Board, the Housing Boards, the Road Transport Corporation, the Warehousing Corporation, and the projected Authority for Industrial Areas, Mining Corporation, Small-Scale Industries Corporation, District Industries Boards, and Corporation for Land Reclamation. Together, these are to dispose of Rs86·71 crores of new expenditure in the Third Five-Year Plan. Adaptation to local requirements and the enlistment of public participation is to be achieved through 'democratic decentralisation'. As part of the plan, legislation will establish elected District Councils and Block Committees in the rural areas. To these will be assigned local government functions, together with 'the execution of certain works and development schemes of the State Five Year Plans'. Once this has been achieved, the central government 'will be able to concentrate on schemes of wider significance involving activities which have a long-range effect or involve heavy outlays, or demand higher technical skills and organisational effort, not within the means of local bodies'. A similar lifting of burdens from the shoulders of the state government will result from the contemplated measures of financial decentralization. Already in Maharashtra, one of the pioneers of co-operative organization, the institutional framework of co-operative credit for agriculture 'meets the bulk of requirements and relieves the government of responsibility'. Further responsibility will be devolved with the expansion of the State Finance Corporation, to meet the needs of small industries, and the inauguration of a Municipal Finance Corporation, to meet those of the town councils (e.g. for water-supply and drainage).

At the same time, administrative methods must be improved and administrative machinery strengthened. The recruitment, promotion, and training of staff require review, and the activities of the 'O & M' Section and of the Work Study Teams need to be stepped up. To improve preliminary surveys and investigations of large programmes, the plan allocates Rs28·65 lakhs for irrigation and Rs50 lakhs for power. The need to secure economies in building estimates, through greater standardization and better planning, is also emphasized. Among the departments of the state government, there is now a more logical division of work; progress has also been made towards a wider delegation of financial powers. These improvements will have to be reviewed from time to time.

Although statistical work is 'fairly satisfactory' down to the sub-district (*taluka*) level, there are a number of major informational gaps to be filled during the course of the Third Plan. Particularly needed for coherent planning are growth indicators, with special reference to production and prices, and information about the tertiary sectors, small-scale industries, the socio-economic conditions of labour, the production of certain crops, population movements, the distribution of incomes, and the incidence of taxation. The compilation of these statistics will facilitate the process of evaluation, which in any case needs improvement. Special studies and surveys will be inaugurated and, in the Finance Department, an Economic Wing created to investigate long-term problems and to liaise with the Bureau of Economics and Statistics on the evaluation of programmes.

Finally, in the appendices to the plan, there is a list of selected physical targets, a region-wise allocation of plan outlays on other than state-level schemes, and estimates of the additional production of important agricultural crops.

In general, the Maharashtra Third Five-Year Plan report explains not only what is to be done, but why and how. In this respect it comes closer than many of the plans of the other states to the method and approach of the national plan. There may be, as we have already suggested, something of the *post hoc* in all this; how much could only be discovered by a detailed and lengthy investigation of the process of plan-making, which is a task now awaiting the attention of some determined Indian scholar. But, at least *prima facie*, the Maharashtra Plan suggests that someone has been doing some real thinking in terms of broad objectives and of the means to their achievement. Thinking of this type is what the Commission hopes to see embodied in all state plans. Although such hopes are often belied, a broad comparison between the Second and the Third Plan reports of the states suggests that there has been some advance.

(vi)

The latter part of the planning exercise described above is repeated, *in petto*, every year. Both the Commission and the states draw up annual plans and, in October or November, the latter bring their proposals to New Delhi for discussion and confirmation. The Planning Commission first indicates 'provisional magnitudes' of total outlay for the forthcoming financial year, both generally and for the individual states, and then, in September, fixes a provisional schedule of dates for discussions. (In 1961, for instance, the discussions covered a period from 15 November to 21 December and each state was allotted three days.) The states, for their part, are required to present the Commission with certain statements. In 1961 these were: (1) a summary statement of state plan outlays for 1962–3; (2) a list of schemes included in the state plan for 1962–3; (3) a list of centrally-sponsored schemes to be implemented in 1962–3; and (4) a check-list of principal projects. The last of these was 'intended mainly for furnishing information in regard to projects which involve considerable construction and use of equipment'. The Commission required this information to enable it to carry out the decision of a conference of state Planning Secretaries that projects costing Rs5 crores or more should be reviewed at quarterly intervals and those costing between Rs1 crores and 5 crores at six-monthly intervals.[73]

As with the quinquennial plans, the Commission provides the states with general guide-lines. Its letter of 17 September 1961, for instance, concluded with a list of 'major considerations in the Plan for 1962–3'. These were:

(1) accelerated progress in agricultural production including intensification of minor irrigation, soil conservation and extension activities, fullest utilisation of irrigation and implementation of programmes for cooperative development,
(2) speedy implementation of all training programmes,
(3) power development,
(4) adequate effort in primary education, and
(5) emphasis on employment-generating and labour-intensive programmes, especially in areas suffering from considerable under-employment.

Information was also provided about the forthcoming expansion of the supplementary rural works programme for manpower utilization, and

[73] No. PC(P)2(2)61, dated 17 Sept. 1961. The corresponding letter of the following year (PC(P)2/62, 'State Plans for 1963–64', dated 3 Oct. 1962) requested two further statements, viz.: 'V—Proposals for advance action in the Fourth Plan; VI—Targets and achievements for selected programmes.' It was announced that the 'advance action' proposals would be 'discussed by the Planning Commission at the time of considering the Annual Plan'.

TABLE 32

Plan Outlay, 1962: Madras (Rs lakhs)

	Head of Development (1)	Third Plan Outlay (2)	1961–2		1962–3		
			Budget (3)	Anticipated Outlay (4)	As Proposed by State Govt (5)	As Recommended by Working Groups (6)	As Recommended by Adviser (7)
I	Agricultural Production	1,066·50	152·93	163·26	218·35	218·35	..
	Minor Irrigation	1,280·00	273·70	221·77	226·42	226·42	..
	Soil Conservation	250·00	44·23	45·18	51·18	51·18	..
	Animal Husbandry	352·25	43·35	38·08	76·70	76·70	..
	Dairying & Milk Supply	275·00	100·69	120·78	84·70	84·70	..
	Forests	212·00	23·59	34·45	40·24	40·24	..
	Fisheries	222·00	32·84	48·00	50·37	50·37	..
	Warehousing & Marketing	40·00	7·30	1·03	7·39	7·39	..
	Agricultural Programme (total)	3,697·75	678·63	672·79	755·35	755·35	715·35
II	Co-operation	471·06	96·71	111·49	121·88	120·00	120·00
	Community Development	2,036·00	363·61	455·86	558·52	474·81	474·81
	Panchayats	10·59				4·82	4·82
	CD & Co-operation (total)	2,517·65	462·32	567·35	680·40	599·63	599·63
III	Irrigation	2,741·85	414·00	505·64	610·12	485·00	485·00
	Power	10,019·00	1,551·00	1,881·37	2,207·30	1,882·73	1,882·73
	Irrigation & Power (total)	12,760·85	1,965·00	2,387·01	2,817·42	2,367·73	2,367·73

IV Large & Medium Industries	335·00	8·78	20·41	16·11	16·11	16·11
Village & Medium Industries	2,016·00	376·84	312·49	518·59	452·75	418·75
Industry & Mining (total)	2,351·00	385·62	332·90	534·70	468·86	474·85
V Roads	1,100·00	187·14	215·00	215·00	215·00	215·00
Tourism	25·00	1·58	2·11	8·00	8·00	8·00
Transport & Communications (total)	1,125·00	188·72	217·11	223·00	223·00	223·00
VI General Education	2,564·09	233·47	179·95	392·06	358·41	358·41
Technical Education & Scientific Research	652·00	116·67	84·04	142·35	142·35	122·35
Health	2,150·00	539·09	603·68	553·51	650·00	550·00
Housing	700·00	121·18	124·01	141·28	141·28	141·28
Welfare of Backward Classes	326·00	54·69	58·03	61·05	61·05	61·05
Social Welfare	51·63	2·66	0·75	3·46	6·32	6·72*
Labour & Labour Welfare	133·00	18·68	7·28	24·18	35·40	35·40
Social Services (total)	6,576·72	1,086·44	1,057·74	1,317·79	1,394·81	1,275·21
VII Statistics	24·44	4·00	4·00	5·00	5·00	5·00
Information & Publicity	35·00	7·70	6·56	6·00	6·00	6·00
Miscellaneous (total)	59·44	11·70	10·56	11·00	11·00	11·00
Grand Total	29,088·41	4,778·43	5,245·46	6,339·66	5,820·38	5,626·78

* Includes Rs40,000 for public co-operation.

states were urged to make district and block plans and to pay special attention to 'the development needs of certain regions which are known to be markedly less developed in relation to other areas of the States in which they were situated'. All proposals for 1962–3 were to be sent (50 copies) to the Commission by 7 November, and copies of the 'relevant proposals' to the 'Central Ministries concerned'.[74]

The discussions in New Delhi closely follow the pattern of the quinquennial discussions. First, there is a general review of the state's financial resources for the current year and an examination of the financial estimates for the forthcoming year: secondly, there is a detailed examination, in working groups on which the relevant ministries as well as the Planning Commission are represented, of the various projects contained in the state's draft annual plan. Madras again provides a *Summary Record*[75] of the second part of these discussions, held on 24 and 25 November 1961, and a table of plan outlay (see Table 32). The main difference between these occasions and the quinquennial ones is that the 'cutting down' process is less severe, because the state, now operating within the limits of its total quinquennial outlay, is compelled to be more realistic in its estimates. Another feature, of some constitutional interest, is that there is no final 'agreement' between state and centre after the working groups have produced their reports. The annual plan, unlike the quinquennial one, finds direct expression in the state's budget; hence, if the state's representatives were to give firm undertakings in New Delhi, they would be by-passing the normal process of financial control.

In Madras's case, a proposed outlay for 1962–3 of Rs63 crores (Rs1·2 crores up on the anticipated plan outlay for 1961–2) was clearly intended to leave room for bargaining. In the preliminary meeting, held in the Planning Commission, the Programme Adviser 'indicated that the overall size of the state's annual plan was to be reduced to Rs55·5 crores and that the state's representatives would indicate in the Working Group's meetings their suggestions for reductions in the outlays for different schemes'.[76] The groups did actually propose a series of cuts for everything except agriculture, which was kept at 7·5 crores, Transport and Communications, which was kept at 2·2 crores, and Social Services, which was raised from 1·31 to 1·39 crores. The grand total which emerged from their discussions was just under Rs3 crores higher than that originally recommended, while the total finally recommended by the Programme Adviser was Rs1·2 crores higher. Clearly, once the original cut has been made, the subsequent operations are fairly marginal.

[74] No. PC(P)2(2)61.
[75] *Summary Record of Discussions held with the Planning Commission in New Delhi on 24th and 25th November 1961* (1961).
[76] Ibid. p. 1.

An interesting feature of the discussions in the Agricultural Working Group, illustrating one of the points already made about central-state relations, is that although the state representatives were prepared to compromise, the central ministry representatives were not. The state considered that a reduction of Rs20 lakhs might be made in the allocation proposed for Agricultural Production, and reductions of Rs10 lakhs each for Minor Irrigation and Soil Conservation; but 'it was . . . emphasised on behalf of the Ministry that these reductions would not be in accordance with the declared objective that if the Plan allocations on important agricultural programmes were spent in the first three or four years, additional allocations would be made available'. Further,

> the pace of expenditure in the State raised the expectation that it was possible to utilize fully the Third Five Year Plan allocations under some of the important sub-heads of development and in fact even to exceed them. The progress with regard to physical targets was also satisfactory. It would not therefore be desirable to reduce the tempo of these and other agricultural programmes.[77]

Naturally, the state's representatives were not going to press their offer to make reductions in the face of the central ministry's resistance. Together, state and ministry ensured that the group should recommend the retention of the state's proposed total, Rs7·5 crores. The Programme Adviser, however, subsequently recommended that this should be reduced to Rs7·1 crores. Evidently, we have here an example of a clash between ministry and Commission.

On Social Services there also appears to have been a ganging up between state representatives and central ministries—although this is less clearly documented in the *Summary Record*.[78] As we have noted, the outlay proposed by the working group was actually higher than that proposed by the state. The Programme Adviser would have none of this and cut the state's proposed outlay by Rs42 lakhs.

The last stage in the annual planning process, for the states as for the centre, is the incorporation of the figures for plan outlay in the budget. They are not allowed, however, to disappear without trace, amid a welter of non-plan expenditure. Each state extracts the 'plan' figures from its budget and publishes them in a separate bulky volume. In this, a summary statement of proposed plan expenditure for the forthcoming financial year is followed by a detailed breakdown of proposed schemes, showing the sources from which they are to be financed. As an illustration, the first page of Andhra Pradesh's 'List of Schemes' is reproduced in Table 33 (p. 380). This volume is accompanied by another, of equal bulk, explaining the purpose and nature of the schemes and setting out their objectives in physical terms. Madras combines this information with a

[77] Ibid. p. 1. [78] Ibid. pp. 26–39.

TABLE 33 *Andhra Pradesh Third Five-Year Plan: Annual Plan for 1962–3* (*Rs lakhs*)

HEAD OF DEVELOPMENT				PROVISION IN 1962–3						CENTRAL ASSISTANCE IN 1962–3			CORRELATION WITH DETAILED BUDGET ESTIMATES, 1962–3		
				REVENUE		CAPITAL									
Srl No.	*Names of Schemes*	*Provision in Third Plan 1961–6*	*Anticipated Outlay in 1961–2*	*Recurring*	*Non-Recurring*	*Loan*	*Non-Loan*	*Total (Cols 5 to 8)*	*Foreign Exchange Requirements in 1962–3*	*Loans*	*Grants*	*Totals*	*Head of Account (Major, Minor & Sub-heads of Account*	*Amount Under the Head in Col. (14)*	*P. No. of the Budget*
(1)	(2)	(3)	(4)	(5)	(6)	(7)	(8)	(9)	(10)	(11)	(12)	(13)	(14)	(15)	(16)
AGRICULTURAL PROD'N ANDHRA REG.															
	Group I Supply Schemes														
1.	Town Compost scheme - distribution of manures	6·60	0·60	..	..	1·00	..	1·00	..	1·00	..	1·00	Q.G. 16(i)	1·00	422
2.	Pilot scheme for night soil compost in smaller villages	6·50	0·50	..	..	1·00	..	1·00	..	1·00	..	1·00	Q.G. 18(i)	1·00	422
3.	Sewage development scheme	1·00	0·20	..	..	0·20	..	0·20	..	0·20	..	0·20	Q.G. 39	0·20	422
4.	Distribution of green manure seeds	0·10	0·02	0·02	..	..	..	0·02	..	..	0·02	0·02	31-P. 31-(f)LXII 140(a)	0·01 0·01	112 122
5.	Other local manurial resources	10·00	2·08	3·33	..	..	..	3·33	..	..	0·33	0·33	31 (e) XXXIX-III	3·33	115
6.	Setting up of seed farms and seed stores	135·00	13·97	0·18	1·27	..	10·00	11·45	1·00	2·80	7·20	10·00	95 (R) D. (1). 31 (f)LXII 5 (a) 31 (P)	10·00 1·00 0·45	241 116 112
7.	Subsidy on distribution of improved seeds of foodgrains including hybrid maize	27·00	4·50	0·10	..	..	..	0·10	..	..	0·05	0·05	31 (f)LXII 46(a)	0·10	118
8.	Concession in price for introd. of improved agricultural implements (rotary push hoes)	1·00	0·20	0·20	..	..	..	0·20	..	..	..	..	31(e)XXXIX-IV	0·20	115
9.	Control of pests & diseases of crops	50·00	9·00	5·00	..	..	2·00	7·00	..	..	2·00	2·00	95(R)(K) 31(e)XXXIX-V(a) 31(P)	2·00 4·00 1·00	241 115 112
10.	Subsidy on manually operated plant protection machinery for sale to ryots (hand-operated sprayers & dusters)	5·00	1·00	1·00	..	..	..	1·00	..	..	0·50	0·50	31(e)XXXIX-VI	1·00	115
11.	Improved agricultural practices	0·66 (token)	..	..	..	..	..	..	..	..	..	..	..	..	..
12.	Intensive district agric. programme (package progr.)	140·00	12·76	13·97	1·48	..	1·55	17·00	2·00	..	12·49	12·49	31(e)XXXIX-X(a) 95(R)-(J) 31(p)	0·83 1·55 14·62	115 241 112

review of the progress achieved during the previous year,[79] but most states publish their 'progress' reports separately. The preparation of these volumes must be both expensive and laborious. It would be interesting to know how much they are actually used at the various levels of state administration. India tends to produce a vast bulk of official papers, and one suspects that their compilation tends to be a ritualistic rather than a utilitarian exercise. The annual plan documents, however, should obviously be of the highest practical importance, and it would be valuable to know how far they are regarded as effectively serving their purpose. So far, no evaluation study has ever been devoted to them.

(vii)

We now turn from the making of the state plans to their implementation. This vast subject could be effectively investigated only through a series of case studies based on prolonged field-work. The annual progress reports, although providing much information, tend to be self-justificatory and to tell us very little about processes as distinct from results.

The broad picture is clear enough. Responsibility for executing the state plan rests on the shoulders of the state's Council of Ministers, its administrative departments, its local government bodies and its *ad hoc* agencies, all working, to a greater or lesser extent, under the guidance and supervision of the Planning Commission, the central ministries, and the multitude of specialized All-India Boards and Commissions. A formidable mass of correspondence flows between New Delhi and the state capitals; conflicts and controversies abound, 'trouble-shooting' missions go in both directions, and innumerable conferences and 'high-powered' committees are called together to sort out current problems. In all this a key role is played by the ubiquitous IAS, without whose intelligence, initiative, and *esprit de corps* little could be accomplished.

Any more specific characterization of the process will have to wait until case study material is more abundant; but there is one crucially important aspect of it: the effect on plan implementation of centre–state financial relations, about which something can and must be said.

Up to 1958, agreement by the Planning Commission for the inclusion of a scheme in a state's annual plan by no means meant that work on it could go ahead. Where central assistance was involved—as in the vast majority of cases—sanction had to be issued by the appropriate central ministry or other central agency. Each of these bodies had its own specific patterns of grants and loans, applicable to different types of schemes; and each insisted on giving 'technical clearance' before any money was released. By the beginning of the Second Five-Year Plan, these arrangements had

[79] e.g. Madras, *FYP(3)*: *Review of Progress for 1961–2 & Programme for 1962–3* (1962).

degenerated into a positive jungle of detailed, meticulous, and time-wasting controls. Designed to ensure administrative efficiency and to prevent the wasting of central funds, they had become entirely self-defeating. Added to other factors, such as the shortage of essential supplies, the paucity of technical personnel, the long formalities involved in the acquisition of land, the difficulty of obtaining foreign exchange, and the inefficiency of the states' own administrative machines, they caused delays so serious as to threaten complete stultification. The Planning Commission—doubtless with the object of securing some reform, as well as of providing the states with much-needed information—published in 1957 a document entitled *Memorandum on Existing Patterns of Central Assistance to States*, which laid out the whole crazy patchwork before the reader's astonished gaze. Yet the ministries, partly from a natural bureaucratic reluctance to disturb established routines, partly from a belief that they alone could protect the public purse from the states' buccaneering proclivities, and partly from a misplaced confidence in their own superior wisdom, remained strongly attached to these 'existing patterns'.

The states, on the other hand, complained loud and long. Among the 'bottlenecks' listed by Punjab, for instance, was 'the uncertainty of central assistance through failure of Central Ministries to give expeditious and firm commitments regarding either the pattern or the quantum of assistance'.[80] Uttar Pradesh, in reviewing the various reasons for the 'shortfalls' in its Second Five-Year Plan, emphasized 'the unduly long time taken by the Union Ministries in the first two years in according sanctions to schemes to be executed in a particular financial year'.[81] As a result, funds for village and small-scale industries, housing and other schemes remained unutilized. Andhra Pradesh referred to 'late sanction' as one of the more important of the many causes of the developmental drag that the state had experienced.[82] Bihar and Mysore claimed that the system involved a degree of uncertainty that was quite incompatible with rational planning.[83]

These complaints seem to have come to a head at the eighth meeting of the NDC on 8 and 9 December 1956. One Chief Minister after another alleged that the critical situation of the Second Plan was at least partly due to the centre's dilatoriness in issuing sanctions for schemes. Bakshi Ghulam Mohammed, for instance, said:

> The provisions for various sectors were discussed with the Working Groups and were approved by the Planning Commission. On the strength of this approval, schemes had also been prepared and work had been started but even after eight or nine months no definite idea was forthcoming about the assistance which would be available for such schemes.

[80] *Rev. of Progress 1957–8* (1959). [81] *FYP(3)*, i: *Rep.* p. 25. [82] *FYP(3)*, pp. 25–26.
[83] Mysore, *FYP(2)* (1955), p. 5; Bihar, *Draft FYP(2)* (1955), p. 9.

This meeting appears to have given the Planning Commission the opportunity for which it was waiting. The 'Summary of Conclusions and Suggestions' stated that the anticipated shortfall in plan expenditure for 1956–7 was due, not only to state reorganization, but to 'delay in financial sanction'. After drawing attention to the states' difficulties in meeting the requirements of the matching procedures, it expressed the hope that 'with the new procedures now being introduced' these difficulties would be diminished, and recorded agreement that the Planning Commission should undertake a review of the whole system.

The forces of resistance to change, however, were too strong for immediate results to be achieved. At the ninth meeting of the NDC, B. C. Roy of West Bengal returned to the charge, saying that the procedure whereby his state was asked to make budgetary commitments without any guarantee of complementary central contributions was 'defective', and that there was too much central interference in the execution of state plans. The subsequent meeting of the NDC's Standing Committee took up the latter point, and suggested that the Planning Commission should work out ways and means of imparting greater flexibility to state plans 'so as to enable State Governments to shift resources within the Plan ceilings from one head to another to meet new requirements or items requiring greater emphasis on account of changes in conditions'.

At last, on 12 May 1958, the Commission, in a letter to all state governments on 'Procedure for Central Assistance for State Plans and Centrally Sponsored Schemes during 1958–59',[84] announced changes which met a substantial part of the critics' case. On financial sanctions the message was as follows:

In the past, Central Ministries have frequently issued specific sanctions to schemes included in State Plans for which Central assistance was made available. It is proposed that these schemes should be sanctioned by the State Governments under their normal procedure and that no financial sanctions as such should issue from the Centre. In respect of new projects or new categories of schemes (as distinct from continuing schemes), however, the following existing arrangements will continue:

(i) In the case of irrigation and power projects, before work is commenced on new projects, they are examined and accepted by the Planning Commission's Advisory Committee on Irrigation and Power Projects;

(ii) Schemes for industrial housing and slum clearance are reviewed from the technical aspect by the Ministry of Works, Housing and Supply before they are implemented;

(iii) For certain programmes the Central Government have set up special Boards or other agencies. These are

(a) for different branches of small industry, the Handloom Board, the

[84] No. Plan/5/2/57.

Small-scale Industries Board, the Handicrafts Board, the Coir Board and the Silk Board;

(b) for schemes of cooperative development other than cooperative farming and cooperative training, the National Cooperative and Warehousing Board; and

(c) for technical education the All-India Council of Technical Education.

The procedures prescribed by these organisations in consultation with the Central Ministries concerned for receiving schemes and giving technical approval to them will not be affected by the terms of this letter except in so far as these relate to the grant of ways and means advances and the final payment sanctions for the year. It may be added that the schemes of the Khadi and Village Industries Commission are altogether outside the purview of this letter.

This was hardly a charter of liberty, but it did mean that over a wide range of schemes (and particularly those promoted by the Ministry of Agriculture) once permission to include in the annual plan had been given no further sanctions were necessary. As for the remainder, the leading-strings had been significantly slackened, in so far as the 'existing arrangements' now applied to *new* schemes only.

Equally important was the acceptance of an agreement reached at the State Finance Ministers' Conference in November 1957 that 'development schemes under each head might be arranged suitably in groups'. The significance of this innocuous-sounding reform was explained thus:

While the total amount of Central assistance to be intimated to State Governments is estimated with reference to individual schemes and the patterns of assistance for them, the intention is that once the State Governments have been informed of the amounts of loans and grants available for the State plans, the final sanctions of payments should be related to the groups specified . . . . Within a group the State Government will be free to regulate expenditure on the schemes without reference to the Central Government.

This, too, was considerably less than a charter of liberty, as the 'groups' were numerous and fairly narrowly defined. But the states were also given permission to transfer funds from one group to another with the concurrence of the central ministry concerned. Furthermore, the groups were arranged under 'Heads of Development' between which *virement* could be made on the following conditions: (*a*) between Heads with which the same central ministry was concerned, 'in consultation with the Ministry with the advice of the Planning Commission'; (*b*) between Heads with which more than one central ministry was concerned, with 'the concurrence of the Planning Commission, . . a copy of the proposal being sent simultaneously to the Ministries concerned'. What this might mean in practice is indicated by the following extract from the appended 'Heads of Development and Groups in which Schemes are Arranged':[85]

Central Ministry	*Head of Development*	*Groups*
Food & Agriculture	Agriculture (incl. minor irrigation & land development)	1. Minor irrigation, incl. tube-wells. 2. Land development & consolidation of holdings. 3. Seed farms. 4. Supply schemes & plant protection. 5. Development of commerical crops, horticulture & fruit preservation. 6. Agricultural education. 7. Agricultural research, information & statistics.
	Animal Husbandry, Dairying & Fisheries.	1. Animal Husbandry, including sheep & wool & poultry development. 2. Veterinary education & rinderpest eradication. 3. Dairying & milk supply. 4. Fisheries.
	Forests & Soil Conservation	1. Forestry schemes. 2. Soil conservation.
	Co-operation	1. Co-operation & warehousing. 2. Marketing, co-operative farming & training.

The third change announced by the Planning Commission's letter was in respect of procedure for the release of funds. The final release, said the Commission, 'will be calculated with reference to the proportion of assistance under loans and grants intimated to the State Government in respect of a group and the total expenditure for the year estimated with reference to that group'. By way of explanation, it added: 'Thus, if for a group of schemes the total outlay accepted is Rs100 lakhs, of which Central grants amount to Rs25 lakhs and Central loans to Rs50 lakhs while Rs25 lakhs are to be contributed by the State Government, grants

[85] For an example of the allocation of central assistance under 'Heads of Development', see App. II, p. 540.

and loans will be given at 25% and 50% of the total expenditure.' To facilitate this procedure, the states were asked to send the Commission (with extracts to the central ministries and a copy to the Finance Ministry) quarterly statements of total expenditure. The third of these statements, in a given financial year, was also to 'indicate the anticipated expenditure for the last quarter of the year'. On receipt of this, the ministries were to 'sanction the final payments of grants and loans', subject to adjustment in the following financial year when the *actual* expenditure for the given year became known.

The above procedure was to apply to state plan schemes. For centrally sponsored schemes the main difference was that they 'required the specific approval of the administrative Ministries concerned', and were subject to rather more stringent financial controls.

All in all, this represented a considerable liberalization and rationalization. It was welcomed by the states for the greater certainty and administrative flexibility which it brought.[86] How far it was responsible for the more rapid progress achieved during the last two years of the Second Five-Year Plan is difficult to estimate; for one must remember that the tight controls operated during the first two years were not entirely the product of procedural constipation; they also reflected the extreme stringency of the financial situation. When this eased, the central ministries could afford to be rather more liberal with their financial sanctions. Nevertheless, there seems to be general agreement that the new system represented a great improvement on the old, which—in the words of a high official of the Ministry of Agriculture—had produced nothing more than 'interminable wrangles and delays which seriously held up plan fulfilment'.

Since the reform of 1958, changes in the procedure for central assistance have been marginal,[87] with one significant exception. The states now receive payments for the first three-quarters of the year in nine monthly instalments; the balance for the last three months is (at least in theory) paid over only when actual expenditure totals are known.[88] Clearly, this is intended as a means of disciplining them financially without (as under the former system) cramping their style. There have also been one or two modifications of the *virement* arrangements, to try to ensure observance of national priorities. Thus it is no longer easy to transfer funds from 'schemes which carry patterns of assistance' to those 'to which specific patterns

[86] Punjab, after explaining the new system in its 'Annual Plan for 1958–9', said: 'The uncertainty about Central Assistance has thus been removed and this is expected to go a long way in accelerating the progress of implementing the schemes' (Punjab, *FYP(2)*: *Punjab State Ann. Plan, 1958–9* (1959), p. 8).

[87] Minor modifications were announced in the following year's 'Procedure' letter (see PC(P)3(2)/59, dated 14 May 1959).

[88] For an example of the 'final payment' calculations, see App. III, p. 544.

are not attached'. Persuasion, too, is used to prevent states from exercising their freedom in a way of which the Commission disapproves. Thus, in a Planning Commission letter of 4 August 1962, we read:

> State Governments have been separately requested to earmark the assistance provided for (i) special schemes for girls' education under 'Education' and (ii) control of communicable diseases under 'Health' for utilisation on these programmes only. In view of the inadequate progress being made in girls' education and the need to undertake the programme for control of communicable diseases as a national programme, it is considered essential that there should be no diversion of funds from these two programmes.[89]

All this underlines the inherent contradictions involved in central assistance, however it may be organized. On the one hand, the relaxation of controls speeds the process of plan implementation; on the other, it makes the enforcement of national priorities more difficult and the effective supervision of expenditure virtually impossible. Those at the centre are now, perhaps, more aware of the defects of the present system than of its virtues,[90] although no one advocates a return to the pre-1958 regime.

At the Ministry of Finance there is a strong opinion, freely expressed in the highest official quarters, that the state governments are now virtually uncontrollable. The 'withholding' of assistance for the last quarter of the financial year is one of those ingenious devices which simply does not work. In fact, the author was assured, the states receive all the money promised to them *before* the end of the year, and the 'adjustments' made during the subsequent year are of a very peculiar kind. If the state's share of the expenditure in respect of a particular group has proved insufficient, then in theory the amount of central assistance for that group is reduced. (It should be noted, incidentally, that whereas overspending on one group does not attract a higher central contribution, underspending on another attracts a lower one.) In reality, however, the state receives compensation, usually in the form of a 'miscellaneous development loan'. The state, knowing that it can rely on this, is not over-worried whether its contribution falls short or not. Admittedly, the 'compensatory' loan carries a rate of interest, but states have by now also become used to receiving further loans from the central government to assist them in paying the interest on

[89] No. PC(P)4/2/62.

[90] A note of alarm is sounded in the *MTA* (p. 66), viz.: 'Because of the limited resources available and large unsatisfied demands from the departments, there has been constant pressure to shift funds as between different heads of development contrary to the scheme of allocations agreed for the Annual Plan. Such diversions have tended to cause setbacks in development in fields like agriculture and co-operation and certain social programmes of high priority have also been affected. In the working of State plans, a measure of flexibility is of course desirable. However, while providing for adjustments in outlays under different heads in accordance with the prescribed procedures, it is equally necessary that diversions of funds such as are likely to upset agreed national priorities should not take place.'

former ones;[91] and in any case the rate of interest is not calculated by the application of any rational principle, but fixed in accordance with the general view taken of a state's resources and repayment capacities. Thus, *de facto*, the central government becomes the 'residuary legatee of all risks'. This is all the more serious in view of the fact that the nature of the risks is now largely at the state government's own discretion. The 'matching' calculations made by the ministries, intended to ensure that funds are used in accordance with certain broad 'patterns', are virtually useless exercises; for the state actually receives global grant-loan instalments, the expenditure of which cannot be effectively supervised.

There is, perhaps, some exaggeration in this plaint. Neither the Finance Ministry nor the other central ministries are really as powerless as it would suggest. The bias of every Finance Ministry is towards strict control of expenditure and it can hardly feel very happy when such control is relaxed. Nevertheless, the problem has become a very real one and some of the best minds in both the Finance Ministry and the Planning Commission are trying to work out a solution. They recognize that attempts at *direct* control have failed and are bound to fail. Automatic financial discipline has also come badly unstuck, although this is for political reasons rather than because of defective technique. Perhaps, with greater courage at the centre, it could be reimposed; but, even so, the problem of *priorities* would remain. To solve this, it has been suggested that the making of lump-sum payments might be combined with a rule that *virement* was to be exercised only in favour of higher-priority projects, centrally defined, at the expense of lower-priority ones. As we have seen, certain tentative moves in this direction have already been made. The question is whether a general procedure could be worked out; and also whether, having been worked out, it could be effectively enforced.

It would be tempting to suggest that the wheel has come full circle, and that dissatisfaction among the states is replaced by dissatisfaction at the centre, but this is still far from the truth. Although, in the implementation of the plan, the states have greater freedom from meticulous financial controls and more discretion in laying out their expenditure, they are still, as we have seen, subject to considerable pressure from the central ministries at the formulation stage. Hence they often find that their new freedom and discretion is in respect of projects which they themselves would not have chosen to adopt and which, at least in some instances, they consider ill adapted to local needs. Of course, if national priorities are to be effectively enforced, it is inevitable that the states should experience this kind of frustration in some measure. It would obviously be wrong, for instance, to permit a state which can easily produce a surplus of foodgrains to divert funds from agriculture to—say—housing or town planning.

[91] See above, p. 329

Indeed, according to the principle of comparative advantage, it may even be desirable to insist that in such a state there should be proportionately *greater* concentration on agriculture than in states where natural conditions are less favourable and marginal costs consequently higher. But although no state can reasonably complain about the enforcement of broad priorities, it can complain with much more justification about the centre's insistence on its adoption of specific means and methods. Such insistence, uninformed by adequate local knowledge, may involve a great deal of 'infructuous expenditure'. How far this has actually happened is difficult to say; but the states themselves are of the opinion that it occurs far too often.

Even at the implementation stage itself, the liberty of the state governments continues to be restricted in some very important fields of development. We have seen that the Planning Commission, in its letter of 12 May 1958, made exceptions to the new general rules in favour of a number of central agencies. These exceptions still hold good, and states complain that the supervision of plan schemes for which the Commodity Boards and the Central Water and Power Commission have central responsibility is still over-meticulous. The CWPC has somewhat slackened the rein, but the Commodity Boards, for the most part, continue to watch the states' performance like so many nervous aunts. As an example, Maharashtra quoted the fact that the staff structure of its projects under the Integrated Cotton Development Scheme was centrally determined.

Hence there is dissatisfaction among the states as well as at the centre. Long after the new system of financial allocations had been introduced, Nehru, at the NDC, recorded a complaint by the absent Chief Minister of Uttar Pradesh that 'too many references and cross-references between centre and states tended to delay matters'.[92] Six months later the Chief Minister of Rajasthan was demanding, at the NDC's sixteenth meeting (12–13 September 1960), that 'rigidity regarding the procedures relating to sanctions and reappropriations should be removed'.

There is no ideal solution to these problems. Inherent in federal government, they are exacerbated by the attempt to plan the economy on a national scale. The tension between centre and states, essentially political in character, will continue to affect planning relationships. So long as there is a scramble for scarce resources, and so long as a high proportion of the expenditure on state plans is met by central subventions, dissatisfaction will be felt on both sides. Such dissatisfaction could be diminished although not eliminated if planning were pushing up the national income more rapidly, so that the resources position became progressively easier. It could also be diminished if satisfactory means of imposing autonomatic financial discipline on the states could be

[92] NDC, 14th mtg, 19–20 Mar. 1960.

discovered and put into effect, if state governments improved the efficiency of their administrations and husbanded their resources more carefully, and if the centre realized that plan implementation by remote control is as ineffective and self-defeating as back-seat driving. As we have seen, some progress has been made towards the realization of these desiderata; but like most progress in India it still lags behind the headlong rush of new problems. This is not surprising, for economic planning in a federation is one of the most difficult of political and administrative exercises. What is surprising is that India, with her enormous size and daunting variety of regional and local circumstances, has brought to its solution the considerable—if insufficient—degree of creativity and flexibility which we have recorded.

A Note on Inter-State Co-operation

In our account of the planning relationships between the states and the centre, we have assumed that the interests of the states themselves—perhaps, for the sake of clarity, one ought to say their 'felt' interests—are competitive rather than complementary. This is only too true, even though linguistic reorganization may have taken some of the bitterness out of inter-state rivalry. Examples of spontaneous co-operation between adjoining states, along the lines of the inter-state compacts in the United States, are very few, so strong is the suspicion felt by neighbour of neighbour. But this situation cannot be passively accepted by the government or the Planning Commission. Both are vitally concerned with the development of a sense of national unity, which requires that the behaviour of adjoining states should be fraternal rather than hostile. Both, moreover, are aware that there are problems of economic development, in the fields of transport, power supply, and the utilization of water resources, which can be solved only by planning for a 'catchment area' wider than that provided by any one state. Both, therefore, are interested in the lessening of inter-state rivalries and in the creation of institutions for inter-state co-operation.

The constitution itself provides the Union Government with powers for this purpose. For certain 'state' subjects, such as highways, inland waterways, industries, mineral development, and the control of inter-state rivers and river valleys, the Union retains regulatory powers. Under Article 252, moreover, Parliament can legislate on 'state' subjects for two or more states, when the legislatures of these states have given it the necessary authority. Under Article 263 the President may establish a Council for (1) inquiring into and advising upon inter-state disputes, (2) investigating matters in which several states, or one or more states and the Union, have a common interest, and (3) making recommendations, in respect of such matters, calculated to secure better co-ordination of policy.

Such powers have been used especially for the purpose of controlling the flow of inter-state rivers and of co-ordinating, for a region embracing several states, the supply of electric power. For the great inter-state river valley projects, two forms of co-operation have been virtually imposed. The first, of which Damodar is the only example, involves the surrender of state's rights to an *ad hoc* body, organized as a public corporation and advised by a committee on which the participating states (West Bengal and Bihar) are represented.[93] The second, of which the most spectacular of many examples is Bhakra, involves the setting up of a Control Board containing representatives both of the participating states and of the central government. To provide the central government with the additional authority it needs to deal with inter-state river problems, Parliament has passed the River Boards Act, 1956, which empowers the establishment of inter-state River Boards, and the Inter-State Water Disputes Act, 1956, which provides machinery for resolving such disputes.

By and large, the Control Boards have worked well—better, indeed, than the Damodar Valley Corporation, which has failed to emulate the achievements of the Tennessee Valley Authority on which it was modelled. In respect, however, of the water disputes that are particularly endemic among the central and southern states, there is much less success to record. The central government has been nervous about using its statutory powers, preferring to leave the states to reach agreement by direct negotiation. Sometimes this has worked, especially where there are obvious common interests. Kerala, for instance, needs the rice that Madras, on the other side of the central watershed, can produce if irrigation facilities are extended. It is obvious common sense, therefore, to divert into Madras some of the waters of the rivers that rush down the western slopes and flow, through Kerala's narrow coastal strip, unproductively into the Indian Ocean. Hence the fraternal settlement of the Parambikulam–Aliya–Shalayar 'waters question', between E. M. S. Namboodiripad's Communist administration in Kerala and K. Kamaraj's Congress administration in Madras, after negotiations in which the Madrasi representatives found the Keralan Communists 'surprisingly' co-operative. But in the much more serious case of the Krishna–Godivari waters, on which Andhra Pradesh, Mysore, and Maharashtra had rival claims, inter-state negotiations produced a dangerous stalemate. When voluntary agreement had proved impossible, the central government appointed the 'Gulati' Committee[94] to investigate, and handed down a decision, which included the appointment of a River Board, on the basis of this body's recommendations. Even so, it is almost certain that the dispute will break out again, for the

[93] For a brief account of Damodar, see IIPA, *The Damodar Valley Corporation: a brief Study;* or Hanson, *Public Enterprise & Economic Development* (1959), ch. 10.
[94] See *Indian Information,* 15 Apr. 1963 and *Asian Recorder,* 14–20 May 1963.

present settlement is founded on the somewhat doubtful view that 'all the projects on hand and contemplated by all three States could be pushed through with sufficient safety margins and suitable adjustments and that the problem, if at all, would arise only after the Fifth Plan when all the schemes would have been completed and other projects had been taken up'.[95]

With the 'linguistic' reorganization of 1956, the central government came to the conclusion that the various forms of *ad hoc* co-operation between states, mostly imposed by New Delhi, should be supplemented by permanent machinery. The States Reorganization Act, therefore, provided for the constitution of five 'Zonal Councils'[96]—one for each of the following groups of states and Union territories:

1. Northern: Punjab, Rajasthan, Jammu and Kashmir, Delhi, and Himachal Pradesh;
2. Central: Uttar Pradesh and Madhya Pradesh;
3. Eastern: Bihar, West Bengal, Orissa, Assam, Manipur, and Tripura;
4. Western: Bombay and Mysore;
5. Southern: Andhra Pradesh, Madras, and Kerala.

Each Council was to consist of (*a*) a Union minister as Chairman, (*b*) the Chief Ministers and two other ministers of the participating states, and (*c*) not more than two representatives from each centrally-administered territory, where such territories were included in the zone. Advisory personnel, with voices but without votes, were to include the Chief Secretaries of the participating states and a representative of the Planning Commission. A secretarial staff was to be provided.

The functions of the Council, as laid down by the States Reorganization Act, were to 'discuss any matter in which some or all of the States represented in that Council, or the Union and one or more of the States represented in that Council, have a common interest, and to advise the Central Government and the Government of each State concerned as to the action to be taken on any such matter.' Without prejudice to the generality of this provision, it might discuss and make recommendations on

(*a*) any matter of common interest in the field of economic and social planning;
(*b*) any matter concerning border disputes, linguistic minorities or inter-State transport;
(*c*) any matter connected with, or arising out of, the reorganization of the States under this Act.[97]

Meetings were to be held at the discretion of the Chairman, rules of

[95] *EE*, 29 Mar. 1963.
[96] The only work which gives a full account of the origin, purpose and early history of these Councils is Joan V. Bondurant, *Regionalism versus Provincialism* (Dec. 1958).
[97] States Reorganization Act, cl. 21.

procedure required the approval of the central government, and decisions were to be by majority vote of the members present.

The establishment of these Councils was welcomed both by those who feared that 'linguism' would disrupt national unity and by those who felt the need for a regional planning area that was larger than any individual state. Others suspected that the zone might become a new source of political authority, which might detract from that of the states or even from that of the centre itself; for although the Councils, as constituted, were advisory only, their more enthusiastic advocates, among whom Nehru himself was to be numbered, looked forward to the conferment on them, when the time was ripe, of appropriate executive powers.[98] In the event, the new institutions neither fulfilled the hopes of their advocates nor confirmed the fears of their detractors. Although vigorously promoted by the Home Minister, Pandit Pant, who became Chairman of them all, they never really came to life. They still exist and still meet from time to time, but occupy such a modest corner of India's political and administrative life that few commentators choose to do more than barely mention them.[99]

Reports of their meetings by the Indian press[100] suggest that, under the impetus given them by Pandit Pant, they showed some initial vigour but soon got into the habit of referring all difficult questions to a maze of inconclusive sub-committees. Some of them appear to have taken useful decisions about such things as co-operation among police forces and the co-ordination of manpower requirements, but their role in the fields of transport development, water control, and electricity supply has been peripheral. To the extent that adjoining states co-operate in these matters, it is still mainly on the basis of direct government-to-government negotiations, the results of which the Zonal Councils may or may not record. The Planning Commission continues to send representatives to their meetings and to raise subjects for discussion, but the importance that it attaches to them may be measured by the fact that it does not even mention them in the Third Five-Year Plan report. So far it has not even taken up the suggestion[101] that the areas covered by its Programme Advisers should coincide with the Zones.

The idea of the Zonal Council, as a planning agency, is administratively sound but politically doubtful. Its success depends upon habits of inter-state co-operation which are absent or weak, and which mere institutional arrangements can do little to promote.

[98] See Bondurant, *Regionalism*, pp. 55 f.

[99] An exception is V. T. Krishnamachari, who devotes a few paragraphs to them (see pp. 20–21, 105–6) in his *Fundamentals of Planning*.

[100] Useful summaries appear in the *AR* from 1957 onwards.

[101] Made, for instance, by V. T. Krishnamachari, p. 105, as one of his suggestions for 'improvements in planning procedures'.

XI

GRASS ROOTS

(i)

IN the last two chapters, we have examined India's attempts to formulate and execute plans simultaneously on two levels, the Union and the state. This is a difficult exercise, and hence many of the problems that it presents remain unsolved. Both Union planning and state planning, however, are essentially 'planning from above'. This does not satisfy the Indians. In their view, it must be combined with 'planning from below', in which every unit, down to the village and the family, plays its individual part, at both the formulation and implementation stages. In the light of what has already been said, in Chapter VII, about the characteristics of Indian society, it will be obvious that to stimulate initiative on this scale and to co-ordinate its results are tasks of positively staggering size. It is not surprising, therefore, that so far the Indian planners have failed to cope with them. This, however, is not for want of persistent effort. 'Public co-operation' has been the subject of innumerable speeches, directives, conferences, exhortations, and committee reports. No subject has more persistently engaged the attention of the Planning Commission or produced more anxious thought among the top men in the Union government. We must inquire into the reasons for this concern, into the ideas which it has inspired, and into the means which the authorities have devised to give the plans that dynamism at the 'grass-roots' level which is regarded, rightly or wrongly, as an essential precondition for their success.

At first sight, the Indian emphasis on the importance of public co-operation may seem the product of false views about social psychology. In the West, we are rather cynically familiar with exhortations to pull together, put our shoulders to the wheel and make that extra one per cent of effort. All this is the current jargon of democratic politics, and no one takes it seriously except in wartime—and perhaps even then fewer than the politicians imagine. We know that, by and large, people are actuated by individual, group, and class interests, and that the unspoken assumption behind every economic plan is that the achievement of its objectives will mainly depend on whether it provides for these individuals, groups, and classes the incentives that call forth effort of the kind required. But elsewhere, and particularly in the underdeveloped countries, belief in our western version of 'economic man' is weaker, especially among the group of intellectuals which provides the main political leadership. The reasons for this difference are obvious. Economic incentives themselves are weaker, or at least differently oriented, in a society which is only just beginning to shift away from its traditional agrarian base, and which is tribal or feudal in organization and outlook, and cemented together with a religious ideology which emphasizes status and de-emphasizes mobility. The comparatively few people who have detached themselves from it to some extent and developed 'normal' economic motivations are not highly respected, nor do they usually merit respect; for the prototype of the entrepreneur is one who seems merely to batten upon economic backwardness, whether as purveyor to a feudal court or money-lender to a village community. To encourage him is neither socially popular nor economically useful. He is the 'rascally merchant', familiar enough to the readers of popular medieval literature, and tends to remain so in public esteem even when—like the Indian Marwari—he succeeds in becoming a producer as distinct from a mere exploiter. Among the bureaucracy and the politicians, in whose hands lies the initiative for economic planning, there is, as we have already noted, a contempt for 'trade' and a belief in the possibility of maintaining and developing a paternalistic relationship between government and people, reminiscent of the 'Young Toryism' of nineteenth-century England. This goes together, perhaps rather oddly, with convictions about the potentialities of popular initiative, once the people have been stimulated to look beyond their narrow horizons to the vision of the promised land of modern science and technology.

These ideas are reinforced, as we have seen,[1] by the fact that a 'new' nation is generally the product of a struggle against alien rulers, in the course of which feelings of solidarity bind together a wide variety of indigenous groups and classes and stimulate a capacity among some of their leading members for altruistic, self-sacrificing effort on behalf of the common cause. It is therefore natural that the political élites should be predisposed to believe that, once independence is achieved, the spirit of 'all for one and one for all' that has inspired the national struggle can be maintained and diverted into constructive, 'nation-building' channels. Moreover, in the heat of the fight for independence and during the period of euphoria immediately following its acquisition, it is not difficult to imagine that the masses possess an inherent idealism and creativity, too long denied an outlet by imperialist tyranny and now ready and eager for self-expression.

Among 'leftists', the correctness of this diagnosis of the situation appears to be confirmed by the experience of the Soviet Union, the most successful of the formerly underdeveloped countries which have raised themselves to power and affluence by dint of economic planning. 'Planning from below'

[1] Ch. VII, pp. 259–60.

and the stimulation of mass enthusiasm have been characteristic of the Russian system since the end of the 1920s. That much of the enthusiasm was bogus is less well understood by the intellectuals of the *tiers monde* than by their counterparts in the West. That 'planning from below' was associated with one of the worst tyrannies of modern times can be easily disregarded, now that the 'cult of personality' has been brought to an end. Whatever the 'mistakes' of the Soviet regime may have been, Russia 'proves' that popular solidarity and initiative open a road to economic development which is not only as viable as, but morally better than, the capitalist road.

Even among those who reject Communism and are free from the grosser illusions about the Soviet Union, Russian experience strongly suggests the importance of a 'turn to the masses'. For if a dictatorial regime could not dispense with popular participation, how much less can a democratic one? If the whip of compulsion is to be withdrawn, what substitute is there for a willing and active consent? From this line of thought there emerges a glowing picture of a regime which possesses all the more attractive features of the Russian and none of its less attractive ones. This is the vision that haunted Nehru throughout his political life.

In India there has been another and even more powerful current flowing in the same direction. Just as the Russian *narodniks* proclaimed the virtues of the ancient *mir*, so the Gandhians proclaimed those of the traditional Indian village. It was not that the village, any more than the *mir*, provided an actual example of these virtues. On the contrary, it was sunk deep in poverty, squalor, apathy, and senseless factionalism. This, however, was due to the deliberate destruction of the village's self-governing institution, the panchayat, by the British. Once the British went, the villagers' sense of solidarity and capacity for self-rule would again find expression. Only the most orthodox Gandhians, of course, believed in the possibility of basing the entire polity on the self-governing village community; but the idea that the rural people, so organized, and with the assistance of modern science and technology, could march unitedly towards higher standards of living and culture has been a constant feature of the Congress Party's programmes, at least since the time when Gandhi established himself as the Party's revered guide. It should be noted, furthermore, that among those who rejected Gandhi's for Stalin's guidance, illusions about the nature of collective farming provided a source of ideological inspiration from which flowed similar conclusions.

These are the reasons why Indian planners have been so insistent about popular participation in the planning process. Before independence, this conception featured prominently in the plans of the 'Nehru' Committee, in the 'People's Plan', and of course in the 'Gandhian' Plan. It can be found even in the 'Bombay' Plan of the industrialists and in the plans of the 'bureaucracy'. By the time that the Planning Commission took up the burden, therefore, it was firmly established. In the First Five-Year Plan report, the Commission gave expression to it in the following words:

> Public cooperation and public opinion constitute the principal force and sanction behind planning. A democracy working for social ends has to base itself on the willing assent of the people and not the coercive power of the State. This leads to the application of the principle of cooperation in all phases of social activity and in all the functions which bring together individuals for the pursuit of common purposes. The people have to cooperate among themselves and with the various agencies responsible for the formulation and execution of the plan. In the way any programme is conceived, offered and carried out, action by the agencies of the government must be inspired by an understanding of the role of the people and supported by practical steps to enlist their enthusiastic participation. Where the administration and the people feel and act together the programme gains in vitality and significance.
>
> The concept of planning has been associated largely with conditions in which a group has gathered in its hands all the power to control and regiment the life of the community and to command and direct its material and manpower resources. What is there in democracy to take the place of this unified direction and the force that will remove obstructions from the path of economic development along a set line? Considering the way democracy works on the basis of fragmented authority and of parties with uncertain tenure, attempting to reconcile all kinds of contrary interests and purposes, no plan, it might appear, can proceed very far. Conditions have, however, developed in the world which make planning not only compatible with democracy, but essential for its very survival. A common social outlook which interprets progress in terms of social justice and the economic and social well-being of the people is crystallising among all who believe in democracy. In fact a major assumption which makes democratic planning real is confidence in the community that the national plan aims at achieving a social order in which economic disparities will be greatly reduced and an equal opportunity afforded to all; that no privilege, no interest is sought to be sustained, even for a period, except in the degree in which it fulfills a larger social purpose. This can furnish the ingredients of social cohesion within the community. We have thus before us here a much wider view of public cooperation in which the interests of the parties are relegated to the background and the common objectives of the nation regarded as a unity are the sole considerations. Certain elements may not agree with the Plan and the aspirations of a section may far exceed the level of achievement set as the target of the Plan for the first few years. But, if the direction of advance is in line with the expectations of the bulk of the people and the rate of progress is not too slow, the essential prerequisites for winning public cooperation will have been secured.[2]

The thesis here propounded is essentially a simple one: that with the progress of planning of the type proposed by the Commission, the objectives that unite people will become more important than those that divide

[2] *FYP*(*1*), p. 144.

them; that, with increasing consciousness of this fact, they will give more of their allegiance to common objectives and less to divisive ones; and that, consequently, an ever firmer basis will be laid for popular co-operation in both the formulation and the implementation of the plan. Basically, the vision is one of a party-less, co-operative democracy.

One might suspect this to be no more than a shop-window put up by the politicians; but this would be to misunderstand the Indian mind. It may be that, today, the vision has become so tarnished as to be unrecognizable; but in 1952 the Commission was serious enough in its statement of principle, whatever after-thoughts it may subsequently have had. If proof is required, it is to be found not only in the great effort devoted to Community Development and *panchayati raj* but in the anxiety that New Delhi has displayed about making 'planning from below' a reality. If success has been evasive, it is not for want of trying. We are therefore concerned with a central, not a peripheral, aspect of Indian planning, and must inquire quite seriously why its results have not been commensurate with the expectations of its authors.

When 'participation' is analysed, we find that it involves three things, viz. (1) the provision of information; (2) the creation of opportunities to take part in the determination of objectives; and (3) the enlistment of co-operation in the implementation of objectives. Clearly, the three must go together. If information is faulty or insufficient, people will not know what they are being required to do. If they play no part in the determination of objectives, it will be difficult to persuade them that the plan is 'theirs' and hence to elicit their active support in carrying it out. If they have no experience of implementing it, they will be at a loss when asked to help in the process of formulation. If they are interested neither in formulation nor in implementation, providing them with information will be a useless exercise. Nevertheless, for purposes of analysis, it will be convenient to keep the three phases separate.

(ii)

On information, we need say little. The means adopted to publicize the plans and to interest people in their progress are described in the three plan reports.[3] In India the means of publicity with which we are familiar in the West play a rather limited role. Newspapers, in a predominantly illiterate country, have a restricted circulation; even the cinema and the radio reach only a minority; and there is no television. Much of the plan publicity, therefore, must be made by word of mouth, supplemented by the pictorial poster. Every local Congress politician, every administrator, every village headman is expected to be, to the best of his ability, a plan publicist. Traditional forms of entertainment, such as the dance, drama,

[3] Ibid. ch. 8; *FYP(2)*, ch. 6, pp. 141–7; *FYP(3)*, ch. 18.

hymn, and song, are enlisted in the cause. The difficulties, of course, are severe. As it passes down the political and administrative echelons, the plan message becomes diluted and distorted. Opposition parties and groups which refuse to accept the government's and the Commission's view of the 'national interest' are making 'unhelpful' propaganda by precisely the same means. (Some, such as the Communists, who have avidly seized on the propaganda potentialities of the dance and the drama, are the pace-makers of publicity technique.) Distances are enormous, the terrain some-times difficult, and funds always short. Hence it is not surprising that the ordinary villager, or even the 'leading' one, often professes ignorance or displays mystification when asked about 'the plan'. The Commission, in its Second Plan report (1956), had to admit that although 'through community participation and the results which have been achieved', the First Plan had 'reached a large number of persons', these represented 'only a small proportion of the population of the country'.[4] In the Third Plan report it said nothing about publicity as such, but made the significant remark that to develop among the people an 'understanding and appreci-ation of the significance, objectives and priorities of the Third Plan' was 'by no means an easy task in view of the growing complexity of the economy and of the many problems to be faced'.[5]

The Commission now thinks more in terms of informing the people through enlisting their participation and places rather less stress than formerly on publicity as a distinct service. For the man in the field or the man at the bench the important thing is that he should know what 'his' plan is; the national plan and even the state plan are beyond his com-prehension, however well they may be explained.

(iii)

In respect of participation at the formulation stage, only the most modest of beginnings were made in the First Five-Year Plan. Over-whelmingly, this was planning from above. There was no time for much else. Even the state governments, as we have seen,[6] could do little more than hastily throw together a few projects and make a rough estimation of financial resources. Nevertheless, in one of the early letters[7] dispatched by the Commission to the states, mention was made of the importance of enlisting the co-operation of local authorities. These, said the Commission, 'have . . . a vital role to play in any scheme of planned development and their plans have to be coordinated eventually to fit in with the plans of State Governments'. A subsequent letter,[8] sent soon after the publication of the Draft Outline, dealt mainly with the role of local bodies at the implementation stage, but also stressed the need to evolve, initially in the

[4] *FYP(2)*, p. 146. [5] *FYP(3)*, p. 297. [6] See above, pp. 349–50.
[7] PC(C)26/51, dated 11 Oct. 1950. [8] Ibid. dated 5 Aug. 1951.

areas selected for intensive development, 'a system of agricultural planning in which all units, beginning with the smallest, can play an active part in formulating . . . programmes'. In this connexion, it drew attention to 'certain suggestions' made in the Draft Outline, of which the most important was for the establishment of Village Production Councils which would '(i) frame programmes of production to be achieved at each harvest by the village; (ii) frame budgets of requirements for supplies and finance needed for fulfilling the programmes; (iii) assess results attained at each harvest.'[9] At the higher levels, there should be (*a*) 'in each group of ten villages a committee working in close cooperation with the official responsible for work in the village'; (*b*) for the Development Block, 'a similar non-official committee'; and (*c*) at the district level, a District Development Board, partly composed of 'leading non-officials from different Development Blocks'.[10]

After the First Plan had begun, the Commission's chief concern was to persuade the states to split up their individual plans 'into programmes for districts and other local areas, such as individual towns, tehsils, talukas, development blocks, villages . . . etc.' in order to get effective co-operation in the process of implementation. It also suggested, however, that only thus could the people become 'partners in the Plan' to the extent of eventually becoming 'associated closely with its formulation as well as its implementation from stage to stage'.[11]

This must be regarded as no more than a notice served by the Planning Commission that in the formulation of the Second Plan 'planning from below' was to be treated more seriously. How sketchy it had actually been in the formulation of the First is revealed in the following passage from a letter of 28 December 1954,[12] dealing with the 'preparation of district and village plans' for the forthcoming quinquennial period:

> Generally speaking States have welcomed the idea of preparing district and village plans, but in some States the aim seems to be to ask district authorities to prepare district plans after ascertaining local opinion in some manner and in the light of local conditions. *While this is an advance on the practice adopted at the time of the preparing of the First Plan*, in the present conditions it is necessary to go further and to ensure that in every State a genuine effort is made to prepare plans from the village upwards and for suitable 'planning areas' within the district.

(iv)

That the Commission was determined that planning from below should become a reality is indicated by the fact that its first letter on this subject,[13] in connexion with the Second Plan, was sent out as early as 28 April 1954—long before even the most preliminary and tentative decisions had

[9] *DO(I)*, p. 88. [10] Ibid. p. 91. [11] PC(P)41/53, dated 11 Mar. 1953.
[12] PC(P)58/54. [13] FYII/CD1/1/54.

been taken about the plan's size and shape. The purpose of this letter was 'to convey suggestions on . . . the manner in which, within the district, the work of planning may be organised and plans prepared for individual villages and groups of villages such as tehsils, talukas, National Extension Development Blocks etc'. It was essential, wrote the Commission, 'that local initiative in formulating plans and local effort and resources in carrying them out should be stimulated to the maximum extent possible. This will help to relate the plans closely to local needs and conditions and also to secure public cooperation and voluntary effort and contributions.'

With a view to gaining experience, it was suggested that plans might be worked out initially for three or four selected districts, each of which might be divided into 'a few convenient planning areas'. At the district level, it was important that the existing development committees, in which 'leading non-officials and the principal social agencies' were involved, should be 'strengthened with a view to the preparation of the second five year plan and the achievement of the targets of the first five year plan'. At the village level, either the panchayat or some *ad hoc* body (where no panchayat existed) should be used to 'express local opinion and help organise local cooperation'. The emphasis in village planning should be on 'agricultural production and activities ancillary thereto, including cooperation', and its aim should be to ensure that: '(i) every family has a plan of improvement for which it works, including agricultural production and subsidiary occupations; (ii) every family is made eligible to become a member of at least one cooperative society; and (iii) every family devotes a portion of its time and resources for the benefit of the community.'

At the end of the year, the Commission sent out a paper[14] on the same subject, drawn up for consideration by the Standing Committee of the NDC, and asked the state governments for their comments 'in the light of experience gained' in the preparation of district and village plans. This document revealed the difficulties which the States were experiencing in carrying out the Commission's previous suggestions. One of these, on which no guidance had been given, was 'how to fit plans prepared in the district with plans prepared by the departments for the State as a whole'. This chicken-and-egg problem was clearly analogous to that affecting the planning relationships between the states and the centre. The Commission had no solution, but nevertheless criticized those states that were attempting to cut the Gordian knot by simply producing 'paper' plans for the lower levels. The view in some states, it wrote,

> appears to be to regard the plans prepared by departments as the real thing and plans prepared in the district as being largely a matter of procedure to support the claim that the people have been associated in the preparation of the plan. For example, in some States it is said that the heads of departments would fix

[14] PC(D)58/54, dated 28 Dec. 1954.

the targets for each District, even in spheres such as village roads, proposals prepared by the people in the district being modified accordingly.

From the dizzy heights of New Delhi, this, no doubt, looked like a grievous malpractice, but one can hardly fail to sympathize with hard-pressed heads of departments in choosing the easy way out of their quandary.

The Commission, however, was equally distressed by another 'deviation', of the opposite kind. There appeared to be a tendency, it said, 'to regard plans for taluks or extension blocks . . . as a summation of village plans'. What was needed was 'that the special problems of each "planning area" should be carefully assessed and should guide the preparation of programmes in villages within the area'.

This was not all. The Commission's suggestions about the part to be played by local bodies in the formulation of development programmes had been 'carried out to a meagre extent only'; village plans were too often regarded as a mere collection of schemes rather than as means of 'organising the resources of the village community'; the guidance given to the villagers was too 'vague'; there was a risk of 'excessive paper work'; and little had been done to ensure that towns should have plans of their own. The Commission, in fact, was not satisfied with the response of the state governments. It also complained that they had not yet sent in 'any accounts of problems and difficulties'.

In January 1955 the Standing Committee of the NDC considered this document, approved its proposals, and asked the state governments 'to send to the Planning Commission some illustrative district and village plans'. In the following month, apparently after receiving some of these, the Commission offered 'further elucidation' on 'the scope and central objectives of the rural development programmes'.[15] This amounted to (*a*) a categorization of specific objectives under three headings, viz. (1) improvements of a permanent or medium-term nature, (2) steady improvements in methods and techniques, and (3) local works programmes; (*b*) a reminder that, in framing village plans, it was important to keep in mind the 'fundamentals of the National Extension movement'; and (*c*) a statement that the goal towards which the villages must be encouraged to strive was a 'doubling of production within a period of ten years'. The letter concluded with the following profession of faith:

> A programme under which every family in a village is offered the assistance needed, in a well-organised manner, with the objective of doubling agricultural production in the country within a period of ten years, and in which every village will be enabled to provide itself with such amenities [as] wholesome drinking water supply, a road connecting it with a main road or a railway station, etc., within a short time, cannot fail to appeal to the countryside and evoke enthusiasm.

[15] FYII/CD1/6/55, dated 22 Feb. 1955.

It was therefore the duty of 'the official and non-official organizations to explain this objective and see that the implications of this were fully understood so that every family in the countryside was animated by a common aim and outlook and public cooperation was secured in the widest possible measure'.

A week later the Commission sent out another letter,[16] containing further criticisms and suggestions, and announcing that discussions with state governments about their proposals for the Second Plan would begin in July. When these were completed, planning from below would have to go, so to speak, into reverse gear.

> After the draft State plans have been reviewed jointly by the Planning Commission with the representatives of each State, the initial proposals of individual departments would have to be amended in some measure. This would, in turn, entail a process of correction down to the district and village level. This task would have to be undertaken by district and taluka committees and village panchayats during the closing months of the year 1955–56. It is desirable that those concerned with the planning in the districts should be aware from now on of this further stage in their work.

There can be no doubt that, in all this, the intentions of the Planning Commission were excellent. None the less, it was a largely futile exercise. Quite apart from the fact that it was based on assumptions about rural India which were rather remote from the reality, it involved asking villagers and non-officials to answer questions to which even the officials, who were supposed to be providing 'guidance', could offer no coherent replies. The general shape and size of the Second Plan was still unknown, the provisional plans of the states were embryonic, and there was no information available about the quantum of central assistance or the manner of its distribution among states and projects. Well might the villager, no fool in matters concerning his livelihood, treat the whole business with some scepticism and leave the formulation of 'his' plan to the discretion of the officials. The latter, being under orders to produce something 'from below', accordingly did so, with a degree of scepticism which probably exceeded even that of their parishioners.

Perhaps, indeed, it was good that the villagers knew so little about the plans that had been prepared in their name; for at least they were spared disillusionment when the axe began to descend on schemes whose cost so greatly exceeded the available resources. How severe that disillusionment might have been, had the hoped-for enthusiasm at the grass-roots level really been aroused, is indicated by the following passage from Mysore's Second Five-Year Plan report:

> The Government . . . took steps to implement the instructions of the Planning Commission in the matter of initiating schemes from 'below'. The result was

[16] FYII/CD1/10/55, dated 2 Apr. 1955.

that the several schemes suggested for inclusion involved an outlay of Rs252 crores nearly. After discussion, the Planning Commission has tentatively fixed a ceiling of Rs85 crores for Mysore. The schemes of development finally included in the Plan have been intimated to the Planning Commission. Steps are now being taken to prepare District Plans and Taluk Plans within the ceiling now allotted.[17]

Other reports occasionally open the door to reality just wide enough to give us a glimpse of the real difficulties that 'planning from below' encountered. A report from the Punjab, for instance, contains the laconic but revealing statement that, although village panchayats are required to participate actively in the execution of plan schemes, 'when there are factions in the village, Developmental Councils are set up with influential villagers as members for proper and timely execution of village plans'. Another document, from the same source, has much to say about public participation in planning and execution, but adds:

> There have been difficulties in the matter of construction of field channels for irrigation water and public cooperation in many cases has not been forthcoming. Necessary legislation has been passed under which water-courses will be constructed at Government level and cost will be recovered from the cultivators concerned. This will be a sort of forced participation of beneficiaries.[18]

It is in the light of this kind of information, which can be almost infinitely multiplied by anyone with the ability to persuade District Officers, BDOs, and Village Level Workers to speak frankly, that one must read the many 'correct' reports made by the states to the Commission, such as the following from Madras:

> Each development committee prepared the plan for the planning unit with the assistance of the local Revenue Officers and Agricultural Demonstrators. The planning area committees approved or amplified the village plans and sent them to the Collector. Each major panchayat and municipality prepared a plan of its own.[19]

[17] Mysore, *FYP*(*2*), p. 12.

[18] Punjab, *FYP*(*3*)*: Rev. of Progress 1957–8* (1959); *Ann. Plan for 1958–9*, p. 11.

[19] Madras, *FYP*(*2*), *Tiruchivappalli Dist.* (1957), ch. 2. See also the following: Madhya Pradesh, Plan. & Dev. Dept, *Draft FYP*(*2*), i: *Memo.* (1956), p. iv; Kerala, *FYP*(*2*) (1958), p. xii; *West Bengal's Approach to the Second Five Year Plan* (address by Dr B. C. Roy, delivered in New Delhi on 26 July 1955), p. 2; Madhya Bharat Plan. Dept, *FYP*(*2*) (1956), pp. 9–10. One of the more distasteful aspects of all this alleged 'planning from below' was the amount of sheer self-deception and deception of the public involved. In the Madras document it was said that 1,487 villages, covering a population of 2,312,921, had been constituted into 960 units, each with a development committee. These, in their turn, had been grouped in 39 'planning areas'. Three years later, a circular about the production of village plans in connexion with the Third Five-Year Plan blandly stated that 'the actual process of working out . . . village plans could not . . . be undertaken till now for want of an organization at the village which could undertake the responsibility for the preparation and execution of these plans' (Madras, Food & Agric. Dept G. O. No. 3792, 16 Nov. 1960). 'Mistakes', apparently, are officially recognized several years after the event, as in Russia.

It is now generally admitted that the 'planning from below' of 1954–5 was a failure. Evidence to this effect was provided by the PEO's sixth report published in June 1959. Only in 44 per cent of its sample of 161 villages was any attempt made to prepare local plans, and even in these 'the village organizations' did not 'seem to have played an active role', as it was the officials who really did the job. At the block level there was a similar picture:

The targets for local development are, in most instances, received from above, and even when the local body plays some part in determining them, the role of the non-official seems to be passive. There is no attempt at an organized assessment of local needs and resources and adjustment of the targets to these needs and resources. In 20 out of 35 districts in our sample, the target is said to be received from above, having been fixed in respect of certain items by reference to the size of the population or some other criterion. Even in the 15 districts in which the local bodies made an attempt to frame the targets, the initiation and the decision are largely taken and made by the District Officers who, of course, use their local knowledge and personal judgement.

Summarizing, the report described the situation as 'far from satisfactory':

The non-official member does not play his proper role and the official member finds it difficult to divest himself, in any large measure, of responsibility for planning. Plans are prepared at the higher and the official level and handed down to lower bodies. Planning by the people at each level in relation to their area has yet to strike roots.[20]

Accepting this judgement, the Commission, in its Third Plan report, stated that 'much more effort would be required' before local plans could 'become a distinctive stage in the initial preparation of a Five Year Plan'.[21] The fact was that the difficulties of the 'planning from below' exercise had not been fully appreciated, least of all in New Delhi. Too much was asked, and too little guidance given. Above all, people were being required to plan in a vacuum, and neither officials nor non-officials had much idea of what was expected of them, except to the extent that they had to 'think big'. Some of these lessons of the 1954–5 experience were brought fully into the open by the 1959 National Conference on CD at Mysore City.[22] Village plans, it held, should be drawn up, mainly for 'activities which involve the fuller use of resources', within the framework of block plans; and no 'lower level' plans should be taken in hand until the state could give the districts and blocks 'an approximate idea of the total resources under each head'. One can perhaps detect in the statement that 'first priority' ought to be given to the strengthening of the programme-*implementing* institutions, viz. the panchayat and the village co-operative,

[20] PEO, *6th Evaluation Rep.* (June 1959), pp. 15–17. [21] *FYP(3)*, p. 334.
[22] Nat. Conf. on CD at Mysore City, *Main Recommendations & Conclusions*, pp. 36–37.

a note of scepticism about the viability of any kind of plan *formulating* at the village level, in the manner originally conceived.

(v)

In the formulation of the Third Plan, some important improvements on previous procedures were introduced. Firstly, the planning tasks assigned to the lower echelons were more clearly defined; secondly, planning from below was delayed until the general size and shape of both the state plans and the national plan could be broadly envisaged; thirdly, states went to much greater trouble to devise planning procedures for the districts, blocks, and villages to follow.

The nature of the tasks became unmistakable as the optimism generated by the 'success' of the agricultural sector in the First Plan rapidly evaporated. At all levels, it was said, there must be concentration on raising agricultural production with the minimum expenditure of scarce resources. This implied the placing of very heavy emphasis on village production plans designed to ensure (*a*) the most effective utilization of the facilities, such as tested seeds, fertilizers, and irrigation waters, put at the agriculturalist's disposal, and (*b*) the maximum mobilization of unemployed and underemployed rural manpower. So urgent had this become that the Commission and the NDC, like the Punjab government in the document quoted above, were now talking in terms of compulsion as well as of encouragement. 'The idea of customary obligations', wrote the Commission in a report to the Council, 'should be extended to activities vital for meeting the new needs of rural development.' This was particularly important for irrigation facilities, the under-utilization and poor maintenance of which were causing great concern. As customary obligations were tending to fall into disuse, said the Draft Outline of the Third Plan, 'there was need for giving greater definiteness to them through legislation'. Such legislation, it suggested,

> should confer power on the village panchayats to enforce these obligations on the part of beneficiaries. If the latter fail to carry out the works in time, the panchayats should carry them out and realize the cost. In the event of the panchayat failing to carry out the works, the Government, or, on its behalf, the panchayat samiti of the block may arrange for their execution, the cost being eventually recovered from the beneficiaries.[23]

Elsewhere in the Draft Outline there were strong suggestions that, in drawing up their plans, the villages would have to be told very clearly what was required of them, rather than be allowed to give free expression to their 'felt needs'. In many aspects of planning, the role of the block received fresh emphasis, often at the expense of that of the panchayat. The following passage, for instance, appeared to imply that the village

[23] *DO*(*3*), p. 69.

was primarily concerned with implementation rather than with the formulation:

> The block plan includes all the works to be undertaken by different agencies through the block organization, such as the programmes included in the schematic budget under the community development scheme, programmes falling within the general plan of the State under agriculture, animal husbandry and cooperation, programmes for large and medium irrigation projects, road development etc. Such a block plan will in turn be split into village plans, and in this form it should be made widely known to all families.[24]

Village production plans, of course, were essential to 'mobilize effectively the efforts of the local community', to enable the extension workers 'to reach all the farmers in the village', and to form a link between block programmes and local efforts;[25] but the suggestion that the block plans should to any significant extent be a summation of village plans was consistently played down, while the idea that the village plan was subordinate to the block plan received frequent emphasis.[26] The Commission, in fact, was at this time becoming uncomfortably aware that contradictions could arise between the 'felt needs' of the people and the demands of the national economy. Experience had, to some measure, undermined faith in an invisible hand which would bring the two together in happy unity. Yet, at the very time when the national demands appeared to be more urgent than ever, an important 'turn to the people' was being made, through the inauguration of *panchayati raj*. Although everyone agreed—or appeared to agree—that this was a good thing, at least in the long run, there were many misgivings among planners and administrators about its immediate effect on economic development. Hence, perhaps, the rather heavy emphasis in the Draft Outline on discipline from above, as a countervailing force to grass-roots initiatives which might not be wholly acceptable. Hence, too, the rather unclear and sometimes contradictory formulations.

Nevertheless, this new emphasis was useful to the extent that the lower echelons were now receiving clearer and more precise terms of reference

[24] Ibid. p. 67. [25] Ibid. p. 156.

[26] The 'democratized' block was the focal point of the 'Balvantray Mehta' Committee's recommendations, while the NDC exhorted the states to treat the block as the basic 'unit of planning and development'—'along with the district', added the Third Plan report. Subsequently, certain writers have attempted to de-emphasize the panchayat still further. Although the village panchayats, writes B. Mehta, Rajasthan's Chief Secretary, 'have been conceived as the primary unit for planning and execution, . . . with the tendency to reduce the size of the panchayat, this is becoming increasingly difficult and centralization in planning is becoming inevitable . . . . The Panchayat will, therefore, be a rural municipal committee and cannot remain a basic unit of planning and development at the village level' (*Community Development, Panchayati Raj and Planning* (Jaipur, 1962), p. 73). None of the Third Plan documents went as far as that, but the tendency was unmistakable.

than they had received during the period when the Second Plan was being formulated.

It was also advantageous that consultation of the lower echelons took place at a time when a fair amount of quantitative information had become available. States varied considerably in their timetables, but serious planning from below did not usually begin until the early months of 1960. This was before the publication of the Draft Outline (June 1960) but not before the broad dimensions of the Third Plan were known. At its meeting on 19–20 March 1960, the NDC agreed to a total outlay of Rs11,000 crores, of which the share of all the states was to be Rs3,650 crores. It was not beyond the wit of a state government, which had also been informed about proposed priorities, to decide in general terms what could be done with the resources likely to be placed at its disposal, and to give the necessary guidance to the divisions, districts, blocks, and panchayats.

Further help was given by a Planning Commission letter of 25 June 1960, on the subject of 'Preparation of District and Block Agricultural Plans in the Third Five Year Plan'.[27] This provided quantitative indications of '(*a*) supply of fertilizers during the Third Plan period, (*b*) phasing of irrigation benefits from large and medium projects, (*c*) overall outlay on minor irrigation, and (*d*) overall outlay on soil conservation'. On the basis of these estimates, it requested the state governments to 'issue the necessary instructions to authorities at the district and block levels for preparing area agricultural plans'. These, it recognized, would not be available to the governments in time for incorporation in their Third Plan proposals to the Commission, but it hoped that, before the finalization of state plans by December 1960, each state would be in possession of the targets 'thrown up in different districts by the area agricultural plans, including estimates of the resources needed and proposals for mobilizing local effort'.

Several weeks before the issue of this letter, some of the states, with the help of material prepared by their working groups, had already attempted to tell the districts what would be expected of them. Uttar Pradesh, for instance, sent out in April tables showing (*a*) the district-wise break-up of irrigation potential created during the First Plan, expected to be created during the Second Plan, and proposed for the Third Plan; (*b*) the district-wise break-up of tubewells proposed for the Third Plan; (*c*) the district-wise distribution of tentative targets for additional food production; and (*d*) the region-wise distribution of requirements for nitrogenous and phosphatic fertilizers.[28] Thus, simultaneously, the necessary emphasis

[27] No. 13/11/60-CD.

[28] No. 2175/XXXV-B. From Shri Satish Chandra, Sec. to Govt & Development Commission to All Dist. Magistrates. Subject: Third Five Year Plan—Preparation of Gaon Sabha, Block & Dist. Plans, App. I-IV.

was placed on food production and the information-hungry districts were given some figures to work with.

To balance the advantage of comparatively abundant information there was the disadvantage of shortness of time. The longer the process of grass-roots consultation was delayed, the more hurried it was bound to be. How tight the programme had become is illustrated by the following time schedule from Uttar Pradesh:[29]

(i)	Issue of instructions to blocks	April 15
(ii)	Preparation of Village Plans	June 15
(iii)	Preparation of Block Plans	July 15
(iv)	Preparation of District Plan	August 15
(v)	Further discussion at the Divisional level and forwarding of recommendations to state government	August 31

In a state of some 70,000 villages, such a schedule rather obviously invited the bureaucracy to prepare 'paper' plans.

Moreover even the comparatively abundant information then available proved to be insufficient. At a review, in September 1960, of the action taken by the states, 'it was ascertained that while preliminary steps had been initiated, . . . local agricultural programmes could not be formulated clearly until the main dimensions of the State plan as a whole had been settled'. It was therefore decided that agricultural production targets should be re-examined *after* the draft plans of the states had been vetted by the Planning Commission.[30] The old chicken-and-egg problem had by no means been eliminated. In fact, the same difficulties were being experienced at the grass roots as during the previous plan-formulation exercise.

(vi)

How seriously the states themselves took their responsibilities for 'planning from below' is not easy to say. That they all paid lip-service to the principle meant nothing; nor did the production of a vast quantity of directions and instructions. Some of the paper that was issued, however, does provide evidence of serious thought as well as of good intentions. Uttar Pradesh, for instance, after classifying the various state programmes according to levels of operational responsibility and sources of finance, attempted to specify in some detail the planning duties of officials, from the District Officer to the Village Level Worker, and of representative bodies, from the *zila parishad* to the panchayat.[31]

Following the suggestions issued by the Planning Commission and the agreements reached at the Development Commissioners' Conference at

[29] Ibid. p. 3.

[30] Plan. Com., 'Agricultural Production in the Third Five Year Plan': paper presented to the NDC, 13–14 Jan. 1961.

[31] Uttar Pradesh, *FYP(3)*, i: *Rep.*, pp. 2–3. The *zila parishad* is the district-level body in the *panchayati raj* set-up. See below, p. 431.

Srinagar, most states—or at least most of those that had already adopted 'democratic decentralization'—treated the *panchayat samiti* (which normally coincided with the Community Development block) as the basic representative organ for planning in the rural areas. But it was expected that 'grass-roots' material for the block plan should be provided by programmes drawn up by the panchayats. As we have noted in the Uttar Pradesh timetable, the issue of instructions to blocks was to be followed by the preparation of panchayat plans. These, a month later, were to become the 'basis' of the block plans 'with such additions and dovetailing as may be found necessary'. How much substance there was in the panchayat plans is very doubtful, and how much genuine democratic initiative went into their making even more so. In one very advanced block in Maharashtra, the author was shown a series of village plans that had obviously been drawn up with great care, and he found that not only the members of the *panchayat samiti* but many of the ordinary villagers knew of their existence and could even explain some of their objectives. This, however, was displayed to him with all the pride that is reserved for the exceptional. In Uttar Pradesh, although he was assured by the Development Commissioner that every village had its democratically formulated plan, he found—not unexpectedly—that even in allegedly 'advanced' villages, no more than a few miles distant from the state capital, the headmen themselves could say nothing intelligible about the planning process. It was, indeed, all too clear that the 'plans' of these villages consisted of figures entered on forms by the Village Level Workers or BDOs. One may surmise, in the light of remarks made by the *Mid-Term Appraisal*[32] on the subject of planning from below, that this Uttar Pradesh situation was far more typical of the greater part of rural India than the situation observed in Maharashtra's 'star' block.

The extent to which the states, in issuing instructions about the drawing up of village plans, recognized the nature of the rural realities with which they were dealing seems to have varied very widely indeed. Punjab, in its document entitled 'The Village Development Plan; its Preparation and Execution', provides an example of utopianism at its most utopian.[33] Each village is asked to pay attention to six aspects of development, viz. agricultural production, village industries, health and sanitation, education, social welfare, and communications, of which the first two are to be given priority. For this purpose the Gram Panchayat is to set up Committees for Agricultural Production, for Village Industries and Communications, for Education, Health, and Sanitation, and for Social Welfare. These are to be constituted with great care, and are to include

[32] See below, p. 419. On the constitution and functions of the *panchayat samiti* see below, pp. 429–30.

[33] Issued on 3 July 1961. In criticizing this document, however, one must remember that it followed very closely the suggestions made by the central govt.

'as many educated and progressive-minded residents' as may be available. Their first duty is to collect 'basic data' on the forms provided. These forms, says the document optimistically, 'may seem tedious, but in fact the information can be quickly collected by a few enthusiastic educated persons'. The Committees, in consultation with the Block Extension Officers (who are assumed to be available at the relevant times), are then to prepare draft plans and submit them to the general meeting of the village for 'discussion and finalisation'. At this meeting 'all reasonable suggestions for amendment of the plans should be incorporated and every effort should be made by the chairmen of the Committees to secure the approval of the majority of persons present to the plans prepared by their respective Committees'. This done, the village assembly proceeds to break up the total programme into the following categories: (*a*) Community Works; (*b*) Group Works; and (*c*) Individual Works. It then assigns responsibilities for implementation to individuals and groups who 'will ensure implementation according to the time schedule laid down in the plan'. Defaulters will be brought to the notice of the assembly, with the concurrence of the panchayat, so that 'popular pressure' may be brought to bear on them. To make doubly sure that everyone is in the picture, each head of family in the village is to fill in 'Pro-Forma IX—Family Survey', in which he gives the following information:

1. Name of Head of the Family
2. Area of land, if any, owned (acres)
3. Area of land under cultivation (acres)
4. Area under the following crops (acres):
   (i) *Kharif*—rice, maize, bajra, pulses, cotton, sugarcane, groundnut, other oilseeds, vegetables.
   (ii) *Rabi*—wheat, gram, barley, pulses other than gram, oilseeds, vegetables.
5. Details of poultry kept; (*a*) number of fowls (i) desai (ii) improved; (*b*) number of ducks; (*c*) number of guinea fowls; (*d*) number of geese.
6. Area under fruit plants, viz. citrus, mangoes, others (plants bearing fruits and young plants separately)
7. Extent of use of improved implements; (1) total number of ploughs—(*a*) furrow-turning ploughs (*b*) soil-stirring ploughs (*c*) wooden ploughs; (2) number of triphalis; (3) number of drills: (*a*) rabi seed drills (*b*) single row cotton drills (*c*) harrows (*d*) threshers.

The futility of issuing instructions of this kind to predominantly illiterate, caste-divided, and faction-ridden villagers, assisted by thinly-spread and overworked Village Level Workers and Extension Officers, needs no emphasis. This was informally admitted, and some states allowed realism to creep into the instructions themselves. Bihar,[34] for instance, emphasized (*a*) that village plans should include only such items on the issued forms as

[34] Bihar, Dept of CD, No. CD.I. A.H.O. 76/61, 6595/CD, Patna, 1 Sept. 1961. From Shri T. P. Singh, Dev. Commissioner, to all Commissioners of Divisions; Subject: Village Plan.

could be 'effectively implemented in the area'; (*b*) that the maintenance of existing assets should have priority over the development of new ones; and (*c*) that village plans should 'as far as possible reflect the total effort to be made by individual cultivators who came forward to improve their production'. Madras, as usual, was 'down to earth' in the most literal sense. The government admitted that hitherto 'planning from below' had been an almost complete failure, both at the block level and the village level, partly for want of a 'durable organization representative of the village people to which responsibility for executing the plans could have been entrusted'. Under the Madras Panchayats Act of 1958, which represented the state's response to the national policy of democratic decentralization, this was being rectified. For each of the 374 development blocks, there was to be a Panchayat Union, performing functions analogous to those performed by the *panchayat samiti* elsewhere. The new system was to be introduced by stages, of which the last was to be completed by October 1961. Thus, said the government,

> conditions are being created whereby Block-level planning can be undertaken for the Third Plan period, by the governing bodies of the Panchayat Unions, as representatives of the village people charged with responsibility not only for the formulation of a Five Year Budget with planned development programmes but also the administration of the Budget and day-to-day implementation of the programmes throughout the Five-Year Period.

As for the panchayats themselves, it was recognized that their specific planning assignments would have to be limited to the all-important subject of agricultural production, and that their planning efforts would need to be phased so that the first village plans could be drawn up with adequate expert assistance and then used as models for the later ones. Thus on 16 November 1960 the following order went out:

> Each District Agricultural Officer will immediately select one Panchayat village in each of the first batch of 75 Panchayat Unions for the preparation of Agricultural Development Plans on the lines set out in the Memorandum of Instructions. The Agricultural Extension Officer of the Block and the Gramsevaks should also actively participate in the preparation of this plan. Based on the model plan prepared by the District Agricultural Officer for one Panchayat village in the Block, the Agricultural Extension Officer and the concerned Gramsevaks should assist the other Panchayats to prepare similar Agricultural Production Plans for all villages in the first batch of 75 Panchayat Unions. The Government direct that the preparation of Village Agricultural Production Plans for every Panchayat in the first batch of 75 Panchayat Unions be completed not later than 31st December 1960.[35]

This procedure might be criticized as savouring more of bureaucratic than of democratic planning, and the time schedule was so tight that

[35] Madras, Food & Agric. Dept, G. O. No. 3792, 16 Nov. 1960.

genuine grass-roots participation must have been difficult if not impossible to achieve. But the principles of limited assignments and phased coverage were sound. They showed that Madras had learnt a lesson which experience was gradually teaching the rest of India—that it was better to arrange for the formulation of a few well-considered and soundly-based local plans, properly related to the villagers' real needs and capacities, than to attempt to ensure that 'every village had its plan' by a certain date, at the cost of giving the representative bodies assignments far beyond their known capacities and reducing the experts and administrators charged with 'producing the figures' to a condition of cynical despair. It is also noteworthy that Madras, in contrast with many other states, went to considerable trouble to explain how the local and area plans were to be meshed with the plans for which the higher state authorities were responsible and to specify as precisely as possible what assistance, material and financial, the organs of democratic decentralization might expect to receive from above. It is not suggested that Madras had found the ideal solution to this latter problem, which causes difficulty all over India, but one may see what progress it had made by comparing its highly detailed specifications with the vague 'indications of availabilities and assistance' included in the previously-quoted document from the Punjab.

(vii)

Whatever specific approaches were adopted by the various states, the major concentration from 1960 onwards was on village *production* plans, with which the concept of 'village planning' was now almost completely identified. Generally, the village was required to give a broad indication of its quinquennial targets[36] and a more specific indication of its targets for each year. In practice, the quinquennial targets were decided for rather than by the villagers, who found sufficient difficulty in thinking in terms of annual periods and were quite incapable of envisaging a situation five years ahead. This meant that the panchayat, with such expert assistance from Village Level Worker upwards as happened to be available, had to organize itself each year for the formulation of the economic objectives which it hoped to achieve within the next twelve months. To enable it to do this, the state governments produced 'Guides'[37] of varying degrees of realism and specificity. The document that contained the Madras Guide (or 'Model' as it was called) has already been mentioned, but as the relevant section is in Tamil—a language which the author does not read—it cannot be used as an example. We will therefore take the

[36] That is, in the *first* annual production plan of the quinquennial cycle.
[37] They were assisted to do this by suggestions produced by the Plan. Com. (see *FYP(3)*, pp. 336–7), by the Ann. Conf. on CD at Srinagar (see *Main Recommendations & Conclusions*), and by a circular dated 23 June 1960, from the Min. of CD & Co-operation (No. 1(77)/59-Agr).

Guide[38] issued by Rajasthan, a state which, although one of the more backward, was the first to adopt *panchayati raj*.

This begins by specifying the planning stages, which are similar to those already quoted from the 'Village Development Plan' document from Punjab, viz. (1) formation of an Agricultural Production Committee in each village; (2) collection of basic data; (3) indication of funds likely to be made available annually to the villages by the relevant *panchayat samitis*; (4) drawing up of a draft village plan; (5) finalization of the plan by the village assembly; and (6) implementation of the plan.

The following members are suggested for the Production Committee: the *sarpanch* (chairman) of the panchayat; the chairman of the co-operative society; one or two progressive farmers; one representative of the local Navak Mandal;[39] the *patwari*;[40] the secretary of the panchayat; and the Village Level Worker. The *sarpanch*[41] is to be chairman, with responsibility for drawing up the programmes of work. The progressive farmers 'should as far as possible represent different land-tenure interests'.

The first step in plan formulation, the collection of basic agricultural data, is to be undertaken, if possible in consultation with the *patwari* and the progressive farmers, by the Village Level Worker (Gram Sevak), who for this purpose has been provided with a lengthy form, containing blank spaces on which 'Existing position in 1960–61' and 'Position expected in 1965–66' are to be entered for each item. The Gram Sevak is also responsible for collecting from the *panchayat samiti* the 'panchayat-wise allocation of funds and supplies (seeds, fertilizers, implements etc.)' and transmitting this to the Village Production Committee. Estimates of funds likely to be available from the co-operatives and from the villagers are to be made by the Committee itself.

Thus informed, the Committee 'will work out a draft village production plan for one year . . . in consultation with the Block Extension Officers of Agriculture, Animal Husbandry and Cooperation'. For this purpose, a form with a long list of items is provided. In using it, the Committee is enjoined to 'select such of the items as are considered useful . . . for increasing agricultural production in the village, giving preference to items based on self help and village community efforts'.[42]

Presumably the Committee transmits the completed draft plan to the panchayat; for the latter body is now required to call 'a general meeting

[38] Rajasthan, Directorate of Agric., Standing Circular No. 6: *A Guide for Preparation of Village Agricultural Production Plan.*

[39] The 'new assembly'. [40] Village revenue official. [41] The chairman of the panchayat.

[42] The emphasis on self-help is very apposite in view of the well-known tendency of villagers to wait for action by the govt authorities. A circular issued on 27 July 1962 (Rajasthan, Panchayat & Dev. Dept. No. F. 149(36) Cont/Coord/DD 62), after drawing attention to the existence of three kinds of resources, viz. (1) those made available by the villages themselves, (2) those obtainable by the village co-operative society, and (3) those received from outside, through the *panchayat samitis,* said that 'greater emphasis' had to be laid on the first two.

of the Gaon Sabha (village assembly), to which all the heads of the families, particularly the cultivators, should be invited'. This assembly, graced by the presence of the Vikas Adhikari (BDO) or his Agricultural Extension Officer, is to 'discuss the data and the draft plan in detail and suggest such changes as they may deem necessary in view of the village conditions'. When agreement has been reached, the Gaon Sabha divides the programme into the three categories of community works, group works, and individual works, and assigns responsibilities accordingly.

In a third form, 'one or two pages' are to be assigned to each item of work and the names of the responsible cultivators entered 'along with the financial assistance or supplies required by them'.

The normal time schedule for this planning process is to be as follows:

1. Collection of basic data	15 March–14 April
2. Preparation of Draft Plan	15–30 April
3. Publication of Draft Plan	30 April–15 May
4. Discussion and finalization of draft plan in the village assembly	16–21 May

Formulation arrangements for the annual production plan are therefore very similar to those widely adopted, on the recommendation of the central government authorities, for a village five-year plan. The narrower terms of reference and the shorter planning period, of course, make the task more manageable; but the problems remain essentially the same. A major presupposition is that the villagers—or at least a few of them—are interested in planning, prepared to do some hard thinking and to keep to a time schedule, capable of mastering the techniques of committee work, and sufficiently united to be able to reach meaningful agreements. There are few Indian villages where these conditions prevail. Consequently, even when technical assistance is concentrated by selecting only a fraction of the total number of villages in the state for the 'production planning' exercise—Rajasthan selected one-fifth for the year 1962–3, while boldly proclaiming that *all* would be covered during the following year—the tendency is for the plan to be drawn up by the block officials, in consultation with a few local notables, to be given purely formal approval by the village assembly, and to remain completely unknown to the majority of the cultivators.

One may admit that adequate generalization on village planning is extremely difficult—indeed the data for it does not yet exist. One may also concede that the 'Model Panchayat' study by the PEO shows that there are some panchayats capable of effective action. But there is now a massive amount of miscellaneous evidence to suggest that the way most of them go about their business is accurately reflected in the following report from Rajasthan:

The meetings of the Village Panchayats have often not been held in a systematic manner. A number of cases have come to notice in which the agenda for the meetings was not issued. At times meetings were held without a proper quorum, and sometimes with considerable delay. From an observation of the meetings of selected Panchayats, it appears that the deliberations of this body are not conducted with sufficient zeal and purposefulness. Usually, most of the time is spent in deciding cases of an administrative nature and very little thought is given to the implementation of the development programmes or the improvement of the socio-economic conditions of the villages. The participation of the Panchas was found to be generally routine in nature. With the constitution of Nyaya Panchayats and the transfer of judicial work to them, the interest of the members in the Village Panchayats has flagged considerably.[43]

What applies to the panchayats must also apply to the panchayat 'Agricultural Production' Committees, except in those cases where a few 'progressive farmers' see in the planning process an opportunity for self-advancement by attracting towards themselves the various financial and technical services which the higher authorities are offering. As for the Gaon (or Gram) Sabhas, these appear to be called together rather irregularly,[44] and even when they are not a prey to faction fail to function as consultative or supervisory bodies. The author well remembers, at such a Sabha meeting he attended in Uttar Pradesh, the blank incomprehension on the faces of the assembled cultivators when the Village Level Worker read out, briefly and rapidly, the annual plan figures for which their approval was required.

Even where enthusiasm can be aroused, and where adequate technical assistance is available, however, the planning process tends to be crippled by the sheer absence of information. As a result, the figures which appear on the numerous forms (and which are transmitted upwards to provide planning 'information' to the higher administrative levels) are frequently the product of sheer invention. The effect of this lack of data is well brought out by an unusually frank and circumstantial report, from

[43] Rajasthan, Evaluation Org., *The Working of Panchayati Raj in Rajasthan* (*Apr. 1961 to Mar. 1962*); *a Rep.* (June 1962), p. 72.

[44] 'The Gram Sabha, which constitutes the base of the Panchayat Raj system, should function as a vital institution and should be able to exert its influence on the Gram Panchayat, if the latter is to function institutionally and in a democratic manner. However, in practice it has been found that the Gram Sabha has not been functioning as an effective institution and that its meetings are not held regularly' (C. Srinavasa Sastry, 'Structure and Pattern of Panchayati Raj'. *IJPA*, Oct.-Dec. 1962, p. 462). M. P. K. Chaudhuri alleges that, during the first year of *panchayati raj* in Rajasthan, not a single meeting of the adult residents was convened, 'by any one of the 7,000 odd panchayats in the State' ('A Year of Panchayati Raj', *EW*, Ann. No., 4 Feb. 1961). This would appear to have been later corrected, according to information provided by *The Working of Panchayati Raj* (see above, n. 43), pp. 72–77. Nevertheless, this document admits that, as an institution, the Gram Sabha is only 'slowly emerging' and has yet to find its plan 'in the fabric of Panchayati Raj' and to function as 'a determining factor in planning and development at the village level' (p. 89).

Madras, of the initial stages of drawing up an agricultural production plan for the Kalyanakkuppam Village Panchayat.[45]

This panchayat, consisting of 220 families, had been selected as one of the 'models'. A well-publicized panchayat meeting was called in the school premises on 19 August 1960, and some 100 people from the village and near-by villages came to observe the proceedings. 'The occasion presented a festive appearance. The farmers of this village were very enthusiastic and evinced keen interest in drawing up production plans.' Exceptional status was given to the occasion by the presence of a positive constellation of officials, including the Development Commissioner, District Collector, Deputy Secretaries to Government for Rural Development and Local Administration, District Agricultural Officer, BDO, Extension Officers, and Gram Sevaks. The main purpose was to secure an increase in the production of rice per acre. To consider ways and means a sub-committee consisting of six of the seven panchayat members was constituted. As, however, no statistics existed of actual rice production or of the inputs required for a given amount per acre, the unfortunate sub-committee found itself floundering in the dark.

> A discussion took place with regard to the production of rice during the previous year and the quantity of rice to be produced during the Plan period. Apart from the particulars available in the karnam's book [i.e., accounting information] . . . no other statistics were available. A panchayat member voiced the view that 10,000 bags of rice could be produced. Another person asserted that it would be possible to produce only 6,000 bags. After much discussion it was concluded that the estimated production would be fixed at 3,000 bags. When a few farmers were enquired [*sic*] as to how much was produced in each acre, their individual replies . . . ranged between 12 and 8 bags. As correct statistics were not available, it was decided that the minimum production of 8 bags of rice should be increased to 12 bags. In view of this, it was decided to increase the target of 3,000 bags of rice to 4,500 bags of rice.

There was a similar absence of information about the amount of manure produced by the village animals and about the extent of the manurial use of groundnut cakes, said to be 'in vogue' among the villagers: 'It was stated by one member that at the rate of three bags per acre about 1,000 bags were used. Another member interfered [*sic*] and stated that only 600 bags were used. By discussion, this figure was reduced to 200. One member expressed the view that 100 bags of groundnut cake were not available. Further, it costs much.'

One should not, perhaps, place exclusive emphasis on this lack of information. It was something to persuade the members of the panchayat

[45] Rural Dev. & Local Admin. Dept, *Guide Book on Panchayat Development in Madras State* (1961), ii. 455–60.

to think in quantitative terms, however vague, and to discuss targets for the whole village, however tentative. Nevertheless, this report illustrates in a graphic way the difficulties encountered by 'grass-roots' planning, even in the most favourable of circumstances, as well as exposing the shaky foundations upon which Indian agricultural statistics rest.

When to lack of information is added the apathy, ignorance, and factionalism of the average Indian village community, it is not surprising that, except in a very few areas, village production plans have as yet made little impact. Indeed, planning even at the block and district levels, where far more expertise is available, is still embryonic, in spite of the amount of emphasis that has been placed upon it.

In an exceptionally able study of 'block' planning, the first scholarly work on the subject, Dr Alice Ilchman has shown that even when it is taken seriously, it appears to have little or no effect on the level of economic performance. She has also emphasized the difficulties of drawing up realistic block plans, closely related to the specific needs of the area, when so high a proportion of the finances are channelled through an excessively rigid 'schematic budget', devised by the CD experts at New Delhi, and through grants earmarked for particular departmental projects. On the basis of an intensive study of nine blocks in Rajasthan and Uttar Pradesh, she gives the answer 'not much' to the question, 'What is the scope for the lower levels to plan contrary to the wishes of the higher levels?'

> The provision of central schematic budgets and departmental programmes limits flexibility. Only 16 per cent in Stage One (31 per cent in Stage Two in a budget reduced by half) of the schematic budget can be diverted. Departmental programmes usually do not have even this much leeway. In addition, departmental programmes suggest where priority should be placed in view of state and national objectives. Budgeting procedure further restricts autonomy.[46]

These restrictions apply *a fortiori* at the village level. Hence, in addition to the local people's ignorance of the planning process and the difficulties they experience in reaching agreement about objectives, there is a justifiable feeling on their part that whatever planning effort they make will have at best a marginal effect. The rigidity of the system of financial allocations, in fact, reinforces their view that in the last resort it is New Delhi and the state capital that prescribe what shall be done.

In a sense, this is inevitable. The basic policy decisions and the consequential financial allocations *must* be made at the higher levels if planning is to have nation-wide and state-wide coherence. But unless, within the

[46] Alice Crawford Stone Ilchman, *Democratic Decentralisation and Planning in Rural India* (Dec. 1964—unpubl. London Univ, Ph.D. thesis), p. 238; *MTA*, pp. 67, 86. The two 'stages' are those into which the CD projects are now divided, replacing the former three stages (see below, p. 423).

broad framework, greater freedom is granted to the localities to decide where the available funds may be most profitably employed, there is an obvious danger that planning from below, already held back by a formidable variety of social obstacles, may never get off the ground.

This, it would seem, is now being recognized to some degree by the central authorities, who are at least under no illusion about the adequacy of planning achievements at the grass roots. Village plans, says the *Mid-Term Appraisal* (p. 68), 'have not yet succeeded in sufficient degree, although useful experience has been gained'. As for district and block plans, the expectation that these 'might serve as an effective means for stimulating economic and social development . . . has so far been realized only to a small extent'. But to improve matters it is not sufficient to demand that 'during the next two years or so, in every State, district and block plans should be made an effective component of the planning process', and to warn that 'otherwise, even in the Fourth Plan, local plans will not have a significant role, and vast development possibilities will remain untapped'. The whole process of planning from below needs to be looked at afresh.

Aware of this need, the Conference of State Ministers of CD and Panchayati Raj agreed in August 1963 to prepare a new handbook 'on the preparation and implementation of district, block and village plans'.[47] This will clearly help, but unless its preparation is preceded by an examination of the present planning relationships between the higher and lower echelons, it is unlikely to have a sufficiently radical impact on procedures and attitudes.

(viii)

So far we have looked at the 'grass roots' solely from the point of view of plan *formulation*. It has already become clear, however, that the lower one descends down the hierarchy of democratically elected authorities, the less sharp is the distinction between formulation and implementation. In spite of the efforts made to build up plans from below, the districts, blocks, and villages are and will remain essentially instruments for adapting to local needs and adjusting to local public opinion planning decisions taken at higher levels of authority, where the plans that come up from the grass roots are regarded primarily as sources of information. In this sense, 'implementation' can be considered as covering the greater part—if not the whole—of the effective activities of the lower echelons. Hence we can deal with it realistically only by looking, in a broad way, at the evolution of local democratic institutions as development agencies—in fact at the process which began in British times and has culminated in *panchayati raj*.

[47] *Main Recommendations & Conclusions*, p. 68.

The involvement of the rural people in schemes for the development of their resources and the general improvement of their living conditions was—and remains—the essential purpose of the CD and NE movement, inaugurated on Gandhi's birthday in October 1952. The 'philosophy' of community development, both in India and elsewhere, is well-known. The community development man does not approach his constituents, in the manner of a government official, with a series of cut-and-dried schemes. He attempts to discover their 'felt needs', to arouse them from their apathy, to extend their vision, and to prove to them that by self-help and co-operative effort they can raise their standards of living and improve their ways of life in a manner that all of them desire. Community development is both paternal and democratic—paternal in the sense that the initiative in breaking the 'cake of custom' comes from above and that most of the 'know-how' and many of the resources are supplied from outside; democratic in the sense that progress is achieved through the enlistment of the willing consent and active participation of the people themselves. Its ultimate objective is a self-liquidating one, to be achieved when the process of development becomes self-generating and self-sustaining. It can be conducted through voluntary agencies or through government agencies or through a combination of the two. When the government is involved—as inevitably it must when the programme is on a state-wide or country-wide scale—there are vast and widely ramifying economic and administrative implications. Massive resources have to be injected in a co-ordinated yet flexible way; new types of administrators, with a variety of technical qualifications, have to be trained; and a new type of relationship between administrator and administered has to be sought.

India is unique in having attempted this extremely difficult exercise on an unprecedented scale. In ten years the whole of the country has become covered with Community Development blocks. But, although 1952 saw the beginning of the *programme*, the *process* was already familiar by that date. During the period of British rule, several experiments in Community Development had been made, both in the provinces and in the princely states, and in some of them the authorities had been fully involved. Among the more famous were Rabindranath Tagore's and Leonard Elmhirst's Sriniketan Project in Bengal, Spencer Hatch's Martandam Project in Travancore, the 'Firka' Development Scheme in Madras State, the Rural Reconstruction Centres in Baroda, and the famous 'Gurgaon Experiment' organized by that veritable rogue elephant among British District Commissioners, F. L. Brayne.[48] All of these had had lessons to teach, both positive and negative. The major positive lesson was that,

[48] A brief account of these projects is contained in Min. of CD, Panchayati Raj & Co-op., *Evolution of CD Programme in India* (1963), which contains bibliographical references.

given sufficient rural welfare workers with the requisite knowledge and dedication and the right approach to the rural people, results—sometimes extremely spectacular ones—could be obtained. The major negative lesson, which emerged particularly from the 'Gurgaon Experiment', was that autocratic methods, while capable of producing rapid transformations, left no permanent deposit. Brayne himself, the autocrat *par excellence* in his devotion to village welfare, finally realized this and lamented:

> Good work, excellent work is going on all over the Punjab. You can travel all day and find nothing that offends either eye or nose. Village after village and zail after zail have been turned into models of the new life. Marvellous changes have been made and there is a feeling of life and movement in the air. Have we found the incentive then? Will this work last and spread? Alas, no! This work is not being done by villagers determined to live a better life but by villagers determined to please their District Officer. A good enough motive in its way but not the motive we are looking for. There is no permanence about this kind of work. What if the District Officer's attention is diverted elsewhere, or he wants something different done, or in a different series of villages?[49]

A serious effort to find a better *via media* between direction and spontaneity was made by Albert Mayer and his associates in the famous Pilot Development Project at Etawah. This project, which still continues, has become the community development man's *locus classicus*: 'What the Rochdale experiment in England is to the world's cooperative movement, what the Tennessee Valley Authority is to the integrated exploitation of the world's great watersheds, this the Etawah Project has fast become to the movement for revitalising the ways of life of the world's peasantry.'[50] It began, under the aegis of the Uttar Pradesh provincial government, in 1948, as a 64 village unit; it expanded within three years to one of 300 villages; it spawned four similar projects in U.P., and finally became the prototype for the CD and NE Service inaugurated during the course of the First Five-Year Plan. By the early 1950s it was considered to have proved that 'there need be no conflict between the two central aims of rural development', viz. 'a maximizing of material production' and 'an expansion of personal and village-organizational resources'. Experience of Etawah was held to show that 'a combination of material and moral elements soon outstrips any more spectacular hot-housing methods in its material results, while yielding also the persistent advantages of human development'.[51] This is still the basic article of faith of the Community Development movement both in India and throughout the world.

[49] Ibid. pp. 34–35.
[50] See Albert Mayer & Associates, *Pilot Project, India* (Berkeley, Calif., 1958), p. xii.
[51] Ibid. p. 131.

It was also regarded as establishing the need for a simultaneous, co-ordinated approach to all aspects of rural development, including the improvement of techniques in agriculture and animal husbandry, the fostering of co-operatives (particularly for the provision of credit), the promotion of rural industries, the organization of community works (e.g. for house building, road building, school building, drainage and village replanning), and the expansion of social and general education. Such a many-sided programme, however, could be brought into existence only by a process of lateral expansion from a series of points represented by the villager's clearly-expressed 'felt needs'. These were found to be 'generally economic, that is, agricultural'.[52]

Administratively, its focal point was the Village Level Worker—a multi-purpose extension agent, in direct contact with the villagers, to act as their adviser and as the channel through which the services of the various technical departments might be brought to bear, in a co-ordinated manner, upon their problems. A necessary corollary was that the technical workers themselves should shed their departmental exclusiveness and function 'as part of the over-all village team, with a feeling of deep interest and participation, so as to invoke and retain the confidence of the village community'.[53] This could be achieved only by a unified direction of their efforts on the level of the project itself, through appointing an official of the type later to be identified as the BDO.

Most fundamental of all was the emphasis placed on helping people to help themselves, so that progressively the responsibility for running the various schemes might be taken over by the villagers' own organizations. With this object, popular participation had to be enlisted from the very beginning.

> No high-pressure methods should be used . . . Discovery and development of local leadership as well as voluntary participation and decision making by the local people in the choice of the programmes, planning and execution should be the key-notes, persuasion and motivation being the only tools in the hands of the Project workers, who should work, not *for* or *on* the people, but *with* and *through* them. In the long run, Community Development should become a people's programme with Government participation and not *vice versa*.[54]

All the basic features of the subsequent India-wide collection of community projects were to be found at Etawah; and it was Etawah's measure of success—which, although by no means complete, was high enough to convince the authorities that they had found the right approach—that opened up the prospect of transforming the whole of India's rural life through this particular type of community development.

[52] Ibid. p. 131–8. [53] Ibid. p. viii.

[54] D. P. Singh, 'The Pilot Development Project, Etawah', in *Evolution of CD Programme*, pp. 55–56.

To do this, a massive training programe for community workers was needed. What was not sufficiently realized, in the atmosphere of euphoria which Etawah had generated, was the degree to which that success was the result of concentrating a number of very intelligent and highly dedicated community workers in a comparatively small area. That Etawah could be indefinitely reproduced was, in fact, too readily assumed.

(ix)

From 1951 onwards the 'generalization' of community development took place with what is now generally considered, with the wisdom of hindsight, to be rash rapidity. First, out of discussions between the Ford Foundation and the Planning Commission, there emerged the proposal to set up 15 further projects of 100 villages each in 15 states, together with 5 training centres for village extension workers. These had hardly been started when, in April 1952, the Commission recommended the establishment of a Community Projects Administration with the initial task of organizing 55 projects of 300 villages each. This recommendation was incorporated in the First Five-Year Plan,[55] which appropriated the sum of Rs90 crores for the purpose. In addition to the organization at the centre, there was to be a Development Committee and Commissioner in each state, a Development Committee and Officer in each district, and a Project Executive Officer in charge of each project, with a staff of approximately 125 supervisors and Village Level Workers. Less than a year later it was decided to inaugurate a permanent National Extension Service for the whole country. For the combined CD-NES programme the unit of operation was to be the 'development block', consisting, on the average, of 100 villages with a population of 60,000–70,000 persons, spread over an area of between 150 and 170 square miles. Each block was to be equipped with a 'schematic budget' and the development programme spread over three stages. The first was called the pre-intensive or NES stage; the second, the intensive or CD Programme stage; the third, during which the people themselves were expected to assume a progressively greater share of responsibility, the post-intensive stage. During the course of the First Plan a total of 1,200 development blocks were inaugurated, covering 122,957 villages with a population of nearly 80 million. By the end of the plan, 900 of these were in the NES stage and 300 in the CD stage. Even in villages which had not yet been brought within the scope of the programme, 'local development works as well as various agricultural programmes' had been carried out, according to the Second Five-Year Plan report (pp. 237–8). In September 1955 the NDC decided that during the Second Plan the whole country should be covered with NES Blocks and that at least 40 per cent of these should be converted

[55] *FYP(1)*, ch. 15.

into CD Programme Blocks. The Second Plan provided Rs200 crores for this purpose, making the money go round by reducing estimated expenditure for a NES Block from Rs4½ to Rs4 lakhs and that for a CD Block from Rs15 to Rs12 lakhs.[56] Subsequently, as we have seen,[57] the dead-line for complete coverage was extended from October 1960 to October 1963. By the end of the Second Plan there were 31,100 blocks serving about 370,000 villages, with a population of over 200 million.[58]

Inevitably, so rapid an expansion involved considerable dilution and distortion of the original conception. The average quality of administrative and technical personnel was necessarily much inferior to that of the handful of dedicated 'servants of the people' gathered together at Etawah.[59] The erection of an elaborate administration meant that Community Development, which was originally intended to transform established administrative procedures, tended more and more to adapt itself to them. Problems of co-ordination proved immensely difficult. While it had been easy in a pilot project to ensure that credit was available for the purchase of seeds and fertilizers or that supplies of these commodities were available to the possessors of credit, such co-ordinative operations were often beyond the capacity of a departmentalized and routine-bound administration charged with looking after the needs of 70 million people. Most serious of all—and indeed most relevant to our present discussion—the programme failed to acquire more than a simulacrum of that popular support and participation upon which it was supposed to be based. Over the greater part of India, the peasants looked upon it as essentially a *government* programme, brought to them by the administration, and not as their programme, in which the administration was assisting and collaborating.

At first, these defects and distortions were largely concealed by superficial 'successes' of the kind that not even a rather incompetent administration, if endowed with sufficient funds, could fail to achieve. Schools and community centres were built, roads constructed, villages cleaned up and wells sunk. The people, said the Planning Commission optimistically,

have participated in a large number of activities, and this has given them a feeling of greater confidence in their ability, with some measure of assistance, to find solutions to local problems. Thus, the construction in project areas of

[56] *FYP(2)*, pp. 241–2. [57] See above, p. 156. [58] *FYP(3)*, pp. 78, 332.

[59] This applies particularly to the Village Level Worker, on whose efficiency and dedication everything, in the last resort, depended. Most Village Level Workers appear to have degenerated into underpaid, under-educated, and under-trained minor officials. The team from the University of Poona which investigated the administration of CD in one of the local blocks reported: 'With a few exceptions, the performances of the gramsevaks failed to impress us. They were the weakest link in the chain of Community Development Administration. Their awareness, consciousness, understanding and zeal for the tasks they confronted did not come up to the expected level' (N. R. Inamdar, *Rep. of Survey of the Admin. of the CD Block Haveli* (Univ. of Poona, 1962), p. 109). Other reports suggest that this situation is general.

14,000 new schools, conversion of 5,154 primary schools into basic schools, opening of 35,000 adult education centres which have imparted literacy to 773,000 adults, the construction of 4,069 miles of metalled and of 28,000 miles of unmetalled roads and the building of 80,000 village latrines are illustrations of local development which have far-reaching social implications. In all these the greater part of the effort has come from the people, and government agencies, notably extension workers, have served as guides.[60]

At a more fundamental level, however, the projects were developing certain alarming characteristics, first pinpointed by the *Third Evaluation Report* of the PEO. Some of the administrative difficulties, such as the inadequate quality of personnel and the muddles created at the block level by 'the dual control of specialists concerned with different subjects . . . by the Block Development Officer and by technical officers at the district', have already been mentioned. More serious, from the standpoint of developing popular initiative, were the virtual monopolization of the Village Level Worker's time by 'constructional' activities, the feebleness or factionalism displayed by most of the panchayats, and the 'excessive emphasis' placed on 'physical and financial accomplishments' at the expense of 'educating the people into new ways of doing things'.[61]

These defects might have been no more than growing pains but subsequent PEO reports revealed that they were getting worse rather than better.[62] The fourth report found that while 'items involving physical change, especially constructional and irrigational activity' had 'contributed in some measure to the production potential and the social overheads of the block areas', those 'involving change in organizational attitudes in the economic field, such as better understanding of the objectives and obligations of cooperation and readiness to make use of cooperative societies for purposes other than credit such as production and marketing', were 'comparatively unsuccessful'. Equally lacking was any understanding of 'the objectives and responsibilities of *panchayat* membership and readiness to use *panchayats* for planning and executing village development programmes'. The vast majority of the rural population still depended far too much on 'Government initiative and assistance' and had not as yet developed a 'strong sentiment of self-reliance and initiative, whether individual or cooperative'. Even at the levels of the block and district, non-official members of the advisory committees had 'still to play the role that was expected of them in the development programme'.[63]

These criticisms simply underlined those already made in the third report; but there were also several new criticisms which seemed even

[60] *FYP(2)*, p. 238.
[61] Ibid. p. 238–9; PEO, *Eval. Rep. on Working of Community Projects & NES Blocks*, Apr. 1956.
[62] See 4th, 5th, & 6th Eval. Reps (PEO Publications Nos 19, 20, 26, 31).
[63] *Eval. Rep. on Working of CP & NES Blocks*, Apr. 1957, i. 19–20. See also Inandar, *Survey of Admin. of CD Block Haveli*, pp. 20, 28–29, 109, 111–12.

more ominous in their implications. The first was the revelation that Community Development was developing in the direction of a class- or caste-oriented programme rather than in that of a people's programme. The relevant paragraph is so important that it deserves quotation in full:

> As regards the benefits of the programme for the economically handicapped classes and the extent of the bridging of the distance between the better off and worse off sections, PEO's reports do not give room for optimism. It is true that some direct benefit has accrued to the handicapped classes by way of employment, drinking water wells, primary education, and rural housing. But these are not, with the exception of the last item and that too only in some areas, peculiar to the handicapped classes. Benefits of these programmes accrue also to the other classes in the villages. In addition, the better off classes get loans, are more easily able to adopt improved practices, and otherwise derive larger benefit from the development programmes. The non-owner classes have not got the status that possession of land alone can give them. Land redistribution still remains in the realm of thought and discussion. Land reforms in the direction of ceiling on holdings, consolidation of holdings, giving of land to the landless labourers, and cooperative farming are still all to be achieved in most of the evaluation block areas. Persons who can use credit productively but do not have the assets that can make credit available are, generally speaking, handicapped by the absence of cooperative institutions lending supplies in kind and arranging for sales and recovery from sale proceeds. This system of what is called 'integrated finances' has been reported from one or two block areas, but is still in an incipient stage . . . . The result of all this is that while some people are undoubtedly benefiting from the development programme and improving their economic and social conditions, these usually belong to those sections in the village who were already somewhat better off than their fellow villagers. This is a matter of concern for the future of the community development programme.

Secondly, where blocks were passing from the 'intensive' to the 'post-intensive' phases, the evidence of a general running down of activities was unmistakable. Panchayats, not having been consulted about works designed for the general benefit and now *in situ*, were refusing to maintain them. Village Level Workers were developing a 'sense of frustration', not knowing what to do with their time now that there was little construction work to occupy it, feeling 'ineffective' because the quantity of funds available for them to distribute to the villages was sharply reduced, spending 'a considerable proportion of their time at block headquarters', and confining 'their contacts to a few people whom they know well'.[64] Their frustration, no doubt, was intensified by the fact that the basic administrative problem of co-ordination—'of combining the horizontal responsibilities of the area specialist with the vertical responsibilities of the subject-matter specialist'—continued to 'defy solution', and by the

[64] Ibid. pp. 18, 22, 26–27.

baffling delays which were the product of 'administrative complexities and over-centralization of financial sanctions'.[65]

Well might the impatient A. D. Gorwala come to the conclusion that the whole CD Programme was based on a 'wrong premise'. The missionary spirit which it was intended to call forth was not, he wrote,

a thing that can be taught. To expect it to operate on a country-wide scale for long dreary years is in any case futile. When it is realised that almost all those engaged for the work are men and women as good or as bad as any others and that if it enabled them to earn a livelihood they would willingly have gone into any other government department they could get into, the folly of regarding them as starry-eyed adventurers on a high mission, and of expecting from them the behaviour of the kind that would be appropriate in such rare individuals becomes obvious.

The whole thing had become 'one of the most wasteful forms of expenditure in the country', of which the most productive side was the 'paper side'. What was needed in the rural areas was not 'community development' but the direct allotment and supervised utilization of funds for specific purposes, such as pure water-supplies, primary education, improvements in agricultural methods and in sanitation and health, &c.[66]

Yet, although subsequent PEO reports—greatly to the scandal of those dedicated but unrealistic souls who equated criticizing Community Development with polluting the Holy Grail—revealed no improvement in the situation, the conclusions officially drawn from this depressing experience were quite the reverse of Gorwala's. His solution to the problem was to go back to the more normal methods of district administration, in conformity with the paternalistic traditions characteristic of the great service to which he had formerly belonged; the official solution, suggested by the Planning Commission, supported by the PEO, developed into a doctrine by the Balvantray Mehta Committee, and eventually accepted by the central government and by all of the states, was to give the people more and not less responsibility. It was out of the stagnation of the Community Projects, in fact, that there emerged the grand panacea of *panchayati raj*.

(x)

The lead was given by the Commission in the Second Five-Year Plan report, where it considered and found wanting the performance of the various advisory bodies, at district and block level, through which the administration was attempting to enlist popular participation in the development process. The whole subject, it considered, should be submitted to a 'special investigation under the auspices of the National

[65] Resolutions of State Agric. Ministers' Conf., Srinagar, 13 Oct. 1957, as reported in *AR*, 1957, p. 1957.

[66] *Mysore Administration*, pp. 72–74.

Development Council'. In the meantime, as a matter of urgency, the state governments should set up district councils and development committees, more broadly representative in composition than the existing bodies but still primarily advisory and supervisory rather than policy-making in function.[67]

Accepting the first of these recommendations, the NDC decided to constitute, under the COPP, a 'Team for the Study of Community Projects and National Extension Service' under the chairmanship of Balvantray Mehta. Promptly formed, this team worked swiftly to produce its three-volume report in November–December 1957.[68]

After accepting the basic 'philosophy' of Community Development, as expressed by various official spokesmen, the report states that the essential requirement of evoking popular initiative has not been met.

> We have found that few of the local bodies at a higher level than the village panchayat have shown any enthusiasm or interest in this work; and even the panchayats have not come into the field to any appreciable extent. An attempt has been made to harness local initiative through the formation of *ad hoc* bodies mostly with nominated personnel and invariably advisory in character. These bodies have so far given no indication of durable strength nor the leadership necessary to provide the motive force for continuing the improvement of economic and social conditions in rural areas.

Immediately it jumps to the conclusion, which represents the foundation of all its subsequent recommendations, that

> so long as we do not discover or create a representative and democratic institution which will supply the 'local interest, supervision and care necessary to ensure that expenditure of money upon local projects conforms with the needs and wishes of the locality', invest it with adequate power and assign to it appropriate finances, we will never be able to evoke local interest and excite local initiative in the field of development.

To the fears, expressed to the Committee by 'many persons', both official and non-official, that democratic decentralization on such a scale would produce inefficiency and corruption rather than development, the report makes brief reply. It recognizes that there may be a fall in efficiency, but considers that this will be no more than temporary, and says that although 'centralization and even autocracy often appear more efficient than decentralization and democracy, . . . in the long run . . . democracy and decentralization assert themselves and succeed better especially in the field of local development and local welfare'. As for the more 'complex' problem of corruption, this can be solved 'only by constant and intelligent vigilance on the part of the citizens', an exercise which is 'possible only

[67] *FYP(2)*, pp. 160–3.

[68] Team for the Study of Community Projects & NES, *Rep.* (New Delhi, COPP, Nov.–Dec. 1957).

if the electorate knows at least by name the persons in whose hands they have placed power'.

There follows a short discussion about the optimum area for the proposed 'representative and democratic institution'. The block, already the basic unit for planning and development, equipped with its own administrative and technical personnel, is the obvious choice, as offering 'an area large enough for functions which the village panchayat cannot perform and yet small enough to attract the interest and service of the residents'. The new representative organ at the block level, christened the *panchayat samiti*, is to be linked with the village panchayat ('whose growth and efficiency it will be one of the functions of this higher body to safeguard') by a system of indirect elections; but while a majority of the *samiti* is to be elected by the *panches* of the village panchayats, there will also be a minority of co-opted members to provide representation for the various disadvantaged sections of the population, such as women, scheduled castes, and scheduled tribes. Special provisions are also suggested for securing representation on the *samiti* of the smaller municipalities 'which lie as enclaves within the jurisdiction of a block' and of the local co-operative organizations.

The functions of the *samiti* should, at least initially, be concentrated 'in the field of development', and should cover

> the development of agriculture in all its aspects, including the selection of the seed, its procurement and distribution, the improvement of agricultural practices, provision of local agricultural finance with the assistance of the Government and of the cooperative banks, minor irrigation works, the improvement of cattle, sheep, goats, and poultry, the promotion of local industries, the supply of drinking water, public health and sanitation, medical relief, relief of distress caused by floods, earthquakes, scarcity etc., arrangements in connection with local pilgrimages and festivals, construction and repair of roads which are of local importance (other than village panchayat roads), management and administrative control of primary schools, the fixation of wages under the Minimum Wages Acts for non-industrial labour, the welfare of backward classes and the maintenance of statistics.

To finance these activities, the Committee recommends that it should be endowed with thirteen sources of income, of which the most important are a statutorily-prescribed percentage of the land revenue, certain 'cesses' on land revenue, a tax on professions, trades, callings, and employment, and grants made by the government. With regard to the last—which experience suggested was likely to be the most important—it is recommended that 'all Central and State funds spent in the block area should invariably be assigned to the panchayat samiti to be spent by it directly or indirectly, except to an institution assistance to which is either beyond the panchayat samiti's functions or its financial resources'.

The officers of the *samiti* will include a chief officer 'and various technical officers in charge of agriculture, roads and buildings, irrigation, public health, vetinerary, cooperation, social education, primary education etc'. These, although responsible to the *samiti*, will not be appointed by it but 'lent' to it by the state government, which will remain responsible for their salaries and conditions of service. The technical officers will be responsible to the chief officer for 'administrative and operational' matters, and to the 'corresponding district level officers' for 'technical' matters.

The village panchayats, constituting the elective base of the *samiti*, should themselves be elected, although there may be provision for the co-option of representatives of women, scheduled castes, and scheduled tribes. Each panchayat is to be empowered to collect a variety of taxes and will receive 'grants from the panchayat samiti on lines similar to those suggested for grants from Government to panchayat samitis'. As far as possible, it should be used as an agency for the collection of land revenue, of which it will be entitled to a statutorily prescribed share. As grants from the *panchayat samiti* are likely to constitute a sizeable proportion of the panchayat's revenue, and as the *samiti* will have the power to approve the panchayat's budget, it will be reasonable to impose on the latter body a number of compulsory duties. These should be:

(i) provision of water supply for domestic use; (ii) sanitation, (iii) maintenance of public streets, drains, tanks, etc., (iv) lighting of the village streets, (v) land management, (vi) maintenance of records relating to cattle, (vii) relief of distress, (viii) maintenance of panchayat roads, culverts, bridges, drains etc., (ix) supervision of primary schools, (x) welfare of backward classes, and (xi) collection and maintenance of statistics.

In addition, it will be required to act as the *panchayat samiti's* agent for executing schemes of development.

Recognizing that 'one of the banes of democratic village administration in some areas has been the intensification of factions and feuds, often also of separatism arising out of caste distinctions', the Committee expresses qualified approval of devices, such as the 'Madhyastha Mandal' already adopted by the former state of Saurashtra, to ensure that, as far as possible, elections to village panchayats shall be unanimous. At the same time, it quotes with approval the Panel on Land Reform's animadversions on 'the dangers which are inherent in unanimity arrived at under pressure'.

Once this new democratic structure has been brought into existence, there will be 'very little left for any higher . . . executive body other than the Government'. Hence the district boards, district school boards, and the various other rather ineffective bodies working at the district level will become superfluous.[69] Their functions, in fact, will be 'performed with

[69] The experience of these bodies is analysed ibid. vol. ii, sect. 1, 'Local Government in Rural Areas—the Present Position', pp. 1–12.

greater efficiency by the panchayat samiti'. However, it will still be necessary to ensure co-ordination, at the district level, between the activities of the *samitis*, and for this purpose the Committee suggests the creation of a *zila parishad*,

> of which the members will be the presidents of the panchayat samitis, all members of the State Legislature and of the Parliament representing a part or whole of a district whose constituencies lie within the district and district level officers of the medical, public health, agriculture, veterinary, public health engineering, education, backward classes welfare, public works and other development departments.

under the chairmanship of the Collector.

This body will not possess executive functions; its duties, nevertheless, are important. It will examine and approve the budgets of the *panchayat samitis*, recruit and post officials such as the Village Level Worker and the primary school teacher, co-ordinate and consolidate block plans, distribute government funds among the blocks, and exercise a general supervisory role.

Unlike the panchayat and the *panchayat samiti*, the *parishad* is to be a body on which officials, with full voting powers, sit side by side with representatives. The Committee concedes, however, that in some circumstances it may have to be wholly or mainly representative, i.e. if 'some of the State Governments . . . find it useful to devolve upon the zila parishads in a progressively larger measure the powers now exercised by them directly through their district level officers'. This need will be even greater if a state government rejects the pivotal role of the *samiti* and considers it 'advisable and convenient to devolve power on to a local body whose jurisdiction is as large as a district'. This the Committee clearly regards as a *pis aller*, as it is convinced that 'devolution of power to a smaller body would be the most effective method of democratic decentralization'. Nevertheless, in view of the strong opinions on this subject already expressed by some of the states, it does not 'refuse to visualize similar devolution to a district body, instead'.

The above summarizes the Committee's major substantive proposals.[70] The remainder of its long report consists of consequential material, studies of particular programmes, and an account of its methods of inquiry and of the reactions of the state governments and central ministries to its draft recommendations.

(xi)

No major report, since India's acquisition of independence, has had more immediate and more radical consequence for the whole process of

[70] Ibid. vol. i, pt 1, sect. 1, pp. 1–23.

planning and development at the 'grass-roots' level. Its recommendations were given general endorsement by the NDC in 1958, and in the October of the following year Rajasthan staked out its claim to be in the van of progress by becoming the first state to pass *panchayati raj* legislation. Andhra Pradesh rapidly followed suit, and by the beginning of 1963 the new system was in various stages of operation in all states except West Bengal, Kerala, and Jammu and Kashmir, and even these three laggards were taking the necessary legislative steps.

While all states followed the fundamental principles of the Balvantray Mehta report, their interpretation of them varied considerably.[71] Inevitably, the powers accorded to each of the three tiers of the new structure and the extent of the supervision that the higher tiers were permitted or required to exercise over the lower ones became matters on which each state government chose to exercise its initiative and ingenuity. The major deviants were Maharashtra and Gujarat, which, rejecting the pivotal role of the *panchayat samiti*, chose to concentrate powers in the hands of the *zila parishad*. There were also wide variations in methods of representation, some states preferring direct or partially direct election of representatives to their *panchayat samitis* and/or *zila parishads* to the indirect election which the Committee had recommended. Prescribed relationships between representative bodies and 'their' officials displayed similar variation. Further to confuse the student of democratic decentralization, no attempt was made to standardize nomenclature. For instance, the body known as the *panchayat samiti* in Andhra Pradesh, Bihar, Maharashtra, Orissa, Punjab, and Rajasthan is called the *anchalik panchayat* in Assam, the *janapada panchayat* in Madhya Pradesh, the Panchayat Union Council in Madras, and the *kshetra samiti* in Uttar Pradesh, while the corresponding body in Gujarat and Mysore, being at the *taluka* and not at the block level, is known as the Taluka Panchayat and the Taluka Development Board respectively. Likewise, the *zila parishad* is called the *mohkuma parishad* in Assam, the District Panchayat in Gujarat, the *zila panchayat* in Madhya Pradesh, and the District Development Council in Madras and Mysore.

These variations, however, are for two reasons not particularly relevant to our present inquiry. The first is that as yet there has been insufficient experience of the working of *panchayati raj* institutions to permit the making of even the most provisional correlations between differences of system and differences of performance. The second is the fact that the problems that have been encountered to date, which are many and serious, seem to be general, i.e. not related in any observable way to

[71] A useful summary of state variants on *panchayati raj* is C. Srinavasa Sastry, 'Structure and Pattern of Panchayati Raj', in *IJPA*, Oct.–Dec. 1962.

specific deviations from the Balvantray Mehta Committee's recommendations.[72]

In spite of the general enthusiasm with which *panchayati raj* was greeted, particularly in political circles, it was realized that the new system was essentially an act of faith. The Committee itself came near to admitting that its introduction *might*, at least temporarily, reduce the efficiency with which developmental programmes were executed, and in several different contexts warned against the deleterious effects that continued 'factionalism' would have on the new institutions. It nevertheless held, without making any serious examination of possible alternatives, that this was the *only* way forward. Basically, its argument was simple to the point of naiveté: community development was in the doldrums because the people's participation has not been sufficiently enlisted: participation can only spring from a sense of responsibility; therefore the people themselves must be called upon to exercise responsibility, through their own democratically-elected organs. The numerous *non sequiturs* in such an argument hardly need to be pointed out, particularly to anyone with some knowledge of the Indian countryside; hence it is not surprising that many of those who were actively concerned with the hard tasks of rural development, such as officials at all levels of the district administrative apparatus, proved hard to convince. There is no evidence that they carried their lack of conviction to the extent of trying to sabotage the system; on the contrary, the majority of them seem to have done their best to make it a success; but their experience of the first few years of *panchayati raj* has tended to reinforce their initial mental reservations.

Whatever else it may or may not have done, there would appear to be evidence that, *except where the officials have retained de facto control*, *panchayat raj* has produced some deterioration in the morale of district administration. Officials have tended to develop two kinds of schizophrenia. The more obvious one is that produced by the attempt to serve two masters: a hierarchical superior and a democratically-elected council. This may not be difficult (e.g. for a *préfet* or a *maire*) in a country such as France, which possesses a unified political culture; but it is liable to be a positively acrobatic exercise in India, where the village's political culture is as different from the state capital's as the latter's is from New Delhi's. The second schizophrenic phenomenon arises from the official's need, not only to operate but publicly to defend a system in which he has no real belief. This is vividly illustrated by certain conversations which the

[72] The most important and acute commentaries on CD and *panchayati raj* are those of Prof. Hugh Tinker. See 'Authority and Community in Village India', *Pacific Affairs*, Dec. 1959; 'C.D.: a New Philosopher's Stone?', *International Affairs*, July 1961; 'Tradition and Experiment in Forms of Government', in Philips, *Politics & Society*; 'The Village in the Framework of Development', in Braibanti & Spengler, *Admin. & Econ. Dev.*

author had, during the course of his tour of the Indian states, with a Development Commissioner (who for obvious reasons, will have to remain anonymous and therefore stateless).

On his arrival at the state capital, he proceeded to put to this official a series of questions about the progress of *panchayati raj*. The official said that everything was going well. The countryside was being aroused from its lethargy; elections were being conducted in an orderly manner; new, vigorous-minded democratic leaders were appearing; the people were beginning to participate and to consider officials as their partners in the developmental process rather than as their masters. A suggestion that democratic decentralization was still in an 'experimental' stage was promptly rejected. Having succeeded, it was no longer experimental.

Several days later, after he had become convinced that the author was a reasonably well-informed as well as sympathetic inquirer, he volunteered information of a very different kind. It now appeared that he was worried to death by the problems which the introduction of *panchayati raj* had raised and very sceptical about the workability of the new system. The fundamental mistake, in his view, was that it had been *presented* to the people, without any demand for it on their part. Hence it very rarely succeeded in producing the 'right' type of leadership. Those who got elected were mainly ex-'feudalists', money-lenders, and party politicians, none of whom had much interest in constructive tasks, being mainly concerned with the enhancement of their own status and influence. Even where a genuinely public-spirited leadership had emerged, this often consisted of humble men, without land, who could achieve very little against the bitter opposition of the traditional leaders of the community, the members of the local dominant castes. In the elections, party politics were rampant. No one openly admitted that the parties were participating, but in fact each party identified itself with a particular local faction, with the result that the factionalism which was the bane of village life and the chief obstacle to united endeavour had become greatly aggravated. So weak was the spirit of democratic compromise and understanding of majority rule that the defeated factions refused all collaboration with the victorious ones. The government's attempt to rectify this situation by giving financial premiums to those units which held 'unanimous' elections had failed; for the unanimity, where achieved, was a bogus one, being the product of a series of unprincipled 'fixings' among the various political groups. He could see no way out of these difficulties, and appeared very depressed.

He was not exaggerating; for by now a whole series of official and unofficial reports have confirmed that, with a few outstanding exceptions, *panchayati raj* does indeed produce these unlooked-for results. Experience might have anticipated them. Even in British days, when statutory panchayats (where they existed), being appointed from among village notables, reflected the established balance of power in the community, such organs rarely competed in popular esteem with the various kinds of traditional panchayat, which were in no way concerned with economic development.[73] The idea that the introduction of the elective principle could generate the necessary unanimity and developmental drive was one that could occur only to people with a deficient sense of reality. Yet the statutory village panchayat provides the basis of the whole *panchayati raj* structure, and therefore gives it its essential characteristics. As A. D. Gorwala said, with heavy but justified irony:

> A village panchayat does not work well. It performs its simple duties most inadequately. But a committee of representatives of village panchayats must do splendidly. Let us call it a 'Taluka Samiti', give it ample powers, repeat the sacred charm of democratic decentralisation and all will be well.[74]

What is now clear is that, as a means of rural development and uplift, local democratic institutions can work effectively only if certain conditions are present. The most important of these, as Tarlok Singh recognized as long ago as 1955, is a 'homogeneous social structure'.[75] This demands the elimination, or at least the considerable reduction, of the differences of social status associated with the institution of caste, and of the differences of economic status associated with disparities in the ownership of land. As neither of these desiderata has been achieved, or is likely to be achieved in the foreseeable future, the original conception of *panchayati raj* is doomed to frustration. It is true that the new panchayat institutions, being endowed with significant powers and having relatively large sums of money at their disposal, cannot simply be disregarded by the leaders of rural society, as the old ones frequently were; it is also true that the existence of elections provides opportunities for the under-privileged groups that they did not possess before and consequently compels—or may compel in the long run—the notables to treat them with greater consideration. But the very fact that the panchayats, *panchayat samitis*, and *zila parishads* are important as centres of political power makes them a focal point, not only for the party struggle,[76] but for the struggle—so accurately reflected by party alignments in the rural localities—between castes, classes, and factions.

[73] See R. H. Retzlaff, *Village Government in India* (1962), ch. 2: 'The Period of British Rule'.

[74] *Mysore Admin.*, pp. 75–76.

[75] As quoted in Retzlaff, p. 6.

[76] Originally it was hoped that the party struggle could be eliminated from *panchayati raj* elections. In spite of a self-denying ordinance taken somewhat hypocritically by the Congress Party, this proved an illusion. On the nature of the party struggle at the local levels, together with divergent views of its significance, see four articles in *IJPA*, Oct.–Dec. 1962, by Jayaprakash Narayan, Harish Chandra Mathur, E. M. S. Namboodiripad, and M. Weiner respectively; also L. L. Shrader & Ram Joshi, 'Zilla Parishad Elections in Maharashtra and the District Political Elite', *Asian Survey*, Mar. 1963.

This may deepen and widen the political life of the rural areas; it may even, in the long run, prove a valuable school of democracy; but its contribution to the cause of economic development, at least in the immediate future, is difficult to envisage. So far, most evidence suggests that its main contribution has been a negative one—at least, if we are to attach any significance to the fact that the introduction of *panchayati raj* has coincided with several years of agricultural stagnation.

(xii)

Precisely why *panchayati raj*, for the present, is irrelevant if not positively hostile to the progress of community development has been explained simply and precisely by a perceptive student of the Indian countryside, John T. Hitchcock. The necessary qualities of initiative and enthusiasm, he says,

> do not exist among the village poor . . . . They do not exist among the landed either, and I would suggest that this is because they, like the poorer segments of the community, realise that issues much more basic than those touched upon by the C.D. programmes are still in abeyance. The landed see the C.D. programmes as part of what they call the 'new order', and this order has meant to them more than just new agricultural methods and hymn-singing: it has meant the attempted abolition of landlordism together with the spread of anti-caste and anti-privilege ideology which threatens further inroads in their dominant position. As a result of these factors there is satisfaction on neither side of the village economic cleavage.[77]

In other words, there is insufficient consensus among the rural people to make democratic decentralization more than a very feeble and halting vehicle for policies of economic development. As a generalization this can be sustained despite the fantastic variety of village social structure throughout the Indian sub-continent. Obviously, the possibility of obtaining sufficient consensus is greater in some areas than in others. Where caste divisions are absent or embryonic, where landlordism is weak and landlessness rare, and where a rough economic and social equality prevails among peasant proprietors or joint cultivators, the chances of obtaining agreement about developmental plans and co-operation in their implementation are comparatively good, particularly if the approach of the administrative authorities or the rural people is reasonably intelligent, sympathetic, and flexible. Unfortunately, these conditions are found more frequently in the tribal areas, where developmental potentialities are low, than in the great agricultural plains where, for reasons of resource-endowment, the main developmental effort has to be made. This is a very

[77] J. T. Hitchcock, 'Centrally Planned Rural Development in India: Some Problems', *EW*, 11 Mar. 1961, p. 440.

broad and inexact correlation, but it tends to be confirmed by most of the village studies so far published.[78]

It does not mean, of course, that the great experiment of *panchayati raj* will have to be abandoned. Gorwala's counter-ideal of a refurbished but still autocratic district administration is as utopian as most of the other solutions that have been suggested. Democratic decentralization, which is supported by all parties, has by now sent down political roots, and the attempt to pull them up would be entirely disruptive. The question, therefore, is how the degree of democratic consensus necessary for its successful operation as a developmental agency can be generated.

One method would be to have a social revolution in the countryside. This would involve the outright abolition of landlordism, the distribution of land to the landless, and the transformation of each village into a roughly egalitarian society of small peasant proprietors, bound together by co-operative credit, purchasing and marketing institutions and perhaps moving on towards a system of co-operative farming, as envisaged by Congress's 'Nagpur' resolution. Such, indeed, is still the official policy of the Congress Party; but at present, despite the abolition of the *zamindaris* and the *jagirdaris*, the imposition of 'ceilings' on landholding, and the various laws regulating tenancies and giving tenants the right of land purchase, India is moving away from it rather than towards it.[79] Administratively, the state governments are incapable of organizing such a revolution, whether suddenly or by stages; politically, the rise to power of what we have termed the 'kulak' elements in the countryside[80] makes it impossible, except as the result of a general rising of the rural under-privileged, comparable with the 'Telengana' revolt organized by the Communists in 1948–52. As there are no signs of such a revolt, and as, should it occur, it would disrupt the political system which provides the present framework for Indian planning (which, in the context of our present discussion, we have to accept), this contingency may be ruled out. One might also mention, in passing, that although rural economic

[78] See, for instance, M. N. Srinivas, ed., *India's Villages* (Calcutta, 1955). One must admit that generalizations on this subject are very hazardous. I should not like to be understood as saying either that no Indian village possesses any sense of unity or even the most faction-divided one on no occasion becomes aware of possessing a corporate identity. Adrian Mayer, after an exhaustive description of a village which contained 'twenty seven different caste groups, each with its barrier of endogamy and often occupational and commensural restrictions', demonstrated that it could 'nevertheless exist to some extent as a social unit' (*Caste & Kinship in Central India*, p. 146). It is noteworthy, however, that *class* divisions in his village were weakly developed. The phrase 'to some extent', moreover, should be emphasized. My argument is simply that, in most cases, whatever degree of unity exists is insufficient to provide a sound basis for the kind of development programme envisaged by the CD authorities and promoted by the government.

[79] This may be confirmed by a comparison of the chapters on land reform in the three Five-Year Plans. For a graphic account of the difficulties that land reform has encountered, see Kusum Nair, *Blossoms in the Dust* (1961).

[80] See above, p. 241.

egalitarianism would certainly provide a better *basis* for consensus than at present exists, it would not automatically solve the problem of caste divisions, so deeply rooted in the Hindu tradition, nor would it suddenly make everybody 'development minded'.

The only alternative method is one that frankly accepts the present trends and attempts to build on them. This involves the recognition that, for the present, the unity envisaged by the community developers is a will-o'-the-wisp, and that the economic development of the Indian countryside, if it is to be achieved at all, will be primarily a matter of individual and family effort rather than collective effort. Such effort will necessarily have to come from 'progressive' farmers and 'improving' landlords, rather than from the village poor. Initially, it may even reinforce caste divisions and exacerbate factionalism. It requires action on the part of the government and district administration, not to equalize conditions in the villages, but to give the maximum encouragement and assistance to all farmers and proprietors, whatever their economic status and caste affiliations, who show the faintest signs of entrepreneurial urge. What is needed, in particular, is that an increasing number of those village people who already have resources capable of development should concentrate on developing them and thereby steadily increase the total pool of village wealth, rather than devote their energies—as all too often happens at present—to the redivision of the existing, miserably insufficient wealth in their own favour. This cannot be facilitated by *panchayati raj* institutions except to the extent that such institutions become dominated by the 'progressive' elements. So long as they remain a battle-ground for rival factions, each primarily interested in the division of such spoils as exist rather than in the increase of the divisible total,[81] panchayats and *panchayat samitis* will be virtually useless as developmental agencies. This would seem to imply that, in default of an almost miraculous transformation of these institutions, there will have to be a direct relationship between the 'progressives' and the administrative agencies concerned with the dissemination of improved agricultural practices, provision of tested seeds and fertilizers, and development of minor irrigation, and that the functions given to the organs of democratic decentralization will become, in practice, far more limited than those they are now supposed to exercise. A *reculer pour mieux sauter* would appear to be on the order of the day.

This seems to be confirmed by the excellent field-work conducted by Professor Retzlaff in a large village in Uttar Pradesh. He found that, as a result of factionalism, the panchayat was almost totally ineffective when it tried to tackle questions of 'land management, maintenance of land records, the right to authorize and enter land transfers, partitions,

[81] One of the best documentations of factionalism, based on a study of a number of villages in Uttar Pradesh, is Baljit Singh, *Next Step in Village India* (1961).

amalgamations and other mutation proceedings'. If that particular panchayat had been concerned, in addition, with questions of agricultural *development*—which apparently it was not—its ineffectiveness might have been even more evident. On the other hand, he records that, before the factionalism that was stimulated by its efforts to deal with matters that actually divided the village completely disrupted its operation as an administrative agency, it had scored a number of notable successes with certain projects that were 'noncontroversial', such as the paving of village lanes and the building of a village community hall and secondary school. On the basis of this experience he gives qualified approval to the suggestion that

panchayat functions be graded into several classes, ranging from the simplest and least controversial on up. Each panchayat would then be assigned a certain class of functions, depending upon the evaluation of the Panchayat Raj officials. Those villages which demonstrated an absence of factionalism would presumably be given the greatest powers.[82]

Obviously, there would be great political and administrative difficulties in operating such a classification, particularly now that one is concerned with the *panchayat samiti* as well as the panchayat, which—since Retzlaff's material was collected before the days of democratic decentralization—was the sole focus of his interest. But, for reasons which he did not make fully explicit and which have been set forth above, this is a line of thought that ought to be taken seriously.

Can one assume that, if the pattern of rural development suggested here is successful, there will be a growing democratic consensus in the rural areas sufficient to warrant the subsequent expansion of *panchayati raj* functions? At first sight it seems unlikely. Indeed, one could easily be accused of producing a recipe for an exacerbated class struggle which would eventually overflow the bounds of democratic institutions. This is certainly a possibility, but not the only one. Already it is being widely said, probably with justification, that the existence of democratic authorities at the village and block levels is causing some change in the balance of political power, in so far as the 'notables', in their anxiety to enjoy the status of *panches* and *pradhans*, are compelled to solicit with promises the votes of the disinherited, who usually constitute a majority of village dwellers. Admittedly, the disinherited are rarely united and often, for reasons of economic dependence allied with traditional deference, merely divide themselves up into supporters of rival higher-caste factions; but this may well be a temporary phenomenon. What prevents them, at present, from deriving any serious benefits from their possession of voting rights is the fact that the village, as a whole, is so poor—the divisible

[82] Retzlaff, *Village Govt*, ch. 6.

surplus, in other words, is pitifully small. If, however, the size of this surplus increases, as a result of the entrepreneurial efforts of their 'betters', the existence of democratic institutions may provide the disinherited with a real opportunity to ensure that they are not left out in the cold. Better tenancy conditions, higher wages, improved access to irrigation waters and wells &c. could be among the various prices which the better-off were called upon to pay for their continued political influence. Moreover one can surely envisage a situation where the rough and hard-fisted village entrepreneur, having acquired a taste for a better mode of living, begins to take an interest, through the organs of local democracy, in the improvement of the social environment—even reaching the point where he is prepared to tax himself and his fellows for the paving of streets, laying of drains, rebuilding of schools, and establishment of health centres.

This vision of the future may well be unrealistic. There is more than a possibility that local democracy will collapse or wither away long before such a point is reached. Nevertheless, it would seem to be much more within the bounds of the possible than the prospect of united democratic effort in the localities, still held out, with increasing desperation, by the more orthodox exponents of the community development and *panchayati raj* ideology.

In any case, there is a choice to be made—one that India's ruling party has so far consistently evaded. The nature of this choice is succinctly expressed by Thomas Balogh, thus:

> The Government can either fully back the successful owners of a viable type and hope for a bourgeois-entrepreneurial type of revolution on the land or it can energetically push the rise of a new cooperative rural organisation, through determined leadership. Only in exceptional regions can both methods be attempted simultaneously . . . . The oscillation between the two policies or rather pious declarations in favour of socialistic-cooperative solutions while actual reliance is centred in privately initiated improvement is likely to continue hampering economic growth.[83]

It was essentially as an expression of preference for the former course of action that *panchayati raj* was introduced. But the full implications of this act of choice were never grasped. If *panchayati raj* was to function effectively, within a reasonably short space of time, as a *development* institution, its introduction had to be accompanied by revolutionary changes in the social and economic structure of the village. As we have suggested, no such changes were feasible within the politico-administrative context which the protagonists of *panchayati raj* had necessarily to accept. Hence there inevitably emerged, as in so many other fields of activity, an enormous hiatus between intention and achievement. Hence disillusion with the new system grew almost as rapidly as it had grown with the old.

[83] T. Balogh, 'Economic Strategy for the Third Plan', *EW*, spec. no., 4 Feb. 1961.

This does not mean that the introduction of *panchayati raj* was a mistake, but simply that, being introduced for the wrong reasons, it aroused false expectations. The purposes which the members of the Balvantray Mehta Committee expected it to serve were many; but the most prominent and urgent of them was the revival of the flagging Community Project. This, for reasons already set forth, the new system was unable to achieve. If, however, the development of agricultural production could be pushed forward by other methods, *panchayati raj* might well become of major significance as a political break-through, and even, *in the long run*, of decisive importance in the context of economic growth. But its contribution towards the solution of the immediate problems has been either nil or negative.

What, with luck and good judgement, the new system may be able to achieve is the expansion and consolidation, at the level where the vast majority of the Indian people conduct their day-to-day activities, of a democratic political consciousness. One of the problems that confronts India is to effect some kind of marriage between the political style of the village, which is mainly traditional, and that of the town, which is comparatively 'westernized'. There is some evidence that this is already happening. On the basis of an analysis of the first *panchayati raj* elections in Maharashtra, Lawrence J. Shrader and Ram Joshi come to the conclusion that 'a basis has been laid for the emergence of new political leaders who may be more closely associated with the general electorate, have extensive experience at the local level, and have potentialities for integrating and deepening the impact of democratic political institutions in the state'.[84] What they suggest is that, although the marriage has not yet taken place, at least the banns have been called. This may be over-optimistic, or based on an experience which is unusual rather than typical; but at least it suggests that, given time, *panchayati raj* may make an important, and even decisive, contribution towards the creation of a unified democratic political culture. What it cannot do is to provide the localities with a unity of purpose which they do not as yet possess, and may never possess, and with developmental ambitions which, for the most part, they have not as yet experienced. Only idealists, such as Jayaprakash Narayan, could imagine that the new institutions could do other than provide national and state parties, caste associations, and village factions with further opportunities for giving expression to their various rival particularisms. If local democracy is on the order of the day, a plurality of purposes and interests has to be accepted as a basis fact of local as well as of national political life. They cannot be conjured away and it is most dangerous to pretend that they do not 'really' exist.

It is with these considerations in mind that one must judge the approach to *panchayati raj* contained in the Third Five-Year Plan report, which

[84] *Asian Survey*, Mar. 1963, p. 156.

presumably still represents the official orthodoxy. 'It is the object of the new institutions and relationships now being established', says this document, 'to help each area to realize . . . to the utmost limits of its resources' the possibilities of economic development. Hence the success of *panchayati raj* will have to be measured by the following 'main tests':

(1) agricultural production as the highest national priority during the Third Plan;
(2) development of rural industry;
(3) development of cooperative institutions;
(4) full utilization of local manpower and other resources;
(5) development of facilities for education and adult literacy;
(6) optimum utilization of resources available to Panchayati Raj institutions such as finance, personnel, technical assistance and other facilities from higher levels, and efforts by them to raise their own resources;
(7) assistance to the economically weaker sections of the village community;
(8) progressive dispersal of authority and initiative with special emphasis on the role of voluntary organizations;
(9) understanding and harmony between elected representatives and public servants to be achieved through comprehensive training and education and a clear demarcation of duties and responsibilities, and progressive increase in competence both among officials and non-officials; and
(10) cohesion and self-help within the community.[85]

First among the various methods suggested for the achievement of these purposes is an 'approach of unanimity or near unanimity' by the Gram Sabha and Village Panchayat, 'so that the various activities are undertaken with the general consent and goodwill of the community'.

Enough has been said to indicate that such expectations are, to say the least, lacking in realism. Yet the Planning Commission, the Ministry of Community Development, and the Development Commissioners continue to use language of this kind in the manner of a magic charm. The gap between theory and reality has now become so wide that no one can fail to see it; but the authorities continue to base their policies on Humpty-Dumpty's principle of 'What I say three times is true'. The Third Five-Year Plan's record in agricultural production shows how dangerous this blindness has become.

The Indian government's attempts to give the plans 'grass roots' have, then, achieved little success. There has been some, but not much,

[85] *FYP(3)*, pp. 338–9. The ninth of these points raises issues which have hardly been touched upon in this chapter, although they have received some attention in the chapter on 'Administration' (see above, p. 307). Paul Appleby, as we have seen, described the administrative arrangements for CD as 'self defeating'. His views have been amply confirmed by the six Evaluation Reps, and by the Ford Foundation's report on *India's Food Crisis* (see particularly the chapter on 'Expansion Work and Community Development'). The assumption we have made in this chapter is that the purely administrative problems are more readily solvable than the socio-political ones.

decentralization of plan formulation to the district and block levels, but hardly any effective popular participation in the process, while the involvement of the people in plan implementation, through the Community Projects and *panchayati raj*, has been patchy and generally disappointing in its results. Even knowledge of the existence of a plan is not very widespread. The reasons for the poor response to a very considerable amount of official effort are to be found partly in administrative difficulties, partly in the overwhelming apathy and ignorance which still characterizes the Indian countryside, and partly in the adoption of approaches insufficiently informed by sociological analysis and even, in some cases, by plain common sense.

To explain this failure is easy; to suggest a better way forward extremely difficult. What might have been avoided was the pouring of resources into schemes, such as the Community Projects, which were based upon insufficiently-tested hypotheses. This is a lesson that some Indians, with their devotion to panaceas and their tendency to disregard reality when it contradicts a favourite theory, have found difficulty in learning. Rather typically, they jumped straight out of the community development frying pan into the *panchayati raj* fire. What now seems to be needed is a thoroughly hard-headed and ideologically-uncommitted reappraisal of the experience of the last ten or eleven years—of the kind that the Balvantray Mehta Committee should have attempted.

XII

PUBLIC, PRIVATE, AND CO-OPERATIVE

AMONG the many controversies that have attended the formulation and implementation of India's plans, the delimitation of the respective roles of public, private, and co-operative enterprise has generated a degree of heat equalled only by that radiating from the centre-versus-state or 'grass roots' issues. That the question of 'who should be responsible for what' in the field of production and trade should provoke acrimonious dispute is not surprising. Not only are powerful vested interests vitally concerned about the answer; upon it depends, to some extent, the whole character of the social order that emerges from India's planning process.

As might be expected, the 'public-versus-private' controversy has been particularly acute since 1954, when Congress and Parliament endorsed the concept of the 'socialist pattern of society'. Closely allied with it is the question of the right methods of regulating, encouraging, and guiding the private sector, so as to enable it to make its maximum 'appropriate' contribution to the cause of economic development. Another associated issue concerns the respective degrees of emphasis to be given to the various kinds of industry, large-scale, small-scale, 'village', and handicraft. Here the persistence of Gandhian ideas about economic organization, even in a diluted form, adds fuel to the controversial flames. Finally, there is the question of the role to be played by co-operative forms of activity, both in industry and in agriculture. Although, in many fields, the usefulness of co-operation is not open to doubt, in others it is no more than a possible alternative to the other two forms of economic organization. In this chapter we shall deal successively with these four major economic and political issues.

(i)

Before considering the Indian government's actual policies for the division of responsibility between the state entrepreneur and the private entrepreneur, it will be useful to recall, and to develop a little, some of the general considerations which were presented in the introductory chapter. In a mixed economy (and even in one that dignifies itself with the name of 'socialist') delimitation between the two sectors is, in the first instance, decided by objective considerations. All underdeveloped countries require heavy infrastructural investments. Some of these, such as investments in roads, schools, and hospitals, will be almost entirely in the public sector, because they yield no direct return. Others, such as those in power, transport, and irrigation, are likely to be mainly in the public sector, if only because even the potentially 'profitable' ones are too slow yielding, technically difficult, or heavily capitalized for the private investor or entrepreneur to be interested in them. Once the government has decided, therefore, on the quantum of resources that must be devoted, over a period of years, to infrastructural investment, it will have predetermined to that extent the balance between public enterprise and private. One should note, however, that this does not mean that it will be able precisely to predict how that balance will change; for, as is well known, public infrastructural investment brings into play two conflicting sets of forces. On the one hand, opportunities for private investment are limited to the extent that resources that might otherwise be devoted to it are withdrawn into the public sector; on the other hand, outlay on the new infrastructural assets provides private enterprise with new markets, and the assets themselves, when complete and in operation, create external economies: thus opportunities for private investment are enhanced.

So far as direct investment in industry and agriculture is concerned, the public share can be made to depend on the answer, derived from experience, to the question of how far private enterprise is capable of achieving the contemplated rate of growth. The two main factors here are partly but not entirely interdependent: the quantity, quality, and distribution of entrepreneurial talent and the availability of funds for investment in private undertakings. Private entrepreneurship is encouraged by the prevalence of appropriate investment habits, by the existence of a market for stocks and shares, and by a pattern of income distribution which enhances the propensity to save. Actual investment, on the other hand, will largely depend on the confidence of the investor in the entrepreneur's ability and honesty. Both will obviously be strongly affected by the capacity of the government to preserve economic and political stability and by its willingness to provide certain incentives. It is in the latter respect that governments are confronted with some of the most difficult decisions. What publicly-provided incentives are likely, in the given circumstances, to prove most efficacious? What is the best combination of such devices as tariff protection, low-interest loans, participation in equities, tax concessions, 'promotional' transport rates, and provision of facilities (e.g. industrial estates, common services &c.)? Entrepreneurial urges and investment habits are such chancy things that no one can answer these questions in advance. If everything fails, then there is no alternative to taking up the desired projects in the public sector. The further question then arises of the capacity of the state to raise the necessary funds and to mobilize the necessary talent—for it cannot be assumed that where the private individual has failed the government can succeed. It may be that, in default of a massive importation of foreign money and skills, very little can be achieved until profound political and social changes take place.

These, then, are some of the objective considerations; but no government, in practice, can allow them completely to determine its policy for economic development—for they rest on the assumption, which no ruling group can accept, that the balance between the public sector and the private sector is a matter of indifference and that therefore, if a desired economic activity can be taken up by private individuals, the state, which has plenty of other work to do, can conveniently and thankfully leave it to them. Even a government with no very strong ideological preconceptions may have to walk warily if public opinion is hostile to the private businessman, which is often the case when business activities have been largely concentrated in the hands of unpopular groups, such as foreign firms or incompletely assimilated indigenous communities. Many governments, moreover, are not unnaturally nervous about leaving to the private sector certain 'key' areas of economic activity whose domination by a small number of wealthy men can create an *imperium in imperio*. The armaments industry is often regarded as coming within this field, and a strong case can be made out, on similar grounds, for state ownership of transport and power facilities. Beyond this, there is the question of the kind of economic and social order envisaged as desirable by the ruling élite and its political supporters. Although the short-term impact of such ideological presuppositions may be negligible—if only because objective considerations are particularly exigent during the earlier stages of economic development—their longer-term impact will obviously be very important. Take the case of a government dominated by the ideal of building up a predominantly private enterprise economy. Such a government may be compelled, at the beginning, to make extensive use of public enterprise, through dearth of private investment and private entrepreneurship; but it will regard its own activities in the public sector as primarily catalytic in character, and this attitude will determine, at least in part, the direction taken by its initiatives. Where it has a choice between creating one kind of asset or another, it will tend to choose that which, by giving promise of early profitability, will be readily saleable to the private investor as soon as possible after its establishment. Where there is the alternative between going into business on its own or in collaboration with private partners, it will unhesitatingly choose the latter. In devising monetary and fiscal policies, moreover, it will lean heavily towards those that provide the maximum incentives to the private entrepreneur and investor, without being inhibited, to a greater extent than may be required by the political situation, by considerations of 'equality'.

By contrast, a government which proclaims its 'socialist' convictions has provided itself—at least to the extent that its convictions are genuine—with a very different set of policy guides. It is saying in effect that public enterprise is not only economically superior to private enterprise, which is a matter for argument, but also morally superior, which is a matter of faith. Economic activity, it holds, should be subject to democratic control of the community, as represented by the organs of the state. This implies the creation of a public sector large enough to play a predominant role in the economy, since effective control of the operations of private enterprise (particularly in comparatively underdeveloped conditions) is notoriously difficult to achieve. Another ultimate purpose, according to most interpretations of the socialist faith, is the establishment of economic equality, at least to the extent that large private fortunes are eliminated and that rewards for services are rationally related to quantity of effort and quality of performance. This, too, requires that the public sector should receive emphasis at the expense of the private, since private enterprise both creates inequalities and demands them as a condition of its effective operation. In practice, of course, such a government may find that wisdom dictates a heavier reliance on the private sector, as an agency of economic growth, than ideological predilections would appear to warrant, just as a government of the opposite ideological complexion may find itself putting an unexpected number of its eggs in the public basket. Nevertheless, the socialist-minded government, when faced with a free choice, will inevitably prefer the public to the private sector, will rarely or never sell public assets to the private investor, will endeavour to ensure that its nominees are firmly in control of whatever 'mixed' enterprises it chooses to establish, will be predisposed to nationalize those private undertakings which appear to be 'failing the nation', and will generally regard the right of individuals to organize production for profit as a privilege conditional upon good behaviour. All this, however, it will attempt to justify, as the British Labour government attempted to justify its nationalization programme, on strictly economic grounds; and a similar type of justification will be attempted by a government whose primary loyalty is to free enterprise. Either may be right, in given circumstances; for the possession of ideological prejudices is not necessarily incompatible with economic rationality.

This is straightforward enough; but what governments intend rarely coincides with what they achieve. Whatever public-private mixture may be initially decided upon, its constituents will almost certainly change in unforeseen ways, as a result of a host of unpredictable problems and pressures which arise during the course of the developmental process. For one thing, only time and experience can tell what are the respective capacities of public and private enterprise—and no government which genuinely has the cause of economic development at heart is going to persist with a mixture which has become patently unviable. For another, the very process of economic development (or attempted development) changes the political balance in the community and calls forth pressures, often hostile to the existing mixture, which the government cannot afford to neglect.

(ii)

Both of these features may be illustrated from the experience of India. Indeed, the Indian government has displayed considerable flexibility in the division of developmental responsibilities between the two sectors. Nevertheless, inspired by certain long-term socio-political objectives, it has also attempted to lay down in advance what tasks shall be given to each, and thereby limited to some extent its own room to manoeuvre. The adoption of the 'socialist pattern' in 1954 was itself a significant declaration of policy, but long before this step was taken the choice between public and private had become a matter of principled decision, through the publication of the Industrial Policy Resolution of 1948.[1]

This resolution was not specifically socialist in outlook. It could not attempt to interpret the quasi-socialist Directive Principles of the constitution, for these were still to be formulated. Its basic assumption was expressed in one sentence: 'The nation has now set itself to establish a social order where justice and equality of opportunity shall be secured to all the people.' The 'immediate objective' which inspired it was to provide educational facilities and health services on a much wider scale, and to promote a rapid rise in the standard of living of the people by exploiting the latent resources of the country, increasing production and offering opportunities to all for employment in the service of the community. To achieve these things a 'dynamic national policy' was required, 'directed to a continuous increase in production by all possible means, side by side with measures to secure its equitable distribution'.

The resolution immediately went on, however, to prejudge these means. There could be 'no doubt', it said, that 'the state must play a progressively active role in the development of industries'. Nationalization (i.e. 'acquiring and running existing units') was rejected, but only because 'the mechanism and the resources of the State' did not 'permit it to function forthwith in Industry as widely as may be desirable'. The state's contribution to the increase in national wealth should be by way of 'expanding its present activities wherever it is already operating' and 'concentrating on new units of production in other fields'. This suggested (*a*) that the development of industry was to be largely the responsibility of the government and (*b*) that private enterprise was to be regarded as no more than a

[1] A convenient source for the text of this resolution is, GB, Commerc. & Export Promotion Dept, *India*, by R. Owen (1949–53), app. I.

temporary developmental expedient. The latter suggestion appeared to be confirmed by the use of the somewhat ambiguous term 'meanwhile' in the sentence: 'Meanwhile, private enterprise, properly directed and regulated, has a valuable role to play'. In so far, then, as precise sense can be made of its distinctly *nuancé* opening paragraphs, the first Industrial Policy Resolution was *implicitly* socialistic in outlook: not more so, however, than the various official and unofficial planning documents of 1945–8 which inspired it.[2]

After these preliminaries, it proceeded to the allocation of tasks. The state was to have monopoly of arms, ammunition, atomic energy, and rail transport, and to be empowered, in an emergency, to take over any industry vital for national defence. This could hardly produce violent disagreement from any quarter. More controversial was the allocation to the state of exclusive responsibility for *new* undertakings in coal, mineral oils, iron and steel, shipbuilding, and the manufacture of aircraft and of telecommunications equipment. Reassurance to potentially frustrated private entrepreneurs, however, was provided by the saving clause: 'except where, in the national interest, the State itself finds it necessary to secure the cooperation of private enterprise subject to such control and regulations as the Central Government may prescribe'. Further reassurance, of a kind that seemed very important in 1948, flowed from the promise that, subject to 'the inherent right of the State to acquire any existing industrial undertaking', all private enterprises in these fields would be free to 'develop for a period of ten years', during which they would be 'allowed all facilities for efficient working and reasonable expansion'. At the end of this period, the situation would be reviewed, but should the state, either then or earlier, decide to acquire any unit, compensation would be 'awarded on a fair and equitable basis'. In effect, therefore, these paragraphs said no more than that for the next ten years the state would participate, to an unspecified extent, in the development of these industries, as well as exercising control over the efforts of private developers.

As for the remainder of the industrial field, this would be open to 'individual as well as cooperative' enterprise; but the state would 'progressively participate' and would not 'hesitate to intervene' whenever the progress of private enterprise was unsatisfactory. As examples of state participation, mention was made of certain enterprises on which the central government had already embarked, such as hydro-electricity, irrigation, fertilizers, essential drugs, and oil from coal. There followed a non-exhaustive list of eighteen basic industries for which 'planning and regulation' by the central government was said to be essential in the national interest. In this field, therefore, the state, while not assuming the

[2] See above, pp. 32–44.

rather ambiguous and highly qualified responsibility for *all* new developments that it had assumed for coal, mineral oils, iron and steel, shipbuilding, and the manufacture of telecommunications equipment, was to promote at least *some* new developments; while the private entrepreneur was to be subjected to sporadic intervention and, in the more important industries, to continuous direction. The impression that the capitalist was a dangerous animal to be kept behind bars was somewhat counteracted, towards the end of the resolution, by rather limited promises of assistance. The removal of transport difficulties, the facilitation of the import of essential raw materials, and the imposition of tariffs to prevent unfair foreign competition were specified as governmental responsibilities. Taxation was to be 'reviewed and adjusted' with the doubtfully compatible objects of encouraging saving and productive investment and preventing the 'undue' concentration of wealth. Rather curiously, there was no mention of the financial services to private industry which the Indian government was subsequently to develop on a large scale.

With the section of the resolution dealing with cottage and small-scale industries we shall be concerned later. There remains to be noted the short section on foreign private capital, which is worded with deliberate vagueness. Foreign capitalists are recognized to be useful, but 'it is necessary that the conditions under which they may participate in Indian industry should be carefully regulated in the national interest'. Each individual case 'of participation of foreign capital and management in industry' will be vetted by the government, and provision made that 'as a rule, the major interest in ownership, and effective control, should always be in Indian hands'. Power will be assumed, however, 'to deal with exceptional cases'. Just how wide a door this opened was, like so much else in the resolution, anyone's guess.

By scheduling the industries that were to be included, wholly or partly, in the public sector, the resolution achieved an appearance of precision. In reality, apart from the reservation of four industries (one of them a public utility) to the State, it left most of the issues fairly wide open. The one reasonably firm promise that it made was that existing private industries, *quamdiu se bene gesserint*, were to be exempted from nationalization for a period of at least ten years. This was necessary, as we have seen,[3] to calm the fears of industrialists who were in a state of uncertainty about the prospects that faced them under the new independent government. It was also clear that the public sector would expand—but that had been clear for a long time, as no one imagined that the Tatas and Birlas, rich as they were, could develop a steel industry on the scale required, and no one doubted that the state would have to undertake further infrastructural investments on a massive scale. Moreover, even the industrialists

[3] See above, pp. 48–49.

who had formulated the 'Bombay' plan fully recognized that, in a country as chronically short of capital as India, a private 'free for all' was inconceivable and that therefore controls along the lines vaguely foreshadowed by the resolution and eventually incorporated in the Industries (Development and Regulation) Act of 1951 and the new Companies Act of 1956 were essential. At the level of principle, all this was common ground to the people who had participated in the production of the reports of Congress's NPC and of the various official bodies that had been so active during the last years of imperialist rule. As for the rest of the resolution, it was obviously intended to give some satisfaction to almost everybody. Nehru could regard it as salving his socialist conscience, in so far as it obviously represented the longest step towards the proclamation of socialist objectives that was practicable at a time when he shared power with the 'reactionary' Patel. To the 'leftists' he could present it as a kind of New Economic Policy which accepted private enterprise as no more than a temporary expedient; to the 'rightists' he could suggest that it offered the entrepreneur and investor even more opportunities than they would actually be able to seize. At the same time it gave him a weapon to use against the 'crude' socialists of the Communist and Socialist Parties, who wanted to nationalize everything at once. Every line bears the marks of compromise, and there is plenty of sheer verbiage designed to paper over ideological cracks. Its authors were trying to produce a formula which would evoke maximum agreement, even at the expense of consistency, and were anxious, at a time when very few of the materials for a national economic plan had been assembled, to keep every possible developmental path as open as possible.

But although the room for manoeuvre that it made available was as wide as anyone could reasonably want in the immediate future, it could conceivably become important as a policy guide as soon as real alternatives between public-sector and private-sector development began to present themselves. For its emphasis on the primary responsibility of the state for the development of *new* units in certain industries, however ambiguously worded, could not be completely nullified by interpretation. In the last resort, the spirit of such a policy statement could mean as much as, or more than, its exact text.

However, its influence on the minds of those responsible for formulating the First Plan seems to have been minimal, although they naturally accorded it the formal respect that any government expects its servants to give to an important policy statement. The plan report said that 'in the transformation of the economy' the state would have to play a 'crucial role' and that an economic development capable of 'satisfying the legitimate expectations of the people' would involve 'a progressive widening of the public sector and reorientation of the private sector to the needs of a planned economy'; but it was careful not to suggest that public enterprise possessed any inherent superiority, still less that there could be serious competition for predominance between the two sectors. On the contrary, the planners were of the opinion that 'the productive capital in industry and services' was 'so small compared to the needs of the country' that the sectors could 'well supplement each other and need not necessarily expand at the expense of the one or the other'. Moreover, as private enterprise was to be given a public purpose and as the 'points of interaction' between the two sectors were 'multiplying rapidly', it was no longer realistic to regard them as 'anything like two separate entities'; they were 'parts of a single organism'.[4] This carried with it the strong suggestion that the public-private controversy was becoming obsolete and irrelevant and that therefore the resolution's attempt to find a *modus vivendi* between them on the basis of a division of territory was not particularly helpful. Later, the planners unmistakably indicated that, in deciding particular cases, they proposed to apply strictly economic criteria, unmodified by considerations of ideology. 'The scope and need for development', they wrote, 'are so great that it is best for the public sector to develop those industries in which private enterprise is unable or unwilling to put up the resources required and run the risks involved, leaving the rest of the field free for private enterprise.'[5] In saying this they were influenced, no doubt, by their awareness of the inexperience of the state in matters of industrial management and by their well-founded belief that the methods of successfully running a publicly owned industry in Indian conditions had yet to be discovered. To help to rectify these deficiencies—which would be serious enough even if the state confined itself to the very minimum of entrepreneurship demanded by the situation—they followed A. D. Gorwala in recommending 'the early establishment of a single central board which will concern itself with the larger problems of policy, management and organisation for the industrial undertakings of the Central Government'.[6]

What interested them far more than the public-private balance was the control of enterprises in the private sector. The Industrial Policy Resolution, as we have seen, had forecast legislation for this purpose. It had been placed on the statute book in 1951, in the shape of the much-discussed Industries (Development and Regulation) Act.[7] This measure applied to 37 scheduled industries. Every existing undertaking covered by the schedule had to register itself with the government, and no new undertaking could be established or existing undertaking substantially extended except under licence. All scheduled industries, new or old, were liable to become subject to a 'full and complete' investigation if the government

[4] *FYP(1)*, pp. 31–34. [5] Ibid. p. 422. [6] Ibid. p. 127.
[7] Act No. 65 of 1951 (as modified up to 1 June 1957).

had cause to believe (*a*) that there had been or was likely to be 'a substantial fall in the volume of production' or a 'marked deterioration in the quality' of the articles manufactured, or a rise in their price, where there appeared to be no justification for such fall, deterioration, or rise; (*b*) that such an investigation was necessary 'for the purpose of conserving any resources of national importance'; or (*c*) that the undertaking was being managed 'in a manner highly detrimental . . . to the public interest'. At the conclusion of the investigation, the government was empowered to issue directions for any or all of the following purposes:

(*a*) regulating the production of any article or class of articles . . . and fixing the standards of production;
(*b*) requiring the industrial undertaking or undertakings to take such steps as the Central Government may consider necessary to stimulate the development of the industry . . . .;
(*c*) prohibiting the industrial undertaking or undertakings from resorting to any act or practice which might reduce its . . . production, capacity or economic value;
(*d*) controlling the prices, or regulating the distribution of any article or class of articles which have been the subject matter of investigation.

In the event of the undertaking's failure to comply with any such direction, the government might take over its management, either directly or through an appointed managing agent (Chs. III & IIIA).

In a further chapter (IIIB), the government gave itself powers to publish orders 'for securing equitable distribution and availability at fair prices of any article or class of articles relatable to any scheduled industry'. Such orders might, for instance, control prices, regulate the terms of sale, compel the disposal of stocks, and regulate or prohibit 'any class of commercial transaction' considered 'detrimental to the public interest'. To enable it to exercise these powers, the government was authorized to enter and inspect premises, to order the production of books and documents, and to examine persons.

Besides equipping the government with this formidable-looking battery, the Act also contained provisions intended to enable the scheduled industries to improve their own efficiency (Ch. II). By order, a Development Council could be established for any industry or group of industries, and required to perform a number of scheduled functions (Ch. II, sch. 2). These included production-targeting, the setting of efficiency norms, the improvement of the utilization of installed capacity, the improvement of marketing arrangements, and the promotion of standardization, training, research, and productivity. Membership of the Council was to consist of representatives of employers and employed, together with persons having special knowledge of the industry and persons appointed to speak on behalf of consumers. A cess might be levied by the government on the value of the goods manufactured by the industry and handed over to the Development Council to cover certain items of expenditure, such as those on research, training, and improvements in design and quality.

By the time of the publication of the First Plan, very little experience of the working of this Act had been accumulated; but it had already become clear that most of the regulatory provisions were intended as 'last resort' powers, to be used only when persuasion had failed. Their existence, the government hoped, would induce private enterprise to improve its standards and to behave co-operatively; their frequent use would clearly be self-defeating. We may conveniently note here that, in fact, the Indian government has had recourse to them only on rare occasions. As for the Development Councils, their effectiveness would depend almost entirely on the attitudes of the owners of the industries for which they were constituted; and subsequent experience has indeed proved that there is little a Council can accomplish if its employer members are hostile or lukewarm.[8] The most important part of the Act, therefore, was that which provided for industrial licensing. Through this device the government could do much to influence the pattern of development in the private industrial sector. And so it has proved, even though, for reasons we have already explained,[9] licensing was of little practical importance until the period of the Second Five-Year Plan, when resources for both the public and the private sector became extremely scarce.

The planners, in their chapter on 'Industrial Development and Policy',[10] summarized the provisions of the Act and proceeded to suggest how the licensing powers that it gave the government should be used and what tasks should be taken up by the Development Councils, which were to be established, initially, for seven industries, viz. heavy chemicals, fertilizers, paper, leather, bicycles, glass and ceramics, and internal combustion engines. Taking into account 'the immediate objectives in view, the resources available and the broad framework of policy in regard to the operation of the public and private sectors', they suggested the following general order of priorities in the industrial field:

(1) fuller utilization of existing capacity in producer goods industries like jute and plywood and consumer goods industries like cotton textiles, sugar, soap, vanaspati, paints and varnishes;
(2) expansion of capacity in capital and producer goods industries like iron and steel, aluminium, cement, fertilizers, heavy chemicals, machine tools, etc.;
(3) completion of industrial units on which a part of the capital expenditure has already been incurred, and
(4) establishment of new plants which would lend strength to the industrial

[8] See below, pp. 484–5. [9] See above, pp. 120–1. [10] *FYP*(*1*), ch. 29.

structure by rectifying as far as resources permit the existing lacunae and drawbacks, e.g. manufacture of sulphur from gypsum, chemical pulp from rayon, etc.

This list was accompanied by specific expansion programmes for forty-two industries in the private sector, which indicated actual rated capacity and production in 1950–1, projected rated capacity and production in 1955–6, and projected capital investment between 1951 and 1956. These, of course, were indicative rather than operative, but, as the Commission said, they had been worked out 'in close consultation with representatives of the industries concerned and of the Central Ministries as also with independent experts and technicians'. They therefore provided rather more than a general guide to the licensing authorities, upon whose procedures the Commission relied to ensure 'an impartial consideration of all issues involved in a substantial expansion of existing units or establishment of new ones'. But as a warning to industrialists, actual or potential, who might be misled into thinking that any undertaking within the forty-two categories and within the investment limits would be automatically approved, the Commission said that 'each concrete proposition for investment that comes up raises a variety of considerations and is likely to secure high priority on certain grounds and relatively low priority on other grounds so that the problem is always to decide as to the relative weights to be attached to various considerations.'

Now that industrial licensing had been added to the already existing control of capital issues, the Commission considered that it would be possible to regulate, in accordance with the priorities laid down, 'the investment of available capital whether it flows through new capital issues or is to be found out of reserve funds'. Regulation, however, was not enough; for while it could prevent the 'undesirable or less desirable' use of resources, it could not of itself 'ensure the flow of capital into more preferred lines'. For this purpose a 'system of specific incentives might become necessary'.

For instance, in the case of projects involving heavy capital investment and the use of new techniques, it might be desirable to extend, after preliminary examination by the Tariff Commission, an advance assurance of protection. For the development of industries consuming minerals or of industries based on forest produce, long-term leases might be granted. Certain new industries might require the supply of power at concessional rates and others might need special Government assistance for securing the technical know-how through international organizations. Capital goods and certain raw materials might be allowed to be imported duty free or at concessional rates. In other words, there are various fiscal and other incentives which can be given by the Government for promoting industrial development along particular lines and these have to be used with judgement according to the requirements of each case.

Once again, it was a matter of following the course of events. All these incentives and many others have been used extensively during the three Five-Year Plans. Indeed, one of the others, low-cost loan finance, was already being organized, on a modest scale, by the newly-created State Industrial Finance Corporations,[11] which were expected to provide Rs20 crores of the Rs707 crores needed by both public and private industry during the First Plan.

It is not perhaps very useful to ask whether the measures taken to implement the First Five-Year Plan were in or out of line with the Industrial Policy Resolution—for the resolution, as we have seen, was drawn up in terms that permitted the government to do almost anything that seemed reasonable. Occasionally the Communists and other leftists, ever fearful that the private sector would be shown excessive favour, quoted it selectively in order to embarrass the government, but the latter rarely had much difficulty in putting up a good case, at least to the extent of proving the consistency of its actions with the resolution's prescriptions. What no one specifically argued, but many must have thought, was that the resolution was largely irrelevant to India's economic needs. The balance between public and private enterprise was at this stage necessarily determined by what we have termed 'objective' factors, in so far as it would have been the height of foolishness for the state, with its severely limited physical and financial resources, either to nationalize existing enterprises or to initiate new enterprises in fields where private capital was willing and able to take the strain. As for controls over the private sector, these had become, with the passage of the Industries (Development and Regulation) Act, fully adequate for all foreseeable purposes, and the immediate need was not so much for control as for encouragement. Only in respect of its attitude towards foreign private capital could the government be accused of violating or misinterpreting the resolution, and it was in this field that it came up against the most severe criticism from the leftists, who were always ready to equate foreign investment in the Indian economy with neo-imperialism.

The resolution's treatment of the subject was, as we have seen, extremely cautious. While recognizing the 'value' of 'the participation of foreign capital and enterprise', it tended to suggest that those who supped with this particular devil should use a very long spoon, and promised legislation to prevent the foreign capitalist from exploiting India's economic weakness. Such legislation, however, was not introduced, because the government felt that the existing controls over capital issues, foreign exchange, and imports already provided it with sufficient instruments of policy. Moreover, as the United Kingdom Senior Trade Commissioner put it, 'practical experience soon showed' that the resolution's 'restrictive tone . . .

[11] See below, pp. 478–9.

was out of line with the availability of external capital for investment'.[12] Accordingly, spokesmen for the government made a series of statements offering the foreign investor terms as liberal as he could reasonably expect of a newly independent state. The first and most important of these was made by Nehru himself in Parliament on 6 April 1949.[13] The resolution's stress, he said, 'on the need to regulate, in the national interest, the scope and manner of foreign capital arose from past association of foreign capital and control with foreign domination of the economy of the country'; but circumstances had changed, and the new emphasis should be on 'the utilisation of foreign capital in a manner most advantageous to the country'. Indian capital *needed* to be supplemented by foreign capital, 'not only because our national savings will not be enough for the rapid development of the country on the scale we wish but also because in many cases scientific, technical and industrial knowledge and capital equipment can best be secured along with foreign capital'. To attract such capital, the Prime Minister gave the following assurances: (*a*) that existing foreign interests would not be subjected to any conditions which were not applicable to similar Indian interests, and that the government would frame its policy 'so as to enable further foreign capital to be invested in India' on 'mutually advantageous' terms and conditions; (*b*) that, subject to foreign exchange considerations, existing facilities for remittance of profits would be continued and no restrictions placed on the withdrawal of foreign capital investments; (*c*) that, in the event of the compulsory acquisition of a foreign enterprise, compensation on a 'fair and equitable basis' would be paid. He then 'interpreted' in the following manner the resolution's insistence that 'as a rule, the major interest in ownership, and effective control, should always be in Indian hands': 'Obviously there can be no hard and fast rule in this matter. Government will not object to foreign capital having control of a concern for a limited period, if it is found to be in the national interest, and each individual case will be dealt with on its own merits.' In this way, without actually saying that the terms of the resolution were unrealistic, he contrived to suggest that what it had treated as 'exceptional' was likely to become quite common.

Later statements on the same subject by the Finance Minister, C. D. Deshmukh, were even more categorical. Addressing the Annual General Meeting of the Indian Merchants' Chamber on 8 April 1952,[14] he stated that it was in India's interest to attract as much private capital as possible, to allow foreign owned industries to 'flourish without impediments' and to expand, so long as all this took place 'within the four corners of the general policy laid down by the Government' and did not involve 'any conditions

[12] GB, *India*, p. 114.
[13] Constit. Assembly (Legislation) Deb., pt 2, iv, 2385–6, reproduced GB, *India*, app. II.
[14] Ibid. p. 114.

injurious to the economic development of the country or its established industries'. A few months later, facing his leftist critics in Parliament, he said:

> I cannot see what an underdeveloped country can do when its own resources are limited without such foreign assistance as that country can receive without detriment to its self-respect and dignity . . . . If once we decide that we shall receive foreign assistance . . . whether it is State assistance or a loan from the International Bank, or *private equity capital*, then we should create conditions in which that flow of assistance will continue.[15]

The only outright attack on this policy came, as was to be expected, from the Communists and the Socialists, who were particularly incensed by the 'concessions' made by the government to the 'oil imperialists', Burmah-Shell and Standard Vacuum, to induce them to establish refineries at Trombay. (Mineral oils, it will be remembered, were among those industries whose expansion was reserved, with qualifications, to the state.) But there was also some uneasiness on the right, among industrialists who feared that Indian-based foreign enterprises, if allowed to expand freely, might drive them out of business. These were expressed, for instance, by a well-known 'business-controlled' newspaper, which demanded that

(i) Foreign capital should be confined to specified industries requiring a high degree of technical skill.
(ii) Foreign capital should not be admitted into spheres in which Indian-owned industries had made reasonable progress.
(iii) A watch should be kept on the expansion of non-Indian enterprises where expansion is carried out by methods (such as the raising of loans) which do not automatically attract inspection and control.
(iv) Non-official Indian representatives should be associated with the screening of foreign investments.[16]

In general, the government succeeded in steering a middle, if sometimes rather erratic, course between left and right. Reporting in 1952, the U.K.'s Senior Trade Commissioner considered that experience of actual cases had indicated that it was applying the following criteria 'when considering whether or not a new enterprise involving external investment should be admitted':

(i) The concern must not be an exclusively financial, commercial or trading enterprise.
(ii) There must be a genuine programme of manufacture.
(iii) The investment must be in a field where indigenous investment is inadequate or technical 'know-how' not available.

[15] LSD, pt 2, ii, 3200.
[16] GB, *India*, p. 115. I have not been able to identify the source of this quotation.

(iv) The investment will help to save foreign exchange by reducing imports or increasing exports.
(v) The project will increase productivity.
(vi) Adequate provision must be made for the training of Indian personnel for senior technical and administrative posts.

These general criteria, he added, had to be 'interpreted in the light of prevailing economic conditions and the climate of public opinion with special reference to the claims of local vested interests'.[17] Broadly speaking, and with due emphasis on this saving clause, it may be said that the government has at least attempted to apply criteria of this kind throughout the period of the three Five-Year Plans. As, however, Owen was writing in the pre-plan period, it must obviously be added that conformity with plan priorities is a seventh criterion, and a very important one.

In this field, the planners were again content to see how things worked out. The section on 'Foreign Capital' in the First Plan report (pp. 437–8) was surprisingly short, although in emphasizing the 'highest importance' of giving the foreign investor suitable conditions it went slightly beyond any previous pronouncements. On priorities it contented itself with the following general statement, which almost exactly reproduced the corresponding passage in the Draft Outline:

> In view of the fact that the investment of foreign capital necessitates the utilisation of indigenous resources and also that the best use of foreign capital is as a catalytic agent for drawing forth larger resources for domestic investment, it is desirable that such investment should be channelled into fields of high priority. The broad principle to be followed is that foreign investment should be permitted in spheres where new lines of production are to be developed or where special types of experience and technical skill are required or where the volume of production is small in relation to demand and there is no reasonable expectation that the indigenous industry can expand at a sufficiently rapid pace.

Again as in the Draft Outline, it gave its blessing to the 'system of joint enterprises by which foreign concerns establish new industries in collaboration with Indian industrialists', as 'suitable for the employment of equity capital'. As we shall see, the joint enterprise has become one of the most important devices for attracting both foreign capital and foreign skills.

(iii)

By the early 1950s, therefore, a series of ideas had crystallized about the balance between the public and private sectors, about the role of foreign capital, and about the methods of controlling and encouraging the

[17] Ibid. p. 115.

activities of private enterprise, both indigenous and foreign, and of relating them to plan priorities. At the end of 1954 a new element entered the situation, with the announcement that India was to have a 'socialist pattern'. This meant—or so it might be presumed—that ideological considerations were to be given greater emphasis. Many highly-placed Congressmen were lukewarm about 'socialism', but of Nehru's devotion to it there could be no doubt—and Nehru, since the death of Patel, had acquired a formidable ascendancy. Moreover, his chosen economic adviser, Mahalanobis, who dominated the early and vital stages of preparing the Second Plan, was an even more unqualified socialist than Nehru himself. The Second Plan, therefore, was to be the first of the overtly socialist plans, and consequently the whole balance and relationship between the public and private sectors would have to be looked at again. Oddly enough, this was not done in a systematic way until the process of preparing the Second Plan was almost complete; for the Second Industrial Policy Resolution,[18] which was to replace the first, was not published until 30 April 1956. It must be assumed, nevertheless, that the planners had actually been working to a policy not substantially different from the one that it embodied.

The resolution began by justifying its 'fresh statement of industrial policy' by reference to the principles laid down in the constitution, the adoption of socialist objectives, and the experience gained during the previous eight years. There followed a rather confused paragraph which suggested that the need to develop heavy industries, to improve living standards and working conditions, to reduce disparities of income and wealth and to 'prevent private monopolies and the concentration of economic power . . . in the hands of a small number of individuals' involved the assumption by the state of 'a predominant and direct responsibility for setting up new industrial undertakings and for developing transport facilities'. Simultaneously, however, the private sector would 'have the opportunity to develop and expand' and the principle of co-operation would be 'applied wherever possible and a steadily increasing proportion of the activities of the private sector developed along cooperative lines'. Then, bringing together in one broad sweep a variety of ideological and practical considerations, the resolution made the following statement of general principle:

> The adoption of the socialist pattern of society as the national objective, as well as the need for planned and rapid development, require that all industries of basic and strategic importance, or in the nature of public utility services, should be in the public sector. Other industries which are essential and require investment on a scale which only the State, in present circumstances, could

[18] Reproduced in *FYP(2)*, pp. 43–50.

provide, have also to be in the public sector. The State has therefore to assume direct responsibility for the future development of industries over a wide area.

There were, nevertheless, 'limiting factors' which required that the state should define its immediate industrial responsibilities with some care and precision. Accordingly, the government and the Commission had decided to classify industries into three categories, 'having regard to the part which the State would play in each of them'.

The first category consisted of industries whose future development would be the state's 'exclusive responsibility'. These were scheduled as:

1. Arms and ammunition and allied items of defence equipment.
2. Atomic energy.
3. Iron and steel.
4. Heavy castings and forgings of iron and steel.
5. Heavy plant and machinery required for iron and steel production, for mining, for machine tool manufacture, and for such other basic industries as may be specified by the central government.
6. Heavy electrical plant including large hydraulic and steam turbines.
7. Coal and lignite.
8. Mineral oils.
9. Mining of iron ore, manganese ore, chrome ore, gypsum, sulphur, gold and diamonds.
10. Mining and processing of copper, lead, zinc, tin, molybdenum, and wolfram.
11. Minerals specified in the Schedule to the Atomic Energy (Control of Production and Use) Order, 1953.
12. Aircraft.
13. Air transport.
14. Railway transport.
15. Shipbuilding.
16. Telephones and telephone cables, telegraph and wireless apparatus (excluding radio receiving sets).
17. Generation and distribution of electricity.

Of these, railways and air transport, arms and ammunition, and atomic energy were to be governmental monopolies. (Air transport, it will be noted, was the only addition to the monopolies in the 1948 list.) As for the remainder, all *new* units would be established by the state, except where their establishment by private enterprise had already been approved. This did not preclude 'the expansion of the existing privately owned units, or the possibility of the State securing the cooperation of private enterprise in the establishment of new units when the national interests so require'. Whenever such co-operation with private enterprise was required, the state would ensure, 'either through majority participation in the capital or otherwise', that it had the requisite powers of control.

The second category consisted of industries in which the state would 'increasingly establish new undertakings', without denying private enterprise its opportunities, 'either on its own or with State participation'. These were scheduled as:

1. All other minerals except 'minor minerals' as defined by Section 3 of the Minerals Concession Rules, 1949.
2. Aluminium and other non-ferrous metals not included in Schedule 'A'.
3. Machine tools.
4. Ferro-alloys and tool steels.
5. Basic intermediate products required by the chemical industries such as the manufacture of drugs, dyestuffs, and plastics.
6. Antibiotics and other essential drugs.
7. Fertilizers.
8. Synthetic rubber.
9. Carbonization of coal.
10. Chemical pulp.
11. Road transport.
12. Sea transport.

The third category embraced all the remaining industries, whose development would be undertaken 'ordinarily through the initiative and enterprise of the private sector'. Even in this category it would be 'open to the State to start any industry'. The state's main role, however, would be to 'facilitate and encourage' the development of these industries, by the provision of services, the adoption of appropriate fiscal measures, and the granting, either directly or by way of assistance to the necessary institutions, of financial aid. Where, in this category, private and public units existed side by side, the former were promised 'fair and non-discriminatory treatment'. Naturally, they would have to fit into the 'framework of the social and economic policy of the State' and remain subject to the Industries (Development and Regulation) Act and other relevant legislation, but in general would be permitted 'to develop with as much freedom as possible'.

After stressing the importance of cottage, village, and small-scale industries (a subject we shall deal with later in this chapter) and of balanced regional development (which we have dealt with in Chapter IX), the resolution made brief mention of industrial training, recommended joint consultation as a means of maintaining industrial peace, and emphasized the need to run public enterprises along 'business' lines and to use them, in appropriate cases, 'to augment the revenues of the State and provide resources for further development in fresh fields'. On the role of foreign capital, it contented itself with a reference to the Prime Minister's statement of 6 April 1949, as an expression of continuing government policy.

Did this new resolution add anything of significance to old one, and did it have any perceptible effect on the industrial policies pursued by the government of India? Certainly, there was a change of emphasis, in so far as the responsibilities of the state were more heavily stressed. But the contrast between the two documents in this respect is not as great as a superficial reading of them might suggest. Both foreshadowed increased state participation, and both indicated that there were limits to what the state could actually do. Both, moreover, implied that private enterprise was to be regarded as an essentially temporary means of achieving national objectives. Even the considerably lengthened list of industries for whose development, as far as *new* units were concerned, the state was to assume exclusive responsibility, is not quite as significant as it appears to be. The first resolution had said that the state would 'progressively participate' in the field normally open to private enterprise; the second indicated that there was room for private entrepreneurs in the field where it had reserved new developments for itself. How was the establishment of new units to be distinguished from the expansion of old ones? What forms of co-operation with private enterprise were envisaged? What were to be the means, *other* than majority capital participation, by which the state proposed to exercise control over the various joint enterprises which were so vaguely foreshadowed? For all its socialist language, the second resolution seemed to leave the public-versus-private issue almost as open as the first one had left it. A possibly significant contrast might be found in the second resolution's emphasis on equality and on the need to prevent the development of private monopolies; but equality was also mentioned in the first resolution, while the prevention of 'the concentration of wealth and means of production to the common detriment', far from being an original idea produced by the framers of the second resolution, was one of the Directive Principles of the constitution. The only contrast which would appear to be of practical importance lies in the formulation of attitudes towards private enterprise. Whereas the first resolution laid stress on its control and regulation, the second emphasized its encouragement—and to this extent might even be regarded as *less* socialist than the first. But what it gave with one hand it promptly took away with the other: for the first resolution's ten-year guarantee against nationalization was not repeated.

One may reasonably ask, therefore, why the Indian government had come to the conclusion that a new resolution was necessary, particularly in view of the fact that, as we have seen,[19] Nehru himself appeared content with the 1948 formulation of policy even after the 'socialist pattern' had been accepted. It did not, after all, give any new guarantees that the private sector might require, or suggest that capitalism was either more or less favourably regarded than it had been previously. Nor did it

[19] See above, p. 124 n. 3.

indicate any fundamentally new orientation of policy, at least over the coming five years; for the general shape of the Second Five-Year Plan had already been decided on. If it was intended as a longer-term statement of intention, it could hardly be taken seriously; for no one could foresee what would be the 'ideal' balance between the public and private sectors in the Third or Fourth Plans, or beyond. One might easily conclude, therefore, that, like the resolution that it superseded, it was just a highly-publicized policy statement which, by its very vagueness and generality, could mean all things to all men and thus help to maintain national unity.

Such a conclusion, however, would be mistaken; for there is evidence that the resolution was *intended* to be operative and that its broad prescriptions were taken seriously. Differences of interpretation there could obviously be, and almost every decision which was designed to give expression to its principles inevitably became controversial. No one was entirely satisfied with it: the business community, for instance, was as critical of its radicalism as the Socialists were of its moderation. But there was no doubt about the kind of guidance it gave to those who had to choose, in a particular field, between public and private development. Its exact wording was less important than its 'socialist' context. Although the government could claim that it licensed an 'empirical' stance in the public-private controversy, the paragraphs that could be made to bear this interpretation had to be read in the light of officially-adopted 'socialist' objectives.

This point was emphasized by the Commission when it proclaimed that the pursuit of socialism meant that 'the basic criterion for determining the lines of advance must not be private profit but social gain, and that the pattern of development and the structure of socio-economic relations should be planned so that they result not only in appreciable increases in national income and employment but also in greater equality in incomes and wealth'.[20] The argument for a large and eventually predominant public sector was, in fact, not merely that it offered a means of more rapid economic growth, but that it helped to create the type of social order towards which the ruling élite had said India ought to be moving. The assumption was that whereas public enterprise almost automatically contributed towards its attainment, private enterprise was at least potentially hostile to it and would therefore have to offer special justification for its own existence. 'Private enterprise, free pricing, private management', wrote the Commission, 'are all devices to further what are truly social ends; they can be justified in terms of social results.'

Such were the views of those who formulated both the Second and Third Plans. Did this *parti pris* necessarily involve the making of decisions in which economic advantage was outweighed by long-term social

[20] *FYP*(*2*), ch. 2.

purpose? This question was never quite honestly faced. Within the framework of overall policy, decisions so weighted were not necessarily irrational, but their rationality was relative to a time-scale, never drawn up, over which the social preferences were to operate. It could be argued, for instance, that the government's own social objectives might be best served by seizing on whatever method of economic growth lay most readily to hand, irrespective of whether it strengthened the public sector or the private sector and regardless of its immediate effects on the distribution of wealth and income. The important thing was to get the economy moving forward, at a pace which made possible significant annual increases in average per capita incomes; the question of how the results should be distributed could be left until there was something substantial to distribute, and that of who should own the assets until proprietorship became as important as productivity. At times, the government appeared to accept this case; at others, fearful lest it should be accused of insufficient ideological fervour, to reject it. This ambivalence is writ large in the plan reports themselves, where potentially contradictory objectives, although recognized and even analysed, rarely become subjected to a clearly-motivated choice. A frequent result is that the worst of motives tend to be attributed to the government, whichever way its decision goes. When it chooses the public sector, it is displaying a stupid preference for unimaginative bureaucracy; when it chooses the private, it is currying favour with the 'profit-makers', probably to induce them to increase their contributions to Congress funds.

Thus the 'socialist pattern', although undoubtedly a source of political support, is also one of confusion. It is in connexion with the pattern's centrally-placed 'egalitarian' component that misunderstanding is particularly common. The noble ideal of equality has not been effectively promoted by the extension of the public sector, and one may reasonably doubt whether any conceivable method of economic growth is compatible, in the immediate future, with a substantial equalization of incomes and living conditions. The government, therefore, constantly incurs the danger of disillusioning its own supporters—many of whom regard 'equality' as an immediate objective which the rapid expansion of public enterprise will bring substantially nearer—as well as of forfeiting the support of those whose enthusiasm for equality is tempered by the fact that they have something to lose by its introduction, and whose recognition of the virtues of public enterprise is tinged with scepticism.

(iv)

The tension between ideology and empiricism which affects decision-making when the public-versus-private issue is on the agenda may be readily illustrated. One example of the triumph of ideology is to be found in the Second Five-Year Plan report itself.[21] After stating that of all mineral extractive industries coal must claim 'first attention', the Commission indicated that production would have to be pushed up from 38 million tons in 1955 to about 60 million tons by the end of the Second Plan. Of current production, the bulk was in the private sector, and the question was therefore whether to rely mainly on a well-established collection of private enterprises to effect the necessary increase, or to concentrate on expanding the comparatively embryonic state-owned collieries. Economic rationality demanded that the Commission should have (*a*) apportioned, in relation to respective capacities, the respective contributions of the public and private sectors to the recorded increase in production from 32·31 tons in 1950 to 38·22 tons in 1955; (*b*) compared the efficiency, actual and prospective, of public and private sector undertakings; and (*c*) divided responsibility between the two sectors on the basis of the estimated yields of the investment projects put up by each. There is no evidence in the plan report, however, that the Commission did any such thing. Instead, it referred to the Industrial Policy Resolution of 1948, and said that the government had decided that the policy, there laid down, 'of retaining all new undertakings in coal in the public sector should be more strictly followed and that the additional coal production required to meet the increased demand during the second plan should be raised to the maximum extent possible in the public sector'. Accordingly, a tentative decision had been made 'that of the additional production of 22 million tons envisaged by 1960–1, 12 million tons should come from collieries in the public sector, either already existing or to be newly opened, and that the balance should be raised by the private sector from their existing workings and immediately contiguous areas'. As the existing *total* production of the public sector was no more than 4·5 million tons, this was quite a tall order. It seems very probable, therefore, that a case could have been made for giving the private sector a larger share, had not the Industrial Policy Resolution and the 'socialist pattern' stood in the way. Certainly, the confining of the private coal undertakings to 'their existing workings and immediately contiguous areas' failed to make much economic sense, whatever political merits it may have had.

In the event, coal production in the Second Plan reached a figure of 54·62 million tons, over 5 million tons short of target. Economic rationality then demanded that the Commission should carefully apportion the blame for this shortfall between the two sectors. This, however, it failed to do, at least publicly. There are some figures in the last of the Second Plan *Progress Reports*[22] which indicate that production in the public sector had risen from 4·5 million tons in 1955 to 6·7 million tons in 1959,

[21] Ch. 18: 'Development of Mineral Resources'.
[22] Available to the author only in mimeo. version.

while that in the private sector had risen from some 33·5 to 40·3 million tons; but in the Third Plan report[23] only total and field-wise production figures are given. All the reader can gather is that, as 'the expansion of production from existing workings . . . did not present any serious difficulty', the main cause of the shortfall was to be found in the new collieries, where 'the establishment of additional production . . . made the task of the public sector a formidable one'. The nature of its difficulties were thus summarized:

> New mines had to be established in practically virgin areas. Legislation had to be passed to enable the public sector to acquire new areas; and these had to be prospected in detail in order to prove the reserves and select the blocks to be developed. In addition the public sector had to build up an organisation practically from nothing and there was a serious shortage of experienced technical personnel fitted to hold supervisory posts. This, combined with initial difficulties in securing foreign exchange for the programme, resulted in rather slow progress during the early years of the Plan.

Clearly, many of these difficulties would also have slowed up the development of new coalfields by the private sector. But the references to building up an organization 'practically from nothing' and to the 'serious shortage of experienced technical personnel' are at least thought-provoking. Could the private sector, by developing its existing organization and expanding its existing personnel, have brought these coalfields into production more rapidly and more economically? This is a possibility that neither the government nor the Commission appears to have seriously considered.

Nor did such dangerous thoughts influence the formulation of coal production targets for the Third Plan. According to the Commission, three factors were borne in mind, viz. (1) the need to 'ensure that the necessary quantities of coking and blendable coals are made available to the steel plants and merchant cokeries and of superior grades of non-coking coal to the railways and other industries'; (2) the capacity of the private sector to expand production from their existing mines and areas near-by; and (3) government's policy which reserves to the public sector the establishment of new mines. As the needed additional production was calculated to be 37 million tons, and as the Working Group on Mineral Resources assessed the potential contribution of private companies at 16·83 million tons, the share of the public sector was put at 20 million tons. By the time of the *Mid-Term Appraisal* (November 1963), however, the public sector (National Coal Development Corporation and Singareni) had increased its production by little more than 1 million tons, from 10·63 million in 1960–1 to 11·66 in 1962–3, while the private sector had increased its production by 7·29 million, from 44·88 million to 52·17 million. This indicated, as the Commission said, that the private

[23] *FYP(3)*, ch. 17: 'Minerals and Oil'.

sector would be able to fulfil its Third Plan target of 61·5 million; it also indicated—as the Commission did not say—that the public sector's 'likely achievement', 28·14 million, was very *un*likely, even though it fell more than 8 million tons short of the original Third Plan target.[24] These figures provided the background and the explanation of Minister Malaviya's statement: 'We want coal and we badly want coal. Therefore whosoever produces it is most welcome to do it'.[25] Such a statement is particularly significant, coming as it did from one of the most left-wing members of Nehru's Cabinet, who was simultaneously opposing the expansion of the private oil refineries.

The oil industry provides another, if slightly different, example of the impact of the Industrial Policy Resolutions and the 'socialist pattern' on a programme of development. In the first resolution oil was not specifically mentioned, although presumably included among the minerals scheduled for 'Central regulation and control'. During the First Plan, development was entirely in the private sector. New refining units were established at Trombay by Burmah-Shell and Standard Vacuum and at Vishakapatnam by Caltex, bringing total capacity up to an annual 4·3 million tons by 1957. Prospection and production were in the hands of the Assam Oil Company (a subsidiary of Burmah-Shell), which made strikes in the Nahorkatiya and Moran areas. By the Industrial Policy Resolution of 1956, however, oil became a 'Schedule A' industry, i.e. one whose future development was reserved, with the various qualifications already noted, to the state. Accordingly, the Commission, in its Second Plan report, announced that proposals for a joint exploration of the Assam area by the government in partnership with the Assam Oil Company were 'under consideration', the company having been granted prospecting licences 'over certain areas adjacent to Nahorkatiya where oil was struck in 1953' in return for agreeing to government participation. In addition, a separate Directorate of Oil and Natural Gas had been set up in the Ministry of Natural Resources and Scientific Research to undertake 'intensive exploration' on the government's behalf and plans were in hand for the training of the necessary personnel. As for refining, the Commission pointed out that the three private sector units did not provide for the production of lubricating oils and petroleum coke, which were of 'considerable importance to the industrial economy', and said that this 'lacuna in the structure of the mineral oil industry' would have to be filled.[26]

During the Second Plan, therefore, state participation in the oil industry was steadily extended. A joint company, Oil India, in which the government's share, originally one-third, was subsequently raised to one-half, undertook the exploitation of the resources of the Nahorkatiya

[24] *MTA*, pp. 134–5. [25] Quoted from *EE*, 26 Apr.1963. [26] *FYP*(*2*), pp. 376, 385, 405.

oilfield. To process the crude oil from this source, the construction of two new public sector refineries, at Gauhati in Assam and at Barauni in Bihar, was begun. In the West Bengal basin the government enlisted the services of the Standard Vacuum Oil Company, to whose expenditure it contributed one-fourth, while a considerable programme of geological survey, geophysical investigation, and exploratory drilling was undertaken by the Oil and Natural Gas Commission in Punjab, Cambay, and the Brahmaputra valley. For the distribution and marketing of oil products, a government agency named the Indian Oil Company was established in 1959.

The Third Plan envisaged an intensification of all these efforts, involving an increase in total quinquennial expenditure from Rs26 to Rs115 crores. For exploration and production, it was announced that the government had invited the participation of foreign firms, 'subject to mutually acceptable terms', presumably similar to those already negotiated with the Burmah Oil Company. Additions to refining capacity however, were visualized to be 'entirely in the public sector', with the possible exception of a plant for the manufacture of 'high viscosity index lubricating oil products', which might be a joint venture. Pipelines costing Rs37 crores were also to be constructed, owned, and operated by the government.

In this case, the influence of the 'socialist pattern' is not quite so obvious. The second Industrial Policy Resolution certainly gave responsibility to the state, but this responsibility was one that obviously could not be discharged without enlisting the services of foreign private enterprise, which was not prepared to collaborate unless it put up a portion of the capital and enjoyed a share of the profits. The alternative, therefore, was either to develop the country's oil resources comparatively quickly by methods which let in the 'oil imperialists', or to develop them comparatively slowly with the exclusive aid of indigenous finance and talent. Not unnaturally, the government chose the first course, in spite of the criticism which it evoked from the left wing. But whether the public-private 'mix' which it selected was deflected from the economically optimum by 'socialist' considerations is a question which still needs to be answered. Evidence that this was so is, in fact, fairly strong. It can be argued, for instance, that the government's insistence first on setting up a joint enterprise in Assam, and then on altering the terms of participation, 'hindered the expeditious exploitation of the Nahorkatiya reserves'. It can also be argued that the expansion of refining capacity has been held back by the government's refusal to permit foreign companies to install new units at existing sites.[27] This much, indeed, was almost admitted by the minister in charge of oil, Malaviya, who led the opposition in the Cabinet to the Burmah-Shell and Esso expansion proposals. One of his

[27] *EE*, ann. no. 1964, 27 Dec. 1963.

arguments was that the extra capacity would be used to extend the distribution of privately-owned oil outside the existing zones reserved to the private oil refineries.[28] In these new areas, he said, Burmah-Shell and Esso would be 'in a better position to distribute than the state-owned Indian Oil Company', which would 'take a few years to put up healthy competition against more experienced foreign oil distributors'. Obsessed as he was by the 'socialist pattern', it did not seem to occur to him that, if this were so, India's scarce capital resources could probably be used, at least in the immediate future, for better purposes than for oil refining. Nor was he in any way impressed by the point that leaving the job to the foreign companies would help to conserve foreign exchange. As, of course, the Indian Oil Company had *already* established refining capacity, he appeared to be on strong ground when he alleged that the further expansion of the private sector would be 'suicidal for our Koyali refinery, for our Barauni refinery'; but this by-passed the question whether the establishment of these refineries in the public sector made any economic sense. The reality behind the controversy was that the government refineries were experiencing 'difficulties' not untypical of the public sector, and making comparatively poor progress towards the realization of their targets.

A third example, steel, again has its distinct features. Socialists have always argued that the steel industry is the key to economic power and therefore must be in the public sector, irrespective of other considerations. In India this argument was reinforced by the practical consideration that the high cost and technical complexity of erecting a large-scale modern steel plant and bringing it into production made adequate development in the private sector inconceivable. This much, indeed, was admitted by the 'steel barons' themselves. Thus J. R. D. Tata, justifying his support for Bokaro, said 'India's economy and the standard of living of our people cannot grow without additional steel and it is clear that the Private Sector, even if permitted to do so, would not be able to undertake on its own a programme of expansion at an average rate exceeding a million tons of new capacity a year'.[29] Nevertheless, the private steel interests were given an important role to play in the Second Plan's expansion programme.[30] A total investment of Rs115 crores (as against Rs353 crores in the public sector) was envisaged, and the two main companies, the Tata Iron & Steel Company (TISCO) and the Indian Iron & Steel Company (IISCO) were expected to raise their combined capacity from 1·25 million to 2·3 million tons. Such an expansion, which slightly exceeded the total projected capacity of any one

[28] LSD, 4th sess., xvi, 9326. See also *EE*, 26 Apr. & 28 June 1963.
[29] Statement to A.G.M. of TISCO, 29 Aug. 1963 (*EE*, 9 Aug. 1963).
[30] *FYP*(*2*), pp. 396–8, 406–7.

of the new public sector units, could be reconciled with the Industrial Policy Resolution only by dint of the rather formal argument that it was all *in situ* and did not involve the establishment of new private sector plants in fresh locations. There appears to have been some argument at the ministerial level about its legitimacy, and there was certainly plenty of criticism of it from leftists of all varieties. But T. T. Krishnamachari, the responsible minister, was not one of the more dogmatic devotees of the socialist pattern. Determined to secure the production of 6 million tons of steel by the end of the Second Plan, he was not very particular about the methods of obtaining it. In any event, he could put forward quite a strong case for his chosen path, even on socialist grounds. The requirement that the public sector should expand faster than the private was obviously being satisfied, and the new enterprises at Rourkela, Bhilai, and Durgapur were not, like Oil India, 'mixed' undertakings, but fully in the public sector, in so far as the massive foreign assistance, financial and technical, which was being enlisted did not go together with foreign participation in equity capital. Hence the very considerable expansion of TISCO and IISCO could be presented as fully compatible with socialism, for the benefit of those for whom socialist criteria seemed rather more important than they did to the minister.

The 6 million tons was not achieved. Bringing the new public sector plants into production proved a harder and longer task than had been expected, and by 1960–1 their combined output was only 0·6 million tons as against a planned 2·0 million. There were also shortfalls in the private sector. TISCO's actual production for 1960–1 was 1,263,000 tons of saleable steel, as against a forecast of 1½ million tons; IISCO's 722,000 tons, as against a forecast of 800,000. Both, however, came within striking distance of their targets, and over the quinquennial period IISCO exceeded its anticipated total production by over 100,000 tons. Moreover, both completed their programmes for the expansion of their capacity more or less as scheduled, TISCO by December 1958 and IISCO by August 1959. At the beginning of the Third Plan their joint capacity was 3 million tons.[31] In the light of this record, it might have been expected, on grounds of strict economic rationality, that the Third Plan would give the private sector even greater opportunities for expansion. In fact, the contribution of the private sector to a steel target of 10·2 million tons of ingots was placed at a mere 3·2 million. Only in respect of pig iron was the policy embodied in the Industrial Policy Resolution somewhat relaxed, to the extent of allowing the establishment of plants in the private sector with a maximum capacity of 100,000 tons a year as compared with a previous 15,000 tons.[32]

[31] Plan. Com., *Programmes of Industrial Development 1961–6* (1962), pp. 3–4.
[32] *FYP*(*2*), pp. 465–6, 458.

By the time of the *Mid-Term Appraisal*, the shortfall in steel production was such that the Commission came to the conclusion that the Third Plan target of 6·8 million tons of finished steel (10·2 million tons of steel ingots) would not be reached until the third year of the Fourth Plan. The delay in commissioning Bokaro, for which the American government was more responsible than the Indian, had gravely affected the prospects of production, but a considerable share of the blame lay in the slow expansion of the three existing steel plants in the public sector. TISCO and IISCO, on the other hand, were doing comparatively well. Recognizing this, the government was in the course of making a few further 'concessions' to the private sector.

> A programme to enable the Tata Iron and Steel Company to remove some of the technical defects and to achieve their full rated capacity of 2 million tons has recently been approved in principle. The proposal of the Indian Iron and Steel Company to expand their capacity to 1·3 million tons of ingots has also been accepted. The foreign exchange requirements of these programmes are expected to be provided by the World Bank.[33]

The above history does not prove that the Indian government was mistaken in developing steel production in the public sector; still less does it suggest that the private iron and steel companies ought to have been given free rein for expansion. Resources for steel production, and particularly foreign exchange resources, are so scarce that a carefully programmed expansion, involving a fairly precise allocation of tasks to the public and private sectors respectively, is obviously essential. What it does suggest is that the balance of responsibilities has not been judged in relation to the respective performances, actual and prospective, of the two sectors. Neither in the Third Plan nor in the Commission's *Programmmes of Industrial Development, 1961–6* is there any clear explanation of why the public sector should have been given a target of 7 million tons of ingots and the private sector one of 3·2, or why the projected rate of expansion of the private sector should be so much slower than that which it was allowed—and that which it achieved—in the Second Plan. It is possible, of course, that economic rationality may have suffered no violation, but there is at least a strong *prima facie* case that the basis of judgement was essentially political and ideological, and there is rather more than a possibility that the development of this essential industry has, in consequence, been slower than it might otherwise have been.

The view that economic rationality has to force itself on reluctant ideologists is supported by the frequency with which plans undergo modification in favour of the private sector. One such modification, of a fairly minor kind, is at present being made for the steel industry, as we

[33] *MTA*, pp. 135–6.

have seen. In fields where the 'socialist pattern' stimulates rather less ideological commitment, the modifications are sometimes very important. One such was provoked by the distressing shortfall in fertilizer production during the Second Plan. The Draft Outline of the Third Plan put the 1965–6 target for nitrogenous fertilizers at 1 million tons, of which 800,000 were to be produced in the public sector and 200,000 in the private. During the discussions that followed, however, different counsels prevailed, with the result that in the final plan document (p. 478) the Commission reported that it seemed 'probable' that the private sector would 'undertake rather more than previously contemplated'. This rather coy phrase reflected the fact that applications from private enterprises to install additional capacity of more than 300,000 tons had already been approved. Curiously enough, however, the government's decision in this instance to rely more heavily on the private sector may have been wrong, for the *Mid-Term Appraisal* (p. 127), reporting that the Third Plan target was not likely to be achieved, ascribed the shortfall to 'the slow process in the implementation of private sector schemes'.

In general, it would seem that the taking of an advance decision, through the Second Industrial Policy Resolution, as to the respective responsibilities of the public and private sectors has not been entirely advantageous, if pace of economic growth is the criterion to be applied. The question that needs to be asked, when each particular case comes up for decision, is whether the public sector or the private offers the more hopeful growing point. This can be answered, very largely, by reference to comparative performance, at least for those industries where units of the two sectors already coexist. Where something is being started from scratch, of course, the decision-maker lacks this kind of evidence and hence has to chance his arm; but if his knowledge of the Indian industrial economy is adequate, he is not deprived of all guidance. There can be no doubt that the planners perform this sort of exercise and that they are prepared to plump for economic rationality, other things being equal. But the 'socialist pattern' means that for the twenty-nine key industries in Schedules 'A' and 'B' of the Industrial Policy Resolution, other things are never equal. When all the exceptions and qualifications contained in the resolution have been allowed for, the terms of reference which it gives to the planners still contain a strong built-in bias in favour of the public sector. Public enterprise is encouraged, private enterprise permitted on certain conditions. Hence the choice, if not absolutely predetermined, is steered in a particular direction by considerations which, while not necessarily hostile to rapid growth, are essentially irrelevant to it.

One cannot say that this is wrong. We have already examined a number of cases, such as those connected with 'balanced regional development', where compromise is obviously necessary between mere economic rationality and stern political prejudice. If an economically rational decision upsets the political applecart, it is not rational at all in the wider context. Where the public-versus-private issue is concerned, we have to remember that 'socialism' has widespread support from the politically more articulate groups and that the private industrialist, generally an unpopular figure, rarely behaves in a way likely to improve his social standing. 'Socialism', therefore, besides being a morally respectable ideal, has its role to play as a slogan. Perhaps an even more important consideration is the danger, of which at least the more socialistically-minded members of the government are constantly aware, of bringing into existence a private enterprise Frankenstein which will use its economic power to dominate the public authorities in such a way as to make the eventual realization of socialist purposes impossible, except at the cost of revolution. Many Indians, indeed, believe that the skewed income distribution which is both the condition and the consequence of a predominantly private-enterprise form of development makes revolution inevitable. Therefore, the argument runs—although it is rarely expressed quite so baldly—let us concentrate on expanding the public sector, which is the essential foundation of a socialist system, more rapidly than the private sector, even though for the present, and until we have discovered the secret of running public enterprise efficiently, the consequential rate of economic growth may be somewhat lower.

The alternative view, as we have already suggested, is that where decisions between the public and private sectors have to be made, optimizing the rate of growth should be given absolute priority. Those who hold it argue that the actual political tensions which threaten to tear India apart have very little to do with who owns the means of production. The caste, communal, and regional antagonisms, which are the ones that have to be held most firmly in check, are basically epiphenomena of the grinding poverty associated with unemployment and underemployment. As soon as a man acquires full-time remunerative employment he sheds the most serious of his frustrations and begins to develop the social and political stability that goes with self-respect. The essential thing, therefore, is to increase employment opportunities as rapidly as possible, irrespective of whether they are in the gift of the public sector or the private. This is the only practicable way of giving satisfaction, at the present stage of economic development, to the demand for 'equality'; for the most grievous and revolution-provoking form of inequality is that between citizens who have regular work, however meagrely remunerated, and those who have none. Optimum economic growth, therefore, makes political as well as economic sense, irrespective of how it is achieved. The longer-term issues, subsumed under the term 'socialism', can for the present moment look after themselves. However 'socialistic' an economy which is characterized by chronic shortages may look, no one will derive much material or even moral satisfaction from the contemplation of its beauties. In any case, 'socialism', in the sense of having a large public sector, is a necessary and inevitable characteristic of the Indian economy for as long as anyone can foresee, for reasons which have already been adequately explained. As for the Frankenstein-risk, this must be squarely faced. It is possible, although not inevitable, that as a result of a type of economic development where the criterion of choice between public and private is simply rate of growth, the 'capitalists' will come to dominate society, which will become set in a grossly inegalitarian mould, characterized by universal materialism and self-seeking. It is possible, too, that this will provoke the masses to make a socialist revolution. If so, one can only say that it is better to have a revolution which is a consequence of growth than one which is a consequence of stagnation. In the first there is something to distribute; in the second, nothing. But, as capitalism grows, it changes. Western experience suggests, that, as wealth becomes more abundant and the labour and trade union movements more effectively organized, the system gradually civilizes itself and develops a whole number of quasi-socialist features. The prospect of its violent overthrow consequently becomes replaced by that of its gradual but by no means imperceptible modification. Such a prospect may seem distant for a country like India, and the temptation to try to 'jump the stages' is correspondingly strong. Nevertheless there is a case for resisting it, unless a jump into Communism is intended; for a 'mixed economy' has its own logic, which imposes constraints which the ideologist and politician disregard at their peril.

These rival arguments have been stated baldly, with few of the nuances and qualifications which ideally ought to be introduced. Enough has been said, however, to indicate that it is with the latter that the balance of the author's own sympathies lie. It would seem that the interpretation placed on the 'socialist pattern' by India's government has sometimes been deleterious to her present and future welfare. Now that a critical stage in her process of economic planning has been reached, the time has perhaps come when the precise meaning of socialism, in the Indian context, should be redefined and when the Industrial Policy Resolution of 1956 should be substantially modified.

(v)

One must beware of exaggerating the tension between the public and the private sector to the point of suggesting that there is irreconcilable opposition. One can argue—as we have argued in the foregoing pages—that ideological presuppositions have tended to shift the balance away from the economically optimum point; but one cannot argue that the decision to reserve to the state the development of certain industries has reduced the private sector to a condition of impotent frustration. There is still plenty of room for the two to develop side by side, and the private sector has, in fact, showed considerable resilience. During the Second Plan its progress was spectacular. Net fixed capital formation in private sector mining, large-scale manufacturing, and power enterprises jumped from Rs298 crores for the period 1951/2–1955/6 to Rs715 crores for the period 1956/7–1960/1. Private entrepreneurs and investors, as is their wont everywhere, complain that they could have done even better if taxation had been lower, state-imposed responsibilities towards the labour force less onerous, and controls (i.e. over capital issues, the expansion of capacity, and entitlement to foreign exchange) more liberally and less bureaucratically administered. They sometimes present a strong case, particularly where the operation of controls is concerned; but the vigorous expansion of the private sector suggests that the overall impact of public policy has been favourable. The frustrations suffered by the industrialist have been less significant than the stimulus given to him by the development of the infrastructure of the economy and the expansion of the market, both largely the product of a massive programme of public investment.

In addition, private enterprise receives from the state a great deal of direct positive encouragement. This has taken many forms, including protection against foreign competition,[34] and a considerable amount of technical assistance, particularly through government-promoted training schemes; but the most outstanding encouragement is the selective provision of finance on favourable terms. This deserves examination in some detail, for, as Venkatasubbiah has said, nothing demonstrates 'more concretely the acceptance by the Government of India that private enterprise has a definite part to play in industrial development than the setting up of a series of financial institutions for extending long term credit to large-scale industry'.[35]

The first institution to be established for this purpose was the Industrial Finance Corporation (IFC), which dates from 1948. Its object was 'to make medium and long-term credits more readily available to industrial concerns in India, particularly in circumstances where normal banking accommodation is inappropriate or recourse to capital issue methods is impracticable'.[36] Specifically, its functions were defined as (*a*) the guaranteeing of loans floated by companies in the open market, (*b*) the underwriting of stocks, and (*c*) the granting of loans and advances. A

[34] Protective measures are taken by the central government on the advice of the statutory Tariff Commission, which both investigates applications and lays down conditions for protection.
[35] H. Venkatasubbiah, *Indian Economy since Independence*, 2nd. ed. (1961), p. 175.
[36] N. Das, *Industrial Enterprise in India*, 2nd ed. (Calcutta, 1956), p. 57.

'mixed' enterprise (but firmly under government control), it was permitted an initial authorized capital of Rs10 crores, of which 40 per cent was to be taken up by the central government and the Reserve Bank, and the remainder by joint-stock banks, co-operative banks, and insurance companies. It could issue bonds to a value of five times its paid-up capital and accept deposits from the public up to a period of not less than five years. The justification for its creation is to be found in the fact that 'even in countries with well-developed capital market mechanisms (which India does not as yet possess), the need for such specialist institutions has been felt for filling the gap . . . that exists between the point where commercial banks leave off and the point where public investors begin'.[37]

It has not been free from the problems that normally complicate the operations of institutions of this kind.[38] Intended to work on a strictly commercial basis, it has found difficulty in gearing its activities to the requirements of the plans. Commercial considerations have predisposed it to provide loans and other forms of financial assistance to large and well-established concerns (which often have little difficulty in raising their requirements on the open market) rather than to the small and struggling ones that really need its services. For similar reasons, it has often tended to look askance at requests from enterprises in the more economically backward areas, to which the planners, for a mixture of political and economic reasons, have chosen to give special attention. This contradiction between commercial policy and planned needs has given rise to two kinds of complaints, both of which were voiced at the IFC inquiry of 1952. When, on the orders of the government, it behaves 'uncommercially' it is condemned for wasting public money in 'infructuous' investments; when it allows commercial considerations to guide its investment policy it is accused of neglecting plan priorities. The contradiction has never been fully resolved—nor could it be unless the statutory basis were fundamentally changed; but in fact the government has ensured that the Corporation gives special attention to 'gap-filling' projects, industrial co-operatives and backward areas.

Its débuts were slow, difficult, and attended by a series of scandals which provoked the appointment of the Inquiry Commission of 1952; but during the Second Plan it made rapid progress, and of recent years has considerably diversified its business. Formerly it concentrated almost exclusively on loans, but nowadays it undertakes what its Chairman describes as a variety of 'promotional' activities, including 'underwriting public issues in the form of equity and preference shares and debentures and also direct subscriptions to such issues'. Up to 1963 it had disbursed financial

[37] IFC Inquiry Ctee., 1953, *Rep.* (New Delhi, 1954), p. 175.

[38] On these in general, and those of the IFC in particular, see Shirley Boskey, *Problems and Practices of Development Banks* (IBRD, 1959).

assistance to the extent of Rs102·57 crores, and its Chairman claimed that as the total cost of the projects that had 'come to fruition' as a result of its assistance was Rs443 crores, it had acted as a catalytic agent for no less than '30 per cent of the total net investment in the organized private sector since independence'.[39] This claim, however, should not be taken too seriously, as it rests on the assumption that the enterprises taking advantage of the Corporation's services could not have found accommodation elsewhere.

To supplement its efforts, there are industrial finance corporations in each of the states. These are intended to cater for the needs of small-scale and medium-scale industries, and are authorized (unlike the central Corporation) to assist enterprises other than public limited companies. Liaison with the central Corporation is provided by the latter's right to appoint a director to each state corporation board and by the fact that the state corporation often acts as the central Corporation's agent for the disbursement of assistance. Public subscription of up to 25 per cent of a state corporation's capital is permissible, and, like the central Corporation, it can float bonds and accept deposits. Government control is ensured by the nomination of a majority of directors by governmental and quasi-governmental financial institutions. A state corporation cannot subscribe to equities, but can make loans and advances for periods of up to twenty years, guarantee loans up to the same time limit, and underwrite stocks, shares, bonds, and debentures.

The state corporations have experienced difficulties not dissimilar to those of the central Corporation. In addition, they are faced with the problem that the small and medium industries they are supposed to help are often unable either to offer adequate security or to present properly worked-out and sufficiently intelligible projects. Hence there is, once again, a bias in favour of the larger and better established undertaking. To some extent, this is corrected by the availability, from other sources, of technical assistance for small-scale industry; but the fact that financial assistance and technical assistance are provided by different agencies creates problems of co-ordination which even now have not been fully solved. The problem of security, moreover, continues to give the corporations a natural prejudice in favour of the comparatively rich and powerful. Hence it is not surprising to find that, of a total of Rs23·5 crores disbursed by the state financial corporations up to the end of June 1961, only Rs4·55 crores had gone to small-scale industries.[40] One should remember, however, that these industries have other sources of

[39] At its 15th A.G.M. (EE, 4 Oct. 1963).

[40] Min. of Finance, *Rep. 1961–2*, p. 41. A recent report says that there is still 'urgent need to use existing institutions—banks, corporations and government agencies—more effectively and to change the general outlook and habits with respect to financing small factories' (Ford Found., Internat. Perspective Planning Team, *Development of Small Scale Industries in India* (1963), p. 11).

'official' finance, such as those provided under the State Aid to Industries Acts.

Originally, as we have noticed, the central IFC was very hesitant about participating in equity capital. Even by 1957 it had 'not taken up any debenture or underwritten any issue of capital or guaranteed any loans of industrial concerns'.[41] This hesitancy was not so much a result of its lack of enterprise as of its own nature. Essentially, a finance corporation waits upon the initiative of others rather than taking the initiative itself. It can, of course, be told to go out and search for business, but this may easily involve it in a schizophrenic attempt to act simultaneously as promoter and banker. The better way is usually to give promotional functions to a separate institution. Such, at least, was the conclusion that the Indian government had reached well before the end of the First Plan. In 1954 and 1955 it brought into existence two new organs, the National Industrial Development Corporation (NIDC) and the ICIC, both of which were to be concerned with strengthening the private sector in its pioneering and risk-bearing functions.

The first was a 'private' limited company, entirely financed by the government and controlled by a Board of Directors meeting under the chairmanship of the Minister of Commerce. Its authorized capital was only Rs1 crore, its paid-up capital originally no more than Rs10 lakhs; but in the Second Plan a sum of Rs55 crores was placed at its disposal. Of this, Rs35 crores were intended for the modernization and re-equipment of the jute and cotton textile industries, and the balance for 'pioneering new basic and heavy industries'. According to the Commission, it had already 'taken up for investigation' foundries and forges, structural fabrication, refractories, chemical pulp, carbon black, and intermediaries for dyestuffs and drugs', and it was expected to 'direct its efforts towards fostering the establishment of a new unit in the aluminium industry and the manufacture of heavy equipment for earth moving, mining etc., and rolls and rolling mill equipment required in ferrous and non-ferrous industries'.[42] Essentially, it was regarded as a gap-filler, intended, in the words of N. Das, 'to tackle the problems of industrialization and unemployment in the country from the angle of shyness of capital and enterprise'.[43] What seemed rather uncertain, right from the beginning, was whether it would attempt to fill the gaps in India's industrial structure by assisting likely looking private entrepreneurs in search of capital, technical know-how, and perhaps foreign collaborators, or by pioneering enterprises entirely on its own account. L. K. Jha, writing in the *Journal of Industries and Trade*, presented this issue as wide open:

. . . if it finds that the private sector will be able to meet the need with or without technical and financial assistance from the Corporation then it might as well

[41] *EE*, Suppl., 1 Feb. 1957. [42] *FYP(2)*, p. 404. [43] *Industrial Enterprise*, p. 64.

decide not to take up the project on its own. On the other hand, it would be equally open to it to execute the project itself or by setting up a subsidiary company, drawing upon Government funds for the purpose to the extent required.[44]

Another open question, initially, was whether, having pioneered an enterprise, it would eventually sell it out to the private investor, as was already being done by Pakistan's Industrial Development Corporation. This was virtually answered, negatively, by the adoption of the 'socialist pattern'. More interesting was the question of the demarcation of its activities from those of the IFC. Its responsibility for loaning money to the cotton and jute textile industries suggested that there might be a considerable overlap. In short, its objectives were by no means clearly defined.

Even in the Third Plan Report, the role of the NIDC remained indistinct. References to it were few and, at least in one case, contradictory. On p. 462 the Commission said that the central government's plan for industries had 'to take into account the resources required to be made available to the Industrial Finance Corporation and the National Industrial Development Corporation to enable them to operate at somewhat higher levels than in the Second Plan'; but on p. 498 it allocated only Rs20 crores to the NIDC in contrast with the Second Plan's Rs55 crores. But despite the Commission's reticencies and ambiguities on the subject, the essential role of the Corporation had by this time become reasonably clear. It was continuing to make reconstruction loans to the cotton and jute textile industries but not extending its loan-making responsibilities to other industries; apart from this, it had become one of the government's agencies for conducting, at the technical level, 'collaboration' negotiations with potential foreign partners, particularly those from the Communist countries. According to the 1960–1 report of the Ministry of Commerce and Industry, it was collaborating with the Hungarians in the field of biogas/fertilizer plants and with the Russians in that of drugs and pharmaceutical plants. The report for the following year mentioned, in addition, its role in negotiations with the Hungarians for the manufacture of aluminium and with the Russians for that of precision instruments, compressors, and pumps. The British had also become its partners in projects for heavy structural fabricating works and heavy plate and vessel works.[45]

Other projects, such as synthetic rubber, rayon grade pulp, and newsprint, it had decided, after study, to leave to the private sector. A project for the manufacture of ophthalmic glass (with Soviet assistance) and one for heavy machine tools (with Czech assistance) it had handed over

[44] Spec. Industries Suppl., Nov. 1955.
[45] Min. Comm. & Ind., *Rep. 1960–1*, pp. 51–53; *Rep. 1961–2*, pp. 59–60.

to the Heavy Engineering Corporation, a public enterprise, for 'further implementation'. Its only 'subsidiary' specifically mentioned was the Pyrites and Chemicals Development Company, registered in March 1960.

As the 1961–2 report said, the Corporation's newly established Technical Consultancy Bureau[46] had become 'the chief agency' through which it worked. This Bureau was generally responsible for 'serving various projects under study or in process of implementation', by developing forms of technical expertise for which 'foreign consultants have at present to be engaged'. Specifically, it was working on preliminary studies, the investigation and selection of sites, the preparation of detailed project reports, and the designing of structures. 'The work of the Bureau', said the 1960–1 report, 'is proposed to be confined for the present to the public sector projects of the NIDC and the Ministry of Commerce and Industry'. The Corporation, therefore, has become an agency very different from that originally envisaged. It is still a 'gap-filler', to the extent that it investigates and pioneers new projects, but no longer a means of stimulating private sector activities, except in so far as it retains its original responsibilities towards the jute and cotton textile industries.

Private sector stimulation, indeed, has become concentrated in the hands of the second of the two agencies here examined, the ICIC, which, in contrast with the 'modest birth and rather hazy objectives' of the NIDC, had 'a spectacular ushering with its clearly defined objectives well proclaimed'.[47] ICIC began with a paid-up share capital of Rs5 crores, of which 70 per cent was held by Indian banks, insurance companies, and the general public and 30 per cent by British banks, Commonwealth insurance companies, and banks, business corporations, and individuals in the United States. Of its working funds, Rs7½ crores were provided by the Indian government as an interest-free deposit (from rupee 'counterpart' funds) and Rs5 crores by the World Bank as a long-term, government-guaranteed loan. Its initial capitalization was therefore Rs17½ crores. Subsequently, this was supplemented by further government allocations and World Bank loans. Of the eleven directors, the Indian government appointed only one. Seven represented Indian shareholders, while the British shareholding interest was sustained by two and the American by one. The 'mixture' thus appeared to be very heavily biased on the private side. Effective government control, the *Eastern Economist* assured its readers, was ensured by the possibility of a publicly-initiated liquidation application if the Corporation defaulted on its loan capital repayments or if its capital became 'impaired beyond tolerable limit considered reasonable in the course of business'.[48] Such control, however,

[46] The creation of the Bureau is mentioned in *FYP(3)*, pp. 490–1.

[47] Venkatasubbiah, *Indian Economy*, p. 177. [48] *EE*, Suppl., 1 Feb. 1957.

is so remote as to be completely ineffective except in the most critical of situations; the real, day-to-day influence of the Indian government on the Corporation's policy springs from the fact that since the nationalization of life insurance, the government is the Corporation's largest shareholder, holding 18 per cent of its share capital.[53]

Like the IFC and the NIDC, ICIC makes straightforward loans, but its major emphasis is on the provision of risk-bearing finance. It sponsors and underwrites new issues, guarantees loans from private sources, and—where needed—offers technical and managerial assistance. Its role is most important at times when the market for private capital is sluggish. The funds that it then provides enable, in the words of its Chairman, 'the flow of investment to continue'.[49] As a well endowed 'mixed' agency, partly controlled by foreign investors, and concentrating exclusively on the stimulation of private enterprise, it has had to meet criticism from those who are less than enthusiastic about the private sector and particularly suspicious of foreign private capital. Justifying the foreign element in its management, its first Chairman, Dr A. Ramaswami Mudaliar, wrote:

> Such participation by foreign investors, and the experience which their representatives would have through being associated with the direction of the affairs of the Corporation, will give them a clear insight into the conditions and circumstances in which private industry is functioning in this country. It will enable them to understand that the fears and apprehensions and even alarmist views that sometimes are spread about the future of private industry, in India and more so in foreign countries, may not be justified . . . . Another advantage which will flow from such understanding is the greater participation of foreign capital not merely through the Industrial Credit and Investment Corporation but outside of it, in assisting under proper conditions laid down by the Government of India the development of Indian industries.[50]

In the Lok Sabha critics have tended to make much of the fact that, through this Corporation, non-interest-bearing funds from Indian government sources are being placed at the disposal of the private sector.[51] The reply—a not entirely convincing one—is that the remission of interest enables loans at 1 per cent below the commercial rate to be made available for projects conforming with the government's approved development pattern. Doubts arise not merely because a non-commercial rate of interest always requires specific justification but because ICIC is almost completely disregarded in the plan reports. In the Second Plan report[52] it receives a bare mention, with no indication of the role cast for it in the development of private sector industries. In the Third Plan

[49] Ibid. 13 Mar. 1964. [50] *Indian Finance*, 23 Jan. 1955, p. 173.

[51] Doubts also arise 'whether the ICIC will shape industry or industry will shape the ICIC' (Venkatasubbiah, p. 178).

[52] *FYP(2)*, p. 389. On p. 405 the planners forecast that loans to industry from the IFC, the State Finance Corporations, and the ICIC will be stepped up from Rs18 crores (1951–6) to Rs40 crores (1956–61).

report, it is not mentioned at all; nor, as far as the author can discover, is there any reference to it in the 706 unindexed pages of the Commission's *Programmes of Industrial Development, 1961–6*. In view of its heavy capitalization and important role, this is rather extraordinary. During the eleven months ending November 1961 it sanctioned net rupee assistance of Rs4·46 crores and net foreign exchange loans of no less than Rs6·28 crores.[53]

One further financial institution deserves brief mention—the Refinance Corporation, established in 1958. The gap that this was intended to fill is thus described by Venkatasubbiah:

> It has become evident in the first year of the Second Plan that the pressure on the funds of the commercial banks . . . had increased beyond their capacity to stretch. Under the impact of an expanding economy their advances rose more rapidly than their deposits. While their funds were primarily meant for short-term financing of trade and industry, in practice an increasing proportion of them came to be locked up for long periods. The balance which they had traditionally maintained between the finance of trade and the finance of industry was also disturbed by economic forces in a way that was unfavourable to the former type of business. On the other hand, the more rigorous control that was instituted on the structure of joint-stock enterprise through the new Companies Act, and the socialistic tax policies followed by successive Finance Ministers, induced a certain shrinking in the traditional sources of finance of industrial enterprises.[54]

To rectify this situation, the new Corporation was authorized to provide discounting facilities first to a limited number of commercial banks and later to all of them. Its share capital of Rs12·5 crores was subscribed by the Reserve Bank, the State Bank, the Life Insurance Corporation, and fifteen 'participating' commercial banks, and the government placed at its disposal the sum of Rs26 crores of 'counterpart' funds. It thus started life with the very considerable total resources of Rs38·5 crores. With its inauguration the network of public institutions for the financing of private industry was, for the time being, completed.

In this field, then, the effort of the government of India has been notable. Whatever complaints the private sector may have, lack of adequate encouragement can hardly be prominent among them. Criticism is inevitable from those who think that the stimulation of private entrepreneurship is *ipso facto* bad; but those who believe that, in a developing mixed economy, the private sector needs this kind of selective assistance to enable it to play its allotted role, feel no doubt about the necessity of the exercise but only about some of the methods that the government has used. As we have seen, the structure has grown piecemeal, by the

[53] Min. of Finance, *Rep. 1961–2*, p. 42.
[54] *Indian Economy*, p. 181.

addition of new institutions to old ones as specific needs have become evident. The result, as in many other fields of Indian economic administration, is that there are too many agencies with fingers in the pie. Co-ordination becomes difficult and it is often possible for the acute private entrepreneur to play off one agency against another. Some attempt has been made at a clearer demarcation of functions. As Venkatasubbiah says:

> Broadly, at one end the Reserve Bank regulates the supply of credit to the banking system as a whole, and at the other the State Bank looks after rural, agricultural and small-scale industrial finance. The other credit institutions look after the middle area of long-term and medium-term finance of industry. Some of them, including the Life Insurance Corporation, support industry's equity capital too.[55]

This, however, is a considerable over-simplification of the picture, as it disregards many other institutions through which industrial finance is channelled, such as the State Industrial Finance Corporations, the Co-operative Banks, the host of agencies catering for the needs of small-scale industry, and, indeed, the state governments themselves. One may therefore echo his view that the multiplication of the country's public credit institutions is 'not an unmixed blessing'. To it we may add the further criticism that these institutions receive little guidance from the planners. The policy of the Commission seems to be to establish priorities and then leave their interpretation to the discretion of the Licensing Committee and their implementation—to the extent that publicly provided finance may be needed—to the various corporations. This certainly has the merit of encouraging flexibility, and one could not advocate its replacement by a system of rigid centralized planning; but it has not worked very satisfactorily.

(vi)

As well as helping to finance the private sector, the Indian government has tried to help it to help itself. The main method has been the formation of Development Councils, under the provisions of the Industries (Development and Regulation) Act, 1951. By 1961 there were nineteen of these in existence—almost twice as many as at the beginning of the Second Plan. Some had had a continuous history since the early 1950s, others had lived a rather chequered and sporadic life. Each was charged with a variety of duties selected from the schedule appended to the Act. The more lively ones met two or three times a year and formed panels or sub-committees to deal with the more specialized aspects of their business.

[55] Ibid. p. 182.

All played some part—although how valuable a part it is not easy to discover—in drawing up the plan programmes for their various industries.[56]

On the whole, they have failed to live up to the government's original expectations. Employers tend to be suspicious of them, partly because they are agencies of a government which is itself mistrusted, partly because the sharing of information which is one of their objects can only with difficulty be distinguished from the giving away of information to actual and potential rivals. In the main, they have acted not so much as a means of industrial self-improvement as one of conveying to the government an industry's collective complaints and requests. Most of the decisions contained in their reports for 1960–1, for instance, are recommendations to the appropriate authorities on subjects such as import and export controls, licensing policy, price policy, the regulation of distribution, taxation, excise duties, infringements of trade marks, and the work of government-controlled research institutions. Industrialists' indifference towards the Councils partly springs, as Venkatasubbiah has pointed out, from the fact that the Act constituting them also contains 'inquisitorial and punitive provisions'.[57]

(vii)

It is to provisions of this kind that we must now turn; for the attitude of private enterprise towards the government is strongly conditioned by their existence and by the manner of their exercise. They can be broadly divided into two kinds, viz. (1) those which regulate the internal organization of enterprises, and (2) those which govern their creation and expansion.

Some of the first kind are to be found in the 'inspectorial' clauses of the Industries (Development and Regulation) Act. Although these provide the government with almost limitless statutory opportunities to interfere, their frequent use would obviously be self-defeating, as it would create among the business community an atmosphere of uncertainty inimical to risk-taking. Their existence constitutes one of those ultimate sanctions the precise effect of which upon business behaviour is always problematical. That the government has clearly understood this emerges from a speech to the Central Advisory Council of Industries by the Minister of Commerce and Industry on the famous 'case' of the United Mills: 'I would like to offer a word of caution . . . if you come to the conclusion that the report indicates gross mismanagement and all that follows thereafter, you cannot ignore the repercussions for better or worse that might be taken [*sic*] on the textile industry as a whole'.[58] Much more practically

[56] Each Development Council issues an annual report, and summaries of DC activities appear in the Ann. Reps of the Min. Comm. & Ind. (now Min. of Industry).

[57] *Indian Economy*, pp. 174–5. [58] Quoted ibid. p. 174.

important are the powers embodied in the Companies Act of 1956, which, together with its amending Acts, constitutes one of the most detailed and stringent codes of business legislation to be found anywhere in the world.[59] It has two main aims: to prevent, or at least reduce, the dishonest practices said to be rife in the formation and operation of Indian companies; and to limit opportunities for effecting undue concentrations of economic power. Some of its more unusual clauses provide the following:

1. That, except with the permission of the Government, dividends are to be paid only out of annual profits, after due provision has been made for depreciation (cl. 205);
2. That overall managerial remuneration shall be limited (cl. 198);
3. That government sanction shall be required for proposed increases in the remuneration of managing directors (cl. 310, 311);
4. That government approval shall be required for the appointment of any managing or whole-time director (cl. 269);
5. That no person shall be a director of more than 20 companies (cl. 275);
6. That no person, except with the permission of the government, shall be appointed managing director of more than two companies (cl. 316);
7. That no managing director shall be appointed for more than five years at a time (cl. 317);
8. That the Government, at its discretion, shall have the power to order a special audit of a company's accounts and, on receipt of the auditor's report, take such action on it as is considered 'necessary in accordance with the provisions of this Act or any other law for the time being in force' (cl. 233A);
9. That on application by a certain number of shareholders, or on special resolution by a company's General Assembly, or on the order of a Court, the Government shall be empowered to conduct an investigation of the company's affairs and, after receipt of report, to initiate a prosecution or make application for winding up (cl. 235, 237, 241, 242).

These and other restrictive provisions were hotly opposed by business interests during the long debates that preceded the passing of the Act. They have certainly kept the Department of Company Law Administration busy. Between 1 December 1959 and 30 November 1960, seven investigations were ordered under Clauses 235 and 237, and during the first ten months of 1960 6,588 prosecutions were launched against 1,009 companies. The corresponding figures for the following year were two investigations and 5,422 prosecutions against 1,225 companies.[60] It

[59] No. 1 of 1956 (as modified up to 1 May 1961).

[60] Min. Comm. & Ind., *Rep. 1960–1*, pp. 188–9; *Rep. 1961–2*, p. 120. The number of prosecutions steadily went up between 1956–7 and 1960–1, and then started falling. According to the Dept of Company Law Admin., it fell from 6,272 in 1960–1 to 3,990 in 1961–2 and 3,690 in 1962–3. Most of the prosecutions of these years are alleged to be 'a result of legacies of the

cannot be said, however, that in view of the prevalence of malpractices and absence of self-discipline in the private corporate sector, the powers conferred by the Companies Act are unnecessary. The Secretary of the Department of Company Law Administration, in an address to a Business International Round Table, justified its 'extraordinary' provisions on the following well-substantiated grounds:

(i) a somewhat narrow and limited acceptance of the principle of social responsibility and social obligations of business in this country . . . .;
(ii) the relatively tardy growth of the sense of fiduciary responsibility in the *average* company management . . . ;
(iii) the absence in this country of strong and well-recognised financial institutions . . . which oversee company flotation and management, thereby rendering statutory regulation in such matters largely superfluous;
(iv) the absence in this country of a strong and reasonably unbiased financial and economic press . . .;
(v) the absence . . . of any strong and well-developed public opinion as regards company matters which is prepared to frown upon unwarranted deviations from accepted norms of company behaviour and practice, and
(vi) . . . the comparatively slow progress so far made . . . towards professionalisation of the management of joint stock enterprises.[61]

Moreover, it does not seem that powers under the Act have been exercised unreasonably. Resented as they often are, they often redound to the benefit rather than to the detriment of the private sector, in that they provide a degree of protection to the ordinary shareholder[62] without which the propensity to invest money in equities would be considerably reduced.

It is only in the provisions which it makes for the regulation of managing agencies (Ch. III, cl. 324–388A) that the Companies Act is really controversial. These agencies, once typical of the Indian commercial landscape, had become extremely unpopular. They were regarded as parasitic, accused of unethical practices, believed to act in restraint of competition, and associated with the evils of 'imperialist' rule. The immensely complex clauses of Chapter III of the Companies Act circumscribed their activities and opportunities so rigorously that the

Department to clear the back log in respect of past defaults'. It is pointed out, moreover, that most prosecutions arise from the violations of the simple rather than the more complex provisions of the Act. About 93 per cent of those for the years 1961–2 and 1962–3 were for 'non-holding of annual general meeting, non-placing of accounts thereat, non-filling of annual returns, balance-sheet and liquidators' annual statements' (Man Mohan Singh, 'Prosecutions under the Companies Act; Some Suggestions to Reduce the Incidence', in Min. of Ind., Dept. of Co. Law Admin., *Selected Articles on the Working and Management of Corporate Sector in India* (1963)).

[61] D. L. Mazumdar, 'A Statement on the Purposes and Objectives of the Companies Act, 1956', ibid.

[62] But not sufficient, hence the government's attempts to promote Shareholders' Associations (see Raj K. Nigam, *The Present and Future Role of Shareholders' Associations in India* (Min. Comm. & Ind., 1960).

whole system, in the opinion of R. R. Morarka, received 'not only a serious set-back but almost a death blow'.[63] Today, comparatively few new companies apply to the government for permission, under the Act, to appoint managing agents. Nevertheless the system has by no means disappeared. Opinion as to the economic usefulness of the agencies underwent a change in the later 1950s, and the government exercised its powers over them with great moderation. By Clause 330 of the Act, it was prescribed that the term of office of managing agents would expire on 15 August 1960 unless before that date the companies concerned decided to reappoint them after obtaining the sanction of the shareholders and the approval of the government. This clause could conceivably have been used to extinguish them; but out of the 1,526 applications to reappoint referred to the Company Law Advisory Commission, only 161 were rejected.[64] Moreover, the government, although from time to time saying that the abolition of managing agencies is receiving attention, has so far failed to appoint the Committee of Inquiry into the system envisaged by its own delegated legislation issued in pursuance of Clause 324 of the Act.[65] Evidently, a growing conviction that the managing agency, with all its faults, still has a contribution to make to Indian industrial development causes the government to stay its hand.

So many 'reserve powers' are granted by the Industries (Development and Regulation) Act and by the Companies Act that it is difficult to say what are the precise effects of these very important pieces of legislation. In general, however it would appear that they have imposed 'desirable order and discipline' on the corporate sector.[66] Their need was emphasized by the 'Vivian Bose' report,[67] which documented a series of unsavoury scandals (all preceding the 1956 Act) in the management of the Dalmia-Jain group of companies. A positive encyclopedia of corporate malpractice, this report made recommendations which have become the basis of a proposed further tightening-up of the company law. Some of the existing loopholes are likely to be closed, but one may be certain that the more slippery members of the Marwari, Gujarati, and Parsi communities will continue to discover new ones.

(viii)

The 'internal' controls that we have so far been examining are important to the businessman, in so far as they affect his *modus operandi*, and

[63] *EE*, ann. no., 7 June 1963, p. 1216. [64] Min. Comm. & Ind., *Rep.* 1960–1, p. 192.

[65] See H. K. Paranjape, 'Government Regulation of Private Industry in India', *IJPA*, July-Sept. 1962, p. 312. For the whole of my section on the regulation of industry I am deeply indebted to this excellent study.

[66] R. R. Morarka in *EE*, ann. no., 7 June 1963, p. 1216.

[67] Commission of Inquiry on Admin. of Dalmia-Jain Companies, *Rep.* (Min. Comm. & Ind., 1963).

to the general public, in so far as they accelerate or decelerate the pace of economic development; but from the point of view of the planning process they are far less important than the second group. Of these, industrial licensing, in accordance with the provisions of the Industries (Development and Regulation) Act, may be regarded as the 'key' control; for it directly influences the size, shape, and purpose of the private sector. Up to very recently, all actual and proposed industrial undertakings employing more than 100 workers and having fixed assets more than Rs10 lakhs in value have been subject to industrial licensing, the operation of which is thus officially described:

> The schemes submitted by entrepreneurs under the Act are carefully examined taking into consideration not only the technical feasibility of the schemes but also certain other factors such as the present and future demand vis-a-vis the Plan targets, availability of raw materials, appropriate location, choice of manufacturing process, economic size of the operations and the importance of the item itself in the light of the priorities fixed in the Plan. The schemes involving foreign collaboration and foreign exchange commitments are scrutinised to ensure that the terms and conditions of foreign agreements are not contracted disadvantageously and the country's holdings are not unduly dissipated.[68]

The Directorate General of Technical Development (formerly the Development Wing of the Ministry of Commerce and Industry), which is staffed largely by engineers and has close and continuous relations with Indian private business, plays an essential role in this licensing process. In scrutinizing proposals for consideration by the Licensing Committee it not only consults the various directorates concerned with the development of specific industries but provides what amounts to an advisory service for the benefit of applicants. After the licence has been approved, the Directorate General keeps watch 'to see whether the licensed schemes are progressing according to the terms and conditions laid down . . .' until such time as 'the schemes are completed and the units are in the regular manufacture of the licensed items'. Where genuine difficulties are experienced by the licensee, further assistance is given; where no progress or insufficient progress has been made despite all possible help action is initiated for the revocation of the licence.[69]

Although the Licensing Committee is now a highly experienced body and the Directorate General one of the more efficient and dynamic agencies of the central government, the licensing process has had serious defects, some of them technical, others more fundamental. The most obvious is the inordinately long period which normally elapses between the presentation of an application and the receipt of a decision. There is a rule that, where a licence is granted, the applicant shall be informed within

[68] Min. Comm. & Ind., Dev. Wing, *Ann. Rep. 1960–1*, p. 46. [69] Ibid. p. 49.

three months; but he who receives satisfaction within this prescribed period is either very lucky or very influential. The Estimates Committee found that a delay of five months was 'normal';[70] the 'Swaminatham' Committee, appointed to investigate the whole licensing process, found that the time taken to deal with eight randomly selected cases varied between 61 and 396 days, and that for six of the eight it exceeded 150 days.[71] This may be partly explained by the failure of many applicants to provide the information required of them or to present their cases in adequate detail; but the practice of extensive consultation with a variety of 'interested' agencies, which—as always—offers so many opportunities for the multiplication of bureaucratic formalities, would seem to be mainly responsible.

Another difficulty is that many of the licences granted are not taken up by the grantees. Quantitative information about 'infructuous' licences is difficult to come by, but the Minister told the Rajya Sabha on 25 April 1962 that 814 licences covering 54 different types of industry were being revoked because the grantees had 'not taken effective steps'.[72] That the number is so large calls in doubt the effectiveness of the scrutiny process; but even if this was as well organized as possible, the practice of obtaining a licence simply as an 'insurance' or as a means of denying it to a potential competitor would surely continue.

Even more serious is the inadequacy of the criteria used by the Licensing Committee. The official list of 'considerations', quoted above, is 'ideal' rather than actual. As Professor Paranjape says, the Committee is mainly guided by 'the targets laid down in the Plan and the capacity already licensed'. Hence licensing becomes 'a mere arithmetical exercise'. Among the factors which the same author holds to be insufficiently considered are import policies, excise policies, and the availabilities of transport, power, and raw materials.[73] These lacunae could, presumably, be filled without too much difficulty. Less easy to deal with is the impact—at present extremely haphazard—of 'non-economic' criteria on the Committee's decisions. Among its aims are to prevent monopoly, to encourage new entrants, and to promote regional diversification. On what principle does the Committee decide between two rival applications, the first from a well-established firm, dominant in its particular field, likely to take up its licence quickly and to produce efficiently, the second from a new entrant whose capacity to make rapid and competent use of the opportunity afforded him is necessarily doubtful, however carefully the 'vetting' exercise may have been performed? We do not know; but we do know

[70] EC 1960–1: *123*, para. 46.
[71] At the time of writing, the only account available to me of the first (interim) report of this committee was in *EE*, Jan. 1964.
[72] Rajya Sabha Deb., xxxviii, 551–3. [73] Paranjape, *IJPA*, July-Sept. 1962, p. 302.

that, for one reason or another, the Committee has adopted a policy of 'promoting uneconomic-scale plants'. We also know that it lacks the means of subjecting proposals to any but the most rough and ready of cost-and-benefit analyses, since it is advised by an agency, the Directorate General, in which engineering rather than economics is the principal skill.[74]

Connected with this is a fourth difficulty: that the licensing process, as at present operated, limits and even—in some cases—eliminates competition among enterprises in the private sector. As Professor Bhagwati says:

> Competition has been virtually ruled out by the detailed target system of planning that is now practised in our country. Foreign competition is ruled out, thanks to the Ministry's heavy reliance upon . . . quantitative restrictions. The adoption of the quantitative target system of planning has led to the elimination of domestic competition as well. Since industrial capacity is closely watched . . . an efficient producer cannot increase output and drive out an inefficient producer, thus ruling out 'actual' competition. (In fact, the rivals themselves are often saddled with equally uneconomic plants under the present system.) Nor can a new firm enter, so that one cannot have even 'potential' competition.[75]

The Licensing Committee, therefore, even while attempting to eliminate monopolistic tendencies by encouraging new entrants and favouring the smaller type of enterprise, is *creating* monopoly—or at least oligopoly—by its policy of trying to relate capacity to potential availabilities and potential demand. As a result, Indian industry is 'feather-bedded' to such an extent that a producer who fails to make a profit has to be spectacularly inefficient, even by the rather low Indian standards of efficiency.

How far can these inadequacies be eliminated? The demand that licensing should be governed by 'purely economic' criteria is unrealistic. Where the location of industry is concerned, for instance, political factors cannot be eliminated; nor is it possible to view with equanimity the indefinite expansion of large firms, even though, in respect of economic efficiency, they may have the edge on the smaller ones. What is needed is a clear realization *when* and *why* the economically optimum is being disregarded, and for *what* precise purposes. As for the elimination of competition, this is difficult to avoid so long as the government is pursuing a policy of administrative rationing of scarce resources; but one would have thought that, even within the limits of such a policy, the diseconomies of competition elimination were a consideration of some importance. What would help in the solution of these problems as well as lessen the seriousness of a number of others, such as those stressed by Professor Paranjape, is the improvement of the advisory service provided by the

[74] See Jagdish Bhagwati, 'Economics of Scale, Distribution of Industry and Programming', *EW*, 1 Sept. 1962.

[75] Ibid.

Directorate General. The lines along which this might be done are thus suggested by Professor Bhagwati, who includes the Planning Commission as well as the Directorate General (Development Wing) within the ambit of his radical proposals:

> Useful planning does not consist in merely multiplying the strength of the Development Wing and the Planning Commisssion with engineers who have no conception of economic planning. The vast staff of bureaucrats who plan industry usually end up being unnecessary nuisances in various ways merely because they have no clue to the type of planning that can improve upon the laissez faire system. We thus get numerous reports, statistics on output and capacity (which mean nothing), meetings and delays. The marginal benefit is almost certainly negative.
>
> It is absolutely necessary that the Development Wing and the Planning Commission's Industries Division be instructed to carry out analytical work to determine optimal location and scales of activities, at least of important items. These exercises would be necessarily expensive, as they would need estimates of costs which, in turn, demand consultation fees. However, once the problem has been viewed, for any industry, and solved in the programming framework, the locations, scales and expansions of plants emerge. The plants could be 'handed over' to the successful applicants who could then be made to bear the expenses of the Ministry's investigations. We would then be able to secure the advantage of rational governmental intervention.[76]

It may be that Professor Bhagwati is unduly contemptuous of the Directorate General as at present organized; it may be, too, that he has excessive faith in the type of 'analytical work' that he advocates. Nevertheless, it is clear enough that if *laissez-faire* is to be replaced by licensing, there must be calculation of a type which, so far, has hardly been attempted. That he should have emphasized this so trenchantly is very valuable.

Proposals such as these, even if accepted, would take a long time to put into effect, since they would make heavy demands on econometric and statistical skills that are in short supply. But present licensing procedure is so obviously unsatisfactory that something needs to be done about it immediately. The closely allied procedures for controlling the issue of capital, for rationing the import of capital goods, and for vetting foreign investment and collaboration proposals[77] are also in urgent need of review. These needs have become so evident during the period of relative economic

[76] Ibid.

[77] Foreign collaboration agreements are almost essential for all but the simpler and better established industries. The number of such agreements underwent a phenomenal increase from 20 in 1956–7 to 425 in 1961–2. Total 'joint ventures' are now some 1,500. Industries for which agreements are welcomed by the authorities are (*a*) 'vital' ones, particularly if they involve large capital investments and complex technical processes, (*b*) those that serve to train Indian entrepreneurs, technicians and labourers, and (*c*) those that improve the foreign exchange position. The rule, originally laid down in the First Industrial Policy Resolution, that Indians should have majority capital-holdings, is now honoured more in the breach than in the observance (see P. K. Srivastava, 'Foreign Collaboration in Indian Industry', *EE*, ann. no. 1964, Dec. 1963).

stagnation between 1962 and 1964 that the government has referred them to a 'high-power' advisory body, the 'Swaminatham' Committee, which was appointed in September 1963 and was still in session at the time of writing. So far, it has made recommendations calculated to eliminate some of the delays in the issue of licences and to ensure that they are taken up by successful applicants within a reasonable time-limit.

Much of the trouble, as we have seen, arises from the need for consultation between the Licensing Committee and a number of other authorities. If the applicant for a licence wishes to raise capital from the public, the consent of the Controller of Capital Issues is required. If he needs foreign exchange to import capital goods, he must apply to the Capital Goods and Heavy Electrical Plants Committee, consisting of representatives of the Ministry of Commerce and Industry, Ministry of Finance, Planning Commission, Chief Controller of Imports and Exports, and the State Trading Corporation. If he proposes collaboration with a foreign firm, he must obtain the consent of the Foreign Agreements Committee, consisting of representatives of the Ministry of Finance, Planning Commission, Controller of Capital Issues, and Ministry of Commerce and Industry. All this, as may be imagined, takes a long time; but the issue of the licence itself is frequently delayed by the fact that the licensing authorities themselves check that the necessary applications have been made and are broadly conformable with the policies currently being pursued by these various officials and committees. What the 'Swaminatham' Committee has recommended, in an interim report, is that the Licensing Committee should issue, within a month of the application, a 'letter of intent' giving a general indication of the conditions attached to the licence and indicating a period (of between six and twelve months) during which the potential licensee should come forward with his proposals for capital issues, foreign collaboration, import of capital goods, &c. If all the remaining applications are not submitted within this time-limit, the letter of intent, and therefore the licence, becomes automatically null and void. For 'key' industries, it proposed that a special procedure be introduced, whereby immediately after the 'letter of intent' has been issued all other 'clearances' will be dealt with simultaneously. In this way, it is hoped not only that unreasonable delays will be eliminated but that the backlog of 'infructuous' licences, with its consequent blocking of capacity, will be reduced. These recommendations have been accepted by the government, which has simultaneously decided to raise the 'fixed investment' limitation under the Industries (Development and Regulation) Act from Rs10 to Rs25 lakhs, with certain exceptions.

After the entrepreneur has gone through these various pre-natal exercises and established his undertaking, he will find his freedom circumscribed in various other ways. He will have to conform, of course, with the laws relating to health, safety, welfare, and labour relations. These apply impartially to all entrepreneurs and therefore will not, in the normal way, involve him in any special disadvantages. If, however, he is operating in certain fields he will find himself subject to controls over production, distribution, and prices. Most of these are embodied in the Essential Commodities Act, 1955, which authorizes the central government to regulate or prohibit the production and control the supply, distribution, and price of certain enumerated commodities and of any other commodities which, by order, may be declared 'essential'. Among the more important commodities at present under regulation and control are iron and steel (production, distribution, and prices), non-ferrous metals (distribution and prices), coal (distribution, prices, and movement), fertilizers (distribution and prices), cinema films (distribution), cotton textiles (production and distribution), paper (distribution), and sugar (production and supply). Powers over these and other commodities, however, are also given to the government by the Industries (Development and Regulation) Act, with the result that there seems to be an excess of statutory authority. In practice, Professor Paranjape tells us, 'the Ministry of Commerce and Industry follows the principle that, wherever power under the Industries (Development and Regulation) Act is adequate, action is taken under that Act; but if the powers are not considered adequate resort is made to the Essential Commodities Act'. This duplication may, perhaps, be convenient for the controllers but it must be a little confusing for the controlled. Prices may also be—and are—regulated by so-called Executive Orders which, although devoid of direct legal authority, are enforceable by virtue of the very existence of the above statutory powers. In addition, the government possesses regulatory authority over specific industries, through legislative measures such as the Tea Act, the Coffee Act, and the Rubber Act.[78]

The total effect on private enterprise of all these controls has never been adequately studied and is extremely difficult to estimate. Most observers, except those who dislike planned economies as such, agree that the government needs the powers of investigation and regulation that it has assumed; but whether it uses them correctly is less certain. Much evidence has accumulated of unnecessary and inhibiting interference by 'the bureaucracy' with the operations of private enterprise. Indeed, on *a priori* grounds one would expect this to happen; for bureaucrats and entrepreneurs in India tend to have different backgrounds and to act on different assumptions. By and large, the entrepreneur is interested in escaping from controls, the bureaucrat in tightening them up. There is very little of that common ground between them such as facilitates the smooth operation of controls in a country such as France. Hence, although

[78] Paranjape, *IJPA*, July-Sept. 1962, pp. 304–10.

one knows that World Bank economists sometimes display excessive enthusiasm for economic 'freedom', one may feel that there is little exaggeration in the following passage from the latest Mission report:

> The activities of industry in India are minutely controlled and supervised by the Government in a manner which is destructive to enterprise and efficiency. Public undertakings are subject to much the same controls as private enterprise. In some respects, indeed, they are more hedged around because of their accountability to Parliament for the public funds entrusted to them. An overworked civil service, which must stick to the rules and avoid mistakes, should not be expected to take what are essentially management decisions. Yet in the last resort it is the Ministries of the Central Government and their subordinate agencies which decide in important cases how large a firm should be, whether or not it should be allowed to expand, what price it should charge for its products, what its wages and salaries should be, where it should obtain its supplies, what foreign exchange it should spend, whether it should go to the market for a loan, and sometimes even who should be its directors. If Indian industry is to operate efficiently, some way must be found of eliminating at least the major of these detailed checks and controls and of decentralising the process of economic decision. The machinery of government in India is simply not designed to carry out the tasks that are being imposed on it, and every year it comes closer to breaking down altogether under the strain.[79]

Perhaps the bureaucracy's back is broader than this suggests; but how broad is industry's? Faced with the deceleration of the rate of industrial growth since 1962, the government is now having second thoughts about controls. Such thoughts are possible because the Congress 'right', traditionally anti-control, has become stronger, because the coincidence of economic stagnation with unprecedented danger from abroad is extremely alarming, and because evidence is mounting that the private sector, which exceeded some of its Second Plan targets, will fall far short of most of those given it by the Third Plan. As a beginning, industrial licensing has been relaxed, the control of capital issues has been liberalized, price controls on some sixteen commodities have been removed, administrative arrangements for dealing with foreign investment proposals have been 'streamlined', and—perhaps most significant of all—the immensely bureaucratic and corruptly organized control over the price and distribution of steel has been partly dismantled.

While, inevitably, there is controversy in the government about this as yet modest 'bonfire', some of the younger and more flexibly-minded ministers are keen enough on stoking it up. Speaking to the Annual Meeting of the Associated Chambers of Commerce, Subramaniam, then Minister of Steel, Mines, and Heavy Industry, questioned whether 'some of the present controls' really served 'the interest of equitable and planned distribution'. Speaking of those measures aimed at encouraging new

[79] Quoted from *EE*, 14 Oct. 1963, pp. 661–2.

entrants into industry and achieving balanced regional development, he said: 'We cannot . . . encourage the proliferation of uneconomic units without rejecting the general progress of industry in the country as a whole.'[80] Such sentiments, together with the actions they have inspired, are naturally welcome to all associated with the private sector of the economy. G. L. Mehta, the Chairman of ICIC, went so far as to say that the setting off of 'inquiries into the functioning of our economic system', such as those headed by T. Swaminatham and V. K. R. V. Rao, was 'a welcome result of the Chinese invasion and the subsequent stagnation of the economy'.[81] But even among the socialists there seems to be a growing realization that the throttling of private enterprise hardly contributes towards the achievement of a just society.

The danger is now, perhaps, that the reaction against controls will go too far. Among the less intelligent businessmen and among members of parties such as the Swatantra and the Jan Sangh there is an insensate ambition to 'scrap the lot' and to deprive the government of the control agencies, including the Planning Commission itself, which must continue to exist if India is to make optimum use of her scarce resources and achieve coherent economic development, consciously directed towards agreed goals. This will have to be resisted, and the government will need to rely for advice far more heavily than in the past on economists, such as Professors Raj and Bhagwati, whose devotion to planning and to socialism is not in doubt but whose intelligence revolts at some of the things being done to the private sector in the supposed interests of the 'planned economy' and in the name of the 'socialist pattern'. That the balance between regulation and stimulation of the private sector now begins to tip towards the latter should be encouraging, not merely to actual and potential capitalists, but to all who find in the current stagnation of the economy a cause for serious alarm. Indian politicians, however, might well bear in mind that a British government which, in the interests of 'setting the people free', got rid of many of its agencies of economic control in the early 1950s began, somewhat hesitantly, to create new ones in the early 1960s.

(ix)

We may now turn to the third of the four issues presented at the beginning of this chapter: the balance between large-scale and small-scale industry, which has already been lightly touched upon in the discussion just concluded.

In dealing with the division of responsibility between public and private enterprise, we distinguished economic from ideological or political considerations. Whereas economic rationality would appear to dictate that each sector shall be given the tasks which it is best fitted to undertake,

[80] Ibid. 13 Dec. 1963. [81] Ibid. 13 Mar. 1964.

ideology demands that the public sector shall be strengthened at the expense of the private and politics demand that the keys of economic power shall be firmly retained in the hands of the government. The same distinction, perhaps rather fuzzy around the edges, applies to the regulation of the private sector itself. Economic rationality dictates that the regulatory agencies should be used solely to economize scarce resources and to gear industry to the requirements of the plan; ideology and politics suggest that they must also prevent 'undue' concentration and promote an 'equitable' regional distribution of industry. Not surprisingly, a similar mixture of considerations affects the government's policies towards small-scale industries. In this case, however, it appears at first sight that the two sets of considerations are complementary rather than contradictory. Economically, it may be argued that small-scale industry possesses, relatively to India's contemporary factor endowment, a favourable capital-labour 'mix'; that it increases employment more rapidly than large-scale; and that it stimulates 'healthy' competition, while large-scale industry breeds 'unhealthy' monopoly. From the ideological-political point of view, one of the advantages of the small-scale would appear to be that it tends to distribute economic power among the many instead of concentrating it in the few. Another is that, by facilitating the geographical dispersal of industry and the industrialization of rural areas, it helps to equalize incomes and conditions of living and to prevent the further concentration of population in large, insanitary towns where 'agitators' can take a full advantage of mass misery. To such alleged advantages may be added those that make a specific appeal to the adherents of the Gandhian ideology, with its hostility to metropolitan life, its quasi-religious exaltation of the small-scale and localized as against the large-scale and centralized, and its belief that the village and small town represent the basic Indian culture on which the political superstructure should be built. In view of this remarkable convergence of arguments from different premises, it is not surprising that the planners should have decided to give small-scale industry special encouragement, both positively, through—for instance—financial assistance and organized marketing, and negatively, through protecting it against 'unfair' competition from the larger units.

To evaluate the policies that have been pursued, one must first distinguish between the different varieties of 'small-scale'. This is all the more important because the planners themselves have failed to do so with sufficient clarity. Much of the discussion about small-scale industry—sometimes confusingly labelled the 'decentralized sector'—appears to assume that considerations which apply to a small factory also apply to a 'back-yard' enterprise or even to one carried on by a single operative in his own house. Such assumptions breed confusion of counsel.

The broadest distinction is that between three kinds of industry: village or cottage, handicraft, and 'small-scale' as such. The First Plan report (Ch. 24) defines a village industry as one engaged in 'the processing of local raw materials for local markets . . . with simple techniques'. As examples, it gives oil pressing, soap making with neem oil, paddy husking, palm gur, gur and khandsari, leather, blankets, hand-made paper, bee-keeping, and matches, for all of which it draws up 'programmes'. Handicraft industry, on the other hand, involves the production, by skilled craftsmen using traditional or quasi-traditional methods, of articles of aesthetic value frequently commanding a national or even international market. The brassware of Banaras, Moradabad, Jaipur, and Tanjore provides a well-known example. Small-scale industry is different from either. Industries in this group, says the Second Plan report (pp. 450–1),

> are of varied types, but their common features at present are their urban or semi-urban location and use of machines, power and modern techniques. They are run by small entrepreneurs or self-supporting workers, and sometimes by cooperatives. Some units in this field, e.g. those manufacturing bicycle parts or sewing machine parts, may be ancillary to large industries but as a rule they are not linked to them by well-established sub-contracting system but as suppliers of products against occasional orders. The working definition adopted by the Small-Scale Industries Board brings within the scope of the term 'small-scale industries' all units or establishments having a capital invested of less than Rs5 lakhs and employing less than 50 persons when using power.

Unfortunately, there are several industries, of great importance to India, which do not fit easily into this neat threefold classification. The most widespread of them are hand-spinning and hand-weaving, which, although of the 'cottage' type, may be carried on in urban as well as rural areas and do not produce exclusively for a local market. Coir manufacture and sericulture are equally difficult to pigeon-hole. Indeed, coir, although listed by the First Plan report among the 'village' industries, has a significant international market, well over half of its products being exported. For purposes of the present analysis, however, it will be convenient to retain all three in the 'village' category.

This type of industry is one where ideological considerations are at their most powerful, as a result of the great emphasis placed on it by the Father of the Nation, Mahatma Gandhi; but it is also a type for whose fostering and development, within the context of a national plan, a strong economic case has been made out. As we have seen,[82] it has been regarded by the planners as a most important method of satisfying consumer demand by labour-intensive methods (and thereby helping to combat inflation) at a time when the nation's scarce capital resources are being mainly devoted to laying the foundations of a modern industrial structure. Even Dhar

[82] See above, pp. 126–7.

and Lydall, who are by no means generally enamoured of the small-scale, admit that 'from the standpoint of saving capital there is much to be said for the traditional village industries—especially when the capital is already in existence'.[83]

The fact that these traditional industries have to coexist with non-traditional ones, however, brings some difficult problems. By and large, the traditional products are inferior—or at least seem so to most consumers—and often their comparative costs are unfavourable. To some extent this can be dealt with by licensing policy. The licensers decide what proportion of total demand is to be satisfied by factory production, license the requisite capacity, and leave the village industries to look after the remainder. Thus, at least some of the demand will *have* to be met by the 'decentralized sector', and the fact that consumers prefer the factory product will push up its price, thereby offsetting the village industry's initial cost disadvantage. Licensing policy has actually been used for this purpose, as first envisaged in the Industrial Policy Resolution of 1948, which promised the cottage industries 'safeguards against intensive competition by large-scale manufacture' and said that the question of 'how the textile mill industry can be made complementary to, rather than competitive with, the handloom industry' would be examined. Pursuing this line of policy, the First Plan report announced and the government attempted to give shape to 'common production programmes' involving, among other things, the reservation of spheres of production to village industries and the placing of limits on the expansion of competitive large-scale (i.e. factory) industries. By themselves, however, these concessions were insufficient, as they presupposed a degree of market perfection which did not exist. Consequently there was added to them price protection and various forms of positive encouragement. Among the items in the First Plan's Common Production Programme were (*a*) the imposition of a *cess* on the products of the factory industry, (*b*) arrangements for the supply of raw materials, and (*c*) the co-ordination of research and training. The importance of co-operatives as a means of organizing and strengthening the 'decentralized sector' was also stressed. As executive agencies for this programme, a series of All-India Boards, with corresponding agencies at the state level, was created: the All-India Khadi and Village Industry Board, the Handloom Board, the All-India Handicrafts Board, the Coir Board, and the Silk Board. Advice on policy was provided by the 'Karve' (Village and Small-Scale Industries) Committee, which reported in June 1955.

Certain aspects of this programme were more controversial than others. Nearly everyone agreed about the importance of village industries in the context of the plan, but there were strong criticisms of the policy of

[83] Dhar & Lydall, *Small Enterprises*, p. 84.

supporting them by curtailing production and raising prices in the factory sector. The mill owners, of course, objected for self-interested reasons, but there were many others, including some distinguished economists, who felt uneasy about something that came very close to the subsidization of technical backwardness and feared that Gandhian enthusiasts, still a significant pressure-group, might persuade the government to carry this policy far beyond the point where it possessed any economic justification. The programme for village industries in the Second Plan (ch. 20) represented a compromise between the rival factions. The total sum allocated was greatly increased, but emphasis, for the first time, was firmly placed on the technical improvement of village industries and on other methods of increasing their economic strength rather than on measures to protect them against their large-scale competitors. This change of emphasis also found expression in the Second Industrial Policy Resolution of 1956:

> The State has been following a policy of supporting cottage and village and small scale industries by restricting the volume of production in the large-scale sector, by differential taxation, or by direct subsidies. While such measures will continue to be taken whenever necessary, the aim of the State policy will be to ensure that the decentralised sector acquires sufficient vitality to be self-supporting and its development is integrated with that of large-scale industry. The State will, therefore, concentrate on measures designed to improve the competitive strength of the small scale producer. For this it is essential that the technique of production should be constantly improved and modernised, the pace of the transformation being regulated so as to avoid, as far as possible, technological unemployment.[84]

Methods were to include training in improved techniques, the supply of raw materials, equipment and credit, and—where appropriate—the encouragement of co-operative forms of organization. Organizationally, this involved the strengthening of the All-India Boards, the creation of state Khadi and Village Industry Boards, the development of the state Departments of Industries, and the appointment of Industries Officers at the district and block levels. One of the inevitable results was a considerable amount of organizational duplication and confusion, commented upon unfavourably in the Third Plan report (p. 437).

In spite of the delays in implementation which were inseparable from an excessively bureaucratic, complex, and slow-moving administrative set-up, the Third Plan report was able to record some impressive progress in the production of handloom cloth, which had increased from about 742 million yards in 1950–1 to about 1,900 million yards in 1960–1, and in that of traditional khadi, which had increased from 7 million to 48 million yards over the same period. 'Fuller employment' had been provided for nearly 3 million weavers, 'employment, mostly part-time' for over a

[84] *FYP*(2), pp. 47–48.

million additional spinners, and 'whole-time employment' for about 140,000 'weavers, carpenters etc'. The progress of other village industries, however, had been less spectacular. Programmes in the Second Plan had provided 'partial relief' to about 500,000 'artisans and underemployed women workers', but the results obtained were 'not commensurate with the expenditure incurred'. Sericulture had achieved modest increases in production, but little technical progress, while the coir industry was stagnant.[85] In all, little had been achieved for the very considerable expenditure of money and effort except in spinning and weaving, and even there it was doubtful how much of the achievement could be attributed to the various programmes. No one could say, moreover, whether alternative uses for the resources devoted to the 'decentralized' textile sector might not have produced superior results, either in production or in overall employment.

Nevertheless, the planners decided to continue with the mixture as before, although total outlay in the Third Plan was to increase only by a small amount.[86] Emphasis was again placed on 'constant adaptation to the conditions of rapid change in a dynamic economy and the adoption of new techniques, methods and forms of organization', while the hope was expressed that with 'the progressive enlargement of programmes of positive assistance'—which, so far as village as distinct from small-scale industries were concerned, did not figure very prominently in the plan—the role of 'subsidies, sales rebates and sheltered markets', could be reduced.

> In the field of khadi, it is hoped to bring about a gradual reduction of prices through technical improvements, pooling of production costs and economy in transport and other distribution charges. Rebates on sales of khadi . . . will be reviewed with the object of replacing them, as far as possible, by suitable management grants. As regards village industries also, it is proposed that the present subsidies and/or rebates on sales in respect of their products should be replaced by gradually tapering management grants. Similarly, in the handloom industry emphasis will be shifted from sales rebates to more positive forms of assistance.[87]

It is clear that in this field a number of fundamental policy questions remain to be answered. The Commission and the government, it would appear, believe that village industries can become economically viable if they receive various forms of assistance designed to enable them, eventually, to stand on their own feet. It is also held that such assistance, costly as it may be, is worth-while to the extent that capital resources are saved, employment is promoted, inflation combated, and the drift away from the villages halted. Whether such beliefs are justified remains to be proved. It is even more doubtful whether the 'positive' approach currently in favour will be sufficient to produce the desired results. The generally

[85] *FYP*(*3*), pp. 429–31. [86] See table ibid. p. 438. [87] Ibid. pp. 426–7, 434.

accepted view, as we have seen, is that permanent protection is uneconomic; but one strongly suspects that, so far, protection has contributed far more to the maintenance and expansion of these industries than all the programmes designed to improve their techniques, strengthen their finances, provide them with regular supplies, and expand their sales outlets. The vital questions, therefore, are how long these protective measures are to be persisted with and whether, as a result of them, the Indian nation will be presented with a collection of assets whose value is in any way commensurate with their real cost. So far, the authorities have failed to give clear answers, and suspicion grows that what may be involved is a long-term or even permanent subsidization of technological obsolescence, which no developing nation can afford. The Gandhian ideology, which regards village industries as good things in themselves, whatever their cost, may no longer have much influence on the minds of the planners; but it has been replaced by a collection of vested interests which, spread throughout the length and breadth of India, are politically of great importance. For this reason, once the policy of protection has been embarked upon, it is exceedingly difficult to discontinue, however unanswerable may be the economic arguments for its discontinuance.

No one would seriously argue that *all* village industries are doomed to become obsolete, and few would assert that the policy of protecting and supporting village industries, in the context of the kind of economic plan that India has adopted, was entirely mistaken as a means of giving certain kinds of temporary relief. The problem is to discover *which* of them, when all economic and social costs have been taken into consideration, have a long-term or even permanent role to play in the economic structure. The 'correct' answer, which can be found only by a combination of econometric calculation with analysed experience, is unlikely to be one that a democratic Indian government will wish to publicize, still less to act upon. For, in this field, the superficial coincidence between the economically desirable and the ideologically or politically acceptable breaks down at too many points. Only if economic development achieves an *élan* where the unemployed and underemployed are absorbed in modern industry at a rate which renders the maintenance of technologically obsolescent but 'employment-creating' forms of industry socially and politically unnecessary can the problem yield to considerations of economic rationality. As yet there is no sign that such a pace is likely to be attained, and one of the vicious circles that makes its attainment less likely is created by the very policy of protecting technological obsolescence.

(x)

When we turn from village industries and allied occupations to handicrafts, we are in a field where the problems are less serious. There is no handicraft 'ideology', comparable with that which has grown up around khadi and handloom. There are, of course, both aesthetic considerations and feelings of national pride which cause people to look with favour on the maintenance and improvement of traditional crafts for which India has become world-famous. But one cannot doubt that these industries also represent important economic assets, if only for their actual and potential contribution to the export trade. Policy in this field must obviously concentrate—as it does—on smoothing the flow of raw materials, maintaining quality, stepping up sales promotion and improving marketing arrangements.

Executive responsibility is in the hands of an All-India Handicrafts Board, concerned with the development of about 40 different crafts. This is particularly interested in extending co-operative forms of organization, establishing handicraft emporia, and improving design. During the Second Plan regional design development centres were set up at Delhi, Bombay, Bangalore, and Calcutta, and over 100 emporia and sales depots in various parts of the country. Through the latter, annual sales were increased from Rs1 to Rs2·5 crores, and in the last three years of the plan handicrafts worth Rs6 crores per annum were exported. These figures may not be large, but they represent a very worth-while contribution made at comparatively low capital cost. Further progress depends on overcoming shortages of technical personnel and raw materials and on improving the flow of credit to artisans.[88]

(xi)

When we turn from cottage industries and handicrafts to consider 'small-scale' industries, as defined by the planners, we enter a different world. The primitive, the traditional, and the technologically obsolescent have been left behind; for the only thing that *essentially* distinguishes a small-scale industry from a large or medium-scale one is its *size*. Although it may be—and often is—technically backward by comparison with the larger members of its species, it may equally well be technically their superior.

There can, however, be no clear definition of a small-scale industry. Any delimitation in terms of number employed or amount of horse-power used is necessarily arbitrary, and the border-line thus fixed is, of course, constantly being crossed by the more successful small enterprises, which are on their way to becoming large ones. This situation makes generalization hazardous. The Indian planners, however, constantly attempt it, and even, as we have seen, try to lump together for certain purposes the 'small-scale' in the village industry sense and the 'small-scale' as we are now using it.

[88] See ibid. pp. 445–6, 431.

Nevertheless, on any reasonable definition, small-scale industry is playing an increasingly important role in the Indian economy. In one year alone, 1959–60, units with 10–49 workers using power or with 20–99 without power rose from 28,417 to 31,336, an increase of 10 per cent. Over the same period their payroll increased by some 6 per cent and their output, in value, by 7 per cent. Figures over a longer period are less reliable, but, as the Ford Foundation's International Perspective Planning Team says,[89] they lend 'strong support to the widespread observation of a very high growth rate in small firm numbers'. Their percentage contribution over the decade 1952–62 to the annual increase in industrial output was hardly, if at all, less than that of large- and medium-scale enterprises, and there is good evidence that in the latter part of the Second Plan they were responsible for spectacularly increasing their percentages of total output in certain lines (e.g. barbed wire, upholstery springs, machine screws, automobile radiators, expanded metal, bicycles, loud speakers, gang condensers, and electric motors) and for more moderate increases in others (e.g. electric irons wire netting, polythene tubing, shoe tacks, and ball bearings) (see Table 34, p. 506). In 1960 small registered factories represented 'over 92 per cent of all registered factories and . . . employed over 1,330,000 persons, or 38 per cent of total registered factory employment'. Their fixed capital amounted to about 17 per cent of the total, and the gross value of their output to 33 per cent (see Table 35, p. 507). In sum, the growth of small manufacturing enterprises 'is among the most significant features of India's recent development'.

This does not mean that the small-scale enterprise necessarily possesses any special virtues *as such* or that it should become the recipient of any special stimulants or encouragements from the public authorities. Nevertheless, for reasons that we have already stated and examined in connexion with village industries, the government and the Commission have decided that it merits such treatment.

The First Plan report,[90] which somewhat darkened counsel by including small industries and handloom under the same rubric, divided these industries into three groups, viz.

(i) those in which small-scale production has certain advantages and is not affected by large-scale industry to any great extent;
(ii) those in which small-scale industry is concerned with the manufacture of certain parts or with certain stages of production in a manufacturing process in which the predominant role is that of large-scale industry; and
(iii) those in which small-scale industry has to meet the competition of the corresponding large-scale industry.

[89] See *Small Scale Industries*, ch. 2: 'The Role of Small Industry in India's Development'.
[90] See ch. 25: 'Small Industries and Handicrafts'.

The only example given of the third was handloom, with which we are not at present concerned. The first group was exemplified by locks and padlocks, wax candles, buttons, *chappals* and badges. These, too, were outside the scope of 'small-scale' as subsequently defined, as the work was usually done 'on an individual basis' and the problem was to organize it 'through groups . . . to facilitate sale and marketing and the financing of production'. As for the second category, of which cycle parts, electrical goods, cutlery, pottery, and agricultural implements were cited as examples, this demanded for its welfare and development a series of 'common production programmes', involving 'a reservation of spheres according to some central plan for an industry as a whole, supported by considerable assistance in finance, organization and training on the part of the Central and State Governments'. At this stage, therefore, the Commission was thinking almost exclusively in terms of using small-scale industry as an ancillary to large-scale, *à la Japonaise*, and of providing it with the means of performing this role. That the large-scale manufacturer might not have much use for this kind of assistance, owing to the difficulty of getting the small-scale man to send him regular supplies of standardized components, did not apparently cross the planners' minds; nor, despite a very brief and ambiguous reference to 'a number of small industries which call for skill and training and, invariably, for the use of power', did the planners conceive of the possibility that small-scale undertakings might be able to function as independent units.

The Second Plan report, which repeated the First Plan's 'grouping' of industries, darkened counsel even further by dealing with 'village and small industries' in the same chapter.[91] It also continued to assume that small-scale industries, now defined as 'all units or establishments having a capital investment of less than Rs5 lakhs and employing less than 50 persons when using power', would be mainly ancillary to large-scale undertakings. The programme for them, however, was more sharply defined, and the allocation of resources for their benefit stepped up to the very considerable figure of Rs55 crores. Under the aegis of the Small-Scale Industries Board, there were to be extensive arrangements for supply, marketing, finance, and technical assistance. In these, key roles were to be played by the recently established National Small Industries Corporation and by the Small Industries Service Institutes. The former was to be mainly concerned with marketing and supply. Through whole-sale depots, it was to purchase goods from small industries for re-sale to retailers; it was to liaise with the Director-General of Supplies and Disposals to secure bulk orders from the government for products of small-scale industries; and it was to make machinery and equipment available to the small-scale entrepreneur on hire-purchase terms. The

[91] Ch. 20: 'Village and Small Industries'.

TABLE 34

Growth in Output of Small and Large Factories: Selected Industries

Industry name	*Years compared*	*Unit*	*Production at start of period*			*Production at end of period*			*Small factory*	
			Small	*Large*	*Total*	*Small*	*Large*	*Total*	*Period start* (%)	*Period end* (%)
Picking stick	58–60	000s	192	11	203	543	13	556	95	98
Industrial brushes	58–60	000s	2,158	134	2,292	2,530	46	2,576	94	98
Electric iron	58–60	doz.	2,183	350	2,533	22,585	550	23,135	86	98
Wire netting & mesh	58–60	ton	6,490	1,579	8,069	7,548	1,279	8,827	80	86
Barbed wire	59–60	ton	4,903	2,289	7,192	10,016	1,947	11,963	68	84
Upholstery spring	58–60	gross	4,600	9,655	14,255	25,431	18,090	43,521	32	58
Oil pressure stoves	58–60	000s	309	134	443	494	221	715	70	69
Polythene tubing	59–60	ton	1,047	854	1,901	2,006	901	2,907	55	69
Toothbrushes	58–60	gross	46,330	26,688	73,018	55,635	26,820	82,455	63	67
Spectacle frames	58–60	doz.	93	101	194	128	116	244	48	53
Electric horns	58–60	no.	6,300	3,700	10,000	13,550	13,450	27,000	63	50
Machine screws	57–59	ton	278	660	938	736	890	1,626	30	45
Shoe tacks	58–60	ton	68	79	147	178	189	367	46	48
Automobile radiators	58–60	no.	809	12,444	13,253	18,029	34,765	52,794	6	34
Taps & dies	58–61	000s	96	132	228	205	418	623	42	33
Air compressors	58–60	no.	209	34	343	830	1,715	2,545	61	33
Nuts, bolts, rivets	57–60	ton	19,770	32,136	51,906	20,744	42,804	66,013	38	31
Expanded metal	58–60	ton	25	1,947	1,972	639	1,758	2,397	1	27
Automobile batteries	58–60	000s	90	350	440	113	509	822	20	22
Bicycles	56–60	000s	26	653	679	228	991	1,219	4	19
Sewing machines	56–60	000s	24	50	74	52	297	349	32	18
Loud speakers	57–60	000s	1	81	82	36	186	222	1	16
Gang condensers	59–61	000s	2	68	70	14	94	108	3	13
Drums & barrels	58–60	Rs lakh	66	410	476	93	633	726	14	13
Ball-bearings	58–60	000s	168	2,126	2,294	468	3,200	3,668	8	13
Electric motors	57–59	000h.p.	21	479	500	70	580	650	4	11
Bicycle free wheels	58–61	000s	37	238	275	72	681	752	13	9
Clocks & watches	57–60	000s	. .	22	22	2	52	54	0	4
Automobile dynamos	59–61	no.	30	447	477	332	16,869	17,201	6	2

Source: Ford Found., *Development of Small Scale Industries in India*, pp. 23–24.

TABLE 35

Employment, Capital & Output in Small Registered Factories by Industry Group

INDUSTRY GROUP		FACTORIES WITH FIXED CAPITAL LESS THAN Rs 5 LAKHS				PERCENTAGE TO ALL REGISTERED FACTORIES			
Code	Title	No. of factories	Persons employed	Fixed capital (Rs. lakhs)	Gross output (Rs. lakhs)	No. of factories (%)	Persons employed (%)	Fixed capital (%)	Gross output (%)
209	Miscellaneous food preparations	3,715	138,238	36,73	2,47,72	87·2	49·6	47·0	51·2
205	Grain mill products	4,255	92,639	16,84	1,82,77	95·6	86·1	84·1	78·8
231	Textile spinning, weaving, & finishing	3,073	146,977	12,12	1,08,74	83·3	12·7	5·4	13·3
350	Metal products exc. machinery & transport equipment	2,080	61,929	10,59	62,40	97·0	66·2	41·5	60·0
010	Ginning & pressing	2,812	104,350	14,83	60,27	95·7	91·9	93·6	88·1
360*	Machinery, exc. electr. machinery	2,599	78,879	15,69	55,54	95·0	51·8	35·1	46·4
220	Tobacco products	2,565	136,171	2,77	51,06	95·3	74·8	34·3	43·0
319*	Misc. chemical products	1,002	42,502	7,22	47,63	89·6	47·1	19·9	28·6
341*	Basic iron & steel industries	709	43,502	5,28	43,11	84·9	31·3	2·7	16·2
291*	Tanneries & leather finishing	413	16,077	1,55	39,87	97·4	77·0	63·7	88·8
280*	Printing, publishing & allied industries	2,466	68,702	14,24	37,97	96·3	60·5	47·4	50·2
399*	Manufac. not elsewhere classified (n.e.c.)	1,028	30,459	6,85	26,89	96·8	83·5	76·9	82·5
342*	Non-ferrous metal industries	267	8,206	2,43	24,68	91·7	36·6	13·9	41·2
250*	Wood & cork except furniture	1,574	40,220	4,67	24,26	97·8	81·9	68·7	82·2
370*	Electrical machinery	485	25,058	8,95	23,04	83·2	28·8	25·1	21·1
339*	Non-metallic mineral products (n.e.c.)	727	33,309	3,48	21,40	95·7	76·2	52·0	63·2
384	Motor vehicle repair	1,174	38,728	6,61	20,17	94·7	72·5	55·3	73·4
300*	Rubber products	257	15,187	6,96	18,20	92·1	38·2	41·5	23·9
239	Textiles (n.e.c.)	778	26,433	1,85	17,96	98·5	86·7	62·0	77·6
311*	Basic industr. chemicals	207	9,110	2,81	17,62	76·9	18·2	3·4	17·9
331*	Structural clay products	604	42,882	10,63	9,57	94·5	70·4	53·2	50·0
332*	Glass & glass products	211	25,041	1,50	8,19	88·6	67·1	24·8	49·9
	All other mfrs.	3,456	113,012	16,97	83,29	..	..	..	..
	TOTAL	36,457	1,337,612	2,11,57	12,32,35	92·1	37·9	17·5	32·9

* CSIO type industry group.

Source: CSO & Indian Statistical Inst., Calcutta, *Annual Survey of Industries, 1960;* special provisional tabulation on census sector; draft National Sample Survey No. 114 on sample sector.

Service Institutes were to be increased in number from four to twenty, so that each state had at least one. Their functions were described thus:

> Institutes will not merely provide technical advice in response to enquiries from small units regarding improved types of machines, equipment and processes, use of raw materials and methods of reducing costs, but their technical staff will contact small units and advise on their problems, thus providing a useful extension service. The Institutes will also arrange to give demonstrations in the use of improved technical services and machines through their own workshops as well as through model workshops set up in centres outside the Institutes and through mobile workshops mounted on trucks. Further they will operate on behalf of the national Small Industries Corporation in regard to the supply of machinery and equipment to small industrialists on a hire-purchase system. They will also provide a marketing service by giving advice and information to small industries on existing and potential markets and on adaptation of their production to suit such markets.[92]

To help in 'providing conditions favourable to working efficiency, maintenance of uniform standards in production and economic utilization of materials and equipment', the sum of Rs10 crores was set aside for the establishment of industrial estates. These would provide the small-scale units which chose them as locations with a variety of common services and facilities, as well as with the other external economies arising from the occupancy of a single site by a number of complementary trades. The distribution of such estates should be such as to discourage 'further concentration of population in large urban centres'. Preferably, they should be 'developed in or near towns of comparatively small size'. Finance for small industries, provided by a great variety of authorities, was to become subject to a 'coordinated policy based on close collaboration between the Reserve Bank, the State Bank of India, state finance corporations and central cooperative banks'.

The Third Plan report[93] was able to record the considerable expansion of small-scale industry which we have already noted; but it did not attempt to estimate how far this expansion was a product of public policies. The projected administrative machinery had been brought into existence, but it was known not to be working very effectively. The planners were obviously worried that their favourite scheme for 'securing closer integration between small-scale and large-scale units over a wide range of industries and the development of small industries as ancillaries' had not made much progress; they were also concerned about the regrettable tendency of small-scale industries 'to concentrate in the larger cities and towns'. Industrial estates, which had proved to be one of the more popular parts of the programme, had been located in a way that reinforced this

[92] *FYP(2)*, p. 451. [93] Ch. 25: 'Village and Small Industries'.

tendency, with the result that 'the objective of establishing new centres of industries' had been 'achieved only to a limited extent'. To correct this deviation, the Commission proposed not only that the 300 new estates to be set up during the Third Plan should be 'located as far as possible near small and medium-sized towns' but that a number of them should be established 'in selected rural areas where power, water supply and other essential facilities are available or can be readily provided'. Without any apparent sense of contradiction, it also said that care would have to be taken 'to locate such estates in areas where there is sufficient concentration of artisans and craftsmen who will be in a position to make use of improved techniques, better tools and relatively modern facilities'. In general, the existing programme was to be intensified with the help of an allocation (Rs84·6 crores), which represented nearly a doubling of the actual estimated expenditure on small industries under the Second Plan. As the allocation for village and allied industries was increased by very little, it was clear that the Commission had come to the conclusion, on the basis of experience, that the small industry rather than the village industry was the horse to back.

The section on small industries in the Third Plan report does not present a very serious evaluation of the complex programme which we have briefly summarized. This, however, has been ably undertaken by two independent inquiries, the first conducted by P. N. Dhar and H. F. Lydall on behalf of the Institute of Economic Growth, the second by the Ford Foundation's International Perspective Planning Team on behalf of the Ministry of Industry. The major value of Dhar and Lydall's survey is that it subjects to analysis the various—and sometimes ambiguous or self-contradictory—arguments that the Commission has used in support of its policy; that of the Ford Foundation's report its use of hitherto unavailable statistical and other information to examine the actual impact of the various services provided by the central and state governments.

Dhar and Lydall examine in succession the five main arguments for the policy of protecting and stimulating small-scale industry as such. The first argument, that small enterprises create more employment than large ones, they quickly and justifiably dismiss, and with it a great deal of irrelevant argumentation that has congested and confused discussion of India's plans.

> It is obvious that, if one wants to increase employment, there is no need to search for industries (or sizes of firms) that *require* a large amount of employment per unit of output. Employment as such can be 'created' by simply adding on extra workers at any point one likes in the productive (or non-productive) process. The important problem, in other words, is not how to absorb *surplus* resources, but how to make the best use of *scarce* resources. If a solution can be found to the latter problem, output can be maximized: and the distribution of

the resulting income between the various members of the population—either by employment or by doles, or in other ways—is a secondary matter.[94]

This, although simply common sense, is a variety of that commodity which still needs to be circulated among those responsible for India's economic policies.[95]

The second argument, that small enterprises are more capital-saving than large ones, is also dismissed. On an examination of the evidence available to them, Dhar and Lydall come to the conclusion that small factories 'use more capital *and* more labour per unit of output than large factories'. The figures they use suggest, furthermore, that 'in general, the most *capital-intensive* type of manufacturing establishment is the small factory using modern machinery, and employing up to 50 workers'.[96] In the light of the Ford Foundation team's study, however, this conclusion may have to be modified; for one of the team's most important findings is that, under the present system of allocation, small factories are seriously handicapped, in comparison with large ones, in their efforts to acquire 'scarce raw materials and imported components'. As they receive lower allocations, in relation to capacity, than the large factories, they have to rely to a much greater extent than the latter on the black market, where they buy at prices which place them at a competitive disadvantage. The team does not attempt to quantify this disadvantage, but considers it to be serious enough to 'override all . . . types of assistance offered to small firms by the Government'.[97] In the light of this finding, therefore, Dhar and Lydall's views about the alleged capital-saving inferiority of the small firm cannot be accepted without further investigation.

Their dismissal of the 'decentralization' argument, however, would appear to be soundly based. Quite correctly, they accuse the authorities of 'a confusion between village industries, which are in their nature decentralized, and modern small factories, which require an urban environment in order to flourish'. They concede that both economic and social considerations are hostile to a further expansion of the major urban centres, but hold that the first task of a serious decentralization effort should be 'to develop several hundred of India's large and medium-sized towns as flourishing regional centres of industry'. To achieve this, the *larger* firms,

[94] *Small Enterprises,* p. 11.

[95] At the same time, it should be remembered that, although a 'secondary matter' in the context of economic growth, provision for the relief of 'technological' unemployment, however temporary, is a matter of great social and political importance. In an underdeveloped country it is anything but easy to arrange. 'Doles' are difficult to distribute efficiently and equitably, while the use of public enterprises as a means of 'making work' has a highly deleterious effect on their efficiency and productivity (see Hanson, *Public Enterprise,* pp. 418–21, and the references there given). Mobilization of displaced labour for labour-intensive public works programmes also presents financial and organizational problems (see ibid. pp. 90–98).

[96] *Small Enterprises,* pp. 19, 84.

[97] *Small Scale Industries,* pp. 2–3, 37–61.

which are less dependent than the small ones 'on the external economies of a good local market, good supplies of raw materials from local dealers, and so on', will have to be used for the pioneering work. Small firms will then follow, 'to some extent automatically'.[98] The Ford Foundation team also condemns the policy 'of trying to implant large amounts of industry in the most backward areas or directly in villages', and suggests that 'the focus for industrial development under a dispersal policy should be neither the metropolis nor the village, but rather the large range of potentially-attractive cities and towns between these two extremes'.[99] Common-sense, it may be suggested, confirms these findings.

Dhar and Lydall then turn to the 'social and political arguments' for small-scale enterprises.[100] The first of these is that the small enterprise promotes a more equal distribution of income. This has some limited validity, in so far as the small enterprise does not generate the large fortune. But the view that it is less 'exploitative' of labour is without foundation, if 'exploitation' is measured by wage-levels. More seriously, the fact 'that the total volume of savings and taxes which is generated by a large number of small incomes is almost inevitably smaller than the volume generated by an equal total income in the hands of a smaller number of people' means that a policy of promoting the former tends to slow the rate of economic growth and thus to postpone, in the interest of a *present* equality of misery, 'the attainment of a higher standard of living for the whole population in the future'.

The other 'social and political' argument is focused on democracy. The existence of a large number of independent self-employed persons, it is held, 'is a guarantee of the maintenance of democratic institutions, an obstacle to the domination of trade unions, and a barrier to communism'. The two authors attempt no detailed examination of this argument, but content themselves with expressing the personal view that 'there is, on the whole, less political stability in those countries in which "self-employment" is most prevalent than in those countries in which the bulk of industry is organized in large-scale enterprises'. Such a view may rest on an impermissible isolation of one factor, but it suggests at least a 'not proven' verdict on the 'democratic' case. Moreover the idea that a solid foundation for democratic institutions can be deliberately *created* by the subsidization and protection of the small producer is contrary to the very substance of the argument, which rests upon the belief that the self-employed man is a sturdy and independent-minded character, contemptuous of all forms of state assistance.

Only the fifth and last argument for the promotion of small-scale enterprise[101] do our authors regard as being of any real importance: that

[98] *Small Enterprises*, pp. 23–24.
[99] *Small Scale Industries*, pp. 12–13.
[100] *Small Enterprises*, pp. 24–27.
[101] Ibid. pp. 27–32.

'there is a shortage of entrepreneurial talent for running medium or large-scale enterprises and that this can be offset by increasing the number of small firms'. They consider, however, that the main policy implication of this shortage is rather one of 'helping existing small firms to improve their methods so as to *grow* into larger and more efficient organizations'.[102] This finding, too, is confirmed by the Ford Foundation team, which considers that 'priority should . . . be given to helping, in depth, those industrialists who have the inherent capability of progressive growth in industries that are most important to the economic development of the country'.[103] Such a policy orientation is particularly important at a time when the deliberate encouragement of *new* small undertakings confronts the obstacle of an acute shortage of raw materials and components. It is obviously more sensible to help existing undertakings, with high developmental potential, to use scarce resources more economically and efficiently than to disperse such resources among a host of 'mushrooms', most of which will necessarily be working well below capacity.

The conclusions which follow inevitably from this analysis are firmly drawn, viz.

that the policy for small modern enterprises in India should not be directed—as it tends to be at present—towards the creation of more small units *for their own sake*, but towards a general improvement in the efficiency of existing enterprises and the creation of opportunities for *enterprising* new firms to be successful and to grow. The emphasis of small industry policy should be switched away from the giving of preferences, subsidies and special measures of protection to small firms, towards measures which *remove disabilities* of small firms and give them a fair chance to compete in the market.[104]

It is in the light of such conclusions—modified to some extent, by a rather more favourable view of the role of small-scale industry as such—that the Ford Foundation team makes its radical policy recommendations.[105] Initial emphasis is placed on the need to reform an allocation system the working of which has virtually nullified all that the Indian government has tried to do on small-scale industry's behalf. The absurdity of this system, which not only raises costs to small firms and delays their receipt of entitlements but actually distorts plan priorities and stimulates the creation of bogus undertakings concerned solely with selling at black market prices the commodities they have bought at controlled prices, is fully and indeed horrifyingly documented. The proposals made for reforming it, although well conceived, are too complicated for reproduction here. They are summarized as 'a phased program toward a single price-tax system for all commodities, supporting an allocation system which will provide priority schedules for high-priority end products'.

[102] Ibid. p. 85. [103] *Small Scale Industries*, p. 6. [104] Dhar & Lydall, *Small Enterprises*, p. 86.
[105] These are summarized in the introductory chapter, pp. 1–13.

Secondly, changes are proposed in the functions of the central and state development organizations, with the object of eliminating 'special financial subsidies or concessional benefits', ending the policy of deliberately multiplying small industrial units, and concentrating official energies on the provision of 'technical assistance programs designed to make existing units more efficient and productive'. These necessarily involve a basic reorientation of the work of the National Small Industries Corporation, the Small Industries Service Institutes, the state Departments of Industry, and their various ancillary agencies. Again, we shall have to omit particulars of the proposed changes, as these can be appreciated only on the basis of a much fuller account of the actual functioning of these organizations than we have been able to give.

Thirdly, the policy of industrial dispersion should be modified in such a way as to eliminate the encouragement given to siting which puts 'additional strain on national financial, transport, educational and other resources without commensurate benefit'. This demands that there should be more 'careful economic analysis before making location decisions, in order that the total national costs may be correctly evaluated in relation to the benefits received and to the effect on accelerated national development'. In particular, further attention should be given to the location of industrial estates, and likewise to the cost of their facilities in relation to expected benefits.

> Analyses should include such considerations as real or effective demand for space in the location; proximity to markets, transport, skilled workers, housing and other worker amenities; construction costs in relation to existing rental levels in the location; availability of equipment and raw material supplies for prospective tenants; and adequacy of power and other utilities.[106]

If the proper criteria are adopted, it is likely that the size of the industrial estates programme in the Third Five-Year Plan will be 'drastically reduced'.

Most of these recommendations are far from esoteric. They are of the kind that would readily occur to any trained industrial economist. The fact that they need to be made again underlines the continuous involvement of the Commission and the government in messy compromises between what is ideologically or politically 'correct' and what is economically efficient. The authorities, in fact, have set out with a prejudice against the large-scale and centralized and in favour of the small-scale and decentralized, and this has tended to cloud their judgement. They have consequently come to devote considerable resources, without ever having made any real cost-and-benefit calculations, to the propping up of inefficient units who do not even possess the merit of genuine labour-intensiveness, yet simultaneously have permitted the virtual wiping-out

[106] *Small Scale Industries*, p. 10.

of this assistance through the idiocies of their allocation policies. They have allowed romanticism to triumph over reason in matters of industrial location, by persisting in foredoomed efforts to create centres of industrial production in rural and semi-rural areas. In spite of the genuine help that small industry has been given, particularly as a result of the training programme, the extension of financial aid and the provision of common facilities, it is more than possible that, *in toto*, government efforts in this field have slowed up rather than speeded up the development of the economy. That this should have been done in the name of the 'socialist pattern' is extraordinary, particularly at a time when western socialists are emphasizing the need to compel the private sector to be adequately competitive and are identifying cartellization and 'feather-bedding' as among the many abuses of latter-day capitalism.

There are, of course, problems which do not yield to mere economic analysis. Competition, although desirable, is difficult to achieve within the framework of a plan which is supposed to be based on the centralized allocation of scarce resources. The preferential treatment of backward areas, even at the cost of a less rapid overall rate of economic advance, is a demand which, as we have seen, has powerful political drives behind it. The fear that too many millionaires may become too influential in government circles is not entirely groundless, and the Gandhian preference for the decentralized and the small-scale and the rural is not yet a negligible force. None of these pressures, all of which tend to deflect the allocation of resources away from the economically optimum, can be disregarded. But it is important that, in deciding whether—or how far—to yield to them, the authorities should count the economic cost and that the public should be made aware of its extent. So far, there has been little counting, and the public, in the main, has been kept ignorant. It is also important that departures from economic rationality should be minimized and made only in the face of *force majeure*. So far, there is little evidence that the planners have persuaded the politicians of the need for strong-mindedness in these matters, and some to suggest that they themselves are ideologically predisposed to follow economically non-rational paths, even when no serious pressures are propelling them in such directions. In promoting small industry, therefore, no less than in dividing responsibility between the public and the private sectors or in regulating the latter, there is an unresolved tension between the indications of economic reason and those of political necessity or ideological presupposition.

(xii)

How far is this tension also experienced in the co-operative sector of the economy—India's *tiers monde* where the public and the private are expected to coexist in interpenetrative unity?

The political élite thinks highly of co-operative principles. For Nehru, co-operation was not just a convenient method of securing certain economically desirable results; it was a way of life. Often, in his speeches, he identified the 'socialist pattern' with the spread of co-operation to all fields of economic activity, and made very little distinction between co-operation as an attitude (i.e. the reverse of competition) and co-operation as a specific form of organization. 'My outlook', he said in 1960, 'is to convulse India with the Cooperative Movement, or rather with Co-operation; to make it, broadly speaking, the basic activity of India, in every village as well as elsewhere, and finally, indeed, to make the cooperative approach the common thinking of India.'[107]

The three Five-Year Plans, as might be expected, give the co-operative movement a great deal of attention, which they justify by a combination of ideological and economic considerations. Ideologically, co-operation is presented as the means to the achievement of a society which will be simultaneously democratic, socialist, decentralized, and planned. The First Plan report, issued before the formal adoption of the 'socialist pattern', puts the matter this way:

> In a regime of planned development, co-operation is an instrument which, while retaining some of the advantages of decentralization and local initiative will yet serve willingly and readily the overall purposes and directives of the plan. This has been amply proved by the recent experience of India, as also of other countries, like the U.K., which have entered upon an era of democratic planning. The co-operative form of organization can no longer be treated as only a species within the private sector. It is an indispensable instrument of planned economic action in a democracy.

A little later the planners carry their enthusiasm for the co-operative principle to the extent of saying that, as the plan's purpose is 'to change the economy of the country from an individualistic to a socially regulated and co-operative basis', its implementation through co-operative organizations must be regarded as one of the criteria by which its success may be judged.[108]

In the Second Plan report the threads of democracy, socialism, decentralization, and planning are drawn together into the following seamless garment:

> Economic development along democratic lines offers a vast field for the application of co-operation in its infinitely varying forms. Our socialist pattern of society implies the creation of large numbers of decentralized units, both in agriculture and in industry. These small units can obtain the advantages of

[107] *Cooperative Leadership in South-East Asia* (a collection of papers read at the Seminar on Cooperative Leadership in South-East Asia held at New Delhi, Nov. 1960) (London, 1963), p. 1.

[108] *FYP(1)*, pp. 163–4.

scale and organization mainly by coming together. The character of economic development in India with its emphasis on social change, therefore, provides a great deal of scope for the organization of co-operative activity. The building up of a co-operative sector as part of the scheme of planned development is, thus, one of the central aims of national policy.

Specifically, co-operation is said to possess, within the context of this policy. certain 'advantages which neither the system of private enterprise nor that of State ownership can match'—in particular, the achieving of socially valuable results 'by drawing equally upon the incentives which are social and the incentives which are individual'.[109] Thus it offers the best of both possible worlds.

In the Third Plan report, these points are repeated, and to them is added the view that a 'rapidly growing cooperative sector' is a 'vital factor for social stability'. The influence of co-operation, we are told, 'extends far beyond the particular activities organized along cooperative lines, and gives to the social structure and national economy balance, direction and a sense of values'.[110]

One sometimes receives the impression, when reading the 'co-operation' chapters in the three plan reports, that this general ideological enthusiasm is constantly straining at the leash of common sense and that the planners would like to 'cooperatize' everything, irrespective of its amenability to the co-operative form of organization. Certainly they freely express their grief when even a healthily developing sector of the economy, such as small-scale (as distinct from village) industry proves resistant to the application of the co-operative principle,[111] or when co-operation shows what they consider to be insufficient development in an area, such as that of consumers' co-operatives, where its adoption could be regarded as entirely a matter of voluntary choice.[112] One might, indeed, feel that there could be a more single-minded concentration on those fields of economic activity where co-operation possesses solid advantages from the standpoint of promoting the maximum rate of economic growth. Such fields, nevertheless, are wide enough, covering virtually the whole of agriculture (apart from the 'plantation' sector) and all those branches of industry dominated by the small, individual producer. Hence the promotion of co-operative forms of organization, despite the difficulties that it encounters,[113] is a policy that hardly requires any specific ideological justification.

Once one has accepted, for instance, the view that the independent artisan has a vital role to play in industrial development, the desirability

[109] *FYP(2)*, p. 221. [110] *FYP(3)*, p. 200. [111] *FYP(2)*, p. 436.
[112] Ibid. p. 229; *FYP(3)*, pp. 211–12.
[113] '. . . the human factors involved in it are complex and in some ways it is much more difficult for the co-operative form of organisation to succeed than it is for a completely socialised enterprise or for an individual entrepreneur' (*FYP(2)*, pp. 221–2).

of introducing him to co-operation follows almost as a matter of course. As an isolated individual, he is unlikely to make good his claim to economic viability. As a member of an organization which enables him and his fellows to present a united front to the supplier and the wholesaler and to obtain credit on reasonable terms, his chances are immensely improved. The services that he requires could, of course, be provided by a public authority over which he had no control; indeed, to a considerable extent they are so provided, as we have seen. But for the independent producer self-help is, almost by definition, better than help that comes from outside. Whereas the state may be prepared to feather-bed him, his co-producers will demand that he contributes his appropriate quota to the cost of the various services. Whereas publicly provided protection tends to breed slackness, collectively provided protection, which he helps to pay for and to organize, tones up his morale and promotes his efficiency. These well-known advantages of co-operative forms of organization for the small producer are rightly stressed by the Indian planners.

The difficulty which confronts them is one that is familiar to the promoters of co-operation in underdeveloped countries. Whereas, in the western countries which pioneered the co-operative movement, the state adopted, at the most, an attitude of benevolent neutrality, doing very little more than provide an appropriate legal framework for the development of co-operative institutions, it can hardly avoid, in a country such as India, involving itself in the positive promotion of co-operation; for, in general, independent producers are too ignorant and too poor to be able to do the job unaided. But once the state begins to take a hand, by engaging in co-operative propaganda, providing co-operative organizers and contributing to 'mutual' funds, the danger is that the voluntary principle will become a mere façade and 'co-operation' no more than a somewhat over-elaborate means by which public services are channelled to their recipients.

The Planning Commission, well aware of this danger, is constantly stressing the need to 'build up the self-regulatory character of the movement and to promote local leadership';[114] but the practice of rushing in with 'temporary' support as soon as a society gets into difficulty has become a habit, with the result that the very means of promotion used by the public authorities tend to become obstacles to the achievement of co-operative self-reliance. The Third Five-Year Plan report offers an excellent example of this practice, from the field of industrial co-operation. After reporting that in the handloom industry, in the coir industry, and in certain village industries co-operation has achieved a large measure of success, the planners say that in general the movement has encountered 'various practical difficulties', which need to be removed. They then

[114] *FYP(3)*, p. 216.

propose (pp. 212–13), as a means of making industrial co-operatives 'a normal pattern of organisation', the application of the following stimulae:

(1) loans from working capital at a concessional rate of interest from Government and central cooperative agencies;
(2) loans to members of industrial cooperative societies for subscribing to share capital;
(3) grants for managerial staff, improved tools and equipment;
(4) subsidising for a limited period specified managerial and supervisory staffs of cooperative banks;
(5) sharing expenditure with State Governments on additional staff appointed to look after the development of industrial cooperatives;
(6) guarantee of advances sanctioned by cooperative financing agencies to industrial cooperative societies for a limited period.

One's immediate reaction, on reading this list, is to wonder whether the ordinary members of the societies are to be given *any* responsibility, administrative or financial. As a programme for state assistance to small industry it has its merits, provided that it is aimed not at feather-bedding them but at making them self-sustaining within a reasonable period. As a programme for co-operative development, it is of more doubtful value. One of the effects of the extension of these and similar concessions is to promote the formation of bogus co-operatives which exist solely for the purpose of enabling their members to qualify for the benefits offered. Many of the 'co-operatives' formed during the period of the three plans have been of this kind. The problem, so far unsolved, is to discover, in each case, how far official regulation and stimulation can go without killing co-operative principle itself. In some cases the need for development may be so urgent that, *de facto*, the principle will have to be sacrificed, at least temporarily. In others, it may be better policy to confine regulatory and stimulatory measures to the very minimum necessary to promote a slower but healthier co-operative growth. What would seem to give the worst of both possible worlds is to *impose* an organization and *call* it co-operative. This is the frequent result of present policies. Overall targets for co-operative growth are set, and then broken down into state, district, and block targets. Officials, expected to 'show results', are therefore under pressure to bring into existence organizations that can be described as co-operative, however remote their resemblance may be to the genuine articles. How much 'infructuous' expenditure of time and energy has been devoted to this purpose would merit careful inquiry.

Problems of this kind are experienced, not only in India, but in all underdeveloped countries where the development of co-operative forms of economic organization cannot be left entirely to voluntary initiative. Serious as they are, they by no means indicate that for the time being co-operation should be put in cold storage; for the co-operative principle remains a sound one, well tested by international experience, wherever the promotion of economic growth depends on the organization of small producers. That the co-operative movement in India, as elsewhere, is endowed with certain powerfully voiced 'ideological' overtones, irrelevant to economic growth as such, should not be allowed to obscure its very solid economic advantages.

The most important area for co-operative development is, of course, agriculture. Where agricultural production depends overwhelmingly on the efforts of millions of small peasant producers, there is virtually no alternative to the co-operative form of organization. Here it is co-operative *credit* that has pride of place. Credit is the peasant's first need. In private hands, it has been used to exploit and even enslave him. But there is no real possibility of substituting a public agency for the village money-lender, as this most hated of rural figures has the cardinal advantage that he is in intimate contact with his clients, with whose strengths and weaknesses he is familiar. The idea of using a horde of public officials as substitute money-lenders is as absurd as it is uneconomic. In the villages the only real alternative to private credit is co-operative credit. If the villagers are not to have their credit-worthiness assessed and their credit-utilization supervised by the moneylenders, they themselves must learn the arts of assessment and supervision.

This is understood by the Indian planners, who inherited from the British a somewhat embryonic and patchy system of co-operative credit dating from the Co-operative Credit Societies Act of 1904. Their aim has been to build a nation-wide agricultural credit structure on these foundations, by stimulating the formation of primary credit societies at the village level and supplementing the meagre funds that such societies can initially accumulate with funds derived from taxation and from public loans. As a result of the Reserve Bank's massive and comprehensive Rural Credit Survey, a complicated, quasi-hierarchical structure has been erected, whereby the primary society is linked, through a Central Co-operative Bank, with a state (or 'apex') Co-operative Bank, which in its turn receives the financial support of the Reserve Bank, which acts as a kind of residuary legatee of co-operative finance. The Reserve Bank has administrative control of the funds earmarked for the development of co-operative credit, some of which are now channelled through a recently formed associate, known as the Agricultural Refinance Corporation. To improve banking and remittance facilities in the rural areas, largely for the benefit of the co-operatives, the State Bank (formerly the Imperial Bank) has been given the task of opening hundreds of new branches. The success of the whole scheme depends, of course, on the efficiency and popularity of its 'grass-roots' agencies, the primary credit societies, in respect of which there were some rather confusing changes of policy during the course of the First and Second Plans.[115] One of the tasks of the district administration, and now of the *panchayati raj* institutions, is to supervise the operations of these societies and to enlist for them such technical assistance as may be available.

The progress of co-operative credit for agriculture has been disappointingly slow, but by no means imperceptible. One may perhaps take with a pinch of salt the Third Plan report's statement that, during the course of the ten years covered by the First and Second Plans, the number of primary agricultural credit societies had risen from 'about 105,000 to about 210,000', with a corresponding increase in membership from '4·4 million to about 17 million'. The statistical foundations upon which these figures rest do not bear serious examination, and one may be certain that some of the societies are dormant and much of the membership nominal. But the reported rise, over the same period, of total loans advanced by primary societies from 'about Rs23 crores to about Rs200 crores' perhaps gives a reasonably accurate indication of the progress achieved.[116] Even the latter figure, however, represents only a small proportion of the total credit advanced from all sources. Except in one or two 'star' co-operative states, of which Maharashtra provides the outstanding example, the rural money-lender continues to dominate.

To break his domination it is necessary, as the Rural Credit Survey itself emphasized, to carry the co-operative principle well beyond the mere supplying of credit. What the rural co-operatives face is opposition 'from a private set-up of trade and finance' which is 'not only much better organized in regard to its technical services but also much more powerfully financed from above'. Contrasting the co-operative set-up (in 1955) with this private set-up, the Committee wrote:

> Financially and structurally, the one is a weak federation of weak units in which the poverty of the rural base is matched by the lack of strength of the urban apex, whereas the other is a strong, powerful and well-soldered projection from a relatively prosperous urban economy at the top into a rural sector of commercial activity and commercial domination at the bottom.

Specifically, there was a close association between money-lending, marketing, and processing, all three being frequently controlled by the same local group, which used its monopoly powers to put a stranglehold on the peasantry. To break this monopoly, it was necessary to extend the co-operative principle to marketing and processing. Otherwise, co-operative credit itself would languish, since credit for production could

[115] These involved principally the size of the basic unit and the question of whether it should be single-purpose or multi-purpose.
[116] *FYP(3)*, p. 203.

not be organized co-operatively while 'finance for marketing and processing remained largely private'.[117]

Accordingly the Second and Third Plans placed great emphasis on the development of co-operative marketing and processing societies. For marketing, national leadership and assistance is in the hands of the National Co-operative Development & Warehousing Board. Through a Central Warehousing Corporation and corresponding bodies in the states, the Board provides the large-scale storage facilities which the primary societies need but, which for the present, cannot be financed, constructed and managed by the co-operative movement itself. Warehousing, as the Second Plan report says (p. 226), provides an 'important institutional link between the activities of credit and non-credit societies', since warehouse receipts may be used as a security for the provision of short-term credit. A further link in the co-operative chain is the use of the marketing societies (and, indeed, the credit societies where appropriate) as distributors of the production goods (e.g. implements, fertilizers, and tested seeds) needed by the cultivators. Co-operative marketing, however, is much less well developed than the more familiar co-operative credit, while co-operative processing is in its comparatively early days. It has a large number of sugar factories and cotton ginning units to its credit, but its achievements in other processing industries are small. One of the difficulties in this field is excess capacity. Already in sugar, as well as in other types of processing, the addition of new co-operatively owned capacity to existing privately owned capacity has become of doubtful benefit. The Third Plan therefore (p. 208) directs attention to the possibility of the 'reorganization on cooperative lines of units which are, at present, privately owned'. In dairying, however, the possibilities of co-operative progress are considerable, given adequate organizational capacity. Here one can bring within a single co-operative fold the organization of milk production and the processing and marketing of the product. In this field of co-operation, as in so many others, the former Bombay state was the pioneer.

Co-operative development along these lines is both realistic and promising. Other fields marked out in the Third Plan are sugar-cane supply and fisheries. Rather more doubtful starters are transport co-operatives, which the planners think should be 'encouraged as a means of providing new opportunities for educated unemployed persons', and co-operatives for the organization of 'a growing range of new activities in industry and services, such as manufacture of implements, printing, supplies of raw materials, provision of common facilities etc'.[118] One has

[117] All India Rural Credit Survey, *Gen. Rep. of Ctee of Direction*, abridged ed. (Bombay, RBI, 1955), pp. 113–14.
[118] *FYP(3)*, p. 215.

even greater doubts about the economic viability of the 'labour-co-operatives' which all three plans recommend with a view to 'gradually diminishing the role of contractors' and utilizing surplus rural man-power.[119] There is the danger here, as we have already suggested, of too great a dispersal of effort and a tendency to allow ideological enthusiasm for the co-operative principle to outrun economic realism. International experience, however, suggests that bold initiatives in the field of co-operative organization frequently pay off.

The experiment which, perhaps, is *least* likely to pay off, at least until Indian rural society undergoes a fundamental change of structure, is co-operative farming. An enormous amount of discussion has been devoted to this subject, with comparatively little result. The desirability of co-operative farming was stressed in both the First and Second Plans, and Congress's 'Nagpur' resolution suggested that a major effort would be made, as land reform and land reclamation proceeded, to persuade the peasants to pool their plots. Since then, there has been a retreat in the face of the enormous social and organizational difficulties involved in this policy. It is now realized, if not explicitly acknowledged, that the co-operative farm, however desirable it may be from the standpoint of the 'socialist pattern', offers no solution to the pressing problem of agri-cultural productivity. The Third Plan (p. 211), it is true, allots Rs6 crores for a series of 'pilot projects in cooperative farming' and another Rs6 crores for 'assisting the development of other cooperative farming societies'. During the first two years of the plan 160 pilot projects, with a member-ship of 19,800, were organized, while 949 new co-operative farming societies, with a membership of 19,462, 'came up outside the projected areas'.[120] The experience of these co-operative farms, which seems to have been generally discouraging, is at present being evaluated by an official committee. It is unlikely that greater effort and wider coverage will be recommended, as the probable consequence of such a policy would be merely to throw good money after bad. If, on the other hand, the decision is to maintain the present rate of progress or to 'consolidate existing gains', co-operative farming may in effect be written off as a serious contribution to the solution of India's rural problems.

In general, the *Mid-Term Appraisal* (pp. 88–92) offers a rather gloomy picture of the development of co-operation. Short-term credit is still the main field of co-operative activity, but even here the rate of progress, outside the six 'advanced' states of Maharashtra, Uttar Pradesh, Madras, Gujarat, Andhra Pradesh, and Punjab, is disappointingly slow, 'despite increased coverage in terms of villages and population'. Arrangements for linking crediting with marketing and with production programmes

[119] Ibid. pp. 213–14. [120] *MTA*, p. 91.

are 'far from adequate'. In the provision of medium and long-term credit[121] there has been even less progress, while co-operative marketing societies, although continuing to increase in number, display deficiencies in organization and management which have become particularly serious now that they are responsible for the distribution of no less than three-quarters of the supply of fertilizers. Except in sugar-cane, the co-operative processing of agricultural products has made only slow headway. Some of these difficulties are obviously the product of the general stagnation of agriculture since the beginning of the Third Plan; others, no doubt, are to be ascribed to the inherent contradictions, which we have already noted, in state-promoted forms of co-operation. But, in addition, there are certain features of Indian society which tend to slow up the rate of co-operative development and will continue to do so until they are gradually eliminated by the process of economic growth. These have been distinguished and defined by Professor D. R. Gadgil, one of the great pioneers of co-operation in Maharashtra, whose knowledge of the Indian co-operative movement is unrivalled.[122]

His thesis is that the structure of Indian society makes the creation of an adequate co-operative leadership very difficult, despite the great attention given by the public authorities to co-operative training. First, the caste system, together with 'the cleavage between urban and rural society', creates an obstacle to the acceptance of leadership tasks by the well-off, competent, and educated. Secondly, the division of the peasantry into caste groups inhibits the emergence of leaders who can take 'a consistently non-partisan view of cooperative affairs' and prevents the growth of that mutual trust between leaders and led which is a basic requirement for stability and efficiency. Thirdly, traditional attitudes of deference, arising from the hierarchical nature of Indian society, are hostile to the democratic spirit which is of the very essence of co-operation. They also involve 'an unequal distribution of benefits of operation', such as the PEO has noted in connexion with the Community Projects: an inequality which is reinforced when 'social ranking and economic strength go together'. Fourthly, there is 'the high degree of specialization of occupations and the tradition of ignoring interests and skills outside a narrow range'. The main effect of this is to create a scarcity of people who qualify for co-operative leadership by combining the sense of social purpose typical of the 'scholar' with the practical abilities characteristic of the businessman.

[121] Such credit is the responsibility of the Land Mortgage Banks, which are not themselves co-operative institutions but which endeavour to do as much business as possible through the co-operative credit organizations.

[122] 'Socio-Economic Factors underlying Pattern of Leadership', in *Coop. Leadership in SE Asia*, pp. 68–79.

These are indeed powerful, but not insuperable, obstacles to co-operative progress. They require more study than they have so far received; for the present reliance on training leaders, enthusing the masses, and offering a variety of financial concessions as a bait obviously provides no more than part of the answer. There can be no doubt that, side by side with public enterprise and private enterprise, co-operative enterprise has an essential role to play in the plans—perhaps, in view of the fact that everything depends on the rapid improvement of peasant agriculture, the most essential role of all. But of all forms of organization it is the most difficult for an underdeveloped country to use successfully. The lesson, perhaps, is that until the economy becomes sufficiently prosperous to permit more weight to be given to considerations other than those of crude growth, co-operation should be used only when there is no alternative.

XIII

THE PLANNING PROCESS: SOME CONCLUSIONS

No one who has followed this lengthy account of the planning process can be under any illusions about the depth of the crisis in which Indian planning has become involved. By the time that this book appears, it may well be that some of the problems of the year 1964 will have been solved, but it is safe to predict that others will have replaced them and that the situation will remain critical. In a sense, the crisis will persist until such time as India enters that longed-for but ever-receding period of 'transition to self-sustained economic growth'. No matter how well the planning may be done, the period rather inappropriately characterized as that of 'run-up' is bound to be one of false starts, miscalculations, lurches away from the course, and general lopsidedness. No one but an innocent (or an economist whose mind is dominated by models, which amounts to the same thing) could possibly expect anything else. But it would be wrong, on the other hand, to attribute every gap between promise and performance to 'natural causes' and to suggest that every disproportion that arises is an inevitable 'problem of growth'. For although the planners can never make the economy develop exactly as they would wish, they can plan well or ill. The difficulty is to distinguish the problems that are genuine problems of growth from those that arise from avoidable miscalculations and misconceptions. Moreover, one needs to discover—and it is not always easy to do so—whether the crisis itself is really a crisis of growth; for it may well be assuming a form that brings growth to a halt. There is, unfortunately, a good deal of evidence to suggest that it may have reached this acute phase.

From 1956, at the opening of the Second Plan, it has shown a general tendency to deepen. Admittedly, the Second Plan itself was partially rescued, but not by the Indians themselves; and the chart on p. 216 shows how far it was from reaching its objectives—a fact largely concealed by the published figures. Moreover, even the comparatively good progress which it registered during its last two years was at the expense of creating bottlenecks which, by the first year of the Third Plan, brought economic growth, as measured by the increase in per capita income, to a halt. The Indians are now experiencing increasing difficulty in maintaining even the modest rate of progress (about $1\frac{1}{2}$ per cent per capita) so far achieved. A genuine diagnosis of the crisis, therefore, has become urgent. The object of this chapter is to see what light has been shed on it by the analysis presented in the preceding pages.

One is not justified as yet in talking of the 'failure' of Indian planning. After all, the period of the three plans has three very important accomplishments to its credit, viz. (1) it has effected a break with economic stagnation; (2) it has significantly raised the national income per head; and (3) it has strengthened the infrastructure of the economy and thereby created some of the preconditions for self-sustaining economic growth. These are great achievements, which can be too easily obscured by an obsession with the present crisis. It could be maintained, however, that they have less to do with planning than many Indians imagine, in that mere government investment in certain sectors of the economy, chosen by the application of informed common sense and rough-and-ready calculation, might have achieved as much at less cost. It could also be maintained, perhaps with greater force, that whereas the accomplishments of the last decade have something to do with planning, the failures are a product of what Marxists term 'the objective situation'. It may well be that however competently the planners do their work, various factors built into the Indian socio-political situation will persistently undo it. In a society as divided and tradition-bound as India, effective planning may be impossible so long as the planners have to operate within the framework of the present political system.

The limitations imposed both by the social and by the political structure are indeed severe. The question is whether they can be transcended. In the long run, no doubt, transcendence will be achieved; but we are here concerned with the shorter run. Experience suggests that in many countries a significant acceleration in the rate of development requires a dramatic break with the old social and political order, and that India may well be one of these. So far, she has experienced no such break. The acquisition of independence was unaccompanied by any kind of revolution. The new constitution was based on the old, and—apart from the abolition of the Zamindars and Jagirdars—the basic social structure remained undisturbed. The introduction of democracy, moreover, gave the manifold interest groups, both old and new, a degree of political influence which would have been denied to them under a more authoritarian regime, and made political stability dependent upon the government's capacity to effect viable compromises between a multitude of conflicting demands. 'Planning by consent', which can never be of the more dynamic kind, therefore became the only kind of planning that could be attempted.

These limitations on the *modus operandi* of the planners have been examined in some detail, and we have frequently reiterated the point that it is futile to condemn a democratic government (or a planning agency responsible to a democratic government) for failing to do something drastic about them. Yet a condemnatory attitude is a very easy one to adopt, as the planners themselves are inclined to indulge in self-flagellation. Their rather fragile belief in their power miraculously to extend the sphere of effective action by the sheer power of words is constantly being shattered, and every time the breast is duly beaten. Such behaviour may look odd to the outsider, but it is the natural reaction of impatient 'developers' who are acutely aware of being pursued by the hurrying chariot of population and horrified by their own countrymen's apathy, for which they feel a vicarious liability. But if they are to be criticized, it is not for their inability to scale insuperable obstacles, but rather for their failure to examine these obstacles carefully enough, in order to find a way round them.

What we have attempted in the foregoing chapters, therefore, is to discover whether, within the limitations imposed by circumstances, some of the more obvious planning mistakes might have been avoided and the whole path of economic development made smoother and less crisis-prone. Some might question whether even this approach is permissible. Time and again we have implied that if knowledge had been completer, understanding better, organization improved, &c. different and presumably superior decisions might have been taken. But one can never be sure that these would have been superior as well as different, nor that different decisions were, under the given circumstances, in fact possible. For the implied dichotomy between the objective situation and the subjective decision-taker is itself suspect. An objective situation, completely described, necessarily includes not only the pressures to which the decision-takers were immediately subject, but the characteristics (i.e. abilities, experiences, prejudices, &c.) of the decision-takers themselves. One may well ask, therefore, what is the precise value of the evidence provided by hindsight.

This difficulty needs always to be borne in mind. Nevertheless, for practical purposes it must be assumed that decision-takers, as rational people confronted with alternatives, have a certain freedom of choice; and it must also be assumed that their minds are open to demonstrable argument and to persuasion based on experience. If this were not so, if they were entirely and deterministically swayed by external pressures and internal motivations, rational planning would be *ipso facto* impossible and the analysis and criticism of planning decisions futile. To ask whether the planners might have done otherwise than they did is therefore pertinent and useful. What one must try to avoid is suggesting that they might have done (or ought to have done) certain things which, in the given situation, were manifestly impossible. Thus, while it is sensible to inquire whether resources might have been better matched with outlay, whether outlay might have been distributed more fruitfully, whether the reactions of the planners to a changing situation were sufficiently swift, or whether their responses to the various pressures bearing in upon them were well or ill conceived, it is not sensible, except in a totally different framework of discourse, to ask whether the country 'ought' to have been placed on a 'war economy' footing, as Anjaria once tentatively suggested.

An inquiry into the *remediable* defects in the planning process, revealed by the experience of the last fourteen years, may begin by attempting to identify faults in the planning organization itself, i.e. in the knowledge, status, organization, and procedures of the Planning Commission.

In respect of knowledge, it seems well endowed. The leading economists, econometricians, and statisticians on the staff of this body and of the associated CSO are men of high ability and exemplary devotion to duty, well acquainted with all the most up-to-date planning techniques. It is they who are responsible for the fact that India, as Professor Wilfred Malenbaum has said, 'has articulated its development programmes at greater length and with greater care and skill than has any other country'. Admittedly, the statistical and other data available to them are defective—grossly so where agriculture and the 'unorganized' sector of industry are concerned; but India is better off even in this respect than most other underdeveloped countries.

Only one major criticism needs to be made here: the failure of the Commission to use the services of sociologists to any significant extent. The social obstacles to economic development in India are so serious that to undertake a continuous and scientific investigation of them, in order to plan their circumvention, would seem to be an elementary requirement. Yet the Commission has no division devoted to this purpose and scarcely any sociologically-qualified personnel. The results of this omission are writ large in the plans. For instance, during the course of reading the 2,000 or so congested pages of the three plan reports, I have never discovered more than a passing mention of India's most important social institution, caste. It would seem that Indian planners, like the majority of her western-oriented intellectuals, regard this institution, which, rightly or wrongly, is held by them to be one of the most formidable obstacles to social and economic progress, as a kind of guilty secret to be swept away out of sight. Although some excellent work has been done, both by Indians and by foreigners, on the recent evolution of caste institutions, there is no evidence that the planners have had any contact with it. Such ignorance has been responsible for many expensive false starts, particularly in the field of rural development.

As for the status of the Commission, this has been subject to powerful attack, as we have seen. We have also seen, however, that there are strong arguments for keeping it as it is. That it has certain disadvantages cannot be denied. The techniques of planning, for instance, tend to get mixed up, at far too early a stage, with the politics of planning, and the power of the politicians on the Commission tends to inhibit the expert officials from producing genuinely independent advice and developing an *esprit de corps*. But these are faults which can be corrected without any fundamental change in the Commission's status. Such a change would make planning less, not more, effective. To remove the ministers from the Commission, to reduce it to the status of a purely advisory body, to deprive it of representation on committees charged with policy execution, and to place elsewhere the responsibility for pruning and co-ordinating the plans of the states would be to sacrifice much that has given Indian planning its admitted superiority over planning in most of the other developing countries.

Structurally, too, the Commission would appear to be reasonably satisfactory. It has been attacked for empire-building and for developing interests rather peripheral to its major purposes. There may be some truth in these accusations, and it may be that planning has suffered from an excessive subdivision of responsibility. One or two of the Commission's divisions, such as that concerned with Public Co-operation, could be dispensed with, and some of the work done in the other divisions unnecessarily duplicates that done in the ministries. But most of the Commission's twenty-five divisions are performing necessary functions, and it can hardly be said that they are over-staffed. With a total personnel (exclusive of clerks, typists, secretaries, messengers, doorkeepers, peons, &c.) of 265, the Commission is not an excessively large bureau to do the planning for a country with a population of some 450 million.

The manner in which it deploys its staff could certainly be improved. Even a superficial acquaintance with Yojana Bhavan is sufficient to show that 'O & M' has never received the high-level attention that it deserves. An atmosphere of amateurism, even of muddle, clings to the Commission's internal organization, and the fact that the institution is small enough for everyone to know everyone else does not provide a sufficient countervailing force. (Indeed, face-to-face relationships sometimes do not help at all.) Records are imperfectly kept, documents are sometimes lost, and there are delays in the circulation of information. More seriously, interdivisional rivalries, in themselves quite harmless and even good for the health of the organization, have in one or two important instances been allowed to develop to the point of obstinate quarrelsomeness; and there is far too much paper—a product of the Indian intellectual's belief, undisturbed by the idiosyncratic examples given by Pitamber Pant and a few of his colleagues, that a document twice as long as another is twice as valuable. These are certainly serious faults, but it is difficult to exemplify and impossible to quantify their effect on the planning process. One's impression is that it is deleterious but not critically so. The work gets done, but at the cost of an excessive expenditure of time and energy.

As for the planning procedures that have been gradually built up over the last thirteen years, these are generally admitted to be highly sophisticated. It may be useful, at this stage, to summarize them.

First comes the formulation by the government, with the Commission's help, of basic political and social objectives. In the light of these, the Commission, whose thinking goes far beyond the conventional five-year period, prepares long-term (15–20-year) targets. Having obtained approval for these, it tentatively formulates the objectives for the five years immediately ahead, and submits these to the examination of the interdepartmental working groups. When these have reported and the necessary adjustments in commodity balances and financial provisions have been made, the Commission drafts a Memorandum, indicating the proposed shape of things to come, for the Cabinet and the NDC. Suitably amended, this becomes the basis of the Draft Outline of the plan, which is published and circulated for general discussion and criticism. For the states, the Draft Outline, which informs them of the general shape and size of the national plan to which their own plans will have to conform, is a signal to go ahead more rapidly and purposefully with their own planning processes, through 'working groups' similar to those used at the centre. When the final drafts of the state plans are ready, they are submitted to the Commission, which conducts negotiations of great political delicacy in order to cut them down to appropriate size. Meanwhile, the Draft Outline is also being considered by the various central ministries, by the large collection of advisory boards and committees with which the Commission surrounds itself, and by interest and pressure groups of all kinds. It is also lengthily debated in the Indian Parliament. Finally, after brooding over the results of this formidable amount of discussion and taking further counsel with the Cabinet and the NDC, the Commission prepares the final plan report, which it once again submits for approval. Confirmed by Parliament, after another lengthy debate, the plan becomes operational. The Commission then has the task of breaking it down into annual plans, of vetting and approving the annual plans of the states, of watching its progress in every detail and of proposing, from time to time, such modifications and adjustments as may seem necessary. For these purposes it receives from the various executive authorities and from the state governments a mass of reports, which it supplements by the maintenance of informal contacts. These reports, of course, also provide basic raw material for the formulation of the next plan, which begins almost simultaneously with the first steps to implement the existing one.

This procedure is easy enough to describe but extremely difficult to operate. Much of it is still experimental, and none of it has crystallized into a fixed routine. One may fairly say, however, that it is both intelligently devised and used with considerable vigour and understanding.

If its end-products show less-than-optimum consistency and realism—which is perhaps the mildest criticism one may make of them—one reason is that it gives the maximum opportunity for interest groups of all kinds, both official and unofficial, to bring effective pressures to bear. Far from being an economic dictator, the Commission leans over backwards to obtain that minimum consensus without which no plan, in a democratic country, can achieve even limited success. The states, the central ministries, and other governmental agencies, operating sometimes on their own account and sometimes on behalf of influential 'clients', function as a complex pressure-group system at the New Delhi level, and there is a similarly complex system, in which voluntary groups play a more direct part, at the level of the state capitals. During the long process of formulating the plan, as well as on the many occasions when the plan has to be adjusted or modified, one of the Commission's main concerns is to give as much satisfaction to the various demands, both actual and latent, as is compatible with the production of coherent and workable proposals. Indeed, there have been occasions when its response to particularly powerful and persistent pressures has been unmistakably at the expense of coherence and workability, as in the autumn of 1958, when, as we have seen, the Commission temporarily accepted target increases urged upon it by the economic ministries without being able to suggest any corresponding increase in resources. Ministries, of course, do not invariably act on behalf of clients; they are important pressure groups in their own right. The governments of the states, as bodies responsible to regional electorates with deeply-felt interests of their own, can make even more insistent and menacing claims. When they do so the Commission has to walk warily; for despite the strong centralizing tendency in Indian federalism, centrifugal forces offer a persistent challenge to India's unity.

That the operation of these pressures is responsible for serious distortions and inconsistencies has been amply illustrated, particularly by our excerpts from the proceedings of the NDC. One could, perhaps, criticize both the government and the Commission for yielding to them too easily, and claim that firmer resistance would, in the long run, bring its own reward, both politically and economically. But it must be remembered that the people in New Delhi have sensitive political antennae and that experience has taught them to judge just how much the various parties concerned are prepared to stand, and to identify the points at which co-operation will be withdrawn. Their conclusions on these matters, therefore, should at least be treated with some respect.

What cannot be maintained, without rejecting the very essence of the

Indian democratic experiment, is that the planning procedures which provide these awkward groups with opportunities for self-expression are *ipso facto* wrong. So long as India remains a democracy, groups will bring effective influence to bear on the planners, and the viability of the plan will largely depend upon their ability and willingness to co-operate. In these circumstances, there is everything to gain and nothing to lose by the organization of consultation. At least it ensures that there is a dialogue, with influence flowing in both directions. It is not only the attitudes of the government and the Commission that are open to modification. At best—although this, one may admit, is rarely achieved—the process of consultation can transform sullen resistance into willing co-operation.

Procedurally, therefore, the work of the Commission would seem to be nearly as satisfactory as one could reasonably expect, given the socio-political setting. There are two criticisms, however, which ought to be made. The first concerns the relationship between the Planning Commission and the private sector. Although this has immensely improved of recent years, it is still not good enough. Perhaps more devoted to the 'socialist pattern of society' than the majority of their countrymen, the officials of the Commission, while recognizing in theory the important role that the private businessman has to play, are in practice inclined to treat him with suspicion and hold him at arm's length. His behaviour, admittedly, all too frequently justifies this negative attitude, but there is much to suggest that the frequent unsavoury scandals that disfigure the record of Indian business are, at least in part, the product of the low esteem in which it is held among bureaucratic intellectuals. Consultation with private business is, as we have seen, both frequent and organized; but, as far as the Commission is concerned, it is perhaps regarded as slightly peripheral activity. Too much of it, one might argue, is left to the Ministry of Commerce and Industry, which has tended to become a 'business' ministry, ideologically oriented towards its clients, and inclined to regard itself as the 'private sector' rival of the 'public sector' Commission. There is now a strong case for a more direct association of private business with the planning process, through devices comparable with the French *Commissions de Modernisation*. In this respect, the planners still have something to learn from Visvesvarayya's proposals of 1934.

The second criticism concerns the organization of reporting. In supervising the implementation of a plan, the Commission is entirely dependent on the regular receipt of up-to-date, accurate, and relevant information. If this is not obtained, adjustments are inevitably belated and sometimes misconceived. There is much to suggest that the rather slow and fumbling responses of the Commission to the deflationary situation of 1953–4 and to the inflationary one of 1956–7 were partly the result of informational deficiencies. Of recent years, the reporting system has been improved, but the Commission's Plan Co-ordination Division holds that it is still not good enough.

Although these faults are not trivial, they weigh lightly against the Commission's manifest merits as an organization. If it cannot be given a clean bill of health, it must be recognized as one of the best conceived and best organized of India's central government agencies.

Why, then, has India's planning reached a point of crisis? In the light of our examination of the political, administrative, and social material with which the planners have to work, this question almost answers itself. One wonders, indeed, how India has managed to get so far and why the crisis is not even deeper. For the crisis-predisposing factors are obvious enough: the weight of tradition, the apathy of a people sunk in deep poverty, the difficulty of squeezing extra savings out of the economy, the stagnation of India's established export markets and the uphill task of developing new ones, the inadequacy of entrepreneurial talent, and the strain placed on the administration by the transition from a night-watchman state to a development-oriented one. When to these we add the difficulty of operating in an economy which is largely non-monetized and which consists, for the greater part, of millions of unorganized or imperfectly organized peasants and artisans, the full magnitude of the task becomes apparent.

To lift this mass out of its traditional ruts, there are two main instruments: the central government and the state governments. Neither, as we have seen, is particularly well-adapted to the task. One could therefore argue that although, within the limitations imposed by the democratic requirements of compromise and conciliation, plan formulation, for which the Commission has responsibility, is competently done, plan implementation, over which it has virtually no control, displays inefficiencies which inhibit the attainment of objectives.

But this would be a wrong way of looking at the problem; for the defects of the implementary agencies are, or should be, part of the data that the plan formulators have to use. Admittedly, a plan which does not place its administrative instruments under some strain is not likely to be much good. Easy assignments are nearly always the less useful ones. To that extent, the planners who argue that the plan should demand of its implementers just a little more than they are capable of giving have reason on their side. A sense of tension is inseparable from serious economic development. Personnel must be keyed up to the point where they are prepared to attempt things formerly regarded as impossible. But that is quite different from demanding of them things that are *really* impossible. Such demands may key people up for the time being, but in the longer run spread slackness and cynicism. If one has no hope of attaining an objective, one might as well cease to make the effort. Yet, as we have seen in so many different contexts, the planners have a persistent tendency to overestimate the capacity of their agents, and to assume that they possess—or soon will possess if they can be persuaded to respond to all the exhortations addressed to them—abilities and attitudes which they neither actually possess nor can readily acquire. Obsessed with achieving the maximum speed of economic development, the planners find it difficult to believe that the whole government service is not equally devoted—or cannot be induced to become so—to the same cause. Prepared to work for long hours at great intensity on the preparation of the plan, they cannot convince themselves that the administrators, once matters have been properly explained to them, will not work similarly on its implementation. Deeply convinced of the need for all the regions of India to pull together for the achievement of comparatively distant but socially desirable objectives, they are constantly surprised and grieved to find that others prefer to pull separately for their own comparatively selfish and short-term purposes. Such lack of realism, of course, is not universal in Yojana Bhavan. There are plenty of hard-headed officials who know well enough what Indian administrators are like. But it has become 'unorthodox' to suggest that grandiose projects should be cut down and tailored to the capacities of those who have to implement them, and 'orthodox' to express confidence that with more effort, more enthusiasm, more intelligence, &c. all will be well.

This fault, which is responsible for the achievement by the Indian administrative machine of *less* than it is actually capable of, has been amply illustrated in the foregoing chapters. We have also related it to the prevalence of certain ideological presuppositions which, because of their lack of realism, throw a veil between planners and people which becomes increasingly difficult to penetrate. Ideology, we have suggested, is responsible for certain irrationalities in the division of responsibility between the public and the private sectors, and for a policy towards village and small-scale industries which has involved the use of massive resources for purposes which contribute little, if anything, to the growth of the economy. Its effect, however, has been far more deleterious in the sphere of agriculture and rural development, where assumptions about the nature of the village community have led the planners to persist in policies which seem to lead nowhere. For of the peasant, far more than of the administrator, they have expected changes of basic attitude which are in the realm of the utopian. In brief, rural development policies have rested on an ideologically-inspired assumption of a degree of unity and common purpose among the peasantry that is at variance with the realities of village life.

To advocate that nothing should be done to *change* attitudes and motivations would be a counsel of despair. The point is that the Commission and the government have based their plans on excessive expectations of such a change—on expectations, in fact, that could be turned into reality only as the long-term result of a social revolution which India's political leadership has neither power nor the desire to effect. Hence the failure of those responsible for agricultural policy to think deeply enough about ways and means of mobilizing *existing* attitudes and motivations in the cause of economic growth. This unrealism, for which Nehru himself was partly responsible, reached its height in the 'Nagpur' resolution of the Congress Party calling for the development of co-operative farming. In this case, brutal facts were allowed to have their way and the schemes of the ideologists quietly pigeon-holed. But the planners are still reluctant to absorb the implications of the fact that the main result of their actual achievements in the countryside, the abolition of the *zamindars* and *jagirdars* and the expansion of services to the agriculturalist, whether through the Community Projects or otherwise, is the creation of a rural *petite-bourgeoisie*.

This is no part of their plan, but unless they treat it as one of their basic planning data, they will run into increasing difficulties—for the 'substantial' peasant is becoming a political power in the land.

The causes of this unrealism, as we have seen, are complex. Partly it is a hangover from the independence movement, partly a product of the misinterpretation of foreign (and particularly Soviet) experience, partly a consequence of the isolation of the Indian intellectual from the Indian masses and his 'alienation' from his own society. But in so far as it involves the attempt to hit Soviet-type targets by un-Soviet-type methods, its source is largely to be found in the powerful pressures, from all but those who have to find the financial ways and means, in favour of setting goals which are far beyond the most optimistic estimates of available resources. Both the Second and the Third Plans displayed a sizeable uncovered 'gap', and both underwent 'upward' modifications during the period immediately after their approval by the Lok Sabha. Ministries and states are unremitting in their demands, while the 'left' opposition parties are always ready to accuse the government of undue timidity and to quote the example of the Soviet Union—and, until recently, that of China—to prove their point. From such 'over-planning' a critical situation rapidly develops, requiring an agonized reappraisal which is anything but good for the public morale on which the government of India sets such great store.

To talk of 'over-planning', in the context of such an urgent need for growth, may sound harsh or even cynical. Yet it exists, in two separate senses. The first is in the setting of targets, for certain kinds of economic effort, at a higher level than a democratic society can reach without disruptive strain. Admittedly, in some respects India might, without in any way endangering her democratic institutions, have done more. The mobilization of internal resources has been sluggish and governments—particularly state governments—have shown a reluctance to use the taxation weapon with sufficient vigour. Moreover, efforts to tap the country's great reserves of unemployed and under-employed labour have so far been feeble. But governments dependent on popular support operate under certain limitations. If agriculture is undertaxed, the reason is to be found in the resistance of the peasantry, who have votes, to any further claim on their resources. Thus, in 1962, the government of Uttar Pradesh was faced with a major political crisis as a result of its proposal to step up the land tax by a very moderate amount. Only the Chinese invasion, which produced a spontaneous enthusiasm for patriotic self-sacrifice, saved the ministry from collapse or retreat. As for the mobilization of rural labour on an adequate scale, this demands a degree of organization that imposes severe strains even on a totalitarian regime. Already the Indian government is making excessive demands on the capacity of administration; further onerous duties might crush the machine beneath their weight.

How to attain an adequate rate of economic development without sacrificing democracy is India's major problem. Perhaps only much greater external assistance can bring a solution. Overplanning, in the sense of setting targets in excess of mobilizable resources does not help except to the extent that it may possibly stimulate foreign powers to mount a rescue operation. Nor does the second kind of overplanning, which consists of a regulation of private enterprise so excessive as to be self-defeating. Congress ideology here combines with bureaucratic predilections to deflect planning from the path of economic rationality. The plans themselves, for all their emphasis on the essential role that private enterprise has to play, very firmly state that unless it is carefully controlled its contribution to the common good is likely to be a negative one; while the bureaucrats who operate the controls are predisposed to believe that anything that they themselves do not regulate will *ipso facto* be working against the national interest. The result is that the 'honest' businessman is one who takes an unconscionably long time to establish his enterprise and who, having established it, finds himself tied up in the formalities of obtaining permits and concessions. Controls therefore effect an identification of enterprise with dishonesty and corruption. This is good neither for public morality nor for economic efficiency, as the 'plums' tend to go not to the most competent and public spirited of the business community but to those who have personal pull with the bureaucrats and politicians and can afford to employ the more expensive contact-men. Moreover, as even the smoothest of machines for easing the passage of the multifarious applications has to be fuelled with time and energy, the pace of economic development, to the extent that it depends on private initiative, is slowed up. As for public enterprise, on which economic development is even more dependent, this too is caught up in the bureaucratic network. There is no complete solution to this problem, as to abolish the controls themselves would be incompatible with the very essence of economic planning. But they could easily be both simplified and streamlined, as the Indian government is now beginning to realize. Unfortunately, it has taken a long time to recognize that the organized inhibition of private enterprise and bureaucratization of public enterprise are not contributions to the 'socialist pattern' that make any economic sense.

It might be argued that all these ideological and political considerations are outside the purview of the planners themselves, who have to work within the terms of reference given to them by the politicians. Such an argument would have considerable substance in a country where 'planning' was confided to a modest bureau, staffed by politically uninfluential econometricians and statisticians. But the Indian Planning Commission is, as we have seen, a highly political body, closely associated with the Cabinet and including among its members the Prime Minister and the Minister of Finance. Its advisory capacity, therefore, may be considered as almost unlimited. But even if it were a less powerful force, it would still have an almost inescapable duty of subjecting a whole series of 'orthodox' assumptions to certain critical tests. It has to accept the constitution and, presumably, the broad outlines of the 'socialist pattern'. Such limitations, however, are not very inhibiting. Within them, it is surely professionally responsible for measuring every policy, actual or proposed, by the yardstick of economic growth. If a policy, however fundamental, is inimical to economic growth the Planning Commission must say so; for no one else can say it with equal authority. If a policy contributes to short-term growth at the expense of long-term, or vice versa, this also needs to be pointed out as clearly as possible. If it tends to slow down growth in the interest of some other objective, this likewise must be known and its consequences precisely assessed. There is always the possibility, of course, that the ultimate political leadership will, in a given instance, reject the 'growth' criterion. The Commission must then accept the *fiat* of its masters and work, within the specific terms of reference, to reduce the economic damage; but not until it has pressed its own view as far as possible.

There is plenty of evidence that the undue respect paid by the Commission to the current orthodoxies, together with some uncertainty on the part of its 'expert' members and officials as to what their assignment really is, has made the work of this body less effective than it might have been. The time would seem to have arrived, therefore, when India needs to take a hard critical look at the Commission itself as well as at the other features of her politico-administrative establishment. For there is an obvious danger that, while everybody goes on behaving 'correctly' according to current notions, planning will go to perdition and economic growth come to an end.

If the final emphasis of these conclusions is on the weaknesses rather than on the strengths of Indian planning, this is not because the plans have been ineffective and as such are unworthy of foreign support. On the contrary, they have established a growth *potential* which did not exist when they began and have justifiably aroused an international interest which ought to increase rather than diminish. Everything that Barbara Ward has said on this subject, in her *India and the West*, is both true and important. Nevertheless, the Indians could both help themselves and encourage their friends by undertaking a realistic reappraisal of their planning experience. What the results of such a reappraisal might be I have not ventured to guess. My sole object, in this lengthy analysis of that experience, has been to shed a little more light on the problems now confronting the economic planners in one of the largest underdeveloped countries in the world, and almost the only fully democratic one.

APPENDIX I

Planning Commission: Statement Showing the Approved Strength in the Various Grades

Division	*Chief*	*Director*	*Asst. Chief*	*Senior Research Officer*	*Research Officer*	*Eco. Inv. Grade I*	*Eco. Inv. Grade II*
Agriculture	—	—	1	2	4	2	3
Economic	—	2	2	6	6	5	7
Education	—	2	1	2	4	2	4
Labour & Employment	1	—	—	1	3	3	3
Health	1	—	1	2	2	2	2
Housing	—	1	—	—	3	1	2
Industry & Minerals	1	1	1	4	4	3	1
Information, Publicity & Publications	—	—	—	—	—	—	1
International Trade & Development	—	—	—	1	2	—	2
Irrigation & Power	—	2	1	2	5	3	—
Land Reforms	1	—	1	1	3	3	1
Plan Co-ordination	—	1	1	2	4	3	—
Programme Administration	1	—	2	3	6	3	6
Public Co-operation	—	—	1	—	1	1	1
Public Administration	—	1	—	—	—	2	—
Scientific and Industrial Research	—	—	—	—	2	2	—
Perspective Planning	1	—	2	4	8	8	8
Social Welfare	—	1	—	1	3	3	5
Transport	—	1	—	2	2	3	3
Village & Small Industries	—	—	1	1	2	2	2
Minister & Deputy Minister's Office	—	—	1	—	3	—	2
Leave Reserve	—	—	—	—	—	—	2
TOTAL	6	12	16	34	67	51	55

Joint Secretaries	3	
Advisers	4	(Planning, Economic, Irrigation & Power and Social Services)
Deputy Secretaries	3	
Under Secretaries	6	
Asst. Information Officers	2	(One for Hindi Section and one for Public Co-operation Branch)
Information Assistants	2	
Publicity Investigators	1	
Officers on Special Duty	3	(Public Co-operation, Scientific & Industrial Research, and Cottage Industry)

APPENDIX II

Outlays & Central Assistance during 1962–3 for Maharashtra State Plan Schemes
(Rs. lakhs)

Heads of Development	Outlay Approved	Central Assistance		
		Loan	Grant	Total
I. *Agricultural Programmes:*				
Agricultural Production	198·00	..	61·00	61·00
Minor Irrigation	270·00	207·60	27·50	235·10
Animal Husbandry, Dairying, & Fisheries	166·00	40·00	18·90	58·90
Forests & Soil Conservation	379·00	220·60	33·80	254·40
Total:—	1013·00	468·20	141·20	609·40
II. *C.D. & Co-operation*				
Co-operation & Warehousing	188·00	68·50	43·20	111·70[1]
Community Development	480·00	141·84	216·00	357·84
Panchayats	44·00	..	..	..
Total:—	712·00	210·34	259·20	469·54
III. *Irrigation & Power*				
Irrigation	1129·00	220·00	..	220·00[2]
Power	1400·00	54·00	..	54·00[3]
Flood Control	3·00	2·60	..	2·60
Total:—	2532·00	276·60	..	276·60
IV. *Industry & Mining*				
Large & Medium Industries	106·00	..	..	..
Mineral Development	20·00	..	..	..
Village & Small-Scale Industries	107·00	61·60	22·40	84·00
Total:—	233·00	61·60	22·40	84·00

[1] Of this Rs88·40 (Rs51·70 lakhs loans & Rs36·70 lakhs grants) will be operated upon by NCD & W. Board.

[2] For Koyna project (Stage I).

[3] For rural electrification.

APPENDIX II (cont.)

V. *Transport & Communications*				
Roads	539·00	..	..	..
Road Transport	100·00	..	..	..
Other Transport	16·00	..	..	..
Total:—	655·00	..	..	..
VI. *Social Services*				
General Education	376·00	..	108·00[4]	108·00
Technical Education & Scientific Research	100·00	..	23·60	23·60
Health	541·00	151·19	161·54[5]	312·73
Housing	243·00	113·66	79·40	193·06
Welfare of Backward Classes	101·00	..	38·00	38·00
Social Welfare	20·00	..	4·75	4·75
Labour Welfare	50·00	..	..	..
Total:—	1431·00	264·85	415·29	680·14
VII. *Miscellaneous*				
Statistics	3·00	..	0·81	0·81
Misc. Development Schemes		679·51	..	679·51
Total:—	3·00	679·51	0·81	680·32
Grand Total:	6,579·00	1,961·10	838·90	2,800·00

[4] Includes Rs1·37 lakhs for the special schemes of girls' education.

[5] Includes Rs110 lakhs for control of communicable diseases.

APPENDIX

Final Payment of Central Assistance for

Head of Development	*Budgeted outlay*	*Anticipated exp. as reported for provisional payments*	*Actual exp. as reported for final payments*	*Excess or shortfall*	*Col. 4 as % of col. 2*	*Central assistance allocated*		
						Loans	*Grants*	*Total*
1	2	3	4	5	6	7	8	9
Agricultural production including minor irrigation & land development	634·54	811·98	635·46	0·92	100·0	194·00	55·30	249·20
Animal husbandry, dairying & fisheries	164·19	182·18	168·06	3·87	102·5	25·10	35·10	60·20
Forest & soil conservation	254·63	287·02	292·01	37·38	110·7	58·10	19·10	77·20
I Agricultural programmes	*1053·36*	*1281·18*	*1095·53*	*42·17*		*277·20*	*109·50*	*386·70*
Co-operation	196·92	202·39	169·77	(—) 27·15	86·2	26·00	27·20	53·20
Community Development	404·84	558·88	491·76	6·92	101·4	76·30	130·60	206·90
Panchayats	146·97	132·60	189·33	42·36	128·8	—	—	—
II Community Development & Co-operation	*828·73*	*893·67*	*850·86*	*22·13*		*102·30*	*157·80*	*260·10*
Irrigation	926·94	1231·67	1394·41	467·47	154·0	—	—	—
Power	645·05	581·14	682·58	37·53	105·8	13·80	—	13·80
III Irrigation & power	*1571·99*	*1812·81*	*2076·99*	*505·00*		*13·80*	—	*13·80*
Large & medium industries	6·00	123·79	3·91	(—) 2·09	65·1	—	—	—
Mineral development	10·75		6·46	(—) 4·29	60·0	—	—	—
Village & small industries	136·20	116·37	186·41	50·21	136·8	23·30	21·70	45·00
IV Industry & Mining	*142·95*	*240·16*	*196·78*	*43·83*		*23·30*	*21·70*	*45·00*
V Transport & communications	*556·98*	*N.A.*	*674·37*	*117·39*	*121·0*			
General education	361·91	811·87	702·62	340·72	194·1	—	94·37	94·37
Technical education	91·39	98·22	49·36	(—) 42·03	54·0	—	8·13	8·13
Health	435·75	332·89	563·98	128·23	129·4	36·80	28·90	65·70
Housing	591·36	615·70	574·00	(—) 17·36	97·0	120·30	125·80	246·10
Welfare of backward classes	131·61	202·20	246·89	115·28	187·5	—	28·00	28·00
Social welfare	33·89	—	15·20	(—) 18·69	44·8	—	—	—
Labour & labour welfare	54·00	—	26·98	(—) 27·02	50·0	—	—	—
VI Social services	*1709·91*	*2066·88*	*2179·03*	*469·12*		*157·10*	*285·20*	*442·30*
Statistics	9·11	8·23	7·98	(—) 1·13	87·5	—	2·10	2·10
Publicity	10·67	—	12·21	1·54	114·4	—	—	—
Others	55·10	—	54·38	(—) 0·72	98·7	—	—	—
VII Miscellaneous	*74·88*	*8·23*	*74·57*	(—) *0·31*			*2·10*	*2·10*
Total	*5918·89*	*6302·93*	*7148·13*	*1229·24*	*120·7*	*573·70*	*576·30*	*1150·00*
Multipurpose project (Koyna)	750·00	1064·19[2]	661·97	(—) 98·03		750·00	—	750·00
Grand Total	*6668·89*	*7376·12*[3]	*7810·10*	*1141·21*	*117·11*	*1323·70*	*576·30*	*1900·00*

[1] Includes Rs 39.50 lakhs for co-operative sugar factories. [2] Includes certain irrigation schemes also.

Note: Figures in parenthesis under cols 10, 11,

III

1960–61 Maharashtra State Plan (*Rs. lakhs*)

Provisional payment sanctions issued			*Central assistance calculated on the basis of expenditure reported*			*Final payments recommended by Programme Administration Division*		
Loans	*Grants*	*Total*	*Loans*	*Grants*	*Total*	*Loans*	*Grants*	*Total*
10	11	12	13	14	15	16	17	18
181·73	50·76	232·49	194·00	55·30	249·30	194·00	55·30	249·30
20·84	30·75	51·59	25·73	35·98	61·71	25·10	35·10	60·20
50·22	16·51	66·73	64·32	21·14	85·46	58·10	19·10	77·20
252·79	*98·02*	*350·81*	*284·05*	*112·42*	*396·47*	*277·20*	*109·50*	*386·70*
75·76[1]	32·02	107·78	22·41	23·15	45·66	22·41	23·45	45·86
65·96	83·43	149·39	77·37	132·43	209·80	77·37	132·43	209·80
—	—	—	—	—	—	—	—	—
141·72	*115·45*	*257·17*	*99·78*	*155·88*	*255·66*	*99·78*	*155·88*	*255·66*
—	—	—	—	—	—	—	—	—
N.A.	—	N.A.	14·60	—	14·60	13·80	—	13·80
—	—	—	*14·60*	—	*14·60*	*13·80*	—	*13·80*
—	—	—	—	—	—	—	—	—
—	—	—	—	—	—	—	—	—
17·48	16·28	33·76	31·87	29·69	61·56	23·30	21·70	45·00
17·48	*16·28*	*33·76*	*31·87*	*29·69*	*61·56*	*23·30*	*21·70*	*45·00*
—	—	—	—	—	—	—	—	—
—	86·00	86·00	—	183·17	183·17	—	104·06	104·06
—	N.A.	N.A.	—	4·39	4·39	—	4·39	4·39
31·85	25·01	56·86	47·62	37·40	85·02	42·93	28·90	71·83
84·32	88·18	172·50	116·69	122·03	238·72	116·69	122·03	238·72
—	28·00	28·00	—	52·50	52·50	—	28·00	28·00
—	—	—	—	—	—	—	—	—
—	—	—	—	—	—	—	—	—
116·17	*227·19*	*343·36*	*164·31*	*399·49*	*563·80*	*159·62*	*287·38*	*447·00*
—	1·55	1·55	—	1·84	1·84	—	1·84	1·84
—	—	—	—	—	—	—	—	—
—	—	—	—	—	—	—	—	—
	1·55	*1·55*		*1·84*	*1·84*	—	*1·84*	*1·84*
488·66	*473·92*	*962·58*	*594·61*	*699·32*	*1293·93*	*573·70*	*576·30*	*1150·00*
600·00	—	600·00	661·97	—	661·97	661·97	—	661·97
1128·16 (1129·31)	*458·49* (439·81)	*1586·65* (1569·12)	*1256·58*	*699·32*	*1955·90*	*1235·67*	*576·30*	*1811·97*

[3] Incomplete.

& 12 are as indicated by state government.

INDEX